Trouble in the Middle

This book will help readers better understand the ethical and cultural assumptions that both American and Chinese business cultures bring to business relationships in China. It analyzes the relationships developed between the two cultures, areas where they conflict, and how these conflicts can be resolved.

These relationships are investigated in three stages. The author:

- describes and interprets American business experience and outlook in China
- describes and interprets Chinese business experience and outlook in China, including interaction with Americans
- compares these two business cultures as they are experienced in China to investigate the relationships between them, centering the cultural analysis on ethical issues.

Feldman's thorough research, in conjunction with historical and theoretical context, gets to the crux of how American and Chinese executives perceive the ethical and cultural aspects of doing business. The result is a book that will prove helpful to all those looking to expertly navigate American-Chinese business relationships.

Steven P. Feldman is professor of business ethics at Case Western Reserve University, Cleveland, Ohio. He was Fulbright Distinguished Lecturer in business ethics at Shanghai International Studies University in Shanghai, China. His Ph.D. is from the Wharton School of Business, University of Pennsylvania. He has held visiting positions at Oxford University, University of Innsbruck, and the University of Minnesota. He has lectured broadly in China on business ethics issues. His previously published books are *Memory as a Moral Decision* and *The Culture of Monopoly Management*. He has published broadly in management journals on ethical and cultural issues. Steve specializes in American-Chinese business relations, business ethics, and nonprofit management.

Trouble in the Middle

American-Chinese Business Relations,
Culture, Conflict, and Ethics

Steven P. Feldman

Routledge
Taylor & Francis Group

NEW YORK AND LONDON

First published 2013
by Routledge
711 Third Avenue, New York, NY 10017

Simultaneously published in the UK
by Routledge
2 Park Square, Milton Park, Abingdon, Oxon OX14 4RN

Routledge is an imprint of the Taylor & Francis Group, an informa business

© 2013 Taylor & Francis

The right of Steven P. Feldman to be identified as author of this work has been asserted by him in accordance with sections 77 and 78 of the Copyright, Designs and Patents Act 1988.

Library of Congress Cataloging in Publication Data
Feldman, Steven P. (Steven Paul), 1954-
  Trouble in the middle : American-Chinese business relations, culture, conflict, and ethics / Steven P. Feldman.
     p. cm.
  Includes bibliographical references and index.
  1. United States—Commerce—China.   2. China—Commerce—United States.
  3. Management—United States.   4. Management—China.   5. Business ethics—United States.   6. Business ethics—China.   7. International business enterprises—Cross-cultural studies.   8. Corporate culture—Cross-cultural studies.   I. Title.
  HF3128.F45 2013
  382.0973'051—dc23
                                                                    2012035535

ISBN: 978–0–415–81877–3 (hbk)
ISBN: 978–0–415–88448–8 (pbk)
ISBN: 978–0–203–38773–3 (ebk)

Typeset in Garamond
by RefineCatch Limited, Bungay, Suffolk, UK

Printed and bound in the United States of America
by Edwards Brothers, Inc.

For John Van Maanen

Contents

Preface

The idea of the middle, when applied to relations between two cultures, denotes a metaphorical space where either ideas and practices are dominated by one side, a compromise is worked out, or communications break down altogether. In the case of American-Chinese business relations, the middle is a little of the first two and a lot of the last one. In fact, the situation is so bad that the Chinese institution of the middleman has become extended into American-Chinese relations to facilitate communications and perform certain functions that isolate and protect each culture, in some cases requiring little direct communication, if any, as long as the middleman makes sure the bribes get paid.

Such is the ground upon which this research is carried out; business in China faces systemic corruption, for historical, cultural, and above all, governmental reasons. It is a difficult environment for foreigners but even worse for the Chinese, since a great many of the benefits of "privatization" have gone to current or previous members of the Communist Party or their families. The "wealth gap" in China has steadily worsened as the "reforms" progress. As for the Americans, these are not their problems; after all, they have their own corruption back home, most recently in the sub-prime mortgage crisis. What is the problem is the lack of trust between the two business cultures. With different values, practices, and institutions, in the context of poor communications, historical anger, and systemic corruption, trust is scarce.

Alternatively, the cultural middle can be a hopeful place where creative efforts are made through compromise to bring two radically different cultures closer so that cooperation can be carried out. This alternative can be seen, for example, in the case of an American purchase of a Chinese state-owned enterprise that maintained a grounds crew of several thousand employees. The Chinese value employment more than the Americans, who value efficiency more than the Chinese. They both compromised. An independent business was set up with start-up funds from the Americans that would sell grounds maintenance to the acquired company as well as in the marketplace. The Chinese maintained some of the employment, the Americans cut costs, and they both appreciated the new entrepreneurial venture.

But typically between American and Chinese businesses there is less compromising and more manning the ramparts in this meeting of two great cultures, one working its way out of oblivion in a tremendous effort of societal transformation, at once finding its past and leaving it further behind, and the other hoping to project its past into the future while fearing it will not be so, due in no small part to the other's rise. As these two great but vastly different cultures collide on Chinese soil, the middleman is found right at the center of this very challenging effort at intercultural cooperation, trying at once to further it along by stopping it in its tracks.

The Chinese middleman was there before the Americans arrived, playing an important role in Chinese (hierarchical) culture, mending slights and inflating face so relations could be maintained and projects developed. But perhaps more to the point, hierarchical culture, real as rain, is impossible. Always in the shadow of power is resistance, and in this case what the Chinese call *guanxi* expands social circuits, installing counterforces in the structure of power itself. Informal networking is at the center of Chinese society, sharing that space with its opposite, authoritarianism. The middleman not only tries to maintain the peace between hierarchy and network, face and friendship, but he is vital to the network itself, introducing new friends, expanding capacities, and getting things done.

With the arrival of the foreigners, in this study the Americans, a second culture appears on the scene with not only vastly different practices for getting things done but vastly different morals for making sense out of what is and ought to be done. The middleman jumps her game, becoming intercultural expert and problem solver. Her trade is no longer just making connections and keeping the peace, but she must now move across two systems of meaning, interpreting one to the other, fixing endless misunderstandings, resolving endless conflicts, ultimately playing a purely instrumental role that forgoes compromise and keeps the cultures apart and whole, doing secretly what must not be done openly in one or both cultures, in order to complete the business transaction.

This research set out to understand ethical and cultural issues in American-Chinese business relations but repeatedly found itself studying the dark arts of the middleman. Because at the center of Chinese-American business relations is trouble in the middle, where shared understanding and trust are in short supply, the middleman steps in to provide understanding and trust, and where that fails, an instrumental fix that makes the relationship possible at all. This book is an effort to understand the middle between Chinese and American cultures, and how they work together with so much historical baggage, power asymmetry, cultural strangeness, and opposing interests.

I would like to thank those who read parts of this book and sent along comments that helped me make improvements. In alphabetical order, they are John Boatright Francis Fukuyama, Qingzhong Kong, Leonard Lynn, Mike Martin, Bill McKinley, Paul Salipante, Michael Santoro, Paul Schroeder, Larry Shotswell, Mike Swain, John Van Maanen, Andy Walder, and Peter Yang.

My Chinese students in China and the United States taught me a great deal about China. In particular my two classes at Shanghai International Studies University were gracious hosts and generous guides during my stay in China. They helped me make initial evaluations of many a data point or vague clue seemingly out of context. In particular I would like to thank Shanshan Gau, James Lee, Iris Ling, Austin Ping, Jane Xingyanheng, Chuanyan Zhang, Dorothy Zhang, and Jesse Zhang.

John Szilagyi, publisher of business and management books at Routledge Publishing, has been wonderful to work with. He was never too pushy, always helpful. I very much appreciate his supportive and light touch. The anonymous reviewers that John put together were very helpful and improved the quality of the final product. Thank you for your professionalism and time.

There were several programs and universities without which this research would not have been possible. The J. William Fulbright Foreign Scholarship Board, which funded my stay in Shanghai, is an outstanding program. It provided not only scholarship funds and placement in a Chinese university but extensive orientation and introduction conferences in the United States before departure and in China upon arrival. In particular, I would like to thank David Adams of the Fulbright Program for this helpful guidance. I would also like to thank the Chinese Ministry of Education for its generous support and for giving me the opportunity to teach and do research in China.

The Chinese university where I taught, Shanghai International Studies University, was very kind and helpful. The staff, both inside the school of management and in the university administration, were good to work with and tried their best to support my efforts. I believe I was the first Fulbright professor to teach at the management school. I hope they learned at least a little bit since I learned so much from them. I would like to thank Dean Angela Yu for her leadership.

I would also like to thank Shanghai University of Finance and Economics for its support while I was in Shanghai and Shanghai Jiao Tong University for its hospitality and interesting discussions. The Chinese university system is developing and I look forward to its continued success in the future.

At the core of my research are the American and Chinese executives who spent so much time and effort trying to help me understand the American-Chinese business relationship. The executives and their companies must remain anonymous. But I greatly appreciate their help and support in enabling me to research this fascinating topic. The research opened up a new world to me, for which I will be forever grateful. I hope this book does the same for others.

The American consulate in Shanghai played an important role in the research by introducing me to a handful of Chinese middlemen in the midst of the research once I discovered their centrality in American-Chinese business relations. Several of these middlemen provided me with key insights into American-Chinese business relations in China.

Finally, I would like to thank Grace Francisco for typing, and Renee Pendleton and Kathy Soltis, who did work on copyediting. Yuting Yan provided some important statistical research. Thank you all.

P A R T

INTRODUCTION

Rationale for and Overview of the Book

The timing was terrible for the Sanlu Dairy Corporation's senior management: After having just been ordered by the government to silence any negative news as the Olympics were about to get under way, the company received irrefutable evidence that its best-selling baby formula product was laced with a deadly industrial chemical.[1] Stuck in the middle between corporate interests and responsibilities on the one hand and the Communist Party's obsession to carry out the games in the best possible light on the other, the board chair ordered a cover-up.

Early the next day, a board meeting was hastily called to approve the executive's decision. Participating in the meeting by phone was a Western executive representing Fonterra, a New Zealand dairy that is a partner and major shareholder in Sanlu. The debate started all over again. The New Zealand executive reported later that after hours of discussion, the board agreed to his demand to reverse the management team's decision and order a full product recall. Despite the vastly different business cultures between China and New Zealand, the Fonterra executive was able to convince the Chinese to put the health of infants over the Communist Party leaders' wishes for China to look spotless as much of the world's attention was focusing on it.

Whatever happened at the board meeting that day, it did not matter. Like all companies in China, indeed all public organizations, the board was part of a giant web-like structure of government officials and, above all, Communist Party committees and overseers. The government of the city where Sanlu was located, Shijiazhuang, and its Communist Party bosses overruled the board and ordered a cover-up of the poisoning threat in order to avoid bringing bad news to the nation's leaders just in their finest hour on the world stage. Hundreds of thousands of babies would become ill, and a few would die.

[1] The account of the Sanlu baby formula scandal presented here follows R. McGregor (2010).

The purpose of this book is to investigate the ethical and cultural aspects of Chinese-American business relations. The term *culture*, as used in this book, is defined as the system of symbols—ideas, ideals, images, notions, standards, in short expressions of any kind—that is historically developed, socially maintained, and individually applied by members of a particular community.[2] The notion of the *cultural middle* will be the central concept used in this investigation. The concept is general; it refers to the difficult social, ideational, and emotional interaction when any two very different cultures attempt to work with each other. Though the notion is general, both the literature and this study's empirical data on ethical and cultural issues in American-Chinese business relations point strongly to specific problems in intercultural relations in China. I think the idea of trouble in the middle has particular moral relevance to cross-cultural business in China because of the Chinese political system.

Intercultural problems can be seen in the Sanlu case. After being informed that local government officials had overruled the Sanlu board, forcing the company to keep a deadly product on the market, Fonterra dithered for weeks until the New Zealand government stepped in and informed the central authorities in Beijing. Fonterra had trouble in the middle; adrift between its values and the Chinese government's desire to squash negative news, it was unable to act.

The Sanlu case also shows a different kind of trouble in the middle inside China itself that is part of the problem Fonterra faced. Once the central authorities in Beijing got wind of the problem—after the Olympics ended—the Chinese government did act. The Sanlu board chair went to prison for life, the Shijiazhuang city mayor and lower officials were fired, the city's Communist Party boss was forced out, and the nation's top administrator in charge of food inspection was forced to resign. All these officials were caught in a dilemma: either squash the news and hurt the nation's children or publicize the news and save the children but fail their superiors' orders. The administrators, all government/Party officials, were stuck in the middle between the Party and Chinese society.

Cover-ups can and do take place in all nations, but not all for the same reasons. In China the ultimate causes of this tragedy were the Party's monopoly power, its insulation from responsibility for its actions, its functioning in a world unto itself, and its shadowy nature behind the government. There is

[2] Geertz 1973

trouble in the middle in China even before the American businesses arrive. Once they do arrive, the considerable cultural differences are only exacerbated by a political situation in which it is unclear who is in charge, the line between business and politics is murky at best, and the reasons behind actions and changes are often not the reasons given.

It is into this labyrinth of political intrigue that American executives arrive, often possessing impersonal financial models and a deep preference for legal resolution of conflict. The trouble in the middle in China is that politics and culture are inseparable. It is in this context that this book analyzes American business culture, Chinese business culture, and how the two try to work with each other in China.

Overview of the Research

1. Research Purpose and Goals. The purpose of this research is to better understand the ethical and cultural assumptions American and Chinese business executives bring to business relationships and how these assumptions affect American-Chinese business relations in China. This understanding will be enhanced by analyses of the relevant literatures and empirical analyses comparing how American and Chinese executives, respectively, perceive the ethical and cultural aspects of doing business in China. Both of these approaches will include analyses of the relationships developed between the two groups, areas where they conflict, and how these conflicts are resolved, or not.

Specific methods will include these: (1) describing and interpreting American business experience in China; (2) describing and interpreting Chinese business experience in China, including experience with Americans; and (3) comparing these two sets of business experience to investigate the relationships between them. At the center of this cultural analysis is a focus on ethical issues,[3] which will involve investigating the different social expectations the two cultures have for business relationships, particularly how they understand and deal with business "corruption" (both business-to-business and business-to-government), with violations of intellectual property rights, and with other business problems and processes; and how they deal with each

---

[3] The field of comparative management has largely neglected ethical issues (Witcomb, Erdener, and Li 1998).

other in regard to these issues. Business corruption in China is broadly seen as a huge problem by both foreigners and the majority of Chinese citizens, with widely varying accounts as to whether it is getting better or worse. American estimates claim it costs U.S. business tens of billions of dollars and tens of thousands of jobs each year.[4]

In addition to providing a detailed description of American and Chinese business experience of business ethics issues and how the two deal with each other in terms of these issues,[5] this study will evaluate existing theory in the area of business ethics and develop new substantive ("grounded") theory, presenting an original concept that arose from study data, that of the *cultural middle.* The cultural middle is the emotional and intellectual space between two cultures, where negotiation, compromise, miscommunication, and conflict take place.

In this context, it is important to note that a great number of business relations and transactions between American and Chinese businesses in China involve third-party "middlemen."[6] This fact has occasionally been noted in the literature but has been given little attention conceptually

---

[4] House of Representatives Committee on Oversight and Government Reform 2009.

[5] Social science descriptions of this sort have not been carried out and are badly needed as a base for research, theory development, and practice in this area. Tsui and colleagues (2004) reported that in 104 papers on Chinese firms published in 20 management journals between January 2000 and June 2003, scholars primarily used existing management theories developed from studies of Western firms in developed economies. Detailed descriptions of business practices in China are needed to improve our understanding of the facts as well as to provide systematized data for theory development. The situation is even more urgent in the area of business ethics, where what little research has been carried out has paid little attention to identifying types of issues that arise in China or how Western firms respond (Brand and Slater 2003). There are reasons for this dearth of data on Chinese firms. As Tsui and others (2004) pointed out, weakly institutionalized Chinese firms and deeply institutionalized interpersonal networks make field research in Chinese firms challenging at best.

[6] China has a long history with middlemen (Redding and Witt 2007). Middlemen were used by colonial powers to help negotiate an environment that was for them quite foreign. During World War II, the Japanese, too, utilized middlemen to run the Chinese economy. Even earlier in Chinese cultural history, middlemen emerged to bridge the gap between the government and society. Government behavior was often unpredictable. To cope with an uncertain environment and the need to co-opt government officials, middlemen began to appear, specializing in what Hofstede and colleagues (2010) called the management of "double trust," inserting oneself between two parties to lower conflict and risk, increase communication, and advance exchange relations. Middlemen are a key adaptive mechanism in low-trust societies characterized by massive and arbitrary government power.

or empirically.[7] If the idea of the cultural middle refers to the ideational and emotional "space" or interaction where two cultures attempt to make sense of each other; then the middleman is a person who specializes in working in this space, in helping each culture understand the other. Hence, analysis of the data on middlemen will be an important source of insight into the phenomenon of the cultural middle.

In the cultural middle, neither culture has priority. Yet cultural disconnectedness must be resolved in this liminal space for business activity to proceed. The problem is at once cultural and practical, but the solution is often entirely practical. Normally a compromise is *not* worked out; the middleman keeps the contending parties apart,[8] absorbing the cultural conflict, providing a third-party solution, that is, doing something inconsistent with one or both cultures behind the scenes. Being a middleman is a "Don't ask, don't tell" function.

In my research on comparing American and Chinese executives' perceptions of doing business in China, especially with each other, the Chinese middleman makes an important appearance. Indeed, one of the major turning points in the field research was when a Chinese consultant educated in the United States, whom I met through a university club in Shanghai,[9] told me,

---

[7] Using mainstream American management theories—transactions cost theory, agency theory, and resource dependency theory—Peng (1998) studied six American export intermediaries. He found that American firms, especially small firms lacking resources, faced daunting challenges to doing business overseas, including the high cost of finding the right transaction partner, negotiating a sales contract involving language and culture differences, monitoring transaction performance for contract compliance, and enforcing compliance when problems arise. The work of intermediaries can substitute for the firm's carrying out its own export functions. Middlemen's knowledge of foreign markets, knowledge of local language and culture, and experience with foreign negotiations can lower the cost and risk of exporting. However, the firm-intermediary relationship is not without risks of its own (Chintakananda et al. 2009). High degrees of information asymmetry and uncertainty may develop between the two parties, leading to exploitation of one party by the other. The exporter can find itself facing monopoly pricing, loss of control over its foreign distribution channels, or both; the intermediary may find its investment disappear as the exporter uses the intermediary-developed relationships to start its own export functions. In my research, "the intermediary" will be examined in its ethical and cultural aspects with specific attention to the bicultural nature of Chinese-American business relations.

[8] Indeed, it is in the intermediary's interest to keep the foreign and domestic firms separate to maximize its own value (Peng 1998).

[9] This is a good example of an incipient *guanxi* (informal connections that provide assistance) relationship. Because of our shared club membership and university affiliation, I was able to call on this consultant for help. The fact that I was leaving China a few months after we met put limits on how much support he would offer because I would not be able to return the favor. The *guanxi* was, so to speak, nipped in the bud.

after hearing about my research focus on American-Chinese cross-cultural business relations, that I should interview middlemen because they have insight into both cultures and are right in the middle of negotiating and resolving the conflicting demands.[10] Sixteen of 33 interviews with Chinese executives I conducted in China in 2007 and five of the 14 I conducted in 2010 were with executives who spent at least part of their time performing middleman functions—that is, individuals who made a business out of helping American and Chinese businesses close the gaps in communications and in conflicting demands, whether over price, time, or bribes to close a deal. Importantly, in terms of bribery, the middleman is involved in morally and culturally conflicted activities. In other words, the middleman is a moral broker of sorts who enables two business cultures with incompatible ethical and legal commitments and constraints to do business together. The description and analysis of the degree of incompatibility and how it is managed is an important contribution of this research.

The prototypical case of middleman behavior is bribe paying. American multinational corporations are, by U.S. law, not permitted to pay bribes to foreign government officials (except to get low-level officials to perform their legitimate responsibilities), and corporate policies are often even more restrictive. In many situations in China, however, it is impossible to do business without paying bribes. In the prototypical case, an American company sells goods to a middleman at a price that enables him to resell the goods to the Chinese buyer at a price acceptable to the buyer, pay bribes to all who require them, and make a profit himself. This is not an easy job, since the middleman, being in the middle, is under pressure from both sides.[11]

The empirical data I collected on the experiences of middlemen have enabled me to develop the concept of the cultural middle with special attention to the ethical aspect. In American-Chinese business relations, the middleman can remove ethical conflict from the cultural middle by removing ethics. The middleman removes the action viewed by Americans as unethical

---

[10] Middlemen also provide practical functions, such as translation and interpretation services, and social and political networking; they can assist in negotiating government regulations and other demands.

[11] Redding and Witt (2007) described the Chinese economy as dominated by large foreign firms that control brands (e.g., Nike) or distribution (e.g., Wal-Mart), and source their supplies from Chinese manufacturers through the use of intermediaries. They argued that much of the value added is captured by intermediaries. According to my interviews, intermediary profit margins peaked years ago and have been in decline, most notably in textiles and apparel.

from American hands and in this way is supposedly removing American responsibility for it. The concept of the cultural middle is used throughout the book to investigate the cultural and ethical implications of the middleman function. Ultimately, however, it is shown that the middleman function is destructive of ethics and culture due to the nearly purely instrumental drive (by all parties involved) to complete the transaction and secure a profit.

In summary, the concept of the cultural middle is the central conceptual contribution this study makes in terms of ethical and cultural issues in American-Chinese business relations. It also has important implications more generally for the theory and practice of "international business ethics." These various levels of theory and practice are explored in the book.

2. The Concept of Culture. Though the business relationship between the United States and China has grown dramatically and is of great importance to each country, surprisingly there has been only limited comparative analysis of the two business cultures.[12] Without understanding the two cultures and their differences, one cannot understand the complex way they interact in the business relationship. As noted, the concept of culture used in this book is defined as the system of symbols through which individuals make sense of the world in which they live and work. Culture is more or less shared among community members enabling them to become intelligible to each other and coordinate their joint efforts. More specifically, the book will focus on *moral culture*, the beliefs about right and wrong, good and bad, that individuals use to develop trust between them.[13]

Francis Fukuyama used a similar framework to carry out a comparative analysis of economic systems.[14] He found that business based on trust comes in two forms: large, autonomous organizations based on society-wide, generalized trust—what he called "spontaneous associability"—most commonly seen in the United States, Germany, and Japan; or family-dominated organizations, usually limited in size because trust is limited to family members, as can be seen in Hong Kong. The ideal economic system has both kinds of trust because it can create both kinds of trust-based businesses: small, flexible, entrepreneurial firms where trust is based on personal relationships and large, bureaucratic organizations capable of complex divisions of labor because generalized trust makes reliable relationships with strangers possible.

[12] See Redding and Witt 2007; Fukuyama 1995.
[13] Rieff 1987; Feldman 2004.
[14] Fukuyama 1995.

The key to creating trust is shared values. Societies differ widely in both the kinds of values they share and the degree to which they share them and thus differ widely in how their workers and managers relate to each other. This disparity can be an important influence on the type of industrial structure that emerges. Without generalized trust, for example, organizations remain small, built on the personal relationship model, or must rely on government control or foreign direct investment to build the large, complex organizations needed to concentrate capital, exploit economies of scale, and create highly complex manufacturing processes or extensive distribution networks. High complexity means high value added,[15] but it requires size, and size requires trust.

Generalized trust in a society is based on the wide diffusion of social virtues throughout a population. The social virtues of honesty, reliability, cooperativeness, and sense of duty are central, being the glue that enables a society to decentralize and create a profusion of intermediate institutions, including businesses that make possible cooperation on a broad scale. Though governments play important roles, in societies with the most effective businesses, autonomous, self-managing organizations and networks, are central. Trust and interpersonal reliability replace hierarchy to a considerable degree in such countries as Germany and Japan, where, compared with England and France, for example, organizational authority in factories is pushed to the lowest levels.

Trust-based decentralization leads to the most effective organizations for several reasons. High-trust interpersonal relations create a strong sense of solidarity among workers. Workers who care about their colleagues and the organization are invested in the organization's success and need less supervision. Their hard work, motivation, reliability, and will to contribute lead to greater efficiency and lower costs. In addition, an organization of decentralized, motivated workers is inherently more flexible than a top-down culture. The organization is more adaptive, innovative, and accepting of change. All in all, the social virtues create dedicated and motivated work groups, without whom large, innovative organizations cannot be built.

It is important to note that the social virtues are not primarily based on rational choice but are maintained in social traditions.[16] That is, they are individual habits broadly held in a society, socially inculcated from one generation to the next through families, schools, and interpersonal relations. They

---

[15] Redding and Witt 2007.
[16] MacIntyre 1984.

are the basis for moral community and, I argue, the basis for decentralized cooperation on any scale above direct personal relations. When one knows others share the same core values, trust is possible without a direct personal relationship.

For Fukuyama, the most dynamic world economies combine the liberal context of the free market with the reliability and honor of moral community.[17] Without the former, decentralization is impossible; without the latter, decentralization is handcuffed for lack of trust.

Low-trust societies, on the other hand, have all experienced strong political centralization in their history—centralization that eliminated all alternative forms of organization.[18] Such a history certainly can be found in China, where dynastic centralization was established in the third century B.C., only to be replaced by totalitarian Communism. The independence of moral community, resulting in autonomous, self-managed organizations, was neither possible nor tolerated. Generalized trust did not develop in China.

China, like the Soviet Union and numerous other politically dominated societies, has an undeveloped civil society, a missing middle. Most, if not all, large businesses are state controlled. Low societal trust results in small, weak, and inefficient private businesses. This state of affairs relates directly to a dominating structure of government power, characterized by many corrupt and ineffective officials, as seen in both the academic and practitioner literature and my own field data on China. This is not to say Chinese private businesses do not have strengths. They are entrepreneurial, hardworking, easy to set up and take down, flexible, and highly adaptive to changing circumstances. But because of its intolerance of separate centers of power, the state maintains a near monopoly on large organizations,[19] keeping private businesses out of complex, capital-intensive sectors of the economy like aerospace, semiconductors, automobiles, and energy.

Small businesses themselves are not necessarily a constraint on wealth creation, as can be seen in northern Italy, Taiwan, and Hong Kong.[20] Small firms can organize labor-intensive activities in markets demanding flexibility, innovation, and fast-changing products, perhaps more effectively than large ones. In industries like apparel, plastics, electronic components, and

[17] Fukuyama 1995.
[18] France and Russia, for example (Fukuyama 1995).
[19] R. McGregor 2010.
[20] Fukuyama 1995.

furniture, smallness is an advantage. Networks between small firms can create economies of scale while avoiding the costly overhead and agency problems of large organizations. Despite having enacted decentralizing reforms in the 1980s, China began in the 1990s to emphasize the growth of state-owned enterprises (See Appendix Two).

The United States, in Fukuyama's framework, is an intermediate case between the high-trust cultures of Germany and Japan, with their large, trust-based organizations, and the lower-trust cultures of Italy, France, Taiwan, and Hong Kong, with their predominance of small (family-based) private businesses.[21] The United States has a long tradition of voluntary organizations, wherein individuals subordinate their interests to those of the organization, resulting in a robust business sector with organizations of all sizes. Also in contrast to the Chinese, Americans have strong anti-statist traditions, their distrust of concentrated power applying to business as well as the state, as can be seen in the Sherman Antitrust Act.

Americans, highly social, were the first to develop the modern corporate structure in the 19th century. Still today, Americans are good at creating large private organizations with committed workers, such as Microsoft and Google. Unlike in Japan or Germany, however, relations between firms in the United States tend to be competitive. Networking is weakly developed. Paradoxically, Americans are highly individualistic and competitive yet capable of forming highly cohesive organizations requiring trust and extensive cooperation.

Citing the work of Robert Putnam, Fukuyama argued that trust in the United States deteriorated badly in the second half of the 20th century.[22] As evidence, he pointed to the deterioration of family life quantified in the highest divorce rate in the world; the breakdown in neighborhoods, churches, and workplaces; the great increases in litigation; and increased expenditures for police and jails. Redding and Witt, however, argued that trust in laws, regulations, and professions is still high in the United States and is key to the U.S. economy's effectiveness.[23] There is evidence that even trust in these areas has declined.[24] In any case, laws, regulations, and professions cannot replace

---

[21] Fukuyama 1995.

[22] Fukuyama 1995.

[23] Redding and Witt 2007.

[24] According to a 2011 Gallop poll survey, Americans' trust in their institutions is mostly down from historical averages (Jones 2011).

general interpersonal trust as the glue of cooperation.[25] Culture is internal and requires emotional commitment that law cannot generate.[26] Indeed, many laws advancing individual rights in the second half of the 20th century have actually undermined community.[27] The unique American blend of individualism and moral community that has contributed to the plethora of private organizations could therefore be in some danger.

In this research, I will use the concept of *moral culture* to investigate the roles of trust, cooperation, and conflict in the American and Chinese field data, and as a framework to compare the ethical and cultural aspects of the two countries' business systems and their interactions. As the literature implies, cultural conflict between the two systems is common. Americans seek trust in stable legal and governmental institutions; to a considerable extent, in China they are disappointed. The Chinese, with their intense reliance on personal relationships and distrust of strangers, feel little obligation toward foreigners.

The foregoing description does not exhaust the cultural disconnects between the two business systems. They will be explored in more detail in later chapters, but a summary review of key issues will be presented here. An important point to underscore is that the differences between the two cultures are old and deep. In a study of differences between Asian and Western thought, Richard E. Nisbett found that cultural differences between the two civilizations have been more or less stable for thousands of years.[28] Greek culture, one of the origins of Western culture, developed a strong sense of personal agency and individual identity. Ancient Chinese culture, on the other hand, emphasized social harmony and defining self through relations to others. From these foundational differences many other cultural differences follow.

Most Western languages are agentic, formulating the self as the center of action. This linguistic characteristic carries over prominently into American management theory, where one of the central theoretical orientations is "agency theory." Agency theory assumes the individual is an autonomous actor and liable to conflicting interest with other actors. Eastern languages, in

---

[25] Fukuyama 1995.

[26] Feldman 2004.

[27] For example, the Housing Act of 1949 mandated slum clearance but replaced slums with expensive high rises that priced many residents out of the community, increased crime, and demoralized residents (Rusk 1999).

[28] Nisbett 2004.

contrast, are nonagentic. They are topic-prominent, emphasizing context over subject or person. These are not just conceptual differences. They literally mean Chinese and Americans see the same reality differently. A Chinese person will, in general, understand a situation in terms of its relation to important others; an American will tend to experience the situation in terms of his or her own goals.

The collective orientation of the Chinese leads them to see the world as complex. They are sensitive to the variety of components in any situation, the relationships between components, and the liability to change given the complexity. Americans, on the other hand, focused on their own goals, block out much of the situational complexity. This gives Americans a much higher sense of control because they focus like a rifleman. The Chinese do not have this sense of control. Indeed, their sensitivity to complexity leads them to coordinate their actions with those of others. It would be hard for them to do otherwise because it is difficult for them to separate objects from the environment. These differences make it challenging for Chinese and Americans to cooperate because the (abstract) goal modeling of the Americans has little relevance for the (concrete) context-minded Chinese.

The different emphasis between American abstraction and Chinese concreteness has several other important implications. The Chinese do not draw a sharp distinction between truth and morality, whereas Americans assume a wide gulf between objectivity and value judgments. To an American, something can be true but bad. Because of their unconcern with abstraction, this distinction has little relevance to the Chinese.[29] They are more interested in reasonableness than reason, that is, in context-specific judgments than logical (abstract) precision. The Chinese tend to favor typicality, plausibility, and desirability over logical analysis.[30] This leads to both communication and decision-making conflicts with Americans, who bury their value judgments in financial analysis,[31] finding Chinese social concerns distracting, inappropriate, and "unprofessional."

Nowhere do American and Chinese cultural differences stand out more than in the area of ethics. Because the Chinese focus on the social whole, they

---

[29] The full extent of Chinese disregard for generalization can be seen in the language, which uses 3,000 different characters to denote a wide range of concrete images, while Western languages use only about 30 separate abstract letters, which are continuously recombined to make words.

[30] Nisbett 2004.

[31] MacIntyre 1984.

tend to emphasize the individual's duties to the group rather than, like Americans, who value individual dignity, emphasizing individual rights.[32] For the Chinese, "rights" belong to the collectivity, a notion that leads to an emphasis on moral virtues, not individual rights. Moral virtues evaluate individual behavior in terms of how well behavior is integrated into the social whole, not in terms of what rights the individual has within the group. Differences arise in how the "social whole" is defined. Americans expect adherence to universal (abstract) principles—wrong is wrong—but for the collective-thinking Chinese, wrong is wrong in context. The Chinese feel fewer moral obligations outside their primary groups.[33] Americans are surprised to find Chinese virtues do not always apply to them. That Chinese can be virtuous is undeniable, as can be seen in their loyalty, trustworthiness, reliability, and self-sacrifice within their networks. Americans, expecting impersonal consistency, mistakenly tend to see the Chinese as lacking in ethics. For the Chinese, it would be unethical *not* to favor in-groups over others.

The differences in abstraction versus concreteness and individualism versus collectivism also determine differences in how Americans and Chinese approach and resolve conflicts. Americans tend to think in terms of universal principles of justice that can determine right and wrong, winners and losers.[34] The Chinese, on the other hand, seek hostility reduction and compromise. Since they value collective harmony over individual rights and abstract principles, the Chinese see wise conflict resolution as improving relationships in the case at hand. Typically the Chinese involve a middleman whose goal is not fairness but conflict reduction through compromise. To make decisions on a case-by-case basis without a consistent standard appears arbitrary and unethical to Americans. To ignore the specific case in favor of general rules seems wrong-headed, rigid, and inhuman to the Chinese.[35] Because of their collectivism, the Chinese are willing to sacrifice fairness for harmony; because of their individualism, the Americans are not.

[32] The wide gap on the individualism-collectivism range was captured in the Individualism Index of Hofstede and colleagues (2010). Out of 76 countries, the United States ranked 1, China 60 (1 = most individualistic).

[33] In collectivist societies, people make exclusive distinctions between in-groups and out-groups. In China, in-groups are limited to family, schoolmates, work colleagues, village members, and *guanxi* relations.

[34] Nisbett 2004.

[35] In regard to focusing on principles over people, the Confucian Mencius (372–289 B.C.) said, "It is the way of animals to have neither father nor brother" (quoted in Bendix 1960, 139).

In summary, this book uses the concept of moral culture to analyze the American and Chinese field data, the role of trust in each business culture, and how the two systems cooperate and conflict in their efforts to do business together in China. Recall that I defined *moral culture* as the system of symbols individuals use to organize the moral demands they make upon themselves so that they become intelligible and trustworthy to each other. When two different business cultures attempt to work together, they need some core, overlapping understanding and agreement on moral demands: the boundaries of practices, the means to negotiate problems, and the ability to generate trust. Without such an overlap, business is fraught with difficulty; a cultural middle is created and expands until potential business partners become like islands with dangerous waters between them. This perspective of moral culture and the cultural middle is of particular relevance in regard to American-Chinese business relations because the cultures are so different, the relationship history so challenging, the change going on in China so radical, and the stakes for both countries so high.

Given this background and foreground, this research seeks to contribute to understanding how the two cultures work together, how they generate conflicts that challenge cooperation or trade, and how these conflicts are addressed, or not. More specifically, the research concentrates on the moral assumptions, moral traditions, and moral frameworks in use, and the range of acceptable compromise of these within each culture. It seeks to illuminate, in the collision between the two cultures, what ethics are shared; what ones managed through compromise and adaptation; what ones rejected and condemned, limiting cooperation and relationship development; and what ones, through the middleman, removed or ignored in the drive toward profit.

It is important to understand the limits of shared moral culture because cooperation can go on outside morality, resulting in higher prices for consumers, lower product quality, issues with product safety, degradation of both countries' business cultures, and attempts by Americans to address problems through the "back door," thus further undermining ethical and legal institutions. Business ethics has economic, political, environmental, and health implications. To better understand American and Chinese business relations in terms of business ethics contributes to understanding the moral challenges and limits of international business, how they are managed, and what can be done to improve them.

The concept of moral culture can make a contribution to the understanding of American-Chinese business relations because both business ethics and international business ethics (especially the latter) involve cultural context, which situates business decision making in an ideational, cognitive, and emotional field that influences how issues are perceived, evaluated, and thus acted on. Indeed, in international business ethics, culture is heightened to the core issue because the problem is exactly how two different cultures communicate, cooperate, trade, and compete in an ethical manner when they have two different definitions of ethics. This research seeks to show the important contribution the concept of moral culture can make to understanding the relationship between culture and international business ethics. The literature on international business ethics is dominated by economic and philosophical models, with little empirically based cultural analysis.[36] The literature on the ethics of American-Chinese business relations is practically nonexistent.[37]

3. Historical Context. To accomplish the goal of carrying out a comparative analysis of ethical and cultural issues in American-Chinese business relations, this study will analyze the historical context from which the current situation has unfolded. It will begin with a brief discussion of Chinese culture and society during the long dynastic history, concentrating on the implications of Confucian hierarchy for social order. Next it will present a brief discussion of Communism, focusing on government-society relations. Particularly important in this regard is the Cultural Revolution, a decisive event in the youth of many current business and political leaders.[38] This will be followed by a brief discussion of the history of cross-cultural relations between China and the West in China, attempting to sketch the difficulty and distance in this history.

Historical context is an important part of the interpretive framework used throughout the book. For example, it is central to understanding the key role of *guanxi* in Chinese business and how Americans, coming out of a legalistic and individualistic background, respond to it. An even more fundamental aspect of the Chinese business system with deep historical roots is the dominating role of the Chinese government. Historical context is an important influence on how the two different business cultures interpret and manage relations with the government. These and other issues are framed in terms of

---

[36] See Chapter 2 for a literature review and discussion of this area.

[37] See Chapter 7 for a literature review and discussion of business relations between Western and Chinese firms from a cultural perspective.

[38] Egri and Ralston 2004.

historical context and discussed from different perspectives—for example, ethical, cultural, political, and economic—in nearly every chapter.

4. *Practical Contributions.* In terms of practical outcomes, this research should help managers, particularly American managers, realize the complexity of Chinese business culture and how it differs from American business culture.[39] I aim to encourage American executives to pause in their ethical and social evaluations of the Chinese, viewing their behavior inside Chinese culture, history, and current conditions to understand the Chinese in terms of their own lives and values, not only the experiences, expectations, and values of Americans. Making both cultures more understandable to each other is a central goal of this research.

A second practical goal of the research is to encourage American executives to consider the ethical significance of using third parties to pay bribes for them. American executives see this as a way to avoid legal culpability under the Foreign Corrupt Practices Act. However, these arrangements are usually carried out by lower-level managers, outside the earshot of higher-level executives, especially top executives back in the United States. This shows that these practices are seen as ethically tainted even by those executives operating with the ethics-as-law model. It is a goal of this research to encourage American executives to reflect on the cultural and ethical costs to their employees and companies of bribery through middlemen. This practice does not build moral culture but instead undermines it by showing that economic ends justify immoral means. It also puts a detour in American-Chinese relations, bypassing the opportunity to develop direct, personal relationships based on trust.

Research Strategy

This research was carried out using an interpretive methodology, following in the tradition of the sociologist Max Weber, the anthropologist Clifford Geertz, and management scholar Melville Dalton. The research method is to immerse oneself in the social system under study over an extended period of

---

[39] For the sake of presentation, I speak here in generalities. Clearly, Chinese or American "business culture" is just a cover term for a range of beliefs and behaviors, some contradicting or inconsistent with others. Nonetheless, the terms are justified by an overlapping set of traditions more or less continuous within each society. Perhaps the central sets of traditions that distinguish the two countries concern collectivism versus individualism.

time in order to develop a descriptive and explanatory framework that is used to discover and make some sense of the key themes motivating the social setting. It is through my immersion in the Cleveland and Shanghai business environments that I discovered and began to make sense of the difficult cultural middle between the two groups of business executives that made business exchange and cooperation so difficult and problematic. The concept of the cultural middle, a concept drawn directly from my field experience and further developed through review of related social science literature, is the organizing principle by which I developed a pattern model of the key themes in the field data. Moving back and forth between the concept of the cultural middle and the field data organized in the pattern model allows the concept to be continuously developed as the field data on ethical and cultural issues in American-Chinese business relations are explained. See Appendix One for more detailed discussion of research methods.

The research is centered in Shanghai, China. Cheng Li has referred to Shanghai as the "pacesetter" city for China.[40] In this sense, it is not representative of all of China, which is, after all, a country of regions. This study compares American-Chinese business relations primarily through the study of the perceptions and experiences of Cleveland and Shanghai business executives. It tells of American-Chinese business relations, but the unique aspects of Cleveland and Shanghai limit the generalizability of the research. Shanghai is the most modern city in China and historically one of the most open to foreign influence. It is also more economically advanced than most of China. Indeed, for these reasons Shanghai attracts the largest amount of foreign direct investment of any city in China.[41] Hence, Shanghai is an excellent choice to study American-Chinese business relations. For a more detailed discussion of Shanghai's economic and political environment, see Appendix Two.

The data were collected through focused interviews with key executives, company visits, company documents, and the experience of living and teaching in Shanghai. The 84 interviews carried out in 2006, 2007, and 2010 averaged between 2 and 2.5 hours each. A handful of the interviewees became key informants and were interviewed multiple times. Living and working in Shanghai in 2007 gave me the opportunity to have my own work experience in China and was invaluable to compare with the data I was collecting through interviews and observations. See Appendix Three for a detailed discussion of the data.

[40] C. Li 2009.
[41] Huang 2008.

It was in the middle of the fieldwork that I learned that Chinese middlemen had unparalleled knowledge of Chinese-American business relations because it was their specialty to negotiate and manage the conflicts between them. I then redirected a large number of interviews to Chinese middlemen, and the research was greatly enriched. Not only did the middlemen's working between the Chinese and Americans enable me to increase my knowledge of the cultural middle, but I learned that the phenomenon of the middleman was a window into Chinese culture generally. Middlemen have been common throughout Chinese history because the culture's collective nature puts a premium on harmony. Middlemen are often used to settle conflicts in order to maintain the collective good. They are also of central importance for expanding and maintaining networks that play a crucial role in protecting the population from a predatory government and a culture that puts a premium on hierarchy. Thus, their role in Chinese-American relations is merely an intensification of deep themes in Chinese culture and institutions. See Appendix Four for a discussion of middlemen's functions and roles in Chinese-American business relations.

In the chapters that follow, the concept of the cultural middle will be used to explore several key themes in American-Chinese business relations. Because the cultures are so different, the changes in China so enormous, and the history between China and the West so fraught with difficulty, trust and even communications are difficult. American individualism and Chinese collectivism often make it difficult, to borrow an image from Wittgenstein, for the two peoples to find their feet with each other. Miscommunications and misunderstanding from both sides are common. These phenomena will be explored in the literature and empirical data with regard to business-to-business relations, business-to-government relations, and intellectual property rights. Special emphasis will be given to cultural conflict, how the differences between the two cultures give rise to conflict, and how it is resolved or not. At the core of the book is the issue of corruption, which gives rise to a great deal of conflict. Cultural aspects of corruption will be analyzed, but the analysis will include economic, political, historical, and legal dimensions.

2

Trouble in the Middle

The Ethics of Cross-Cultural Business Relations

The dichotomy between universal moral truths and ethical relativism closes off much more fruitful approaches that recognize the paradoxical tension that exists between them.[1] Assuming such a thing as life itself from which all human creatures try to scratch out an existence does not preclude us from recognizing that we do so in different places, at different times, in different ways, with different mind-sets. The abstractness of philosophical reasoning needs to be tethered to the everyday activities wherein moral decisions actually get made if we are to understand one another and get along in a diverse world.

Such it is for ethics in business and, more to the point, for ethical relations between different business cultures, especially ones that are vastly different, as is the case between those of the United States and China. It is in this context that I would like to reintroduce the concept of the "cultural middle," the ideational space between two established cultures where they can potentially work to understand each other. When things are not going well, the cultural middle is a place of conflict, miscommunication, and misunderstanding; when things are working well, it is a place of adoption and fusion, where cultures can somehow work with each other, each making sense of the other in its own terms, the only way sense can be made. One does not become the other but somehow, short of agreeing on universal truths, finds the other not so strange but enough like itself that some categories can more or less be shared and recognition of the other through one's own categories can be made.

This chapter will bring this line of thinking, using the concept of the cultural middle, to bear on a review of the literature on "international

---

[1] Geertz 1983.

business ethics." It will begin with the business ethics literature that deals explicitly with culture, exploring the implications different cultures have for business ethics. This will lead to an examination of how business ethicists have dealt with the universalism-localism puzzle, the major questions that have been raised, and the answers given. It will then take a look at how business ethicists have evaluated the international business system, with special attention to the role of multinational corporations (MNCs) and the explosive growth of the phenomena often summarized as "globalization." This will be followed by a review of how business ethicists have debated the ethical responsibilities of MNCs and the various practices they use to address ethical issues. The chapter will end with a discussion and critique of the literature on international business ethics from the point of view of the concept of the "cultural middle," further developing the concept and demonstrating its usefulness for understanding relations between culturally different business systems.

To provide an empirical backdrop for this analysis, I will use American-Chinese business relations from which to draw my primary examples, though the concept of the cultural middle can be used to explore relations between any cultures. With that said, two distinct cultural phenomena must be mentioned about business in China. First, though found in all business systems and especially in emerging markets,[2] middlemen are pervasive in American-Chinese business relations in China. Middlemen are mostly Chinese people who speak both English and Chinese, know something of both business cultures, and sell their services as intermediaries to bridge the cultural and business problems Chinese and Americans face in attempting to do business with each other. The middleman is particularly relevant to the study of the "cultural middle" because her specialty is to operate within it.

The second issue that must be mentioned about China's business culture is that, like the economy itself, it is emerging. So this is not a story about relations between two established business cultures, say the United States and Japan. In China the "business culture" is changing fast, its future uncertain; indeed, given the central role played by the Chinese government in business it is an open question whether the idea of "business culture" aptly applies. This uncertainty has profound implications for the applicability of the concept of the "cultural middle" because the concept assumes two established business cultures, whereas in this case there is an established business culture

---

[2] Chintakananda et al. 2009.

and an emerging one, "emerging" under and along with the Chinese government.[3] But this circumstance leads back to the role of the middleman and the concept of the cultural middle, because it is exactly the differences in the China market that bring into strong relief the conceptual and practical challenges of doing business between cultures.

International Business Ethics and Business Cultures

1. Ethics, Business, and Culture. There is no international consensus on standards for business conduct.[4] This is hardly surprising. Velasquez states that contemporary ethical theory is not capable of offering moral principles that can even theoretically address moral differences that arise in cross-cultural contexts.[5] The goal is to create a conversation that leads to consensus, but to get to a consensus on, say, an appropriate concept of justice, people from different cultures will have to bring their cultures closer to each other. They will have to share some common assumptions. The situation is paradoxical: To develop consensus, consensus is required. In practice, this dance toward consensus has not been easy. It requires profound cultural change for one side or the other, or both.

In any case, consensus can go only so far. People must be able to respect cultural differences; Donaldson calls this respect a crucial ethical practice.[6] At the end of the day, decisions must be made in a cross-cultural context where there will never be a perfect cultural consensus. A perfect consensus would truly require the end of history, which is a fairy tale. Nonetheless, people must be willing to go some way toward finding or creating something in common. Creating something in common requires adoption by one side or the other, or fusion, where previously there had only been strangeness. One ethical principle that can contribute to the creation of commonality comes from Confucian ethics, which subordinates economic policy and practice to

---

[3] In the case of the meeting of an established culture and an emerging (weaker) one, the established culture will dominate, in keeping with the enormous role of power in relations between societies. In the case under discussion, however, the tables are somewhat turned because this study focuses on the American-Chinese business relationship in China and because of the central role of the Chinese government in the Chinese business system.

[4] Donaldson 1996.

[5] Velasquez 2000.

[6] Donaldson 1996.

how best to promote a humane community.[7] Confucian humanism, or some type of humanism, is needed to encourage business competitors to seek moral agreement.

The situation in practice, though, is far from simple. Business cultures are very different. For example, in a survey asking if profit is the only goal of business, 40 percent of Americans answered yes while only 8 percent of Japanese did so.[8] Perhaps the central issue where Western and Asian cultures differ is the degree of individualism versus collectivism.[9] Take for example the Western emphasis on "human rights." It assumes some level of individualism independent from the community. "Rights" are defined in terms of personal goals, personal welfare, and the ability to choose without regard to the community.[10] These assumptions are, however, shared by only a minority of societies.[11] In Confucian societies, for example, there is little or no conception of individual rights. In Asia, rights inhere in the collectivity.

Santoro cites a study that found Western companies doing business in China influenced the Chinese in terms of economic prosperity, merit-based hiring, information sharing and teamwork, and leadership values, and that these practices had an "elective affinity" with human rights.[12] In other words, American firms can bring the Chinese around to Western values. On the one hand, this is an interesting example of cultural change whereby one culture adopts the cultural practices of the other. This kind of influence is undoubtedly going on in China. One the other hand, thousands of years of Chinese culture are not going to disappear. Instead of an "elective affinity" for human rights, a syncretic process bringing together elements of both cultures is both more likely to resolve cultural differences and more sound.[13]

East and West may seem to share a commitment to utilitarianism, yet closer inspection reveals two different conceptions of utilitarianism. In the

[7] Koehn 2001.

[8] Donaldson and Dunfee 1999.

[9] In Hofstede and colleagues' (2010) Individualism Index, out of 76 countries, the United States ranked first, the United Kingdom third, Germany 19th, Japan 36th, China 60th, and South Korea 65th, for example.

[10] Velasquez 2000.

[11] Nisbett 2004.

[12] Santoro 2009.

[13] Outside of scientific knowledge, syncretism is the most positive outcome possible when two cultures clash (Shils 1981)—an idea captured in the old saw that cultures never die, they get married.

West, utilitarianism bases value in the individual. A decision that leads to the greatest happiness for the greatest number of individuals is ethical. A democratic ethos can be seen here. In China, however, the Communists make decisions based on the collective good with much less emphasis on aggregating individual happiness. The collective good is understood more in terms of the nation as a whole, with individualism as a subsidiary concern.

The principle of justice, likewise, is subject to two different conceptions in Western and Asian business cultures. What constitutes a just business exchange in terms of benefits and costs? Western cultures emphasize the relation between benefits and individual effort. The exchange is just if the benefits are seen as adequate to the effort. Eastern cultures, however, put a much stronger emphasis on equality. The exchange is fair if the benefits are more or less equally distributed between the participants.

Thus "international business ethics" is a misleading phrase. Ethics are embedded in cultures. And the basic orientations of Eastern and Western cultures have been stable for thousands of years.[14] This is why, to avoid intractable cultural issues, international business conflicts are usually addressed through legal agreements negotiated by governments. Often, however, as is the case in China, the cultures still hold sway and the legal agreements are far from satisfactory. Hence, cross-cultural management skills remain very important.

2. *Localism versus Universalism.* Ethicists have approached the cultural divide problem in a number of ways. At the center of these approaches is the debate between the integrity of local culture and the importance of universal truths. Communitarians have argued that local traditions and cultures are the source of core values and should take precedence over abstract notions of rights or justice.[15] Werhane has been particularly sensitive to the tension between economic growth and cultural integrity.[16] She argues that business activity must be modified so as not to damage local cultural integrity and the social goods it values. Economic growth cannot ethically assume that it trumps all other goods; it must respect goods as locally defined. For example, host-country employees should not be forced to follow all the values and

[14] Nisbett 2004.
[15] Etzioni 1993.
[16] Werhane 2000.

policies of foreign corporations if they conflict with local values.[17] Foreign corporations must adjust their systems to consider local traditions.[18]

Sensitivity to local traditions immediately raises ethical issues. How does a company respect local traditions without giving up its own ethical commitments? This is what Hartman calls the "great challenge" of globalization.[19] A company cannot simply respect all traditions without falling into logically and ethically indefensible relativism.[20] Some way is needed to ethically decide which local traditions to respect and which ones to reject.

The other approach to cultural conflict is universalism, a commitment to universal moral truths that apply to all situations in all cultures. Many writers, especially philosophers, take this position, arguing that cultures may differ but there are some basic overriding moral values.[21] Donaldson lists core human values as the right to good health, education, and safety, the right to economic advancement and an improved standard of living, the requirement to treat people as one wants to be treated, and the requirement to support and improve the institutions upon which the community depends.[22] Without some type of transcultural moral standards such as these, it is argued, there is no way to address moral differences between cultures.

Velasquez argues that out of the three most prominent universalist frameworks—human rights, utilitarianism, and principles of justice—human rights seems to have the best chance of providing a basis for moral principles that can apply across cultures.[23] His argument is intuitive, that surely all people have human rights that must be respected by all cultures, but it is based on an individualism that is not shared by all cultures.

Unlike Velasquez, Werhane finds her universals in negative terms, arguing that cultures do not agree about what is the good life, only what is the bad

[17] Donaldson 1996.

[18] American companies are the most likely to use home-country policies as worldwide templates (Hofstede et al. 2010).

[19] Hartman 2000: 211.

[20] The argument that since all cultures have different moral values, all moral values are equally valid is invalid because disagreement about moral values does not demonstrate that all moral values are equally valid (Rachels 2003). Further, moral relativism makes it impossible to criticize racism, sexism, and other repugnant practices.

[21] Green 1994; Sen 1999.

[22] Donaldson 1996.

[23] Velasquez 2000.

life—what is to be avoided.[24] All people want to avoid human suffering, abject poverty, preventable disease, high mortality, violence, indecencies, violations of human rights, and so on. These are the moral minimums and should be the foundation for a universal business ethics. This line of reasoning points out another problem with trying to define universal values. Though no culture would desire the items on Werhane's list, different cultures would value the trade-offs between evils differently. Impoverished farmers in China might accept the risk of preventable disease for a chance at economic development. Most contemporary Americans would not. The main point is that culture is not abstract; it is historically developed, socially maintained, and inseparable from the particular desires and ambitions of particular lives.

Other writers think there will be a convergence of values but have different reasons for thinking so. Boatright argues that differences between different business systems are likely to narrow because everyone will be competing under the same conditions.[25] In order to compete, participants will be forced to adapt to dominant trends or become less competitive. He thinks the system they adapt to will probably be the Anglo-American one. From a more theoretical perspective, Scherer and McKinley argue that firms in the same field come to resemble each other out of needs for legitimacy, to reduce uncertainty, or out of similar training and professionalization.[26] Both Boatright and Scherer and McKinley seem to assume the dominance of bureaucratic capitalism over entrepreneurial capitalism, since the former gives rise to more homogeneous firms.[27] Yet even in state-dominated China there are some 30 million private businesses, most of them small, family-dominated firms.[28] Even on the MNC level there are limits to homogenization as cultural identities continually reassert themselves.

Vogel, in contrast, sees only some truth in the expectation of movement toward uniformity in business practices, even between close allies such as the United States, Europe, and Japan, because even between these countries there

---

[24] Werhane 2000.

[25] Boatright 2000.

[26] Scherer and McKinley 2007.

[27] Baumol, Litan, and Shramm 2007.

[28] In 2005, these firms employed 200 million people and accounted for 49.3 percent of GDP (Tsai 2007). The number of small businesses in the United States was 23 million in 2010, employing around 81 million people (Dunn and Bradstreet 2011), accounting for 44.5 percent of GDP (U. S. Small Business Administration 2012).

has been limited convergence in regard to business ethics.[29] He notes that when MNCs adopt one set of ethical standards across all their foreign subsidiaries, these standards do not remove cultural differences; indeed, national differences continue to overshadow systemic standards. Hefner agrees that the tension between international standards and local culture is irremovable.[30] Hence, ultimately there has not been and will not be convergence toward a single market culture. The forces of history are simply too deeply rooted.

For these reasons, I would disagree with those like Santoro, who argue that MNCs have a moral duty to work to develop the rule of law in China.[31] Santoro's argument seems to be that a "rights-respecting nation" with an independent judiciary is needed to protect Western property rights; and the Chinese, he says repeatedly, are on the "wrong side of history."[32] Many of Santoro's goals are admirable—workers' rights, product safety, Internet freedom, and so on—but his insistence that China adopt Western values and institutions, and his confidence that the future belongs to Western culture, completely ignore the social and historical immensity of Chinese culture.[33] Achieving some of the ends Santoro seeks will involve a great deal of change in Chinese culture, but this change cannot and will not take place, if it does take place, without transformation of Western culture and yet-to-be-created East-West cultural amalgamations. This is not to say that Western institutions will not have influence but that Chinese culture will surely be a stronger influence on Chinese institutions.

Perhaps even more relevant for the critique of universalism, there are differences not only between cultures but also within them.[34] This is an important point in the debate on convergence because participants in the debate tend to assume homogeneous national cultures. But there is significant diversity inside national societies. If cultural diversity internal to a society is pervasive, the meaning of "universal values" will need to be reconsidered. Values do not define themselves. They receive their meaning through

[29] Vogel 1992.

[30] Hefner 1998.

[31] Santoro 2009.

[32] Santoro 2009: 126.

[33] It is true that Japan has adopted Western institutions, but the fact that Japan was under American military occupation influenced this development. And even today it is very difficult for Western firms to gain access to the Japanese market. In any case, the size of China, its regional diversity, and its role in the world make it a very different situation from that of Japan.

[34] Hefner 1998.

relations with other values; values exist in a system.[35] The number of relations makes the establishment of a value's meaning very complex. Hence, when a culture "adopts" a value from another culture, the value's meaning changes as it is brought into new relationships in the new cultural context; indeed, to some extent the receiving culture also changes from the new addition.[36] The "marketplace" of ideas can be very fluid, with different streams of ideas moving closer together and further apart simultaneously. The idea of cultural convergence misconstrues culture by overfocusing on "practice" at the expense of meaning and experience.

A related point can be seen in the discussion of "cross-pressures" in the negotiation literature.[37] Cross-pressures bring out conflicting aspects in a single culture during negotiations between two different cultures. For example, the Chinese are less individualistic than Americans, so they are less assertive in conflict resolution, but since they are more masculine than Americans,[38] they simultaneously become more assertive. Thus, not only can different aspects of a culture emerge in different situations, conflicting aspects of a culture can emerge in the same situation. Cultures are complex.

Another related phenomenon mentioned in the organization theory literature is "cross-convergence."[39] Cross-convergence happens when national culture and business culture interact to create a new and unique value system. Thus business culture is seen as having some autonomy from the national culture. This could be because of the specialized nature of subcultures and because the marketplace introduces new ideas from foreign actors that impact local businesses in specific ways not involving the national culture generally. In any case, business culture is partially autonomous from national culture and the two can interact to create new cultural forms. Since these new forms can have input from foreign cultures, the cultural distance between national culture, local business culture, and foreign business culture is reduced in some areas. These new forms are not "universal values" but local developments that are different from country to country, context to context. Nonetheless, the process shows how values can develop in local contexts that have sources in

---

[35] Geertz 1973.
[36] Shils 1981.
[37] He, Zhu, and Peng 2002.
[38] Hofstede et al. 2010.
[39] Ralston, Holt, Terpstra, and Kai-Cheng 1997.

foreign cultures, creating overlapping meaning and likely reducing cultural conflict. There are many and complex relations between cultures.

Something mentioned in both the philosophically oriented literature and the management-practice literature is cultural compromise, the realization by two different business cultures that to resolve a conflict between them by finding a compromise they can agree on, each must help the other understand its counterpart. As He, Zhu, and Peng put it, "adaptation has to take place when it comes to practical resolution."[40] They argue that compromise is the most effective way to resolve conflicts in cross-cultural settings.[41]

As to standards to determine whether a compromise is ethical, Brenkert argues that a compromise is permissible if it does more good than bad, tries to limit the bad as much as possible, and does no more bad than is necessary to achieve the good.[42] This puts the compromise inside a utilitarian framework for evaluation. One suspects that it would be difficult always to determine the quantities of "good" and "bad" in every situation. Another approach would be to combine the utilitarian framework with a core values approach. One would not compromise core values, but once core values were met, a utilitarian framework could be used to justify lower-level compromises; the problem of commensurability would still apply, though it would be on a lower level.

The idea of cultural compromise brings to light two issues about cross-cultural business ethics that are not given adequate attention in the philosophical literature, which emphasizes rational argument and universal justification. First, for cross-cultural business conflict to be resolved, not only

---

[40] He, Zhu, and Peng 2002: 144.

[41] This is different from Donaldson and Dunfee's (1999) social contract approach because they posit universal "hypernorms" that cannot be compromised. Only once the hypernorms are met do firms face a "moral free space," where they can decide to compromise because their basic values are not at stake. Donaldson and Dunfee's framework operates on all four levels of cultural commitment: local, foreign, compromise, and universal values. Velasquez (2000) argues that the social contract framework fails because the universal component is impractical and culturally biased, and the compromise component is impossible to implement because a just compromise cannot be determined. The latter point is a good example of the philosophical approach. Velasquez cannot find a position from which to secure a just compromise because he requires a universal (outside) justification. But if two cultures do in fact compromise, it can be argued that it is just for them. Philosophical reasoning is an important means to evaluate thought and action, but the self-justifying nature of culture must be considered too.

[42] Brenkert 2008.

respect for local culture is required but also specific knowledge of local problem-solving styles and business expertise.[43] Even more important is to build up mutual confidence and trust. This process involves not only intellectual understanding but also empathy and emotional investment. The latter takes time to develop. For example, in China, Americans sometimes use licensing and franchising contracts to cut costs and lower risks, but the Chinese see in these mechanisms a lack of commitment to the relationship.[44] To build trust in China, Americans not only must understand the Chinese reciprocity rule, but they must make an effort to develop a personal relationship through gifts, dinners, and personal interest. If the Chinese are interested they will respond in kind.

Second, cultural compromise requires to some extent accepting the values of a foreign culture. To be able to do this in a constructive way requires self-confidence based in a secure relationship to one's own culture.[45] The accepting culture needs to be able to compromise and accept new cultural forms without completely destroying its old forms. In other words, the existing culture must be securely established and act as a foundation into which new cultural forms can be integrated. Otherwise, compromise can be destructive. Compromise requires both cognitive and emotional integrity. Given China's humiliation at the hands of foreigners in the 19th and 20th centuries and its own more recent history of cultural and political turmoil, accepting foreign cultural forms could add to the disorientation and loss. China's cautiousness in doing so is thus a sign of health.

Globalization and Ethics

1. Ethics and Free Trade. The ethics of the current system of international free trade is hotly debated. Its critics describe a system of MNCs operating with new levels of autonomy unrestrained by anything other than their own search for profit. Cragg states that by operating worldwide, multinationals have been able to choose (and alternate between) the legal systems that govern their operations.[46] This leads governments to weaken their legal requirements

---

[43] Shenkar and Yan 2002.
[44] Su and Littlefield 2001.
[45] Erikson 1964.
[46] Cragg 2000.

and regulations to attract business. Cragg calls this "a race to the bottom."[47] Specifically, NAFTA and WTO put multinationals beyond the effective reach of any single country's legal system by setting up weaker international regulatory systems. Multinationals exploit this vacuum.

A second way globalization undermines ethical practice is by separating the economic and political realms from the values that sustain communities.[48] Similar to what happens with regulation, the establishment of international systems consigns specific communities to a second-class status, one removed from the decision-making level. Decision making thus does not give adequate representation to communities—often disproportionately disenfranchising poor and less developed communities. One outcome of this mechanism is the much-criticized sweatshops, recently found at Foxconn in China which makes over 40 percent of the world's electronic products.[49] Sweatshops often pay below minimum wage, mandate overtime, and outlaw unions. Even worse, child labor can be found and safety is lax to nonexistent, with thousands of deaths reported. While large numbers of workers suffer, a small number of owners become immensely wealthy. The system is expansive because an ethical company that does not use sweatshops is at a competitive disadvantage.

Another example of the splitting of economic and political processes from community values through globalization is government corruption. The primary form of corruption associated with MNCs is bribery,[50] whereby developed-world businesses pay off government officials in developing nations for competitive advantages. On the other hand, the United States has been active in trying to reduce corruption in developing nations.[51] Environmental damage is also mentioned as a major problem in the ethics of globalization.[52] All these problems—sweatshops, corruption, pollution, and the like—are

---

[47] Cragg 2000: 209. Even when governments do not weaken their regulatory systems, smaller governments find themselves overmatched by sophisticated and powerful MNCs (Scherer and McKinley 2007).

[48] Gamer 2002.

[49] Duhigg and Greenhouse 2012.

[50] Ryan 2000.

[51] The U.S. Foreign Corrupt Practices Act of 1977 makes it a crime to offer anything of value to foreign officials with the intention of changing policies or achieving the suspension of a legal norm (Sanyal 2005). An amendment was added to the law in 1998 that permits bribes for, say, speeding up legitimate actions by lower-level government officials. Using the act, the Justice Department extracted nearly $2 billion in penalties in 2009 and 2010 (Bussey 2011).

[52] Boatright 2000.

pervasive in China—"the world's workshop"—where nearly all of the world's largest MNCs go in search of ever lower manufacturing costs.[53] Hence, all of these problems result not only from the behavior of MNCs but also from the demand for ever lower prices in the developed world's markets.

All of these ills have led to criticism of the global economic system as a whole. Boatright points out that globalization has created such fierce competition based on rapid product development and intense cost cutting that ethical considerations have little room to influence decision making.[54] Profitability is the one and only concern. Cavanaugh sees this mind-set as selfish and laments the fact that no countervailing sensibility exists on the global level.[55] It is like 19th-century Darwinian capitalism all over again. Cragg adds that this atmosphere is not good for capitalism because by damaging communities and not sharing the benefits, it will hurt economic development in the long term.[56] Ethically, too, this state of affairs cannot be justified if the social good is the ethical criterion.[57]

The free trade camp counters the critics of globalization by arguing that growth in national income will lead to better labor and environmental standards as well as social security.[58] Higher per capita income, they argue, is perceived to create a less bribe-friendly climate, and higher income among government officials also appears to decrease bribery.[59] Further, it is argued, economic growth leads to democracy.[60] A growing middle class will demand a say in how they are governed. Free trade advocates tend to ignore human rights violations in trading partners, saying they have no right to force Western morality on non-Western cultures. In other words, the free market camp is universalist when it comes to economics but relativist when it comes to ethics.

The market also works, some argue, to enforce ethical values through the sheer fact that intensifying competition provides choices for consumers and

---

[53] Harney 2008; Hessler 2006.

[54] Boatright 2000.

[55] Cavanaugh 2000.

[56] Cragg 2000.

[57] Sherer and McKinley 2007.

[58] Sherer and McKinley 2007. It is true that as China has developed over the last three decades it has passed improved labor and environmental laws. However, still today it is very difficult to find the laws enforced (Pan 2008; R. McGregor 2010).

[59] Sayal 2005. However, repeated double-digit pay increases for Chinese government officials have not significantly lowered government corruption in China (Huang 2008).

[60] Sherer and McKinley 2007. However, after three decades of economic development there are few signs of democratization in China (Pei 2006).

because countries with endemic corruption "are increasingly paying a price in the loss of investment."[61] This latter point, too, is certainly untrue in China, which exhibits widespread corruption but has the world's highest level of foreign direct investment.[62] Some economists argue that corruption is actually better for the social good when compared with no corruption accompanied by economic stagnation, or compared with market-restricting clampdowns on corruption.[63] Apparently, even corrupt profits increase the flow of capital through the economy, adding to the economic pie for the benefit of all, as opposed to economic stagnation, which does not help anyone. This utilitarian perspective at the least ignores issues of justice as well as the entrenchment of corrupt officials, which undermines both political institutions and the efficiency of capital investments to the detriment of the weakest groups.

2. Global Standards and Regulation. The first and most important level of ethical responsibility resides with the MNC. Werhane argues that MNCs cannot merely apply their ethical codes but must try to understand what impact these codes will have when applied in a foreign setting.[64] What are the local social structures and local community relationships? What social goods does the community value? How will family, religious, and community traditions be affected by the MNC's practices? At what point will the MNC's practices harm the local culture, the identity of its people? Given the economic power of MNCs, they have moral responsibilities not to cause social and economic changes that lead to cultural harm.

Werhane is one of many voices expressing concern about the impact MNCs are having worldwide. In 1999 this concern led the United Nations to call on MNCs to adhere to principles expressing the importance of human rights, labor standards, and environmental protection.[65] This is an attempt to expand the ethical mandate of MNCs to fill the regulatory vacuum created by their worldwide operations. To some extent, the UN is pushing for MNCs to act like the church in its global moral concern or the state in its domestic moral responsibility. This goes far beyond the traditional wealth-producing functions of business limited only by the negative responsibility not to break the law.

---

[61] Boatright 2000: 5.
[62] Huang 2008.
[63] Ryan 2000.
[64] Werhane 2000.
[65] Sherer and McKinley 2007.

In a study of the ethical practices of MNCs, Enderle found four types: conforms to local customs, applies home concepts, does both (that is, follows uncompromisable national ideals but beyond that respects local customs), and has global values.[66] All four types seem to imply that MNCs seek clear ethical codes and the responsibilities that follow from them. They seek to reduce moral uncertainty. This is quite different from Werhane's recommendations, which assume moral ambiguity and managerial indifference, and call for MNCs to analyze and study local cultures and their impact on them.

Cragg presents an even more critical view of MNCs' codes of conduct,[67] arguing that their primary purpose is to protect the firm from costly acts by unethical employees and to present a positive (ethical) image to the public. Generally, all aspects of the corporation (including ethics) are designed to contribute to the bottom line. This is why, for example, codes of conduct are seldom extended to cover human rights.

This view of MNCs' codes of conduct is similar to Santoro's critique of corporate social responsibility (CSR).[68] Santoro argues that many MNCs adopted CSR as a reaction to negative publicity from labor rights activists and nongovernmental organizations. Many MNCs do not wholeheartedly implement CSR, and the ones that do are dependent on outside firms to carry out CSR audits in their supplier networks, many of which are ineffective and erroneous.[69] Nonetheless, the audits continue because they provide MNCs with "plausible deniability."[70]

Because MNCs are sticking to traditional (narrow) wealth-producing missions, moral regulation will have to be sought elsewhere. The two most likely alternatives are national governments and international bodies. National governments are responsible for making sure the economy serves the interests of the society as a whole, but this is no easy feat. Wealth gaps between rich and poor have worsened over the last decade in both developed and developing economies. Democratic political systems should work to benefit the

---

[66] Enderle 1997.

[67] Cragg 2000.

[68] Santoro 2009.

[69] See the Epilogue for a recent example of the unfair and self-centered use of audits in China by an American firm.

[70] Santoro 2009: 29.

majority, but this process is hampered by the self-protecting role of corporations in the political process.[71]

This leaves it to international bodies, specifically public interest groups and nongovernmental organizations, to address ethical issues involving MNCs. These organizations can, for example, provide information to the public about MNC practices that will bring public pressure on MNCs to act ethically.[72] Because of the Internet and other advances in communications, MNC corruption is more exposed now than at any time in the history of MNCs.

From this point of view, the solution to unethical practices by MNCs requires that international bodies have the power to enact and enforce rules applicable in all countries.[73] This in turn requires that nations subordinate their own interests to cooperation with other nations and transnational agencies.[74] Only transnational agencies can address worldwide problems. For example, the Apparel Industry Partnership is a collaboration of individual companies, human rights organizations, and the U.S. government to establish a code of conduct and monitoring to regulate sweatshops and human rights violations.[75] Companies have an incentive to join because they receive the "No Sweat" label, which brings marketing advantages with consumers. Santoro, however, argues that certification processes like the "No Sweat" label have not worked.[76] Among the reasons for their failure are that the social audit process has repeatedly been shown to be unreliable at best, there are too many certificates, and the certification process has failed to develop a brand that has value in the marketplace. In general, companies have found that marketing ethics is not a big winner, though association with unethical behavior is definitely a big loser.

Conclusion: The Middle Alternative

Two very different business cultures find it difficult to develop business relationships. A natural development in this situation is the use of "middlemen"

---

[71] Barley (2007) reports that a few years before the 2008 financial crisis the financial industry actually wrote the language for the Bankruptcy Abuse Prevention and Consumer Protection Act of 2005. Not surprisingly, the legislation actually weakened consumer rights.

[72] Boatright 2000.

[73] Boatright 2000.

[74] Hartman 2000.

[75] Boatright 2000.

[76] Santoro 2009.

who specialize in developing relationships with both cultures so as to bridge the relationship chasm.[77] But from an ethical point of view, the situation does not develop community; like a diplomat shuttling between two antagonistic countries, the middleman keeps the two business cultures apart.[78] Since the ethical context for each culture is different, keeping the sides apart keeps the seeds of a new moral community from developing through interaction between the two separate business cultures. Even assuming the two parties share the value of profit maximization,[79] the use of the middleman does not provide the basis for a new moral culture; on the contrary, it keeps the parties wary and distrustful.

Moral culture is a delicate flower even within a single business culture, always under pressure from self-interest, greed, ignorance, competitive threats, and difficult economic cycles. Maintaining a moral business culture even within a single firm takes continuous vigilance and is not common.[80] When companies from two different societies engage each other, the problem is exacerbated because their moral values can be profoundly inconsistent or incommensurate. Some of the literature tries to address this problem by creating moral universals, but universals are abstract, often lacking the affinity with local cultures that would allow them to be culturally integrated and internalized by individuals. They are perhaps a starting point for discussion, but for the most part they are of limited usefulness because they are introduced into a social field that is characterized by intermittent meetings, instrumental goals, and different cultural norms and business practices. This is not a context in which moral values are internalized; it bears more resemblance to a context that requires legal rules that must be monitored and enforced by external authority.

In addition, many participants in this intercultural affair have little background or training to encourage intercultural exploration, let alone the empathic responses needed for intercultural understanding and cooperation. Creating a shared moral culture from two different business cultures is necessarily a slow process that requires identifying different meanings,

---

[77] Peng 1998.

[78] Indeed, if the two come together the middleman will lose his job.

[79] Even this assumption can be questionable cross-culturally since, for example, many public and private Chinese firms are more concerned with employment than profits (Lieberthal and Lieberthal 2003).

[80] Feldman 2007b.

understanding the context in which these meanings make sense, and either adoption by one side of the values and practices of the other, or the working out of a compromise between the two. In either case, much trial and error is required.

More commonly, however, time is of the essence, awareness of cultural processes is limited, and Western firms, following Western traditions, seek consistent legal processes and constraints to control the behavior of the culturally diverse participants. This dependence on the legal system works as long as there are Western legal institutions available with jurisdiction over the relevant parties. Such institutions are, however, far from universal. China, for example, shares neither legal philosophy nor legal institutions with the West, except where the WTO has jurisdiction.[81] Inside China, Western attempts to use contracts or to enforce contracts through the Chinese courts have led to frustrating and inconsistent results. Even though some writers say the Chinese legal system is improving and adopting Western procedures and processes, the improvement is slow, and it is still uncertain where it will end up and when.

Another cultural approach is to accept local cultural norms out of the belief that all cultures are equally valid, none able to demonstrate moral superiority. This is not a moral argument; it forfeits the whole field of ethics in the effort to remove the conflict between different cultural systems. The argument recognizes difference but not reason or humanity, claiming that culture, as the final frontier not penetrable by human knowledge, simply must be accepted as is. But in a world of continuous social interaction where cooperation is ever more required, the idea of each culture giving up its own commitments whenever it crosses into another country is not workable. Giving up one's ethics whenever abroad will undermine one's culture at home, leading to the destruction of all ethics. A commitment is only a commitment if it is taken seriously and attachment is maintained. Intermittent attachment will result in intermittent feelings, intermittent feelings in declining commitment. Instead of increasing intercultural cooperation, this cycle will increase

---

[81] The United States has recently filed several complaints against China with the WTO. In a number of them the WTO has ruled in favor of the United States. But it is still unclear what will be the final results of these rulings because the process takes years and enforcement is still an open question. The fact that China negotiated for 15 years to gain WTO membership (K. Yu 2009), which in turn has brought a continuous stream of accusations that China is violating WTO policies, shows the limits of the legal approach in cases of broad cultural differences.

intercultural conflict because there will be less, not more, moral restraint. Relativism, in seeking to resolve intercultural conflict, will not only increase it but will increase intracultural conflict as well.

With formal systems such as law not universally applicable and influenced by the same cultural differences as ethics, with relativism apt to do more harm than good, and with "universal values" a currency difficult to integrate universally, we end up back at the same problem: two different business cultures unable to communicate with and trust one another. This situation can be referred to as "trouble in the middle," as the two stare across a culturally barren "middle ground" unable to work out their differences. In the present state of American-Chinese business relations, Chinese "middlemen" attempt to bridge the differences to make business activity possible.

The current state of affairs is "precultural" in that little consensus is developed; the middleman is a specialist in instrumental problem solving, helping to move the two parties to a mutually profitable exchange as best she can. Indeed, it is exactly the two established cultures that are the problem; to solve the problem, the middleman seeks to isolate them and make them inoperative as far as the relationship is concerned. Hence, the situation is instrumental in a hard-nosed sense: Social norms and moral values are deliberately isolated so as not to cause conflict, avoiding moral values indeed.

The potential for manipulation of both American and Chinese businesses is quite high because of the asymmetrical information between the middleman and either business.[82] The Americans, for example, do not know what the Chinese are really asking for and must rely on the middleman for this information, and likewise for the Chinese. Thus, not only are the two moral cultures rendered inoperative, but the new structure itself creates ambiguity and the opportunity for exploitation. The new structure is each man for himself, an odd solution to social and cultural conflict but one that improves the situation because conflict is isolated, clearing the way for an overriding instrumentality. The fact that instrumentality takes center stage is another reason moral hazards increase. It is a risky way to do business but still better than no business at all. The risk is tempered by the trustworthiness of the middleman, which is one of her central sources of value added. In this sense, moral virtue is introduced into the middle. But risk remains from the fundamental fact that there are no agreed-upon moral principles at work. For the

[82] Chintakananda et al. 2009.

Americans, low-cost labor, materials, and infrastructure, and access to a potentially huge market compensate for the high risk in social exchange.[83]

An important point to note is that despite the middleman's acting as a "bridge" between two incompatible cultures, his role as moral translator is limited because the "bridge" does not function to help the two cultures understand each other better. It is not a moral bridge. The instrumental goals lead the middleman to do what needs to be done, to satisfy the two parties, to meet their needs, but these tasks do not require building a better relationship between the two parties. Indeed, the middleman phenomenon is a substitute for a direct relationship between the two parties. As noted earlier, the middleman has an incentive not to contribute to improved relations since his work would no longer be needed if relations improved sufficiently. The middleman thus operates in the gray area, doing the deeds neither side can nor wants to do itself. This is clearly seen in the middleman's bribe-paying function.

The middleman is pragmatic, practical, and instrumental. He connects two incompatible cultures, absorbing the moral failures between the two systems unto himself. The connecting does damage to both cultures, despite the fact that the two parties do nothing wrong, because their moral faculties are suspended as the middleman transforms the lack of trust, cultural conflict, and possible moral violations into instrumental success.

The alternative is the dominance of one side or the other, or a compromise between the two. The latter would represent not "universal" values but a complex local development generated out of repetitive social interaction in a certain place at a certain time. This development assumes stable, enduring interaction.[84] The middleman might play an important role by helping the two principals develop their own relationship. The middleman could benefit from this role by using the connections, capital, and goodwill created by helping the two principals to generate new business or expand into new areas: for example, to provide middleman services to new customers, suppliers, or partners, or to take on new functions within the new relationship or for either principal, such as a customer, supplier, or partner.

---

[83] The utter fear that competitors will gain competitive advantages that will apply worldwide is also an important factor in decisions by foreign companies to enter the China market.

[84] Hofstede and colleagues (2010) report that it is not uncommon for executives working in foreign cultures to experience culture shock for the first year or more before acculturation begins to set in.

Building a new local culture requires compromise. Participants in the two cultures can seek cultural compromise as an intentional and practical solution to the incompatibility between the two cultures. The participants will need to learn about each other, identify conflicting expectations, and enter into discussions on how the two conflicting sets of requirements can be compromised to create a new set of commitments. The context of this discussion will be structured around business goals and the type of business transactions the two parties might engage in, but the virtues of care, empathy, and self-understanding are required as well. Where these virtues are missing, the goal of building moral community will not be reached or will not last. Building trust is required for such endeavors. Excessive self-seeking or insincerity will put a quick end to the process. Cultural approaches to moral conflict resolution are fragile and time consuming. In addition to their practical value, they also provide the possibility for moral growth and thus better relationship-building capacities. From a legal or economic perspective, regulations or incentives make quicker exchange possible and put less demand on scarce supplies of self-understanding and empathy. Though they too have their downsides, regulatory regimes are liable to manipulation or avoidance, and incentive systems assume shared values the lack of which is the problem needing resolution in the first place.

Compromise also requires a stable cultural base from which to compromise. Without an integrated culture, cultural change can be destructive, causing social instability and personal disintegration. A stable cultural base is notably missing in China, where so much cultural, social, political, and economic change has left many Chinese unclear about their core commitments. This is one reason intercultural business conflict is so intense in China: Not only did the Cultural Revolution leave people traumatized, disoriented, and desperate to make up for the "lost decade," but no one knows what the new rules are for "market socialism with Chinese characteristics" or how long they will last. Those seeking to build a new moral community will need no small amount of patience.

The MNC entering China and other developing nations arrives with not a moral mission but an economic one. In fact, its arrival implies that it sees economic opportunities that in developing nations can include weak regulatory, tax, and moral constraints. But these weak constraints cut both ways: They both lower and raise costs. In terms of the lack of moral business culture, MNCs have no choice but to turn to the foreign government for help. This too cuts both ways because often the local government is the biggest source of corruption.[85] So the long-term strategy of building new moral communities with local business partners is further complicated by the fact that the government might not have any interest in seeing these communities built.

The resulting tension has led MNCs to develop close ties with local government elites. These ties can be seen in China, where MNCs have had little choice but to become involved in corrupt "privatization" processes that enable high-level Communist officials to reap the lion's share of the benefits from "privatization". Bribery has played a central role in this process.[86] Hence, MNCs have been on their own in China with little Chinese government support to enforce ethical behavior. Furthermore, the marketization of Chinese firms and the mass arrival of foreign firms has resulted in fierce competition that has made ethics seem like a luxury few could afford. Committed above all to profit maximization, Western firms have little incentive to take on the difficult project of attempting to develop new moral cultures with Chinese partners.[87]

The economic growth argument in the literature on MNCs says this is all OK because economic growth will raise the standard of living, resulting in a decline in corruption, pollution, and labor exploitation; the claim is that it will in fact lead to democracy. There is no need to worry about intercultural conflict and ethical depravity, because economic growth will transfigure culture by generating economic rationality, which precludes culturally or economically induced unethical behavior. On the contrary, however, there is little evidence this is working in China after 30 years of economic growth. Indeed, corruption and authoritarianism are firmly in place. Even in the United States, which has a long-established democracy and the largest economy in the world, there is no shortage of unethical business behavior. Democracy hardly guarantees ethical business conduct. Business culture cannot be dismissed as an important explanatory variable.

So for now there is trouble in the middle as two incompatible business cultures transfer instrumental needs to "middlemen" who do what it takes to make transactions possible. The economic argument simply says foreign firms are not responsible for what local firms do in their home countries; that

[85] Scheifer and Vishny 1998.
[86] Sun 2004; Pan 2008.
[87] General Motors has had some success in building a relationship with Shanghai Automotive Industry Corporation (Terlep 2012). Relationship building is integral to GM's business goals. The Chinese government is intimately involved in this relationship.

would be moral imperialism. This argument is universalist in terms of economic growth—free markets are the only option—but relativist in terms of ethics—local culture cannot be judged by outsiders. Is this coherent? If corrupt cultures undermine free markets, which they do in terms of both efficiency and justice, then the economic justification for the behavior of MNCs is self-contradictory.

Competition is not the answer for all problems. In China, great competition goes hand in hand with great economic growth, great corruption, and great tyranny. Clearly the West is focused primarily on the economic growth, as the huge increases in foreign direct investment demonstrate. At what point do Western firms increase the profile of ethics in the world's fastest-growing economy? So far, as long as economic growth has remained robust, most firms do little more than try to stay out of trouble—that is, avoid getting caught paying bribes.

But to practice business ethics, MNCs must go beyond the moral minimalism of pursuing profit without breaking the law. In the case of intercultural business conflict, this means they must proactively attempt to understand the other culture and develop moral relations with it. Black-box business transactions through bribe-paying middlemen are not a moral option. Given China's situation of great cultural change and confusion, what responsibilities do Western firms have? This is a very difficult question not only because a history of Western exploitation in China has made the Chinese untrusting, even vengeful, but also because an endless string of ethical failures in Western economies makes them both economically and ethically ill positioned to provide moral leadership.

Still, problems must be addressed. Facilitating bribe payments through middlemen harms both business cultures in moral terms. Moral character is developed through virtuous behavior, not avoiding legal prosecution. MNC ethical codes must be seen in this light; they are mechanisms to limit unethical (illegal) activities by employees. They are most often self-interest-oriented rather than driven by moral ideals. At best, they seek to reduce moral ambiguity that could obstruct decision making or lead to unethical activity. At worst, they seek little more than to avoid prosecution, enhance profits, and generate a positive public relations image.

To be ethical in the international arena, MNCs must work with local companies to create new moral forms that are acceptable to both parties. This is something that should be done locally and will vary from country to country. It is unlikely that governments can take the lead in this endeavor because the core participants are business firms.[88] Governments have their own agendas. At bottom, the middle needs to become a creative space where new business relationships can develop. Western firms must enter the middle, involving middlemen as facilitators of relationships, not black-box specialists in bribery. This may not be possible where bribes are required by government officials, but it should be the ideal.

---

[88] Though, again, in China, the boundary between business and government is anything but clear.

P A R T

CULTURE AND HISTORY

3

Central Control and Its Shadow

A Brief History of Chinese Culture and Institutions

In a story told by Hill Gates, a tax collector in mid-nineteenth century China, who is rounding up individuals who have not paid their taxes, has run out of chains by which to secure the prisoners to the wagon; needing a solution to his problem, he uses nails.[1] I mention this story to make two points about Chinese culture. First, it has long been true that the state in China exercised great power over the Chinese people. The exercise of power was often cruel and brutal, and the effects of the brutality were not always limited to small numbers of victims. Great centralization of power is not unknown in world history; what is unusual about China is the continuity of the authoritarian state over 2,000 years. Even though Chinese history is filled with struggle between central authority and those it seeks to dominate, the authoritarian state stretches across Chinese history to the present day.

Second, one reason the authoritarian state has lasted so long is that it ruthlessly prosecutes any alternative forms of authority. The emperor was at once the political leader and the Son of Heaven, combining politics and religion into a single structure. This unparalleled hierarchicalization of society left little more than families, kin groups, and villages facing the state, which was represented by the best-educated part of the population, the literati, who administered the realm. Without autonomous organizations of any significant size, or self-governing cities,[2] a civil society based on shared values did

---

[1] Gates 1996. Weber (1951: 234) describes ". . . patrimonial fiscalism which everywhere proved a training ground for dishonesty. For both in Egypt and China the process of tax collection involved raids, flogging, assistance of [kin] members, howling of the oppressed, fear of the oppressors, and compromise."

[2] Chinese cities were imperial fortresses governed by a prince for the purpose of central government administration, especially administration of the rivers and tax collection (Weber 1951). Unlike those living in the villages, city residents lacked autonomy and self-government.

not develop. The result was an impersonal society in which, at even small distances outside family groups, fellow feeling for strangers did not exist. This depersonalization can be seen in the extreme in the tax collector's behavior, in which a shortage of chains results in unthinkable barbarism.

In this chapter, I will address the historical relationship between the state and society in China, outlining its general features and most common cultural forms. The central themes I will explore are the relationships between state authority, the role of hierarchy, and the personalism that developed an informal under-system within the structure of authority in order to protect small groups and individual interests. I will follow this thread generally through the imperial era, briefly examining the role of religion, ethics, culture, politics, and economy. I will continue the analysis in a brief examination of the communist state, specifically the role of politics, the people's perception of the government, the Tiananmen Square massacre, and the issues raised by economic reform and modernization. Finally, in an extended concluding section, I will summarize the key themes, and relationships between themes, that have surfaced in the analyses and will make some general conclusions about the inner dynamics of authority and its role in Chinese society. I will concentrate on its dual nature, that is, the hierarchy-personalism nexus.

I. The Imperial System

1. Religion. Religion in Chinese history was not the primary source of ethical values as it was in the West.[3] In China, the major role of religion was magical, to induce the gods and spirits to help men and women with their problems.[4] As such, it contained no universal validity. So it sat alongside and intermingled with secular moral systems. There was no clear line separating the world of spirits and the world of people—likewise between the worlds of the living and the dead. In fact, ancestor worship was the universal religion of China, the central link between the world of people and the world of the spirits.[5] It permeated every aspect of Chinese society, above all cementing the great bonds of the Chinese family. It was key to the central cultural ideal in Chinese

---

[3] C. K. Yang 1961.

[4] Buddhism, Confucianism, and Taoism all rejected any notions of a supreme deity or heavenly salvation for individual souls (Hoiman and King 2003). In Chinese religion, the highest ideal was human order as sacred order. Its innermost goals were social order and harmony.

[5] Hsu 1981.

civilization, filial piety, which structured all human relations into superior and subordinate, beginning with lifelong dedication to one's parents.

Confucianism, arising out of centuries of violence during the Warring States period (481–256 B.C.) and more a philosophy than a religion, also developed a moral system emphasizing hierarchical relationships.[6] Confucian ethics was practical in the sense that it abhorred abstraction, focusing the individual on his or her concrete obligations as manifested in extensively detailed ritual behavior towards others.[7] Since the Confucian was constantly oriented toward social adjustment and harmony with others—not systematic consistency with abstract beliefs as in Judeo-Christian religion—there was no tension between other-worldly ideals and this-worldly social life.[8] The individual lacked an ideal base from which to evaluate and criticize others as well as his own behavior. To this day, Chinese experience shame when their misbehavior is known to others, more than guilt in the privacy of their inner voice.[9]

Two important practical implications follow from this religious orientation. First, since the individual was oriented toward gaining magical power through connection to the spirits, he had no desire to transform this world.[10] This follows both from Taoist contemplative mysticism, which sought emptiness, not action, through traditional ritual; and from Confucian rationalism, which sought order and equilibrium, both personal and social, thus reducing tension with the world (and the will to change it) to an absolute minimum.[11] Hence, both Confucianism and Taoism led to traditionalism—indeed, to a fear of innovation, for that would disturb the spirits that desired the same order and harmony as did the people and Heaven.

Second, because the individual believed he had access to the spiritual world, thought he lived within it, yet was required to exhibit great self-control to get along with others, the family, the others closest to him, took on the

---

[6] Fairbank and Goldman 2006.

[7] Nisbett 2003. Taosim and Buddhism also emphasized harmony and discouraged abstract thinking.

[8] Weber 1951. Hence, the Chinese moved back and forth between gods and ancestral spirits, depending on their particular needs on a given day. Chinese religion is still polytheistic. No one actually knows how many gods there are in China (Hsu 1981). The distinction between good and evil is thus relative in China. The very idea of evil has little importance in this context.

[9] Hofstede et al. 2010.

[10] Weber 1951.

[11] C. K. Yang 1963.

importance of the spiritual world. Ancestor worship presented the family as part of a sacred domain. This sacredness justified and enforced Confucian ethics.[12] In an agricultural society, this religious structure supported the functional needs of the family. Family and filial values were raised to absolutes, becoming the "ethical cum sacred foundation" of Chinese culture.[13] This is the master trend in Chinese culture. Historically, religion was confined to sanctifying these values, remedying their fallibility in practice.

Family is always the core building block of society. But in China, because the family's grip on the individual never loosened,[14] trust outside and beyond the family never developed.[15] This left kin groups island-like, competing for resources with other kin groups in an uncaring social world.[16] Ironically, Confucian humanism left Chinese social life without community. Outside the kinship group, only the state had deep roots.

The magical nature of Chinese popular religion was despised by the Confucian literati, whose training in rational self-mastery led them to disparage the world of spirits.[17] But they supported it nonetheless, because it was the foundation for the official cults that ultimately guaranteed the structure of power by which they prospered. Hence, Chinese religions assisted in enforcing moral values—while not providing the premises for them.[18] The magic garden of Chinese religion provided the supernatural sanction for both the political and moral systems, yet the priesthood, having no other-worldly system of belief, exercised no moral authority. Priests were merely stewards of ritual for religious ceremony. In China, religion fit into and supported the structure of political power.

2. *Ethics.* Up to the twentieth century, the Confucian system of ethical values had served as moral orthodoxy for the Chinese people for 2,000 years.[19] The key reason for its success is that it met the practical needs of everyday life,

---

[12] C. K. Yang 1961.

[13] Hoiman and King 2003: 345.

[14] Weber (1951) also mentions that since, in Chinese religion, magic was used to explain misfortune, it led to an inhibition of sympathy in Chinese culture.

[15] Fukuyama 1995. The Chinese equal-division inheritance rule played a huge role in maintaining the family's grip on the individual (Hsu 1981). Likewise, since sons did not have to leave the land, non-kinship organizations remained weak.

[16] Redding and Witt 2007.

[17] Weber 1951.

[18] C. K. Yang 1963. For example, Buddhism tacitly accepted secular (Confucian) values in everyday life even when they were in conflict with Buddhist values (C. K. Yang, 1961).

[19] C. K. Yang 1961.

particularly the needs of the kinship system at the structural core of the agricultural society.[20]

The central moral imperative of Confucianism is filial piety, the obligation of loyalty to key people, especially the parents.[21] Outside the family there are decreasing levels of ethical responsibility, where little moral obligation is felt; because of this there has been widespread corruption in the history of Chinese business.[22] Family relations are blood relations, not a universal value that requires responsibility toward broader social groups.

Because Confucianism had no metaphysical foundations, its basic interest was everyday life.[23] Confucius did map the relations between heaven, earth, and man but this narrative developed mostly into a magical theodicy used for everyday affairs. Without a universal moral orientation, Chinese spiritual life remained fragmented or pluralistic. An individual could be a Buddhist, Taoist, and Confucian while also practicing magic whenever he felt it would do him some good.[24] Perhaps this accounts for the Asian capacity for tolerating cultural and moral complexity where Westerners see confusion or contradiction.

From magic also followed tradition, as the Chinese used tried-and-true ritual to ward off evil, cure sickness, or win success in business. Such premonitions still exist today, as it is not unusual for Chinese to correlate their options to magical dates or patterns before making a decision. In terms of ethics, Confucius does not distinguish between custom, morality, and justice.[25] One must simply learn to act well, that is, follow acceptable behavioral forms. The notion of an exemplary individual is central to Confucian thought. Hence, Confucianism repeatedly confirms the status quo. Social life is governed by an immeasurable number of rules and rituals. There is no end or goal by which to confront or criticize social custom. Adaptation is everything.

[20] In 1980, 80 percent of China's labor force worked on farms; in 2010, the number was down to 30 percent (Gang 2010). However, 49 percent of the population still lives in rural areas (Wines 2012).

[21] Chow and Ding 2002.

[22] Nonetheless, as Hsu (1981) points out, neither the Japanese government nor Chinese business has ever reached the level of corruption found in the Chinese state. Hence, not Confucianism but dictatorship wins first prize in corruption. This is still the case today.

[23] C .K. Yang 1963.

[24] C. K. Yang 1961.

[25] Koehn 2001.

The prevalence of social custom in determining Chinese social ethics followed from what Weber calls Confucianism's "radical world-optimism," the perfectibility of man and society by human effort.[26] Confucianism saw all things in the universe as interrelated, indeed as harmonious. The individual's self-cultivation is meant to help him fit into and adapt to the world. Thus, the individual is never seen as an individual per se, but always in relation to something else—e.g., individual to family, to organization, to society, to empire, ultimately to cosmos.[27] Confucian ethics is a collectivist ethics, focused primarily on the welfare of the broader polity.[28]

The core Confucian ethical value that anchors this system is *jen*, universal benevolence.[29] It orients the individual outward toward others, encouraging generosity, kindheartedness, tolerance, gentility, reticence, self-restraint, and the like.[30] This attitude deepens human relationships through acknowledging and respecting other people. It is cultivated through self-discipline, a sense of equality, respect for order, and, above all, the maintenance of traditions.[31] One still sees this central aspect of Confucianism in Chinese culture today in courtesy, indirectness, and the carefully controlled expression of self-importance and self-indulgence. Selfishness is sin. Ironically, the decline of communism reawakened Confucian values in Chinese society as, almost simultaneously, the arrival of capitalism weakened them through the growth of individualism, especially among the young.[32]

Because Confucianism led to such great emphasis on external control as opposed to internal belief, Weber argues that the Chinese personality never developed an inner core, a unified way of life flowing from internalized ethical demands.[33] The Confucian's constant self-control and continuous enactment of ceremonial conventions led to an abundance of useful traits, but not a systemic moral unity. Moral autonomy was not cultivated in this system. Self-discipline manifested itself in the control of external gesture and manner for

---

[26] Weber 1951: 235. This is in strong contrast with Western transcendental ethics, which creates tension between ideals and everyday life, between God and a sinful world.

[27] Ropp 1990.

[28] This contrasts with Aristotle's ethics, which is defined in terms of the happiness of human individuals (Broadie 1991). Likewise, Taoism, Buddhism, and ancestor worship are religions of the group, while Christianity and Judaism are individualistic religions.

[29] C. K. Yang 1961.

[30] Koehn 2001; Redding 1995.

[31] Koehn 2001.

[32] Redding and Witt 2007.

[33] Weber 1951.

the purpose of keeping "face," a socio-political psychology that regulates both one's self-esteem and status position within the group. This behavioral system is more aesthetic than moral—primarily, in Weber's terms, negative and devoid of moral content.[34] It was another primary source of distrust in Chinese society because everyone knew behavior was only externally controlled, not internally motivated. Community was not a community of believers based on shared values, but a community of ritual based on shared behaviors. Nonetheless, the ideal of propriety was broadly accepted (and enforced). It worked to socialize the masses and brought a remarkable endurance to Chinese civilization.

C. K. Yang has criticized Weber's view, arguing instead that proprietary norms were based on unified ethical principles and, far from mere external conformity, contained definite and positive emotional attachment.[35] It seems clear that Yang is right to correct Weber's exaggerations of the internal emptiness of Confucian conventions. The bonds between parents and children in Chinese society are visibly strong and their emotional energy flows into the channels set by Confucian ethics: as Confucian ethics shapes the form of these feelings, the feelings internalize the forms.

The more fundamental problem appears more sociological than psychological. Defining, regulating, and enforcing moral authority was jealously guarded by the government, particularly Confucian scholar-officials.[36] From the beginning, their power had deep moral authority. They were the best-educated group in society in the area of ethics. But through the authority to tax and other such powers, they also controlled the primary means to wealth in agrarian China.[37] Capitalism was political capitalism; that is, officials accumulated capital through the use of their office. Hence, the people in charge of moral law were also prone to the abuse of power. It is a characteristic of government-society relations in China that is difficult to overestimate to this day. It was (and is) another source of dishonesty in Chinese society because the abuse of authority in government bred dishonesty across society as a

---

[34] Weber 1951.

[35] C. K. Yang 1963.

[36] C. K. Yang 1961.

[37] "For two thousand years the emperor and his bureaucrats were China's biggest spenders. . . . few individuals outside government offices earned more than a skilled laborer" (Hsu 1981: 188). Clearly the economic system was structured by and for the benefit of the emperor and his officials.

whole. And this dishonesty is another source of the universal distrust in Chinese society discussed above.

Officials had little choice but to sell justice, offices, and favors and to skim tax revenues—because they were underpaid and had to spend heavily for gifts to superiors in order to receive positions and hold onto them once they had them.[38] Not buying extravagant gifts for superiors was political suicide. The practice was so widespread that officials regarded public monies as a legitimate source of private income.

The government passed more candidates through the examinations than there were positions to put them in. Thus competition for positions was intense. The hierarchy was such that once in a position, superiors could arbitrarily remove subordinates. This not only kept subordinates completely dependent on superiors and continuously transferring wealth to them; it kept the whole bureaucratic structure dependent on the emperor, with the individual unable to develop an independent power and status position. In this way, the continuous pressure to undermine the patrimonial system and return to a feudal order was kept in check.

The Confucian ethic deified wealth. Along with tremendous population density, the Confucian belief that wealth is a universal means to moral perfection led to "a calculating mentality and self-sufficient frugality of unexampled intensity."[39] The Chinese social environment has always been brutally competitive.[40] Most economic mobility in China was downward due to government exploitation, famine, and war.[41] For those rare families that were able to get a family member into the class of officials, the prospects improved.[42] The life of the Confucian official was dedicated to the cultivation of "moral perfection."[43] This required wealth, and partly explains why moral "perfection" existed side by side with the abuse of power.[44]

---

[38] Hsu 1981.

[39] Weber 1951: 242.

[40] China's population exceeded 300 million by 1800 (Rong 2003).

[41] Gates 1996. "At least one-third of the Chinese farmers existed on a calorie count that was below the minimum for subsistence" (Hsu 1981: 300). The situation for farm labor was even worse.

[42] Most often this would be a family that was already wealthy, because the cost of supporting a son through the education and examination process was considerable.

[43] This meant, among other things, not getting involved in implementation, rather restricting one's efforts to policy pronouncements (Bendix 1960). This distaste for labor is common among aristocratic classes.

[44] As happened with Christianity, Confucian benevolence never fully won over the power interests of the leadership classes.

3. *Culture.* The ancient development of Chinese culture is inseparable from the ancient development of Chinese religion. Key themes in early Chinese culture are Confucian optimism about ultimate questions of nature and man's place in it, deep concern for order and harmony, reliance on bureaucratic organization to maintain order, and emphasis on the collectivity over the individual.[45] Implicit in this list are two underlying themes: the passive and traditionalist nature of Chinese culture promoted by Confucian and Taoist values and the patrimonial state, and strong kinship organization through which these values are implemented and maintained.[46]

It is impossible to imagine the longevity of both Confucian values and the patrimonial state without recognizing the particular character of the Chinese family and its role in Chinese society as the model of Chinese organization and the carrier of the Confucian ethic. The Chinese family is a system of roles with the father at the fulcrum.[47] Each role has duties; personal interests are sublimated. The emphasis is on obedience. Obedience is the source of power. Rules or rights play a secondary role at best. This leaves the father as a near-absolute authority. Unlike the situation in the West, this system was (and is) primary over what is still a rather undeveloped legal system. Chinese law gave legal status only to relatives, not strangers. A few steps outside the family there is a harsh and cold social environment. Inside the family there is the domination of the father.[48] Since the child was so tightly bound inside this unit, independence and individualism were discouraged.

This is the Confucian family; it is the basic building block of the Confucian world. It seeks a peaceful, harmonious, ordered society.[49] It combines discipline with benevolence. Almost all the individual's needs were met within this unit. Discipline was instilled through role socialization. Within the roles, benevolence is possible. This system was fully enforced by the state. Indeed, the family can be seen as the state in microcosm, and the state as a super-family.[50] The problem with this structure, as mentioned above, is the missing middle, civil society. What the Chinese gained in terms of collective stability, they lost in terms of individual autonomy.

[45] Ropp 1990.

[46] C. K. Yang 1963.

[47] Redding 1995.

[48] Though there are other adult authorities as well, since Chinese children often receive considerable care from grandparents. Hsu (1981) argues that the grandparents have more authority than the parents, while aunts and uncles are often equal to the parents in authority.

[49] Redding 1995.

[50] Redding and Witt 2007.

The security and solidity of the Chinese family led to social resignation. The existence of slavery (until recent times), infanticide (still a problem), opium addiction, and the exploitation and inhumane treatment of workers (still a problem in some industries) never aroused popular outrage.[51] Female foot binding was universally practiced until it was stopped under Western influence. The Chinese family was so all-encompassing that moral responsibilities and rights did not extend much beyond it. When the government became too oppressive, there was mass revolt. But when the new government was created, the same authoritarian structure was accepted. The people returned to their families and tried to avoid the government as much as possible. As long as government benevolence was greater than abuse by the government, there was no effort to improve it. This is why China was blessed with long periods of peace. Tradition ruled the land.[52] Family relationships were the core of tradition.

Family structure is mirrored in all types of organizations throughout society. These organizations, as is true of Chinese society generally, can be characterized as having strong vertical order. Nuanced rituals pervade interpersonal relationships defining public behavior toward a superior, an equal, or an inferior in terms of extending greetings, speaking, taking a seat, drinking, and so on.[53] These rituals express status, respect, and bonding in *formal* terms. Sensitivity to the "face" of others, as well as the carrying out of obligations of mutual rights and duties, is crucial to the regulation of the system; otherwise, the system can generate conflict.[54]

The system is focused particularly on those who control vertical mobility, i.e., bosses and teachers.[55] Because organizations continue the hierarchical order inculcated by the family, other types of organization control are needed to a much lesser degree. Individuals accept hierarchical positioning; subordinates cultivate dependence to gain the support of superiors. The hierarchical relation is actually one of mutual dependence. Compromise is preferred over

---

[51] Hsu 1981.

[52] Because of the sanctity of agriculture, rulers never challenged the private ownership of land, but the situation with business was another story (Hsu 1981). Merchants suffered for centuries from government predation. Their best defense was to cultivate relationships with officials and get a family member into the government.

[53] Steidlmeier 1999.

[54] Steidlmeier 1997.

[55] Redding 1995.

conflict. Positive feelings are used to influence.[56] One problem with this system is that vertical order is so strong that horizontal relations remain weak. There is little room for organizational initiative between equals. This is another reason the system resists change. A second problem is that the culture of mutual dependence is so strong that it leads to nepotism and corruption. It is assumed that it is only natural that one will prefer family and friends over others. Thus strong hierarchical order in China comes with an escape hatch through the "back door," which undercuts to a great extent the respectful formality so exactingly enacted in public.[57]

Going through the "back door" is a subcategory of the centrality of primary relationships. Not only is it a counterweight to the strong formal vertical order; it is the result of centuries of subsistence living and a government that has been (and can be) cold, harsh, and unpredictable.[58] Dependence on family and friends is a way to build essential bonds of trust in a political and social environment of terrible mistrust. Whereas in the West civic traditions replaced blood relationships to a considerable extent, in China the norm remains the fact of blood relationships coloring personal relationships. The Chinese tend to be very secretive towards people outside their social circle. Inside their social circle, among friends, they believe relationships should be completely trustworthy, selfless, and dutiful.[59] Armed with these bonds, people can construct amazingly sturdy alliances in order to survive or prosper in an intensely competitive and hostile environment characterized by many *other* sturdy alliances and an always-lurking predatory state.

Friendship is defined through ritual categories, not merely through "natural" attraction. This goes back to Confucian dyadic types, i.e., father-son, emperor-official, husband-wife.[60] A "friend" who does not share membership in an important category such as village, school, or workplace is ambiguous or unusual because that person cannot be defined in terms of an archetypical category at least analogously. In this case, the relationship runs the risk of being defined as purely instrumental, and thus morally discounted.

In China, the individual's position within the group is important because it determines how much of the group's resources one can legitimately demand.

[56] Hsu 1981.

[57] Hwang 1987.

[58] Redding 1995.

[59] Harvey 1999.

[60] There are five dyadic social ties (*gang*) to which broadly significant behavioral rules apply, each of which has its archetypical manifestation in the domestic family (Bell 2000).

The more "face" one has, the more deference, respect, honors, and gifts one receives.[61] For these reasons, face-saving is extremely important.[62] It pays to avoid criticizing or disappointing others, especially key leaders in the group. Skill in flattery, indirectness, equivocations, circumlocution, entertaining, and so forth is important in this system. By doing face work, granting face to others, one is demonstrating one's power because position in the group determines not only how much face one has but also how much face one can grant to others. Face work can thus be seen as a game in which interpersonal positioning can determine one's influence and rewards.

The ubiquitous Chinese practices of gift-giving and feasting can be seen in this context.[63] Both are used to encourage reciprocal obligation. If a gift is accepted, a gift is owed. If the accepter is of high status, any gift he or she gives should reflect this status. The process is negotiated, but it is also delicate. Group harmony and group integrity are always the goals. Distributive equity is much less a factor. But the system of power is important. Gifts from those with little face or power can be ignored. Despite the central ideal of mutual dependence, the role of hierarchy limits equality in Chinese culture.

Nonetheless, it is difficult to exaggerate the importance of reciprocity in Chinese relationships. Reciprocity involves a robust notion of equality. The notion of equality is much more highly developed in Chinese culture and more tightly bound to reciprocity than in many other cultures.[64] This means equality is closely related to expectations for repayment.[65] Chinese culture is a culture that cherishes the importance of repaying favors. Indeed, typical parents expect their children to repay parental care. This system would work only in a relationship-based (traditional) society, where relations are expected to last.[66] Hence, a gift can be seen as a single link in a potentially continuous series of gift exchanges going on for years. Because of the group-oriented nature of Chinese society, to not repay a favor is to damage not just a relationship, but one's position in a whole network of relationships outside of which

---

[61] Steidlmeier 1999.

[62] Hwang 1987.

[63] Hwang 1987

[64] Steidlmeier 1999.

[65] Hwang 1987.

[66] The one-child policy in effect since 1979 has put great pressure on the Confucian family because the virtual disappearance of large families has made care of aging parents much more difficult (Redding and Witt 2007).

it is difficult to accomplish anything. Because one cannot move between networks as easily as in the West, one is much more dependent on this system. Even moving to another city requires references from overlapping networks in order for one to get started in the new network.

Thus the boundary between the in-group and what is outside it is of enormous importance to the Chinese.[67] It is not just the pervasive lack of trust characteristic of Chinese society, the heavy hand of the government, and the culture of hierarchy that send people burrowing into personal relationships; it is also the lack of a reliable system of property rights.[68] Even where there are laws protecting property rights, the courts continue to enact government preferences and protect government officials or protect the friends and family of government officials.[69]

In spite of the government's abuse of power, the Chinese have an overpowering sense of *being* Chinese; there is nothing equivalent to it in the West.[70] It is not unknown to hear openly racist comments from educated Chinese. So on one hand, Chinese society is socially fragmented and intensely competitive and corrupt; on the other, it is capable of almost instant collective single-mindedness which can boil over into collective acts of aggression toward stigmatized out-groups.[71] These two sides of the Chinese mind are related: collective aggression against out-groups reunifies the country, limiting the damage from conflict between in-groups.

4. *Political History.* A striking characteristic of Chinese political history is its continuity. The idea of China has been documented almost continuously since 841 B.C.[72] China was unified by the Qin Dynasty in 221 B.C.[73] The Han Dynasty collapsed in the third century A.D. and was followed by several

---

[67] "Distrust and fear of strangers, or even of those who are simply outside the circle of kin, are striking characteristics of Chinese people. . . . This distrust is vividly dramatized in the near-universal Chinese anxiety about ghosts. Ghosts represent perhaps the ultimate fear in Chinese life, that of being alone in an exacting, competitive world, with no economic base. . . . The chasm between the household and the outer economy is built into China's highest ethics, and into its deepest fears" (Gates 1996: 34).

[68] Redding 1995.

[69] In a recent court case concerning abuse of power by provincial government officials, one official stopped the trial, while he was on the witness stand, to take personal calls on his cell phone (Pan 2008).

[70] Redding 1995.

[71] Hwang 1987.

[72] Tu Wei-ming 1994.

[73] Fairbanks and Goldman 2006.

centuries of disunity, only to be reunified by the Sui Dynasty in 589 A.D., which more or less resulted in imperial unity until 1911.[74] Cultural unity had been achieved by the feudal states even before political unity, and thus was an important reason for the political continuity. Also, as has been mentioned, religious functions were carried out by the emperor and his officials. This eliminated the need for a powerful religious class, which could have challenged the state. There was considerable tolerance for religious diversity for much of Chinese history, but religions were left pluralistic and unorganized. Diversity was permitted as long as it did not lead to dissenting beliefs, politics, or family disruption.[75] The Chinese state has long been obsessed with the suppression of unorthodox thought. It rejected both new ideas and competition between ideas, so as to undermine the impetus for improvement or even change.[76] The political and cultural unity was free to feed on itself. For all practical purposes, China remained a closed civilization to foreign influences until the middle of the nineteenth century.[77] This, too, greatly supported continuity and stasis.

The primary means of state control was the central bureaucracy. Highly educated and well-trained officials have operated impersonal bureaucracies for the past two thousand years. A very demanding examination system was used to guard entrance to officialdom.[78] Bureaucratic organization was never extended outside of government. Despite the rationalization of bureaucracy, corruption, nepotism, and inefficiency still existed within.[79] This reflects its existence as a tool of patrimonial power.

Along with responsibility for canals, irrigation systems, and roads, for example, the bureaucracy was used primarily for control of the population. Officials differed from the rest of the population as much as if they were a different biological phylum.[80] Indeed, the bureaucratic system had a weak relation to local life.[81] There was thus a discontinuity with local control,

---

[74] Ropp 1990.

[75] Gates 1996.

[76] C. K. Yang 1963. This is why intellectuals have had such a harrowing existence in Chinese history, as can be seen especially during the Mao-led period and still today.

[77] Spar and Oi 2006.

[78] These examinations tested knowledge of the classical literature, primarily focusing on the practical problems and status interest of the patrimonial bureaucracy (Weber 1951). Propriety was stressed, while skills in logical reasoning were not.

[79] Sterba 1978.

[80] Gates 1996.

[81] To keep officials dependent on the central government, they were transferred every few years (Gamer 2003a).

which was filled by the gentry,[82] who did not develop rationalized administrative structures. Central government officials operated in their own economic self-interest. High taxes on agriculture were common.[83] Continuous agrarian crisis and land redistribution characterize Chinese history. The latter was used to address the former, or to wring more taxes out of the population. Officials became experts at social control, breaking the population into ever smaller units and co-opting the bodies that escaped fragmentation.[84] The magistrates were not above terrible savagery; control of the population was their goal above all else.[85]

Guild-controlled small workshops received the same exploitation.[86] So much energy was taken up in meeting government demands or defending against them that economic development was impossible. Until only very recently, merchants were held in contempt by the government upon which they depended for protection. Even during the early stages of industrialization in the late nineteenth and early twentieth century, much capital had to be expended on patronage to government officials.[87] This is why the position of an official was by far more attractive than that of an entrepreneur or businessman: the former could protect his wealth.

Wealth thus accumulated in the hands of ruling officials. They spent it to fortify their tax-collecting privileges, to defend from internal or external attack, and to maintain the system of Confucian discipline that kept the population in voluntary compliance with their authority and directives.[88] Given this system, there was never any need for the officials to improve their performance. They remained generalists, rejecting further rational development through specialization.[89] One important consequence was the lack of codification of law; it remained unpredictable and inconsistent on the local level. Ethical and ritualistic norms were used to create and interpret law. This served well the power, prerogatives, and ethical goals of the patrimonial rulers,

[82] Tu Wei-ming 1994. Perhaps here is a primary source for the ubiquitous Chinese middleman: Gentry tried to serve the central government, protect the local population from government exploitation, and profit for themselves (Hsu 1981).

[83] Wong 2003.

[84] Redding and Witt 2007.

[85] Spence 1990b.

[86] Wong 2003.

[87] Boisot and Child 1996.

[88] Gates 1996.

[89] C. K. Yang 1963.

but it blocked off precise forms and procedures needed for legal rationalization and calculability. In this situation, the highly particularistic kinship groups were left to fend for themselves, and did so. The practice of law as an autonomous profession never developed. All in all, outside the family the authority of officials was nearly boundless.

5. *Economic History*. China's economic history is inseparable from its political history. Unlike Europe, the Chinese state never allowed free merchant cities to develop.[90] As has been mentioned, Chinese society had two basic social classes, commoners and officials; economic units were mostly small family groups; and these were kept small through high levels of taxation.[91] Through its legal stance, the state protected the private property of these small family units, but not other forms of enterprise.[92] The whole system was designed for political control, not economic growth.

The Chinese state's relationship to business was far from unambiguous. In addition to holding the merchant in low regard, for most of Chinese history the state stayed aloof from business.[93] This did not, however, stop officials from doing side deals with local merchants or setting up state manufacturing monopolies when income could be had.[94] In any case, the state's primary relationship to its subjects was extractive. This is why kin groups bound together to protect economic activities from a predatory government. The government was not completely against personalism, since it checked the impersonalism needed to develop large-scale organization, a potential threat to the state.[95] To be sure, the state blocked impersonalism by not providing legal protection for contracts. Without reliable contracts, business organization remained small-scale.

As a petty-capitalist class slowly emerged in what was primarily an agrarian society, it became a direct competitor to the state. Since all other potential competitors had been successfully neutralized—e.g., church, nobility, powerful guilds, and strong local government—the petty-capitalists met strong resistance.[96] Ultimately, merchants had no social space, no social

[90] Redding 1995.

[91] Gates 1996.

[92] Redding 1995.

[93] But by enforcing gender and kinship hierarchies within the family—that is, by making women and children second-class citizens—the state maintained political control over household enterprises (Gates 1996).

[94] Weber 1951.

[95] Gates 1996.

[96] Gates 1996.

legitimacy, in a fundamentally agricultural system defined by two classes, officials and families.[97] Since wealth could not be privatized beyond the family, money wealth had to be hidden or in some way protected. This is why merchants invested capital in land, titles, or attempts to get their children into officialdom. Nonetheless, petty-capitalists were always objects of suspicion from officials and families. They were outside of government and half outside of family, because they did not need family labor as farmers did.

Since merchants were politically impotent, they could never gain power beyond their domestic circle.[98] To grow beyond this scale would invite attack both from the state and from others upon whom they would need to depend for expansion. Under these threatening conditions, successful merchants became pragmatic, frugal, and hard-working. They also carefully cultivated relationships and their reputation for honesty in their local area so as to secure credit outside official channels.[99] Like kin groups generally, Chinese businessmen learned to look out for themselves and avoid officials. They did this by developing a flexible organization under their direct control, with movable assets (avoiding large capital investment) and deep reserves.[100] Economies of scale could not be achieved because management and capital could not be concentrated. This is one reason the Chinese became energetic experts at low-technology techniques, developing little aptitude for radical technological innovation.[101]

As stated earlier, this system was highly stable. In an agrarian context, it was also successful. Until the fifteenth or sixteenth century, many scholars believe, China was more advanced than the West in science, economy, politics, and culture.[102] Per capita income and internal trade may have been greater than Europe's at the beginning of the nineteenth century.[103] But the system did not change; that is, it did not improve. In the eight centuries

---

[97] Guilds produced practically all manufactured goods sold in pre-twentieth century China (Gates 1996). The guilds were kin dominated. The absence of legal guarantees for guild privileges kept the guilds in check (C. K. Yang 1963).

[98] Gates 1996.

[99] Redding 1995.

[100] Gates 1996.

[101] Redding 1995. Weber (1951: 226) emphasizes a religious explanation for the same facts: "[I]n the magic garden of heterodox doctrine (Taoism) a rational economy and technology . . . was simply out of the question."

[102] Gates 1996.

[103] Ropp 1990.

before 1900, it increased, added more of the same, but did not develop.[104] Small-scale economic activity meant that productivity remained trapped. Isolated from foreign influence and exploited by the ruling elite, commerce never evolved into industry.

By checking the natural tendency of free markets to produce ever larger pools of capital, to concentrate risk in the hands of a single entrepreneur; by making arbitrary interventions in fiscal policy, sometimes reversing directions, at other times completely restructuring the agrarian economy; by supporting a dominating kinship organization with little market development outside the reach of personal relationships, hindering work discipline and a free market for labor; by practicing self-serving interpretations of law depriving economic decision making of systemic order and predictability—the state and the traditions it fostered for two millennia created an economic environment of brutal competition, small-scale organization, and risk avoidance.

II. Communism

It was not a random accident that Marxism–Leninism–Maoism grew on Confucian soil.[105] Both focus on human rather than transcendental reality. Both have humanistic goals, but result in authoritarian control. Mao's cult of personality follows the emperor's Son of Heaven charisma. Despite great differences, the shadow-land of collective authority flows through both.

1. Political System. In 1949, Mao Zedong announced the beginning of the People's Republic of China, a communist state. The government was intent on joining the most developed countries in the world. One way the communists went about doing this and securing control of society was through the totalization of the political process; very little was left private for the individual.[106] A work-unit system was devised that included a great proportion of workers, both agricultural and industrial. Autonomy in the spheres of economics, ethics, and culture was greatly reduced; politics ruled all; to a significant extent the individual's whole life fell under the sway of the Communist Party.[107] There was practically no social space left for other power bases or even other sources of ideas, let alone ideals. This experiment

---

[104] Gates 1996.
[105] Hoiman and King 2003.
[106] Munro 1977.
[107] Hanafin 2002.

in totalization was very violent. Almost immediately upon taking over, the communists killed over two million landlords.[108] This was an effort to radically and immediately change the ancient nature of Chinese society.

In spite of the stated policy during Mao's reign that intellectuals were supposed to be leaders of the nation, they were persecuted mercilessly. Ironically, they were crushed after the "Let a Thousand Flowers Bloom" movement in 1957, when intellectuals had been invited to criticize the Party. This was immediately followed by the "Anti-Rightist Campaign," in which practically all prominent intellectuals were purged. Most intellectuals came from families with landed wealth and were seen as contaminated and a threat to the new regime. In any case, what would have been seen as common Confucian expressions of political protest in imperial China were high-risk under the communists.[109]

The "Great Leap Forward," taking place between 1958 and 1960 and intended to increase economic productivity, led, in combination with natural disasters, to mass starvation—killing an estimated 20 to 30 million people.[110] Power struggles inside the Party as a result of these failures led Mao to attack the Party itself. He did so by instigating teenagers to forcibly and violently punish anyone even suspected of doubting communist ideals.[111] This became known as the "Cultural Revolution" (1966–1976). At least hundreds of thousands more died as primitivist and fundamentalist sentiments were released within communities, even within families. In Tu Wei-ming's words, "[N]ationalism degenerated into cannibalism."[112] During this decade-long savagery, societal values were severely damaged. A whole generation not only lost opportunities for education and professional practice, but was left disillusioned and cynical.[113] The following generation, those in their twenties during the 1980s, grew up in this disillusionment and cynicism.

[108] Gamer 2003a.

[109] Tu Wei-ming 1994. To be sure, both Confucian and communist regimes had put a straitjacket on dissent and an emphasis on socialization practices (Pye 1988). But communist mind control was something new.

[110] Fairbank and Goldman 2006.

[111] The teenagers, known as the "Red Guards," actually broke into two factions and started fighting each other in open warfare within cities. One faction was from educated families, the other the less educated but upwardly mobile children of Communist Party members and government officials (Fairbank and Goldman 2006).

[112] Tu Wei-ming 1994: 29.

[113] In the aftermath of the Cultural Revolution, there has been long-term damage to government administration, factory management, and the education system (Wong 2003).

The Communist Party is responsible for the Great Leap Forward and the Cultural Revolution and other disasters, but it has never been held accountable. This has been managed in several ways. First, collective and individual amnesia is a striking characteristic of Chinese society.[114] From personal experience, I can say that I seldom came across undergraduate students in Shanghai in 2007 who knew much about the Cultural Revolution. The Communist Party is able to enforce this amnesia through the strict control of public information and of the education system, punishing those who do not toe the Party line.

Second, Maoist doctrine teaches that the distinction between private and public domains must be minimized, the human mind is highly plastic, and people learn through imitation and peer respect.[115] Hence, omnipresent state involvement in society attempts to ensure that all information, education, and role models lead to the acceptance of social duties and collective goals *as defined by the Party*. The notion that political leaders should structure the population's belief system for collective purposes carries on Confucian traditions of how best to achieve social harmony and stability.[116] The result is not only intense socialization starting in the first years of school, but also the use of informers throughout the education system, indeed throughout most organizations.[117] From among those who remain recalcitrant, individuals are picked as negative examples or chosen for selective punishment, sometimes severe, as further education about the right path and as a reminder about the costs of crossing the Party.

Third, having insufficient legitimacy of its own to back up its power, the Party continues to use coercion, including outbursts of violence, to maintain control. Its leaders also continue to use public shaming and a ubiquitous presence to create fear in the population.[118] The army reports to the Party, not the government, so government officials are afraid to confront the Party or the army. The army and provincial and local Party members are typically involved in illegal money-making operations such as prostitution networks, child labor,

---

[114] Tu Wei-ming 1994.

[115] The goal is to achieve a grand unity that by definition minimizes disparities between people (Munro 1977). This reflects the ideal of equality in socialist theory.

[116] Lampton 2001. The importance and effectiveness of social conditioning are easily grasped in a Confucian society, where ritual is a basic part of social interaction (Ropp 1990).

[117] Of course, socialization is already under way in the family. The child is not permitted to express any feelings of hostility towards parental authority (Pye 1988).

[118] J. McGregor 2005.

and theft of state-owned assets, and so on.[119] The legal system, too, is controlled by the Party, thus offering little help in prosecuting corrupt officials. Basically, the ruling elite is subject to almost no accountability.[120] Its primary purpose appears to be to maintain power. This can be seen clearly in its shift to "market socialism"—after decades of strict ideological commitment to Marxism.

The switch to "market socialism" has allowed the Party to maintain power in four ways. First, as the economy has been "privatized," the Party has positioned itself as an essential partner in wealth-producing opportunities.[121] Little can be done economically without government involvement in myriad ways.[122] Second, in addition to the need for the state's cooperation, obedience is predicated on fear—fear of exclusion from participation in economic growth.[123] Third, as economic growth has increased so has government corruption.[124] This has enabled the Party to maintain its hold over the many officials who enforce its edicts by allowing them to grow rich at public expense.[125] Fourth, the government directs people's attention away from itself by drawing attention to foreign threats.[126] Because of foreign domination in the nineteenth and twentieth centuries, the Chinese are already nationalistic and sensitive to foreign threats. But even more basic than the "lost century," China's ancient and enduring civilization naturally has a strong sense of itself. The Party merely takes advantage of these historical identities to encourage fear of foreign nations, and thus support for itself.

2. *Chinese Perceptions of the Government.* The Chinese people's perception of their government is complex, but more negative than positive. On the positive side, the central government still enjoys considerable support.[127] This support deteriorates rapidly as one descends down the government hierarchy. The population's loyalty to the central government is related to the great tradition of Confucianism and the great strength and durability it has lent to Chinese political culture.[128] The Chinese tend to respect ultimate authority,

---

[119] Pan 2008; R. McGregor 2010.

[120] R. McGregor 2010.

[121] Pei 2006.

[122] Indeed, arbitrary intervention by the Chinese government remains a constant danger to many firms (Peng and Luo 2000).

[123] Krueger 2009.

[124] Sun 2004.

[125] Pei 2006.

[126] R. McGregor 2010.

[127] *Economist* (March 3, 2006).

[128] Pye 1988.

even in the form of despotic government.[129] For many Chinese, the Confucian principle of order is their top concern. They want a strong government to maintain order. Many also do not seem to understand or even conceive of possible alternatives. Dickson found, in a survey of business people, that many believed China already had a multiparty system.[130]

On the negative side, a telling fact is that many successful Chinese either leave or plan to leave China.[131] The reasons for the Chinese people's dissatisfaction with their government begin in fear—fear of an unfair legal system, of a network of informers, of officials dangerously removed from the consequences of their actions, and of ignorant, selfish, or cruel economic decisions that can result in years of hardship, including death.[132] Another cause of great bitterness is the blatant and cynical corruption of government officials.[133] Finally, among those of the Chinese who have participated in the country's economic growth, they want more protection of their property, i.e., a government and legal system that protects them.[134] That so many leave or plan to leave suggests that they are not getting this.

Perhaps a more important aspect of society-government relations is manifested in how the Chinese people see themselves because of how they see the government. There is a pervasive sense of cynicism in Chinese society. Since 1911, no institution of significance, from universities to the press to civic organizations, has lasted more than a generation.[135] Even the Communist Party has been so radically reoriented that its own members are cynical and uncertain; hence, their corruption. When the Party introduced market reforms, it lost whatever moral legitimacy it had left following repeated episodes of incompetence and violence.

[129] Madsen 1995.

[130] Dickson 2003. Tsai (2007) found that both officials and entrepreneurs did not think of democracy in terms of elections, rule of law, and protection of individual and minority rights. In a graduate seminar of 25 students at a university in Shanghai in 2007, I was told that China had a democratic political system (Feldman 2007c).

[131] A survey published in April 2011 showed that almost 60 percent of wealthy Chinese have arranged for or are considering emigration (Page 2011).

[132] Pan 2008; Harney 2008; R. McGregor 2010.

[133] Sun 2004; Pei 2006.

[134] Between 1999 and 2004, the number of self-employed businesses in urban areas in China dropped from 31.6 million to 23.5 million (Huang 2008), as a result of rising government fees.

[135] Tu Wei-ming 1994.

When Deng Xiaoping introduced market reforms in 1978, high-level officials scrambled to get as much as they could for themselves, rather than for the good of the nation. This was not a secret. The Chinese people wondered why their culture had not produced leaders who are moral and ethical.[136] They could not help thinking that their corrupt leaders were right: self-indulgent materialism *is* all there is to life. After all, the same leaders who were warning about spiritual pollution were the ones who were stealing the most! What else did Chinese culture have to offer the world?

Not much, it seemed. The committed cadres who had believed in the communist ideals were left with nothing but despair.[137] People strongly committed to a country's values play an important role in any society, because they maintain and transmit the society's traditions.[138] They hold the center together. In China, such persons suffered a double blow: Marxism savaged Confucianism, and "market socialism" replaced Marxism.[139] Culturally, the Chinese live among fragments with the ancient obsession with acquisitiveness currently holding center stage.

3. *Tiananmen Square.* In 1989, decade-long on-again, off-again protests against the government came to a violent end in Beijing, on the central symbolic ground of Chinese public life, Tiananmen Square. The protests centered on the unfair distribution of job and income opportunities and on the general theft of state assets by government officials that emerged simultaneously with economic reforms.[140] Most protesters were Beijing workers demanding protection from the insecurities of the newly introduced market economy, but unemployed peasants from rural areas also participated.[141] Students from top Beijing universities and, over time, from other universities all over the country, were deeply involved and rose to leadership positions. Students were concerned that good jobs kept going to relatives of political leaders: where would that leave them? Hence, though much of the language

---

[136] Madsen 1995.

[137] Madsen 1995. The battle between those wanting to return to China's Maoist past and those wanting to proceed with societal reforms is still raging as can be seen in the recent downfall of Bo Xilai (Garnaut 2012).

[138] Shils 1981.

[139] Tu Wei-ming 1994.

[140] Bribery cases rose almost fivefold in absolute numbers between 1988 and 1989 because of the central role of bribery in the use of public office for private gain during this period (Sun 2004).

[141] Madsen 1995.

of protest focused on freedom and democracy, the deeper sentiment was anger against government corruption, arbitrariness, and unfairness.[142]

The classes that were not benefitting from the "reforms" were on the square. Gates reports that even some government workers and military and security people supported the protests.[143] The core issue was this: Could the communist state continue to monopolize the distribution of public goods? Importantly, one class not on the square and not supporting the protests was the business people, the majority of whom were small-scale. The Party had needed them to implement the move to marketization, and they had benefited. To attack the government would be to attack themselves, because their success was based on a close working relationship with government officials.[144] Certainly the government saw in the protests a threat to its power, but business people saw a threat to the order necessary for their success, and to the system through which their success had been possible. Because the citizenry never debated these questions—Who was on the square and who was not? What were their motivations, and how were these related to the societal changes taking place? What role did government dictatorship and corruption play?—any future fundamental political reform will have to begin with a reassessment of the Tiananmen Square protests and the government's violent response to them. At this point, in China, the government blocks the words "Tiananmen Square" from Internet access.

4. *Economic System.* According to Gates, much of the improvement in China's economy between 1949 and 1978 can be traced to the socialist accomplishments of the 1950s.[145] At first, Mao stated that the communists needed the private business sector, what he called the "national bourgeoisie," given the country's stage of socialism.[146] But this did not last long. In 1951, the communists launched the "Three Antis" program, and then the "Five Antis" program in 1952, attacking the "national bourgeoisie" for tax evasion, bribery, theft of state property, stealing state secrets, swindling the government on contracts, and so on. This was followed by mass trials, psychological terror, and forced confessions. Some 450,000 private businesses were investigated. Most accused business people were fined or sent to reeducation camps.

---

[142] Madsen 1995.
[143] Gates 1996.
[144] Tsai 2007.
[145] Gates 1996.
[146] Tsai 2007.

It is estimated that 200,000 suicides took place. The largest private businesses were forced into joint private-state enterprises. Between 1953 and 1957, these joint enterprises were nationalized.[147] Between 1950 and 1953, private wholesale trade declined from 76.1 percent of the economy to 30.3 percent.

Even more draconian measures were taken in the agricultural sector. Starting in the late 1950s, enormous agricultural communes were created that resembled military organizations more than industrial organizations.[148] Government economic policy ignored basic laws of economics, psychology, and management, and basic processes of exchange.[149] This was the period of the "Great Leap Forward" mentioned above, when tens of millions died of starvation.

The goal of these changes was to use the economic system to achieve total political control. Totalization, however, is never absolutely achievable. Though the application of this method to industrial organization did not lead to mass death, it did lead to perverse results. State-controlled industrial organizations developed a highly institutionalized network of patron-client relations between superiors and subordinates.[150] The original intention was to use industrial organization to gain complete control over workers by making workers completely dependent on the organization. Their every need was met: from food, housing, and medical care to education and entertainment. By making the individual dependent on the enterprise and the enterprise dependent on the Party, Party leaders sought total control over the citizenry. To secure this system, each work unit had a Party branch coterminous with it, as well as security personnel and informers. In this kind of structure, each individual is monitored; each individual has a life-long file containing his

[147] At the same time, retailers were merged into cooperative teams and rural private markets were forbidden (Tsai 2007).

[148] Spar and Oi 2006. In the countryside, where the majority of the population lived, 26,000 "communes" were created, each consisting of two to ten thousand families (Hsu 1981). Each commune was subdivided into several "production brigades," which themselves were subdivided into several "production teams." In most areas, the "production teams" were the traditional villages. The local government controlled the various levels of the commune structure. The local government reported to a commune people's congress, elected every two years. The whole structure was paralleled by the Communist Party structure, all the way down to the work teams. Importantly, since the traditional villages remained intact, the ancient kinship and village ties remained foundational. From the beginning, free-riding crippled commune efficiency (Fukuyama 1995).

[149] Redding and Witt 2007.

[150] Walder 1988.

superiors' *political* evaluations of him.[151] Superiors thus exercised great control not only over salary and promotions, but over the individual's whole social and material life.

It is here, however, in the superior-subordinate relationship, that the system of total control takes a detour. In these relationships, instrumental-personal ties were enacted.[152] While the goal of totalization is to establish the individual's very identity—gain authority over the whole person—in the end, the superior is still dependent on the subordinate for help in meeting the superior's goals; thus, an illicit personalism crept into the relationship, so that each helped the other somewhat independently of top-down edict.[153]

The individual, instead of internalizing all political commitments, develops a "calculative attitude" for getting what he wants from his boss.[154] The organizational context is one of continuous politicization, i.e., continuous political indoctrination through study groups, discussion groups, challenge groups, and so on. Because the *context* is so politicized but the *individual's* interests are personalized in her relations with her bosses, the individual learns to say the right thing publicly while remaining skeptical privately.[155] The presentation of self is continuously evaluated, thus becoming ritualistic—ironically similar to Confucian deference to authority figures. Yet the external matters. Joining the Youth League, Party, and so on, leads to a better material

---

[151] It was not just the individual's behavior that was monitored and recorded. The individual's "class background," based on the work done by parents and other relatives, was also part of that person's evaluation even though he or she had no control over it. This latter point shows how system domination went beyond behavioral control to categorization and definition of self (Foucault 1979), the purpose of which was to change society from the inside out.

[152] Walder 1988.

[153] Interestingly, Weber (1951) argues that the origin of personalism in Chinese relationships derives from provincial officials' development of personal relationships with local people to resist administrative centralization by the central government. Walder's analysis of communist industrial organization is analogous. This is contrary to much of the literature, which sees personalism as a defense against government predation. The fact that personalism originates with mid-level officials—or SOE managers in Walder's data—demonstrates how Chinese government could be overbearing even upon itself.

[154] Walder 1988: 149.

[155] In collective culture, there is always a tension between the individual's identification with the group and her inner sense of self, even though the sense of self arises primarily from the group (Pye 1988). The centrality of individual interests in Walder's data not only points to central control and its shadow, but the primacy of group over society, and thus the limits of fanaticism even in a society organized around collective values, with a government committed to totalization.

life because one is more closely aligned with Party ideology. Hence, externally the individual must meet expectations, but internally he maintains some autonomy based on his interests. Thus, shadowing the formal hierarchical structure and its ideologically determined rewards and punishments is a system of interpersonal and informal networks where the hierarchy is softened, the ideology is lightened, and a much more complex transaction economy is set up within hierarchical relations.

In this system of external conformity and internal calculation, it is vital never to take risks.[156] Violations of the external order were not tolerated because they not only challenged totalization, they also exposed the systematic lies upon which it stood.[157] The political always dominated the economic, though underground personal interests flowed continuously contrary to political edict. Hence, though productivity was always a desperate goal and desperately needed, it was always secondary to control. Sleeping on the job, reading the newspaper, or drinking tea was common because workers were neither self-motivated nor self-directed, but were sitting subdued in a hierarchical system where to do anything not ordered by one's boss risked violating the external order by which status was ascribed, control maintained, and culture proclaimed.

Within this system, some were more ambitious, playing the game more intensely, since success at it led to promotions and a better material life. This was the choice of the "activists."[158] Undoubtedly some percentage of activists internalized communist ideology to a great extent and their personality was structured by it. In any case, activists created tension with the rank and file who were not oriented toward ideal commitment, either sincerely or in order to get ahead. The rank and file was more passive and defensive when it came to ideology. They mistrusted and disliked the activists. The social life of the activist was difficult because there was intense competition between activists to outdo one another in terms of correct behavior, development of relationships with powerful superiors, and work productivity. In addition, the teasing and cold shoulder from the rank and file separated these activists from large numbers of their peers. Nonetheless, activists were still central in the factory

---

[156] Walder 1988.

[157] The magic garden of irrational wishes and leadership worship was part of Mao's power base. Trying to overturn the applecart could get a person involuntary admission to a mental hospital (Pan 2008).

[158] Walder 1988.

power system. They aspired to be in the center, and in so doing they supported the center's values and power. The ideological system and the continuous indoctrination efforts of the Party were inconceivable without the activists' dedication, whether emotionally charged or feigned.[159]

Following Mao's death in 1976 and the economic reforms of 1978, the state industrial sector underwent continuous downsizing—even though in 2012 it still employed 46 million workers. The culture of the state industrial sector has also changed, from ideological to paternalistic.[160] One must still support the Communist Party and its central beliefs and programs, but productivity is slowly becoming a relevant value under the threat of plant closings and job loss. But one is no longer asked to sacrifice for the ideal socialist society.[161] Instead, the state attempts to secure worker loyalty through material benefits such as job security, health insurance, pensions, and numerous perks.

Activists are still central to the factory power system through their support for their bosses. Loyalty is still central, but loyalty by itself is no longer enough; workers must be loyal *and* qualified. Hence, the hierarchy is still in place but ideology has a much smaller role in defining it and productivity demands increasingly influence decisions. The subculture of instrumental-personal ties thrives and has even expanded with the decline in ideology. But the Party's goals are still paramount; it will not hesitate to use escalating threats and violence in the face of resistance.

Finally, in order to fully understand the communist system of industrial organization, we must point out its relations to, and continuities with, pre-communist forms of Chinese social organization. There is an important continuity with Confucianism. The impersonal ideological commitments demanded by the Maoist state and the personalism that existed alongside them transform but continue the Confucian (feudal) ideal of combining

---

[159] The activist's ideological role was not easy to carry out (Walder 1988). One not only had to understand the theory to correctly commit to it, but one had to keep up with continuously changing, sometimes reversing theoretical positions, organizational policies, socialist values, and "facts." If one was said to have the wrong "class background," one had to agree with the charge, no matter how preposterous, and confess to having received capitalist orders to sabotage socialism.

[160] Walder 1988.

[161] Nor is the ideal socialist society sacrificing for its workers. Tens of millions have been thrown out of their jobs, losing promised pensions and health care after a lifetime of work (Pan 2008).

loyalty to filial virtues with direct loyalty to superiors.[162] Commitment to filial virtues channels loyalty to superiors, while service to superiors results in benefits to the subordinate. Communism attempted to replace the filial virtues with a terrifying total politics covering every aspect of the individual's life; yet personal benefit still arose in the inextinguishable directness of the superior-subordinate tie.

In addition to feudal virtues, patrimonial social organization pervades Chinese socialism.[163] The communists inherited a patrimonial bureaucracy that they never successfully eliminated from socialist organization.[164] The patrimonial (Confucian) bureaucracy was run by a non-specialized class of literati. Communist organization was built around activists who also lacked specialized training. Without specialized training, neither bureaucracy successfully institutionalized universal rules; both demonstrated an abundance of personal interpretations of rules based on individual self-interest.

Perhaps the most important continuity of all is that both the imperial bureaucratic state and the communist socialist state were based on predatory relations towards their society.[165] Both governments extracted revenue from their citizens by institutionalizing discipline through a hierarchical vision of personal relationships. The fact that such continuity existed over such long periods of time, and across such different systems, confirms the profound importance the hierarchical-deference system has in Chinese culture. Indeed, even the escape clause of individualism that is common to both systems, in the personalism ethic,[166] further details not only how hierarchical culture functioned and adapted, but how utterly central it is to Chinese civilization.

5. *Modernization.* When looking back over the last two centuries of Chinese history, some have argued that the tortured attempt to modernize is the central issue in Chinese culture.[167] Indeed, as just described in the

---

[162] Gates 1996.

[163] Even though feudalism and patrimonialism are the two most prominent forms of traditional authority, they are distinctive. In Weberian terms, feudalism always involves a contract between free men, whereas patrimonialism is an extension of the ruler's household and as such the ruler's officials are dependent on him (Bendix 1960). Feudal vassals as a group follow a code of honor defined by filial loyalty and brotherly affection, whereas in the patrimonial system the ruler seeks to make his will the ultimate authority, merely using officials to extend his rule.

[164] Boisot and Child 1996.

[165] Gates 1996.

[166] Hefner 1998.

[167] Pye 1988.

discussion of the Chinese economic system under Mao's version of socialism, China faces many obstacles—including its continuous re-creation of feudal values and patrimonial social organization. Many societies have been able, to some extent, to rewrite their kinship rules; but in China the state, even unwittingly, as under Mao, continuously recreates the patrilineal core.[168] As a result, China entered the twenty-first century having more continuity with its ancient past in culture, politics, and economics than any of the other ancient states. Compared with the states deriving from the Roman Empire, for example, China still maintains more sexism, political authoritarianism, and shackled capitalism. For Hill Gates, state-supported kinship relationships are at the center of this continuously re-created pattern.[169] For this reason, the overwhelming majority of Chinese intellectuals believe Chinese identity is incompatible with modernization, defined as a commitment to democracy and free markets (i.e., individualism).[170] This has led them to dismiss their Confucian heritage as a relic of the outmoded feudal past.[171]

It is true that if modernization is defined in terms of democracy and capitalism, the Chinese system has a long way to go—because, even in regard to capitalism, despite the great economic growth in China, the Chinese state still calls the shots. As long as the Communist Party maintains its dictatorship and markets are allowed to develop only to the extent that they meet Party needs, the freedom and individualism associated with capitalism in the West will likely *not* develop.[172] This is the great question: Will markets continue to develop to the point where they will throw off the yoke of dictatorship, or will dictatorship continue to use markets for its own ends? The latter seems more likely, since the former will require not only the transformation of the state, but also the transformation of the kinship culture which supports the state. True modernization, even accepting a broad definition that included non-Western forms, will require interrelated changes in political, cultural, and economic systems.

As was graphically demonstrated in the Tiananmen Square massacre, the Chinese state has made little progress toward political liberalization. Indeed, as was mentioned previously, the state does not even allow the memory of

[168] Gates 1996.
[169] Gates 1996.
[170] Tu Wei-ming 1994.
[171] Tu Wei-ming 2002.
[172] Friedman 1972.

Tiananmen to be transferred to the next generation. And in the generation that experienced Tiananmen directly, there is complacency and escapism.[173] Hence, Chinese culture is fragmented, but the fragmentation is concealed by the state's suppression of freedom of speech. One would think that as China continues to invite in the West, the pressure for change will only grow, as more and more Chinese are exposed to new ideas and alternative world views. But, as we have seen, it is not only the communist dictatorship that controls Chinese social life; it is also Confucianism. Marxism–Leninism could wither away—indeed has—with but little change in the culture of hierarchy.

What "modernization" means in this context is unfolding before our eyes. It means increasing cultural fragmentation, economic development, and materialism. How long moral decline can continue before some kind of political change takes place is unclear. It is hard to think that materialism offers a long-term answer to moral decline because materialism addresses very little of the aggregate of deeper human needs.[174] This is so even though materialism does fit well with the intense acquisitiveness, deeply embedded preference for family business, and intense competition characteristic of Chinese cultural history. But the family business ethic was always supported by the Confucian emphasis on the family. For now, great energy is focused on materialism, perhaps partly as a response to the great hardships experienced during the Cultural Revolution, and also because there are few other avenues open.[175] Maybe in the longer term there will be a resurgence of Confucianism. In any case, Confucianism and the intense kinship relations that it gives rise to *must* be the cultural raw material out of which any changes emerge.

III. Conclusion

A culture is not a simple or consistent thing. It has different parts created in different periods for different reasons that relate, more or less, to each other. Every culture is different, of course; some are better integrated than others. China is an ancient culture of enormous complexity. It has its share of paradoxes: it is at once of almost unparalleled continuity and great fragmentation;

---

[173] Pomfret 2007; Goldman 2006a. Complacency and escapism have given way to an irreverent nihilism in the following generation. This mixes with the nationalism stoked by communist propaganda and the pride in China's remarkable rise.

[174] Humans need moral order, an order that provides coherence, continuity, and justice (Shils 1975).

[175] Egri and Ralston 2004.

its outstanding feature is the importance of hierarchy, yet interpersonal networks operate outside, through, and in contradiction to hierarchy. In this conclusion, I will try to make some sense of Chinese culture in terms of the historical context it presents to political and economic reform and the development of free markets within China.

One of the defining features of Chinese culture is its optimism about the human world, as opposed to the idealization of a heavenly world that stands in contrast to this world and is critical of it. Chinese religion and philosophy posit the human world as the right one, where man, nature, and heaven can live in harmony. Harmony is both a central goal and the expected practice. Throughout Chinese history, there has been less debate about other worlds and ideal kingdoms than about the earthly Kingdom and its regulation. This has led to a great emphasis on right behavior in the here and now, to maintaining harmony with others. It is an applied philosophy of the whole or, in other words, a collectivist ethics. The emphasis is on the external over the internal; the concrete over the abstract. Inevitably, tradition and ritual play important roles as effective mechanisms to provide predictability, order, and harmony.

Above all, the key structure holding the system together, allowing it to function with a minimum of conflict, is hierarchy. From top to bottom, everyone has their place. This is what makes harmony possible: all relationships are defined within a right order, and at the center of this order is hierarchy. From the relationships of citizens to emperor, from family members to father, hierarchy is the core organizing principle. Loyalty is thus the key virtue. Superiors expect loyalty from subordinates; subordinates want to offer loyalty and in return receive security from superiors. This is true in both Confucianism and Chinese communism.

Loyalty implies another key feature of Chinese culture, the personalism ethic. Continuing relationships become personalized, as opposed to regulation through shared values. From the intense, involuted relations inside the family to the subordinate's relationship to her boss, personal loyalty is expected; personal respect must be expressed upward as personal benevolence should be expressed downward. All this is ritually regulated within a vast complex of cultural instructions. Making loyalty personal makes it particular and concrete. One person owes loyalty to another. Abstract ethical codes that apply to categories such as "customer" or "citizen" are secondary at best. This gives Chinese society a strong tendency toward decentralization, as personal networks of direct relationships play a very strong role in social organization and social interaction. This is a source of the much-commented upon Chinese dishonesty, because people outside one's network receive much less consideration and care. Within the network, however, intense feelings of obligation and responsibility can abound.

Hierarchy as the central organizing principle of Chinese culture has led to great concentrations of power through all spheres of Chinese life. Nowhere is this seen more clearly than within the government. From the imperial system to the communist, great power was concentrated both in a single individual at the top as well as in the structure as a whole. In dynastic history, scholar-officials controlled religion, law, and administration, which gave them enormous power over the population. This concentration of power inevitably led to abuse. Scholar-officials used their offices as rent-producing systems just as, to this day, government officials routinely demand bribes just to carry out their official duties.[176]

Even though government corruption led to corruption generally, as the population either protected themselves from government exploitation by dishonest means or just followed the government's lead, government rent-seeking was an accepted part of Chinese society. It was accepted up to the point, that is, when it became too oppressive it led to open rebellion. Until that point was reached, political capitalism has repeatedly been a systemic, expected, and legitimate part of government behavior in China.[177] A government position was, and still is, though to a lesser extent, a respected and coveted job in Chinese society. It is coveted and esteemed for its job security, benefits, reasonable work demands, financial opportunities, and rent-producing capacities as well as its position in the central structure of power.[178]

The fact that government office was the primary means to wealth in agrarian society shows the dominance of government in Chinese life. All other categories of livelihood, from landholding to farming to merchants to

---

[176] To be sure, historically it was common worldwide for officials in patrimonial bureaucracy to use their offices to generate personal income. The problem is patrimonial patterns still penetrate Chinese bureaucracy. Though, even without patrimonial bureaucracy, government corruption is common worldwide in other emerging markets.

[177] This is undoubtedly still the case today, though it is no longer legitimate. "Corruption thrives in sectors with heavy state involvement and considerable room for administrative discretion: customs, taxation, the sale of land, infrastructure development, procurement and any other sector dependent on government regulation" (R. McGregor 2010: 141).

[178] In 2008, out of the top ten government jobs that received the most applications, eight were in provincial tax bureaus and two in customs bureaus, all of them along the prosperous east coast (R. McGregor 2010).

guilds, were suppressed by the government so that they could not challenge government dominance. This kept the government on top and society in a more or less continuous condition of stasis. Society grew, but did not develop.[179] With this kind of practically unchecked power, Chinese rulers were prone to corruption throughout their long history, up to and including the communists.

But no hierarchy is absolute. Indeed, at the point of becoming absolute, a hierarchy destroys its subordinates and thus itself. Power cannot exist without resistance. In the Chinese case, a fundamental feature of Chinese culture developed along with the principle of hierarchy—namely, resistance to it. In fact, it was the very personalism at the center of hierarchical culture that gave rise to resistance through interpersonal networking, known in Chinese as *guanxi*. These personal relationships developed into almost unlimited networks that worked through, under, and in contradiction to the hierarchical structure.

The hierarchical structure is a stiff, inflexible system with benefits flowing to the upper levels. *Guanxi* is in some ways the opposite: extremely fluid, flexible, and creative. The Chinese say, "There is always another way." This is a reference to the enormous fluidity and creativity within *guanxi* networks, allowing members to bring in new people, to utilize new resources, to create new options.

On the surface of Chinese life, harmony, respect, and deference behavior are expected; but below the surface, completely different networks of social relations dominate, based on different principles of exchange, reciprocity, and obligation. Hierarchy has its shadow. Personalism is Janus-faced; it infiltrates and strengthens hierarchical relations, while simultaneously spreading into interpersonal networks that are outside of and undercut hierarchical structures.

Guanxi is yin to hierarchy's yang. It, too, plays a central part in Chinese corruption. Not only did *guanxi* networks help themselves at the expense of government, society, and other networks, but their very antithetical relation to hierarchy meant that "going through the back door" was at the center of their purpose and function. Hierarchy can squash individualism only so far

---

[179] It is true today that there are large "private" businesses, but these businesses are either dependent on or partly owned by the Party (Huang 2008). And in cases where this does not give the Party enough control over private owners, a number of the wealthiest businessmen have been put in jail.

before its capacities are exhausted and the very structure of hierarchy—in this case, personalism—becomes part of exactly what it is meant to oppose, i.e., independence. In Chinese society, this double system, seemingly at odds with itself, has long been the taken-for-granted core of Chinese culture, no doubt partly because it works efficiently: indeed, so much so that Boisot and Child considered it—i.e., "network capitalism"—a new form of capitalism competitive with Western rational-legal types.[180] In any case, either yin or yang, hierarchy or network, both systems are prone to corruption; indeed, each stimulates corruption in the other.

It is a striking fact that both Confucian moral philosophy and Mao's utopian socialism led to similar ritual enactment of hierarchical relations, with backdoor behavior sprouting in both cases. This again shows us the profound role of hierarchical structure in Chinese society and the unavoidable development of anti-hierarchical systems and routines to express individual ambition or the aspirations of suppressed groups, and just to get things done efficiently. The fact that this happened with two very different systems, indeed opposed systems, shows the deep attachment to external form and ritual in Chinese culture. By giving such great emphasis to public expressions of deference, Chinese culture guaranteed the importance of secrecy and fragmentation.[181] It is a great irony that a culture, under two different political systems, so committed to public order and public control developed such pervasive hidden networks of informal, and at times illicit, behavior.

This is particularly apparent in the totalitarian period. As harsh and uncaring as some dynastic systems were, it is true that the communists produced an obsession with control that reached new heights of totalization and new lows of primitiveness.[182] Never before had there been an effort to control the *internal* nature of the individual to such an extent. China during the Mao period is a major example of totalitarianism. Yet despite the great efforts to centralize, indoctrinate, and control, interpersonal relationships still developed within organizational hierarchies, based on common mutual needs. The so-called patron-client relationships relaxed the hierarchy, marginalized the ideology, and created a human space for human sentiments.

---

[180] Boisot and Child 1996.

[181] The Chinese have a long history of "secret societies" (Fairbank and Goldman 2006). They also have a long history of spies and informers to counter them, still today. In fact, secret societies are on the rise.

[182] Arendt 1950.

That patron-client relationships were broadly institutionalized in communist industrial organizations indicates the failure of the socialization of ideology over feelings and desires. It had to fail because success would have required removing individual interests from social existence. Though the communists are certainly right that human nature is plastic, there are limits to it. Totalization is one such limit. It has never succeeded fully. There is no better evidence for the impossibility of totalitarianism than the systematic development of patron-client relationships at the center of communist industrial organization. The essence of patron-client relationships—interpersonal bonds and exchange—is a reversal of the effort to collapse the individual into the collective.

The double system at the center of Chinese hierarchical culture is practical, externally oriented, and centered in the political system. Though religion played a foundational role in sanctifying the political system, it was never rationalized under a single value, a single god. Thus many religious ideas and beliefs were practiced in Chinese society; without a central godhead, the inconsistencies between them were accepted as the normal state of affairs. Whereas political diversity was harshly repressed throughout Chinese history, religious diversity was not—as long as it did not interfere with the religious sanction of political power. The lack of separation between religion and politics gave the political system great authority and power; the lack of rationalization of religion left religion fragmented and the culture firmly centered in the political system.

This structure was amazingly stable; it lasted two thousand years. But that stability lasted only until external threats and pressures proved the system no longer adequate to fend off modernized competitors. Given the dynastic-Confucian history, it is not surprising that communism won the battle for control of China under the mandate of modernization. After all, communism's collectivist ideology fit well with Confucianism's collectivist philosophy. But communism had no heart for Confucianism's reliance on tradition. Mao quickly attacked the "four olds"- old ideas, old culture, old customs, and old habits.[183] The communists also attacked *guanxi*—though their performance was so poor that they actually fostered its increase.[184] So

---

[183] Fairbank and Goldman 2006.
[184] M. Yang 2003.

the double system at the center of Chinese culture lived on, and lives on today as the heavy hand of government ensures its existence.

Just as the communists continued the tradition of intolerance of competing political positions, they also ruthlessly suppressed, and continue to control, religion. Nonetheless, in their drive toward ideological totalization, they created their own cultural fragmentation. Here, too, the limits of power as an organizing principle can be seen. Under the communists, cultural fragmentation continues through the repression of history. When the communists throw their whole institutional weight—through the schools, media, and public expression—against the memory of, say, the Cultural Revolution or the Tiananmen Square massacre, the memory disappears only from the surface of public life. Below the surface, the memory exists—repressed, hidden, but still active, only reemerging distorted, altered.[185] Repression is no final solution to trauma. Eventually, the truth will come out. In the meantime, the Party tries to stoke economic growth to stay one step ahead of the missing memories of human and cultural destruction.

Thus, as the communists reach the limits of power in trying to control what their citizens know and think, their suppression of information and knowledge drives untenably apart the public-private domains and, in some cases, the conscious-unconscious spheres. Their repression of history and suppression of freedom of speech create cultural fragmentation. Add to this the transition from a planned economy to "market socialism"—a transition that cut at the core of communist legitimacy—and the center of Chinese culture is left fragmented and disoriented.

The dual system of hierarchy-*guanxi* is still in place, but the hierarchy has nowhere near the legitimacy it once had, and both hierarchy and *guanxi* are complicit in corruption. The gap between rules and action has grown so wide that rules hang limp on the robust body of economic expansion, and most people know this to be the case. Holding the culture together are a sputtering Confucianism, an ancient but questionable materialism, and a government-supported nationalism. Where a moral core will emerge from is still unclear.

Confucianism should not be counted out. China has more continuity with its ancient past than any other ancient culture. Indeed, sexism against women is actually on the rise, renewing a traditional practice. Authoritarianism, though down from the levels of the totalitarian period, still fills the body of

[185] Feldman 2004.

dictatorship. It is far from clear when, or if, this will decline. In spite of the introduction of "*market* socialism," the system currently supports dictatorship more than it expands freedom. Up to a point, a resurgence of Confucianism, especially its emphasis on the collective over the individual and deference to authority, can easily support dictatorship as well. Confucianism is still a dominant force in the Chinese family, and it is there that the attitude toward authority is established. All in all, much is in place for the continuation of the hierarchy-*guanxi* culture centered in a dictatorial political system.

If some change away from dictatorship is to happen, from a cultural perspective this would seem to require a transformation of Confucianism. Confucianism would have to incorporate other cultural elements in order to heighten respect for the individual *and* respect for diverse political positions. This would be a slow process—if change is going to be brought about through the *cultural* sphere. It seems more likely that a resurgent Confucianism will refill the old channels of authoritarianism and collectivism. But because human social life is so much more than culture, political or economic change could much more rapidly push the country in new directions.

4

Confused Motives and Deep Ambivalences

A Brief History of American-Chinese Cultural Relations in China

In her book *The Clash of Empires: The Invention of China in Modern World Making*,[1] Lydia H. Liu discusses a conflict that arose between the English and Chinese governments, during the negotiation of the Treaty of Tianjin in 1858, when the English insisted on translating the Chinese sign "yi" as "barbarian" and demanded the Chinese not use it to refer to the British government.[2] The Treaty of Tianjin was signed after the Chinese lost the "Opium War" in 1842 and a second war in the 1850s. The treaty after the loss of the first "Opium War" gave the British the island of Hong Kong in perpetuity, access to five Chinese ports, extraterritoriality (foreign jurisdiction over foreign citizens), indemnity (Chinese responsibility for damage to British assets), limits on tariffs and access to customs officials, most-favored-nation status, and freedom of trade with all participants.[3] The Chinese were coerced into signing the treaties after both wars and for this reason dragged their feet on implementation until the British and French occupied Beijing in 1860.

With all the valuable concessions won by the use of force including the occupation of Chinese land, one wonders why the British would be trifling with the meaning of the Chinese sign "yi." In fact, the British demanded a provision be inserted into the Treaty of Tianjin defining the sign "yi" as "barbarian" and thus outlawing the Chinese use of it in their communications with the British government.

---

[1] L. Liu 2004.
[2] The sign "yi" can also mean "stranger," "foreigner," or "non-Chinese."
[3] Fairbank and Goldman 2006.

Exactly who the barbarians were in this situation—the "Opium War" was fought partly for British rights to sell opium in China against the Chinese government's will—is not my main concern. The episode's relevance for my purposes is that it demonstrates the unhappy historical relations between China and the West, the history of misunderstanding—the Chinese relentlessly disagreed that "yi" meant "barbarian"—and the unsettling psychological dynamics between the two cultures that easily devolved into disrespect. Indeed, the West was well on its way in the nineteenth century to using "science" to demonstrate Chinese inferiority.[4]

In this chapter, I will briefly examine the history of Western and Chinese cross-cultural relations in China, with special emphasis on American-Chinese cross-cultural relations. The chapter will have three main sections: Western views of China, Chinese views of the West, and an extended conclusion. The section on Western views of China will show how the close connections between Western political, economic, and religious interests shaped Western perceptions of China and how changes in these interests led to changing images of China. Ultimately, Western views of China will be seen to show more about the West than about China. The section on Chinese views of the West will focus on the West's impact on Chinese culture, the relation between Chinese modernization and Westernization, the Chinese critique of Western culture, and the role of culture in political relations. Here I will emphasize the tension between Chinese collectivism and Western individualism. In the conclusion, I will review the difficult relations between Chinese and Western cultures in terms of the West's forced entry into China and its lasting effects. In this context, I will discuss the current transformation of China and the stresses and strains it creates, with a focus on China's changing cultural dynamics. I will explore some forms of resolution of China's cultural challenges and how these can potentially contribute to better relations between countries.

---

[4] "By the middle of the nineteenth century, when the treaties of Tianjin were being signed, the European scientists and writers had correlated the shapes of Chinese skulls, facial angles, the inner constitution of the skin, and the racially distinctive shape of the hand with arguments about the intelligence and moral failings of the Chinese, who changed from "white" to "yellow" in all European languages during this time" (L. Liu 2004: 62). As will be shown, Americans, too, expressed fears of racial contamination during periods of Chinese immigration (Jespersen 1996).

Western Views of China

I. Early Western Views of China

1. Origins. Westerners began going to China in the sixteenth century.[5] Their early interests in Asia were primarily economic.[6] They sought to outflank Muslim power; monopolize the spice trade; import textiles, tea, and other goods into Europe; find markets for European manufactured goods; and find opportunities for the advantageous investment of capital.[7]

Pannikar argues that from the beginning of the sixteenth century, China was, in effect, subjected to a naval blockade that stayed in place until the middle of the nineteenth century.[8] With this blockade, the West imposed a commercial economy over Asia's agricultural production and internal trade that radically changed almost every aspect of Chinese life.[9] There was a shift of economic and political power from inland areas to coastal cities, as well as the rising of a Chinese commercial class in alliance with foreign business. As the West dominated Asia politically, a doctrine of European racial superiority took root.[10] By the end of the eighteenth century, Western religious organizations, namely Protestant sects, became interested in evangelization in Asia,[11] a development that was connected to and synchronized with Western political domination.

The awkward marriage between Western political and economic domination and religious enthusiasm continued into the nineteenth century.[12]

---

[5] Ropp 1990.

[6] American trade with China has been more or less continuous since 1784 (Isaacs 1958). The first treaty between the two countries was signed in 1844, after China lost the Opium War.

[7] Panikkar 1953.

[8] Panikkar 1953.

[9] For most of China's history, the Chinese had little contact with the outside world (Gamer 2003b). When the West forced its way in during the middle of the nineteenth century, the result was the fracturing of Chinese culture (Tu Wei-Ming 1994). The effects of these fractures are still relevant today and can be seen in Chinese swings between rejection of the past and fervent nationalism. These fractures are still not understood.

[10] Dawson 1967.

[11] Panikkar 1953. The Roman Catholic Church sent missionaries to China as early as the sixteenth century but had relatively little success (Hoiman and King 2003).

[12] British behavior in China, for example, was simultaneously recklessly greedy and intensely religious (Spence 1998). In general, business interests used Christianity to justify colonial exploitation, and the Church supported business if it contributed to the expansion of Christianity (Hoiman and King 2003).

Western religious beliefs, religious goals, and religious disagreements all entered into Western perceptions of China.[13] Images from the New Testament figured prominently in the way missionaries viewed China.[14] By Christianizing their own perceptions of the Chinese, missionaries made the task of conversion look less than insurmountable.[15] Reality on the ground, however, was less than brotherly. The wife of an American missionary wrote in 1889,

> We are shut and locked in a compound that is surrounded by a wall fifteen feet high. This is the way everyone lives in China if they can afford a wall.[16]

The Protestant missionaries had little success in their attempts at conversion. The Chinese language proved inhospitable to the spread of the Gospels, and the deeply embedded Chinese traditions resisted Christian conversion.[17]

Western misperceptions of China go back 400 years, typically lacking historical context or understanding. Like the missionaries, Western writers simplified and distorted China.[18] Western audiences did not want to understand China; they wanted to use China's opacity as a screen onto which they could project their own emotional needs.[19] Over several generations, the same old themes have never been condemned, just constantly refurbished and reused.

---

[13] For example, in the seventeenth century Europe sought to use Confucian classics to prove the accuracy of the Bible, which was coming under attack from science; in the eighteenth century, French Enlightenment thinkers argued that China was an ethical society that was completely non-Christian to support their attack on the role of the Catholic Church in Europe (Spence, 1990b).

[14] Spence 1998.

[15] Spence 1990b.

[16] Spence 1998: 119. Indeed, the fiction of this period routinely portrays the inconsistency between Western Christian claims of fraternity and the aloof contempt Westerners expressed towards the Chinese (Turnbull 1990). In the 1950s, a report by the American National Council of churches concluded that missionaries had typically been arrogant, culturally insensitive, and isolated by affluent lifestyles (Madsen 1995).

[17] Dawson 1967. The unconditional belief in the reality of the Christian God, the Holy Trinity, and eternal life for individual souls had little affinity, if any, with Chinese religious experience (Hoiman and King 2003).

[18] Ezra Pound's representations of Confucius around 1915, for example, attempt to universalize Confucianism's appeal, but in so doing ignore his judgmental character, which is one of his defining strengths (Spence 1998).

[19] Spence 1990a.

Many of these themes as used in Western fiction were cruel and ignorant.[20] The experience of Western businessmen in China was more complex, however. Some made friends with Chinese; others focused on the cruelty and deceit in Chinese life.[21] After the defeat of Chinese armies by the British in 1842 in the Opium War, China's weakness bred contempt. By the early twentieth century, hysteria over the "Yellow Peril"—China awakening from her slumber to overrun the white man's world—appeared in Western fiction.[22]

American experience with China is consistent with Western experience generally, but has its own specific emphases. Americans have long felt that China is a country that needs America's help.[23] In the nineteenth and early twentieth century, missionaries had the strongest influence on American images of China.[24] Missionaries believed bringing Christianity to China would lead to democracy—because democracy was the Christian way of life.[25] Armed with the truth about the nature of man, his duties, and his destiny, the missionaries imagined in the Chinese person a close resemblance to the ideal American. So for China to improve, it would need to become more like America. It was a paternalistic view of China based on an American-Christian-liberal developmental ideology. America would help bring China into the modern world—and coincidentally bring business opportunities to America.

2. First Half of the Twentieth Century. Over the first half of the twentieth century, some American perceptions of China remained the same; others changed. China as a future Christian nation remained central. Henry Luce, chief executive of media giant Time Inc., played an important role in "explaining" China to the American public.[26] Luce became a strong supporter of Generalissimo Chiang Kai-shek, leader of the Nationalist government,

[20] European comic books in the nineteenth century, for example, portrayed Chinese as loathsome (Dawson 1967).

[21] Spence 1990b.

[22] Arthur S. Ward, the author of the Dr. Fu Manchu stories (1910) read by millions of Westerners, describes his protagonist: "[T]he green eyes, eyes green as those of a cat in the darkness, which sometimes burned like witch lamps, and sometimes were horribly filmed like nothing human or imaginable, might have mirrored not a soul, but an emanation of hell. . . ." (Spence 1998: 140).

[23] Jespersen 1996.

[24] Isaacs 1958.

[25] Jespersen 1996.

[26] Jespersen 1996.

which was attempting to unify China beginning in the late 1920s. Chiang created the New Life Movement, a hybrid of Confucian principles and Christian ideals; Chiang and his wife converted to Christianity. Luce focused on these developments, arguing that China was becoming more like America. Luce saw America as an exceptionalist nation, obligated to expand its influence, and China as a land of boundless opportunity, heading toward a democratic and Christian future.

According to Jespersen, Luce's view of America was idealized, and his view of China misleading.[27] Chiang's New Life Movement continued the ancient Confucian tradition of dependency on the ruler-father, tending more likely to lead to dictatorship than to democracy.[28] Luce's notions were romanticized at best, but they had a great impact on the American public's perceptions of China. This can also be seen in Luce's portrayal of China's war against the invading Japanese. *Time* magazine combined the war against Japan, and China-as-a-future-America, into a single image. In describing a retreat from the Japanese, *Time* said that Chinese government officials, soldiers, and students embarked upon a "covered wagon trek to their Wild West."[29] America is portrayed in idyllic nineteenth-century imagery, and thus the Chinese become innocent Americans fleeing the evil Japanese.

As in the worldview of American missionaries in nineteenth-century China, the *Time* narrative relates Christianity and democracy to business opportunities. In the late 1930s, *Fortune* magazine, also part of the Time Inc. stable, argued that Chiang would help American businesses realize the potential of the China market.[30] Part of modernizing China to help the Chinese people would require American businesses to modernize Chinese industry. What was actually happening, or likely to happen, in China was ignored if it

[27] The universal esteem Americans had for China in the 1930s came from missionaries, the writings of Pearl Buck, and the war against Japan (Isaacs 1958). As we have seen, however, the missionaries' reports varied in accuracy. According to Jespersen (1996: 26), Pearl Buck's book, *The Good Earth*, was also misleading: "The exoticism of Asia came home to Americans in the form of a central character whose attachment to land closely resembled Jeffersonian ideas about a virtuous class of yeoman farmers. . . . [T]he great popularity of her work was clearly tied to its cultural and historical resonance with Americans' ideas about themselves and their heritage as settlers, pioneers, farmers, and frontiersmen. . . ."

[28] Spence 1998. Indeed, Hsu (1981: 185) states that the New Life Movement was "a mixture of Christianity, Confucianism, the YMCA, and Nazism."

[29] Jespersen 1996: 40.

[30] Jespersen 1996.

did not fit Luce's image of the future Christian-capitalist China—that is, of an Americanized China.[31]

Given this history, it is interesting to see how American images of China changed after the Communist takeover in 1949. The change from China as a weakling among nations, whose non-warlike nature required America's help to fight the Japanese and advance out of backwardness, to China as a highly warlike people threatening to overrun world order took place with remarkable rapidity.[32] The Korean War saw the resurrection of the "yellow tide" imagery that had previously appeared during high levels of Chinese immigration in the nineteenth century. Whereas Chiang Kai-shek was *not* seen as backward and dishonest, these characterizations did reappear in regard to Mao and his team. It seems that Americans have a warehouse of China images, using some while suppressing others, depending on their reaction to current events.

Isaacs argues that American images of China are a "hall of mirrors."[33] Writing in the 1950s, he identified six historical periods, each with its own dominant image of the Chinese: Respect (eighteenth century), Contempt (1840–1905), Benevolence (1905–1937), Admiration (1937–1944), Disenchantment (1944–1949), and Hostility (1949–?).[34] In addition to closing out the Hostility era in 1978, perhaps we can add a seventh historical era, Excitement (1978–?), as Western businesses rush into the China market, hoping to finally capitalize on that most elusive of prizes. These historical eras and the sets of images they contain become activated in kaleidoscope fashion as the American media and other institutions shape the information they make available to the public at any given time—and, importantly, as Americans' emotional needs go through constant changes. As Isaacs's "hall of mirrors" metaphor characterizes them, American perceptions of China tend to be a self-involved and distorted affair.

---

[31] This is a good example of the role of power in Western perceptions of China (Said 1979). Concrete empirical reality is bypassed in favor of generalizing images of both China and America, with the latter dominating and transforming the former to satisfy cultural and material desires and interests.

[32] Isaacs 1958.

[33] Isaacs 1958: 215.

[34] These historical era designations create images and reuse images from previous historical eras. Many of these images contradict one another. For example, the Chinese are seen as highly intelligent, industrious, pious, peaceful, and stoic, but also cruel, barbaric, inhuman, inscrutable, overwhelming, and threatening (Isaacs 1958). These contradictory images play off one another, rising and falling depending on the perceiver's emotional need.

II. Post–1949 American Views of China

1. American Motivations. Americans have a long history of misperceiving China for many reasons. One is that leaders of American institutions tend to perceive China in ways that advance their own institutional interests. In the 1970s, as Vietnam and Watergate led to challenges to Americans' beliefs about their own institutions, those institutions created a myth about China as an emerging liberal society that reflected positively back onto America's liberal values.[35] This gave the institutions newly valid purposes: new worlds to discover, new people to convert, new markets to open. American institutions seized Nixon's "Open Door" policy to advance their own interests. But the liberal myth they created ignored the terrors of China, focusing only on the good. It was not only naïve and self-serving; it assumed there existed a universal model of the good society and assumed that American society and Chinese society were basically homogeneous. These assumptions misled the American public, the main consumer of this information.

Before Nixon's historic visit, American views of China were more complex, struggling with contradictory images of China as "Red Menace" or "Revolutionary Redeemer" of the working class.[36] By the time of Nixon's visit, an older image of China as "troubled modernizer" was brought out, dusted off, and crowned the current winner in the competition. What we saw in China was what we needed and wanted to see at that time.[37]

In addition to challenges to our institutions, there were other reasons Americans refocused on the "troubled modernizer" myth about China. The "troubled modernizer" myth implied China needed our businesses to help them modernize.[38] This theme has been around since the beginning of our relations with China. In the early 1970s, it led to an unrealistic optimism that greatly exaggerated the opportunities existing in China. Closely related to the economic motivation for the liberal-China myth were religious and political motivations.[39] As in the past, American economic involvement in China occurred simultaneously with religious and political activities and was rationalized in these terms. In any case, the differing American motivations left the liberal myth Janus-faced, the better to adapt to changing political needs:

[35] Madsen 1995.
[36] Madsen 1995.
[37] Spence 1990b; 1998.
[38] Madsen 1995.
[39] Lampton 2001.

China is an emerging liberal society, so we should help it, and China is so dangerous and backward that we are justified in confronting it.[40]

The "troubled modernizer" myth also provides us with a way to admire ourselves. Having offered to help makes us superior.[41] The myth allows us to invest strong feelings in *China* without too carefully attending to *the Chinese*.[42] In a word, our images of China tend to be narcissistic. Thus, to the extent that our images of China have had any effect on China, they have been harmful. Another example of this tendency can be seen in American academic institutions. They, too, seized on the "troubled modernizer" myth to justify their interest in expanding research, teaching, and recruiting opportunities in China.[43] Ironically, contradicting their own research interests, they not only assumed that they already knew China—but that their presence would make China better.[44]

America's underlying purpose was to make China like America—Christian, democratic, capitalist, respectful of human rights, and so on.[45] All the Americans had to do was expose China to American practices, and China would recognize their superiority and adopt them. This is what the liberal myth implied. The key ingredients in the myth were progress (modernization); recognition of universal, rational principles; rational application of these principles; competition; and a good dose of individualism.[46] The idea of endless "progress" was unquestioned. That this myth did not exactly fit Chinese culture and history was not relevant to the ahistorical Americans. Americans like to see themselves as *making* history,[47] not limited by it. Indeed,

---

[40] Dawson 1967.

[41] Hsu (1981: 359) writes as late as the 1970s ". . . that while American television, comic book writers, and movie makers are now busy giving favorable (and even heroic) roles to blacks, they continue to cast Chinese as slant-eyed, opium-smoking white slavers. Or Chinese appear on the periphery as laundrymen and restaurant operators with queer accents. If they do not fall into these two convenient slots, they are hopeless figures oppressed by native Communists, eventually to be rescued by an American like Steve Canyon in the comic strip."

[42] Madsen 1995.

[43] Madsen 1995.

[44] In 2007 at a Fulbright conference in Guangzchou for incoming American Fulbright professors, we were told by several representatives of the American State Department that we were there to help bring democracy and democratic values to China (Feldman, 2007c).

[45] Steidlmeier 1997.

[46] Madsen 1995.

[47] Nixon and Kissinger dubbed the planning for their historic trip to China in 1972 "Polo II" (Spence 1998).

it is part of the *American* myth that Americans see the world "objectively," without any historical or social biases.

The liberal-society myth that Americans promulgate presents many challenges even for American society. Commitment to endless "progress" uproots communities, brings out a destructive level of competition, and has tended to produce corrupt and cynical elites.[48] With "progress" often replacing moral traditions, an ends-justify-the-means ethic is pushed to extremes, with dire consequences as we see currently—for example, in the subprime mortgage crisis.[49] Another problem resulting from the liberal myth is that the value of "freedom" has also led to extremes. Indeed, it is a common view among American business executives that the only constraint on their actions they will acknowledge is legal constraint. Many actions that contributed to the subprime crisis, however, were legal but not ethical. This can be seen in American business education, where business ethics classes have increased in numbers over the years, but have been met with considerable ambivalence, even inside business school faculties.[50]

Ironically, even though individual freedom is central to both Americans' self-definition and their understanding of capitalism,[51] capitalism leads to ever larger concentrations of capital—and thus huge organizations where freedom is considerably restrained.[52] Americans voluntarily accept these bureaucratic roles; they are not forced into them. But the result is much the same: considerable conformity. As long as the organizations pay well, Americans take their freedom on the weekend. This would suggest that for many Americans, it is not so much freedom that they love, as wealth and status.

In any case, the cultural complex known as American "individualism" or "freedom" is hardly a direct fit with Chinese social life. Chinese individualism is much more deeply buried in social relations; and competition, though intense, is hemmed in by family commitments and personal networks much

---

[48] Hedges 2010.

[49] Feldman 2004. Angelo Mozilo, CEO of Countrywide Financial, for example, started out trying to increase American home ownership, but joined in a race to the moral bottom resulting in massive mortgage defaults and the loss of tens of billions of dollars (McLean and Nocera 2010).

[50] Swanson and Fisher 2010.

[51] Friedman 1972.

[52] Fukuyama 1995.

more than in the United States. Indeed, these networks mediate the individual's relationship with the broader society. In the U.S., the law performs this function to a much greater extent. Even behavior inside large bureaucratic organizations is different. Americans demand fair treatment in terms of organizational rules; the Chinese follow the orders of superiors independent of rules. To say that the Chinese are becoming like us denies the very essence of the Chinese.

2. American Distortions. Chinese culture challenges American presuppositions. China has emerged as a major industrial power in the world economy, but its political system remains authoritarian. Americans see the market economy and democratic politics as fundamentally related, two foundations of individual freedom. Central characteristics of Chinese culture are intense familial relationships and a weak sense of community; another is broad-ranging mistrust. In this culture, is an American-style democratic system possible? The important role nonprofits play in American society, in between private business and government, is relatively unknown in China. There are fundamental differences between the two societies which suggest that differentiation will remain an important part of their future relations.

The disinclination to grasp the fact that Chinese culture is fundamentally different from American culture has led to shallow, but continuously changing, American conceptions of China. Spence has identified three recent phases of American perceptions in just a twenty-year period, between 1970 and 1990: reawakened curiosity (1970–1974), guileless fascination (1974–1979), and renewed skepticism (1979–1989).[53] These phases are based on a shallow understanding of China and tend to change easily usually in reaction to the latest headlines. Lampton notes that American television coverage of China in crisis (e.g., the Tiananmen Square protests) is "like looking at China through a straw."[54] Like most American reporting, it focuses on the negative.

The reality is that China changes much less rapidly than America's superficial understanding of it. In 1988, China received sixty-four minutes of air time on American network news.[55] After the Tiananmen Square massacre in September 1989, coverage rose to 881 minutes. The massacre caused

[53] Spence 1990b.
[54] Lampton 2001: 278.
[55] Lampton 2001.

literally an overnight shift in American public opinion. Americans were shocked. They were shocked partly because China's economic liberalization had led them to assume that political and cultural freedoms were soon to follow, if not already under way.[56] This is why Tiananmen upset Americans so much, out of proportion to the actual cost in lives or the rollback of any real freedoms. It contradicted the American understanding of what is good, what all people want, and what ideas inevitably must go together. It contradicted Americans' understanding of themselves, and the belief that the future belonged to them, to individual freedom.[57]

Outside of American corporate leadership, American public opinion is quite different. As American corporations are making money in China or hope to be, their rank-and-file workers are losing jobs to Chinese workers. Fifty-four percent of Americans believe the emergence of China as a major power would be a threat to international peace.[58] One-third of Americans surveyed thought China would soon dominate the world. These exaggerated fears also exist within the American government, as seen in actions to block Chinese efforts to buy American companies.[59]

Thus American executives appear to have distorted perceptions in a positive direction, while a broad sampling of Americans appear to have distorted perceptions in a negative direction. Some executives ignore or downplay China's oppressive bureaucracy, the widespread corruption by government officials, the arbitrariness of government authority, the intolerance towards even minimal political dissent, the history of brutality against intellectuals, and the rampant sexism.[60] At the same time, rank-and-file Americans focus only on Chinese manufacturing prowess, low cost labor, government involvement in the private sector, and competitive success. Both groups are resuscitating old American stereotypes about China, albeit contradictory ones, as the images of "one billion customers"[61] and a faceless mass/threatening horde demonstrate. As Edward Said documented about Orientalism

---

[56] Madsen 1995.

[57] The American myth is not dead. It shows up repeatedly in my interviews in 2006 with American executives on their business experience in China (see Chapters 6 and 8).

[58] *Economist* (March 25, 2006).

[59] The United States government has been strictly enforcing national security laws in regard to the Chinese even in cases where it is difficult to see the threat to national security (Davidoff 2011).

[60] Madsen 1995.

[61] J. McGregor 2005.

generally,[62] the long career of these images in the American psyche, say more about American than Chinese culture.[63]

Chinese Views of the West

1. Western Impact before 1978. Based on the loss of the Opium War and the West's ability to force concessions on China in the middle of the nineteenth century, it was clear to all that China had fallen far behind technologically and militarily. From this time forward, Chinese elites debated the issue of how to come to terms with the West, which they clearly could no longer avoid. Thus began China's torturous journey along the road to acceptance of "modernization" and its inseparability from "Westernization." This journey can be divided into five periods: the reform movement during the second half of the nineteenth century as the Qing dynasty declined; the "May Fourth" movement which began in 1919 during the "Republic of China" period; the Kuomintang modernization efforts of the 1930s; the communist transformation period after 1949; and the "market socialism" period after 1978.

The Westernization movement in the middle of the nineteenth century was the beginning of China's efforts to modernize.[64] The Chinese wanted to modernize because they believed they had fallen behind the West economically and culturally, and because they wanted to throw off the yoke of colonialism. Thus, modernization and independence from the West are linked in Chinese history. This is the origin of China's still-active debate with itself about its own identity, the identity of the West, and how the two are related. The problem at the core of this debate is a contradiction: China must modernize to get free from the West; China must learn from the West in order to modernize.

After the fall of the Qing dynasty in 1911, the ancient structure of Chinese society was open for change. A key event in the context of modernization came on May 4, 1919, when, ironically, the Western powers negotiating an end to World War I at Versailles left the German concessions at Shandong

---

[62] Said 1979.

[63] Anticipating J. McGregor's (2005) *One Billion Customers*, in 1937 Carl Crow published a book titled *Four Hundred Million Customers*. The quantitative mind-set inherent in American capitalism is on display here.

[64] F. Yu 2009.

under Japanese control.[65] Student protests sprang up in Beijing, which came to be known as the "May Fourth" movement. Intellectual leaders of this movement came to represent a Chinese Enlightenment, promoting an anti-feudal revolution to throw off the yoke of tradition in favor of science and democracy.[66] The May Fourth intellectuals embraced Western culture fully. For them, modernization and Westernization were the same thing.

On the ground, however, the country's direction was far from clear. National unity fell to pieces, with warlords taking control of different parts of country. By the 1930s, the debate over modernization had grown more complex. Even though it was acknowledged that Westernization was the dominant force in the world, some argued that modernization and Westernization were not the same thing. Some thinkers started arguing that Chinese and Western civilization could be combined. Others argued that modernization could be achieved without Westernization. Some seeking combination sought to incorporate Western technology and democracy, but rejected Western "spiritual degeneracy."[67] These writers wanted to preserve Chinese traditional culture.

But the process of cultural assimilation proved to be less controllable by the Chinese than these writers had thought. Even though attempts by Protestant missionaries in the nineteenth and early twentieth century failed to convert even one million Chinese,[68] Western technology and consumerism were broadly accepted in the cities—which had unintended consequences. A Chinese intellectual commented in the 1920s,

> [W]hat we have taken over from the West most rapidly are the forms of existence. The cinema, electricity, mirrors, phonographs, all have seduced us like new breeds of domestic animals. For the people of the cities, Europe will forever be only a mechanized fairyland.[69]

Technology and consumerism impacted culture. The eternal yesterday of Chinese tradition was disrupted by the new "forms of existence." The cinema introduced new ways of seeing the world, new values. Mirrors encouraged a focus on self. Technology could not help changing feelings of power and

---

[65] Fairbank and Goldman 2006.
[66] F. Yu 2009.
[67] F. Yu 2009.
[68] Madsen 1995.
[69] Spence 1998: 189.

stimulating fantasies about power. Confucian emphasis on important others could not avoid impact from Western culture once the use of Western technology altered forms of thought and relations between people.

As China struggled to find itself after the fall of the dynastic system, trying to figure out what to accept from the Western world and what to keep from its own past, the fragmented political system fell into open warfare as local warlords sought to expand their domination. These conflicts were settled when the communist forces won on the field of battle in 1949. For the next 30 years, influence from Western technology was reduced to a minimum as China and the West became antagonists.

Marxism-Leninism, however, a form of Western collectivism, transformed the patrimonial (bureaucratic) state, diminishing further the role of Confucianism.[70] In fact, it attacked Confucianism, trying to remove it altogether from Chinese culture. The onset of Marxism-Leninism-Maoism affected every aspect of Chinese life. It was the most important influence on China in the twentieth century. It appears to mark the high point in nearly two centuries of Chinese alienation from its own history.

2. Reforms and Ongoing Debate. In 1978, two years after the death of Mao, China again made a radical change in direction, introducing a market economy in what had been almost completely a state-controlled society. Its own identity, as well as its relationship with the West, was radically changed. The modernization of Chinese traditional culture again became a consensus goal for the first time since the May Fourth movement of 1919.[71] It was seen very clearly in China, for example, that the nature of Chinese traditional culture is incompatible with the rule of law. But cultural modernization has met great resistance from political elites, especially in the area of political reform. In China, the question of cultural modernization is inseparable from the more basic question of political reform.

Debates on cultural modernization continue, reaching a level of "cultural fever."[72] They exhibit extreme complexity. Some participants argue for the modernization of traditional culture, others advocate cultural globaliza-tion, others cultural localization. Some criticize localization as cultural

---

[70] Tu Wei-ming 1994. Confucian morality is feudal in origin and social purpose, but it survived the unification of China and decline of feudalism in 221 B.C. It was incorporated into the dynastic (patrimonial) system (Weber 1951).

[71] F. Yu 2009.

[72] F. Yu 2009.

nationalism, while others worry about the decline in national identity and advocate for the preservation of national culture. Still others argue for innovation to take place within traditional culture, and others for a revival of traditional culture, and so on.

The question of integration with the West is at the center of these debates. For some, integration of and conflict with other cultures can lead to the development of culture. So questions of how much integration, in what areas, and how to safeguard Chinese nationality and cultural independence are intensely debated. Some feel that the Chinese must have a strong sense of cultural self-consciousness in order to know who they are, what is worth protecting; otherwise, cultural integration can be destructive. The integration of "bad" aspects of foreign cultures can hurt China.

All these debates take place within the context of Western-led globalization. Many Chinese intellectuals consider globalization the leading trend in the world today.[73] The primary vehicle for globalization is economic integration. For China, globalization and modernization are inseparable. They are key to understanding the social transformation taking place in China.

Globalization both hurts and helps China. On the positive side, it helps China realize that it shares a common future with other nations and should participate in developing a consensus on global issues. Yu believes this helps people to identify with basic values such as freedom, equality, justice, security, welfare, and dignity.[74]

On the negative side, globalization threatens China's domestic economic security if foreign companies can monopolize key technologies and markets, force China's government to abide by international treaties that favor the West, and undermine Chinese culture as Western culture is exported along with its capital, technology, and products. Globalization means less economic and cultural independence for China. From China's perspective, Western countries are trying to use their economic and technical superiority to force Western culture on the whole world. As a result, developing-country cultures either weaken or collapse. Some Chinese feel it is of the utmost importance to have a cultural strategy to develop China's national culture and make sure foreign cultural influences serve China's purposes.

[73] F. Yu 2009.
[74] F. Yu 2009.

3. Wealth and Change. Materialism from the West has again become a major influence on China. According to Madsen, the reemergence of Western materialism has had a negative impact on Chinese culture by undermining the virtues of self-discipline and social responsibility.[75] These virtues had been at the core of Confucian morality, and their decline left the Chinese adrift in a rapidly changing social environment. By turning their backs on Confucianism in favor of consumerism, the Chinese lost their distinctive identity in the world. This is not a small matter. Not only does it leave them with little psychological anchorage, it means they have little to teach others. Without the ability to teach others, they further devalue themselves. They run the risk of being overwhelmed in the world, resulting in either further cultural implosion or a tendency to hate others for reflecting back on them their own emptiness.

At this point, the Chinese are still on the materialist honeymoon. There are signs of a resurgence of Confucianism and an increased interest in religion, but these are still marginal developments.[76] Most Western observers believe the obsession with wealth is a reaction to the state having blocked most other avenues of human endeavor, especially participation in the political process. But materialism in China has profound forces propelling it: China's huge impoverished rural population; the decades of horrible economic performance under the communists, including the worst man-made famine in human history; the cruel hardships, shortages, and disruptions during the Cultural Revolution; China's irrepressible entrepreneurial energies; the intense competitive pressures from an enormous population; the cultural belief that wealth is required for status; and the deeply ingrained (and nearly universal) sense that wealth is needed for security in an unpredictable world.

Simultaneous with the spectacular growth in consumerism, Chinese youth have become intoxicated with Western popular culture, particularly television shows like *Desperate Housewives* and *Prison Break*. Teaching at universities in China in 2007, I hardly met an undergraduate or graduate student who was not intimately familiar with these programs; they believed the shows *were*

---

[75] Madsen 1995.

[76] Over the last three decades, Christianity has been the big winner. There are now about as many Chinese Christians as Communist Party members, about 60 million (Pomfret 2007). If the Chinese religious traditions had remained strong, Christianity could not easily have taken root (Hoiman and King 2003). The Chinese government has supported a renewed interest in Confucianism.

American society. They expressed great emotional interest in and attachment to the characters in these dramas.[77] Older Chinese expressed concern at what they saw as a decline in moral character among young people.

Within this broader cultural change, the Communist Party monopolizes the political process and keeps tight control over dissent and even public expression. The Party appears to have no intention of giving up power in the foreseeable future, and thus its members are in need of legitimacy to govern. Nationalism is one card they play.[78] The Chinese have strong national identity and pride, but see the last 150 years as a time of humiliation and exploitation at the hands of the West.[79] In the highly political and economically competitive world of today, the Party has a natural platform on which to build up nationalist passions against outside forces and thus solidify its hold on power. In this context, there are growing forces inside China against Western culture and influence.[80] Many Chinese feel the West is trying to keep China from taking its rightful place as a great nation.

A third impact of the West on China is the great increase in business competition and productivity as Western firms flood into the China market with capital, manifold expertise, and products. Economically, this has been great for China, as it has achieved the largest increase of population ever brought out of poverty in human history—as well the rise of tens of millions of people into the middle class. But culturally the outcome is less clear. On the positive side, entrepreneurial creativity and self-expression, plus the independence from increased wealth, have provided vast improvements in the quality of life. The Chinese are traveling more, sending their children to better schools, and consuming healthier foods and better products of all kinds.

On the negative side, the rise of economic competition in a society not prepared for it has led to excesses in the form of corruption and brutal

[77] Jacobsen (1998) reports that Chinese university students had the same strong attachment to American popular culture in the 1980s and 1990s that I saw in 2007.

[78] But they play it warily, because national pride is in the nation, not necessarily the Party, and could turn against the Party (Osnos 2008).

[79] A popular Chinese television series, *Deathsong of a River* (Su Xiaokang and Wang Luxiang 1988), portrays China as unequipped for modern life and describes the West as a hostile power that attacked and exploited China (Madsen 1995).

[80] Osnos 2008. Numerous widely read books appeared in the 1990s criticizing American culture and encouraging the Chinese to value their own culture (Jacobson 1998).

disregard for others and the environment.[81] Western capitalism has been imported into China along with its destructive potential; and China not only does not have adequate government regulation, it also does not even have an adequate legal system. But the main point is the cultural damage. Confucianism encourages humility, deference, and social harmony. As this ethic declines, competition does not replace its moral role. American capitalism does not offer a moral vision, only endless wealth creation. Thus, the Chinese run the risk of economic success coupled with moral depravity.

4. *Critique of Western Rationality.* The Chinese are ambivalent toward the West for both historical and contemporary reasons.[82] They admire, reject, and are both seduced and threatened by the West. Western economic culture in particular has come under criticism. Some Chinese argue that China must be made safe from the impersonality and coldness of Western capitalism.[83] Chinese society, with its emphasis on human relationships and interpersonal obligations, can only be undermined by a system built around legal contracts.[84] Western neoclassical economic theories do not recognize the great variety of ways economies are socially embedded in different historical forms and social institutions. China needs to learn from the West, it is argued, but also needs to develop its own form of capitalism.

Other Chinese intellectuals have gone further and produced a critique of the Western Enlightenment. They argue that all major institutions in Western societies—i.e., science, technology, market economy, democracy, mass communications, multinational organizations, and research universities—are closely bound to the values of the Enlightenment.[85] Central among these Enlightenment values are liberty, equality, human rights, private property, privacy, and due process of law. But these values are not up to the task of inspiring human community in an interconnected world because they grow

---

[81] "Dotted across the Chinese landscape are 'cancer villages,' towns full of widows whose late husbands worked in the same toxic industries, enclaves where women give birth to babies with deformed limbs and other disabilities" (Harney 2008: 57).

[82] During the Maoist period, America was particularly identified as China's antithesis. In 1957, for example, there were only twenty-three Americans known to be in all of China (Isaacs 1958). More than any other people, Americans were kept out.

[83] M. Yang 2002.

[84] Confucian culture encouraged merchants to hold their customers through friendship and treat their employees like extended family (Hsu 1981). Since mutual dependence was the rule, profits and competition were lowered.

[85] Tu Wei-ming 2002.

out of an outdated anthropocentricism. Because of commitment to individualism and individual cultures, Enlightenment values lead to a minimalist ethics, it is argued, well short of the global ethics that is needed. Providing little more than a universal "human rights," Western ethics cannot overcome cultural relativism.[86]

In addition, the Enlightenment's anthropocentric rationality has led to aggressiveness toward nature and, at best, inattention to spiritual matters.[87] These Chinese intellectuals call for a comparative cultural approach emphasizing ethical and religious values which would include Confucianism. Confucianism has several things to offer the West. Confucius extends the story of the cosmos into an inclusive humanism, as opposed to an exclusive anthropocentrism. This could liberate the Enlightenment mind from its drive to dominate nature and ignore spiritual matters. For Confucius, the secular is sacred. One must respect everyday existence in all its aspects. The individual can be encouraged toward self-cultivation, as opposed to the pursuit of endless wealth and material progress.[88] This could lead toward harmony between the individual, community, and spirit.

A key part of Confucian self-cultivation is the developing of the self as a center of relationships, not as an autonomous, self-interested participant in the competition that is society in the Western view. The ethic of reciprocity is fundamental to this project. The individual must empathize with others on their own terms. Difference should be respected because it authenticates and empowers the other. We can cultivate ourselves only by helping others cultivate themselves, because it is through difference with others that we grow and change.

These parts of the Confucian ethic can help address the ethical challenges brought on by globalization. Globalization has created conflicts between trade, finance, information, migration, and disease, on one hand, and

---

[86] This is a philosophical critique of Western values from a Chinese point of view. A more culturally hostile critique can be seen in a 2009 commentary by a high level Chinese military leader in the prestigious Chinese Academy of the Social Sciences, where "freedom, equality, and human rights as the universal values of humankind" were said to be nothing more than the "fantasy and hegemony of the Western capitalist classes" (R. McGregor 2010: 109). The comments were accompanied by photos of prisoner torture at the Abu Ghraib prison.

[87] Tu Wei-ming 2002.

[88] This means promoting community harmony over economic growth and individualism (Koehn 2001). But Lee Kuan Yew, one of the founders of Singapore, claims Confucian virtues of discipline and work are at the source of Singapore, Hong Kong, Taiwan, and South Korea's economic success. *The Economist* (January 21, 2012), interpreted Lee Kuan Yew's view of Confucianism as a mixture of family values and authoritarianism.

ethnicity, language, land, class, age, and religion, on the other hand.[89] To address these conflicts, all participants must enter into dialogue with one another. Chinese traditions, far from being obsolete, have much to contribute to this cross-cultural dialogue on how to move forward with the globalization phase of modernization.

5. *Political Relations.* The Chinese see American foreign policy toward China as hypocritical and self-interested, despite all the moralistic language on human rights.[90] The Chinese resist demands for improved human rights, arguing that they are culturally formulated within the Western paradigm and conceal self-interested goals.[91] Anglo-Saxon culture is seen as having no moral high ground to stand on, with Westerners having massacred American Indians and traded Africans as slaves.[92] No high-level Chinese officials would portray the U.S. as contributing to world peace. Many Chinese who read English or travel to the U.S. see an anti-China bias in the American media.[93] This is in line with the already established view in China that China has been victimized by the West and the West continues to try to humiliate the nation.

China has a strong desire to regain international respect and recognition as a world power. Its growing success and aspirations, coupled with its sense of past victimization, have led to a sense of entitlement. The Chinese feel entitled to what they have lost (e.g., Hong Kong), what they have yet to regain (e.g., Taiwan), and perhaps "face" in the world not just for their accomplishments but to make up for their past suffering.

Conclusion

According to Panikkar, the West started putting pressure on China as early as the sixteenth century in order to meet its own expanding political and

[89] Tu Wei-ming 2002.

[90] Lampton 2001.

[91] Confucius does not mention human rights (Koehn 2001). Indeed, he rarely writes about justice. Confucianism is a collective ethic that gives priority to the community as a whole.

[92] Britain's forcing of opium into Chinese markets against the Chinese government's will during the nineteenth century can be added to the list (L. Liu 2004).

[93] Large numbers of Chinese were outraged by the way the Western media covered the conflict in Tibet and the related conflict over the Olympic torch protests (Osnos 2008). The Virginia Tech massacre took place in 2007, when I was teaching in China. The initial reactions from my Chinese graduate students expressed outrage—because they believed the American media had mistakenly identified the shooter as Chinese, not Korean. I did not see this mistake in the American news reports I read, however (Feldman, 2007c).

economic interests.[94] It was not the other way around, and this is exactly the point: the West industrialized before China, and this gave the West power over China. The imbalance grew worse during the following centuries. The West saw in China a great opportunity and tried to take it. The uninterested Chinese delayed Western inroads, but could not prevent them.

Chinese civilization was set in an agricultural economy and a patrimonial political system—as well as a feudal culture that for many reasons stopped developing, especially in science and industry. Though inside China the quality of life was at least equal to that of the West, say, in 1500, by 1800 it had fallen behind in terms of wealth, technology, and military power. Nondevelopment is exactly the issue: Chinese rulers wanted to stay the way they were and sought to keep the West out; but the West had the power to force the Chinese to accept its terms. By the middle of the nineteenth century, the West was colonizing Chinese land and forcing the Chinese to enter into economic and political relations.

The changes that started in the sixteenth century changed the very nature of Chinese society. The agricultural economy was forced into international trade; commercial structures, commercial classes, and commercial interests were greatly expanded. In other words, the Western model of development was forced on the Chinese political and social systems. In the West this is called "modernization" and refers to the development of capitalism, democracy, and science as the central institutions around which society is organized.[95] Chinese culture did not provide fertile ground for these three institutions, and the struggle with capitalism and democracy continues to this day.

In any case, once the West arrived, it stayed until the communists finally threw it out in the middle of the twentieth century.[96] Different parts of Chinese society reacted to what the West had to offer in different ways. In 1911, the ancient imperial political structure was overthrown and an attempt was made to recreate Chinese society along the lines of modern (Western) institutions. This led to civil war inside China as different modernist camps fought for their vision of how a modern China would be organized—and who would benefit. The communists won the struggle and in 1949 announced the formation of a communist state organized along the lines of Marxism-Leninism, a form of Western collectivism.

[94] Panikkar 1953.
[95] Gellner 1992.
[96] Of course, the British retained Hong Kong until 1998.

Despite some early success, intense struggles continued within the Chinese political system. By the time of Mao's death in 1976, the Communist Party had lost a great deal of legitimacy and the Chinese economy was in tatters. In 1978, Deng Xiaoping reversed the communist course and introduced "market socialism with Chinese characteristics" and an "opening" to the West in order to get help in developing industry and technology in China.

Throughout the history of these attempts by China and the West to come to terms with one another, the West focused more on its own goals, rather than actually try to understand China as China understood itself. Because China did not develop as had the West, Western nations saw China as backward. At other times when they did look closely at China, they transformed what they saw to meet their own needs, as when in the seventeenth century the Europeans used Confucianism to demonstrate the truth of the Bible. This same process goes on today when American executives see the Chinese government's "gradualism" strategy for introducing markets as being based on the country's economic goals, not the Communist Party's political interests.[97]

The tendency has been for the West to vacillate between seeing the Chinese as budding Westerners or impenetrable others. One aspect of this is the changes occurring in images of China to express the West's emotional or political and economic needs at a particular time. A striking example is the spike in the expression of American racial prejudice in the late nineteenth century during rising Chinese immigration and competition for jobs. Similar behavior can be seen today as the loss of American jobs to Chinese manufacturers appears to increase American perceptions of China as a threat to world peace. As China gets stronger and more competitive, American anxiety about economic loss is displaced onto fears of military threat.

This process takes place with all foreign competitors, but the history of distortion with China is particularly strong. This seems to be related to the distinct differences between Eastern and Western cultures.[98] Since the two are so different, they do not easily identify with or recognize themselves in one another. This makes it particularly easy to use the other as a *tabula rasa*, as a screen to project one's feelings and needs onto.

The alternative would be to take the time and make the effort to understand the other. This has not been seen in American relations with China

[97] Pei 2006.
[98] Nisbett 2003.

historically. Americans take a short-cut; they project their own negative and positive emotions, bypassing the longer route of actually understanding the Chinese in their own terms. A clear example of positive projections is seen in the Luce-led Time Inc. media empire, which for decades portrayed the Chinese as budding Americans, or heading in that direction. There is something very selfish about this behavior—especially since it is always closely related to American profits. The reasoning seems to be that America should help the Chinese because they are good people who need help and have, or will soon have, the same values as we do and, by the way, Americans can make money in doing so.

In the Luce case, Christian love and capitalistic self-interest are portrayed as being in the very nature of the Chinese. Both China's differentness and the inability to grasp Chinese culture easily encourage these projections. Depending on whether the Chinese represent opportunity or threat at a particular point in history or to a particular group, the Chinese are seen as very "smart" or very "barbaric." Currently many American firms are making profits in China's booming economy; so, among the business classes, the dominant perception is one of Chinese "smartness."

Inevitably, perceiving the other according to one's feelings and needs brings a great deal of volatility to the image of the other. This is why American views of China change so often and produce so many contradictory images. It is understandable that Americans had a strongly negative response to the Tiananmen Square massacre, but the fact that right before the massacre they had perceived China as moving toward democracy demonstrates their detachment from the situation in China and the need to see China as less threatening.[99]

Perceiving the other in terms of one's feelings and needs inevitably reflects more of one's own culture, not the culture of the other. We can see several components in the American perceptions of China. First is the liberal developmental ideology; that is, that history inevitably moves toward individual freedom expressed in capitalism and democracy, as they are manifest in the United States. Historically, there was also a strong Christian component in

[99] That is, threatening both politically in terms of competing interests, and psychologically in terms of rejecting American values. Judging from the way Americans treat other Americans who hold different political values, we seem to be becoming less tolerant of difference as we become more diverse. This will make it even more difficult for us to deal with foreign competitors, including the Chinese.

this ideology: the Christian God is the one true god. The future of China must be like the present America. America is the exceptional country; it is the end of history.

Second, the liberal ideology presents America in unitary and ideal terms. America's racial and social tensions are taken out of the picture, as well as the messy process of democratic politics and the destructive aspects of free enterprise. Americans debate the pros and cons of democracy and capitalism; different groups have different opinions. These are, of course, institutionalized in the two main political parties. But in perceptions of China, China gets a thumbs-up or thumbs-down depending on whether it measures up to an idealized image of a happy, free, prosperous America. Americans use a high level of abstraction in the process, enabling swift and absolute judgments. The abstraction, simplification, and absolutism are hallmarks of a process driven by emotion.

It would appear, too, that involved in this process of abstraction and absolutism is concealment, the hiding of something about self in the idealization of society. Because life is difficult and uncertain, people use idealization to conceal or distort uncomfortable and threatening experiences.[100] The economy falters, wars are engaged in, race relations become inflamed, youth becomes angry or self-destructive; all the hardships and uncertainties of life question a society's beliefs continuously in one area or another. Under external conflict and internal anxiety, belief systems harden; views of self and other become idealized to remove the troubling parts. The American-Christian-liberal developmental ideology becomes a protected port in a stormy world. The problem is, this port does not exist; and, in the case of China, the wrong-headed expectations it creates make the world even more stormy, not less.

The idea that China was so backward that it needed our help to modernize is a myth, an over-simplification.[101] The myth is inseparable from our economic self-interests. If China modernized, it meant profits for American business—as is plainly the case now. Throughout the West's 400-year relationship with China, China's potential for helping Western economic growth has always been a very important part of Westerners' dreams. More often than

---

[100] Chasseguet-Smirgel 1985.

[101] Even though myths are fictions, they are essential to social life in helping a people understand itself, grasp moral dilemmas, focus on common goals, and maintain hope (Madsen 1995). But if myths lead away from self-understanding or understanding the other, they can be harmful—which is the case with seeing China as backward.

not, China has not met Western needs or gratified Western fantasies, because Western expectations about China were not realistic. They were based on Western lives, not the lives of the Chinese.

From the Chinese side, the West was always received with a great deal of ambivalence, sometimes outright hostility. That the Chinese were not able to defend themselves against the West's economic, technological, and military power has left a deep scar in the Chinese psyche to this day. The Chinese see the West as dangerous, exploitative, arrogant, and humiliating. They also admire the West's strengths and want to learn from them to make China stronger. Currently, more than anything they want Western technology and, to a lesser extent, business know-how.

The social system that will emerge from the great transformation China has embarked upon is as yet unclear; perhaps it will not be clear for a long time. Perhaps there will be many stages of change over many decades. Currently, the phase of communism seems to be in decline and unlikely to re-emerge as the core value system. It was a great experiment that failed. Confucianism declined under communist indoctrination; even though it is re-emerging, it is in some ways also declining as capitalism takes hold, separating families, weakening loyalty, and stimulating individualism. Perhaps Confucianism will re-emerge as the central value system, as in Singapore, but Chinese culture seems to be growing more diverse, not more unitary.[102]

Certainly the Chinese have ample opportunity to observe American individualism as they work with Americans in China, watch American television shows, visit American websites, and travel in the U.S.; but even though it does appear that the Chinese want Western wealth, technology, and legal protections, it is less clear that American individualism is equally attractive. That would radically change the nature of the Chinese family, Chinese social relations, indeed the hierarchical nature of Chinese culture. Chinese culture would not be Chinese culture without the centrality of hierarchy and deference as it plays out through ritual in the daily lives of the Chinese. Hence, one would think that there are limits to individualism in China. While it is true that individualism does express itself through consumerism, deeper manifestations of individualism in China are buried in social relations, in family relations, and any change must come out of these materials, out of the Confucian vortex. Consumerism is thus just a superficial manifestation.

---

[102] China's size, diversity, and different institutions make Singapore a poor model for predicting China's future course.

However, there are signs of deep trouble in Chinese culture. According to the World Health Organization, the female suicide rate in China is the third highest in the world.[103] I can only speculate as to what might have led to this. Chinese sexism against women is on the rise. This is a traditional part of Chinese culture, and as the market economy has weakened socialist ethics, sexism has increased.

Another profound change in Chinese society is mobility. It is estimated that 100 to 200 million Chinese have left their villages to seek work, mostly in coastal cities.[104] Even though women were brought into the workforce in huge numbers under the communists, most of them still remained in their villages, in their local areas, near family and community. Despite the radically new ideas the communists brought into Chinese life, the fact that people were not allowed to move kept a great deal of traditional culture intact in the lives of many Chinese. In addition, communism was puritanical and had much in common with traditional culture despite its attack on the "four olds."[105]

From the rise in the female suicide rate, it can be speculated that mobility and the undermining of traditional culture and traditional roles have done more damage to women than to men. In the coastal cities, young couples can have premarital sexual relations much more easily than they could have had in the communist era or even in their villages today. Freedom without commitment can lead to inner despair, or what Durkheim called "anomic suicide," when the culture is no longer able to make life meaningful, to make it worth living.[106]

The increase in the female suicide rate seems to suggest that the woman's role in Chinese society has changed in such a way as to make life less worthwhile for some women. It is evidence that wealth and individualism have in some ways made Chinese society worse, undermining the culture that provides the socio-psychological materials that make life meaningful and the personality robust in the face of hardship and change. There is evidence that some

---

[103] Out of 105 countries, only Sri Lanka and the Republic of Korea have a higher female suicide rate (World Health Organization 2011).

[104] Harney 2008.

[105] Old ideas, old culture, old customs, and old habits.

[106] Durkheim 1934. Jianlin and colleagues. (2001) found premarital sex in the context of a failed love affair a factor in the female suicide rate in China. Women faced stigma and loss of face from premarital sex that did not lead to marriage because traditionally women are expected to remain chaste and faithful before marriage.

changes in Chinese society are hollowing out Chinese culture. Men and women do not—cannot—survive on bread alone.

Besides individualism, nationalism has increased in China and is observable in many parts of Chinese society. If individualism does not become a central social orientation and Confucianism does not re-emerge as a central way of life, nationalism could fill the void. Pride in and love for one's nation are positive human emotions, up to a point. When they become a cover for feelings of inadequacy and compensation for self-loathing, they can become exaggerated and dangerous. The Chinese have several potential sources of self-hatred. One is the century-long humiliation they suffered at the hands of the West as the West forced its way onto Chinese land and into Chinese markets. The Chinese still remember this period acutely, and it no doubt contributes to the fact that the word "foreigner" has negative connotations. Second, under Mao, China had fallen further behind the West. When the reforms and "opening" began in 1978, China was woefully behind the West in economic and technological development. Perhaps its great success since 1978 has tempered this source of feelings of inadequacy.

Third, perhaps the most important potential source for a dangerous level of nationalism is the loss of other sources of cultural integration. The void in Chinese cultural life left by the decline of communism, the personal and cultural destruction that communism left in its wake, communism's prolonged attack on traditional culture, the Party's continued suppression of religion, widespread and severe government corruption, and the great social changes sweeping China leaves the Chinese in great need of a center that could make sense of the world and provide them with the capacity to know and trust each other. With so much need and with traditions so badly maligned, China could grasp onto an exaggerated nationalism to fill the void.

The Chinese family is still fundamentally Confucian. If these moorings continue to decline without the development of cultural resources that hold the family together in a humanly fulfilling way, the family could be drawn into and damaged by political chaos, like that seen during the Cultural Revolution when children turned against parents. Further, if the family continues to weaken, Chinese culture itself, characterized by involuted family relations, strong interpersonal networks, and a weak sense of community, could also provide an opening for an exaggerated nationalism. Right now, *guanxi* in the service of wealth production has stepped into the void as purposeful ties among "friends" have increased to take advantage of the sudden and enormous economic opportunities that have become available.[107] But either economic downturn or increased state control over the economy could marginalize *guanxi* networks. With large numbers of people looking for a meaningful life and the Communist Party able to hold on to the levers of power, the Party may be forced to increase nationalist propaganda as its only means of control.

Given the government's central role in corruption, however, an increase in nationalism could turn back on the government. Perhaps the population's respect for central authority will keep the government in good enough standing. This is an open question. In any case, nationalism is usually more a political movement than a moral one and does not necessarily supply the moral orientation and restraints needed for a society to live peacefully with itself and its neighbors.

Some Chinese intellectuals argue for a return to Confucian moral philosophy, not just for China but as a contribution to a new global ethic.[108] Advocacy for Confucianism's contribution to a global ethic is predicated on the Western (Enlightenment) failure to provide a holistic ethic for human life. Specifically, Western individualism, making man the center of moral philosophy, has led to a disregard for the natural environment and for society as a whole. In place of commitment to ultimate values, the West has over-emphasized law, as if relations between people can be regulated by external means alone; this assumes personal integrity is a private matter and can take care of itself. Thus is the legacy of Western individualism.

This has led to a minimalist ethics, in life, in business, in global relations. In particular, the centrality of individualism has led to cultural relativism as the only means to understand relations between cultures. The result is an inability of one culture to judge another or to resolve conflicts between cultures. Likewise, Western individualism has enshrined materialism and endless wealth production as the ends of life. This has weakened communities and added to environmental degradation.

Some Chinese intellectuals argue that Confucian humanism can contribute to resolving these problems. Confucianism can address cultural relativism because it incorporates nature and spirit into its worldview, going beyond the Enlightenment's anthropocentrism. It can work with Western pre-Enlightenment spiritual commitments to cultivating ultimate values for human life

---

[107] M. Yang 2002.
[108] Tu Wei-ming 2002.

that go beyond materialism. For countries to live peaceably in an intensely interconnected world, global values of justice and of what constitutes the good life are needed. It will take not only a cross-cultural dialogue to arrive at shared values, it will take a fundamentally different philosophy from the individualism that cares so little for political and social wholes.[109]

Confucian self-cultivation as an end in itself is an alternative to materialistic individualism.

Confucian self-cultivation encourages the search for knowledge, for understanding of life, and for cultivation of value commitments. Western individualism takes itself as the ultimate value, seeing value commitments as a form of power, of oppression.[110] But morality requires commitment, commitment beyond the individual; and this is even more the case in the relations between cultures, where synthesis is required.

Difference is a building block of ethics in several ways. Different cultural forms must confront one another to investigate the strengths and weaknesses of each form in the new context. Ideally, one would demonstrate moral superiority or a new synthesis would be created or a compromise would be worked out. In these cases, there is some kind of moral development. In situations where basic assumptions are incompatible and cannot be prioritized, but simply suggest different worldviews, difference still has moral value.

In the Confucian commitment to self-cultivation, difference is needed in order to define self. Thus empathy is important out of respect for the other, to understand the other in one's own terms. Once we understand the other in our own terms, we can use this understanding to explore our own selves through difference, to learn from the other, and to sharpen self-understanding through identification of otherness. The search for knowledge is not a finite act; it is a continuous journey through a changing and an endlessly complex world. Appreciation of and empathy for the other, even in difference, at least demonstrates tolerance. Tolerance must be the touchstone for understanding, development, compromise, and acceptance in a world of difference. At bottom, a "global ethic" must do business under these conditions.

---

[109] It cares little, that is, until it is confronted by holism, which arises from individualism's own emptiness. As was seen in the twentieth century, individualism untethered to moral community can become fodder for totalitarianism's final solution (Dumont 1986).

[110] See Foucault 1980.

PART

3

GOVERNMENT AND CORRUPTION

5

The Turtle and the Hare

An Essay on Political and Economic Reform in China

According to myth, the turtle wins the race with the hare because his slow, consistent pace is more effective than the hare's short bursts of speed. Despite the myth of Chinese gradualism, it is unclear whether the Chinese political turtle will even bother to finish the race. In fact, the rabbit-like speed of Chinese economic growth is a win for the political turtle. The rabbit, it turns out, instead of pulling democracy in its torrid path, may well supply the Communist Party with the resources and legitimacy to maintain its dictatorship into the foreseeable future.

This chapter examines the Chinese economic reforms and "opening" over the last three decades, with special attention to the type of economic system that is developing and its relationship to the political system. Some of the key themes taken up are the centrality of the Chinese government in business, how its role has changed and not changed, its view of business as a tool for economic development and for its own political interests, and its role in business corruption and what significance this role has for the type of economic system that is developing in China.

Despite remaining central in business behavior, the Communist Party did an about face to remain in power. To create economic growth, it had to decentralize its powers to city, province, and village levels of government as well as allow private ownership.[1] But in so doing, it significantly weakened its power base and control. To remain in power, the Party had to give up power. Yet it did not give up power by enforcing the rule of law or implementing a robust regulatory and monitoring system. It decentralized through the Party,

---

[1] The extent of decentralization is significant. The local share of government expenditure in China is 68 percent, highest among 20 Organisation for Economic Co-operation and Development (OECD) countries (Redding and Witt 2007).

keeping control through licensing, taxation, ownership (direct, indirect, and ambiguous), control of land, and access to capital.[2] The result has been widespread corruption. It is this history and what it tells us about Chinese economic reform and the Chinese economic system that is examined in this chapter.

Economic Reform in China

1. The Privatization Process

China's transition to a market economy is widely considered highly successful. Unlike the Russians, the Chinese are using a gradual and incremental strategy, thereby limiting the disruptions to their social and economic system. This success is partly because China was better positioned for change right from the start than Russia, having a less industrialized and less tightly planned economy, and a population that still remembers the pre-1949 business environment.[3] But also the Chinese leadership demonstrated great flexibility, pragmatism, and entrepreneurial style by first decentralizing the communes and setting up a successful incentive structure for the towns and villages.

Tsai argues, however, that most formal institutional change was first brought about by entrepreneurs and officials acting informally and only later made into policy by the government.[4] In fact, according to her, most privatization was brought about in spite of the government. For example, in 1988 the government approved private enterprises with more than eight employees. But some such firms were active as early as 1976.[5] Many of these larger firms concealed themselves by registering as collective enterprises or as units of state-owned enterprises (SOEs). This was so common it had a name, "wearing a red hat."[6] It is estimated that 500,000 such enterprises existed by 1988. Still others registered as foreign firms. Indeed, also in direct violation of the law, profit-oriented businesses were run out of government offices. Tsai estimates

---

[2] In this context, without clearly specified property rights in China (North 2005), it is not obvious what "privatization" means. Boisot and Child (1996) claim the dissociation of marketization from private ownership is a distinctive feature of Chinese economic development.

[3] J. Wong 2003.

[4] Tsai 2007.

[5] Tsai 2007.

[6] Tsai 2007: 53.

that 15.3 percent of private businesses do not register at all.[7] Goldman, too, found that reform of the communes was started by individual farmers well in advance of government decollectivization.[8] It is in this context that the "gradualism strategy" must be understood.

The key to the gradualism strategy was the postponement of the "privatization" of state industry until the late 1990s, which averted sudden spikes in mass unemployment.[9] Prior to 1978, the SOEs dominated each sector of the economy, getting their production plans from the national government.[10] Below these were enterprises controlled by provincial, municipal, and county governments. Lifetime employment and extensive organization-based welfare programs were the norm in this system. Citizens did not apply for jobs; they were assigned to particular jobs in particular organizations. Many of these workers were hardly ready to compete in the marketplace.

Initially, the government focused on the expansion of the private sector through joint ventures; special enterprise zones; and collective, private, and local enterprises, hoping to force discipline on the SOEs from the outside.[11] The town and village enterprises (TVEs) were a big success. They had been outside the central government's planning system and thus were both more nimble and without the legacy costs of providing housing, health care, pensions, and the like, as did the SOEs. The TVEs were allowed to set wages, make investment decisions, and retain profit.[12] As their name implies, they were collective in ownership but largely capitalistic.[13] They paid taxes (and in many cases dividends) rather than producing products for the state. Through the 1980s, output grew at 30 percent per year and exports increased at a rate of 65 percent per year.[14] After 1984, the dual-price system the government had created for the planned economy and the market economy was moved beyond agriculture to a broader range of products, opening the door to its

---

[7] Tsai 2007.

[8] Goldman 2006a.

[9] Nonetheless, between 1995 and 2001, 46 million workers lost their jobs at SOEs (Tsai 2007).

[10] Spar and Oi 2006.

[11] Goldman 2006a.

[12] Spar and Oi 2006.

[13] Actually a proportion of these firms were private firms "wearing the red hat." Local TVE officials were happy to allow private firms to register as collective enterprises because the TVEs could use these firms' assets as collateral for bank loans (Tsai 2007).

[14] Spar and Oi 2006.

abuse by both private firms and state companies, which both tried to buy at government prices and sell at market prices.

Yasheng Huang argues that the key to economic growth in the 1980s was *rural* financial liberalization, particularly decentralization of the management of local savings and loans, and allowing private entry into the financial service sector.[15] These changes had a big effect on small businesses in the rural economy, promoting private-sector development and entrepreneurship. There were also political reforms at this time: mandatory retirement of government officials, strengthening of the National People's Congress, legal reforms, attempts at rural self-government, and some loosening of control over civil society groups. Huang calls this period the "entrepreneurial era" and argues that these types of economic and political reforms that favored entrepreneurship took place between 1980 and 1988.[16]

In 1985, China opened four coastal cities to foreign trade.[17] Special economic zones were created in and near these cities to attract foreign companies. By the late 1980s, these zones were very successful. Importantly, during the 1980s almost 70 percent of investments in these zones came from overseas Chinese. One reason for this investment was that the Chinese leadership was imitating the success Hong Kong, Singapore, and Taiwan had had in growing their economies by focusing on consumer goods industries and international trade. This focus, along with family networks and cultural know-how, made China a good fit for the overseas Chinese.

In 1994, the government accelerated the process of "privatization."[18] It auctioned off many TVEs, often to factory managers. Local governments often remained as shareholders, however; in other words, the Communist Party remained on the board of directors. The Party played central roles in other ways too. It became a "privileged agent," acting as gatekeeper for access to land, buildings, labor, and bank loans, and vitally, as protection from the central government.[19] With such a central position, not much business took place without local officials grabbing a piece of the action. According to Redding and Witt, local governments became "de facto the board of a

---

[15] Huang 2008.
[16] Huang 2008.
[17] Spar and Oi 2006.
[18] Spar and Oi 2006.
[19] Redding and Witt 2007.

conglomerate whose subunits were local TVEs."[20] Officials interpreted state policies favorably for firms in which they had a stake and implemented them strictly for firms in which they did not. The result was extensive tax evasion. The successful firms were run clan-like, with strong family ties bringing together officials; entrepreneurs; bankers; and those with connections to markets, technology, suppliers, and whatever other services were needed. Thus, collusion was involved from beginning to end of the massive "privatization" of wealth that took place.

Since officials controlled access to land and capital, collection of taxes, and much else, they were the wheeler-dealers at the center of the "privatization" process. This fact brought into play rivalries between Party cliques on local levels for the most lucrative opportunities and on the regional level for the biggest investments, and jealousies between officials and the new entrepreneurial class.[21] Officials sold their power into the market, collecting fees, bribes, and ownership stakes. This period in the 1990s is referred to as "the seven golden years."[22]

The other side of this equation was that in addition to exploiting local success, the central government explicitly rewarded and demoted officials based on economic growth and foreign investment in their jurisdictions. In other words, Beijing created competition between officials and between political units such as cities and towns.[23] The tax system itself was decentralized, allowing local officials to use it as they pleased to attract business once they met target amounts for Beijing. This resulted, however, in a market for tax rates. Incoming businesses benefitted and officials benefitted, but a conflict of interest was created between the interests of officials and the communities for which they were responsible.

By the late 1990s, the government had begun the gradual "privatization" of some parts of state industry. An important result of this process was that

[20] Redding and Witt 2007: 118. More generally, R. McGregor (2010: 177) writes, "every jurisdiction is a company, and every company a jurisdiction" to capture the pivotal organizing and directing role played by local governments in business development within their areas. The army, too, entered the conglomerate game big time in the 1990s, perhaps becoming the largest conglomerate in China (Goldman 2006a).

[21] Redding and Witt 2007.

[22] Redding and Witt 2007: 119

[23] R. McGregor (2010) argues that this competition is so intense it is the primary driver behind China's extraordinary economic success. It also explains why there is a "constant civil war" among the provinces for control of the center (K. Yu 2009: 162).

many government officials ended up as owners of "privatized" state assets. Pei reports that almost 66 percent of the 6.2 million owners of private firms had formerly been officials in government agencies or executives in SOEs.[24] Some officials kept their government jobs and took second jobs in newly created private firms that had business ties with their government positions. The latter points to a general characteristic of the "privatization" process: Most large private firms are descendants of SOEs.[25] Their connections to the government give them advantages over smaller firms, which usually have fewer connections and less bargaining power with the government. Indeed, small firms are institutionally discriminated against in terms of taxation, bank loans, registration access, and fees, and are generally subjected to more frequent intervention and hindrance.[26]

In general, the government plays a central role in business in China. Constantly changing regulations, bureaucracies, and reporting relationships make business planning very difficult.[27] For example, it took Coca-Cola three years to get approval for a new bottling plant,[28] and its concentrate production volume must be reauthorized every year. The central government still controls resource distribution, investment size, industry structure, bank loans, access to infrastructure, and business formation in strategic sectors.[29] In addition, the state is the biggest shareholder in the country's 150 largest companies and has significant influence in thousands more.[30] It appoints 81 percent of managers at SOEs and 56 percent of all enterprise managers.[31] In 50 percent of restructured SOEs, the board chair had previously been the

---

[24] Pei 2006. Tsai (2007) found in a 2002 survey that 47.2 percent of private businessmen had been employed in collectives, SOEs, or the government.

[25] Park and Luo 2001.

[26] The situation gets worse if one compares private with state-owned companies. Private firms are systematically denied state bank loans; are prohibited from entering multiple sectors; are charged higher rates of taxation than SOEs, collectives, and foreign-owned firms; face higher levels of corruption; have less access to land and must pay more for it; are charged higher rates for electricity; and face more uncertainty about the security of their property and the trajectory of reforms (Tsai 2007). Note in 2011, efforts were made to move toward tax parity.

[27] Lieberthal and Lieberthal 2003.

[28] Enright 2005.

[29] *Economist* April 21, 2012.

[30] *Economist* April 21, 2012.

[31] More importantly, the Party controls all top and mid-level executive appointments (R. McGregor 2010). This is the key mechanism for its control of the country.

organization's Party secretary.[32] In 6,275 restructured SOEs, the organization's Party committee became the board of directors 70 percent of the time. The state keeps state-owned monopolies in most key industries. Local governments also keep ownership stakes in and provide protection for lower-level SOEs in their jurisdictions. In this way, the various levels of government secure revenue streams and resources that they can use for patronage and thus control.

China has a long history of blurred boundaries between private and public sectors, between state and society. For example, in a study of 158 venture capital firms, Batjargal and Liu found companies where the state simultaneously played the roles of shareholder, fund manager, and auditor.[33] In this situation, investment decisions were often influenced by noneconomic factors. Doing business with companies like this creates high uncertainty. In another example, Pomfret describes the development of a "private" retail area in Nanjing.[34] A government official had control of everything, down to the design of restaurants, even though 84 percent of the area was in "private" hands. The government official in charge ordered bank loans, randomly confiscated goods, dictated sales policies, and decided who prospered and who did not.

In this context, relationships with government officials determine not just profit or loss, but firm survival or failure. In China, the government has the upper hand over the rule of law. Property rights thus remain ambiguous. At the center of Chinese business is interpersonal networking, especially with government officials. Boisot and Child have called the situation "quasi-capitalism,"[35] whereby government officials introduce their desires for money, power, status, public infrastructure, and their own career development into (private) business decision making. This is particularly true on the provincial and municipal levels of government, especially outside the major cities. Property rights are much more a negotiation between public officials and private interests than an enforceable legal construct.[36] This situation is

---

[32] Pei 2006.

[33] Batjargal and Liu 2004.

[34] Pomfret 2007.

[35] Boisot and Child 1996.

[36] This state of affairs explains why there is a shortage of data on economic policies and institutions, and the nature, context, and activities of economic actors (Huang 2008). It is practically impossible to know the ownership structure of most firms in China. This obfuscation is done deliberately as a means of power both against the government and other stakeholders, and by the government against society and foreign businesses.

completely consistent with age-old patrimonial bureaucracy, with its hierarchical ordering and the intense interpersonal relations that unavoidably grow
up around and through it to accommodate the complex array of passions,
interests, and powers that exist outside the hierarchical structure.

Importantly, the "privatization" of many SOEs in the 1990s took place
simultaneously with the reversal of the 1980s' liberalizing reforms of the rural
and small business/entrepreneurial sectors. Yasheng Huang calls this the
"state-led era" that took place between 1989 and 2002.[37] Huang argues that
growth of rural household income in the 1990s dropped by more than
50 percent from its 1980s growth levels and the share of labor income to
GDP fell in the 1990s, reversing its rise in the 1980s. Furthermore, the size
of government during the "privatization" phase of SOEs increased substantially in the 1990s in terms of the number of officials and the value of fixed
assets it controls.

In addition to reversing rural political and financial management—that is,
recentralizing them—"privatization" policy during the 1990s had several
other distinct characteristics. Even though there was an emphasis on SOE
restructuring, there was little in the way of penalties for mismanagement,
poor decision making, and financial loss.[38] In fact, corruption by high-level
SOE executives and government officials was enormous during the restructuring process. This will be discussed in more detail below. Also, in the
1990s, nationwide "land grabs" increased 15-fold on land near and around
cities.[39] Again, there was enormous corruption involved, which will be
discussed below. Part of this land was needed for economic expansion,
including large-scale infrastructural and urban investment projects. But also
included were lavish office towers that appeared to primarily benefit real
estate developers, builders, and government officials. This use of capital could
represent massive opportunity costs for society. In any case, the emphasis on
urban as opposed to rural development led Goldman to comment that the
government created a transition less from socialism to capitalism than from
rural to urban.[40]

[37] Huang 2008.
[38] Sun 2004. So even though competition was introduced into the state sector in the 1990s,
manufacturing value added per worker per year actually fell from $3,061 in the mid-1980s to
$2,885 in the late 1990s (Huang 2008).
[39] Huang 2008. News reports show this is still going on in 2012.
[40] Goldman 2006a.

A third leg of the "privatization" process of the 1990s was a great emphasis on foreign direct investment (FDI). Chinese laws and regulations provide a more favorable operating environment for foreign-registered firms than for domestic private firms. In particular, foreign firms can deduct wages from taxes at a much higher rate than domestic private firms.[41] This is an example of the severe restraints on domestic private firms.

The FDI model relies heavily on export processing and has low domestic valued added; thus, a significant amount of profit remains with the foreign firm.[42] Ninety percent of Chinese exports in electronics and IT products are produced in foreign-owned factories with limited supply chains within China.[43] In 2005, 22 percent of industrial value added originated in the domestic private sector while 28.8 percent originated in foreign firms.[44] One must ask why the Chinese government favors foreign firms over domestic private firms to this extent, given that this practice stifles growth of the domestic private sector.[45] Pei argues that the Chinese government favors FDI because it fears growing domestic private capital.[46]

There are several possible reasons why the Chinese government reversed course on privatization in the 1990s. It appears the Tiananmen Square events of 1989 played a role. In the 1980s the annual growth rate for the private sector was 19.9 percent, but in the period 1990–1992 it fell to 2.6 percent.[47] Even though it increased to 12.4 percent in the period 1993–2001, the "privatization" process, as has been shown, changed course. It appears the government rethought economic development after Tiananmen Square in that private-sector growth was cut back and investment in the state and collective sectors was expanded.[48] Decentralization and liberalization were

---

[41] Several of my Chinese interviewees used a relative in a foreign country to register their firms.

[42] Huang 2008.

[43] Redding and Witt 2007. Foreign firms account for 55 percent of all Chinese exports.

[44] Huang 2008.

[45] Zhejiang has the most successful entrepreneurial economy in China, and it attracts very little FDI (Huang 2008). Furthermore, Hong Kong, Taiwan, and South Korea all developed strong export economies without significant FDI.

[46] Pei 2006. The government has since created the "indigenous innovation policy," which seeks to increase domestic innovation at the expense of foreign firms (Peng and Heyue 2010), though much of this benefit may go to SOEs.

[47] Huang 2008.

[48] Other factors that led to recentralization were an alarming drop in central government control from the reforms and a great increase in corruption.

cut back, government control increased. As the population ecology theory of organizations might predict, the government reverted to its central planning instincts after the experimental 1980s.[49] Certainly adjustments were needed and will continue to be needed in a situation of such massive change, but the story at this point is that the government is retrenching into its earlier forms.

In summary, as the Chinese government successfully began a transition to "market socialism with Chinese characteristics," it kept itself centrally involved not only in the regulation of business but as a partner in business decision making and the rewards that it generates, on the levels of both the government as a whole and individual officials. An independent legislature and judiciary were not developed, nor were fair and transparent laws with impartial enforcement.[50] Reliable public financial information is not available. Brutal and ruthless competition has been unleashed, with government agencies and government officials participating in every conceivable role. Trust in commitments, information, contracts, and the quality of goods promised has not developed. Instead, personal relationships based on shared interests between public and private individuals play a huge role in how things get done and who benefits.

2. The Economy

The idea of "market socialism with Chinese characteristics" is really just that of a mixed economy, commonly found the world over, with various balances between government involvement and free-market exchange.[51] The more uncommon feature of the Chinese economy is its growth rate. Since 1980 the Chinese economy has multiplied 14-fold, adjusted for inflation.[52] In 2008, it grew by 9 percent.[53] Industrial production has risen by an average of 16 percent annually for the last five years. Since the early 1980s, the private sector has been growing at an annual rate of 20 percent.[54] Between 1999 and

---

[49] Freeman et al. 1983.

[50] S. Li 2005. The problems still exist in 2012.

[51] J. Wong 2003.

[52] Areddy 2009.

[53] However, this growth should be seen in context: Even before reform, China's economy grew at an average of 5.7 percent per year between 1952 and 1978 (J. Wong 2003).

[54] Goldman 2006b.

2009, entrepreneurs have created 5 million businesses with at least eight employees, creating 75 million jobs.[55] The private sector accounted for about two-thirds of the $11 trillion GDP in 2011.[56]

The key driver of growth is industrial production. This represents a huge shift from agriculture. In 2004, agriculture still accounted for 46.9 percent of employment but only 14.6 percent of GDP; while industry accounted for only 22.5 percent of employment, it contributed 50.8 percent of GDP.[57] Wong reports that 80 percent of China's economic growth is generated by domestic demand[58] to supply a huge population growing wealthier. A key driver of the increase in wealth has been exports. In 2003, 50 percent of all exports were from the processing trade, that is, assembling and packaging products in China from imported components.[59] Foreign firms have flocked to China to take advantage of the massive pool of inexpensive labor. Changes, however, are occurring. In 2009, Areddy reported that 40 percent of China's GDP traces to factory construction and other kinds of fixed-asset investment.[60] The tremendous growth in factory production shows how far and how fast China is moving beyond assembling and packaging.

In addition to inexpensive labor, the Chinese market offers other attractions, such as increasing demand from Chinese consumers and manufacturers. Ninety-five percent of the world's largest 500 companies have set up operations in China.[61] This, combined with the increasing number of Chinese manufacturers, has made the Chinese consumer market the most competitive in the world.[62]

As the private sector has experienced dynamic growth, government expenditures have correspondingly declined, from 32 percent of GDP in 1979 to 23 percent in 2012.[63] Likewise, the SOE sector has seen its percentage of

[55] Areddy 2009.

[56] *Economist* April 21, 2012. And according to some estimates, 75-80 percent of the profits (*Economist* March 10, 2011).

[57] Spar and Oi 2006.

[58] J. Wong 2003.

[59] Lieberthal and Lieberthal 2003.

[60] Areddy 2009.

[61] Moody 2010.

[62] J. McGregor 2005. Yet the fact that the Chinese government has instituted rules to force the transfer of technology from foreign firms to Chinese firms shows that Chinese firms cannot compete technologically with foreign firms.

[63] Heritage Foundation/Wall Street Journal 2012. In recent years Chinese government expenditures have been increasing as a percent of GDP.

GDP decline from 77.6 percent in 1978 to 33 percent in 2009.[64] These statistics are misleading, however, if the role of the government-controlled banking system is not considered. Central government debt in 2010 was a significant 80 percent of GDP.[65] Many of these loans are to SOEs, rural cooperatives, and towns and villages. There are still 153,800 SOEs employing 65.16 million workers[66]; more than 30 percent of these SOEs are not profitable.[67] The Chinese government continues to provide them with capital as a way to regulate unemployment. Also contributing to the debt crisis is corruption and a poor understanding of risk.

The banking system is funded by the high savings rates of the Chinese people, some of the highest in the world, upwards of 40 percent of income.[68] Anderson argues that the outstanding growth performance of the East Asian economies is due to extremely high rates of capital creation from savings.[69] Regardless, the high savings rate is key to China's economic growth strategy. High savings are used to make large investments in high-export growth industries, which leads to significant GDP growth.[70] The weak spot in this strategy has been the loan defaults as rising output led to declining retail prices, to which the noncompetitive SOEs could not respond.

Financial capital flows are so critical to economic functioning that a closer look at the financial system is worthwhile to deepen our understanding of the complex (and murky) vicissitudes of the Chinese economy. Chinese banks are directed by Party-controlled supervising committees, resulting in a close correlation between Party goals and bank loans.[71] This has led to excessive industrial capacity, endemic waste, and poor financial controls. In 2009, about 85 percent of bank loans went to SOEs.[72] Between 2003 and 2008, the

[64] OCED 2009.

[65] *Economist* June 2, 2011. Political scientist Victor Shih, however, estimated Chinese government debt to GDP at 150 percent in 2010 (*Economist* June 28, 2011).

[66] *National Bureau of Statistics of China 2012.*

[67] In 2006, 30 percent of the SOEs were not profitable (*Economist* March 25, 2006).

[68] J. McGregor 2005.

[69] Anderson 2006.

[70] J. Wong 2003. "Using these high savings for development is basically theft. The use is made available because the government is not providing an adequate social security net. Some 300 million people are without health insurance and, contrary to popular notions, school tuition is not free. People have to save their money against rainy days" (Schroeder 2011).

[71] Redding and Witt 2007. Foreign ownership of banks has been capped at 20 percent, further restricting the flow of funds.

[72] *Economist* April 21, 2012.

ratio of gross industrial output to GDP rose from 90 percent to 160 percent; virtually all of this increase in overcapacity came from SOEs.[73] In 2009, private firms accounted for only two percent of official outstanding loans.[74] Private firms also have very little chance of getting listed on Chinese stock exchanges. The stock exchange listings are almost all SOEs, and even then the government withholds most shares for itself.[75] So here too access to capital is difficult for private firms.

The hybrid sector (which includes TVEs) is a somewhat different case. In a study reported by Redding and Witt of 17 hybrid firms, 45 percent received their start-up capital from banks.[76] Once they were established, financing changed from banks to private credit agencies (28 percent), friends (24 percent), and overseas Chinese (15 percent).[77] In general, the hybrid (sometimes called "collective") sector self-funded from retained earnings for the majority of its capital needs. Its role in the economy, however, declined significantly after the late 1990s.

It is important to note the role of the overseas Chinese in regard to capital financing. Between 1985 and 2005, 47 percent of FDI came from Hong Kong and 12 percent from Taiwan.[78] The overseas Chinese also brought technological and manufacturing skills as well as access to global markets. Their long-standing entrepreneurial traditions were key in starting initiatives involving local families and local governments (registering the firm as a foreign entity meant tax rates would be 50 percent lower than regular rates). Furthermore, overseas Chinese capital was not just used for business financing; coming from foreign bank accounts, it was used to bribe local officials to get additional financing from local banks and other advantages.

[73] European Chamber of Commerce in China 2009.

[74] *Economist* April 21, 2012.

[75] Redding and Witt 2007.

[76] Redding and Witt 2007. Eighty percent of the entrepreneurs running the hybrid firms had prior experience in SOEs or TVEs.

[77] In Tsai's (2007) study, some entrepreneurs were paying "friends" 2 percent per month interest on loans. Illegal money houses were charging up to 4 percent per month. According to research reported in *The Economist* (March 10, 2011), in the city of Wenzhou 89 percent of the population and 57 percent of its enterprises borrowed outside the banking system, paying interest rates as high as 10 percent per month. Established businesses received the better rates of 1.5-2 percent per month.

[78] Redding and Witt 2007. In 2009, non-financial FDI was $54 billion from Hong Kong, $6.6 billion from Taiwan, and $3.6 billion from the United States (The US-China Business Council 2012).

In summary, from bank loans to stock market listings to a declining hybrid sector, the government limits domestic private firms' access to capital markets. This mechanism supports the earlier analysis of the "privatization" process, which showed increasing government control over the economy compared with that of the 1980s.

In 2008, the world economy went into a severe recession. The Chinese export machine has been hurt too. China's 2008 fourth-quarter growth slowed sharply to 6.8 percent; industrial production dropped severely to 3.8 percent.[79] This is the first contraction the post reform generation of entrepreneurs is having to face. Tens of thousands of plants are closed. The number of unemployed rose to 35 million.[80] This exposes a contradiction in China's high savings–high investment export industries strategy. Without increased domestic consumption, China will be subject to boom-bust cycles of export demand. Furthermore, at some point the world economy will become saturated with low-tech Chinese manufactured goods. So in addition to reducing savings and increasing domestic demand, China needs to develop high-technology products. But with the government's declining support for private entrepreneurship, can this be done?

3. Winners and Losers

China's high-growth economy has helped many of its 1.3 billion people. Per capita income increased by 2,800 percent from 1978 to 2010. Per capita GDP went from $153 in 1978 to $4,260 in 2010.[81] The infant mortality rate was 46 per 1,000 in 1975, 16 per 1,000 in 2010.[82]

But many groups are suffering greatly under China's economic reforms. While the coastal areas have done well, the interior has done less well; while there are many new entrepreneurs, there are many laid-off SOE workers; while urban workers have prospered, farmers' incomes have stagnated.[83] The central problem is that the government has presided over a "successful" but harsh, self-serving, and unfair transition to a market economy.

---

[79] Areddy 2009.

[80] Santoro 2009. Out of 5.6 million university graduates, 1.7 million cannot find jobs.

[81] The World Bank 2010.

[82] UNICEF 2010.

[83] In developing countries, urban GDP is rarely more than twice rural GDP; in China, urban GDP averages four times rural GDP (Santoro 2009).

After Mao's death in 1976 and the ending of the Cultural Revolution, Communism in China was significantly discredited. Mao's successor, Deng Xiaoping, developed a vision to move China forward primarily through the increase in economic freedom and the wealth it would generate while keeping the Communist Party in firm control of the state. Pan calls this vision "authoritarian capitalism."[84] It resulted in what *The Economist* calls "Dickensian capitalism."[85] The problem was and is that without a democratic process that gives representation to vulnerable groups, these groups are exploited. In China trade unions are illegal.[86] Only recently has the government allowed some workers to strike. By making its members and their families, friends, and allies wealthy, the Communist Party became dependent on Dickensian capitalism to stay in power.

Take for example the private mining industry. According to Chinese government figures, for every million tons of coal produced, 4–5 miners are killed.[87] This compares with 1 death per million tons in Russia and 0.5 in the United States and Great Britain. In China, the government limits the amount of money the family receives from the loss of a miner to $1,200–$6,400. At this rate, the mining companies, which have close relations to local and provincial officials, choose not to buy safety equipment. Pan reports 13-year-old girls working in mines pushing coal carts.[88] When I was in China in 2007, children, some mentally retarded, had been kidnapped by mining companies and forced to work in mines as slaves.[89]

A more widespread problem is unemployment. Pan reports that during the late 1990s and the following decade, layoffs were 5–6 million per year.[90] By 2002, 40 million jobs had been eliminated. In rust belt cities, 30 percent to 60 percent of all state workers had been laid off or were not being paid. In 2006, *The Economist* reported that 25 million people were unemployed.[91] Of

[84] Pan 2008.

[85] *Economist* March 25, 2006. By one estimate, Chinese manufacturing workers earn less than handloom operators in mid-19th-century England (Harney 2008).

[86] There is one trade union in China, the National General Trade Union. It is controlled by the Communist Party.

[87] Pan 2008.

[88] Pan 2008.

[89] Feldman 2007a.

[90] Pan 2008.

[91] *Economist* March 25, 2006. J. Wong (2003) argues that 200 million people (including migrants) are unemployed or underemployed.

SOE workers who still had jobs, many lost their pensions and health care and had their salaries reduced, frozen, or not paid.[92] Many state workers who lost their jobs had spent their lives working for the state and its "iron rice bowl" welfare system. Many were not able to adapt to market reforms and fell into poverty. These people are very bitter that they did not get what they had been promised under the Communist system after a lifetime of work.[93] The government, trying to keep a lid on mass dissatisfaction, brought large numbers of people into government employment. Pei reports that the government's administration expense rose from 5.3 percent of the national budget in 1978 to 18.6 percent in 2002.[94] In Pei's view, the cost of government overstaffing is an important cause of government corruption.

Despite government attempts to quiet dissatisfaction, widespread protests have been accelerating across the country. The reasons for protests are many: widespread corruption; official abuse of power; burdensome local taxes; demolition of housing for development of modern infrastructure; layoffs at failing SOEs; unpaid health care, pensions, and wages; air and water pollution caused by unregulated industrialization; and confiscation of land without adequate compensation.[95] In 2003, security forces were trying to contain an average of 160 demonstrations each day.[96] In 2004, Goldman reported, 3.76 million people took part in 74,000 protests.[97] In 2011, the number of protests was estimated at 100,000, with many going unreported.[98]

In regard to labor disputes that went to arbitration, the number leapt from 19,000 in 1994 to 184,000 in 2002.[99] In the late 1990s, some protests by SOE workers led to large-scale riots.[100] As SOE workers lost jobs, health care, and pensions, they could see government officials, their families and friends, and private entrepreneurs growing enormously wealthy. These huge disparities aggravated the losses SOE workers were experiencing. Under socialism,

[92] Goldman 2006a.
[93] Pan 2008.
[94] Pei 2006.
[95] Goldman 2006a.
[96] Pan 2008.
[97] Goldman 2006a.
[98] Kaiman 2011. Page (2011), citing figures leaked from the Chinese government, put the number at 127,000 for 2008.
[99] Hualing and Choy 2004.
[100] Goldman 2006a.

their positions carried high status and were high paying. By 2008, the number of disputes reached 295,000; in 2009, the number reached 318,600.[101]

Another group of workers who expressed complaints was that of migrant workers. On the one hand, in the 1990s, the Mao-era restrictions forbidding peasants to leave their villages were lifted. This meant that by 2003 upwards of 120 million rural residents were migrating to cities seeking jobs in the expanding private sector and associated services.[102] In 2005, the average monthly wage of migrants from the countryside, working mostly in manufacturing, was $150.[103] These jobs carried no health care or pensions, and could not be unionized. Despite the low pay, as the numbers suggest, it was still better than staying in the countryside. On the other hand, the low wages, discrimination by city residents, and abuse in the form of wages not being paid, or being paid in part, and unsafe working conditions led to protests.[104]

Private property rights, despite being enshrined in the constitution in 2004, have continued to be an object of conflict. In Beijing and Shanghai, for example, families were evicted from their residences in the city center and assigned apartments on the city outskirts worth a fraction of their former homes, which in many cases had been in their families for decades.[105] Likewise for farm land. As cities expand, peasants' land is seized and they are compensated for its agricultural value, which is one-tenth its market value.[106] Tens of millions have lost land without any compensation. In some cases, village leaders sell the land and do not share the proceeds.[107] Many times individuals with connections to the government are able to buy the land at very low prices and sell it immediately, making enormous profits. Fifty out of the 100 wealthiest people in China have made their fortunes in real estate. The

---

[101] E. Wong 2010.

[102] Goldman 2006a.

[103] *Economist* March 25, 2006. In 2011, the average monthly wage for migrant workers rose to $325 (Xin and Edwards 2012). Many economists attribute the rise to a shrinking labor pool. Migrant workers are not covered by China's new minimum wage laws.

[104] Cumulative wage arrears for migrant workers stood at 100 billion yuan in 2003 (Huang 2008). Urban residents disrespectfully refer to migrant workers as "blind flow" (Santoro 2009). For lawyers, representing migrant workers in court can result in harassment by the government to the point of disbarment and imprisonment.

[105] Pan 2008.

[106] *Economist* March 25, 2006.

[107] Gamer 2003a.

number of rural protests has been increasing and those over the illegal seizure of land have been severe.[108]

The economic reforms have hurt the rural population in other ways. Despite their being the poorest part of the population, their tax burden has increased, in some cases to oppressive levels.[109] Also as the state sector has declined and government revenues along with it, the government is purchasing fewer goods from the rural population at lower prices, while simultaneously both peasants and workers are paying higher prices for goods.[110]

Despite the fact that the economic reforms have brought 200 million people out of absolute poverty, there are still 700 million people living below the poverty line by Western standards.[111] The middle class is growing, but the poor are a bigger group and growing faster. In 2005, the poorest group saw their incomes decline despite the torrid pace of economic growth.[112]

The Communist Party is concerned about both urban and rural unrest. Over the last few years it has increasingly earmarked funds for rural infrastructure, including roads, schools, and hospitals. Efforts are being made to lower school fees and provide some sort of medical care.[113] Top leaders have increased their visits to rural areas to try to generate goodwill. The government's response to urban labor protests is more combative. It arrests leaders and in some cases gives them lengthy jail terms, while trying to co-opt followers, many times successfully.[114] It further divides followers by paying some and not others. If there is still a problem, the government scapegoats a few of its own to decrease the confrontation.

Fear also plays a role in how far protesters will go to confront the government. The middle-aged and older workers remember the Tiananmen Square massacre. They know that at some point, without warning, the government

[108] Spar and Oi 2006. R. McGregor (2010) states that 60 percent of all protests are over the selling of land for development by local governments.

[109] Gamer 2003a.

[110] According to a Chinese survey published in 2008, the number one concern for both rural and urban residents is the rising price of consumer goods (Santoro 2009).

[111] Three hundred million people in China are living on less than a dollar a day (Santoro 2009).

[112] Spar and Oi 2006.

[113] Increased school fees for rural residents in the 1990s led to an increased dropout rate, which resulted in an increase of 30 million illiterate Chinese adults between 2000 and 2005 (Huang 2008).

[114] Pomfret 2007; Pan 2008.

will not hesitate to kill them. Torture of prisoners is common. More generally, both the government and the population fear chaos, in an almost instinctive knowledge of China's long history of public disorder. This cognizance keeps significant segments of the population sympathetic to a strong role for the central government in society and keeps the government ever ready to crush any opposition. The growing gap between rich and poor creates a tension with the desire for order and has many times in China's history led to disorder.

4. Reforms and Government Corruption

With the Communist Party's credibility in tatters after the Cultural Revolution, the Party pinned its future on marketization. It attempted to use economic growth to justify its grip on power. But this states the case too broadly. More precisely, "market socialism with Chinese characteristics" means Party officials or their families and friends have grown rich by being the first to benefit from "privatization" and from making sure whoever else benefitted also contributed to the Party's grip on power. Perhaps the fear of disintegration, as was probably heightened by the disintegration of the Soviet Union, also helps keep the Chinese Communists in power.

In any case, the reforms had a big impact on the central government both economically and politically. The state has been continuously weakened since the 1992 reforms. The central government's budgetary revenues declined from 35 percent of GDP in 1978 to 12 percent in 1998.[115] The central government's share of public outlays fell from 47.4 percent in 1978 to 34.7 percent in 2000.[116] At this point, China is one of the most decentralized countries in the world in terms of paying for social services.[117] One of the consequences of these changes is decreased expenditures on education, health care, and infrastructure, especially in rural areas.[118]

The balance between centralization and decentralization has always been difficult for China. Its huge size, topographical barriers, and vast economic differences between regions are continuous challenges to governance.[119]

---

[115] Goldman 2006a.

[116] Pei 2006.

[117] *Economist* March 25, 2006.

[118] Goldman 2006a. As noted earlier, these expenditure shifts also represent a shift in policy away from private, rural economic development to public, urban economic development.

[119] Boisot and Child 1996.

During the Mao era an intense centralization had been implemented. It was not a period that emphasized personal wealth, and much of the central government's revenues had been used for public goods. But once the reforms were implemented during the post-Mao period, they required a great decentralization, which left the central state weakened. For one thing, under marketization, the number of transactions and the number of people involved increased exponentially. The state is relentless though less than successful, for example, in trying to maintain control over the Internet.[120] State power was also curtailed by the increasing independence of some of its own agencies and agents, who developed their own agendas.[121] Even more debilitating were local agencies' and officials' seeing financial opportunities and pursuing them no matter what the central government dictated. This led to intellectual property (IP) theft, tax overcharges, corruption, and labor exploitation.[122]

The original idea was that decentralization would incentivize state agents and thus increase productivity. It was decentralization in property rights.[123] But the central government did not have a clear understanding of property rights. It decentralized without controls.[124] This led to asset stripping and a plethora of other abuses. For one thing, central government officials had always done whatever they wanted. So once the city and province governments gained power, they did likewise. There was less reason than ever not to. The reforms themselves were yet another blow to Communist ideology,

---

[120] Pomfret 2007.

[121] Sun 2004.

[122] Goldman 2006a.

[123] Pei 2006.

[124] There were policy ambiguities, absent supervision, and weak rule of law (Sun 2004), which turned "decentralization" into local protectionism, with local governments and organizations trying to get the most for themselves. One problem was that the government did not develop any new controls for these massive and radical changes, so decentralized assets instantly became spoils. Another problem was that established supervisory and regulatory offices had no independence to carry out their responsibilities. If a corrupt official had a rank higher than or equal to that of the regulators or was protected by someone with higher or equal rank, he was untouchable. This demonstrates the dominance of the status hierarchy over the rule of law and the government's own rules and regulations. Actually the biggest threat to corrupt officials was that if Party power dynamics were such that their benefactor lost power, the officials themselves became vulnerable (Pan 2008). They stole with abandon but never knew when the curtain might fall. Their very success led to jealousies and the constant risk of betrayal by or report to other government officials outside their networks (Pomfret 2007). A system based on personal power is a breeding ground for corruption, though the very fluidity of power dynamics makes corruption not without uncertainty and risk.

which under Mao had been a central pillar of power. The Communist Party made a deal with the devil. Decentralization kick-started economic growth and co-opted upwardly mobile groups, but it opened up the flood gates of corruption, further undermining the state economically and politically.

Why has the central government been unable to address official corruption? For one thing, it does not get any help from the media or civic groups because the government represses them. The media are given some freedom under reforms as long as they stay away from political topics. Likewise, nonprofit organizations have been allowed to exist as long as they do not address political issues.[125] A second problem is that the courts have been kept subservient to the government, so it is nearly impossible to prosecute government and Party officials.[126] Hence, local officials have run their jurisdictions as personal fiefdoms for their own benefit. A third factor is that with the lifting of restrictions on foreign travel, no small number of officials steal and run. Access to travel has lowered the risk of stealing.[127] A fourth reason is weak supervision and practically nonexistent whistle-blowing. The exploitation of office takes place through networks. So a whole agency could be involved. Even if one individual merely tries to avoid participation, he can be scapegoated and put in jail (or a mental hospital). Fifth, there is a high probability that abusers will not be prosecuted even if they are reported; if prosecuted, that they will not be convicted; and if convicted, that they will not be punished.[128] Finally, and most important, because the people who are stealing are essential to the state's own power structure, systematic punishment of corrupt officials would undermine the reforms and undermine the central state.

Corruption in the Communist Party and government appears to involve all levels of officials, though top levels are particularly noticeable. *The Economist* reports that top Party leaders have amassed fortunes in foreign bank accounts.[129] An internal Party document reports that 78 percent of

---

[125] Pei 2006.

[126] Pan 2008.

[127] The Ministry of Public Security announced publicly in May 2004 that more than 500 corrupt officials had fled China with more than 8 billion dollars; an official news agency reported 4,000 individuals had fled the country with 50 billion dollars (Pei 2006).

[128] For example, only 6.6 percent of officials found guilty of corruption between 1993 and 1998 received sentences (Pei 2006).

[129] *Economist* March 25, 2006.

fraud cases of more than $600,000 involve senior Party officials.[130] Many of these senior Party leaders are also top executives at SOEs. Pei reports that 40 percent of "number-one leaders" prosecuted for corruption were CEOs of SOEs and 30 percent were grassroots-level rural cadres.[131]

Sun found that corruption tended to follow typical patterns, which changed over time as the reforms changed.[132] In the 1980s, the main form of corruption involved exploitation of reforms to open up the command economy. SOE executives were given new discretionary power for a two-track system of prices. The purpose was to allow some percentage of goods to be priced by the market, but executives used the two-track system to sell controlled goods at higher market prices and take advantage of supply shortages for private gain. In some cases, they set up private companies to siphon off goods from state companies just for this purpose.

Starting in 1992, the state created new forms of public power to further privatize the economy. This in turn led to new forms of corruption. Power over sales of state assets or asset shares, bank loans, social welfare funds, tax benefits, development and infrastructure projects, levies and fines, regulatory and judicial fees, sale of land, appraisal of state assets, regulation of business disputes, licenses and permits, and so on, all created opportunities for illegal profits. Whereas the primary source of corruption in the 1980s was SOE executives, after 1992 it included Party and state executives, law enforcement agencies, judicial officials, and economic governance agencies. Sun states that the chief executives remained the largest group of corrupt officials because corruption now went beyond the declining manufacturing SOEs to include nonmanufacturing SOEs in investment, banking, stock exchanges, property development, and insurance.[133] As reforms went beyond input-output

---

[130] Gamer 2003a. It is also common, though, to see relatively low-level officials arrested for stealing funds or assets worth millions of dollars (R. McGregor 2010). The largest theft on record is $12 million by a vice-mayor in Suzhou. The number of officials involved is apparently quite large, as evidenced by the Chinese having given them a name, "the new black-collar class."

[131] Pei 2006. J. McGregor (2005) states that more often than not, successful CEOs of SOEs open up offshore bank accounts or siphon off shares when their SOE is listed on a stock exchange.

[132] Sun 2004.

[133] Sun 2004. Fifty to 60 percent of economic crime cases involved SOE executives, while 25–33 percent involved state executives, law enforcement agencies, judicial officials, and economic governance agencies.

regulation to involve revenues, assets, and loans, the average age and rank of officials participating in corruption increased and the monetary values involved went up dramatically.

A favorite conspiracy that was used repeatedly throughout China was the forcing of SOEs into bankruptcy by a cabal of executives and officials in order to sell off assets to their own family and friends at pennies on the dollar.[134] In the process, workers would not receive years of back pay, promised pensions, and health insurance or unemployment payments as executives drained the firm of funds and anything of value. Needless to say, the law was completely ignored.[135] According to Pan, former officials or their children were the biggest beneficiaries.

The full integration of government, private business, family, and organized crime in rapacious corruption can be seen in the case of the city of Shenyang.[136] The mayor and more than 100 officials were detained for corruption, including the deputy mayor, the city's chief judge, the chief prosecutor, the head of the tax bureau, and the manager of the state assets agency. The mayor's first wife, second wife, brother, daughter, and chauffeur were also arrested. At the center of the scandal was a mafia boss who not only sat on the city legislature but was also responsible for 30–40 murders. The mayor had corrupt relations with the police, banks, and construction bureaus; he was involved in smuggling, extortion, sale of official positions, rigging of state contracts, embezzlement, and using public funds to maintain mistresses.

There are different theories as to why the Communist Party allowed corruption to get started in the first place.[137] One is that corruption automatically results when privatization of state assets is carried out by an authoritarian government.[138] The temptation is simply too great for those with unchecked power not to make themselves enormously wealthy. Another theory is that if officials were not given great incentives to carry out the reforms, they would never have gotten out of the bureaucracy.[139] McGregor thinks the Party allowed leaders' families to exploit the "privatization" process

---

[134] Pan 2008.

[135] In one case involving an SOE, an accountant who reported embezzlement to the government was put in jail for 19 days (Pan 2008).

[136] Pan 2008.

[137] Pei (2006) argues that local government corruption likely cut central government revenues by 25 percent.

[138] Pei 2006.

[139] Pan 2008.

so they could keep their status in what had become a commerce-oriented society.[140] For this reason, the government will always be ambivalent about rooting out corruption.

All in all, the Party apparatus came to resemble an organized crime network, with autonomous profit-making subunits, rivalries, and rules for dividing up state assets and the revenues state office makes possible.[141] The state not only used its security apparatus for bullying and intimidating, but for the more underhanded or publicly offensive activities it employed thugs. When workers went missing during labor protests, for example, families did not know whether they had been arrested, kidnapped, or murdered because police had ties with organized crime. Like the situation in Shenyang, local governments became so closely aligned with criminals it was difficult to tell them apart. In some cases, this arrangement went on for years.

The prototype case of private sector–government collusion involving not only criminal activity but criminal organization is probably the real estate industry. Private developers offer bribes or promises to build roads or municipal buildings or apartments for city employees or just to help the career of an official in exchange for land-use rights. But to make the big money, the private developer must evict residents living on the land in order to demolish their homes and build the much more profitable high-rise buildings. The problem is, of course, that the residents do not want to leave their homes. So the developer hires criminal gangs to intimidate and bully the residents while the police look the other way; the courts refuse to consider the matter; and the public utilities cut off electricity, water, and heat.

There are other forms of government corruption. Since so many Party officials run businesses,[142] other businesses find themselves competing with and regulated by the same individual. Or in regard to foreign businesses, as McGregor points out, if the regulator is not the competitor, he is helping the competitor.[143] Another form of government corruption is giving preferential treatment to state firms or newly privatized firms, with which the government shares in the proceeds, while levying high taxes and fees on entrepreneurial start-ups, with which they do not have such relationships.[144] Related to this

---

[140] J. McGregor 2005.
[141] Pan 2008.
[142] Pomfret (2007) says it is more than 150,000.
[143] J. McGregor 2005.
[144] Pan 2008.

practice, the government allows firms with which it has connections to break the law. In one case, the CEO of a private bottled water company, who had close connections with the Communist Party, was able to cover up the deaths of three girls from poisoned water.[145] Importantly, many Chinese businessmen prefer this system to one in which laws are fair, impartial, and enforced.[146] Their reasoning is that bribes cost less than taxes, pollution regulations, and worker safety rules.

There are several obvious costs to a corruption-based economic system:

1. It continually corrodes government authority.
2. It weakens the state financially. Much of the ill-gotten gains going to Party officials correlate directly with a loss of state revenues.[147]
3. The weak and poor, who are dependent on the state for support, suffer because the state has less revenue from which to allocate to them.
4. It raises costs for all businesses and prices for all consumers.
5. It results in underinvestment in education, health care, and public safety.[148]
6. It undermines reforms.
7. It discredits law enforcement and the judicial system.
8. It undermines small businesses and farmers.
9. It disorganizes and corrupts state agencies.
10. It misallocates societal resources.
11. It undermines the solvency of the banking system.
12. It leads to extreme income inequality, undermining social stability.[149]

---

[145] J. McGregor 2005.

[146] Pomfret 2007.

[147] Goldman 2006a.

[148] In 1988 public expenditure on education was 2.6 percent; in 1998 it was 2.2 percent (Huang 2008). By 2000 the growth in tuition and child care costs exceeded the consumer price index by 30 percent. Between 1992 and 2002 GDP per capita grew by 50 percent but per capita spending on hospital/clinic visits increased by just 2.15 percent and spending on hospitalizations increased by only 3.76 percent. Huang claims that during this period 65 percent of the rural population needing hospitalization did not go because of skyrocketing costs. In 2003, 20 percent of the rural population received publicly financed health care; in the 1970s the proportion was 90 percent.

[149] China is one of the most unequal societies in the world, with a Gini coefficient (which measures inequality of income distribution) of 45 in 2002; India's Gini coefficient was 32.5 in the late 1990s (Huang 2008). This inequality, along with the unpaid salaries, pensions, and health care of SOE workers and the unfair land sales and forced evictions for property development, led to increasing social unrest.

5. Reforms and Society

The relationship between government and business is a two-way street. Government officials are the big winners in the reform period, but many entrepreneurs seek out government benefits. For example, many entrepreneurs in rural areas set themselves up as "collectives" so as to more easily get help from local governments.[150]

In general, the Communist Party pays close attention to co-opting entrepreneurs and business people. Business people were first admitted to the Communist Party in November 2002.[151] By accepting, organizing, and co-opting the new rich through opportunities for wealth and status, the Party hopes to stop pressures for reforms.[152] Clearly the Party intends to control all areas of society, as can be seen in the 2001 comment by Jiang Zemin, general secretary of the Communist Party, about the "three represents," which defined the Communist Party as representing the most advanced forces of production, the most advanced cultural forces, and the broad masses.[153] The Party's prominence does not, however, accord with a survey that found that 99 percent of Party officials thought the status of entrepreneurs was getting better while only 41 percent felt their own status had improved.[154]

Like all others in business, entrepreneurs must work closely with government officials.[155] Hence, their attitudes toward reform and the Communist Party are relevant for the success of the reform agenda. In Dickson's sample, 16.1 percent of candidates in village elections were entrepreneurs and 72.5 percent of these were Communist Party members.[156] Goldman found that 33 percent of businessmen were Party members and the percentage of

---

[150] This type of relationship was common in the 19th century (Goldman 2006a).

[151] In Tsai's (2007) 2002 survey, 43.5 percent of entrepreneurs expressed an interest in joining the Party. Redding and Witt (2007) report that Communist Party membership among entrepreneurs is between 15 and 34 percent.

[152] Dickson 2003. The Party has penetrated the new business associations, which will likely undermine their ability to represent business (Redding and Witt 2007). Both entrepreneurs and officials believe that if a businessman who is not a Party member is elected to a low-level government post, he should join the Party (Dickson 2003). Given this attitude, it is difficult to see where challenges to the Party will come from.

[153] Tsai 2007.

[154] Dickson 2003.

[155] Peng and Luo (2000) found that relationships with government officials were more important than relationships with other businesses.

[156] Dickson 2003.

Party members among large entrepreneurs was even greater.[157] Dickson found entrepreneurs tend to be elitist:

> The longer entrepreneurs have been in business, the more likely they have been a candidate for village chief or council; the more likely they believe that ambition and skill determine economic success, that rich people should have more influence on policy, that what is good for business is good for the community, and [that] diversity of individual views and groups is a threat to stability.[158]

Thus, their views do not support democratization. Ironically, they also do not give strong support for free markets; 44.7 percent of the entrepreneurs in the more developed counties and 88 percent in the less developed counties believe competition is harmful.[159] This seems to imply that they prefer stability over change and receiving rewards because of their status rather than earning them in the marketplace.

The same pattern is found in the attitudes of entrepreneurs toward authoritarian government; 51.3 percent of entrepreneurs with a primary education agree that the government alone should initiate economic reform, while 75.6 percent with a university education think the same.[160] Also, Dickson found that support for reform tended to decrease in the more developed counties. Pomfret tells of a university lecturer in computer science who led student marches against the government in 1989.[161] Now he is a successful entrepreneur selling technology to the security services. He is wealthy and supports the Communist government. Of course, one's choices are limited. Pan reports that a prominent agricultural tycoon was jailed for five months for criticizing the Party.[162]

Nonetheless, China is undergoing great social change. The reforms have brought personal, social, and cultural freedom. This has gone some way to improving (and, unfortunately, burying) the damage from Mao's ideological fanaticism. In its place one can see the beginnings of a civil society wherein

---

[157] Goldman 2006b. Tsai (2007) reported that entrepreneurs who were members of government-sponsored political organizations had large numbers of employees, had Party branches in their organization, and were likely to have access to bank credit.

[158] Dickson 2003: 135.

[159] Dickson 2003.

[160] Dickson 2003.

[161] Pomfret 2007.

[162] Pan 2008.

citizens have a communal life related to but independent of the government. Not only is Mao's totalitarian state mostly gone, but the authoritarian state has been significantly weakened.

Signs of civil society take many forms. There has been significant growth of the news media independent of the government.[163] Even the government media are bolder in how they cover the news. In addition, the Internet is expanding exponentially. The Chinese people are getting more and better information than ever before. Religion is experiencing a revival.[164] Expanding markets have contributed to these freedoms by increasing the flow of information and social interaction. The increase in wealth is also leading people to seek a more meaningful life. The number of nongovernmental organizations (NGOs) has greatly expanded, though they are closely watched and their scope limited by the government. Donations by entrepreneurs to help their communities have increased.[165] Hence, the economic reforms have led to more than economic freedom. But how far this development will go is an open question. With the current level of government repression, it is limited. Chinese history is characterized mostly by a blend of private, public, and state institutions rather than the state-society dichotomy more common in the West.[166] This history will play an important role in China's future development.

There are other obstacles to the development of a civil society in China. The intense bonding inside the Chinese family is an obstacle.[167] It developed under the duress of a predatory state after the latter "eviscerated" intermediate groups.[168] This state of affairs is supported by Confucianism, which does not posit universal moral obligations, making relationships a few steps away from the family impersonal. In China, ties of reciprocity, not a trust in shared values, are key for the development of relationships, thus limiting

---

[163] Osnos 2009.

[164] Sixty to 80 million Chinese Christians go to church every Sunday; China now has more Buddhists than any other country in the world; and folk religion is making a comeback (Johnson 2011). To be sure, much religious activity is still suppressed by the government.

[165] The most common contributions go to local construction projects and social welfare efforts (Dickson 2003).

[166] Goldman 2006a.

[167] The Chinese male "will be much admired as an example of a good son and a good man if he has few outside associations and devotes his entire energy toward working [for] and pleasing his parents" (Hsu 1981: 115).

[168] Fukuyama 1995: 98.

relationships beyond family, close friends, and *guanxi*.[169] Beyond these direct, personal relationships, the social environment is seen as dangerous and uncertain. Without more generalized feelings of trust, it is difficult to see how a broader civil society develops. Indeed, along with the government's jealous control over the institutions of law, finance, administration, and communications, the return of paternalism in all relationships of authority, replacing the obsolete Communist ideals, makes the development of voluntary organizations difficult at best.

The return of paternalism also makes the development of a market difficult at best. Tsai reports that in 1986, Chinese scholars concluded China is in an early stage of socialism, so it will be impossible to avoid developing the private sector.[170] But to fully develop the private sector, the Chinese will need to develop large private businesses and independent professions of accounting, law, and journalism to go beyond low-tech production and remove government politicization and corruption from business decision making.[171] If the Chinese indeed see the development of the "private" sector as temporary, as in "market socialism," that would explain the tight control the state maintains over the economy—because without more autonomous institutions and a sense of shared values, the trust needed to create large, complex, private organizations will not develop.

Recent changes in Chinese culture are also not encouraging. As mentioned, the breakdown of the Marxist-Leninist-Maoist system has led to increases in nationalism, consumerism, and religion. Consumerism is most observable. It results from exposure to Western culture and living standards, disillusionment with the deprivation experienced during the Cultural Revolution, and the lack of any ability to participate in the political system.[172] Consumerism is related to a focus on self. The focus on self is so extreme in many cases that it has led to a widespread concern for the health of Chinese morality.

Pomfret has noted that these cultural changes have changed the use of language.[173] In the 1980s, *frugal* was a compliment; now it is a put-down. *Open-minded* now means "promiscuous," *miss* means "hooker." The universal *comrade* has all but disappeared and been replaced with words more precisely

---

[169] Redding and Witt 2007.
[170] Tsai 2007.
[171] Redding and Witt 2007.
[172] Goldman 2006a.
[173] Pomfret 2007.

denoting status. In these examples, the focus on freedom, self-expression, and how one is different from others is apparent. The influence of Western culture is also apparent. When university-age men and women were asked where they would like to take someone on a date, the majority of them said out for Western fast food.[174] Individual choice, consumption, and personal status have become more important since the economic reforms and opening.

The exaggerated focus on self has had some negative effects. Rising expectations; rising crime; perceptions of declining moral standards; widespread corruption; and a staple of capitalism, envy, what the Chinese call the "red-eye disease," are all challenges the Chinese face as a result of economic liberalization in the Chinese context.[175] All of these are threats to Chinese culture and social integration.

One place in particular that shows the moral decline brought about by the reforms is the role of women. Chinese society has long been structured by patrilineal kinship organization, wherein women receive second-class status. Even after the Communist Revolution, when equality became a universal organizing principle, in many rural communities the new commune system merely "revivified lineage segments as production brigades and teams, further monopolizing power in the hands of clusters of male agnates."[176] Similar results were obtained in all other types of organizations. The gender bias can also be seen in the one-child policy, whereby most of the birth control enforcement falls on women. Nonetheless, under Communist equality job opportunities and advancement for women did improve.

Under reforms, the situation for women has deteriorated dramatically.[177] Female workers are paid 21 percent to 28 percent less than male workers for the same types of jobs.[178] When families sell land in rural areas, women family members receive six-tenths as much as men.[179] Their access to business opportunities are more limited than and unequal to those of men.[180] Lam found occupation segregation by gender higher in new private firms than

---

[174] Pomfret 2007.
[175] J. Wong 2003. Before reforms, the Communists had removed the "four pests" of drug abuse, prostitution, gambling, and secret societies (K. Yu 2009). Under reforms, they have all come roaring back.
[176] Gates 1996: 247.
[177] He, Zhu, and Peng 2002.
[178] Lam 2002.
[179] *Economist* March 25, 2006.
[180] Dickson 2003.

older SOEs, pointedly showing a decline in the status of women under the economic reforms.[181] Further, the decline in social welfare programs under reforms has hit women and the elderly in the countryside more than men.[182] In 1990, 70 percent of the illiterate population was female.

The other side of the decline in the status of women is the rise of male dominance and chauvinism. This has left female entrepreneurs cut off from the male world of connections.[183] Men indulge in endless banqueting, typically involving competitive drinking, from which women are excluded. Female entrepreneurs remain backstage, while male family members or employees work the male networks. This shows how the traditional patriarchal system is reemerging under economic liberalization. Female entrepreneurs run their businesses as "inside people," just as their grandmothers and great-grandmothers ran the family.[184]

Tens of millions of women from rural areas have become even more alienated. While the reforms have brought improved economic opportunities, for these women they have also brought dire social and psychological experiences.[185] They leave their families and villages, where they have lived in close, traditional relationships, to seek monotonous jobs in toy, clothing, shoe, and electronics assembly factories in coastal southern China. They have little support in their new situation beyond possibly a relative or mate from their village. They often live in crowded factory-owned dormitories, purchasing their meals in factory-owned cafeterias. Typically they work a six-day week, and overtime on top of this is common. Their pay is around $70 per month, a third of which they send back to their families.[186] Their boss is usually a male, and exploitation is common.[187]

---

[181] Lam 2002.

[182] Goldman 2006a.

[183] Hefner 1998. Nine out of 10 entrepreneurs are men (M. Yang 2002).

[184] Hefner 1998.

[185] Santoro 2009.

[186] Santoro 2009. In 2012, the Fair Labor Association published a study of 35,000 Foxconn workers (Duhigg and Greenhouse 2012). Foxconn has 1.2 million workers in China. At one plant, average wages were about $440 a month. About half the workers stated that they were unable to pay for health care or education at this wage. There were numerous instances of employees working more than 60 hours a week and sometimes more than 11 days in a row. Chinese law prohibits employees from working more than 49 hours a week. Forty-three percent of workers said they had experienced or witnessed accidents. The study found dormitory rooms crowded.

[187] Hessler 2006.

It seems certain that these developments for women, especially those in the previous paragraph, contribute to China having the highest female suicide rate among the world's major economies.[188] The suicides are usually women from rural areas who have some education. Poverty is usually not a factor. They are mostly women whose lives have been improved economically but who have experienced great social and psychological change. Like the poisoning of air and water, the speed and consequences of the economic reforms have been deadly for culture too.[189]

6. Reforms and Political Change

Along with the economic reforms, there have been some improvements in China's political system. Generally, the Communist Party is less repressive than during the Mao era. The legislature is more active and there are some signs of improvement in the legal system. Despite the harsh crackdown on protesters in the spring and summer of 1989, political reforms begun earlier have been continued.

Perhaps the most hopeful changes have been the introduction of elections at lower levels. Beginning in 1980, multicandidate elections were permitted for local-level people's congresses. This practice was expanded during the late 1980s to elections for village leadership. In most cases, however, the village Communist Party secretary won.[190] Elections for Party posts usually have only one candidate.[191] All in all, the process is still carefully controlled by the Party, which explains why elections have done little to reduce rural protests.

The chance of democracy spreading in China seems slim at this point. China's post-Confucian neighbors did evolve into democratic systems. But China does not have a well-developed education system or a professional bureaucracy committed to the rule of law, and decentralization has already proceeded to the point where it will be difficult to reverse.[192] Furthermore,

---

[188] World Health Organization 2011.

[189] Jianlin and colleagues (2001) study of suicide in China found rural females 20-25 years old to be the group most prone to suicide in China. While 18 percent of the population, they account for 50 percent of total suicides. The primary cause was the low status of women in family and society, as manifest in constrained opportunities and cruelty from husbands and in-laws. This has been exacerbated by weakening family ties resulting from economic reforms.

[190] Goldman 2006a.

[191] *Economist* March 25, 2006.

[192] Pei 2006.

according to Pei, no Communist government has ever evolved into a democracy.

Certainly there are strong political forces against democracy in China. Political and cultural elites fear democracy could lead to domestic chaos, result in their loss of power, engender vicious conflict among leaders, lead to the rise of demagogues, create an opening for foreign influence, break down multiethnic relations, and embolden poor and resentful social groups.[193] Further, the political culture is characterized by a low degree of tolerance for mistakes, institutional inertia, a lack of strong incentives for leaders to make bold reforms, and an obsession with stability.[194] More broadly, entrepreneurs, intellectuals, and political elites widely share the belief that the masses are too ignorant to participate in democracy.[195]

Above all, even though the Communist Party's repressive tendencies have declined in comparison with Mao's ideological fanaticism, the Party is still predatory; it feeds off of and exploits Chinese society through its monopolization of the means of power. The reforms have actually solidified the resolve of some to maintain the Party's dictatorship because its high profits have made it easier to buy off competitors.[196] Despite the appearance of increasing economic development, predation actually undermines both society and policy by undermining the delivery of public goods, property rights, and the fair and just application of law. For a while, as society gets wealthier and the Party more self-confident, a sort of financial thrill develops that distracts from the deeper political and social problems.

But the underlying problems do not go away. *The Economist* reported in 2006 that the Chinese government had changed little in the previous six years:

> China remains politically almost as secretive, just as risk-averse, nearly as dictatorial and every bit as determined to crush any organized dissent as it was at the turn of the decade.[197]

---

[193] K. Yu 2009. In regard to fears of a loss of elite privilege, a powerful example is the "wicked coalition" formed by officials and business groups to stop political and economic reforms in the real estate industry, where they are making vast fortunes (C. Li 2009).

[194] C. Li 2009.

[195] Tsai 2007.

[196] Pei 2006.

[197] *Economist* March 25, 2006: 13.

It is difficult to see how substantial change will arise in this system. It is still easier to rise in the government than to rise in the Communist Party.[198] At the center of the government is the Party and even though the fanatical commitment to ideology is gone, an absolute (martial) demand for loyalty remains. It is difficult to see how this structure willingly gives up its dictatorial power. Indeed, *The Economist* reports "intensive indoctrination among Party officials."[199]

Looked at in broader perspective, China has one of the earliest and longest-enduring bureaucracies in the world.[200] There is much continuity between the behavior of the Communist Party and China's long history of imperial dynasties. State predation is not new with the Communists. Gates considers predation a foundational principle throughout the last thousand years of Chinese history.[201] Even religion was closely aligned with state power, never developing an autonomous institutional space of its own. Likewise now, the Communists jealously control religious worship just as they narrowly restrict NGOs. For Pei, corruption is getting worse.[202]

No matter who takes over in the once-in-a-decade leadership change in 2012, there is little choice but to keep economic growth and development as key priorities. For one thing, economic growth is essential for China's security.[203] But, as has been shown, economic growth does not occur in a vacuum no matter how hard the Communist Party tries to keep it in one. There are inevitable social, cultural, political, and ecological effects to which society must adjust. This adjustment has been greatly hampered by the rigid and repressive Communist Party in key areas such as the environment, education, cultural and ethnic pluralism, economic and political decentralization, rural development, stemming of corruption, investigative reporting, local elections, NGOs, and labor and peasant protests.

There are other serious pressures and problems. For one, the developed economies work in a more or less shared system of legal, economic, and administrative institutions. Without continuing innovations in civil law,

---

[198] Gamer 2003a.
[199] *Economist* March 25, 2006: 13.
[200] Chen, Chen, and Xin 2004.
[201] Gates 1996.
[202] Pei 2006.
[203] Gamer 2003a.

banking, election processes, and administrative procedures, China will not be able to sustain its developing role in the world economy.[204] Even more importantly, with the decline of Marxism-Leninism, China is to some extent flying blind at the same time that increasing cultural diversity is putting great pressure on societal integration. Without new political institutions that provide a more inclusive political life, and procedures and processes to work out conflicts, the country could face endemic conflict. Economic growth cannot and will not meet all of China's needs.

Conclusion

The Chinese economic reforms and opening have greatly changed Chinese society in many ways, including contradictory ones. Their impact will continue to be felt for decades to come in many unforeseen ways as different issues arise and different parts of Chinese society react differently. It is a situation of great complexity and importance, producing significant accomplishments and offering hope for further improvements for the huge number of Chinese people, many of them in great need of opportunities and support.

The exact nature of this great experiment in economic development has attracted much attention, particularly how it compares and contrasts with Western capitalism. It has been given many names as writers try to describe and explain how it functions. Boisot and Child's reference to "quasi-capitalism" focuses on the lack of rational-legal bureaucracy in the Western sense, that is, without impersonal rules and relationships that drive decision making and action.[205] This view highlights the much-commented-on *guanxi* relations, where trusted personal relationships inside extensive interpersonal networks account for the inner mechanism of organized action. This view leads to claiming that Chinese economic organizations are not "modern" but feudal, because fiefdoms and hierarchies, long organizational forms in Chinese history, dominate organizations. Nonetheless, China's economic success cannot be denied, so Boisot and Child create a second name, "network capitalism," to categorize this new form of business organization, separating it from Western capitalism, indeed showing that

---

[204] Gamer 2003b.
[205] Boisot and Child 1996.

Western capitalism is just one type of capitalism among potentially many others.[206]

Harney's name for Chinese economic organization is "athletic capitalism."[207] This name connotes the great energy the Chinese people bring to the opportunities that have opened up in their country. Indeed, an estimated 100 million to 200 million people are on the move inside China's borders, moving from rural areas to cities in search of work. It is said this is the greatest movement of human beings in history. Harney's name also connotes the intense competition that has developed as all these people, plus the great influx of foreigners, try to capitalize on the new opportunities. Less visible in this metaphor is China's poverty and desperation. Tens of millions of people are on the move not only because of opportunities but because, in the worst case, some of them are starving. Athletic capitalism, the great competition, is both great hope and great tragedy. The competition is so intense because the stakes are so high. The stakes are so high because some of the competitors are starving and no one knows if or how long the window of opportunity will stay open before political change shuts it. This is the story of Chinese history and this is the field upon which "athletic capitalism" is played.

This leads to another metaphor for Chinese economic organization, "authoritarian capitalism."[208] Authoritarian capitalism captures the central (dominating) role the Chinese state plays in economic activity, everything from capital allocation to regulatory approval to ownership to extortion. Indeed, "privatization" must be put in quotation marks because the government has in many ways maintained control of "privatized" assets. The government is the major player in the business system in China, and to do business in China means to do business with the government more than any other entity. So even though the economy has been "reformed" and "opened," the government on all levels is still much more involved than in the West.[209] The

---

[206] Boisot and Child 1996. In fact, "Western" capitalism is a misnomer. Redding and Witt (2007) discuss five types of capitalism: shareholder capitalism (e.g., United States), coordinated capitalism (e.g., Japan), collaborative capitalism (e.g., Germany), state-led capitalism (e.g., South Korea), and network capitalism (e.g., Hong Kong). Hong Kong's "network capitalism" is nearly a pure type of market competition (Huang 2008), whereas China's "network capitalism" refers to small networks operating under and through a predatory state.

[207] Harney 2009.

[208] Pan 2008.

[209] This is still true even after the financial crisis in the United States, which resulted in unprecedented government involvement in the U.S. economy.

decentralization of the market means something different in China than in the West; it means the government must approve business transactions for a host of reasons, interests, government interests, and many times the interests of government officials. The Chinese government does not just regulate business, it uses it. For the government, business is still a tool of policy and exploitation, not a semi-autonomous part of civil society.[210]

The relationship of the government to law in China parallels that of the government to business. The government is above the law as it is above business. The law is not used to impartially define and regulate the different parts of society and their interrelationships. It is a tool of the government, a tool of power. Authoritarian capitalism means business under a political dictatorship.

Hence both the great benefits for and great costs to Chinese society from economic reform. A dictatorship sports a significant concentration of power. This power has allowed the Chinese government to make huge changes, fast, in everything from infrastructure to capital allocation to regulatory regimes to labor allocation to education and training. A democratic system would make decisions slower because it would include conflicting interests. The more singular nature of the Communist Party allows it to make faster decisions because many fewer voices are included in the process. Unlike Russia, which introduced "capitalism" through a change in government, China began to change its economic system without a change in government. The Chinese thus avoided the political chaos that undermined economic reform in Russia and led to oligarchic capitalism.[211]

Unfortunately, however, the Chinese government also ignored the well-being of large segments of the population. These people simply did not have a voice in the decision-making process. This is what another metaphor, "Dickensian capitalism," alludes to.[212] While the Chinese miracle brought tens of millions of people out of poverty, it also increased taxes on the poorest parts of the population while withdrawing health, education, and retirement supports. It broke its commitments to millions of state employees who had worked decades for the Communist system contributing to Communist goals. Dictatorial powers forced the removal of millions of people from their

---

[210] There is an overlap here with South Korea's state-led capitalism, less China's endemic corruption.

[211] Russia too has a large state-led dimension as well as a criminal component. The latter Sun (2004) refers to as "booty capitalism."

[212] *Economist* March 25, 2006.

homes at a fraction of their value to "modernize" cities and similarly remunerated farmers at a fraction of the value of their land. It enabled the government to pursue industrialization at breakneck speed without regard to the environment, resulting in the death and illness of millions.

Dickensian capitalism is a no-holds-barred competition, where IP theft, fraud, lies, lack of legal recourse, and material theft are part of the "competitive" landscape. Perhaps most important of all is the level of official corruption, particularly the distribution of public assets to the families and friends of government officials. In other words, one part of society, the government, is allowed to grow rich at the expense of other parts. The loss of wages, health care, and pensions from SOE workers relates directly in many cases to the sudden wealth of SOE leaders and officials who have control over these assets. Dickensian capitalism is an out-and-out war of one class against other classes, where the weakest suffer the most, the ones unable to adapt to an unfair, uncaring environment defined by opportunities for those with the best connections to officials or the skills to develop them.[213]

Of the five metaphors cited, perhaps the most applicable is "authoritarian capitalism." The reason is not the government's heavy regulatory role nor the highly centralized (opaque) decision-making process controlling infrastructures, banks, and key industries nor the continuing widespread government ownership of "private" companies nor the high number of government officials who have purchased government assets at fire sale prices nor the seizure of land and housing without fair remuneration nor the widespread corruption involving huge sums of money and criminal organizations, but all of these combined. The summary effect of all these activities and others makes the government, its role in the economy, its decision-making style, and its governance the central dynamic in Chinese "market socialism." To use another metaphor, this time from Max Weber, Chinese "market socialism" can be called "political capitalism" because of the centrality, power, and predatory role of the state in business.[214]

---

[213] The size of government employment roughly doubled over the last two decades (Huang 2008). This increase is probably related to an effort to reduce unemployment among the 40 million state workers who lost their jobs between 1995 and 2005, showing that there are limits to government exploitation. If the government makes things too bad for too many people, it could lose control of the country.

[214] Weber 1951. The terms "crony capitalism" and "booty capitalism" are also used in this context. The key point of contrast with American capitalism is the extent to which, in the latter, private individuals freely participate in exchange relations. In China, political power has a much stronger influence on all levels of economic decision making.

The government's motivation for introducing markets into a centrally planned economy was to try to legitimate itself after the disastrous Mao years and to develop the economy, which had fallen far behind many market-based economies. But the facts are that in implementing the "market" reforms, the government kept close control of the economy and officials on all levels used their positions to extract rents. This demonstrates the government's underlying character. It is an elite class with monopolistic power. Hence, it is unlikely to give up power, change its predatory disposition, or introduce significant democracy. The government may have had little choice but to introduce markets to address growing dissatisfaction among the population and destructive conflict within its own ranks, but nonetheless once it did implement them, it did so to both enrich and entrench itself. Ultimately, "market socialism" is political capitalism, profits and power for those in power.

Even though systemic corruption appears to be an "unintended consequence" of the reforms, it still results from deep causes, which grow out of an ancient authoritarian culture. A second "unintended consequence" of the reforms is the weakening of the government. To introduce markets, the government had to make a deal with the devil. To remain in power, it introduced markets to develop the economy and detract attention from its own oppression, cruelty, and incompetence. But as the devil gave with one hand, he took with the other. The government was able to stay in power but in a weakened condition. Ironically, the decentralization required for marketization actually increased authoritarianism and corruption at lower levels of government. This weakened the central government in terms of revenues, power, and status. So even though the country has grown stronger economically, simultaneously the central government has grown weaker. Hence, there is a growing need for alternative political mechanisms to replace declining government capacities in the increasingly complex nature of Chinese society. To date, the limited governance changes made by the government are inadequate. They are not able to address corruption, environmental destruction, growing protests, ethnic conflicts, and the like.

One thing that seems certain about the Communist Party's strategy for economic reform and opening is that it is too narrow; it does not address China's broader problems. Not only does China have problems beyond the economic sphere, but changes in the economic sphere have caused changes in the other spheres—for example, politics, art, education, culture, social behavior, gender relations—and the relations between them. Yet the government is attempting to stop or control change in the other spheres, especially in the decisive sphere of politics, where it has made no fundamental changes.[215]

The lack of political change and attempts to control change in other spheres, both in the face of emerging strong forces for change, is leading to dangerous cultural problems. One of these is the increasing mistreatment of women, the result of the reemergence of patriarchy. It is a great irony that as the Communist Party attempts to modernize the economy, the treatment of women is becoming more patriarchical. Political repression is involved here. As forces for political change are blocked, they are redirected to the repression of women, which both repeats past cultural patterns and enables males to take advantage of the politically weaker gender in the societal competition for resources and status. It is an unhealthy sign when societal economic growth is paired with a decline in economic opportunities for women. The reemergence of patriarchy suggests deep support for the authoritarian state.

The stark increase in female suicide rates is, of course, not just a political issue. It also signals that societal changes are leading to psychological despair and impacting most demonstrably the vulnerability of women. Under the Communists women had gained some measure of equality, which they are now losing. Traditionally, they have been the emotional center of the family. With departure from traditional village life, participation in harsh manufacturing jobs, growing materialism, the one-child policy, and rising male domination, women are losing the cultural coordinates of their social identity. This loss leads to inner despair and, at worst, suicide.

The rise in the female suicide rate is the most profound example of a broader problem. The decline in the culture of Communism after the Communists' decades-long assault on Confucianism and other aspects of traditional culture has left China culturally disoriented. Add in the dizzying rate of economic and technological change and harsh political repression by a technocratic, materialistic political elite, and China's cultural disorientation can be seen as deep indeed. The country is flying blind to some extent at the same time that its economic and military power is growing rapidly. This is

---

[215] The Party is also making a monumental effort to control access to information on the Internet (Chao 2009). In some areas, however, the government is not attempting to stop change. In the erotic sphere, for example, the abbreviation "ONS" (one-night stand) has become part of everyday parlance. Like consumerism, the government permits sexual freedom as a distraction from and release of the pressure built up by political repression.

particularly true of the political elites, who have little to believe in other than their own self-interests. Thus, the Communist Party leadership must allow generous payola to its cadres for the political center to hold, while not enraging the population so much that public order breaks down altogether.[216]

This line of analysis is further supported when the new entrepreneurial elites are considered. As Dickson found in his survey of entrepreneurs, they do not support democratization or, ironically, even strongly support free markets.[217] In fact, the more educated the entrepreneurs, the more they support government control; and the more developed the counties, the more they are against political reform. This is consistent with the work of Pomfret, who found highly educated and successful businessmen supporting the government.[218]

What is shown here is a mind-set. Businessmen want the government to keep society stable and happily work with officials for their mutual benefit, while at the same time they manipulate, distort, and ignore government rules, again for their mutual benefit.[219] The arrangement is a strong support for the Communist Party. It also shows an elitist perspective. In a hierarchical culture, entrepreneurs see themselves as superior. They consider it natural that the ones who are superior should be in control.[220] Self-interest is also a factor. Their success is inseparable from their relationship with the government. They are against political reform because it would undermine the system they know and through which they prosper.

It might seem surprising that they are against free markets since, as businessmen, they prosper through trade. But this finding shows how deeply the Chinese understand "markets" as government controlled. Markets are no different than anything else in China; the government regulates and monitors

---

[216] This balancing act can be seen in the fact that the salaries of officials were raised five times at double-digit rates between 1989 and 2001 (Huang 2008). Raises both buy loyalty from officials and lower the incentive for official corruption. Unfortunately, the latter has not worked. The opportunities are too big and the risks too small.

[217] Dickson 2003.

[218] Pomfret 2007. This is what I found, too, in my 2007 Shanghai interviews, but in my 2010 interviews, Chinese executives expressed much more dissatisfaction with income inequality, health care costs, and housing costs.

[219] Tsai 2007. This is more typical for large private firms; small private firms tend to suffer in this system.

[220] The idea that all people are equal does not enter into their thinking, showing how little the Communist idea of equality had been internalized in the thinking of elites.

the public sphere (and beyond). There are two reasons this system is seldom questioned. One, it is all the Chinese know. To the extent they are aware of Western markets—and this awareness is certainly growing—it is not at all clear to them that Western markets are better than what they have. Their markets are new and successful. They have been told all their lives that Western systems are inferior. It will take major failures in their own markets before they might question them—failures that have not happened, yet. Indeed, during the massive failures in Western markets in 2008 the Chinese economy held up relatively well. With Western governments increasing their ownership in and regulation of their own economies, Chinese confidence in the Chinese approach has observably increased.

Another factor in Chinese perceptions is fear. Questioning the government is not a healthy business to be in. Ultimately, fear influences how Chinese consciously and unconsciously see their government's role in society. When Chinese entrepreneurs support the government or think the Party should be the sole decision maker regarding reforms, they might just be expressing a fact: This is how it is, so they accept it.[221] Questioning it could lead to a loss of benefits, jail, or worse.

For these reasons, Chinese do not have high expectations in regard to political reform. Individuals who do seek political reform are regularly put in jail. The groups who protest unfair treatment have their leaders jailed, and their success is limited. Most people focus on economic opportunities, which remain hugely improved from what was available to the previous generation. Indeed, the decades of shortages, rations, and deprivation can only sharpen the drive to material improvement. Added to this, the Chinese feel the window of opportunity can be shut; the government could change direction; they must take while the taking is good.

In any case, they have little alternative. Different cultural spheres such as religion and philosophy have only recently received attention. For now, cars, cell phones, and consumerism generally are the low-hanging fruit. This too is partly a symptom of cultural disorientation. With all belief systems discredited, materialism shines brightly as the lowest common denominator across a materialistically underdeveloped society. The attitude toward materialism, forever a Chinese obsession inside a predatory state with great population density, will be a key "measure" to gauge the future development of Chinese ethics and culture.

---

[221] Chinese culture has a strong tendency toward fatalism (Redding 1995).

In this context, where a predatory dictatorship governs society in its own interest but great economic development has improved the lives of hundreds of millions of people, for many there is little to complain about. As long as the economy grows, corruption is tolerated by most, accepted by many, and relished by some. But for those who have been left behind, who have lost their old position or are falling behind in their new one, government self-involvement, incompetence, and corruption are glaring defects in the current state of affairs. Indeed, they are the central causes of their problems. This is the great balancing act: Can the government continue to provide opportunities to greater numbers of people than it displaces and leaves behind with its actions? One way leads forward, toward economic growth without political change, the other to increasing dissatisfaction and political conflict.

6

Business-Government Corruption in China

Americans Suffer Only the Half of It

In the middle of an engaging interview with a smart and experienced 40-year-old Chinese entrepreneur, I asked him about business-government corruption. His eyes opened wide and he said he had forgotten what he knew in this area and I should remind him about the different types of corruption. I said I had heard bribery at customs facilities is very bad. There was a long silence, and then he said, "A man says he is against prostitution, but he comes home and they put the prostitute in his bed. He has no choice but to have sex with her" (Mr. Ch20).

His comments surprised me. They seemed to have come out of nowhere. I ask him what exactly he meant, but he would say no more.

It was another two months before a second Chinese entrepreneur's forthright comments on government-business corruption enabled me to hazard a guess about the prostitution analogy. The second entrepreneur told me the driving force in government is conflict over money within and between the different levels of government: central, provincial, and municipal. Each level tries to retain as much money as it can. Secrecy and corruption are the natural results of this continuous battle over money. It almost does not matter whether the official steals the money outright or uses it to carry out his legitimate responsibilities and advance his career.[1] The main point is that

---

[1] In either case, the businessman still has to pay bribes to receive required government approvals. However, if the official steals the money, the cost to the businessman is usually lower than if he pays for both the government service and the bribe (Shleifer and Vishny 1998). The latter case is also riskier for the official because an increase in the businessman's cost might prompt him to report the bribe request to the official's superiors. In the former case, corruption tends to spread because both bribe seeker and bribe payer benefit—the resulting loss is to the government. It is this situation that Pei (2006) believes is the usual case in China. He takes the loss of government revenues as evidence that China's "gradualism" is not working and will eventually undermine economic development because of government incapacity.

government officials seek money and the Chinese businessman has become a prime source for providing it. It might be said that the Chinese government wanted money, so it created business.[2]

Thus, one reading of the prostitution analogy is that the prostitute is the government official. The businessman has no choice but to pay bribes because the government has positioned itself in such intimate proximity to the businessman that he cannot make a move without paying off an official. This is how the system works. There is no way out. Business-government relations mean bribery.

Into this situation come American and other foreign companies, a vital economic stimulus to jump-start economic growth. The government faces a dilemma: If it puts the prostitute in the foreigner's bed, the foreigner could leave.[3] Also, foreigners have access to their own media; the Chinese government cannot keep its rent-extracting machine out of the foreign press. So despite their complaints, American companies get off light.[4]

But the Chinese government's rent-extracting machine is not to be denied; in regard to the Americans, it merely goes further underground. The key to understanding ethical and cultural issues in American-Chinese business relations is the "middleman." Middlemen, or "intermediaries" or "third parties," pay bribes for American companies. In this way, American companies do not *pay* bribes—which they cannot without violating their own policies and possibly American laws—but Chinese government officials and others *receive* bribes. In this context, the middleman operates in the cultural middle—an amoral space between two incompatible cultures—to end-run legal and ethical obstacles to business transactions.

[2] Gates (1996) argues, and my data support, that free enterprise is not seen as a way of life in China; that is, it is not viewed as rooted in values of freedom and private property, but as an instrumental means to the problem of economic growth. Without cultural support, commitment to economic reform can more easily be reversed.

[3] Foreign direct investment does not shy away from corrupt markets (Habib and Zurawicki 2002). Companies still make money while paying bribes. In this sense, bribery is just one of many costs that need to be considered in an investment decision.

[4] Indeed, as noted in footnote 1, bribing a government official can be profitable if the bribe costs less than the price of the government service. This situation can be called *profitable bribery*. If the bribe adds to the price of the government service, it can be called *unprofitable bribery*. Finally, as in the situation now being discussed, when the government restricts bribery because it cannot control the negative consequences, such as bad publicity from the American media, it can be called *restricted bribery*.

This chapter follows the activities of the middleman from both American and Chinese perspectives as well as explicating other aspects of business-government corruption in China, including the role of the courts, state-owned enterprises (SOEs), and the various forms of bribery. The chapter begins with a description and interpretation of the perceptions of American executives, followed by a description and interpretation of the perceptions of Chinese executives. The ensuing discussion compares and contrasts the two sets of perceptions, followed by some concluding remarks.

American Perceptions of Business-Government Corruption

I. General Perceptions of Business-Government Corruption

1. Central Government Corruption. American executives generally believe there is considerable corruption in the behavior of Chinese government officials: "If I look at the imperial system, it's subject to one kind of corruption or another. When you concentrate power, you'll find abuses pluralistic societies won't tolerate" (Mr. Am27). It is telling that Mr. Am27 refers to the Chinese government as the "imperial system." The word *imperial* implies an empire and an emperor, as in China's long dynastic history. In other words, the connotation is premodern, not the view one would expect for a modern Communist state.[5] The executive's insight is, I think, correct. The Chinese government's bureaucratic form has significant continuity with premodern forms of Chinese governance, most importantly its predatory nature, the extreme autonomy of its power base, and a social class of government officials who live off this base.[6]

The Chinese have a different view of the central government. My Chinese interviewees repeatedly told me the central government is trying to do the right thing but cannot control corruption on the municipal and provincial levels. When I mentioned the Chinese view to an American executive, he said,

> I am surprised to hear that. Maybe the central government lets them criticize the province and city levels as long as they don't criticize the

---

[5] Boisot and Child (1996) argue that the Chinese Communist state never fully made the transition into modern forms of bureaucratic structure based on rational and legal authority. On the contrary, it inherited a patrimonial bureaucracy, feudal in its operation, functioning through fiefdoms and personalized networks.

[6] Gates 1996.

central government. It is inconceivable to me that the central government does not have corruption. However, I would say that a high-level central government official in finance has been excellent. Also, many of the mayors have been excellent.

(Mr. BD1)[7]

This executive's comment that the central government "lets" citizens criticize provincial and city government as long as they do not criticize the central government implies that he believes the central government can control public criticism, but provincial and city governments cannot.[8] In any case, he recognizes that freedom of speech does not exist in China.[9] Further, even though he undoubtedly thinks the central government is corrupt, he mentions that some central and city officials are excellent, in line with the view that China has made some progress in professionalizing its government officials.[10]

2. Corruption on the Mayoral Level. The American executives interviewed had had various experiences with the mayors of Chinese cities. One executive mentioned that though there is "huge corruption" in China, international firms tend to steer clear of it (Mr. Am30). Requests for bribes tend to come from lower-level officials, not top ones. Nonetheless, good relations with mayors or their representatives are central to doing business in China. Meeting with them, taking them to dinner, and so on are required. There is "bound to be corruption in this process" as the interests of officials enter the mix (Mr. Am30).

---

[7] "BD" stands for *business diary.* These data are the result of observations made at American operations in Shanghai, in contrast with the "Mr. Am" or "Ms. Ch" data, which were collected through interviews.

[8] To be precise, the army and security services report to the Communist Party in China, not the government (Walder 1988). But the Communist Party is so integrated into the structure of governing, it makes little sense to say local and provincial governments cannot enforce obedience.

[9] In 2011, calls for a "jasmine revolution" in China inspired by Middle East uprisings led to the strongest attack on dissidents and activists in years (Branigan 2011). Dissidents were rounded up and jailed, some well-known rights lawyers were placed under house arrest, and some were badly beaten (Johnson 2011). Generally, security forces imprison and torture activists perceived to be a threat to the state in violation of Chinese law (E. Wong 2012).

[10] Currently there are 672,531 officials above the county level, 90% of whom have degrees equal to or above the associate's level (K. Yu 2009). In 1981, the proportion with degrees was 16%. On the other hand, American executives from Fortune 500 companies are treated much better by officials than most Chinese citizens.

Ms. BD8 provided a substantial example of what these interests might look like on the mayoral level and how they manifest themselves, as a city mayor controlled decision making inside a private company:

> I worked for a year to get a private company to buy our product. The manager of the company decided to do it. The company had just invested in a new $5 million production line. But the mayor said if you stop buying products from my son, you will have a lot of trouble with government permits. We will shut down your new line. So the private company canceled the order with us and fired the executive who ordered our product.
>
> (Ms. BD8)

The important point here is that the company succumbed to the mayor's threat. It had no choice, being inside a government-controlled society that is the only game in town. The courts, the media, the regulators are all controlled by the mayor. A second important point is the role of family and "friends."[11] Officials use their office to steer business to family or friends, through which they receive a piece of the action. It is these personal networks that play such a central role in state-society relations in China, as will be discussed later on.

3. Extent of Corruption. As to the extent of government corruption, two views emerged in the interviews. The view that it is widespread can be seen in the comments from an American official at a U.S. consulate office in China:

> Since the 1978 reforms, the Chinese government has emphasized the problems of corruption a little. But it helps the greasing of the wheels, so they have not emphasized it too much. Some anticorruption campaigns have been politically motivated to remove competitors. Some government leaders have amassed huge fortunes.
>
> (Mr. BD10)

The view that anticorruption campaigns can be used to remove competitors is widely held among Chinese executives. Mr. BD10's comments portray

---

[11] The Chinese use the word *friend* extremely broadly. It seems primarily to connote reliability. Pye (1988) argues that ambivalence toward intimacy is a central issue in Chinese culture, partly because Chinese social structure leaves little room for privacy, associating it with secrecy, which in turn is identified with illicit activities. Thus, developing "friendships" becomes a management skill used to expand one's network of personal ties for pursuing instrumental goals.

an intensely political bureaucratic system where the boundary between public office and private benefit is weak indeed. American business executives, however, were a bit more positive about declines in government corruption, though, like Mr. BD1 earlier, they saw improvements in some areas and not others:

> In the 1990s asking for bribes was rampant. There was open asking for money, especially from government officials. Today it is not as blatant. The early '90s were like the Wild West, unbridled capitalism. We are not exposed to it as much now [2006]. Then we could not get our product in or out of customs in Xiamen. Every town has its own customs. A container was held up. You had to send someone cigarettes to get it released. Once we had dinner with a customs official. He told us if we hired him as a consultant, then there would be no problem with customs. It still exists today, but it is less blatant. It's occurring in the rank and file. What's unethical to us is not to them.
>
> (Mr. Am9)

Mr. Am9 makes several points about corruption. First, he sees corrupt profit seeking as pure capitalism. He equates it with the American "Wild West," thus equating the Chinese present with the American past—a lawless, purely capitalist past. This identification of the corrupt Chinese present with the corrupt American past implies that Mr. Am9 has an emotional identification with the Chinese—one based on ruthlessness and greed. Present-day Chinese and past Americans are ruthless and greedy. It also implies that the lawless Chinese will become like the law-abiding present-day Americans. This view of the Chinese of the future—that they will become law-abiding and democratic—is common among American executives.[12]

Second, every town has its own customs, with rules and procedures varying from one place to the next. It is all decentralized and personalized.[13] In one place one must send cigarettes as a bribe; in another place it is not required.

---

[12] The same view can be found in the literature on business ethics (Hanafin 2002). Based as it is on an economic determinism—that is, rationalization in the economic system will lead to rationalization in other parts of society—it strongly underestimates not only the roles of power and culture in human affairs but also the role of irrationality. Indeed, as Pei (2006) notes, the Chinese government has used its newfound wealth to buy the loyalty of new-rich entrepreneurs, whereas basic social services like health care and education have been cut back for the general population.

[13] Boisot and Child 1996.

This lack of universal standards is a key characteristic of the Chinese market.[14] Third, multiple levels and types of Chinese officials regulate and monitor private-sector businesses, much more so than in the United States. Permits, fees, approvals, evaluations, taxes, and so on are required.[15] It is when dealing with government officials in regard to these requirements that bribes are requested.

Fourth, according to Mr. Am9, what is unethical to us is not to them. This is a moral judgment of the Chinese based on idealized American standards. Certainly if we have learned anything about American business in the last two or more decades, it is that its ethical standards are far from ideal. Nonetheless, there are differences between the two societies. The Chinese are much more identified with their families and "friends," the Americans more with principles and codes, even if they do not live up to them. Mr. Am9's judgment does not demonstrate an understanding of these differences. He appears to judge the Chinese by ideal American standards. The judgment is thus invalid because of both the misapplication and the idealization involved.

4. Geographic Differences in Quality of Officials. One American businessman points to the unevenness in quality of government officials from one area of the country to another:

> Corruption among the province officials depends on the quality of the official. In the last two years [2004–06], there have been very public prosecutions of corrupt officials. On the east coast and in the south you are usually dealing with classy, high-quality politicians. Most can speak English. They have had some experience in the United States and Europe. In Hubei province [central China], however, they are not very sophisticated. They want invitation letters so they can get visas to the United States.
>
> (Mr. Am10)

Mr. Am10 sees corruption decreasing in some parts of China. Public prosecutions—even executions—of corrupt officials certainly have a deterrent effect. In addition, this businessman finds it easier to deal with Chinese officials who

---

[14] Lieberthal and Lieberthal 2003.

[15] Excessive government requirements for various approvals and reviews are a classic characteristic of a corrupt government acting against the interests of society (Shleifer and Vishny 1998).

speak English, have visited the West, and understand Western business practices—a far cry from the local Communist Party officials American executives used to meet with a decade earlier, who did not speak English, had never been out of China, and were wearing Mao suits. The latter situation still exists in western provinces, where top officials are like princes ruling over their fiefdoms and corruption is more common than elsewhere. Still, American executives find themselves increasingly traveling to these provinces in search of cheap labor as labor rates rise in the east and south.

5. *The Ambiguity of Chinese Politics.* To do business in China is to do business with the government, but the government is very difficult to deal with. Even the very successful leader of Singapore, Lee Kuan Yew, lost a great deal of money investing in China:

> We went in with Lee Kuan Yew, the past [prime minister] of Singapore, to a new industrial park in Suzhou in 1996. The industrial park was a mini-city modeled after Singapore—one square mile given by the Chinese government. It was supposed to be the only one in the area. We bought it hook, line, and sinker. We did a joint venture [JV] with a Chinese chemical company. It was an SOE. In typical Chinese fashion, however, in 1998 the Chinese announced a new industrial park 20 miles from ours and a carbon copy of ours. It was open to everyone. We lost a great deal of money. This is typical Chinese business style. They see nothing unethical. As far as their culture, it's okay. No legal recourse if you want to protect your patent or JV. Unless you have a strong JV partner tied into the Communist government, you're in trouble, particularly if you're manufacturing and exporting.
>
> (Mr. Am19)

Mr. Am19 too sees "their culture" as corrupt. He expresses no understanding of Chinese culture or history, only that it is different than American business culture and corrupt in that sense. He too is assuming an ideal version of American culture. More specifically, he points out that in China, unlike in the United States, there is no legal recourse against corruption,[16] though he is aware that in China these problems can be worked out with the right connections. Hence, instead of drawing the conclusion that it is a different

---

[16] The lack of a fair and reliable legal system is a common theme in the management literature (Tsui et al. 2004; Lieberthal and Lieberthal 2003).

culture with different rules, he condemns it morally based on his ability to file a lawsuit against corrupt practices in the culture he is familiar with—not exactly a logical conclusion.

Mr. Am19 knew the China market was difficult and dangerous, so he entered the market along with Lee Kuan Yew, past prime minister of Singapore, attempting to use political connections to succeed in China. Unfortunately, they proved to be the wrong political connections when Lee Kuan Yew lost more than $30 billion on the Suzchou city-state investment.[17] Hence, Mr. Am19 tried to play by the right rules but lost anyway.[18] His anger over losing leads him to condemn the Chinese morally. Perhaps Mr. Am19 should have entered the China market more slowly so as to understand it better and avoid sustaining such huge losses.

6. Dictatorship and the Reforms. American executives gave two reasons for the continuing corruption in Chinese government. First, government pay is low, so officials try to supplement their income (Mr. Am23). An official from an American consulate in China said the average salary of a village chief is 6,000 renminbi (RMB, about $769) per year. Second, "everyone knows" politicians, government officials, and SOE executives convicted of fraud get light penalties; they go to a special jail in Beijing that is like a country club (Mr. BD2).

Both Mr. Am23 and Mr. BD2 give economic explanations for Chinese corruption.[19] Mr. BD2's comments support the U.S. consulate official's view that the Chinese government does not try very hard to stop corruption. This

---

[17] Lee Kuan Yew told CNN the Chinese had promised him "special attention" to open up a Singapore-style special trade zone in China and then opened up a second Chinese zone nearby with a fraction of the overhead (Studwell 2004). In 2001, the Singaporeans sold out to the Chinese.

[18] *Guanxi* may lower risk through interpersonal trust, but *guanxi* relations are continuously renegotiated as crossing and countercrossing commitments ebb and flow in the pull and push of interpersonal relations (Hwang 1987). Outsiders working through the *guanxi* system are necessarily operating blind to some extent. By the nature of *guanxi*, advantage goes to the insider.

[19] Using a similar economic framework, Pei (2006) points out that prior to the 1990s corruption was frequently associated with the "59 phenomenon"; that is, officials approaching the mandatory retirement age of 60 increasingly committed crimes because they had less to lose from job loss. However, in recent years the age of officials prosecuted for corruption has been dropping significantly as officials try to generate income as fast as they can, out of fear that the reforms will take away their rent-creating positions.

view suggests that corruption is intrinsically related to government strategy, culture, or both.[20]

If the government is intrinsically corrupt, then why does it prosecute some corrupt officials, even occasionally holding a very public execution?[21] As noted, many believe prosecutions are politically motivated. The core problem is the predatory nature of the Chinese state, which has only intensified as a result of the current economic reforms.[22] The increase in corruption results from the massive decentralization of property rights from the central government to the local governments, local governments' transfer of a significant proportion of these assets into private hands, and the massive inflow of foreign direct investment. The government is intrinsically corrupt because, as a dictatorship, it relies heavily on power to stay in office. During a period of economic reform, it is only natural for a system accustomed to near absolute power to use its power to secure its own position as well as the personal positions of its members. Indeed, the Tiananmen Square crisis can be seen as a failed attempt by those not benefiting from government corruption to try to force their way into the corridors of power and wealth.[23]

II. Approaches to Bribery

1. Refusing Bribe Requests. The interview data show that some American companies paid bribes and some did not; clearly, then, not paying bribes could result in loss of business to a less scrupulous competitor. In this case, not only would ethics not pay, it would lose money. American executives reported many requests for bribes:

[20] As was mentioned in footnote 12, this is Pei's (2006) argument: The government uses rents from corruption to buy off important subgroups and thereby maintain their support for the government. Thus, currently, economic growth actually blocks the development of democracy under the "gradualism" approach to societal change.

[21] Violence against individuals selected as examples has long been a means of control used by Chinese Communists (Walder 1988) and, it might be added, by the emperors before them.

[22] For example, between 1992 and 2002 the lowest bribe prosecuted by authorities was almost double the highest bribe prosecuted during the previous decade (Sun 2004).

[23] Madsen (1995) states that Beijing workers seeking economic security made up the biggest group of participants at the Tiananmen Square protests. There were also significant numbers of unemployed peasants from rural areas, as well as students angry about their inability to benefit from the considerable opportunities made possible by "privatization." The protests were motivated by the fact that many of these opportunities were being gobbled up by Party members and their families.

I went to a meeting. The top Chinese silicone chemists were there. They say, "We know how to get the shipments approved. But we need five things." I am told to step out of the room. When I come back in, I'm told they want five gold Rolexes. They cost $5,000 each. I told them to fuck off. If I okay this, I could go to jail from the U.S. Fair Trade Act. The following week I saw [another American company] working with them. This is culturally common: graft, corruption, sweetheart deals developed with the state.

(Mr. Am19)

In the previous section, Mr. Am19 tried developing relationships with the Chinese (through working with a well-known politician from Singapore and establishing a joint venture with a Chinese SOE) and still got burned. Here he got burned for not developing relationships. These are some of the challenges and frustrations of doing business in China.

2. Deciding What Bribes to Pay and Not Pay. In the previous example with Mr. Am19 and the following two examples, American executives refused to pay two bribes, but paid one. It appears the bribe that was paid was illegal and possibly one of the ones not paid was not illegal. Expediency and risk seem to be factors in deciding what bribes to pay or not pay. Several executives said it was very common to have to pay bribes for business licenses, export licenses, electricity, water, business permits, and the like:

Corruption is more or less with the government. It is not unusual to lose electricity for a day or two without warning. They do not have the capacity to fill the needs. We don't have electricity but the guy next door does. He paid off officials. It's at all levels of government. They are cracking down, but it's the way they do business.

(Mr. Am8)

Several executives mentioned that a need for special approvals could make a company particularly vulnerable to bribery requests:

In general, doing business in China is unbelievably cheap. But if you are dealing with a deadline, it could be costly. We once paid $16,000 to run a telephone line 50 feet. The flip side is the building was cheap, a fraction of what it would cost in Taiwan. That's just how it was. I guess that individual was looking for some money.

(Mr. Am9)

These two executives describe another dimension of bribery in China: The influx of so many large foreign companies, all of which need services, presents potential new sources from which to seek bribes. Despite their vulnerable situation, some companies pay the bribes and some do not.

The three decisions described here illustrate a variety of such vulnerabilities and responses: Mr. Am9 paid $16,000 to run a telephone line 50 feet, but Mr. Am19 refused to pay $25,000 to get his shipments approved and Mr. Am8 did not pay a bribe to keep the electricity running. The deciding factors seem to be expediency (Mr. Am9 was in desperate need of telephone service), flexibility (Mr. Am8 was willing to accept down time for his plant), and fear of prosecution (Mr. Am19 cited legal risk as the reason he rejected the Rolex bribe request). Decisions on whether to pay or not pay bribes thus appear to be context specific.

3. *Using Middlemen to Pay Bribes.* The main way American companies protect themselves from violating their own policies—and potentially U.S. law—is to use third parties to pay bribes: "Facilitator payments are made. Everyone uses brokers and agencies for exporting and extraditing shipments. We have no direct knowledge of it. We hear a lot about it. We don't encourage it" (Mr. Am29). Americans' use of middlemen to pay bribes in China is an important ethical issue that will be discussed in detail later. Mr. Am29 takes the position that everyone knows it is going on but he has no "direct" knowledge of it. "Direct" must refer to knowledge of a specific bribe payment. He says he does not "encourage it," but clearly he knows that the "brokers" he uses pay bribes. "Encourage" must refer to explicitly instructing the broker to pay a bribe. Even though he knows that brokers pay bribes, he reasons that if he does not give explicit instructions, the mere fact that he uses a broker cannot implicate him as encouraging or participating in bribe paying. This denial that his involvement is an ethical issue is typical of American businessmen in China.

4. *Using Consultants and Employees to Pay Bribes.* Some American companies go beyond using middlemen to pay bribes; they hire Chinese employees whose job is to pay bribes:

> Over there you go through intermediaries. It could be a consultant or an employee. We have an employee, local guy. He is connected to the ministries, has lots of contacts. It's the name of the game over there. He is approached on the basis of gift giving. Our company says no. We don't even know. He handles it. Gifts are part of their culture. We have rules that limit gifts. If you do not give the gifts, it would cost you business.
>
> (Mr. Am2)

Mr. Am2's statement that "consultants" and Chinese employees are used for "gift giving" is surprisingly frank. In an even more unexpected disclosure, he reveals that his company hires Chinese employees with connections to high-level government ministries for the purpose of "gift giving." Even while acknowledging that his company prohibits such gifts, he claims, rather disingenuously, "We don't even know." Like Mr. Am29, he is splitting hairs, even though his approach is much more direct than Mr. Am29's approach of using "brokers" despite a general knowledge that such brokers pay bribes.

When Mr. Am2 characterizes "gifts" as part of Chinese culture, he means that American businesses have no choice but to give "gifts" that violate their own policies. Notwithstanding these two businessmen's linguistic contortions, it is clear that American companies violate their own policies and American law to do business in China. Their choice is to violate their policies or forgo the business. The pursuit of profit determines behavior.

III. Navigating the World of State-Owned Enterprises

1. Relationships with SOE Executives. An American executive working in China for the past 15 years stated that the most corruption is in the SOE sector but that some SOEs are reformed (Mr. Am29).[24] Salaries have been increased in some SOEs, resulting in less corruption. Other American executives apparently worked with the unreformed SOEs, finding there a culture of alcohol and prostitution:

> You need heavy entertainment to do business with SOEs, trips, after-hours entertainment, payoffs. It means you take the guy to KTV [karaoke bar], to disco, and buy a girl for him. This is how you develop a business relationship. The biggest customers of KTVs are government employees and Taiwan businessmen. An American executive working with a Chinese steel company told me, "The Chinese say you have to develop a relationship with them and then tell you how much money they want to trust you. That's how they 'get to know you'".
>
> (Mr. Am28)

---

[24] Of "number-one leaders" prosecuted for corruption between 1993 and 2003, 40 percent were CEOs of SOEs (Pei 2006).

The dilemma in which American businessmen find themselves in China is seen clearly in their dealings with SOEs.[25] Some American executives not only feel obligated to take their Chinese counterparts to KTVs where prostitution is available but also feel considerable pressure from them to consume large quantities of alcohol. Some American executives feel getting extremely drunk with the Chinese is required if the Chinese are going to do business with them. One American explained that it is a way for the Chinese to "accept us as one of them."

In a drunken state, self-control is obviously decreased.[26] That SOE executives value sharing this condition with their American counterparts points to it as perhaps an initial test to see if the Americans might be willing to forgo other types of control such as rules against expensive "gifts" or conflicts of interest. Mr. Am28's "relationships" with SOE executives focus on money. One has to buy "trust." Sharing large quantities of alcohol and women who sell sexual favors is a way for the Americans to signal the Chinese that they are on the same page: pleasure first, rules second.[27]

2. Loss of Business. American companies who refuse to pay for women, alcohol, and other things for SOE executives say they lose business:

> The real risk for corruption is SOEs, particularly as customers. It concerns the Foreign Corrupt Practices Act. Not blatant bribery things, but blurring between gift giving and bribery. We can control this and we do. But what effect does this have on business? It hurts business. It still exists today.
>
> (Mr. Am30)

If one does not cooperate, one can lose business, but since SOEs are government owned, gift giving to SOE executives could violate U.S. law. The

[25] Despite privatization, in 2010 there were still 153,800 SOEs in China employing some 65.16 million people (*National Bureau of Statistics of China 2012*). SOEs are responsible for about 35 percent of GDP. Eighty percent of firms on Chinese stock exchanges remain subsidiaries of state-owned group corporations (*Economist* January 21, 2012). Boundaries between the state-owned and the "private" in China remain blurred in many cases.

[26] In a culture where the direct expression of one's true sentiments is extremely rare (Pye 1988), alcohol offers a means to probe behind the screen of propriety.

[27] Chinese men practice the same drinking patterns among themselves as a ritual of male bonding, a way to become friends and build trust. Bonding is probably a goal in the relationship with American executives, too, but the importance of money is heightened because of the real and perceived wealth of American firms and the tendency for these relationships to have a shorter duration.

problem is not blatant, Mr. Am30 says, just a "blurring" of the line between gifts and bribes. Other American executives, however, say it is blatant; it can easily go from thousands to millions of dollars on large transactions.

3. *Communism and SOE Culture.* American companies buying or entering JVs with SOEs found organizations that were worlds unto themselves, a mixture of central planning and local self-dealing:

> We bought an SOE. It had what it called a "white business" and a "gray business." They were retaining a small amount of goods not marketed through government channels. They were selling these goods through the back door. They used the money for a secondary payroll, divvying it up between employees. Since it was for everyone and a small amount of output, it was seen as "gray" and had the connotation of something redeeming. We had to explain we will not do this. We had to educate. As long as you pay reasonable wages and take care of them, they don't steal from the company. It is a challenge.
>
> (Mr. Am27)

The Chinese saw the "backdoor" activities not as unethical but in fact as "redeeming" because the profits were shared among all employees. This attitude reveals the localism of the Chinese. They did not see in this sort of arrangement any conflict with principle or even with the broader planned economy of which they are a part. This anecdote also points up the value of equality. Since profits were shared, the practice was good—importantly, however, equality was not applied beyond the walls of the SOE. Communist bureaucratic culture is thus more bureaucratic than communist. This is what the "dictatorship of the proletariat" always comes to mean.

Mr. Am27 saw the second payroll as stealing. He tried to set up an American-style wage and benefit system but said it was a "challenge."[28] SOE culture is built around high levels of dependence, vertical loyalties, and personal ties.[29] American bureaucratic culture is less rigid, having more

---

[28] Having carried out his study of business organizations in Shanghai in 1995, Guthrie (1999) concluded that a process of rationalization was occurring in Chinese firms and particularly that it was being influenced through relationships with foreign companies. My research, carried out primarily in Shanghai 12 years later, does not show strong support for either of these conclusions. On the contrary, culture clashes in American-Chinese joint ventures are the norm.

[29] Dependence is the key to Communist Party control in China (Walder 1988).

emphasis on organizational performance and individual salary.[30] Mr. Am27 said his firm had to educate. But changing this culture will take much more than education. It will take changing a way of life; it will take years.

4. *SOEs and Communist Power.* SOEs have been a central pillar of Communist Party power, yet they are now being shut down, reformed, and sold. American companies are right in the middle of this uncertain experiment:[31]

> In the JV with an SOE we entered into, we found they were paying employees a low salary base but lots of benefits, a long list of allowances. They received an allowance for altitude! The state provided almost everything, like a parent providing for a child. This is taxable income, but they were not paying taxes. We changed this into compensation and paid taxes. We wanted to put practices in place that were in line with local law. But the ownership of the JV was 50–50. We took a lot of resistance. We had to take majority ownership, but at the end of the day it was resolved.
>
> (Ms. Am31)

Large SOEs provide a great many of life's essentials to employees—salary, housing, health care, education, pension, recreation, and so on. Ms. Am31 refers to it as a parent-child relationship.[32] In this case, a low salary was offset by many allowances—some approaching the absurd, such as the one for

---

[30] The societal cultures in which these two different bureaucratic cultures operate are very different. Out of the 40 countries Hofstede (1984) studied, the United States obtained the lowest score for collectivism; China was among the highest. Hofstede's results exaggerate the cultural dimension of collectivism in China, however, because much of it is enforced through power. So too with the work of Boisot and Child (1996), who attributed the lack of rational-legal authority in Chinese bureaucracy to premodern personalistic ties. But Communist ideology is also a factor in the lack of rational-legal authority, and it is antipersonalistic (Walder 1988). Ideology is different than rational-legal authority and personalism. It is an extreme form of dichotomy that seeks total commitment to the "truth." It is not a stable social pattern and breaks down to commitment to the boss. But this aspect of Chinese industrial authority should not be seen as the same as "fiefs" and "clans," because as long as the Party maintains dictatorial powers, a relapse into political idealism is always possible. This tendency is seen in the current power struggle going on in Beijing, which centers on neo-Maoist Bo Xilai's support of "red culture" (Branigan 2012).

[31] Indeed, the experiment was significantly reversed in the 1990s (Huang 2008).

[32] Perhaps the parent-child analogy is not strong enough. The Communist state seeks to establish the worker's whole social identity (Walder 1988), to establish its authority over the whole person. Even most parents wish some autonomy for their children.

"altitude," even though this SOE was located in a low-lying area far from any mountains. Importantly, when the American company tried to bring compensation practices in line with local law, they met fierce resistance.

The violation of law many times seems to mean little in China. American executives complain repeatedly about the lack of consistent and reliable court proceedings.[33] The Chinese say there is always another way to solve a problem. If you know somebody who knows somebody, you can find ways around laws. But the SOE is government owned: Why would it not pay its taxes? After all, Communist Party officials are literally part of each SOE's management structure. Allowing the SOE not to pay all its taxes is a way to maintain the workers' support for the government. It can be seen as a bribe to the whole organization. It is evidence that the government's legitimacy is in question; its priority is securing its own power base, not collecting taxes. So when Ms. Am31 tried to tax workers' full compensation, she was violating the social contract by which the workers had accepted the "reforms."

The government and the SOE are parts of an interlocking power structure. The Communist Party is now slowly trying to alter the nature of this power structure without losing its own power. It is a difficult balancing act. Millions of SOE employees have lost their jobs, but huge revenues have been created through economic reform.[34] So far the economic reforms continue and the government's power position is little changed, but the loss to state revenues due to corruption has significantly increased. It would appear that the government is in a serious dilemma. If it does nothing, corruption will undermine the reform process. If it cracks down on corruption, it will undermine its power base.[35]

[33] This lack is not just the result of political control and corruption but also of the culture itself. Chinese culture values harmony. Saving face is more important than protecting individual rights or discovering the "truth." Nonetheless, the slow-moving reform of the legal system suggests the Communist Party is more focused on maintaining power than reforming society.

[34] Pei (2006) reports, however, that the central government's share of public outlays fell from 47.4 percent in 1978 to 34.7 percent in 2000. Much of this money ended up in the hands of local governments and has been wasted or stolen, he says. This is one of the major problems with China's decentralization; it was carried out without the necessary institutional changes and controls (S. Li 2004, 2005). Or perhaps it is carried out the same way as SOE taxes.

[35] This is perhaps one reason the Party has reversed course on privatization, to hold on to revenues and its SOE power base.

IV. The Legal System: The Court of Law as Government Agency

The court in China reports to the government in the same way as any other government agency:

> The Chinese courts are much less sophisticated than in the U.S. The judges are really poor quality and subject to corruption, except in big cities. There is even mild corruption like judges asking to be taken to dinner. In the U.S., we solve everything in court. In China courts don't deal with many things. There are no rules defining the court's responsibilities. In the U.S., you can appeal a bad court decision. In China the government can make life difficult. The court is just like any other government agency and is subject to influence from other agencies. So we must maintain good relations with the court. Long-term there is a big focus on fixing this. It is a big hindrance to local commerce. Without a court system, it's harder for local commerce to have the predictability it needs.
>
> (Mr. Am30)

The authoritarian nature of the Chinese government can be seen clearly in the court system. In Mr. Am30's description, the court system is a government agency reporting to political authorities instead of an independent judiciary autonomously interpreting and applying a body of law to resolve conflict—application of which might require the court to conclude the government has violated the law. It is unthinkable that the court would criticize the government in China. This is one reason the court's responsibilities are left undefined: the better to change them as government interests and policies change. The court, like the media and other institutions in China, is an instrument of the government, pursuing the government's ends, both general and specific.

The behavior of judges mirrors the behavior of other government officials and SOE executives: They expect to be taken to dinner. Outside of large cities they are less trained and more inclined to seek bribes. As in other areas of Chinese life, the courts can be influenced by personal relationships.[36] All of this

---

[36] S. Li (2004) tells the story of the owner of a manufacturing company who hired a manager to run his company. But the manager set up a second company using resources from the first company, took out a $146,000 loan for the second company by forging the owner's signature, and conspired with a local court to issue a court order to seize 10 truckloads of equipment from the first company. When the owner found out, he consulted lawyers and was told the forgery is a misdemeanor at most, and the seizure is not a crime because the court approved it. The bank, whose loan was not paid back, sued the owner based on the use of his forged signature—and won.

leaves American businesses without the legal conflict resolution system they rely on so heavily back home. Contracts, for example, are routinely broken in China and cannot be enforced. Like many other American executives in regard to many other aspects of the Chinese marketplace, Mr. Am30 claims some improvements have been made in the court system and hopes they will continue.

Even without the legal foundation of American capitalism, business prospects in China are so promising it is worth the trouble anyway.[37] So a legal system is not necessarily central to capitalism. After all, the legal system in the United States did not stop any of the massive business frauds of recent decades, and even when it does rectify matters, it is at quite a cost in time, money, and attention. Despite the roar of complaints, American firms are adapting to business in China without Western-style courts. They are learning new tricks and strategies. Ultimately, the only question that matters is, can they profit? So far the answers are *yes, no,* and *I hope so.*

In summary, the American executives I interviewed saw some signs of professionalization of government officials despite widespread and systemic corruption. A majority of executives were mildly optimistic about the China market, others exceedingly frustrated. Dealing with bribery in one form or another and on one level or another was constant. Some Americans paid bribes, some did not, others used middlemen to pay bribes for them. Middlemen were seen as a needed reality; the inconsistency with the Americans' own values and company policies was very seldom even noticed. Some Americans learned to live and even prosper without an independent legal system with clear legal standards. They engaged SOEs as customers, suppliers, owners, and partners. In the latter two capacities they sought to implement American management systems, themselves becoming centrally involved with the transformation of the Chinese economy and the uncertainty of its future reform.

Chinese Perception of Business-Government Corruption

I. Central Government Not Corrupt

1. Professionalization of Government Officials. Not all but most Chinese executives said that the central government is not corrupt and is trying to stop corruption at the province and city levels.

---

[37] Orit, Philip, and Till (2007) argue that not only will China's explosive growth continue for decades, but companies that do not compete in China will fall behind competitors who develop new skills, strategies, and products in China and apply them globally.

The central government has tried to stop province and city government corruption. Now they have systems for reporting if an official's kids are in overseas schools and if an official's family is in certain types of businesses. Government officials are benefiting more than before. Now the government is paying higher salaries and benefits so officials do not have to have bribes. The government just ruled certain level officials must fly economy class and use designated hotels. Government officials have become more efficient. In old days, different units used different rules. When you deal with local officials, it's a lot of headaches. Overall, the provincial government is trying to make changes. Even the mayor of Shanghai was brought down. He had a lot of success. He overstated himself.

(Mr. Ch24)

Mr. Ch24 is a successful entrepreneur. He is wealthier than he ever expected to be. He watches the economy carefully and observes that the central government does many things to support and stimulate economic growth. The idea that the central government is basically corrupt seems incredible to him. Mr. Ch24 lists many improvements the central government has made to discourage corruption. He and other Chinese executives in Shanghai say that government at all levels is becoming more professional, more consistent, and less subject to personal relationships.

2. Democracy Leads to Chaos. Some Chinese executives do not think democracy will resolve China's problems.

There is corruption in all systems. If corruption is revealed in China, it will be punished. But it happens in the U.S. too. It happens in China more often. We can see generally the country has developed. The U.S. has a lot of corruption. If you do something in China, one day it will be revealed. Corruption is worse in Taiwan among their many parties, and in South Korea and Thailand. Generally, the economy is growing quicker than before. More punishment and people will be afraid to do corruption.

(Mr. Ch33)

The arrest of the Shanghai Communist Party chief is often mentioned by the Chinese, but there are two different views of the matter.[38] Some, like

[38] In September 2006, Shanghai's Communist Party chief, Chen Liangyu, was arrested for pension fund fraud, furthering the economic interests of illegal entrepreneurs, protecting his staff who violated laws, and furthering the interests of his family by taking advantage of his official posts (*China Daily* 2006). In April 2008, Chen was sentenced to 18 years in prison for taking bribes and abusing power (Barboza 2008).

Mr. Ch24, take it as a sign that the central government seeks to stop corruption. Others, like Mr. Ch33, believe the arrest is the result of a political conflict between high-level leaders because, as he says, many people are corrupt but only some are arrested.[39] Indeed, the corrupt activities of the Shanghai Party chief were known for a long time before he was arrested.

Mr. Ch33's reference to corruption in Taiwan "among their many parties" is a rejection of democracy. He comments that Taiwan's economic performance too has decreased since the introduction of democracy. Mr. Ch33 is not impressed with democracy, believing it does not decrease corruption. Like many Chinese, he wants a strong central government that can ensure stability. He pointed out that fistfights on the floor of the Taiwanese Parliament are hardly a sign of progress. He is happy with the political stability and economic growth China enjoys and sees no advantages, only disadvantages, to democratic systems. To the extent corruption is a problem in China, stricter punishments will decrease it. For Mr. Ch33, economic growth is the key issue. Political participation is not something he desires.

II. Local Government Improving: A Tolerance for Government

Looking at some of the same facts the Americans discussed in their interviews, the Chinese executives saw a benign, improved, and even relaxed government. It is clear that their expectations for government are vastly different than those of the Americans.

Chinese executives gave several different reasons why corruption did not affect them or was improving on the local level. First, if one follows the rules and meets labor laws, there is no problem. Even these executives, though, said one must be flexible and take officials to lunch. They felt Shanghai has a good system. Second, as long as you ask only for what is required by the government and not for special favors, you do not have to worry—though they added that you might have to wait for it.

Third, some executives felt the Chinese people are more tolerant of government than people in other countries. In any case, the government today is

---

[39] Despite the great increase in corruption during the 1990s, the number of investigations of government officials actually dropped (Pei 2006). Only two percent of provincial leaders are punished each year for corruption. Arrest for corruption as the result of political battles is the conclusion reached by R. McGregor (2010) in his study of the Chinese Communist Party.

much more open than it was in the past. Nevertheless, they acknowledge that in China "the law can be gotten around." It is not like the United States, where one cannot talk one's way out of a violation. In China everyone argues with the police; in fact, there is a general looseness about rules all through Chinese society, evidence that the government is not so oppressive. Fourth, the government is now very strict and one can get into dire trouble taking bribes. Bribes are from the old days, 5 to 10 years ago. Even relationships do not help much anymore, a fact that the older generation does not understand. Fifth, corruption is mostly relegated to the rural areas. Bigger cities are much better managed.

These executives presented a conflicting picture of the level of government corruption in Shanghai. For instance, some indicated that anything required by law is unlikely to involve corruption. The fact that one must still take local officials to lunch can, after all, be seen as a relatively harmless local custom. Yet even these executives acknowledge that the law can be ignored. Likewise, some executives said as long as one does not ask for favors, there is not a problem with corruption. But even these executives added that one might have to wait for the government service or approval. Of course, this is exactly the problem: Time delays are often costly, and bribes are needed to get timely service.

Some executives said the Chinese people are more tolerant of government than other peoples, and anyway, the government is much more open than it used to be. Both these points are true on their face, but the fact is that living under a dictatorship, the Chinese people have little choice than, out of fear, to "tolerate" their government.[40] The increased openness of the Chinese government is a positive development, but it must be remembered that increased corruption has accompanied the increased openness. Ideological mobilization was relaxed as "privatization" was introduced, but "privatization" was pervaded with official exploitation. Thus, while the population gained economic freedom, they lost public assets. What does this amount to? Is there less dictatorship? No. Increasing corruption while increasing openness means the dictatorship merely changed its outer form from mass mobilization to massive theft.

Some Chinese executives welcome the informal, relationship-based system they have, citing a general looseness in Chinese society that allows government

---

[40] Gates 1996.

rules to be negotiated. What they do not seem to acknowledge is the many negatives inherent in this type of organization: bribery, kickbacks, conflicts of interest, and so on. There is also the problem of justice. In-groups prosper while out-groups, undoubtedly the majority, gain little or nothing, or even lose position.[41] Such a system, where the primary competition is for relationships, not goods and services, tends to increase interpersonal dependency, lower creativity, and ultimately decrease the quality of goods and services.

Finally, some executives claim that bribes are a thing of the past, yet this is not quite true even for them, because their companies pay bribes to buyers too. They share the view of some of the American executives that things used to be worse and the government is now very strict.[42] But even according to many Chinese, corruption among officials on the provincial and municipal levels is bad. Indeed, this is a central problem. Given the size and geographical dispersion of cities and provinces, the central government could not fully control them even if it wanted to without destroying the decentralization that is essential to the reforms. So even if the perceived decrease in local corruption has some basis in fact, the decrease is from astronomical levels. With its basic political, structural, and cultural supports still in place, corruption has simply moved into the shadows.

III. Government-Business Relations

1. Government Is Involved in Everything. In the process of "privatizing" state assets, the government has maintained direct or indirect involvement with businesses at all levels.

> Higher-level government evaluates local levels by how much money they make and how much they build. Thus local government must have good relationship with local companies. This exists at every level of Chinese government. In local government or small town, cooperation

[41] In Shanghai, for example, despite massive growth in GDP relative to the national mean, household income has experienced almost no growth relative to the national mean (Huang 2008). Rural areas have actually declined from 1980s levels.

[42] In general, this does not seem to be true. In the late 1990s, the conviction rate for Party members prosecuted for corruption was only 5.6 percent (Pei 2006). By 2004, the rate had fallen to 2.9 percent. Moreover, only 6.6 percent of all officials found guilty of corruption receive sentences.

with business is more direct. In big city you cannot be so secretive because government is too big. In small city it is easy to hide. In Shanghai they do it; it is big money. Money is taken from government pension fund and put into real estate development and stock market. We do not have efficient supervision of government behavior. The media are controlled by the government. All governments work together; there is no balance of power. So if we talk about economic growth, it leads to discussion of politics because the government is involved in everything.

(Mr. Ch29)

In the United States, government regulators and the companies they regulate can develop close, mutually beneficial relationships. In China, a much more enmeshed relationship is a fundamental characteristic of the economic system. Governments use their powers to infiltrate or control businesses; businesses work hand in glove with governments. Businesses pay kickbacks to or carry out construction projects for government officials.[43] Consistent with the concentration of power in small cities and in the countryside, by all accounts this process is both more secretive and more widespread in these locales than in the larger cities.

As Mr. Ch29 notes, the economic reforms have brought about new tasks and responsibilities for government officials, such as managing a pension fund with significant inflows of money and expectations to invest it successfully. Due to their inexperience with this type of work, officials often make mistakes. Added to this burden is a lack of oversight.[44] Changes have taken place so fast that the system's ability to keep up with them is overwhelmed. So corruption may be pervasive, but a lack of experience and oversight, as well as incompetence, are also important contributors to the problems businesses face. Government control of the media and, as Mr. Ch29 points out, non-existent balance of power in government make it difficult for problems to be publicly identified and resolved.[45]

[43] S. Li 2004.

[44] Sun 2004.

[45] The lack of civic organizations, particularly public-interest ones, is also part of the problem (Pei 2006). More recently, however, the media have become more aggressive in their reporting—for example, the high-speed train accident in Wenhou and the rise of Twitter-style microblogs (Dean and Page 2011).

This level of economic and bureaucratic change would overwhelm any administrative system. In China, we see how an authoritarian system adapts to the challenge. Decentralization, indeed, took place in the extensive redistribution of government revenues and delegation of responsibilities to city and province governments, "privatization" of state assets, and increase in private-sector activity. But, as Mr. Ch29 remarks, the government at all levels is still intricately involved with all levels of economic activity.

Curiously, many American executives express deep respect for the Chinese government. They are impressed with the levels of social and economic stability that have been maintained,[46] the level of economic growth that has been created, and the vast improvements in infrastructure that have been accomplished. Most American executives do not dwell on the lack of human rights in China, while many Chinese are either satisfied with China's human rights or at least see rights as much improved from former times.

2. Government Does Not Like the Businessman. In response to a question about the government's commitment to free enterprise, Mr. Ch23 said, "I'm not so confident. Everything is still planned. The government does not like the businessman; they like the businessman who gives money." Mr. Ch23 sees the government as still firmly in charge and tolerant of business only to the extent that the latter funds government projects and pays off officials. This is a very different view than that of the American executives who think the government will steadily move away from dictatorial control. Mr. Ch23's view implies that there are strict limits to how much power the government will give up. From this perspective, American executives who admire the Chinese government are hypocrites. While their belief in capitalism is supposedly based on respect for human freedom and dignity,[47] their dealings in China reveal an interest only in wealth, especially their own. Their respect for the Chinese government is disturbing because it amounts to respect for the role a dictatorial government can play in making capital productive—that is, respect for the lack of freedom of speech, freedom of association, right to representation, and so on.

---

[46] As noted in the previous chapter, there are more than 100,000 protests per year. If some of these protests become organized nationally, then the stability could be gone.

[47] See Friedman 1972.

IV. Corruption and Privatization

The Communist Party benefits during the entire process of "privatizing" state assets—beginning, middle, and end:

> In textiles a lot of SOEs turned private. There was a lot of corruption. My friends became bosses. Total assets for one SOE were 1 billion RMB [$80 million]. He bought it for 4 million RMB [$500,000]. He also accepted the SOE's debts. If it had stayed as SOE, it would go bankrupt. This happened everywhere during the last 15 years. There were no bidding processes. My friend was made managing director of the company. He had been the former Party secretary of the company. He had good relations with local government. Local government must approve the sale. I believe there was some agreement between local government and my friend. For example, he had to make some donation to government, build road, etc. Also, when government wants to send delegation abroad, he will pay the bill. This is not corruption, just cooperation between private owner and government. These two figure out how to make local economy grow.
>
> (Mr. Ch29)

Mr. Ch29's story about his friend, the company's Communist Party secretary, "buying" the company for a fraction of its value without any competitive bidding process, is instructive on many levels. First, the Party basically sold public assets to itself. In this case, the company Party secretary merely exchanged his title for that of "managing director"[48] but remained the same person embedded within the same Communist power structure, continuing to work closely with government officials.[49] The difference is that "privatization" has a chance of increasing efficiency and profits, but the resultant increase in wealth benefits fewer people. The formal reporting relationships to multiple levels of government are removed, but only after local officials cut deals at the point of "privatization" to ensure their benefits will continue. Thus, either through becoming private owners or securing

---

[48] This is not unusual. Fifty percent of company Party secretaries became the new CEO in restructured SOEs (Pei 2006). In 6,275 restructured SOEs, the Party committee became the board of directors 70 percent of the time.

[49] Boisot and Child 1996.

benefits from the owners, Party officials have been the main beneficiaries of "privatization."[50]

Second, the fact that as part of the deal a textile mill had to agree to build a road seems curious. Why did it not agree to make uniforms for police, for example? Herein lies the tremendous flexibility of the Chinese socioeconomic system. It is not literally the textile employees who would build a road, it is the human and technical resources that the new owner of the textile mill could marshal through his position in a network of relationships.[51] In this sense, as Mr. Ch29 commented earlier, the Chinese system is indeed flexible, efficient, and robust through social ties.

A downside to this system is, of course, the potential for corruption. Mr. Ch29 deems the sale of state assets during the "privatization" process to be corrupt, but he sees the side deals arising out of these sales—to send officials abroad, for example—as cooperation, not corruption. Government and private enterprise must work together, in his view, to create economic opportunity and growth.

The problem with side deals is their lack of transparency and the in-group control of public benefits that they afford (such as the opportunity to travel abroad). Since the arrangements are hidden, there is no way to know if the money is well spent or even if it is spent for public benefit at all.[52] Since it is in-group controlled, in-group networks benefit.[53] Outsiders might be more qualified or deserving of traveling abroad, for example, but they will not have the chance. Mr. Ch29 does not realize these problems because, being Chinese, he sees it as natural to look out for one's family and friends.

Other executives also reported observing corrupt processes of "privatization"—what some call "black deals"—but most felt these deals were becoming less common because it has become more difficult to conceal them. In their view, there is increasing pressure against corruption. Corruption of

[50] In a survey of private business owners in 2002, more than 65 percent of the 6.2 million owners of private firms had formerly been officials and executives in SOEs and government agencies (Pei 2006). Pei also reports on "double-dipping," whereby officials keep their government jobs but take a second job in a private firm that does business with the government.

[51] Boisot and Child (1996) argue that the depth, intensity, and social embeddedness of Chinese networking are the defining features of Chinese "capitalism."

[52] S. Li 2005.

[53] Warren, Dunfee, and Li 2004.

privatization was a phase the country went through, they reason, but the corruption will fall away and private ownership will bring moral, political, and economic benefits for years to come. It is hard to justify this level of optimism except maybe in theory. Indeed, not only does Mr. Ch29's experience make it clear that the authoritarian government is still in charge, but Mr. Ch29 sees this as a good thing and the appropriate model. Perhaps "black deals" must now be concealed, but blackness is a defining feature of the personal-ties culture. The Chinese are intensely secretive, and the personal-ties system is built to provide channels for such secrecy. So, from where will the moral and political improvements come? Why and how will private ownership weaken government control and alter the secrecy of the personal-ties culture? The personal-ties culture and authoritarian government are hand in glove in Chinese history. It seems more likely the government will keep a grabbing hand in the business system, and the personal-ties culture will last another thousand years if a day.

V. Corruption in the Government-Business System

1. Corruption and the One-Party System. The following is a response to a question about the view that the central government is not corrupt and is trying to clean up corrupt local and provincial governments:

> The overview is correct, but the real reason for corruption is the government system is not watched by an independent party. The central government wants profit from local and regional governments. All policy is made to share such profit. They always argue and fight between themselves to get more profit, but no one is watching, the people are not watching. The central government says they want to clean up corruption, but they cannot do so because if they try, it would destroy the whole system. If the central government wants to perform professionally at all levels, then it will destroy their system because more and more illegal subsystems would be discovered. The only way to do it is have an independent media and court.
>
> (Mr. Ch23)

Mr. Ch23 rejects the "gradualism" strategy of political reform. The Communist Party's fundamental purpose, in his view, is to remain in power. It cannot fully attack corruption because to do so would destroy its structure of power. So what we have seen for the last three decades, the on-again, off-again, highly publicized attack on corruption, is the end product. The Party will not, cannot go beyond this approach. Without profound decline in corruption, of course, serious institutional change cannot be brought about. The ultimate question, then, is when or if a tipping point will be reached that creates power bases outside the Party.

2. *Officials as a Class unto Themselves.* Like the Mandarins before them, Communist Party officials exist in a world separate from the population, focused primarily on each other.

> People in general do not complain about government corruption. They don't realize it's their money. The government has never been transparent. The people think government corruption has nothing to do with them. Though in China, officials do think it's their money. The government has not really changed. A president of a tobacco company was sentenced to death for corruption. People do not really understand this because they think he made huge growth for the company and his salary was very little. In the past, everybody was equal. Right now China has changed this. Right now government officials are not paid a lot, but paid much in government account. It is a problem with the system. It cannot do long-term things. The subordinate must show the superior how great he is. Many cities build buildings to show face, face projects. Nobody invests in the long term. The short term is to help get promoted. It is the one-party system.
>
> (Mr. Ch24)

Mr. Ch24 describes how deeply ingrained the culture of corruption is. The population does not care about corruption, in the same way the fish does not know it is in water. It is also not in one's self-interest to focus on it. Criticism of the government will easily invite a visit from the security services. The government is the center of society and society belongs to the government. The people see it this way and the government sees it this way. It has always been this way. There is also the problem of government control of information. For example, my Chinese graduate students told me that China is democratic. They did not seem to know democracy involves freedom of speech, freedom of assembly, free elections, and so on.

One manifestation of government ownership of society is "face" projects. "Face" projects are construction projects using public funds whose primary purpose is to make an official look powerful or productive. The projects often look good on the outside but are cheaply finished on the inside.[54] They help build an official's career inside the government but are often not needed by the public. In fact, in some cases they can be dangerous because the emphasis on "face," coupled with widespread bribery among key participants, encourages substandard construction.[55]

Similar to Mr. Ch23, Mr. Ch24 attributed these results to the one-party system: Without checks and balances, without independent parties, without external observers with a voice, corruption flourishes. Another important aspect of this situation, as Mr. Ch24 noted in regard to the tobacco company president, is that many people do not "understand" the extent of corruption. Mr. Ch24 implied that *personal* repression supplements public repression. Meanwhile, government officials are wasting vast public resources for their own advancement. Corruption is only the illegal part; the amount of waste is even more damaging to society. Because of the one-party system, there is no self-corrective mechanism. The citizens either deny it or accept it; only a few protest it.

3. Corruption as a Team Enterprise. Corruption is seldom the work of a single official:

> Government officials all share their bribe money as a team. They thus protect each other. Their crime will not be discovered. If an official does not accept such money, he will be out of the department. I know honest officer who won't take bribes. He is in jail to silence him. We have no independent media. The story cannot be discovered. No court can accept a lawsuit against a government official. I cannot sue him if he comes here and asks for money. I can only give money or close my company. If you expose him to his boss you end your business. No other government official will negotiate with you. It is teamwork. They will destroy your business. Sometimes they have special case. They will take official to jail, but requests for bribe money continue every day.
>
> (Mr. Ch23)

---

[54] Pomfret 2007. Face projects are examples of a broader category in Chinese culture. The Chinese will spend 120 percent of their yearly salary for a car, but furnish their entire apartment for $15,000 (Doctoroff 2012). The difference is the car is seen in public, the inside of the apartment is not. The Chinese define themselves through others.

[55] A case in point is the high-speed rail network, which has been plagued by deadly crashes and corruption. Liu Zhijun, head of China's Ministry of Railways, was removed from his position in February 2011 on corruption charges involving billions of dollars (Dolinar 2011; Ramzy 2011). Other officials and business executives are also under investigation. Substandard workmanship on the rail line is widespread.

Since there is no one inside the department able to blow the whistle and there are no independent parties outside the government, corrupt behavior is unstoppable. Ultimately, it comes back to the one-party system. The party in power controls everything, including investigating its own corruption.[56]

There is no outside to this system, only an inside, and the businessman is in it. Once illicit funds are requested, the businessman must pay or his business will be shut down, either directly by the government or indirectly through an inability to function without government cooperation. In the worst-case scenario, he can be put in jail on trumped-up charges, for example, of tax evasion. Paying off officials is the only solution. The only question is how much it will cost. My data show a range from a few percent to a high of 30 percent of profit. It appears the amount of money demanded is related to firm profitability.[57]

VI. Bribery

1. The Locus of Bribery. The highest concentration of bribery requests in my field data involved the need for high-level government approvals for projects or products that involved high dollar amounts. Mr. Ch23, a middleman assisting American firms to sell expensive technology products in China, summarizes his experience: "If the government official helps you, he wants money. Friend to friend. You must share your commission with the key man" (Mr. Ch23). There are many ways Chinese firms must work with the government: business registration, weekly or monthly tax payments, annual audit, building plant permit, plant expansion permit, business expansion permit, material certificate approval, business project approval, budget approval, advertisements approval, plant inspection, land purchase approval, price approval for imports, order approvals, change in budget approvals, and on and on. For any of these approvals, "mutual benefit" may be required.

---

[56] Disciplinary agencies are equal in rank with those they supervise; thus they cannot prosecute without approval from higher-level agencies (Sun 2004). The decision to investigate is a political decision, not a legal or moral one (R. McGregor 2010). Overall, the monitoring system lacks organizational resources as well as political and financial independence.

[57] For this reason, "People are afraid of getting famous, just as pigs are afraid of getting fat" (Tsai 2007: 15). Tsai reports, for example, a large, private firm in a community paying 70 percent of profit for community needs such as teachers' salaries, food for the elderly, and the like.

2. The Case of Serial Bribery. Mr. Ch23, assisting an American technology company to build a plant and import technology for it, describes the seemingly endless need for government approvals and the bribe requests that accompany them:

> My American customer needs approval to build a plant. The customer tells me the name of the government man for me to visit to pay my portion. So I put extra money into the government pot. But now the budget for the plant has gone over, so the customer needs approval for new budget. So the same officer or a second officer wants a new bribe for the new budget. The budget is then approved but the budget does not include the price for my product. Now I have to negotiate with the customer and the government on the price because the government has final approval on the price of my product because it is imported. The final step is to get the order and the last department comes to approve the order. Also, sometimes things happen at the last minute. You must share more profit. You deliver the product and the product is running. They ask for another 10 percent "security deposit." The American company does not know about this. Seventy percent of my business is the result of this procedure. I hate this procedure. I'm tired out to control it. In the open market, I would have more opportunities.

> [Researcher: Why do some Chinese executives refuse to believe government corruption is this bad?]

> If small business maybe you miss this. If big business it is normal procedure, especially if you do business with government institute. If I'm selling to Motorola factory in China, no such procedure, more professional; we make deals by e-mail, easy. But we give Motorola 24-hour service. The government does not ask for service. They don't care. Our government is also concerned not to do too much illegal with American companies because American companies have American media to expose corruption.

> [Researcher: Why do some Chinese and American executives say bribery is declining?]

> Some businessmen do not see the real procedure. If you deal with decision level you meet this. But if you only discuss with technical level, you do not meet such problems.

> [Researcher: What percentage of your profit do you pay in bribes to the government?]

Thirty percent. They think I have enough. I had dinner with an official last week. I have a $2 million order next week. He told me he is sending his daughter to the U.K. for a six-year education. He needs 400,000 pounds. So, the order will need to be $3 million. The government will buy at this price.

According to Mr. Ch23, government corruption is systemic and has gotten worse because Chinese businessmen have more money for officials to extort. In his story, even though the approvals are required by government regulations, there is much uncertainty as to what their final costs will be. If new officials enter the process, new bribes might be required. All the bribes involve lengthy negotiation. Mr. Ch23 estimates that 70 percent of his time involves negotiating bribes and approvals.[58] It appears that bribery is one of the largest costs of business for Mr. Ch23. His central business skill is controlling the cost of bribery so he can make a profit.[59]

The American customer knows Mr. Ch23 is paying bribes for the plant approval because the American tells Mr. Ch23 to whom to pay the bribes. This is a clear example of the intimate involvement American companies can have in bribe paying without literally paying the bribe. Indeed, since Mr. Ch23 refers to paying "my portion," the American company is probably orchestrating a whole series of bribes by other middlemen involved in other aspects of the project.

The American company becomes even more involved when negotiations start over the price of the American product that Mr. Ch23 is importing to run in the American plant. Mr. Ch23 starts negotiating with both the American company and the Chinese officials over the price of the imported product. Mr. Ch23 never owns the product; he just helps manage the process of importing it. His primary concern is negotiating a "price" high enough to

---

[58] This is standard practice in corrupt governments (Shleifer and Vishny 1998).

[59] This situation raises questions about the often stated belief in the management literature that weak management is a major constraint on the competitiveness of Chinese business (e.g., Lieberthal and Lieberthal 2003; Redding and Witt 2007). The argument goes that decades of Communism have ingrained political skill over management skill. But the case of Mr. Ch23 shows that political skills are needed to survive in a government-dominated economy. Hence, political skills are far from obsolete in "market socialism." It is practically impossible to exaggerate the importance of middlemen in Chinese "market socialism," and for the middleman, political skills are hugely important. Management writers bemoaning the lack of "management" skills appear to be forgetting about some central characteristics of Chinese market socialism.

cover his bribery costs and make him a profit. Apparently the Americans are aware, when Mr. Ch23 is negotiating with them over "price," that a major factor in these negotiations is the bribe Mr. Ch23 is paying to import the product as well as the other bribes he is paying to help the Americans get their plant built.

Mr. Ch23 mentions that the Americans do not know about the 10 percent "security deposit" he pays once the machine is running. Importantly, they do not know because he does not tell them. Mr. Ch23 runs a delicate operation trying to avoid upsetting either the American company or the Chinese officials, either of which could delay or scuttle the project. Mr. Ch23's job is exhausting. He does not tell the Americans about the additional 10 percent bribe, perhaps because he has already put extensive pressure on them to compensate him for the other bribes he paid. He absorbs the 10 percent loss to his profit to get the job done, keep his relationship intact, and do business again another day. Ultimately, the government has the upper hand. It demands bribes, and both the Americans and Mr. Ch23 go to extensive lengths to push the project through while attempting to minimize bribery costs.

According to Mr. Ch23, this process is typical if a lot of money and high-level government officials are involved.[60] We also see how American executives can say they are not approached for bribes: Middlemen carry out the negotiations. Mr. Ch23 cited American media as the reason high-level Chinese officials do not ask American companies directly for bribes. In one sense, then, the Americans remain outside the one-party system; but in another sense, through bribe-paying middlemen, they are inside and in support of the corrupt system. At best, they are half ethical.

Middlemen are thus not only a bridge between two different business cultures, they constitute a moral no-man's-land between Communist power in the form of secrecy and extortion, and capitalist power in the form of publicity and public criticism. Middlemen receive a rent for mediating between these two powers and working out a compromise whereby both groups can accomplish their goals. Chinese officials receive bribes and can maintain their secret activities, but American executives do not pay bribes and can claim they are not violating their principles. Hence, middlemen not only speak English and have a driver's license to travel to and communicate with the different parties, they transform American principles into Chinese

---

[60] R. McGregor (2010) says it is common with mid-level government officials as well.

corruption. They are cultural alchemists who operate in a murky borderland where irresolvable conflicts are taken underground, separated, rechanneled, and resolved. Positioned between two incompatible systems, their work is purely instrumental. Their pervasive role and particular function is powerful evidence that the "market" in Chinese "market socialism" is far from free.

Finally, Mr. Ch23 said he runs into no such problems when selling to American companies. The American companies want service while the Chinese government institutes want bribes. Since a significant and growing part of China's economy is SOEs,[61] issues of productivity must be a problem.[62] Corruption and inefficiency are related in two ways. First, bribe payments detract from productive uses of capital. Second, to the extent that executives are focused on bribes, they are not focused on organizational goals. Corruption not only wastes resources, it crowds out and misdirects incentives. Dictatorship can support markets by making decisions that improve transportation and communication systems, for example, but dictatorship in China has not shown an ability to separate itself from corruption.[63] Only an open political system with separation of powers can address corruption.

VII. Guanxi and Bribery

1. Favors, Relationships, and Efficiency. Some Chinese executives maintained that their relationships with government officials protect them from pressure to pay bribes:

> Bribery takes two. If you ask for a favor, you are open to bribery. Otherwise, you have to stand firm on your principles. It is important to expose yourself to many officials so they know you know other people. Risky, if you know only one and ask for special favor. If you know

---

[61] My 2010 data shows the SOE sector expanding in Shanghai. See Huang (2008).

[62] When taking into account cheap capital, free land, and the like, the *Economist* (January 21, 2012) reports the average real return on equity for SOEs between 2001 and 2009 was 1.47 percent.

[63] Pei (2006) argues that inefficiency and corruption are endemic to China's approach to reform. The gradualist strategy itself is inherently inefficient because it consists of partial reforms. Its primary purpose is to keep the Communist Party in power. Corruption is inherent to the government's approach because it needs to buy off supporters. Corruption even undermines the partial reforms of the gradualist strategy. Hence, the level of corruption is the key measure of China's progress toward reform and the key predictor of its future development.

others, they won't deliberately delay for long time because they risk trouble from higher levels. In China you know you can always go around another way. Relationship building is key skill.

(Ms. Ch15)

Part of Ms. Ch15's position depends on the meaning of "favor." Rules are one thing; in the implementation of rules there is always room for interpretation. So it is unlikely that avoiding asking for "favors" is as black and white as Ms. Ch15 suggested. In any case, even if one avoids asking for favors, according to Ms. Ch15, one must still develop relationships with many officials to protect oneself. So it is not just asking for favors that is the problem. Ms. Ch15 mentioned specifically that if you know a variety of officials, one official will not purposely delay providing service—or at least will not purposely make a "long" delay. According to Ms. Ch15, then, the situation is delicate; delays of various lengths are common and one must ask for "special favors" to expedite the process, making one vulnerable to bribery requests; but one can minimize the potential problem through *guanxi*, through a network of people in positions of authority, or those who know people in authority, or those who know people with means to influence people in authority.

How does this system work? Ms. Ch15's position is consistent with the view that many officials are corrupt, but one can develop mutually beneficial relationships with some of them, who can be called upon to help resolve problems with others in expectation of future payback.[64] The more "friends" and resources one has, the more one can be a successful player in this type of system. So in a sense, "corruption" is not unethical in this type of system because ignoring rules and exploiting one's position are accepted assumptions about how the system works. The potential chaos that could result from these assumptions is countered by the quick willingness of players to develop relationships with each other that are supportive and trustworthy. Hence, there are two levels of social interaction, one between strangers that is exploitative and one between "friends" that is supportive. It is the latter level that Mr. Ch24 meant when he said, "If you know an official, the Chinese system is the most efficient in the world."

Well, maybe not. It is "efficient" for the in-group. Those without relationships lose out in this system. It would also seem to favor the wealthy and

---

[64] The key to *guanxi* is reciprocity (Hwang 1987).

powerful, who find it easier to attract others into mutually beneficial relationships. This raises moral questions about whether the system leads to social harmony, the government's stated goal. It is hard to see how this leads to social harmony, since the whole point of the system is in-group advantage.[65]

In any case, as can be seen perfectly in Ms. Ch15's and previously in Mr. Ch24's statements, the whole system is predicated on the centrality and monopoly of government in business. Because all important and many less-than-important business activities must be approved by the government, and because the government is corrupt, *guanxi* is needed to grease the wheels of government. Take away the government's centrality and corruption, and *guanxi* begins to resemble networking as found in the West. *Guanxi* is the child of power.

2. Personalization of Office. The official's arbitrary power is key to how the system works.

> Individual officials can control the interpretation of policies. That's why *guanxi* is still so valuable. If you have a good relationship with the government, you can get a lot of economic benefits. In China, local or province officials will come to the factory. They find something wrong and give you a ticket or ask your support to help the government. This is why you need relationships. If you do not have relationships, you are at a disadvantage. But with personal relationship, they take the ticket back. But if it is corruption, they still get some payoff. This is unfair business war. But it's getting less. In the West it can still be a problem.
>
> (Mr. Ch13)

Mr. Ch13's comments suggest, counterintuitively, that one can use *guanxi* to have a government fine for a rule violation canceled but not to completely cancel a bribe request. One might think it would be easier to have a bribe request withdrawn than a fine for violating a legitimate government rule. That the opposite is true demonstrates the centrality of the officeholder over the office, personal power over the rule of law. The legitimate fine does not enrich the official, and thus there is less resistance to nullifying it. But the bribe does enrich the official and at best can only be reduced.

---

[65] It does not promote competition but instead undermines it because there is no stable set of ground rules. Secrecy is dominant; information is extremely fragmented and monopolized through relationships.

VIII. Corruption and SOEs

1. Bribe or Gift? Bribery at SOEs mirrors what has been described in govern-ment.[66] What is the dividing line between bribery and gift giving?

> I get an order from an U.S. company. I want the order produced at a big SOE. But at that time production is tight. They cannot achieve the lead time I request. I go to the production manager and invite him to dinner and give him cigarettes and ask him to move my production forward. The cigarettes cost 2,000 RMB [$256]. The dinner costs 3,000 RMB [$384], though usually dinners cost 1,500–2,000 RMB [$192–$256]. Ten people at the dinner: production manager, group leader, shift leader, and skillful key employees. This is very common in my industry.
>
> (Mr. Ch29)

Here we see one version of *guanxi*: gift giving. To get his order produced, Mr. Ch29 pays $640. But he does not give cash. He buys the manager ciga-rettes and dinner. Are the cigarettes a gift or a bribe? Their function is to draw the plant manager's attention to Mr. Ch29. It is the potential start to a rela-tionship. So the cigarettes are a gift. They are accompanied by dinner. The dinner is a social event. Part of the value of the dinner is to enjoy each other's company—that is, to develop a relationship. Thus, even more clearly than the cigarettes, the dinner is a gift. If the dinner is successful and a bond is sparked, it can have long-term implications for their relationship, especially beneficial if Mr. Ch29 seeks to have more orders produced at the plant. Hence, the dividing line between gift giving and bribery in the *guanxi* system is whether the payment is to develop a relationship or to achieve an immediate gain. In this case, all the hallmarks point to relationship building.[67] This ritual is common in Chinese business and especially common in the SOE sector, where financial rewards are more limited.

2. SOE Wastefulness. Because the government is not accountable for its actions, the SOE sector has been prone to extreme wastefulness.[68] "At one

---

[66] Quantitatively, it is actually worse. SOE managers account for 75 percent of all violations of corruption laws (Sun 2004).

[67] In this case there is an immediate gain, too, but because the types of payments lead to relationship building and bonding, they meet the Chinese definition of *gift*.

[68] Policy makers overseeing the SOE sector have limited skills, are generally chosen through relationships, and are subject to the self-serving political interests of central government minis-tries, regional bodies, and the Party (Redding and Witt 2007).

power plant, different high-level managers each had connections to different paint companies. So when they built 16 storage tanks, 16 different paint companies provided the paint. It was unclear how they would maintain quality, but relationships dominated" (Ms. Ch30). This case highlights the enormous power of personal relationships over decision making in the SOE sector. The power plant executives apparently had little incentive to be efficient, so they cared little about savings from bulk purchases, controlling paint quality, or ensuring reliable maintenance. Precisely because they had little incentive to be efficient, their behavior was in a sense rational. It was in their interests to reward those with whom they had personal ties, from which they will benefit in the future, and stiff the faceless society that paid for the paint. The enormity of the waste reflects the enormity of their power. They are accountable to no one.

The case also highlights a system in which personal ties are dominant over all other ties. Here the personal ties are wasteful and self-serving, but next time they could be efficient and beneficial to the collectivity; indeed, some portion of the time they are both self-serving and collectively beneficial. But the 16 different paint suppliers illustrate the general problem: The system of personal ties is prone to extreme wastefulness and blatant disregard for the public good.[69]

3. Declines in SOE Corruption. There have been reductions in the amount of SOE corruption; the improvements come, however, from political and economic changes, not cultural ones. Mr. Ch20 noted that 10 years ago most export licenses and export quotas were controlled by state-owned trading companies, leading to a lot of bribery as mills and private trading companies sought to export. But since China entered the WTO, more and more quotas have been lifted, leading to a decline in corruption. However, there are still quotas, still state-owned trading companies, and still corruption.

A second development that has led to a decline in SOE corruption is better incentive pay. Ten years ago, state-owned trading company salesmen asked for a five percent bribe from the mill or manufacturing plant because the salesmen controlled the orders from foreign customers. The mill or plant could not contact the foreign customer directly because its personnel did not speak English. As more and more private companies are established, salesmen leave SOEs in search of private-sector wages. To keep salesmen, SOEs started

---

[69] Snell and Tseng 2001.

offering commissions on sales. Also, as more SOEs have to compete to survive, they offer bonuses to motivate salesmen. For both these reasons, there are fewer requests for bribes.

In summary, the Chinese government is "involved in everything" and many Chinese executives think that is how it should be to maintain societal stability. Reforms have introduced a market economy in China, but it is seen more as a means to economic development than a refiguring of dictatorship. This attitude is apparent in the systemic level of official-led corruption that is a central feature of the reforms. Government officials have been the central group to benefit from "privatization" by channeling state assets to family and associates at pennies on the dollar and by using their offices to force bribes from the newly established private sector. The collective nature of Chinese society is seen both in the team organization of official corruption, as whole departments share in the illicit funds, and the reemergence of *guanxi* to provide both cover for and protection from the tidal wave of extortion. The higher the level of government approvals needed and the larger the dollar amounts involved, the worse the corruption. American firms are spared direct confrontation with this system because of their access to external political powers and media, and their ability to exit. Instead, Chinese middlemen pay bribes for them. In other words, the Americans are bowing to authoritarianism, not introducing civility.

Discussion

American and Chinese executives experience business-government relations in China quite differently. This section details the two sets of experience in regard to bribery, the role of middlemen, *guanxi*, human rights, and perceptions of the Chinese government. It also offers an evaluation of the ethical assumptions surfaced, actions taken, and justifications given.

1. Two Faces of Bribery. The semi-secretive world of bribery in China affects Chinese and Americans differently. Chinese businesses operate fully inside an authoritarian political system.[70] Requests for bribes can be made directly in

---

[70] Except, of course, to the considerable extent that they avoid paying their taxes and fees, hide their money abroad, and participate in illegal schemes to rip off the government. The bribery door swings both ways: Businesspeople are oppressed by bribe-seeking officials, but they can also gain large fortunes through bribing officials.

the face of Chinese businessmen. If they are selling to a government depart-ment, they might have no alternative than to pay bribes. The department is a self-protecting system that has self-protecting relationships with other depart-ments. Refusing to pay bribes can result in various punishments, up to having one's business shut down.

American companies are not usually subjected to this level of abuse. The Chinese official making the bribe request knows he does not have the same level of control over the American company. For one thing, the American company can report corruption to the American media. This kind of publicity will hurt China's reputation and provoke negative reactions from higher-level Chinese officials. The government seeks foreign direct investment and cooperation, and thus must control mistreatment of foreign companies so as not to damage relations. This balancing act usually gives American companies somewhat of a buffer against the full brunt of Chinese corruption.

In this sense, Chinese firms operate at a competitive disadvantage in the Chinese marketplace.[71] This is especially true for small firms that do not have relationships with high-level government officials. The situation is the opposite for American firms. Americans report bribe requests coming mostly from low-level, not high-level, Chinese officials. For Chinese entre-preneurs, it is exactly the high-level officials who extract the largest bribes and pose the greatest threat because they are connected to other high-level officials and can therefore mount the most severe retaliation for efforts to resist them.

The situation puts a premium on developing relationships with govern-ment officials to build up a mutually beneficial network of relationships, the much-noted *guanxi* system. Americans are not immune to this system and also benefit from having relationships with government officials at all levels. But when large amounts of bribe money are at stake, *guanxi* is no guarantee of protection. Like almost everything else, the outcome is situational, depending on factors including industry, region, business size, product cost, profit margin, government departments involved, personality, and so on.

---

[71] SOEs also have advantages over private Chinese firms, such as near interest-free loans, bailouts when they falter, huge stimulus injections, and other monopolistic supports (Wines 2010). It appears the government does not want to give the private sector too much support; the better to keep the Chinese people dependent.

Guanxi is a Chinese power game.[72] Americans are seldom first-line players because they seldom have the same depth of relationships. Luckily, their connections to the American government and American media give them some measure of protection. For the Chinese, playing *guanxi* means asking for favors, making commitments, giving IOUs, and being locked into an ever-changing, dynamic system of dependencies. There is no free lunch. Receiving bribe protection from a "friend" one day means expending resources to help the friend on another day. It is a continuous process of negotiation. The assistance is more or less helpful, the future obligations more or less costly.[73]

2. The Ethics of Middlemen. American companies may be buffered from high-level bribery pressure to some extent, but the pressure does not disappear, it merely becomes indirect and disguised. This creates an ethical dilemma for American companies: If they want to do business in China, they must use "third parties" or "middlemen" to pay bribes for them, but paying bribes is against their own ethics codes. Almost all the American executives interviewed did not see this as an ethical dilemma because they did not personally hand over bribe money. They either took a legal perspective—"we are not legally responsible for the bribes"—or they claimed to know little about them.

American companies have little choice but to use middlemen for many reasons: the middlemen speak both English and Chinese, have relationships with local businesses, know local rules and customs, have connections with local government officials, and so on. Importantly, they can pay bribes that the Americans cannot pay without violating their own policies and, in some cases, American law.

American companies are under intense pressure to enter and succeed in China. The China market is very difficult and highly competitive, even

---

[72] Since one's power and status, as perceived by others, can determine how many social, political, and material resources one can muster, maintaining "face" inside one's social network is no mere ego game (Hwang 1987).

[73] There is a great deal of debate whether the *guanxi* system is in decline, whether business relations are becoming more instrumental and less affective (Guthrie 1999; M. Yang 2002). I see plenty of instrumental *and* affective ties in China. Like all cultural forms, the *guanxi* system changes over time. But I doubt we can anticipate its disappearance any time soon. Cultural forms do not exist independently. They exist embedded in current practice and shared values that go back in time and forward into the future. *Guanxi,* for example, has ties to Confucian social practice and philosophy (Bell 2000). For *guanxi* to just disappear, it would be like part of a ship sinking while the rest remained afloat.

without the ethical challenges. The ethical dilemma of whether to use middlemen to pay bribes and thereby directly or indirectly violate company policy, or not use middlemen and fail in the China market, never gets beyond the questions of legal liability and top management deniability. If ethics matter to the Americans, it appears they have decided ethics are a luxury better suited to less difficult and more profitable environments.

3. *Middlemen and* Guanxi *Relations.* The American use of middlemen resembles the Chinese use of *guanxi* relations, but only to a certain extent. In both cases, a third party enters the picture to negotiate a conflict or set up a deal. In the case of *guanxi*, the third party is a "friend" and is connected to the individual requesting the help through a system of mutual dependencies, IOUs, and in some cases, bonds of genuine warmth. The American relationship with a middleman is not usually a friendship, does not usually involve strong expectations of future obligations, and does not usually develop the emotional glue of mutual dependency. Hence, the American use of middlemen is more a pay-as-you-go relationship, similar to a business relationship in the United States. It is an instrumental substitute for the *guanxi* relationship—the Americans' way of adapting to Chinese culture in order to do business.

This adaptation works for most Americans because they have neither the cultural orientation nor the emotional disposition to truly bite the apple of mutual dependency. The middleman is exactly the middleman because he understands the American orientation, accepts it, and prospers by it. He enters into an instrumental tie with the American as the American's representative and then engages with the Chinese in the full dress of *guanxi*. This change of clothes, so to speak, is the unique talent of the middleman. His work is processed through a cultural warp, doubly negotiated, instrumentally with the Americans yet inside the intense reciprocity dynamic of the Chinese.

Seen in this light, through the Janus nature of the middleman, the individualism in *guanxi* is exposed. China is a "collective" society. The Chinese people have strong group attachments and strong group orientations.[74] *Guanxi* demonstrates this collective nature in that the essence of *guanxi* is reciprocity and obligation. But through the agency of the middleman, one can see more clearly the entrepreneurial (individualistic) dimension of *guanxi*. The middleman is an entrepreneur of relationships and, to some extent, of

[74] Hwang 1987.

politics. This entrepreneurial function operates to a lesser extent in *guanxi* relations in general.[75] The middleman is particularly entrepreneurial because she operates in a creative space, betwixt and between two very different cultures. But this just amplifies what is in *guanxi* generally, an individualistic capacity to develop relationships based on shared interests and values for the purpose of personal benefit.

A *guanxi* relationship is an entrepreneurial resource. It is a creative resource in that it can be endlessly reused and reapplied to new situations as economic and social capital is reconnected in new ways to new people for new purposes. *Guanxi* is a culturally intense form of social entrepreneurship.[76] Whereas American entrepreneurship is more typically individually creative—indeed, the American entrepreneur is celebrated as a social rebel who makes it on his own—*guanxi* requires a different type of individualism and entrepreneurship, embedded in relationships that work with and against a system of power wherein hierarchy is patterned deeply into social behavior.

The individualistic aspect of *guanxi* works hand in glove with the collective nature of Chinese society. Indeed, after being ridiculed under Communist ideology, *guanxi* is increasing under economic reforms, in part merely because there are many new opportunities to bring people and resources together in new ways to meet needs and advance interests.

Mao's attack on Chinese customs and culture was partly an attack on *guanxi* and the hidden individualism in it, which is antithetical to the fanatical Communist goal of a purely collective identity. In this context, bribery can be seen as an act of freedom. Yet it is a terrible price to pay for freedom, because it undermines norms of fairness and reliability that people need in order to trust one another. Indeed, widespread distrust exists in Chinese society. All societies must balance collective needs with individual freedom. Just as Communism is condemned for its collective excesses, bribery must be condemned for its individual excesses. It is no accident that Chinese Communism stimulated *guanxi*;[77] the individual never died even during the

---

[75] "The art of *guanxi* lies in the skillful mobilization of moral and cultural imperatives such as obligation and reciprocity in pursuit of both diffuse social ends and calculated instrumental ends" (Smart 1992: 399).

[76] China is an ideal place for the American with a budding interest in "social entrepreneurship" to study its principles and develop its practices. In China, Americans will quickly learn that "doing well by doing good" is not without its tensions, trade-offs, and ambivalences.

[77] M. Yang (2002) says *guanxi* increased during the fanatical Cultural Revolution.

darkest days of fanaticism, it only more and more limited its activities to trusted associates. That individualism in China operates primarily through *guanxi* relations demonstrates the collective nature of Chinese culture (and the iron fist of dictatorship).

4. *Middleman as Moral Void.* If, as one American executive said in regard to economic liberalization in China, "the genie is out of the bottle" and cannot be put back in, then this optimistic faith in China's future must contend with what else came out of the bottle: excessive greed, bribery, and myriad other forms of corruption. If it is indeed true that liberalization will continue beyond the economic sphere to the cultural and political spheres, then destructive individualism will need to be addressed. With such strong political repression currently in place in China, it is hard to appreciate this position. Yet it is no doubt true that widespread bribery, kickbacks, and fraud are common aspects of current Chinese business practices.[78]

This is exactly the problem American businesses face. By pitching their tent at the boundary with the middleman, their bribe-paying, corruption-abetting associate, they are complicit in the middleman's work. The middleman amounts to a moral no-man's-land, a liminal space betwixt and between American legal constraints and Chinese bribery patterns, transforming American business standards into Chinese bribery practices. The Americans are "doing as the Romans do," which, of course, most of them say they never would.

The fact that the middleman transforms American business standards into Chinese business practices is a manifestation of the vast cultural divide between the two cultures. The middleman's work, however, is not without its side effects; it damages both cultures. It lowers both through their connection to the pure instrumentality of the middleman's function. The opportunity to learn about and from each other is lost. The opportunity to develop a shared moral ground is foreclosed. This is a measure of the distrust between the two cultures. The middleman boxes out the distrust by keeping the parties separate yet consummating the business transaction. This is the middleman, a cultural buffer zone, keeping American and Chinese business cultures at arm's length from each other, just as American executives live in the Shanghai Ritz Carlton or the gated, expatriate communities in order to keep China out, the

---

[78] Harney (2008) tells of "falsification engineers" whose whole business is to teach Chinese manufacturers how to falsify their pay and work records to pass social responsibility audits required by Wal-Mart and other American corporations.

better to tolerate being there, with all the spitting, differentness, and crowds. The middleman can be a double detour, where two eminent cultures avoid each other to the loss of both.

5. *Human Rights.* Human rights issues in China do not require a middleman to negotiate between American and Chinese cultures. The Americans run their factories the same way they run them everywhere else, except at lower cost, the original reason for going there. The Chinese strive to work at American firms for better pay, for better working conditions, to learn advanced business practices, and to get an American firm's name on their resume. But outside the factory walls, some bad things are going on. For starters, the government does not allow free speech, an independent media, or an independent legal system. As has been described, these facts contribute to the widespread corruption documented in this book.

American executives do not dwell on these issues. They focus on business, trying to scratch out a profit. Many Chinese think they have human rights or think things are not so bad, that certainly public repression has lessened. No longer is everyone wearing a dark Mao suit and hollowly reciting the latest political "truths."[79] Most of their newly won freedoms are in the economic sphere. Many have more money, there are more things to buy, and the Chinese do a lot of shopping.[80] The marketplace is very exciting for them after decades of rations. So from their perspective, things are much improved. The mass mobilization (totalitarian) era, and its particularly pathological manifestation in the Cultural Revolution, are not talked about much by those who experienced them and are not even remembered by many of those who did not experience them.

Americans and Chinese thus have two different experiences of human rights. Given that Americans see the Chinese government's record on human rights as poor at best, does American business have any ethical responsibility

---

[79] Walder (1988) argues, however, that though the Communists have lightened up on intense ideological indoctrination, they have merely substituted an intense paternalism in its place. He sees this as two versions of the same pattern of authority: dictatorship, one way or the other.

[80] On biographical cards my students filled out on the first day of class, 15 percent of my Chinese students listed shopping as one of their favorite hobbies (Feldman 2007c). With my American students, this phenomenon would be almost nonexistent.

to address human rights issues in China?[81] Or does paying wages and taxes, and providing industrial and consumer goods pay the full bill of moral obligation? Is business some kind of socially autonomous wealth-generating mechanism that need not care about people outside of business roles and relationships?[82]

Certainly American businesses do not say they have no responsibilities beyond the economic sphere. In fact, many American companies claim "social responsibility" as one of their core beliefs. Then why do American executives ignore human rights issues in China? They do so to avoid conflict with the Chinese government. And they do so because they understand corporate social responsibility to mean doing things for the community that are consistent with, or even advantageous to, their own profit motive.[83]

American business has its hands full in China just competing in a challenging environment. It is there to make money. Its presence has created many benefits for the Chinese. Its people are not social workers. But does this justify ignoring human rights issues? No, I do not believe it does. American executives say they are committed to capitalism and democracy, and to the values of human freedom and dignity that these commitments assume. To be consistent, then, they cannot work and prosper in a repressive environment without at least expressing their beliefs. Going mute is not morally justifiable because it contradicts their own beliefs and, indeed, weakens them.

6. Perceptions of the Chinese Government. Both the American and the Chinese executives interviewed expressed mixed perceptions of the Chinese

[81] Similarities to Western traditions of human rights are not usually found in Asian cultures, given their focus on authority and conformity to social roles (Krueger 2007). Koehn (2001) recommended that since Chinese ethics do not speak about rights, the West should not approach China with the language of human rights.

[82] Santoro (2009) argued that American corporations do have responsibilities to address human rights issues in China because the idea of human rights would be meaningless if there were not duties associated with them. In terms of specifying these duties, he made four points: One, the closer the relationship is with the victims, the stronger the duty to help. Two, the greater the chance that one's help will be effective, the stronger the duty to help. Three, the greater the capacity to withstand retaliation from the Chinese government or others, the stronger the duty to help. Four, the more uniquely the corporation is positioned to help (relative to others), the stronger the duty to help.

[83] A Chinese nonprofit executive in Shanghai told me she had trouble getting both financial and volunteer support from American firms. She said they preferred to give money to government-run charities so they could win favors in return. As for volunteering, in her experience, they only wanted to volunteer once per year so they could claim they were doing it, but obviously they were not committed to the cause.

government. On the one hand, a minority of Chinese executives expressed disapproval and distrust toward the central government, believing strongly that it is a self-serving and very dangerous dictatorship. Some American executives, too, said they did not respect the central government, characterizing it as corrupt and committed to little more than maintaining its own power.

On the other hand, most Chinese executives expressed respect for the central government, saying central officials try to do the right thing but the corrupt provincial and city governments make it difficult to do. Many American executives also expressed respect for the way the Chinese government is managing the reform of the economy, comparing the approach favorably with that of Russia, as more thoughtful, careful, and successful. They expressed belief that the "gradual" approach to reform implies that the ultimate goal is to create a liberal democratic society, comparable to that of Western liberal democracies.

The Americans who respect the Chinese government also expressed appreciation for the government's ability to make fast decisions and implement them across the whole economy. For example, an American CFO working in China told the story of American investment bankers coming to China, carrying out analyses, and concluding the Chinese economy could not possibly continue growing at its current rate but would run into serious problems with inflation and other economic maladies. The CFO said he tried to explain to the investment bankers that the government simply would not let this happen, but they did not believe him. The government's extensive level of control, he believed, could stop or alter economic forces.

This CFO and other American executives appreciated the Chinese government's ability to act unilaterally, cutting off debate and resistance. Those who had worked in India complained about the prolonged decision-making process in that country's democratic institutions and the resulting disrepair of infrastructure. In China, on the contrary, massive infrastructure projects are planned, implemented, and completed with astonishing speed and success.

These American executives who respect the Chinese government respect it because it is good for business. Their companies see opportunities in China with this government and pay these executives well to pursue these opportunities. In my view, however, these executives have tunnel vision. They can leave China whenever they want and do not concern themselves with the limited rights of Chinese citizens or the brutal and corrupt practices of the Chinese government.

Many Chinese executives also respect the Chinese government for very similar reasons, even though they live permanently in China.[84] They are impressed with the considerable economic growth that has taken place and continues to take place in China. Several of them predicted, with certainty, that the growth will continue without interruption for 10 to 20 years. They are wealthier than they ever dreamed. They have more freedom than their parents had. What is not to like?

In fact, their primary concern was not for more freedom but for more wealth and, even more, for stability so that what has been accomplished can be maintained and continued. It is very common to hear that a strong government is needed because China has "56 different minorities" that could threaten the country's stability. In my interviews, there was never any expression about the rights of these minorities. One Chinese executive told me, "Taiwan must come back to China. The Chinese are patient, but Taiwan must return. What the Taiwanese want is not relevant" (Ms. Ch32). Hence, for Chinese executives, "stability" and "harmony" mean central control.

The American executives who respect the Chinese government for the successful economic development it has orchestrated also do not concern themselves with the rights of the 56 minorities. Their tunnel vision reflects a selfishness that is not good for America because it makes one American value, free enterprise, the only American value relevant in China. Many American businesspeople at home have the same view. It is even supported up to a point by some versions of economic theory that posit private businesses as having no social responsibilities other than to obey the law.[85] It is the government's responsibility to take care of society; after all, government, not business, has been elected for just this purpose.

This theory never reflected reality in the United States,[86] and it applies even less in China; after all, China does not even have elections. So the tunnel

---

[84] Their respect for the government has not, however, stopped a significant percentage of them from leaving or getting second passports for themselves and their families as an insurance policy (Page 2012).

[85] The classic statement of this view is by Milton Friedman (1970).

[86] A healthy society requires more private institutions than just the free market—private schools, religious organizations, professions, and so on. With so many different types of public/private organizations, the virtue of civility is required—that is, to some extent citizens must care about each other and society as a whole—from all parts of society, including business (Shils 1997). Hence, a society cannot function adequately with only self-interest, law, and government "benevolence."

vision some American executives practice at home loses even its limited moral basis in places like China. For this reason, concerning themselves with only the Chinese government's *economic* policies is not ethically justifiable.

Some American executives justify their participation in the China market with the belief that it is moving toward a liberal democracy in one form or another. This optimistic vision is a naive American tradition going back 200 years.[87] It has more to do with American desire than Chinese reality.[88] It has repeatedly been proven false, but American executives have little historical perspective on current affairs, substituting instead the abstract models of free markets as inevitably creating freedom and democracy.

Some Chinese executives, too, see the economic reforms in positive terms, even though they are well aware that government officials sold government assets to their families and "friends" (especially their Communist comrades) at fire sale prices as part of the "reform" process. They see the close relations between the officials and their old comrades as a sound approach for building society, using private enterprise. Other Chinese executives look at the same situation and see inbred, irremovable, and unstoppable corruption. When they look into the future, they see the same dictatorship and corruption as in the present.[89]

In summary, there is a dearth of business ethics in the China market, for which all participants have some responsibility. The key factor explaining American business relations with the Chinese government is the Chinese middleman. The Americans use middlemen to pay bribes to government officials, supporting the Communist Party and enriching its members. Americans for the most part deny the ethical dilemma that forces them to choose between paying bribes and losing business. There is a general tendency among both Chinese and Americans either to focus on the government's success in generating economic growth or to imagine a natural evolution toward liberalization, views that require tunnel vision for the Americans and denial for the Chinese.

[87] See Chapter 4 for a discussion of this history.

[88] Madsen 1995.

[89] China has a long history of significant integration between public and private spheres, with the public sphere dominant. The Tiananmen Square protests challenged the structure of power and the distribution of wealth resulting from it. The way these protests were resolved certainly has an impact on how the government is seen and talked about now. So in terms of attitude toward economic reforms, the positive group uses the values of wealth and stability to evaluate the government; the negative group uses the values of freedom and fairness. How the memory of Tiananmen influences these perceptions was not addressed in my research.

Conclusion

The complexity of the variables that will determine the future makeup of business-government relations in China renders the outcome unknowable. Yet many American executives see a liberal democracy emerging on the distant horizon and claim this is the intent behind the "gradualism strategy." This view is, in my opinion, naive or self-serving or both. At best, it reveals a grave misunderstanding of the government's motivation for moving slowly. The "gradualism" strategy enables the government to tightly control sales of public assets, divert public assets to family and "friends," use the proceeds to buy off key subgroups, and above all, maintain its grip on power. The American vision also ignores the eternal yesterday of authoritarian governance in China. The yoke of dictatorship is hand in glove with Chinese history and culture. This is not an insight commonly recognized by American executives.

The key theme in my data for understanding the nature of business-government relations in China is the fact that massive government corruption has accompanied economic "reform" every step of the way. One of the reasons for the corruption simply has to do with the fact that there is more to steal. Another reason is the transfer of central governmental authority to provincial and municipal governments without adequate controls. On the provincial and municipal levels, local relationships have a huge influence on decision making.

But the central reason for corruption over the last 30 years is the Communist Party's monopoly on political power, whereby, practically speaking, checks and balances are nonexistent. So when the reform process was initiated, the gates of corruption were opened. The more the economy was "reformed," the more corruption increased, signifying that decentralized, market-based behavior can coexist with one-party, authoritarian domination in China, at least up to a point. Will one-party domination lead to a freeze or rollback of economic freedom, or will increasing economic freedom lead to a breakdown in one-party domination? There is no way to know. Either one is possible (as well as somewhere in between), depending on many internal and external factors.

One thing is clear: The fact that it could go either way draws attention back to the current state of affairs. Currently, the dictatorship is well entrenched and has the power and structures of control to stay that way. A moral challenge for American executives who are using the fantasy of future liberalization to accept and participate in corruption is to call a cat a cat and confront these issues. American companies *as a whole* need to develop positions and plans to address corruption in China. It would be good to include Chinese companies with the same mind-set, but this would not be acceptable to the Chinese government—which is exactly the problem.

But government control does not absolve American businesses of their moral responsibilities. They need to address issues such as the role of middlemen, human rights, and the many faces of corruption. The ostrich strategy of insulating themselves through the use of middlemen leaves them a handshake away from criminal activities. It also further ingrains these problems in the China marketplace, precludes mutual learning and problem solving, prevents the development of shared moral values, and weakens American commitments to resist corruption.

Ultimately, these two great cultures have much to learn from each other. It would be a shame if Chinese dictatorship and American denial or greed combine to prolong the problems rather than address them—problems that under the best scenario will require attention over the long term.

P A R T

CULTURE AND CONFLICT

7

Ones, Twos, and Threes

The Roots of Cultural Conflicts in American-Chinese Business Relations

A few months into my fieldwork in Shanghai, I was having difficulty securing the number of interviews I needed with Chinese executives. I contacted a high-level executive I knew at a large American company back in Cleveland for help. He contacted a mid-level manager at his company's plant in Shanghai with instructions to assist me. The mid-level manager was a Chinese national. He immediately turned me over to a low-level administrator at the MBA program from which he had just graduated with a request to help me secure interviews with Chinese executives.

After several meetings with the MBA administrator, weeks of delays, and two introductions that led to unhelpful interviews, one of which required me to eat a second dinner an hour after I had finished my first, I felt frustrated. I fired off an e-mail to the mid-level manager saying he was not helping me as his boss had instructed him. I immediately received an e-mail back from him and, to my surprise, from the MBA administrator, both blaming me for the whole situation.

Noteworthy in this sequence of events is that upon being asked to help me, the Chinese mid-level manager turned the request over to someone in his network. I never did meet the mid-level manager, even though he had agreed to do an interview with me. So he not only did not introduce me to Chinese executives in his own network, he did not participate in my research himself. What I had hoped would be a productive relationship turned out to be an unhelpful contact with a low-level university administrator. In the United States, in contrast, a request from a high-level executive to one of his subordinates would most likely have been carried out.

I tried to shake things up with my e-mail, implying that I was going to report the mid-level manager to his boss back in Cleveland. Despite the immediate response—the two e-mails blaming me—my complaint did work because the mid-level manager then introduced me to a manager at the American consulate who secured some excellent interviews for me with Chinese executives.

The point relevant to this chapter is the mid-level manager's use of third parties in his network to respond to my request. What I had hoped would be a good (two-way) relationship between the mid-level manager and me turned into a three-way relationship between the mid-level manager, the MBA administrator, and me; and even though I thought I had developed a warm relationship with the MBA administrator, I received a critical e-mail from him once I criticized his contact, the mid-level manager.

I had intended to develop good one-on-one relationships with these two individuals, but in reality I was dealing with a network that had clearly defined boundaries and rules for behavior. At all levels, individual, dyad, and network—ones, twos, and threes—social organization in China was different than in the United States.

This chapter explores the roots of cultural conflict in American-Chinese business relations. It begins with a review of Chinese business culture, focusing on central aspects of Chinese culture as they relate to business management and organization. Next it reviews American business culture, focusing on ethical and management issues in the context of doing business in China, including Western views of Chinese business ethics. The third section discusses the different thought-worlds involved in the two different cultures, with special attention to managerial interaction, conflict resolution, and joint ventures. Finally, an extended conclusion explores central differences between the two cultures—collectivism versus individualism, *guanxi* versus the rule of law, and authoritarian versus democratic government—to examine how such significant cultural differences and challenges are managed. Key in understanding this process is the role of the middleman, its ethics, and the solutions it provides.

Chinese Business Culture

1. Business Context. The most significant feature of the Chinese business system is the role of government. Very little gets done in business in which the government is not involved. Large businesses, especially, invariably have strong ties to the state.[1] The process of "privatization" many times leaves

[1] *Economist* April 21, 2012.

business-government ties murky. Still, the key principle of organization is interpersonal relationships, which are fluid. The roles the government, especially the local government, plays in business are those of organizer, banker, protector, supplier, partner, regulator, customer, and so on. With such central roles, the government claims a cut of the profits or some other benefits, many of which go to individual officials, not their agencies. Corruption is a pervasive and, by some accounts, growing dimension.

Even under the post-Mao economic reforms the situation is not exactly new; there are many similarities to business-government relations that go back centuries.[2] Because of the high risk and uncertainty from a history of government exploitation in the economic sphere, Chinese entrepreneurs have developed a robust work ethic and intense focus on opportunities and successful transactions.[3] The threatening behavior of the government is one reason it is hard to define and locate organizational boundaries.[4] Businesses rapidly morph from one name, location, and business activity to another as a defense against exploitation and taxes. Even though laws protecting property rights were passed in 2007, they have had little practical effect as of yet. In addition, most markets in China remain local or regional,[5] further encouraging local government intervention. Without reliable legal protection, property rights are maintained through personal relationships, often involving family members or other trusted relations, in what Boisot and Child refer to as a "communal definition of property rights."[6]

To make matters more uncertain, there are no constitutional rules that define the division of authority between various levels of government,[7] leading to runaway autonomy by the lower levels during the reforms. The central

---

[2] Gates 1996.

[3] Redding 1995.

[4] Tsui et al. 2004. That's not all that's hard to find: Private companies typically have three sets of financial records, one each for the government, the bank, and themselves (Huang 2008).

[5] One reason for localism is that the Communists built self-sufficient regional command structures, fearing attack from the Americans and later the Russians (Fairbank and Goldman 2006). A second reason is that Chinese private firms remain small (the reasons for which will be discussed below) and thus do not have the supply chains, brands, marketing, distribution, managerial resources, and so on to develop national markets (Fukuyama 1995).

[6] Boisot and Child 1996: 14. This mechanism can be seen clearly in Fujian and Guangdong provinces, where capital primarily from Hong Kong and Taiwan going to family- and lineage-based networks stimulated much of the significant economic development (Fukuyama 1995). Trust in these networks functioned in the place of property rights.

[7] Lieberthal and Lieberthal 2003.

government tries to regulate relations with lower levels through policy pronouncements, but since policies change constantly there are no clear administrative directives or controls. And given that the lower levels have different interests than the central government, they many times simply ignore central government directives.[8]

China has never relied heavily on the rule of law, the Confucian heritage having influenced courts to seek friendly resolution to conflicts[9] rather than evaluate cases against formal standards or case history. Historically, the state used law to advance its policies for the organization of society, not to resolve conflicts between private individuals. Instead of using the court system to resolve disputes, China relied more heavily on government administrative edict or communal censure. Thus, in collectivist-oriented Chinese society, both parties in a legal dispute are viewed with suspicion by the court.

Given the conflicting relationship between levels of government and a disinclination to use the court system to consistently interpret and apply a relatively stable body of law, it is not surprising that business relationships and contracts remain ambiguous at best, often fading into a labyrinth of interpersonal relationships and networks. This lack of a stable and enforceable legal system undermines business competition in many ways. From protectionist measures taken by local governments to a practically complete unwillingness to rein in intellectual property (IP) violations to severe price competition from state-subsidized firms to counterfeiting operations run by local governments,[10] business in the China market is difficult to say the least. When labor costs rise and 10 percent growth in GDP ends, without institutional changes Western firms will find it much more difficult to scratch out a profit.

2. Guanxi and Relationships. One of the main cultural categories in the practice of Chinese management is *guanxi*, interpersonal networking. The traditions of *guanxi* go back to the origins of Confucianism in the sixth century BC, when the intense emphasis on family and primary relationships was first systematized.[11] There are many components to *guanxi* as a cultural system. Confucianism established hierarchy as a central principle in Chinese

---

[8] Though they only ignore central government's vital interests (e.g., Tibet, Falun Gong) at the risk of personal harm (R. McGregor 2010).

[9] Koehn 2001.

[10] Lieberthal and Lieberthal 2003.

[11] Park and Luo 2001.

society,[12] meaning that a pronounced distance always exists between the generations. *Guanxi* to a degree compensates for this lack of vertical openness by intensifying particular horizontal relationships. Also, in a society in which family and other primary groups are so central, trust is often lacking outside these groups. As Li puts it, "In a relation-based society there is a dearth of public information and low levels of trust. Laws, financial regulations, accounting rules are merely ink on paper. Bringing a company public is an opportunity to loot outside investors."[13] *Guanxi,* then, is a way to develop trust in a treacherous social environment. Interpersonal networks or working with a friend of a friend lowers the hazard considerably.

There is thus a great emphasis on developing relationships and joining networks in China. The goal is to set up "networks of mutual dependence and manufacture of obligation and indebtedness."[14] Once a relationship has started to develop, a request for a favor in time of need has a better chance of being heard, though nothing is promised.[15] Bell likens a well-developed relationship to a premium paid for residential fire insurance.[16]

The sense of obligation at the center of *guanxi* is best understood in terms of a range. Park and Luo describe the obligations as utilitarian, not emotional.[17] If they make economic sense they survive; otherwise, they do not. Hofstede and others, however, understand *guanxi* in terms of collectivist society, where individual identity is based on in-group membership.[18] This view relates *guanxi* more to trust and friendship than to just advantage, with obligation taking on a moral weight. McGregor, too, notes the moral obligation in a request from a friend, making it very difficult to refuse.[19] In any case, in China not meeting one's obligations is quickly registered in one's reputation, making it difficult to gain trust and function in society.

With the highly social Chinese, gifts, favors, and banquets play a special role in the development of relationships and the building of trust. A gift is not for a particular favor. It is a way of developing positive feelings to get the

[12] Redding 1995.
[13] S. Li 2005: 299.
[14] Millington, Eberhardt, and Wilkinson 2005: 257.
[15] Bell 2000.
[16] Bell 2000.
[17] Park and Luo 2001.
[18] Hofstede et al. 2010.
[19] J. McGregor 2005.

relationship started. Repeated gifts and favors deepen the relationship, developing trust.[20] Along with trust, personal feelings can develop, leading to friendship.[21]

But China has a hierarchical culture, not a democratic one. Cutting across the positive feelings and instrumental advantages is the issue of status or "face." Thus, gifts are acts not only of friendship but also of respect. When one gives a gift, it is not only with the hope of a future benefit, but more immediately it provides a symbolic gain.[22] Giving a gift demonstrates one's economic power, thus increasing face[23] and rendering the giver the moral and symbolic superior.[24] Simultaneously, however, the gift pays respect to the receiver, thus giving face.[25] This is a more complex moral dynamic than discussed earlier.

The subtle dynamics of face demonstrate the issue of power in *guanxi*. The receiver gains face but also accepts obligation for repayment. The receiver owes the giver. Thus the giving of the gift is an act of power in that the receiver, in owing the giver, is now subordinate. If the receiver does not return the favor when it is requested, the receiver will lose face,[26] undercutting his power base within the network. Hence, the Chinese do not give gifts to everyone. They give gifts to those who have face, specifically to those who can help them. It becomes enormously important, then, to protect one's face, one's reputation. Having face will influence whether your gifts will be accepted, whether others will want relationships with you, whether your requests for favors will get serious attention. Those with face can develop extensive networks involving up to several hundred people,[27] extending their power, resources, and effectiveness. So much of Chinese social interaction takes place within the *guanxi* system that one has little choice but to develop relationships to get things done. Connections are always needed to develop

[20] Smart 1993.

[21] Su and Littlefield 2001.

[22] M. Yang 2002.

[23] Su and Littlefield 2001.

[24] Smart 1993. This is quite different than in the United States, where gifts usually come from a superior to a subordinate to gain support for the superior's goals (Hsu 1981). Gifts from a subordinate would also violate the value of equality, which formalizes and restricts hierarchical authority in the United States.

[25] Snell and Tseng 2001.

[26] Su and Littlefield 2001.

[27] Redding and Witt 2007.

further connections, to know who knows whom in order to get assistance when and where it is needed. Otherwise, one will not get access to the levers of power, or will pay too much for them, or will damage one's face by failing or looking inept.

Key to maintaining face and key to the system of *guanxi* is the principle of reciprocity, which must be culturally ingrained in the society for *guanxi* to work, though it must remain tacit. If the obligation to return the favor becomes direct and immediate, instrumentality will undermine the feeling-state of obligation and *guanxi* will become nothing more than economic calculation. For *guanxi* to maintain its cultural force, instrumentality must be subordinated to relationship. Otherwise, the "gift" is a bribe. Indeed, in China, norms of reciprocity are intense.[28]

This is not to say instrumentality is not an important part of the motivational structure, but the principle of reciprocity is a cultural force, a sort of cultural invisible hand, that makes possible group effectiveness and identity over time. It is a partly preconscious collective value that provides glue to social relationships. One "knows" that if one keeps face within the network one will have access to support and resources. The Chinese rely heavily on relationships to define themselves. From the earliest age they are trained to repress their aggressiveness and fit into the group. The dynamics of face and the principle of reciprocity enforce and channel the group orientation—though, as noted, this is a particular kind of group, one with a strong sense of hierarchy. The reciprocity rule enforces hierarchy in that the individuals with the most status and resources can secure the most favors because they can return the most. *Guanxi* thus tends to distribute resources according to the social status system.

Culturally, the principle of reciprocity is situated in an enormously complex system of behavioral ideals and norms of mutuality and right relations that are themselves rooted in a Confucian understanding of righteousness and commitment to benevolence.[29] The Chinese feel very strong commitments to their friends. But, as in all societies, conflicts arise as the trials and tribulations of a relationship influence the ongoing understanding of obligation; further, conflicts with other commitments in other networks leave the situation fluid and open to continuous evaluation and negotiation.

[28] Hwang 1987.
[29] Steidlmeier 1999.

Networks themselves are hierarchically prioritized. The three general categories of relationships are family, familiar people, and strangers.[30] To family, obligations are unconditional and moral. Even the principle of reciprocity is weaker here, duty to kin being primary. To friends, obligations are moderate, influenced by the rule of reciprocity and pragmatic calculation. To strangers the Chinese can be surprisingly indifferent. The middle category of "friends" tends to group into schoolmates; colleagues; distant relatives; friends of friends; and people from one's hometown, alma mater, or work unit. In other words, personal attachment as the driving force tends to be the exception without some type of shared social identity. This is why Chinese can feel so little for strangers; without a shared social identity it is as if they are unknowable and thus not trustworthy. Without universal values, Confucian personalism keeps social networks small. So much the better for authoritarian government.[31]

3. Guanxi *and "Market Socialism."* Interpersonal relationships are important in all business systems. The difference in China is that they are ubiquitous, playing a pervasive role in interfirm relations,[32] so much so that it is not uncommon for connections to dominate hiring decisions.[33] Boisot and Child conclude that *guanxi* makes the Chinese business system a "distinctive institutional form—network capitalism."[34] The distinctiveness resides in the fact that the Chinese carry out decentralization with a minimum of bureaucratic codification, relying instead on a complex, historically developed system of interpersonal rules.

The research on whether China's economic development is increasing or decreasing *guanxi* is mixed. Millington, Eberhardt, and Wilkinson found that in relations with private Chinese firms *guanxi* plays a stronger role than in relations with state-owned enterprises (SOEs),[35] suggesting that market development is increasing *guanxi*. On the other hand, Park and Luo found

---

[30] M. Yang 2002.

[31] For this reason Hsu (1981) says the Chinese manage their relationship with the government through respect and distance, as opposed to Americans, who consider themselves equal to their officials.

[32] Luo 2000. In a survey carried out by Li and Filer (2004) to measure the centrality of relationships (as opposed to institutions) in a country, China received the highest score, ranking 48 out of 48.

[33] Warren, Dunfee, and Li 2004.

[34] Boisot and Child 1996: 2.

[35] Millington, Eberhardt, and Wilkinson 2002.

businesses with advanced skills and resources to be less dependent on *guanxi*,[36] suggesting that there is an entry point in Chinese "market socialism" for competition to undercut *guanxi*. Guthrie similarly argues that the arrival of Western firms and the impact of their business practices is decreasing the role of *guanxi*.[37] However, Yang makes the interesting argument that the arrival of Western firms has actually increased the use of *guanxi* as these firms struggle to "elude state power and gain its collusion."[38] Given the pervasive and costly role of the state in China's marketplace, the latter argument cannot be easily dismissed.

4. Ascribed and Achieved Guanxi. The discussion as to whether *guanxi* will increase or decrease with the arrival of economic reforms is not exactly on target because *guanxi* has always had an element of the impersonal. Once out of the family, *guanxi* relationships grow more impersonal and calculated. Hoiman and King talk about two types of *guanxi:* ascribed *guanxi*, based on goodwill and compassion, and achieved *guanxi*, based on strategic calcula-tion.[39] The balance between the two had already been changing before the introduction of the economic reforms. During the intense politicization of everyday life and corresponding shortages of goods and services during the Cultural Revolution, ascribed *guanxi* increased as a means to establish community and secure needed goods in a hostile environment.[40] After the increase of "privatization" in 1992 and the corresponding increase in rent seeking among government officials, however, ascribed *guanxi* diminished while achieved *guanxi* increased.[41] Snell and Tseng describe the increase in achieved *guanxi* as dishonorable because of its role in corruption.[42]

The distinction between ascribed and achieved *guanxi* needs to be kept in mind when considering the advantages and disadvantages of *guanxi*. Six advan-tages were found in the literature. First, *guanxi* creates efficient relationships.[43]

---

[36] Park and Luo 2001. Similarly, Redding and Witt (2007) concluded that those who control technology and market access are gaining power vis-à-vis those with political connections. My 2010 interviews support this conclusion up to a point.

[37] Guthrie 2001. This is supported by Millington, Eberhardt, and Wilkinson (2002), who found *guanxi* plays little part in the supply relationships of U.K. companies.

[38] M. Yang 2002: 468.

[39] Hoiman and King 2003.

[40] Sun 2004.

[41] Sun 2004. See also Hefner (1998) and Snell and Tseng (2001).

[42] Snell and Tseng 2001.

[43] Warren, Dunfee, and Li 2004.

Employees with *guanxi* can minimize their employers' costs, especially for government procedures, requirements, taxes, and fines. Connections add a significant measure of flexibility and freedom inside an authoritarian political system. Second, related to the first point, *guanxi* provides considerable savings through dispensing with lawyers, extensive record keeping, and other bureaucratic control mechanisms.[44] Third, subcontracting, alliances, and mergers all depend heavily on *guanxi*[45] to lower the risks in organizational interdependence and to mitigate environmental uncertainty and threats.

Fourth, *guanxi* is particularly useful to entrepreneurs who lack resources but can secure favors to create a start-up.[46] Indeed, *guanxi* is an art and can be seen as a scarce entrepreneurial skill in this context. It can be critical to minorities or others facing obstacles to capital, labor, or market access. Fifth, *guanxi* has been used to increase sales by calling on people who owe favors.[47] In other words, purchases are made not for the product, but because of relationship position in a network.[48] Finally, ascribed *guanxi* can lower bribery costs by allowing one to gain support based on long-term relationships.[49] In China, the definition of *bribery* is using impersonal means to attain an immediate, instrumental goal.[50] The bribery transaction takes place outside the enveloping commitment to a long-term relationship and the ethics of reciprocity—and it usually involves cash. Ascribed *guanxi* is different; it puts favors in a moral context.

The negative implications of *guanxi* are also plentiful. First, the line between *guanxi* and bribery is not always clear. Cases show that *guanxi* leads to the edges of unethical activities and beyond.[51] Because it is based on

---

[44] Redding and Witt 2007. Given that the legal system is used by the government as a control mechanism and can be unfair, arbitrary, and inconsistent, *guanxi* opens up an alternative channel for action. I think this is why the Communists were against *guanxi*, not because it blocked "modernization."

[45] Boisot and Child 1996.

[46] Tsai 2007.

[47] Warren, Dunfee, and Li 2004.

[48] Such purchasing practices highlight another difference between Chinese and American cultures. Because the Chinese are usually nested in their primary groups, their attachment to things is moderated, whereas American individualism leads to identification with things as a means to define the self (Hsu 1981). Conspicuous consumption expresses the American's personal worth, for the Chinese, his social place.

[49] Sun 2004.

[50] Snell and Tseng 2001.

[51] Snell and Tseng 2001.

in-group interests, it is by nature secretive[52] and inevitably leads to collusion.[53] Second, since the reforms, the joining of authoritarian government with large-scale, private business has transformed *guanxi* into bribery because the huge amounts of money involved have made financial calculation the core of the relationship.[54] This is different than meeting interpersonal needs based on a long-term relationship that involves values of benevolence, friendship, and reciprocity. Third, there is a moral dilemma at the heart of *guanxi*. While *guanxi* may increase interpersonal trust and develop moral values on the small-group level, it simultaneously runs the risk of violating procedural justice and trust outside the *guanxi* network.[55] For example, *guanxi* relationships have contributed to the terrible pollution problems in China as in-groups ignored public welfare to maximize their own profits.

Fourth, related to the previous point, *guanxi* undermines business competition in several ways. Relations with government officials open backdoor channels to government contracts; passing of favorable laws and policies; special access to government-controlled real estate; expedited approval processes; favorable execution of laws; less-stringent review of projects; bypassing of export and import rules; and evasion of regulatory requirements, fines, taxes, and the like.[56] Similarly, in the government-controlled banking system, relationships can steer credit away from lower-risk, productive accounts to the higher-risk accounts of family members and "friends." Some analysts argue that these "suboptimal" investments will leave China behind in the competition between nations. But, as was noted above, "network capitalism" has advantages too.

Fifth, *guanxi* sets up particularly sharp employee conflicts of interest. The commitment to the *guanxi* network can cause employees to run afoul of employer rules and policies.[57] Park and Luo found that *guanxi* appears to be more strongly related to sales growth than to net profit.[58] In other words, *guanxi* leads to kickbacks or other schemes that raise sales levels but not profits.

---

[52] S. Li 2005.

[53] Su and Littlefield 2001. Hofstede and colleagues (2010) argue that in-groups are inseparable from collective culture, so inside these cultures, giving preference to in-group members is natural and ethical.

[54] M. Yang 2002.

[55] Chen, Chen, and Xin 2004.

[56] Warren, Dunfee, and Li 2004.

[57] Warren, Dunfee, and Li 2004.

[58] Park and Luo 2001.

Paradoxically, employer efforts to control *guanxi* through job rotation and purchasing systems based on multiple bids undermine not only *guanxi* but all long-term relationships that are important for many aspects of modern business systems.[59] Sixth, internal to the organization, *guanxi* can result in hiring and promoting less qualified individuals, negatively impacting the morale and motivation of other employees. Even without established *guanxi* relations, *guanxi* is still part of the culture, potentially leading to job opportunities and promotions not being given without some promise of unspecified payback.

5. Strategy and Organization. In 2011, *The Economist* quoted a Communist Party official as saying there are 40 million private firms in China, employing 92 percent of Chinese workers.[60] The article cited a source arguing that return on equity for unlisted private firms is 14 percent (compared with 4 percent for state-owned firms). Most private firms are small and controlled by a single individual. Capital for these businesses comes from personal savings, retained earnings, and informal credit.[61] The key to understanding Chinese management and organization is its development through a long history in relation to a predatory state. This explains why private businesses tend to stay small and rely closely on family to maintain trust.[62] Family is a fortress against an authoritarian, interventionist, and demanding state,[63] explaining in part why Chinese family relationships are intensely involuted. Family as defense was the only option left open by a state that supported Confucianism, with its marked emphasis on piety, first and foremost in the family. This situation led to both technological stasis and robust population growth in Chinese economic history.

With the intense focus on family in the context of a dominating state, communal and cooperative values were stunted. This is another reason why Chinese firms tend to remain small. Trust is an endemic problem in Chinese society. *Guanxi* is a solution to this problem but basically exacerbates the broader distrust by limiting trust to relationships with "friends." By staying small and utilizing limited networks, Chinese firms maximize strategic flexibility, keep their business focus narrow, and ruthlessly keep costs low in

[59] Millington, Eberhardt, and Wilkinson 2005.

[60] *Economist* (March 10, 2011). According to this source, this would leave three million cooperative and state-owned firms.

[61] Less than 4 percent of the loans given out by three of the four largest banks are to small and medium-sized enterprises (*Economist* March 10, 2011).

[62] Redding 1995.

[63] Gates 1996.

the pursuit of profit.[64] This model tends to work best in labor-intensive, fast-changing, highly segmented, small markets,[65] such as textiles and apparel; commercial trading; electronic components manufacture and assembly; commodities; real estate; and small-scale manufacturing in metalworking, furniture, plastics, toys, paper products, and the like.

The weaknesses of the model are several. Low trust and small size mean little corporate development. Chinese firms tend to be undeveloped in product design, marketing, brand management, distribution, supply-chain logistics, research and development, production logistics, organization of decentralized structures, and so on.[66] In short, reliance on family means no professional management; lack of professional management limits organizational development. This is also why there are so few Chinese brand names; without large, enduring organizations capable of economy of scale and extensive marketing programs, brands remain beyond reach.[67] For the same reasons, there are few private Chinese multinational corporations (MNCs). Without professional management beyond family resources, it is impossible to expand abroad. To be sure, it is not merely a lack of personnel; it is a lack of trust. There is not enough delegation and autonomy to build the requisite level of organizational complexity for a large-scale, efficient, competitive business.

The record of innovation in Chinese businesses is a case in point. Though Chinese firms have had some success at process innovation in manufacturing, they still typically lose out to Western firms in product design and marketing.[68] In addition, the lack of adequate funding,[69] seen in the sources of capital listed above, contributes to the focus on labor-intensive, low-cost, low-margin products. Further, because of the low-trust, uncertain environment, there is a disinclination to invest in expensive machinery and capital goods to expand production, make more sophisticated products, or improve labor productivity. These investments would create employee and government risk that would be practically unheard of in the United States.

Importantly, these factors—a low-trust, high-risk environment; obsession with cost; and lack of access to capital markets—have led to little

---

[64] Redding 1995.
[65] Fukuyama 1995.
[66] Redding and Witt 2007.
[67] Fukuyama 1995.
[68] *Economist* March 10, 2012a.
[69] Huang 2008.

understanding of the cost of capital. Chinese businesses never developed capital accounting.[70] Cost of capital was simply not part of their business thinking.[71] Needless to say, the result is an inefficient use of capital and an ineffective straitjacketing of strategic thinking.

Given the low-investment, small-organization, network-based model, Chinese firms tend to make frequent changes in business activities as opportunities present themselves.[72] As labor costs increase and international pressure forces appreciation of the yuan, millions of small Chinese firms will face increasing international competition.

6. Management and Leadership. Private Chinese businesses are primarily family businesses with the father as the leader and other family members as key employees. Lineage members traditionally staff the next level of responsibility. The whole system works in a highly centralized, hub-and-spoke manner.[73] In a collective society, most business owners work to accumulate wealth for the family and perpetuate the family name.[74] Indeed, family identity is so important many families keep records over centuries recording their lineage. Owner-managers typically are committed to Confucian values of social harmony, hierarchy, respect for knowledge, family, personalism and its obligations, and security.[75] Because many entrepreneurs come from poor sections of society and others suffered deprivation during the Mao era, especially during the Cultural Revolution, they and their families work extremely hard.

The owner's leadership style is despotic. The hierarchical implications of Confucian social philosophy and the heritage of an extremely aloof, elite group of scholar-officials have influenced the nature of leadership in Chinese society. The aloof, authoritarian father of the Chinese family is the model for leadership in Chinese organizations.[76] McGregor describes the typical entrepreneur as secretive, highly critical, controlling, and feared.[77]

---

[70] Redding and Witt 2007.

[71] Contributing to the lack of understanding of the cost of capital are the rarity of concentrations of capital due to government taxation (Weber 1951) and equal inheritance among male heirs (Fukuyama 1995).

[72] Huang 2008.

[73] Fukuyama 1995.

[74] Redding and Witt 2007.

[75] Redding and Witt 2007.

[76] Redding 1995.

[77] J. McGregor 2005.

Related to authoritarianism is the indivisibility of leadership because it is identified totally with the person, not the job or role.[78] This too limits the size of the organization. Leadership is not shared. Strong subordinates tend not to be promoted. The leader surrounds himself with nonthreatening, trustworthy subordinates. Because so much authority is concentrated in a single individual, control systems are not needed. All control is exercised through relationships. The system is cost-effective, but it limits the scope of the organization.

To his core group of extremely loyal subordinates, the CEO modifies his authoritarianism to fit the personal nature of the relationship.[79] He becomes less a dictator and more a teacher. This highly personal system cannot work if the organization grows beyond the capacities of the CEO's personal relationships.

The decision-making style that goes along with the father/emperor model of CEO leadership is aloof and intuitive. Seldom does the CEO rely on research. His "strategy" is usually vague, flexible, and open ended.[80] Because those around him are highly dependent on him, he can call on them for information or for special effort when needed. Other than that, their job is to carry out his will. They seldom have much information other than what they need to carry out his orders. To the extent that the CEO explicitly formulates plans, he keeps them to himself. Obviously communication in this system is very poor.

Redding's research found that most Chinese executives believe in luck, some believe in fatalism, and many rely on portents to guide their fortunes.[81] Unlike Western culture, Confucianism emphasizes accommodation to the world rather than control of it. Chinese do not personalize their mistakes;[82] fate was simply against them. This attitude encourages risk taking and entrepreneurship.[83]

The father/emperor model of leadership is not limited to family businesses but is a universal characteristic of Chinese organizations. Moreover, the current group of business leaders descends from the same social orders that

[78] Redding 1995.
[79] Redding 1995.
[80] Redding 1995.
[81] Redding 1995.
[82] J. McGregor (2005) mistakenly saw this attitude as not taking responsibility for one's actions.
[83] This is consistent with the high level of optimism J. McGregor (2005) observed among entrepreneurs.

ruled imperial China, were brought up during the Mao era of intense politicization, and in some cases, were Red Guards who went from peasants to bullies to bureaucrats to businessmen; little in their background prepared them to lead private firms.[84] Nevertheless, entrepreneurship is booming in China. Millions of businesses have been created. Since 1980, the economy has grown 14-fold, adjusted for inflation.[85] Jun Yeop Lee of Inha University, South Korea, concludes that Chinese firms not majority-owned by the government account for about 70 percent of GDP.[86] Clearly, Chinese culture is a fertile ground for entrepreneurship.

Underneath the leader in these organizations, subordinates must balance carrying out the leader's commands, developing a place in the organization, and satisfying their own personal goals. Employees arrive at the organization predisposed to a dependency relationship that started in the family.[87] They are prepared to give loyalty, respect, and caring but want to get the same in return. Because of the highly personal nature of the leader-follower relationship, promotions and innumerable other types of rewards are seen as personal gifts that imply unspecified reciprocal obligations, further deepening the dependency relationship. Unlike in the United States, the personalization of hierarchy is based on socially accepted behavior, not fear. Despite the strong hierarchy, there is less worker alienation in China than in the United States because Chinese workers seek compliance, not individualism.[88]

Nonetheless, tensions exist. The lack of a system of authority outside the CEO creates cliques and factions in the organization (though these are normally not observable from the outside).[89] And within the authority relationship, the personalism ethic requires constant interpersonal work. Expressions of loyalty must be continuously communicated. Dependence vertically, distrust horizontally, and vague responsibilities and goals organizationally create insecurity and anxiety for the employee,[90] stifling initiative, creativity, and commitment.

---

[84] Gamer 2003a.

[85] Areddy 2009.

[86] Cited in *Economist* (March 10, 2011).

[87] Redding 1995.

[88] The desire for compliance is the result of the Confucian household and, some argue, the exacting discipline that is needed to master the written Chinese language.

[89] Redding 1995.

[90] Hsu (1981) argues that American self-reliance leaves relationships transitory and unsatisfying. Self-worth is found through endless competition, leaving the individual fearful and alone, or through joining status groups, which creates resentment and guilt in a culture of self-reliance.

These factors also reinforce the tendency for the leader to surround himself with a small group of very loyal followers, usually family members. Employees not in the inner circle easily suffer from frustration and poor morale.[91] A focus on personal reward over company gain, debilitating politics, and unethical activity are common in Chinese companies.[92]

External forces also influence the culture of the Chinese business organization. Decades of government indoctrination and domination—far from nonexistent today—have ingrained political skills over management capabilities.[93] So there is a shortage of management skill in addition to a tendency to distrust the managers who are available.[94] Thus outside the inner circle, owners do not always treat employees well. They tend to pay the minimum the market will bear; hire skilled personnel when they need them and fire them when they do not; and reward only key personnel who are essential, usually some technical people.[95] Worse, those who are easily replaced are easily mistreated. Needless to say, there is little skill development in this system with its high employee turnover due to firings, job hopping, and employees leaving to be their own boss. Still, because of the huge supply of workers, productivity is maintained despite the poor working conditions.[96]

But it is a certain kind of productivity. The educational system does not cultivate creativity or independence. Though the Chinese are highly disciplined, trainable, and flexible at the top of the organization, their social structure has made it difficult to develop efficient large-scale organizations, innovative cultures, autonomous and motivated middle management, and skill at the important tasks of systems integration and optimization.[97] They are good at mass production of low- to mid-technology products, wherein jobs can be highly standardized and specialized.[98] Indeed, in a 2004 survey,

---

[91] Chen and Chen 2005.

[92] J. McGregor 2005.

[93] Walder 1986; Lieberthal and Lieberthal 2003.

[94] Ironically, the collective nature of the Chinese family makes the business a family yet divides employees' loyalty because of their commitment to their own family and friends (Hofstede et al. 2010).

[95] Redding and Witt 2007.

[96] My 2010 interviews and conversations with managers in Shanghai found a much higher percentage of dissatisfaction with career conditions, career opportunities, and life situation than in the 2007 interviews.

[97] Lieberthal and Lieberthal 2003.

[98] Redding and Witt 2007.

Chinese organizations had a 99 percent on-time delivery rate and 98 percent rate of meeting specifications on the first try,[99] both higher than the scores of U.S. organizations. But they are not good at products dependent on consumer taste; rapid technological change; complex production systems requiring initiative and cooperation; or complex assembly tasks that need to be coordinated with design, marketing, and new science.[100] On the contrary, the Chinese do a great deal of product copying and imitation.

There is some debate in the literature as to whether the reforms and the arrival of Western firms are having much impact on Chinese firms as they have been described here. Guthrie, for example, argues that Chinese firms are moving toward formal rational systems of organizational authority due to their interaction with Western firms.[101] Lam offers some evidence for this claim in his finding that foreign-invested enterprises (FIEs) and private Chinese firms discriminate against women less than SOEs and collectives because they are more subject to market forces.[102] The use of written contracts, however, is higher in SOEs and collectives than in private firms, suggesting that private firms are still relying heavily on interpersonal networks to conduct business.

7. Business Ethics and Business Corruption. Traditionally and even today, people will uphold their agreements because the gods require probity, because they want to protect their reputation and future creditworthiness, and out of fear that repayment can be forced on them through government or private muscle.[103] But since the reforms, the situation has become more ambiguous. Confucian values of loyalty and reciprocity, selflessness, the golden rule, proper conduct, and orderly relations are still relevant. Indeed, they are deeply ingrained in the Chinese psyche through the socialization of an acute sensitivity to significant others. The Chinese government, following Singapore, has even begun to encourage the use of Confucian values in business alongside socialist equality as an alternative to Western market culture.[104]

But despite the Confucian cultural context, the introduction of the market economy has led to weakened professional morality, decreased social

---

[99] J. McGregor 2005.
[100] Redding and Witt 2007.
[101] Guthrie 1999.
[102] Lam 2002.
[103] Gates 1996.
[104] Hefner 1998.

responsibility, and increased money worship.[105] Another ethical challenge is Confucianism itself, which historically has tended to provide those in positions of authority with unquestioned discretionary power.[106] This model is prone to degeneration as individuals unrestrained by checks and balances are inclined to pursue their own interests. But most relevant now is the effect the introduction of the market economy is having on monitoring and enforcement. With the rapid growth of economic opportunities and the new permission to travel, it is easy to change jobs and hide past transgressions.[107] Employee referral and background checking systems are in their infancy. As discussed earlier, the court system too has not developed to keep up with changes in business activities. Nor have weak management and accounting systems done much to deter filing false expense reports or using company funds for personal advantage or to help friends.[108] Presumably, over time some of these systems will be improved.

A more serious problem is the role of ethics in Chinese culture. As shown in the discussion of *guanxi,* the family is a fortress against a predatory government and a highly competitive, often hostile, social environment. In this context, social morality is what serves the family or the *guanxi* network. There is little concern for others outside these personal relationships. Decisions are made purely for results. Confucian ethics is a luxury afforded only to friends. With a predatory government on one side, a network of personal relationships on the other, and nothing in between, business transactions are dangerous. Not only is there little ethics in the business world, but many Chinese do not recognize any problem with this lack.

Given this cultural context, Chinese society, as has been observed for centuries by foreign visitors, is prone to corruption. In today's private business sector this means a substantial number of fraudulent financial statements,[109] widespread kickbacks to purchasing managers and salesmen,[110]

---

[105] Harvey 1999. Hefner (1998) argues that the market has clearly increased the utilitarian aspect of *guanxi*, undercutting Confucian values of loyalty, benevolence, and respect. On the other hand, there has been a significant increase in religious belief (Johnson 2011) and some writers see nascent stirrings of professionalization and moral autonomy (Kleinman 2010).

[106] Snell and Tseng 2001.

[107] Chen and Chen 2005.

[108] Ironically, a strict hierarchy tends to result in unethical behavior at both high and low levels (Hofstede et al. 2010) because excessive hierarchical control undermines personal commitment.

[109] Firth, Mo, and Wong 2005.

[110] J. McGregor 2005.

pervasive IP violations,[111] misrepresentation and dishonesty in negotiations,[112] lying to the government,[113] and pervasive bribery of government officials.[114]

There is some evidence that corruption in China has declined. Transparency International's corruption index gave China a rating of 40 on a 41-point scale in 1995, but 75 out of 183 in 2011.[115] McGregor argues that Hong Kong and Taiwanese businessmen have largely been responsible for reviving corruption in China.[116] It is true that due to a lack of capital and private-sector management experience in China, Hong Kong and Taiwanese executives have played an important role in the country's developing private sector.

All in all, it is not possible to lay blame for China's corruption on one sector or with one group. Decentralization without adequate controls was certainly a big factor, whether one sees it as inevitable once the government decided to privatize or as the result of official greed. Given the government's involvement in corruption, the media could play a powerful role by investigating it and bringing the facts to the public's attention—but this is generally not the case. Business news is commonly as corrupt as any other aspect of business. Journalists take bribes for helping inflate a company's stock price or discrediting the stock of a competitor.[117] Except for a brief period in the early 1980s, the government has kept tight control over investigative journalism.[118] With good government connections, private businesspeople or SOE

---

[111] For example, it is estimated that 77 percent of the software in China is pirated (*Business Software Alliance 2012*).

[112] J. McGregor 2005.

[113] For example, a survey found 66 percent of Shenzhen's 35,000 companies lie to the government about their business activities (Gamer 2003b).

[114] Bribery of government officials in particular has played a huge role in the post-1992 "privatization" process. Sun (2004) reports that in government prosecutions between 1992 and 2002, the percentage of corruption cases involving bribery rose from 35.6 percent to 58.2 percent while both embezzlement and profiteering declined. One study estimated that bribes account for 3–5 percent of business operating costs (Su and Littlefield 2001) though for some businesses they can rise much higher.

[115] Transparency International 2011.

[116] J. McGregor 2005.

[117] Pan 2008.

[118] Except for coverage of foreign companies, which J. McGregor (2005) says is a "media free zone." Though, as noted in Chapter 5, the recent high speed rail disasters have been covered aggressively in the media (Dean and Page 2011). This coverage was "permitted" perhaps because of the large number of dead and injured that could not be concealed, the high profile nature of the accident, and its relation to government corruption.

executives can get government help to force editors to retract unfavorable stories or, if that is not enough, to put editors and journalists in jail or worse.[119]

Western Business Experience in China

1. American Business Culture. Before examining American business experience in China, a brief review of American business culture is in order. In the United States, 60 percent of business capital is raised through the equity or debt markets, based on the firm's quarterly results.[120] Capital as a percent of GDP is an extremely high 160 percent, suggesting a highly liquid and efficient financial system. Most large businesses are publicly owned. Their stock is actively traded in stock markets. Government agencies and the legal, accounting, and journalism professions generally ensure availability of reliable business and financial information. Thus shareholders are the key stakeholder in American capitalism, compared with employees in Japan or the government and labor in Germany.

In addition to shareholders who buy and sell shares, boards of directors and professional managers are the other two pillars of American business governance.[121] Theoretically, both boards and professional managers serve the shareholders. Without a doubt, they serve each other; at many U.S. companies the CEO is also the board chair.[122]

Top management is central to this system because it is responsible for firm financial performance and is monitored by the board and the financial markets to this end. Because of this centrality, managers' power and status are significant. Their pay packages are the highest in the world, twice that of British executives, the next-highest-paid group.[123]

The other side of the coin from management is labor, which has much less status, power, and pay. American firms tend to have high task fragmentation and standardization.[124] The relationship between management and labor tends not to be a happy one. Loss of work days to strikes, for instance, is

---

[119] Pan 2008. Large Chinese companies also write their own scripts, which are then reported by the government media as if they were reports by journalists (R. McGregor 2010).

[120] Redding and Witt 2007.

[121] Young et al. 2008.

[122] De Kluyver 2009. Warren Buffett has for many years complained that boards overpay mediocre CEOs (Buffett 2006).

[123] Ossinger 2006.

[124] Redding and Witt 2007.

astronomically higher in the United States than in Germany or Japan. Thus American management culture tends to be hierarchical and technocratic. Because of the concentration of power and the culture of continuous ratio-nalization—focus on short-term profit maximization and cost reduction—firms tend to have a high capacity for coordinating complexity. American firms are more innovative, especially on advanced levels of applied science and knowledge creation, than those of any other country in the world. However, they tend not to be as good in areas where labor is central or where close relationships with the customer are important, such as automobiles, consumer durables, and consumer electronics.[125]

But this is not the whole story. In addition to corporations, there is a thriving entrepreneurial sector of small companies. American individualism, combining both self-reliance and antiauthority values, has produced wave after wave of innovation. Hence, paradoxically, American culture has produced both large bureaucratic organizations and small entrepreneurial ones. Strength in both areas is its greatest strength. Americans as a whole are both self-reliant *and* group oriented.

The explanation for this paradox is to be found in American civil society.[126] Civil society is a social arena where people organize and cooperate in more complex arrangements than the family, but independent of the government. Businesses as well as nonprofit educational, religious, medical, labor, and philanthropic organizations are examples of entities that operate in this "middle" or intermediate social space. Because of the traditional strength of civil society in the United States, Americans have been able to cultivate both individualism and trust in each other, what Fukuyama calls "spontaneous sociability," which allows them to create large private organizations.[127]

Countries that do not have a strong civil society must rely on government to create large organizations and play a significant role regulating the relations between them. The fact that Americans could create both large organizations structured on bureaucratic principles and small organizations driven by families and single entrepreneurs gave the economy significant decentralization

---

[125] Redding and Witt 2007.

[126] de Tocqueville 1969.

[127] These capacities and tendencies originated in sectarian Protestantism and the Enlightenment, where shared beliefs in both freedom and community developed (Fukuyama 1995). These doctrines gave the community substantially more authority than the family, compared with the reverse in China.

and diversity, making it highly adaptable and creative. Historically, these attributes have been a key source of American competitiveness. In the last half century or so, however, American civil society has weakened due to excessive individualism and what Edward Shils calls "collectivistic liberalism," a set of beliefs that emphasizes the role of the government at the expense of civil society.[128]

2. *American Business Ethics.* Americans arrive in China with their own traditions of business ethics, though these traditions vary and are far from consistent.[129] Ethics in business quickly involves the businessperson in questions of trade-offs, where difficult, values-based decisions are required. There is very little consensus on how to rank these values. Margolis and Walsh argue that the neoclassical economic view of the firm as a legal entity with legal responsibilities is the dominant model.[130] Milton Friedman is the most influential proponent of this model.[131] One key ethical assumption in this model is that the purpose of business is to maximize profits for its owners, constrained only by the law and specifically avoiding fraud and deception. Other than that, the firm has no "social responsibilities." After all, the firm is already paying taxes, employing citizens, and producing goods and services for societal consumption. If society needs more help with social problems or environmental issues, the government is responsible, not business.

The main competitor of the neoclassical business ethics model is "stakeholder theory,"[132] which argues that the firm is dependent on the participation of its stakeholders—employees, customers, stockholders, communities, suppliers, governments, and others—and it is the ethical responsibility of management to make decisions that balance the interests of the various stakeholders. This line of reasoning suggests that democratic values should be the moral basis of the firm. Though prominent in the field of business ethics education, stakeholder theory has not displaced the private-property, legal-responsibility view in business education generally, let alone in business practice.

---

[128] Shils (1997) argues that the expansion of the government to solve "social problems" has often weakened social networks, and the considerable expansion of "rights" has pushed "emancipationism" to the point of undermining community. At some point the promotion of diversity in organizations, for example, undermines the shared moral culture that is needed for trust and thus cooperation and commitment.

[129] Hollender 2004.

[130] Margolis and Walsh 2003.

[131] Friedman 1970.

[132] Freeman 1984.

A third view of American business ethics focuses on the role of business in American society and culture. Because of the early influence of Protestant moralism and the central role business plays in the American way of life, Americans have always expected businesses to act with a high level of social responsibility.[133] No other capitalist nation is as persistent or as intense in its moral concern for business conduct as the United States. But despite these high standards, a gap exists between theory and practice. Americans routinely enter the competitive arena of business with great ambition and often ignore their own moral beliefs. Nonetheless, American moral expectations for business have led to a plethora of laws to regulate business that are strictly enforced. In addition, American journalists aggressively seek to expose business corruption. The result is that many more businesses are exposed for unethical and illegal practices than in other countries.

There is a second reason for the legalistic approach to business ethics in the United States. Even though Americans see the individual as the central source of business responsibility, not the group or the corporation, they also see the individual as autonomous and free to choose her own value commitments. So instead of indoctrination, Americans rely heavily on the law to represent collective interests. The United States has the most lawyers and is the most litigious society in the world. Ironically, then, despite positing its values as universal, liberal individualism leads to conflict.

In practice, because of the ambiguity that results from the lack of agreed-upon moral standards for business, many executives use the law as their "ethical" standard to resolve the ambiguity and work within the lowest level of constraint. Internationally, this means the Foreign Corrupt Practices Act of 1977, which makes it a crime to bribe foreign officials. Because of their accustomed legal approach to business, many Americans abroad find themselves bitter and disoriented when they are unable to resolve their conflicts through a foreign legal system.

3. Western Perceptions of Chinese Business Ethics. Western managers working in China see the business ethics environment as very challenging. In a study of 31 Australian managers in China, Brand and Slater found that virtually every manager cited "considerable and often significant examples of corruption."[134] In this environment, it is inevitable that Western companies will

---

[133] Vogel 1992.
[134] Brand and Slater 2003: 12.

suffer losses due to corruption. MNCs in particular complain that because they are required as a matter of corporate policy not to engage in corruption worldwide, they lose significant profits in China.[135] Western managers find themselves in moral conflicts because they cannot reconcile Western codes of ethics with the demands of doing business in China.

Westerners complain that the Chinese think it is "morally okay to rip off foreigners—it is almost sport," according to one manager.[136] Some Westerners are not quick to understand the dangers. They arrive in a foreign culture intending to be polite and respectful, but it turns out they are also gullible to local Chinese who are "good at hoodwinking expats."[137] In general, the Chinese see foreigners as wealthy and in China to exploit the Chinese.[138] For the Chinese, the traditional rule of reciprocity does not apply to foreigners.

In the literature, Westerners have given a variety of explanations as to why the Chinese environment is so corrupt, several of them cultural. One is the distinction between friend and stranger in Chinese culture. The Chinese will do anything to help a friend, but "if they don't know you, you are worthless."[139] Loyalty is particularly strong in family relationships; for instance, Western executives are often asked to find employment for relatives of current employees. Another explanation is that the Chinese only focus on consequences; they have little regard for rules. So if there is an advantage to be had, rules will be bent. Third, the Chinese are subject to shame if caught doing something wrong in front of others, unlike in the West, where internalized rules can create guilt in the individual when the rules are broken. As a result, McGregor reported, "the Chinese can feel pretty good about doing almost anything as long as they don't get caught,"[140] from which he concluded that Chinese culture leads to the need for a strong state.[141] A fourth cultural explanation for Chinese corruption deals with the reciprocity rule. Most managers in Hutchings and Murray's study said that although they were able to refuse requests for bribes, they still had to provide services or purchase goods for

---

[135] Hutchings and Murray 2003.
[136] Hutchings and Murray 2002: 6.
[137] Hutchings and Murray 2002: 6.
[138] Smart 1993.
[139] Hutchings and Murray 2003: 7.
[140] J. McGregor 2005: 11.
[141] Alternatively, a predatory state may have undermined the development of shared values through its policy of isolating families and discouraging the development of autonomous communities.

anything the Chinese did for them if they wanted to maintain ongoing relations.[142]

Some Western managers do not subscribe to cultural explanations, instead simply believing the Chinese are corrupt.[143] Some British managers reported a belief that the rapid change in Chinese society had led to a decline in morality.[144]

Western managers reported encountering several different types of corruption. In Brand and Slater's study, bribery was the type most often mentioned.[145] Millington, Eberhardt, and Wilkinson found that 70–80 percent of British suppliers gave Chinese purchasing managers vouchers or ATM cards in exchange for purchasing their products.[146] According to Western managers, Chinese purchasing managers at Western companies think these types of "gifts" are justifiable. Through "gifts," the salaries of Chinese employees can increase by 200–300 percent. Relatedly, costs of inputs for MNCs can triple. More than 65 percent of the MNCs surveyed found or suspected under-the-table activities in their purchasing departments.[147]

Western managers, try to defend against corruption in multiple ways. In terms of stopping kickbacks, Western firms fire violators, develop supplier approval procedures, require more than one employee to sign off on purchases, rotate staff to curtail relationship building, split up sourcing and purchasing into two different departments, and require non-Chinese managers to approve supplier selection and countersign purchase orders.[148] Steidlmeier recommended offering training in valuable skills such as marketing in place of bribes or using the fact that bribes are against Chinese law to argue against them.[149] The latter suggestion is basically an effort at enlightenment according to Western values. It is similar to attempts to convince the Chinese that respecting Western IP rights is to their advantage.

Finally, Western managers reported widespread abuse of IP rights. To defend against it, Lieberthal and Lieberthal recommended keeping critical

---

[142] Hutchings and Murray 2003.
[143] Hutchings and Murray 2003.
[144] Millington, Eberhardt, and Wilkinson 2005.
[145] Brand and Slater 2003.
[146] Millington, Eberhardt, and Wilkinson 2005.
[147] Millington, Eberhardt, and Wilkinson 2005.
[148] Millington, Eberhardt, and Wilkinson 2005.
[149] Steidlmeier 1999.

technologies and production processes that can be pirated out of China, compartmentalizing production know-how, using wholly foreign-owned enterprises instead of joint ventures (JVs), and automating the manufacturing of complex products.[150] Ultimately, however, due to reverse engineering it will be difficult to stop IP theft until the Chinese want to play by the same rules as the West.

4. *Western Management in China.* Australian managers described their experience with *guanxi* as follows:

> Nobody does anything for nothing. Even where something is entirely legal and granted through policy with an official signature, you need to know how the favor is expected to be reciprocated. . . .
>
> You must pay back +1. In China you do not know where you stand but must remember who you owe. It starts with lunches and karaoke and builds from there—the Chinese will not do business with you until the barriers are down.[151]

These Australian managers felt that *guanxi* is more relevant to small businesses than large ones. They said it is of little relevance to MNCs; in fact, it is not much different from the need to develop good relationships in Australia. For small firms, however, *guanxi* is vital. The Australians' explanation for this difference is that large firms automatically have *guanxi* (that is, have access to networks) because of their resources, whereas small firms have to build relationships. Australian executives also believe that as the Chinese private sector has expanded, the importance of *guanxi* has declined for larger companies.

With all the ambiguities and challenges of the Chinese marketplace, it is not surprising that some Western executives have negative views of the Chinese. Two Australian managers commented,

> The Chinese are the most racist country on Earth – they are tough people . . . like a separate race. They are not Westernized at all. The stupidity of these people is difficult. They are brought up as followers, not leaders.
>
> You need to form strategic drinking alliances. Chinese do not trust Westerners—they were clapping in our office after the September 11 incident in the United States. They are a very racist people—their

---

[150] Lieberthal and Lieberthal 2003.
[151] Hutchings and Murray 2003: 10.

government policy is as well. Negotiations are frustrating—they are trying to rip you off because you are a Westerner.[152]

Yet with all the difficulty and animosity, 95 percent of the largest 500 firms in the world have set up operations in China, some of them very profitable.[153] General Motors, for example, sells more vehicles in China than anywhere else in the world.[154] But there are other reasons Western firms flock to China. A Goldman Sachs portfolio manager has predicted that China will have the largest economy in the world by 2027 or sooner.[155] Another argument about the importance of China is that it is a "lead market,"[156] meaning that China is not only a major opportunity for profit but also a potential threat that can be ignored only at one's peril. MNCs must defend their market positions in China to stop upstart Chinese firms from developing experience, cost advantages, and scale in China and then spreading worldwide. Already there is consolidation among Chinese firms, often with government support, with powerful global firms, like Haier and Huawei, emerging. Competing against these firms in China is no easy matter, since not only do they often have government protection but they also have language, culture, and connection advantages. It is argued, though, that Western firms have little choice since soon enough they will be competing with Chinese firms worldwide.

This difficult and demanding situation calls for cultural adaptation on the part of Western firms. Some Australian managers living in China became attuned to the culture and accepted it.[157] To a considerable extent, the managers in Hutchings and Murray's study self-selected to go to China.[158] This would more often than not predispose them to arrive with a positive attitude toward Chinese society and the challenges it presents. On the other hand, many of the managers in the Hutchings and Murray study came from small and medium-sized companies with less international experience than the MNCs and were therefore more apt to be surprised by what they encountered.

The Australian managers in Hutchings and Murray's study found burdensome the continuous banquets and drinking that were necessary to develop

---

[152] Hutchings and Murray 2003: 10.
[153] Moody 2012.
[154] *Bloomberg* (August 28, 2011).
[155] O'Neill 2011.
[156] Gadiesh, Leung, and Vestring 2007; Perkowski 2012.
[157] Brand and Slater 2003.
[158] Hutchings and Murray 2002.

relationships with Chinese executives.[159] In Australia the business focus is on business success, but with the Chinese a much higher priority was placed on enacting the correct social process. The Chinese were less impatient with the process, less focused on immediate results.

On a deeper level, Western managers confront two particularly difficult challenges. One is the lack of trust between the two cultures. Some of the central causes of mistrust are the Chinese memory of foreign exploitation in the 19th and 20th centuries, the pronounced antagonism with the West during the Mao era, and the current environment of corruption in the China market. Another problem is cultural distance. The two cultures have trouble understanding each other, a difficulty made worse when a translator is involved. Conversations take place in which neither side knows what the other side really means. Westerners have tried to address the trust problem through audits and contracts. Since Western firms have arrived, there has been explosive growth in the number of external audits.[160] Contracts present their own difficulties of enforcement.

After trust, the other big cultural challenge has been the Chinese cultural complex of "face." Managers in Hutchings and Murray's study thought Chinese face was markedly different than anything they had experienced in other parts of the world.[161] Face is a form of social standing in the group with significant social, political, economic, and psychological implications. In Chinese culture, one needs to be conscious of giving face (adding to the status of another), saving face (protecting another's public reputation), and above all avoiding causing loss of face. To cause loss of face in business is to make it practically impossible to do further business with that individual. It also lowers one's own face because of the damage to one's network. Westerners not only arrive in China unaware of the subtleties of face, but they can also overdo it by exaggerating their expressions of respect.

Sometimes it is nearly impossible to do business in China because of language, culture, government, social, corruption, and regulatory challenges. This is where the middleman comes in, a Chinese person who speaks both languages and has connections, strong entrepreneurial drive, and experience. The middleman can dramatically reduce transaction costs, especially in regard

---

[159] Hutchings and Murray 2003.
[160] Firth, Mo, and Wong 2005.
[161] Hutchings and Murray 2003.

to the time it takes to reach agreement with suppliers, government, and others.[162]

There are, however, important ethical issues involved in using middlemen. First of all, one of the core purposes of the middleman, beyond communicating in Chinese and utilizing an already developed network, is the paying of bribes, particularly to government officials.[163] Indeed, McGregor reports that contracts with middlemen are limited to one copy printed with black ink on red paper, making it impossible to photocopy.[164] Higher-level American executives are routinely not told about these arrangements so they can deny knowledge of them. The bribes paid through middlemen can involve anything from prostitutes to gambling to large cash payments to damaging the business prospects of a competitor.

Other forms of Western corruption in China are not unknown. According to Park and Vanhonacker, two-thirds of MNCs that claim to be losing money in China are using transfer pricing mechanisms to take profits out of the country.[165] One American tactic is to overcharge JVs for technology and book profits in the United States, while claiming losses on the JV. These types of mechanisms lower the amount of taxes owed to the Chinese government. In 2012, Avon Products, Inc., fired its vice chairman (it had fired four executives in 2011) when it found out the company was paying bribes to government officials.[166] AIG admitted its agents were illegally selling insurance policies in China.[167] When Morgan Stanley set up operations in China, it hired the inexperienced children of Communist leaders at multimillion-dollar salaries.[168]

More generally, the relationship between Western business and the Chinese government raises questions. The government is notoriously corrupt, especially at the provincial, city, and county levels. Officials are not paid enough to discourage corruption—and they cannot be, given the large number of officials.[169] In any case, the nature of government is such that no serious effort

[162] Smart 1993.
[163] Su and Littlefield 2001.
[164] J. McGregor 2005.
[165] Park and Vanhonacker 2007.
[166] Pavlo 2012.
[167] Park and Vanhonacker 2007.
[168] J. McGregor 2005.
[169] R. McGregor (2010) reports a conversation in 2007 in which a government minister reported he made $1,350 a month and a cabinet member $1,450 a month. These are very high-level officials.

has been made to stop official corruption. For government officials, the biggest worry is not getting caught taking bribes but the rise of new power cliques that will use the law to remove them from office, or worse, as a means to expand their territory.

Foreign businesses both benefit and suffer from government corruption. If they have good connections, they can benefit. Regardless, foreign business leaders, both Western and Asian, seldom criticize the Chinese government for its corruption[170] because they fear retaliation. Foreign business leaders seek stability and know pressing for political reform could upset the applecart. Even less so do foreign business leaders criticize China's political repression. Madsen says American business leaders justify their silence by arguing that they cannot do anything about it, so there is no point in damaging profitable business relations.[171] Morally, the argument is weak because it ignores the Americans' own Western values.

Cultural Differences in American-Chinese Business Relations

1. Two Very Different Thought-Worlds. In *The Geography of Thought: How Asians and Westerners Think Differently . . . and Why,* Richard E. Nisbett argues that Westerners and Asians not only have different world views, they literally view the world differently.[172] This section explores these different world views and different worlds. One fundamental difference that will appear over and over in different ways is Asian collectivism versus Western individualism. Asians emphasize harmony with others, not liberty. The world is seen as complicated—things are interrelated, connected not as pieces in a pie but as ropes in a net.[173] In this world, the person is defined through his or her relationships with others. Self-control is very important. Given the complexity of the world, control over outcomes is seen as difficult at best. Collective agency is highly valued. In fact, carrying out one's role in an organized hierarchical system is seen as the correct way. Virtue in this system is getting along with others; self-esteem is dependent on it. Success is group success.

---

[170] Shenkar and Yan 2002; Gamer 2003b.
[171] Madsen 1995.
[172] Nisbett 2003.
[173] Nisbett 2003.

In the West, things are different indeed. In Nisbett's words, "Westerners are protagonists of their autobiographical novels; Asians are merely cast members in movies touching on their experiences."[174] In Nisbett's research, American children refer to themselves three times more often than Chinese children. In another experiment, Americans worked best when they thought they were working alone; Chinese worked best when they thought they were working with others.

The differences go beyond social behavior. Western individualism leads Westerners to see reality in terms of their individual goals, blocking out much of the context. In attempting to discover reality, they work backward from the goals they want to achieve to causes that will achieve them. This leaves Westerners more likely than Asians to commit the fundamental attribution error, exaggerating the importance of individual intention and overestimating the predictability of human behavior.[175] Americans do the same thing when trying to understand history; they start with the event and then work backward in search of a cause. This type of thinking reflects a people confident in their personal agency; it reflects a sense of individual centrality and control.

Since the Chinese see themselves in terms of others, they are more sensitive to context, complexity, relationships between parts, and tensions between parts. Their root metaphor is part/whole, not one/many as in the West.[176] For the Chinese, everything is connected; to get anything done others must be involved. For the West, objects are singular, like individuals, and can be manipulated by individuals. The Chinese have other views and strengths. They see the big picture. They are good at seeing relationships between events in their environments—so much so that they have difficulty seeing objects separately. Americans literally see fewer objects because of their focus on causal relationships between objects.

Since the Chinese tend not to see objects out of context, they tend not to generalize. The Chinese language is strikingly concrete, no "whiteness", only a white swan.[177] In tests, Asians found it hard to recognize changes in objects while Americans found it difficult to recognize changes in background. Hence, the Chinese tend to excel in applied sciences, where the individual

---

[174] Nisbett 2003: 87.

[175] Nisbett 2003.

[176] Nisbett 2003. A one/many organization of knowledge encourages inference from the single case; a part/whole organization does not.

[177] Nisbett 2003.

and concrete is key, but not in fields like philosophy, where abstraction is central.[178] Where Westerners can confidently make predictions about behavior based on abstract modeling independent of context, Asians are apt not to generalize but to seek reasonableness, common sense, plausibility, or typicality.

The difference between American abstract reason and Chinese concrete reasonableness has several other implications. Because the West developed a thought-world assuming individual objects, it developed the law of identity (*A* and *not–A* cannot be the same) and the law of noncontradiction (a proposition cannot be both true and false); whereas the Chinese, more focused on complexity and relationships, look at things dialectically: *A* and *not–A* have to get along with each other. When faced with a strong contradiction, Americans look for a rule to follow to decide what choice to make; Asians, on the other hand, look for compromise. The Asian preference for the middle way can weaken both logic and decision making; but the West's contradiction avoidance can lead to seeing things as black-and-white when in fact they are far from it.

2. Managerial Implications. The management literature comparing American and Chinese cultures focuses mostly on the different nature of hierarchical relations and the different emphasis on collectivism and individualism. Hwang describes the role of hierarchy:

> The Chinese national culture of social orientation consist[s] of conformity, unoffensive strategy, and submission to expectations and authority. . . . In comparison with their American counterparts, Chinese subjects tend to be less autonomous . . . more submissive . . . more conforming . . . more subservient to authority . . . and more susceptible to the influence of powerful others.[179]

As can be seen in the following studies, several implications follow from these different orientations to hierarchy. In a study of 523 subjects (150 Chinese employees in SOEs, 50 Chinese employees in Sino-American and Sino-French FIEs, 150 American expatriates, and 73 French expatriates), the FIE and SOE employees scored highest for a dominating style of management.[180]

---

[178] Hofstede et al. 2010.

[179] Hwang 1987: 959. Kleinman (2010) argues, however, that under pressure of globalization the Chinese are becoming more individualistic and overtly self-interested.

[180] He, Zhu, and Peng 2002.

Americans scored lowest for power-distance (a measure of dependency). In another study of 604 managers from the United States, Russia, Japan, and China, Chinese managers had the highest score for submission to authority and the lowest score for self-direction.[181]

Related to the different attitudes toward hierarchy is the collectivism-individualism dimension. Of the 76 countries in Hofstede's study of collectivism, the United States ranked 1 (least) and China ranked 60.[182] The Chinese word for *role* is *fen*, meaning "portion or share of the whole."[183] This contrasts strongly with the American idea of *role*, which assigns role status to the individual; the *individual* assumes the role expectations while maintaining a distinct set of rights as an individual. The hierarchical structure of Chinese society suppresses individualism, while the emphasis on individualism in American society limits collective attachment.

He, Zhu, and Peng found the Chinese were less open than Americans to the free exchange of information and to satisfying all parties in a conflict.[184] In other words, the Chinese have very strong subgroup boundaries, whereas Americans are more open to the broader community. A key reason for this difference is the way individuals make attachments in the two societies. In picking "friends," the Chinese use a nonobjective combination of cost, quality, and relationship, with different elements interpreted differently at different times.[185] The "personality" of the person is a less important concern for the social evaluation of the individual. This relates back to the hierarchical nature of Chinese society. Hierarchy puts a premium on knowing others in important positions to acquire favors and resources. Americans, in contrast, rely more on personal qualities to develop relationships because in a more individualistic society these qualities enhance cooperation and communication.

Ironically, even though the Chinese pick their "friends" for pragmatic reasons, these relationships tend to become more personal and long-lasting compared with those of Americans. Americans rely on contracts and ownership rights to regulate exchanges with business partners, but the Chinese rely

---

[181] Ralston et al. 1997.

[182] Hofstede 1984.

[183] Bell 2000.

[184] He, Zhu, and Peng 2002.

[185] Hwang 1987. This analysis applies to the third circle of *guanxi* relationships, not the first circle of family relations or the second circle of relatives, classmates, and the like.

on personal connections.[186] Interpersonal trust based on reciprocity is key in Chinese business relations and without it, business is difficult to conduct. Relationships take longer to develop than in the West and tend to be more binding.[187] American networking is more fluid and based on short-term expediency, resulting in higher uncertainty, even litigation.[188] The courts in China are inconsistent and unpredictable, encouraging the Chinese to fall back on personal relationships to lower their risk.

Because the Chinese personalize business relations as opposed to relying on contracts, the Chinese are more particularistic than Americans, who rely more on rules and principles.[189] This difference leads to different decision-making styles in the two countries. In a study of fiction, Weber, Ames, and Blais found that the involvement of recognized others inhibits calculation-based decision making in Chinese but not American novels.[190] In other words, Chinese novels promote the value of protecting one's friends. Furthermore, calculation-based decision making results in fewer bad decisions in American novels, whereas in Chinese novels it always leads to bad outcomes. The importance of social context hints at the complexity of decision making in Chinese business, as the effects of decisions on various layers of relationships and networks, many long term, must be considered.[191] This contrasts with American business decisions, where the impersonal nature of both financial discipline and bureaucratic control sharply limit emotional and social commitments, and long-term considerations as well. The different styles of decision making also reflect the institutional environment, for in China environmental uncertainty leaves Chinese executives highly risk averse (compared with Americans), embedding themselves deeply in social networks to blunt the effects of rapid change, fierce competition, and a predatory government.

3. Conflict Management. Americans go to court to resolve conflicts more often than residents of any other country in the world. In contrast, the

---

[186] Boisot and Child 1996.

[187] Hutchings and Murray 2003.

[188] Boisot and Child 1996. Hsu (1981) argues that American self-reliance accounts for the transitory nature of relationships: Americans seek to reduce the number of restraints, abandoning one set of relationships when a new set is taken up.

[189] Chen, Chen, and Xin 2004.

[190] Weber, Ames, and Blais 2004.

[191] Indeed, a significant amount of management attention goes toward meeting agreements and maintaining interpersonal relations (Redding and Witt 2007).

Chinese use mediators. In fact, there are more mediators per 100 individuals in China than there are lawyers per 100 individuals in the United States.[192]

Not only is mediation important in China, but the type of mediation differs strikingly from that used in the United States. The Chinese avoid confrontation during mediation because it would violate their overriding belief in social harmony.[193] The American overriding belief in equality, however, allows the open expression of disagreement during conflict resolution. In hierarchical Chinese society it would lead to an unacceptable loss of face. Individualistic Americans, on the other hand, are quite willing to sacrifice harmony for fairness.[194]

American mediation also assumes the open pursuit of self-interest, which leads to confrontation and competition, behaviors the Chinese would see as selfish and that would also lead to a loss of face. The Chinese are unlikely to express their true thoughts publicly.[195] Chinese executives tend to avoid public conflict to the point of making false promises or just withdrawing from the problem altogether. In addition, the Chinese tend to become emotional during disagreements, perhaps because their feelings are so often tightly controlled, leading to outbursts.

For these reasons, the Chinese take their conflicts to middlemen, whose goal is not fairness but restoration of harmony. So for the Chinese, two people in negotiation are seen as an incomplete structure because they are vulnerable to win-lose or lose-lose outcomes. Confucius says whenever there are three persons, there is always a teacher.[196] The mediator is seen as a teacher. She is there to remind the conflicting parties that their views will be evaluated in terms of the community. The emphasis on the community is quite different than American conflict resolution, which seeks to integrate interests, not maintain relations.[197] Americans tend to focus on each side's underlying interests, synthesizing multiple interests to produce a creative resolution by balancing gains on high-priority issues with losses on low-priority issues. The Chinese tend to focus less on interests than on the social network and especially the preferences of high-status individuals within the network.[198]

---

[192] Jia 2002.
[193] Jia 2002.
[194] Nisbett 2003.
[195] Chow and Ding 2002.
[196] Jia 2002.
[197] Chow and Ding 2002.
[198] Outside of these networks, however, the Chinese engage more easily in conflict with strangers than do Americans (He, Zhu, and Peng 2002).

In the process of resolving conflict between two parties through the vortex of the broader social network, the Chinese concept of face is of central practical importance. If the middleman fails to resolve the conflict, all three parties will lose face—indeed, will lose significant status in the network.[199] If the network sends in its own representatives to mediate and they fail, the network will lose face with the state. Normally, the parties in the conflict will resolve or pretend to resolve the conflict to avoid loss of face and the anxiety that goes with it, and/or to protect the loss of face of more powerful patrons in the network. In the United States, there is much less concern for a harmonious outcome; instead, the goal is to remove the conflict and let the parties resume their individual interests. The whole emphasis on the relational network is much less pronounced.

For the Chinese, managing face in the process of conflict resolution means that all the "right" relations are maintained; that is, each person receives the deference he deserves given his place in the hierarchical system.[200] When the "right" relation is challenged, the person challenged cannot respond directly because this would be a lowering, a loss of face. This is why middlemen are indispensable and their practices are indirect and behind the scenes. Regardless, when slights to face are experienced in a conflict, it can make the conflict enormously difficult to resolve. Such is the case when self-esteem is held publicly, that is, when collectivism is the dominating organizing principle for culture.

4. Joint Ventures. JVs have declined since the Chinese government began to permit wholly foreign-owned firms in China. In 1985, JVs accounted for 35 percent of foreign direct investment; in 2010, they accounted for 26 percent.[201] Another reason there has been a decline in JVs is that they do not work very well; they create a lot of conflict and usually produce unimpressive financial results. McGregor describes the typical JV as based on completely divergent visions, resulting in destructive internal politics.[202] The Chinese tend to ignore the rules set up when the JV is created, and the Americans, in a rush to get into China, do not bother to do the groundwork for a successful JV; most importantly, Americans usually do not take the time to develop relationships and a shared vision. Often this haste infuriates the

---

[199] Jia 2002.
[200] Gamer 2003a.
[201] This represents 5,270 projects in 2010 (The U.S.-China Business Council 2012).
[202] J. McGregor 2005.

Chinese, but the Americans are unaware of this because they misinterpret Chinese politeness as agreement.

From the Chinese side, they do not trust the Americans.[203] They think the Americans are trying to take advantage of them. The purpose of a JV as the Chinese see it is to bring capital, business expertise, and technology to China.[204] The Chinese expect that as the natural result of the learning process, control of the JV will go to or be taken by them.[205] The foreigners, on the other hand, often feel Chinese management skills are so poor that if given control they would destroy the JV in short order. The Chinese government is always involved in the formation of JVs. Its goal is to build up Chinese manufacturing capabilities and supply chains, for which the country needs foreign help, but the government has no intention of allowing foreign firms to dominate an industry.[206] Foreign firms, on the other hand, want access to the huge Chinese market.[207] They know they are training future competitors, but for one reason or another the JV is the best option for entering the Chinese marketplace. Hence, for both sides the JV is a compromise right from the beginning, and both sides understand that more than likely the arrangement is temporary, though the exact life span is unclear.

Another issue is conflicting interests among the different levels of government involved. While the central government is trying to develop the economy, local governments can have much more parochial interests. These interests get played out through local executives who represent the local government in the JV, leading to conflicts with the foreigners, who are focused only on the JV's business prospects. Since the local governments have powers and resources needed by the JV, the JV as a whole can be undermined and its assets used for other purposes, benefiting the JV's Chinese executives and their allies in the local government.

Many other conflicts emerge between Chinese and foreign JV partners. MNCs sometimes want to reinvest profits to expand domestically, while the Chinese either want to earn foreign exchange through export or merely

---

[203] Yan and Gray 1994.

[204] J. McGregor 2005.

[205] A "squeeze-out" of the Western partner is sometimes part of the original plan (*Economist* September 3, 2011).

[206] Recently, the Chinese government has demanded "indigenous brand" JVs with rights to technology and exports (*Economist* September 3, 2011).

[207] China was the largest car market in the world in 2011 and its expansion is expected to continue, for example (Terlep 2012).

dominate the local market, in either case taking profits out.[208] A second conflict is that MNCs want continuous performance improvement, while the Chinese, sensitive to government goals, seek ways to maintain or expand the labor force. A third conflict is that the Chinese are desperate to bring the latest technology into China, while foreign firms are desperate to protect their IP by either not bringing it in or searching for ways to keep it out of Chinese hands. A fourth conflict involves different business styles.[209] Western firms insist on signing contracts to clarify terms and verify commitment. The Chinese see contracts as an expression of distrust toward them and unwillingness on the part of MNCs to commit to long-term relationships.

Fifth, American firms do not understand the political needs of Chinese JV executives. Chinese executives must show the government that the JV is contributing to China's economic reforms so they can win promotions in the public-private Chinese system.[210] The American executives primarily focus on the business aspects of the JV. In general, Western executives and Chinese executives do not understand each other very well. Many times there is so much haggling over the structure of the JV that by the time it is established the relationship is already damaged.[211] Language itself can be a problem. When translators are used, the translators can inject their own interests and the interests of their families into the negotiations.

Sixth, even when the structure is established to the satisfaction of both partners, the agreement is unstable. Over time substantial learning by one partner or both leads to a reevaluation of each side's needs as well as to what the other side has to offer.[212] Satisfaction with the original agreement decreases, resulting in increasing demands. If a process of renegotiation is not assumed up front, the JV soon falls apart.

All this conflict and misunderstanding inflames what is a power imbalance to begin with. At one JV, the Chinese referred to the American CEO as

---

[208] Lieberthal and Lieberthal 2003.

[209] Su and Littlefield 2001.

[210] The reason a number of JVs in the car industry appear to be doing well is that the senior Chinese executive does not rock the boat, satisfied with employment and profit levels as he waits to return to a government post (*Economist* September 3, 2011). This alignment of interests is rare and perhaps happens because the high-profile car industry receives ample attention from the central government.

[211] Shenkar and Yan 2002.

[212] Yan and Gray 1994.

"General Patton."[213] Maintaining face is extremely important to the Chinese, yet the Americans have the know-how, the technology, and much of the capital. The Chinese expect to be treated as equals even if they are not. Chinese feelings of inferiority in this situation need to be addressed, but few American firms do so. Chinese executives are caught between feelings of inferiority in front of MNC executives and fears of change in Beijing that might paint them as corrupt. This inevitably leads to secrecy on their part—not a good base for developing a relationship with their new partners.

Conclusion

It is an interesting irony that *guanxi*, the socially intense system of informal relationships that undercuts and reverses formal Chinese institutions, is itself a subcategory of the central principle of Chinese culture, hierarchy. *Guanxi*, in a word networking, connects the individual to a social network of "friends" who can be called upon for favors when needed. These social networks, however, pay tribute to the status of their members. The social status of each member in the broader community is respected within the social network. Yet the exact purpose and function of *guanxi* is to bypass formal hierarchical systems, institutions, and demands for obedience in the broader society. These intense obligations of respect, required and mapped out in detail in innumerable interpersonal rituals and mannerisms, make efficient action difficult. *Guanxi* addresses this problem by enabling relationships to develop new types of bonds based on trust and mutual advantage and thus new channels for action. *Guanxi*, then, is an outgrowth of hierarchy that simultaneously turns back against it, undermining its directives while maintaining its integrity. It maintains its integrity by both respecting hierarchical status within *guanxi* networks and contributing efficiency to rigid hierarchical structures.

Western businesspeople walking into this system find it difficult to master because they see only two opposite extremes. Many times they experience only chaos. On one hand, the Confucian principle of hierarchy is nowhere more observable than in the government-society relationship. The government is authoritarian and makes extensive if not enormous demands on business, some portion of which can be classified as abuse of power. On the other

[213] J. McGregor 2005.

hand, every rule the government passes, every demand it makes, can be gotten around with the right connections. So simultaneous with the enormous power of the state is a system of relationships that regularly ignores state edicts. Indeed, state officials are right at the center of this system, playing both sides as loyal bureaucrats, "friends," and rent-seeking individuals.

Some of the main disadvantages Westerners face in this situation are their language, culture, and outsider status, leaving them less than expert players in the *guanxi* system, which, for all practical purposes, is an escape hatch in a hierarchical society. Here enters the third party, the Chinese middleman. Westerners, especially big companies that can put steep incentives into play, work with Chinese middlemen, utilizing their already developed networks. So, for example, if an SOE is not paying its bills, a Western firm can ask its middleman "friend" to contact his friend in the provincial ministry to put pressure on the SOE to pay its bills. If the minister sees the Western firm as potentially helpful to his own goals, all the better. In this way, the Western firm, through the middleman, has entered a *guanxi* network. Without the middleman this would have been nearly impossible. The fact that the Western firm is able to utilize the *guanxi* network shows the utilitarian aspect of *guanxi*. It is not all bonding, brotherhood, and obligation.

Perhaps the most important aspect of this situation is the *rule of three*. There is the Western firm, the middleman, and the government official. The dyad, a direct relationship between the Western firm and the official, is highly unlikely. An essential aspect of *guanxi* is that for A to win a favor from B, many times a third party, C, is needed. This need for a third party demonstrates the intense personalization and informalization of collective action in China; it also highlights the lack of trust and fear of dishonesty.

The rule of three grows out of the collectivist nature of Chinese society. Individuals attach themselves to groups and work through groups. This is a corollary to the *guanxi* principle. The hierarchical nature of Chinese society strongly limits individualism in the Western sense, instead channeling individual effort informally into groups and networks. Both hierarchy and its resistant child, *guanxi*, are forms of collectivism. The difference is that hierarchy, in pursuing collective goals as decided upon by top leaders, gives rise to informal, secretive *guanxi* networks to accommodate individual and outgroup interests, though these networks still operate collectively and hierarchically.

It cannot be otherwise because all Chinese cultural forms emanate from the principle of hierarchy, even *guanxi*, which directly challenges it. Hierarchy infiltrates *guanxi* through the principle of face. Face is the status one has in the network. It is extremely important in regulating interpersonal relations. A person of a certain status has expectations for how he should be treated. If these expectations are not met, conflict will result.

This is why the rule of three is so important in Chinese culture. A third party can enter into a dyadic relationship, separating the two parties and damping down the emotions, helping to manage and safeguard delicate and sensitive issues of face. Face is the blood of collectivism, infusing and enforcing hierarchical status throughout the social body. The middleman too is thus part of the hierarchical and collectivist system, ensuring its smooth functioning by creating distance and indirectness, social forms badly needed in the rigid and conflict-prone nature of hierarchy.

For Westerners, profoundly dependent on the use of middlemen in Chinese business, middlemen do more than offer connections and translations, they also manage issues of face to avoid an escalation of conflict between Westerners and Chinese. Westerners are typically ill equipped to be sensitive to the face needs and expectations of Chinese executives. The middleman can take the intention of the Westerner and formulate it such that it is acceptable to the Chinese, in terms of not just economic value but also social form. Western culture and Chinese culture are so different that both sides are typically made anxious by the ambiguity and foreignness of the other. The middleman, speaking both languages and having familiarity with both cultures, reduces this vulnerability to miscommunication and stress.

One area of particular importance and especially liable to conflict is that of ethical norms. The middleman is hired to take the Western firm into a *guanxi* network that exists exactly for the purpose of avoiding rules, laws, taxes, and regulations. The legally minded Westerners are disinclined to enter the Chinese no-rule-unbent universe directly for several reasons, not least of which is liability to prosecution under the Foreign Corrupt Practices Act. Bribery, the central form of corruption in China, is handed off to the middleman so American executives can wash their hands of it.

The middleman, then, is a bit of a magician. He can involve American firms in business transactions that require bribery even though the American firms have specific laws and policies against paying bribes. The expectations of Chinese officials or managers are met even though they directly and fully contradict the requirements of the Americans. The middleman operates between two cultures and, in a sense, in no culture. His specialty is having no cultural allegiance while participating in two different cultures. Thus

American and Chinese business cultures are paradoxically connected and remote. From the American side, the paradox makes apparent the breakdown of American ethics, because ultimately the bribes are paid. The "magical" middleman in the "middle" transforms American business values into Chinese business practices. In reality, he creates a social conduit through which money flows but the law does not follow.

Thus when American firms utilize the rule of three, which they regularly do, they are participating deeply in Chinese culture. This is evidence, contrary to the view of Guthrie for example, that Western firms in China are more influenced by Chinese business culture than the reverse. This is an empirical question that requires more research and also time to answer. In any case, the rule of three has Western firms adapting to and participating in Chinese business culture. Using middlemen is accepting a teacher, someone who instructs and educates Western firms on how to do business in China. Using a middleman is not merely an impersonal transaction. It is a dependent, appreciative, and many times long-term relationship. In other words, it involves social and psychological elements of Chinese culture.

If ascribed *guanxi*, relations based on goodwill and compassion, and achieved *guanxi*, relations based on calculation and self-interest, are seen as two ideal end points by which to evaluate informal business relationships, Western relations with middlemen usually will mark out closer to the achieved pole. Given that *guanxi* relations are often used to avoid formal rules or change them, it is difficult to see how achieved *guanxi* can be morally justified. Indeed, Snell and Tseng lament that the large increase in achieved *guanxi* during the "privatization" process in the 1990s was dishonorable—that is, based merely on self-interest while hurting the broader society.[214] Unlike ascribed *guanxi*, which builds community by bringing moral values like benevolence, reciprocity, and caring into the relationship, achieved *guanxi* does not have any such moral counterweight to offset its self-interested, anti-government, and anticommunity intentions. Western involvement in *guanxi* relations, since they are seldom of the ascribed *guanxi* sort, therefore raises moral questions.

But even if Westerners were to develop ascribed *guanxi* relations, can these relationships really be morally justified given that they operate only on the subgroup level? In the West, core values—freedom of speech, equal

---

[214] Snell and Tseng 2001.

opportunity, the right to vote, privacy, equality before the law, and so on—are considered "human" rights and thus are considered morally universal. *Guanxi*, on the contrary, is exactly designed to give insiders more rights than others. Thus, *guanxi* and universal rights are incompatible. Hence even ascribed *guanxi* cannot be morally justified according to the principle of universalization.

In practice, however, the principle of universalization does not work perfectly even in the West. Clearly, people with money or power have better opportunities in the marketplace or better chances in court, for example. Is there really such a big difference between *guanxi* and "human rights" as they are *practiced* in the West? Yes, there is. In the West, failures to honor human rights are continually debated and efforts are made to improve them; in the *guanxi* system, honoring relationship over principle is the nature of the system.

This is the difference between a democratic culture and a hierarchical one. The individualism inherent in a democratic culture pushes toward universal rights; this tendency is missing in a hierarchical society, which puts a much stronger emphasis on the whole. The problem is that *guanxi*, hierarchy's other half, undercuts and hurts the whole in favor of the subgroup. Though *guanxi* can lead to the development of strong bonds, bonds often missing in the West as individualism becomes an end in itself (narcissism) and leads to impersonalization and selfishness, the cost of *guanxi* is high, as is evident in widespread corruption and damage to public goods such as water and air in China. Even though *guanxi* addresses the evils of unchecked power, it merges with power and creates its own abuses.

It has often been noted that individualism too is prone to abuse, but, unlike hierarchical society, a democratic society is hedged around with checks and balances so that both public and private action are more subject to public, political, and legal review. In a hierarchical society, all processes of review are subordinate to one, the political. Hence, Western businesses operating in hierarchical societies cannot morally justify full participation in hierarchical culture without violating their own values. When they enter into *guanxi* relations, they may easily be entering into unethical activities according to their own beliefs.

This is not to say Western values are superior to Chinese values. The Chinese have low trust in impersonal relations and high trust in personal relations, while the West has higher trust in contracts and the ability to enforce them when they fail, and less reliance on personal relations. Is the latter "modern" and the former feudal or less developed? Is universalization the test of development and ethical superiority? Maybe so in the economic sphere, where the single criterion of efficiency can be used as a universal measure to evaluate action. But it is less true in the political sphere, where complex goals involving diverse values make universal (rational) criteria less relevant because continuously shifting contexts and multivalued actions make it impossible to universalize the criteria of evaluation.[215] Hence, since the economic and political spheres are interrelated, not to mention the value-laden religious, cultural, esthetic, and personal spheres, it is impossible to judge a social system merely according to its "modernization." Profound moral choices and trade-offs are involved in any life order, requiring moral evaluation to be multilayered.

In addition, it is important to keep in mind, when comparing Western and Chinese cultures, that there is much to respect in both. In hierarchical culture, the emphasis on social harmony and respect for others—especially parents, teachers, leaders, and elders—is noble and has good consequences. But, as was mentioned, hierarchical culture often leads in practice to abuse of power. Western culture relies more on formal structures such as laws and rules, not personal relations, to provide order in society. But just as *guanxi* can benefit the subgroup at the expense of the community, the expensive and overused legal system in the United States is evidence of a destructive (selfish) individualism that concerns itself little for the good of society. Neither Chinese collectivism nor American individualism lives up to its own ideals of the good society, particularly the need to care for the whole. Each society in its own way evidences an imbalance toward benefiting subgroups and individuals at a cost to others and the whole.

In the West, however, legal competition to address the imbalance works more effectively than does reliance on the good character of leaders in hierarchical culture. Institutionalized checks and balances have proven more reliable than the good graces of absolute power. On the other hand, hierarchical (Confucian) culture has made possible huge and densely populated cities, such as Shanghai and Beijing, where the crime rate is relatively low compared with that of New York, Chicago, or Los Angeles.

In the abstract, neither a culture developed around the core category of individualism or one developed around the core category of collectivism is superior to the other. Indeed, all cultures must have both categories. It is a

[215] Gellner 1992.

question of emphasis. In this regard, both China and the United States can learn from each other.

This conclusion does not remove the moral challenges faced by Western businessmen working in China. There is widespread corruption on the different levels of Chinese government, and the government represses its own citizens. Western businesspeople cannot morally ignore these facts if they are committed to the democratic values upon which Western societies are based. The argument that it is morally justifiable to do business in China because Western businessmen cannot do anything about the behavior of the Chinese government is not valid. One cannot support unethical activities without sharing some responsibility for them. Western business is, at a minimum, required to express its own values and protest values it finds unethical. One cannot benefit from business activities in China without taking some moral responsibility for them. Otherwise, Western business is caught in a contradiction between its own values and its behavior in China, undermining Western values for itself and others. Considering the risks of protesting is valid, but it is not sufficient. Moral deliberation involves multiple aspects; in addition to risks, responsibilities to and consequences for others must be considered.

Western businesspeople face a dilemma. China's growing role in international business, and the opportunities for and threats to Western business in China, make it nearly competitively impossible not to do business in China. Yet the moral challenges cannot morally be ignored. Ethics is not just a nice thing we should do if we can afford it. It is part of social reality and has concrete consequences. Ignoring Chinese government transgressions strengthens these transgressions at the same time that it weakens Western ethics. It encourages both the Chinese government and other governments to violate human rights and exercise unrestricted power, which can only contribute to the suffering of its people and a more dangerous world for everyone else. Poisoned food products and medicines coming out of China are not unrelated to government corruption in that they are the model for other types of corruption. Complete resolution of the dilemma is not possible; thus a compromise is called for. It should be worked out both collectively and individually by Western businesses. It should involve, at the least, a statement of principles that expresses Western business values, defines what practices are acceptable and what ones are not, and outlines sanctions for Western businesses that violate these principles.

8

Culture, Corruption, and Business in China

The Conflicting Worlds of American and Chinese Executives

Corruption in business is not unusual. Competition, the internal driver of business and much of the rest of life as well, puts a premium on deceit.[1] When business takes place away from one's home country, especially in the developing world, where differences in language, culture, business custom, and income levels are significant, the problem of corruption can become widespread and deep.[2] This means the costs can be punishing and the problems intractable, even to the point that it is not worth the candle.

The case of China is mixed. On the one hand, increasing numbers of American businesses are going to China and making ever-larger investments, trying to benefit from China's low manufacturing costs and high rate of economic growth; on the other hand, corruption in China is pervasive and costly.[3] This chapter investigates how the two business cultures perceive and manage the difficult opportunities between a growing market and corruption. In particular, it explores the different perceptions each culture has of the Chinese marketplace and of the role of business-to-business corruption in it, as well as how these perceptions affect business relations.

In the context of both general perceptions of corruption and specific issues such as bribery, kickbacks, stealing, misrepresentation, and dishonesty, the chapter examines the current American use of Chinese "middlemen" to pay bribes on their behalf. This practice is common, but its ethical significance has received very little attention. The phenomenon of the middleman is a strikingly rich aspect of a broader phenomenon in international business, what I call the "cultural middle." The cultural middle is the space between

---

[1] Knight 1997.
[2] Sanyal 2005.
[3] R. McGregor 2010; Sun 2004.

two dramatically different cultures, where communication, cooperation, and meaning must be negotiated if business between them is to take place. This chapter, therefore, focuses on what can be learned about the cultural middle under conditions of extensive corruption.

My approach to the study of business ethics is cultural.[4] This chapter therefore analyzes and evaluates both American and Chinese perceptions and behavior in terms of the ideational and emotional structures through which each group makes sense of its experience. For example, American views on the difference between a "bribe" and a "gift" in China are primarily determined by American corporate rules and American legal statutes. Chinese views, however, are primarily determined by a complex social philosophy of relationships.[5] As might be expected, the two different approaches do not lead to intercultural understanding.[6] This chapter analyzes the gift-versus-bribe data by explicating the cultural contexts of both American and Chinese executives, exploring the conflicts their different perspectives create.

The chapter has three main parts. First, it describes and analyzes American views and experiences of corruption in the China market, followed in the second section by a description and analysis of Chinese views of corruption in Chinese business. The end of this second section presents data from two university classes I taught on business ethics to Chinese students in Shanghai in 2007, analyzing the students' ethical preferences to provide some hint about the unfolding development of Chinese business culture. The analysis of both the American and the Chinese data includes quotations from interviews and observations so the reader can see the participants speak in their own words, followed by my interpretations of and commentary on these views.

The third section compares the American and Chinese data and my interpretations of them, surfacing and exploring intercultural conflicts, misunderstandings, dilemmas, and contrasts with the goal of discerning aspects of American-Chinese business relations that are hidden when looking at the relationship from only one side or the other. Concluding remarks address the challenges of intercultural business relations.

---

[4] Feldman 2004. See Chapter 2 for a review of the literature on international business ethics.

[5] Steidlmeier 1997.

[6] Su and Littlefield 2001.

American Perceptions of Business Corruption in China

I. General Perceptions of Corruption

1. Business in China as Ruleless. Many American executives experience the Chinese business environment as having few or no rules:

> Chinese culture is 5,000 years old so they must have some ethics. But it appears to me as if they do not follow any rules. . . . It's like crossing the street. Did you ever try crossing the street in Shanghai? You could get killed. They don't obey any rules. A senior Chinese executive told me I would understand China when I learned how to cross the street. You must look in every direction.
>
> (Mr. BD1)[7]

This executive has worked in many parts of the world. His comment that the Chinese do not follow any rules despite the great age of Chinese society is essential. He views China not as a country in the midst of extensive social change but as one that exists in a condition of chaos. The crossing-the-street symbol stresses the danger in the Chinese business environment. To protect oneself, one must look for danger in every direction. Further, this speaker implies that the Chinese are not comprehensible; their behavior is not rational or trustworthy.

2. China Market as the "Wild West." The metaphor used most often by American executives for the rulelessness of Chinese business is the "Wild West."[8]

> The '90s was like the Wild West. Anything could happen. In China it's unregulated. It's pure capitalism. Our capitalism formed over centuries. China had no history of capitalism. Enron is classic Chinese. It is more typical for China.
>
> (Mr. Am9)

---

[7] "BD" stands for Business Diary. Data in this diary are from observations at American facilities in Shanghai and other episodic data collection opportunities. Quotes attributed to Mr. Am or Ms. Ch, for example, are from semi-structured interviews. See Appendix 3 for more discussion of data collection.

[8] Metaphors have a surface meaning and a deep or hidden meaning (Turner 1974). Analysis can unpack the hidden meaning, bringing to light implicit aspects of social and psychological experience.

The "Wild West" symbol is culturally richer than the China-as-ruleless symbol. It brings to mind a chain of images of cowboys, gunfights, lawlessness, hardship, and self-reliance. It adds to the rulelessness motif the hardened individualism of the American frontier. Some American executives experience the Chinese business environment as consisting of rugged individuals who potentially must fight or flee to protect their plans and property. With business relations lacking regulation by a consistent application of the rule of law, some American executives experience the Chinese and themselves as cowboys.

Mr. Am9 describes China as like the Wild West in that it is "pure capitalism." Like Mr. BD1 above, who described Chinese business as ruleless, Mr. Am9 puts his perspective in historical terms: American capitalism is old, having formed over centuries, whereas Chinese capitalism is new. Historically, however, this is not true: Chinese capitalism is not new.[9] But the more relevant (and ironic) point is that the relatively young American nation is seen as old, while the ancient Chinese civilization is seen as young. The reversal is telling,[10] casting the Chinese as inferior to, or behind, the Americans. Indeed, Mr. BD1 and Mr. Am9 are both saying that since the Chinese do not play by American rules, they have no rules. Both offer a historical explanation for this conclusion, but neither portrays Chinese history accurately. The Americanization of Chinese history shows Americans needing to see China in their own shadow, as not measuring up to what some Americans see as universal values of freedom, democracy, and markets.[11]

Mr. Am9 makes a second reversal in his comment that Enron is more Chinese than American. He places American corruption in the American past (the Wild West) or in China ("Enron is classic Chinese"), based on an assumption that China is corrupt and America is not. Mr. Am9 is trying to make sense of his experience in China, but he needs to purify himself to do so. This reversal shows the discomfort some American executives experience while doing business in China, suggesting that they are involved in business practices they feel the need to deny.

[9] Small-scale, highly competitive capitalism is 1,000 years old in China (Redding 1995; Gates 1996).

[10] Reversal in this context is a distortion of reality. It enables the American executive to ignore Chinese history.

[11] Seeing China as backward is a common theme throughout the history of American-Chinese relations (Jespersen 1996).

3. Chinese as Cowboy Entrepreneurs. Some American executives simultaneously disdain and admire Chinese corruption, and in so doing express their ambivalence about the role of ethics and law in American business culture:

> Chinese entrepreneurs, it's like the Wild West. They put up 10 percent of the money to start a company; the banks loans them the balance. The biggest problem is underperforming loans. The entrepreneurs double their business in one year. They make their money back. The banks had not done enough due diligence. The loans were made through connections. After two to three years the entrepreneur walks. He does not pay the loan back to the bank. It's not cultural, it's the entrepreneurial spirit. It's not really cheating. This is very different than [a specific Fortune 500 company]. We seek 10–15 percent profit. We take years before dollar one is invested. By the time we're ready, the opportunity is half passed.
>
> (Mr. Am23)

Mr. Am23 even more precisely identifies the attributes of the Chinese businessman with those of the cowboy, describing the former as using rulelessness to make money, a trait he seems to admire. Both Mr. Am23 and Mr. Am9 understand the Chinese in terms of *pure* economic self-interest, that is, self-interest without any ethical or legal constraints. This fantasy is not only exciting to the American executives, it *is* American, though they posit it in America's past. But the fantasy is not in the past; it is in the present and it is distorting American perceptions of the Chinese.

Mr. Am23 realizes not paying back bank loans is bad for Chinese society, but he does not condemn the practice. He even notes that the whole process is possible because of connections, that is, because of culture. But he does not connect the cultural aspect with the economic aspect, with profit. The culture may have made the profit-seeking behavior possible, but the behavior is lifted from its cultural context and understood in the realm of an imaginary "Wild West."[12] In severing economics from culture, Mr. Am23 severs economics from morality, highlighting a theme that occurs in American business culture: the idealization of profit seeking and individualism coupled with an insensitivity to the moral and institutional context that makes profit seeking possible.

---

[12] America's need to mythologize China is rooted in efforts to repair its own faltering cultural institutions (Madsen 1995).

4. American Lack of Adaptation. Some American executives interviewed had not been successful in China and blamed their lack of success on Chinese corruption. Mr. Am28 complained that even the translator he hired was trying to get a cut. "It's all part of the way they deal," he said. Mr. Am19 remarked on how difficult it is to learn to do business in this type of environment: "You need to get screwed two to three times to learn, or have a high-demand product or connections to the Party or sweet deals for hard currency."

These two executives were bitter about their experiences of doing business in China. Mr. Am28's company had invested a large amount of money in China but was not making a profit. He said his company was at a competitive disadvantage because it would not pay bribes. Mr. Am19 was bitter because under his leadership, his company had made many investments in China and had lost a lot of money. He blamed these losses on the Chinese propensity to break every rule, to pursue self-interest by any means possible, no matter how unfair.

Both of these American executives were unable to adapt to the Chinese business environment. They played by one set of rules and the Chinese played by another, to the Americans' loss. Yet Mr. Am19 was clear about how to avoid getting "screwed." The three ways he mentioned, and the success of other American companies, demonstrate that the Chinese are willing to participate in mutually beneficial business dealings, but only if one develops enduring personal relationships with individual Chinese, either as a partner or as an advisor and helper. Unfortunately, it is a time-consuming and labor-intensive process. Mr. Am19 did not put the time in to understand Chinese society. Not understanding *their* rules, he played by his own and got "screwed." Being fast and aggressive, he found, does not work in China. American impersonalism cannot substitute for Chinese personalism.

5. American Frustration as a Cause of Misunderstanding. American frustration can lead to anger and misunderstanding, as is apparent in Mr. Am19's experience. Although extensive change is happening in China's business environment, not everything is changing; indeed, in a "transition" economy, if everything changed equally, the economy could not function. The fact that the intense centrality of relationships[13] is more or less continuous in China

---

[13] *Guanxi* is an ancient pattern of relationship building developed as protection from a predatory state (Gates 1996). The Communists tried to squash it (Kruger 2009), it has surged since reform (Sun 2004), and some researchers now find it less emotion-based and more instrumental (Weller 1998). Indeed, M. Yang (2002) argues that *guanxi* is now regularly transformed into bribery as business calculation impacts Chinese culture. Interestingly, in Yang's view, multinational corporations are using *guanxi* to elude state power and embed capitalism in China.

tells us something about the nature of the transformation: that it primarily concerns the production and distribution of economic goods, while the cultural and political systems are changing less rapidly.[14] The focal point of development is economic action. For the Chinese, all is not chaos—far from it. For the Americans, however, whose only reason for being there is to make profit, it is a country without rules, where profits in many cases are difficult and elusive. The "Wild West" metaphor is as much a reflection of American frustration as of Chinese reality. It tells us Americans find China exciting, exciting in a way that allows them to feel adventurous and brave, though also ashamed and vulnerable.

American frustration at times leads to anger. Mr. Am28 often tells this joke: "The Chinese people are upset about corruption. They are upset when they don't get to participate." It is, of course, a joke unfriendly to the Chinese, intended to make the American listener laugh. It reverses the relationship between corruption and character.[15] Corruption is normally considered upsetting because of the *loss* it creates, but in the joke, the Chinese are upset about corruption when they do not *gain* from it. This reversal makes the Chinese different from "us." Portraying the Chinese as children, unaware of right and wrong, the joke makes them corrupt not only in practice but also in character. This put-down of Chinese as uncultured children is what is "funny" in the joke and also what allows it to express both anger and moral superiority.

II. Bribery

1. Misunderstanding Chinese Gift Giving. American executives said in interviews that bribes and kickbacks are commonplace in Chinese business, many citing a five percent kickback as the norm in negotiations.[16] Numerous American executives said the Chinese did not think bribery was wrong:[17]

> I'm concerned about the local Chinese practice of gifts. In the U.S., if a supplier asks me to go to a baseball game, I ask myself if going will

---

[14] Pei 2006.

[15] Freud 1963.

[16] In a study in Hong Kong, Su and Littlefield (2001) found bribes and gifts averaged three to five percent of operating costs.

[17] Witcomb, Erdener, and Li (1998) found that 59 percent of Chinese students did not consider it unethical to bribe.

affect my decision in business later on. The Chinese do not have this thought process.

(Mr. Am9)

Mr. Am9 claims the Chinese do not reflect on the business significance of gift giving. In reality, however, the Chinese thought process about gifts is highly sophisticated and complex. In particular, gift giving is related to respect and face,[18] group membership,[19] reciprocity,[20] status,[21] and long-term relationships.[22] Given the Chinese tradition of gift giving, it seems their experience of it is much less instrumental than that of Americans, though, as mentioned in footnote 13, there is evidence that instrumentality is an increasing aspect of Chinese gift giving.

There is a subcontext in the gift example Mr. Am9 chooses, tickets to a baseball game; baseball is, after all, an American competitive sport with many distinctive rules and rituals. But it is unclear exactly what "thought process" Mr. Am9 thinks the Chinese are missing when it comes to gift giving. Presumably Americans too give gifts for business advantage, but Mr. Am9 believes these gifts are customarily at arm's length or only indirectly related to a business decision, while he thinks Chinese gifts are *directly* related to such a decision and as such are unethical. To the extent that this is true, of course, it represents a breakdown in Chinese culture and ethics. That Chinese culture and ethics are under considerable stress is certainly true.[23]

Mr. Am9 worries that his Chinese employees might be accepting gifts for their own benefit rather than that of the company. Mr. Am9 is a high-level executive; he has more to gain from company success than do low-level Chinese employees. He knows how baseball is played; it is a team sport. He has succeeded in the American (team) system. Most Chinese, in contrast, do not see themselves as part of a team system. They see immediate individual benefits, and it makes sense to them to take them. They are living in the Chinese system, where opportunities have rather suddenly become plentiful (and, from their perspective, could just as suddenly disappear). They are not missing a "thought process"; they are living in a different social context.

[18] Snell and Tseng 2001.
[19] Bell 2000.
[20] Hwang 1987.
[21] Steidlmeier 1999.
[22] Smart 1993.
[23] Witcomb, Erdener, and Li 1998; Harvey 1999.

Mr. Am9 does not understand this social context; instead, he sees inadequate moral judgment. This disinclination to understand the other in his own terms makes working with different cultures more difficult.

2. Personalism in Chinese Gift Giving. Many American executives are uncomfortable with the personalism ethic in Chinese culture. Mr. Am30 gives an example:

> We give gifts in the U.S. We can accept dinner and go to the game, but cannot take tickets for the game. An unreasonable gift goes to the person, not the customer, not benefitting the company, but the person. It's also unreasonable if given at the point of business exchange. These lines are unclear in China. If you give a $20 gift, then you are selling the product for $20 less. The customer would rather get the product for $20 less than let the buyer get the $20. In the U.S., it is built into the fabric that we take the buyer to lunch. In China it is a gift. This makes it more cloudy.

Do different types of gifts in different cultures imply an ethical breakdown? In themselves, not really. Like Mr. Am9, Mr. Am30 measures Chinese practices against American standards,[24] which leads him to fear a breakdown of the boundary between individual interests and company interests.[25] But the problem is not the type of gifts; it is the personal ethic in Chinese culture. American business relationships are more impersonal. The problem is not that the Chinese give a wide variety of gifts or that they are unethical; it is that Mr. Am30 does not agree with their personalizing business relationships. But that is who they are. I doubt the Chinese will ever balance personal relationships and organizational relationships in the same way Americans do.[26] Part of cross-cultural management skill is learning new ways to manage because one must consider, and to some extent incorporate, different cultural forms.

[24] But the Chinese have different standards. The value of a gift is related to the value of the friendship, the wealth of the giver, the status of the receiver (Snell and Tseng 2001), and the power of the giver in the network (Hwang 1987).

[25] Many Chinese businesses have very strong family cultures where this breakdown would be rare (Redding 1995). Given the strong personalization of authority in Chinese cultures, however, large organizations could be vulnerable to a breakdown in organizational commitments.

[26] The convergence thesis, which postulates that China's business culture will take on Western values and norms, vastly underestimates the historical and psychological basis of culture and cultural change (Shils 1981).

3. Judging Chinese Behavior by American Standards. American executives have difficulty knowing how to evaluate the behavior of Chinese subordinates. Mr. Am20 found out his Chinese salesmen were taking kickbacks. He forbade the practice, with the result that many of his salesmen quit. Mr. Am20 then quietly accepted the practice in order to staff his sales office. In this case, the kickbacks are not part of long-term relationship building. They are, however, common in China. Are they ethically justifiable? No, unless wages do not provide a minimum level of economic welfare.

Did Mr. Am20 manage this situation correctly? He could not sell his product in China without Chinese salesmen, and he could not find Chinese salesmen who did not take kickbacks. To take the ethical high road, he should offer his salesmen some economic incentive to forgo kickbacks, along with training so they can understand his philosophy. His acceptance of the kickback situation should be temporary.

The bigger challenge for American managers is understanding the cultural meaning of Chinese actions; misunderstanding will misdirect their response. Consider Mr. Am30's ruminations on "form" and "substance" in Chinese culture:

> Our sales guy goes to a distributor and asks him to stock our product. The distributor asks for a 20 percent discount for himself and receives it. We find out and fire our sales guy. In the U.S., it is clearer it is wrong to participants. The Chinese are willing to allow form to control substance. They will accept labels. They label it as "just a gift," rather than look at the substantial implications.

Mr. Am30 is engaging in cultural analysis, but instead of recognizing a different cultural system, he sees a moral failure. For him, "substantial implications" means economic outcomes. Mr. Am30 believes economic outcomes should dominate social behavior. After all, in American (democratic) culture, norms of equality require no such gift rituals.[27]

Mr. Am30 implies that the Chinese are either corrupt or shallow to "allow" ritual to interfere to such an extent with business transactions. But the Chinese are not bad Americans, and they do not "allow" form to dominate substance; "form" (in this case gift giving) is an essential part of their culture.[28]

---

[27] de Tocqueville 1969.

[28] Innumerable proprietary rules of interpersonal behavior, whose origins go back thousands of years, are central to Chinese culture (C. K. Yang 1963).

So even though the salesman's "gift" is not ethically justifiable because its purpose is not relationship building, Mr. Am30's understanding of Chinese culture misses its target. It is not that form dominates substance, it is that form has a different role in a different social life.

4. *American Use of Middlemen to Pay Bribes.* For all their concerns about Chinese bribery, American companies routinely use third parties to pay bribes for them:

> Our company uses middlemen of one kind or another for export, import, and sales to the domestic market. And basically these middlemen pay bribes. Do we care? No, because the middleman is its own legal entity.
>
> (Mr. BD2)

Americans have come to China to do business and make money, so they try to find a way to get the job done. Mr. BD2 takes a common American position: The law is the only standard.[29] This despite the fact that Mr. BD2's company has extensive formal and informal ethical standards, one of which, promulgated both formally and informally, is that the company does not pay bribes because it has ethical standards. For all this company's talk about "ethics," its "ethics" is to avoid violating the law. As long as the law is not violated, executives are free to do business.

They are not free, however, to inform corporate headquarters that middlemen are used to pay bribes:

> All foreign companies say they don't pay bribes but they sell to an agent who sells it to the customer with a bribe. Corporate headquarters does not know they do it. The company is clean. Somebody has knowledge but there is no paper trail. I was in an expat training seminar. Forty percent of the participants said they used brokers or agents.
>
> (Mr. Am28)

So even though American executives rationalize third-party bribe paying in terms of its legality, they still keep the practice hidden from superiors.[30]

---

[29] This position is consistent with Milton Friedman's (1972) view of business ethics, though Friedman also argues deception is unethical. Is it deceptive to use third parties to pay bribes? It certainly is the case if American companies are instrumental in setting up the bribe. According to my data, sometimes they are.

[30] J. McGregor (2005) reports that even executives in China go out of their way not to know what is going on in their own sales departments.

Clearly, if they did not think the practice was wrong, they would have no reason to keep it hidden. Indeed, they go to great lengths to hide the practice. J. McGregor reports that contracts with middlemen are restricted to one copy printed in black ink on red paper so it cannot be photocopied.[31] The fact that they participate indirectly in bribe paying, even though they know it is wrong, is a compromise in the face of an intractable problem. To the extent that companies are not working to remove themselves from these compromises, the compromises are unethical.[32]

III. Nonbribery Corruption by Chinese Employees at American Firms

1. The Conflict between Impersonalism and Personalism. Sometimes even if Americans understand the cultural differences, corporate rules force them to make unfair decisions, such as this one:

> In China things are different. We call it TICB: "This is China, Baby." I fired a Chinese woman last month because she changed our company bank account to another bank, where her husband works. We got a better deal at the new bank, the husband got a huge bonus, but it involved a conflict of interest and it was against company policy. She said she did not understand that she did anything wrong, even though she had been told the policy. Her boss actually had to approve the change, but she got the boss's assistant to chop [officially stamp] the change. This showed me she knew she was doing something wrong, so I fired her.
>
> (Mr. BD1)

I spoke with the boss whose chop was used in the above story, and he added a few details:

> I know the woman and she is honest. She has high integrity; she did not think what she did was wrong. All she had to do was disclose that her husband worked at the other bank, but she chose not to. She had been trained by the company. She should have known.
>
> (Mr. BD2)

These two comments illustrate the dilemmas American executives face in managing Chinese employees. Mr. BD1 says the Chinese accountant was

---

[31] J. McGregor 2005.
[32] Brenkert 2008.

fired for inappropriately approving the transfer, but Mr. BD2 says she was fired for not disclosing that her husband worked at the bank. It appears she was *not* fired for inappropriately approving the transfer because it involved Mr. BD2's chop and he certainly would have known if his chop had been used inappropriately. Mr. BD2 wanted to protect his employee, who he thought had high integrity, but did not because she did not disclose her husband's relationship to the bank. Mr. BD1 is Mr. BD2's boss. He made the firing decision and justified it by citing the accountant's alleged deceptive use of the chop; otherwise headquarters might raise questions about who else was responsible.

It appears Mr. BD1 and Mr. BD2 were protecting themselves. Mr. BD2 says the accountant did not know she was doing anything wrong but should have because of her training. If indeed the accountant was honest and had made a mistake while working in a foreign culture, this can be seen as a gray area. Additional training possibly could have removed the potential for more mistakes. Mr. BD1, however, afraid of either looking bad or not following company procedures, felt he had best fire her.

This was a case of culture conflict. The Chinese accountant was living in two different worlds: the American, where conflict of interest is forbidden, and the Chinese, where a wife's support of her husband is morally required.[33] Firing an honest employee for a first offense where there is no loss and cultural conflict is involved seems harsh. The dilemma Mr. BD1 faced was that the impersonalism of the American rules put him at risk if he did not fire her. In effect, the accountant acted to meet her cultural responsibility; Mr. BD1 fired her to meet his. Importantly, they both would have had different problems had the accountant not transferred the bank account or Mr. BD1 not fired her for it.

2. Middlemen and Nonbribery Corruption. Middlemen carry out multiple unethical activities for both Americans and Chinese. Mr. BD2 provides an example involving employee theft:

> We caught a purchasing manager overcharging us because another Chinese employee reported him. We looked into the purchase file and the guy was so dumb he had left the original invoice from the supplier in the file, which was one-half the final payment. The guy got a

---

[33] In Confucian social philosophy, a wife's obligation to her husband is the second of the Five Cardinal Relationships (Snell and Tseng 2001).

middleman to claim the middleman had assembled the product. The product was a forklift. This was ridiculous to me. The employee had cut a deal with the middleman to overcharge for the forklift.

It was shown in the previous chapter that middlemen play a moral role in Chinese society; they can be used to resolve conflict between two individuals for the purpose of communal harmony. It was also shown, however, that in American-Chinese business relations, middlemen regularly pay bribes on behalf of the Americans. In the example above, we see a middleman as an accessory to fraud. Hence the middleman as an institution is degraded when it functions between American and Chinese cultures as opposed to within Chinese culture. This is not to say middlemen do not do unethical things within Chinese society or ethical things in American-Chinese relations. But in the latter case, it appears middlemen function significantly to both resolve and exploit cultural differences.

In American-Chinese relations, the middleman is not a representative of the community because now two different communities are involved. The middleman is now a "third party," with neutrality as its defining characteristic. It is the neutrality that degrades the institution, removing its moral base as representative of the community, turning it into an institutional black box whose pure instrumentality is key in resolving conflicts between two incompatible moral cultures. That the cultural middle in this situation is defined by neutrality and instrumentality measures the moral degradation of the marketplace. The middleman currently functions to keep it that way.

IV. Honesty and Reliability

1. Government Domination and Chinese Business Ethics. Most American executives do not find Chinese executives to be honest, perhaps because they seldom understand Chinese motivation. The following comment is from an American executive who purchases textile and home furnishing products in China for import to the United States:

> The Chinese are cutthroat and will do anything for an order. They don't have very good ethics. They show the customer what he wants to see. I have close Asian friends, some employed by us, some not. For the most part, Asians are not two-faced, but they are driven to extremes by opportunity. They will do anything for an order. I see a lot of bait and switch. Procter & Gamble cannot cut quality. Crest is Crest. But in

Asia, a lot of corners get cut. If the buyer pushes hard to get a price, the Chinese will take the order and cut quality. To me, people with high ethics will not do this. Most Chinese will do it: 99 out of 100 will take the order. Then there are claims and issues down the road. In my world, Chinese factories do whatever it takes to land an order.

(Mr. Am20)

This executive's belief that the Chinese are obsessed with landing an order because they are unethical shows little understanding for the Chinese context. The Cultural Revolution (1966–76) left a whole generation of Chinese demoralized, destitute, and desperate to make up for their losses in life any way they could.[34] In addition, not all Chinese trust the reforms. Some want to make as much money as they can as fast as they can, so if the government cuts back on economic liberalization, they will have capitalized on the opportunity before the window closes. American executives typically misunderstand the Chinese because of their lack of historical knowledge and empathy.[35]

2. Incongruence between American Standards and Chinese Context. American executives routinely apply American standards to Chinese contexts where they do not fit. An American executive reported a discussion he witnessed among Chinese about loyalty to friends:

I was in an EMBA [executive MBA] program in China. During one class, the students were asked, if they were driving with a friend and the speed limit is 30 miles per hour and their friend is driving 50 miles per hour and hit someone and killed them, would they testify against their friend in court. The vast majority of Chinese said no. When asked what they would do if they had to testify, the majority said they would lie.

(Mr. Am28)

Mr. Am28 provided this example as evidence of the inherent immorality of the Chinese compared with his own American values of respect for the rule of law, the sanctity of life, and honesty. The Chinese students, however, seemed to be applying a different value, moral responsibility to friends; and this in a societal context where power and relationships, not the rule of law, determine court cases.[36] In other words, the comments by the Chinese EMBA students

---

[34] Pomfret 2007.
[35] Madsen 1995.
[36] Pan 2008; Santoro 2009.

reflect a context in which relationships determine outcomes. In this case, to portray the Chinese as unethical or inherently corrupt is to misunderstand the context and to inappropriately apply American standards to the hypothetical question.

V. American Corruption in China

1. The Chinese View of a History of American Exploitation. Both the past and the present make it difficult for the Chinese to trust Americans. An American executive explains:

> I set up the first JV [joint venture]. During the negotiations, the Chinese put much emphasis on what technology we were going to bring. They wanted specifics. I couldn't figure it out. It turned out, before me people brought in second-generation technology and sold it as first-generation. The Chinese felt they got screwed. If you understand the people you're dealing with, they are no different in behaviors and motivation than people anywhere else.
>
> (Mr. Am27)

Mr. Am27's comment shows some of the problems the Chinese face in doing business with Americans. In general, the Chinese have less international business experience than the Americans. This leaves the Chinese vulnerable to deception, especially in complex areas such as technology transfer. The Chinese have a long history (and memory) of mistreatment going back to the nineteenth century when European and American powers forced the Chinese to accept Western occupation and trade.[37] Both the reality of this exploitation and fear of its recurrence still influence Chinese reactions to American businesses. Distrust on both sides makes it very difficult to work together constructively in the cultural middle.[38]

2. The Hidden Meaning in the "Wild West" Metaphor. The Chinese are not the only ones who break rules in China. Mr. BD3 explains:

---

[37] Lampton 2001. As will be discussed later, a Communist education in China familiarizes students with the history of foreign aggression but not with the history of Communist aggression.

[38] Note that in his last sentence, Mr. Am27 seems to deny the existence of a cultural middle, indeed to deny that there are cultural differences. This denial makes it impossible to "understand the people you're dealing with."

There is much pressure on American business in China to become like the Chinese, which means to be unethical. There is much pressure for profits. The only way to make profits, for most American companies, is to cheat on paying fees and taxes to the Chinese government. The biggest part of doing business in China is with the government. The Taiwanese companies cheat the Chinese government to make profit. The Chinese government has a range of enforcement. They enforce their policies more against foreign companies than Chinese companies. Most American companies are not making a profit.

(Mr. BD3)

These comments highlight one aspect of American misbehavior in China, that involving the government. The Chinese marketplace is highly competitive and difficult, and one part of the difficulty is extensive government involvement,[39] to which some American businesses respond by cheating on taxes and fees.[40] Mr. BD3 says Chinese businesses, under pressure themselves,[41] also commonly cheat the government, an assertion borne out in my interviews with Chinese executives.

Other comments, reported earlier, show American companies directly and indirectly paying bribes, most of which go to government officials. As in the Wild West, American companies go to China in search of new business opportunities. A costly high-level American executive, along with a supporting organization, is sent to China to set up a business with the purpose of making money.[42] Once there, many face considerable and long-term challenges, making profit frustratingly elusive. The "Wild West" metaphor used by American executives implies, of course, that the Chinese are not the only ones

[39] The 2011 China Business Climate Survey by the American Chamber of Commerce found government red tape, discriminatory licensing processes, an unfair regulatory environment, and ineffective protection of intellectual property rights (American Chamber of Commerce 2011).

[40] See the Epilogue for a discussion of American tax-avoiding strategies gleaned from the 2010 interviews.

[41] Margin pressure on Chinese firms is only increasing due to government phaseout of subsidies to industry, relaxation of energy price controls, mandated wage increases, and tightening of environmental standards (*Economist* December 9, 2010).

[42] In the conference room of the China headquarters for an American Fortune 500 company, a framed *Time* magazine cover depicting the upcoming Olympics sat on a window ledge overlooking Shanghai. On the magazine cover was a handwritten note from the board of directors, "Bring home the gold" (Feldman 2007a).

breaking the rules. When in China, many do as the Chinese, another layer of meaning in the "Wild West" metaphor.

3. Bribes Going to Americans. American purchasing managers have substantial power over Chinese suppliers, enough that they can extract bribes from the Chinese in a variety of forms. Mr. Am20, an American middleman, describes the variations:

> If we go to dinner with Wal-Mart, they go Dutch. They pay for their own water! I never met a Wal-Mart buyer who takes anything. At [large American company] it's massages, Morton's Steak House, etc. [Said company] has a policy of accepting no more than $25 in gifts in the U.S. Wal-Mart wants to go to Denny's because they are paying. Most American buyers typically want drinks, dance clubs, and a lot of buyers want hookers. We don't do the hookers. We draw a line. Karaoke bars are borderline because of different levels of service. You rent a room for the night. The hostess comes in, brings beverages, and will do sexual acts. Twenty girls will come and you pick a girl and do anything. CVS cracked down a couple of years ago. A couple of buyers were fired because they started a second family in Asia. Their Asian family was funded by a supplier.

Again, we see the dark side of the "Wild West" metaphor. Some American purchasing managers behave in China in ways in which they would not behave back home. Perhaps some companies turn a blind eye toward executives willing to work in such less than comfortable conditions.

The "second family" example reveals another aspect of American exploitation. A "second family" is possible both because a supplier is willing to pay the bribe and because the cost is low enough that it makes sense relative to its benefit to the supplier. Indeed, it demonstrates the value of an American customer relative to the aspirations of a Chinese family. The "second family" American executives are exploiting the difference in economic development that makes the cost of living in China so much less than in the United States. Moreover, this type of indiscretion is a relatively easy thing to conceal because China is still opaque to the outside world and one can "disappear" in cities where the population can be upwards of 20 million. For the most part, Westerners live and socialize in "expat" communities, the basis for another derogatory meaning in the "Wild West" metaphor: Outside of their racially walled-off enclaves, Westerners see primitiveness.

In summary, the cultural middle between American and Chinese executives in China is a difficult, troubled space where "middlemen" both resolve and exploit cultural differences. The focus on money making and economic opportunity trumps the establishment of a business ethics environment. Self-interest faces few enduring constraints. There are historical, political, cultural, and demographic reasons for this situation, which resembles more a military standoff, where each side launches disparate harassment raids on the other's supply lines, than a mature market, where shared norms of exchange are at least known, if not always followed.

Chinese Perceptions of Business Corruption in China

I. General Perceptions of Corruption

1. Corruption, Careers, and Cultural Context. Some Chinese executives point to a culture of corruption in China:

> In a Chinese company, salary could be low, maybe 3,000 renminbi [RMB, about $384] a month. But the real money could be higher by manipulating expense reports.[43] Chinese employees may be proud of how they get money from different channels. This is a culture. Most people are doing it.
>
> (Mr. Ch1)

Mr. Ch1, interestingly, now works for an American company. He says the Americans taught him and he now counsels others to take a long-term view of one's career. Cheating on expense reports is not really worth it when compared with the risk to long-term career success. In other words, one should avoid cheating not because it is wrong but because it is not profitable; it does not maximize long-term financial benefit.[44]

Mr. Ch1 is 30 years old. The American company he works for offered him a long-term career plan, but like many upwardly mobile Chinese, he quit anyway for a higher-paying job. He was lured back when the company

---

[43] Chen and Chen (2005) found it was common practice for Chinese employees to turn in false expense claims.

[44] The extreme instrumentalism of Mr. Ch1's view is important. It is similar to the instrumentalism common in authority relations in Communist industrial organization (Walder 1988), but without the extreme dependence. Cynicism, too, seems common to both. These continuing patterns demonstrate that some aspects of Chinese economic culture are not changing.

promised additional long-term opportunities.[45] (Like most American companies, it was trying to reduce extremely high turnover of Chinese employees.)

Chinese employees working for Chinese companies usually do not have these opportunities. So even if Mr. Ch1 is right that not thinking in the long term about their private-sector careers leads the Chinese into corruption, it is also true that they have no experience that would lead them to think in the long term. In a business environment experiencing explosive growth, many Chinese go after the most lucrative opportunities even if it means changing jobs every few months or even weeks. In a sense, then, corruption and turnover are related: They both reflect a disinclination to make long-term career commitments, which in turn reflects a society unsure of not only its future but also its past. Freed to some extent from total dependency, many Chinese have stepped into a moral void.[46]

2. The Cultural Revolution and the Next Generation. The Cultural Revolution is having ongoing influence on business management:

> In old times, people were not able to get an education, especially during the Cultural Revolution. Now it is too late to teach them everything. They want to make up for their life by working hard and making money every way, no matter how indecent or bad that way is. Small part of the people that generation, ages now 41 to 51, they believe it not fair that they were born at that time. They want to catch up. They feel they deserve more from life. They do everything they can to get it.
>
> (Ms. Ch14)

The influence of the Cultural Revolution on management has already been discussed briefly. An important point to add is that in this troubled generation are the parents of the young employees now doing the intense job-hopping. It is unlikely that the younger generation was counseled early in life by their elders to pass up opportunities in favor of long-term commitments.[47]

---

[45] After transferring to the company's U.S. headquarters in 2008 as part of his career development plan, Mr. Ch1 quit again and moved to Canada in 2009.

[46] Madsen 1995.

[47] Cheung Yan, the 52-year-old founder and CEO of the Nine Dragons Paper Company, is one of the wealthiest entrepreneurs in China. During the Cultural Revolution, her father was branded a "rightist" and jailed for three years. The family was reduced to poverty. As a child, Cheung had to quit school to support eight brothers and sisters. She summed up her attitude toward the future: "We only have a certain number of opportunities in our lifetime. Once you miss it, it's gone forever" (Osnos 2009: 2).

Long-term commitments assume a stable social environment that the previous generation never experienced. Furthermore, almost all of my Chinese students knew little about the Cultural Revolution. Hence, not only were they encouraged to seize opportunity but they lacked any historical knowledge that could have led them to reflect on their careers and their parents' advice differently. The loss of historical memory, enforced by the government to maintain its legitimacy and control over the population, is a key characteristic of Chinese culture.[48]

3. Chinese Business Efforts to Stop Corruption. Many Chinese executives feel that corruption in Chinese business is declining:

> Metro [a large German retailer similar to Wal-Mart] opened several years ago and business was very poor. Their invoices listed everything, prices and quantity. Purchasing managers from companies did not like the invoices because they could not turn in padded expense forms. So they did not use Metro. They like small shop. But now many companies insist on buying from Metro because of clear invoices. Metro's business is much better now.
>
> (Ms. Ch10)

Even though Ms. Ch10, the president of an auto parts manufacturer, said corruption is common in China and difficult to control, she did not think it would continue much longer because Chinese companies are getting "very strict on corruption." She said that in 2007, her customers, Chinese manufacturers, sent her notices requiring her to "declare we will not pay bribes to their employees." If she breaks the agreement, she will be taken off the manufacturer's list of suppliers.

Ms. Ch10 has an MBA from an international business school in Shanghai. What she reveals about Metro and the Chinese auto parts industry are examples of efforts Chinese businesses are making to try to curb padded expense reports and bribery of purchasing managers. Of course, the efforts themselves demonstrate the corruption they are designed to address. Since

---

[48] Wei-ming 1994. The seize-the-moment ethic, material deprivation, and loss of historical memory are three important reasons consumer culture has so easily become a preoccupation of the Chinese in areas where wealth has increased. Consumer culture teaches endless consumption, not the moral discipline needed for social responsibility or even for commitment to work (Bell 1978). This culture is a recognized problem in the United States; the intense job-hopping and widespread corruption shows it to be an even bigger problem in China.

requiring a no-bribe statement was just started in 2007, it is apparent that the battle against business-to-business corruption is in its early stages.[49]

II. Bribery

1. Denial of Corruption. Some Chinese executives believe bribery is contained or limited. Ms. Ch14 said in the chemical industry "rumors would spread if you take bribes," hurting one's business opportunities. Mr. Ch33 said, "If someone takes bribes, he will eventually be caught and punished." He adamantly rejected the idea that corruption is widespread in China. Ms. Ch14, a distributor, said her company paid bribes to only 5 out of 100 customers. She explained:

> Both Americans and Chinese would fire an employee immediately for taking bribes. Even an SOE [state-owned enterprise] would fire. In my circle, no one will dare take money back from customers. Some engineers will take money but not salespeople. In my company, we have a rebate to salesman if you meet quotas. We give 10 percent of net profit. It's all on the table. I have experienced engineers who want kickbacks. We sell at 22 RMB per unit and give 2 RMB to the engineer. Both in SOE and privately owned. We are not selling commodities but specialty chemicals and we have a good margin. Kickbacks are not common but possible.

Clearly, Ms. Ch14 and Mr. Ch33 did not experience business in China as anything analogous to the American executives' experience of the "Wild West."

But another executive, also in the chemical industry, saw things differently:

> There are many types of corruption in China. Over 30 percent of purchasing managers ask for bribes. Companies trying to cheat customers or lie to them to get them to commit to a purchase and then raise the price are over 50 percent. Giving away confidential

[49] Three years later, in a 2010 interview, Ms. Ch10 said the situation had gotten better. However, she gave credit for the decrease in corruption to stricter central government punishments, though she also said large companies have to pay to support government activities. Tsai (2007) found that entrepreneurs spent up to 70 percent of their profits on government fees and bribes.

competitive bidding information is over 30 percent. Chinese would not even consider this wrong. It is normal to help friends. They would only be offended if someone used their power to make millions of RMB. They would think this is very unfair. They would draw the line based on huge amounts.

(Ms. Ch30)

In evaluating the different perceptions of corruption between Ms. Ch14 and Mr. Ch33 on the one hand, and Ms. Ch30 on the other, it can be said that the American data, the academic and practitioner literature, and even a strong majority of the Chinese interviewees support Ms. Ch30's views. So how can Ms. Ch14 and Mr. Ch33's views be explained? In one of three ways or a combination of them: First, their views were consistent with their experience. For some reason they had not encountered widespread business corruption in their work. Second, they feared telling the truth because they worried they could get in trouble with the government or peer groups. Third, pride in China's development led them to minimize the dark side of this development.

Even though the data show that different businesses and different industries face different levels of corruption, it seems unlikely that Ms. Ch14 and Mr. Ch33 escape it for the most part. Indeed, Ms. Ch14 is in the same industry as Ms. Ch30. The third option—pride in country—seems unlikely too, because there is much to be proud of even with corruption. Hence, it seems most likely that their denial is primarily based on fear of what others might think or do if it became known that they criticized China to a foreigner who is writing a book.

2. Equality and Corruption. Perhaps most interesting in the previous views on corruption is Ms. Ch30's statement that there is a moral limit against using one's position to amass sizable wealth. This is a conservative quantitative ethic. It implies the moral value of equality. In other words, corruption is okay if the results are more or less equally shared. But when huge wealth is amassed by a single individual or small group, a moral offense has been committed.[50]

---

[50] In Chinese culture, equality is interrelated with the norm of reciprocity (Hwang 1987). Expectation of reciprocity is a driving force in Chinese social relations. Great wealth achieved dishonestly violates both of these values.

Equality is the central value in a collective society,[51] and corruption is the exception that proves the rule. It permits an escape from suffocating equality, thus making equality more tolerable up to the point where large-scale corruption threatens to destroy equality.[52] Corruption, then, is acceptable up to the point where it violates the vague but powerful sensibility of equality. It follows that as the opportunity for large-scale corruption increases due to capitalist wealth creation, and as the predatory nature of the Chinese state goes unchecked, the culture of socialism in China will be squeezed to extinction.[53]

3. China, Asia, and Corruption. Some Chinese executives saw widespread corruption as a common feature not only of Chinese firms but of Asian firms generally:

> I seldom see corruption with American and European companies. But with Asian companies there are many. If the decision maker is the owner, then no. But for other decision makers, 60 to 70 percent are corrupt. Foxconn [Taiwanese electronics producer and Apple's OEM], their purchasing managers ask for commissions. Samsung, LG, and other Korean companies ask for commissions.
>
> (Mr. Ch17)

The implication that Taiwanese and South Korean companies are as corrupt as, or more so than, Chinese companies is not supported by Transparency International's 2008 Corruption Perceptions Index. Taiwan ranked 39 and

---

[51] China is a collective society in a number of different ways. It has a long history of a strong and repressive central state that enforces its will across the whole population (Gates 1996). A central tenet in Confucianism is piety toward key relationships, which accords strength to the kinship system and undermines individualism (C. K. Yang 1963). Finally, the Communists have tried to minimize the private person altogether, seeking to create a grand unity wherein all are one (Munro 1977).

[52] This view is consistent with Walder's (1988) analysis of a personalistic "sub-culture" developing below strict Communist bureaucratic impersonalism in the operation of large SOEs. The "sub-culture" was essential to get anything done, and as long as it did not grow too unruly, it was an essential aspect of Communist authority. If it did get unruly, as is the case with corruption today, the security forces, as is the case with corruption today, stepped in.

[53] Western businessmen might find this prospect appealing, but to the extent that a nihilistic (atomistic) individualism results (Arendt 1950), a repeat of something like the Cultural Revolution or worse is possible. This point was recently made by Premier Wen Jiabao when he pointedly referred to "such historical tragedies as the Cultural Revolution" in the context of condemning the fallen neo-Maoist Bo Xilai (Garaut 2012: 1).

South Korea 40 out of 180 countries. China was ranked 72. Thus, corruption in China is perceived to be significantly worse than in Taiwan or South Korea. Mr. Ch17's perceptions of the United States and Europe are generally validated. The United States ranked 18, Germany 14, and France 23. However, his blanket statement about "Asian companies" is not validated: Singapore ranked 4 and Hong Kong 12.

China is part of Asia, but Mr. Ch17 did not give examples of Chinese corruption. He mentioned specifically that he does not like South Korean companies. It is not uncommon for Chinese executives to express negative feelings toward companies from Japan, Taiwan, and South Korea.

Despite Mr. Ch17's blaming culture for corruption, it is known that corruption is the outcome of a complex interaction between economic conditions, cultural values, and the state.[54] In China, the state plays a central role in the level of corruption, and the level of competition arising from population density is far from insignificant. Mr. Ch17's blanket statement was probably an effort to deflect attention from the level of corruption in China—or perhaps to show the interpreter he was toeing the Party line.

Interestingly, it appears that growing democratic influences and increasing wealth have lowered corruption in Taiwan and South Korea. In terms of the three causes of corruption mentioned above, only economic conditions have seen much improvement in China (indeed, political relations and cultural values may be in decline),[55] so it is unlikely there will be a steady decrease in corruption in China any time soon.

4. Two Types of Chinese Bribery. Bribery in the private sector is less brazen than bribery in government, according to this account:

> It would not be uncommon for middle managers at Haier to ask for bribes. It is against company policy and they would lose their jobs if caught. But they are careful to ask for bribes only from people in their group, people they can trust. They check you out, take you to dinner, and see if you are thinking like them. It would not be uncommon for public companies trading on the Chinese stock exchanges to have middle managers asking for bribes.
>
> (Ms. Ch30)

[54] Shleifer and Vishny 1998.
[55] Pei 2006.

In contrast, several executives said bribery in government is systemic and thus cannot be stopped. In many cases, there is no one to whom to report the bribe because either the whole organization is in on it or those requesting the bribe are capable of severe retaliation, or both.[56]

The Haier example, however, suggests that private-sector bribery, not being systemic, is therefore less prevalent than government bribery—though the comparison is relative because Ms. Ch30 says bribery would not be uncommon among large Chinese companies. Of course, it must be remembered that many large Chinese companies are government owned or partly government owned.[57] This fact, combined with extensive government regulation of business, results in intertwining of corruption in business and in government. In any case, the 2009 antibribery law has leveled the playing field to some extent, forcing bribe seeking underground as government officials, like their private counterparts, seek bribes only with caution.

5. A Case of Idealism. Ms. Ch32 learned Communist ideals as a child, protested for political freedom at Tiananmen Square as a college student, and now seeks to run an ethical business. Her story is tragic. Here she speaks of her ethical idealism:

> Some businesspeople bribe government to get better channels. But my company wants to show a quality product. If we are only successful through relationships, friends will look down on you, you will not be respected by society. Maybe your family will still accept you. Bribery is not a good way for me. Fifty percent of the people are like me. Many of my friends in business are successful. The more successful they are, the more bribery they use. Bribery creates many opportunities. For me, money is not the most important thing. One should show dignity in making money. I want to live gracefully. We want customers to respect us. We want to prove our value.
>
> (Ms. Ch32)

When Ms. Ch32 was a student leader during the Tiananmen Square conflict, nine of her student followers were killed. It is likely she went through

---

[56] In 2009, the government expanded the anti-bribery laws to require citizens to report corrupt activities to the government. However, the process of enforcement is still subject to the whims of powerful officials (Barboza 2009). Some executives say the level of corruption has decreased. See the Epilogue for a discussion of the law in the 2010 interviews.

[57] State-owned companies make up 80 percent of the value of the stock market in China (*Economist* January 21, 2012).

a "re-education" process at the hands of the government.[58] It is hard to think that these experiences did not have a profound effect on a 20-year-old student.

At 20 years old, Ms. Ch32 was idealistic in politics; at 40 she is idealistic in business. The first idealism sought to change the political system; the second seeks to "live gracefully." This change in idealistic ends is a move from external control to internal control. Ms. Ch32 says 50 percent of Chinese businesspeople are like her. Whether that number is right or not, it is certainly true that Tiananmen, the Cultural Revolution (Ms. Ch32 was separated from her parents as a child and lived for years with inadequate food and clothing), and an untold number of lesser events affected the outlook and character of many of the new entrepreneurs. For them, corruption, whether in business or government, is far from their deepest fear; their deepest fear is of government brutality.[59]

We have seen that personal relations dominate communal relations in China;[60] accordingly, Ms. Ch32 mentions that she would still be respected by her family if she was successful through bribery. Her experience, however, has led her to go beyond personalism. She wants to do right by society. Communism attacked family bonds, encouraging citizens to make their primary attachments to the state. Ms. Ch32's concern for society, then, is not the result of capitalism[61] but possibly the residue of early Communist idealism, the "re-education" experience, or both. It does suggest that a capitalist role can fit neatly inside the Communist end game. The question is

[58] A Chinese professor of political science pointed this out during a conversation with me (Feldman 2007c).

[59] Wei-ming (1994) reports that no Communist official has been held accountable for the government's countless acts of brutality. Gates (1996) writes that the Chinese are fearful of a personalistic legal system, informers, and cruel government decisions. Madsen (1995) describes the Communist Party as cruel and incompetent. Most wealthy entrepreneurs Tsai (2007) interviewed had made arrangements for their families to live abroad to protect them from government predation.

[60] Kinship relations and the state are both enormously powerful in China. Personalism dominates in everyday affairs. The idea of community with unknown others is a much weaker force (C. K. Yang 1963).

[61] Of course, in *The Wealth of Nations* (1974), Adam Smith concludes that trying to do good for others usually leads to trouble. Good comes from everyone's pursuing self-interest through trading freely with others. Following this line of thinking, Milton Friedman (2005) concludes that "social responsibility" for business is unethical.

still open: How far will the Communist Party allow capitalism to cultivate individualism in China?[62] The case of Ms. Ch32 is one possibility.

III. The Younger Generation

One way to further investigate Chinese perceptions of corruption is to consider the views and values of university business students. I taught two classes in business ethics at a university in Shanghai in the spring of 2007, one an undergraduate course in which the students were all 21 years old, the other a graduate course with an average age of 24. There were 25 students in each class. The students were from all over China. I recorded my classroom experience in a university diary, often comparing the Chinese students' views with those of American students I have taught.

1. Corruption, Law, and the Media. Chinese students, socialized into a very different culture and institutional context than American students, often see their ethical responsibilities very differently as well:

> Taught my first undergraduate class today. I presented the introductory case of a vice-president at a chemical company who is told of a toxic chemical spill at his company. The safety manager assures the VP that the spill was contained before "too much" chemical was released into the ground, and she assures the VP there is no danger to the public. The media finds out about the spill and wants to interview the VP. The corporate attorney tells the VP that the company will undoubtedly be sued and under no circumstances should he admit liability. I tell the students to take the role of the VP and decide what to tell the media. The students come up with three options and vote on them: give all information to the media (2 votes), avoid talking to the media (9 votes), lie to the media about the spill (11 votes).
>
> (Feldman 2007c)

The number of students who voted to lie surprised me. I often use this case with American business students and the option to lie never receives many

---

[62] Sennett (1998) argues that American capitalism's effect on individual character is corrosive. Thus, the choice is between two pathological extremes: the extreme individualism of the United States and the oppressive authoritarianism of China. Can these societies learn enough from each other to move away from extremes and toward an autonomous individual who also cares about others?

votes.[63] I mentioned this class activity and its results to Ms. Ch3, a high-ranking executive at a huge Chinese SOE, who explained that there are "historical reasons" the Chinese people give the least possible amount of information to the media.

Of the undergraduates who voted in my class activity, 50 percent had no moral problem lying to the media in order to protect their company and themselves. Many of my American students in this situation would also want to protect the company and themselves. They, too, have very little love of the media, viewing them as untrustworthy and unethical for hurting business. But my American students are wary about lying to the media because they know, whether in court or in the public arena, the truth might become known. Hence, my American students usually find some clever way to avoid reporting the spill without overtly lying.

In China, the media are not an independent investigative institution or even a government investigative unit; they are a vehicle for government propaganda. Hence, "lying to the media" in China is trying to avoid getting tangled up with an arbitrary and all-powerful state. It is more a political act than a moral one. Morally, the Chinese feel primarily obligated to their boss and colleagues, creating a problem for business ethics because business organizations have little concern for the country as a whole. There are similar tendencies in the United States, but the context is entirely different: The government is buttressed by an independent media and an independent legal system that can potentially raise the costs to businesses that stray too far from communal interests and values. In China, the legal system, like the media, is just another arm of the government. Ultimately, this lack of autonomy limits oversight and, as we have seen, encourages corruption. This is the system into which current Chinese students have been socialized.

2. Ethics, Power, and Education. Another classroom situation involved a graded student presentation given by four undergraduates and a comment on it by the Communist classroom monitor. The students and the monitor are

---

[63] Witcomb, Erdener, and Li (1998) conducted a survey with both Chinese and American students. One of the questions asked the respondents if they would be willing to exceed the legal limits on air pollution to gain an advantage over competitors. Chinese students were more concerned about getting caught, 35 percent compared with 20 percent for the Americans. On a second question, the students were asked whether they would blow the whistle if their company was making a defective auto part that could result in injury. Of the Americans, 33 percent said yes, to 18 percent of the Chinese. It appears the Chinese are more self-protective.

grappling with the tension between ethics and law. In the shadow, however, is the role of power in the education system.

> The students presented the case of a CEO at an SOE dairy, which was being bought by a Chinese company that was 60 percent foreign owned. The CEO illegally used the dairy's own capital for a management buyout. He did this out of patriotism to keep the dairy industry from foreign dominance. All four students said this is an example of illegal but ethical behavior because the CEO was motivated to protect the "dignity" of China.
>
> (Feldman 2007c)

The Chinese students are very sensitive to issues of national sovereignty and pride,[64] caring deeply about national dignity. At the conclusion of the presentation but with the class still in session, I asked the 26-year-old Communist monitor who sits in on each class to comment on the case. She responded,

> I can understand the CEO's behavior. I am in a similar situation. If the class will give me 1,000 RMB ($128), I could do something good for the university. If I do not get the 1,000 RMB, another university will benefit and we will lose out. I cannot tell you what the money will be used for [implying it was not aboveboard]. This is justified because it is good for the university.
>
> (Feldman 2007c)

Whereas the students were willing to violate the rule of law to protect the country from foreign ownership of one of its assets, the Communist monitor was willing to violate moral principles to advance local interests. In both cases, the particular trumps the general, the political the moral. In societal terms, the students do care about the whole, but at the cost of society's legal integrity. This class discussion exemplifies the Chinese tendency to politicize what in the West would be nonpolitical institutions, in this case the legal system.[65]

Importantly, these are 21-year-olds. Despite China's current growth and development, its students learn only what is in the power interests of the

---

[64] This sentiment is common among Chinese businesspeople generally (J. McGregor 2005).

[65] Since time immemorial the Chinese state has kept the law flexible to support its power interests (C. K. Yang 1963). The Communists continue this tradition.

Communist government: the history of foreign aggression, not the history of Communist aggression.[66] An implication for business is that future Chinese business leaders may misconstrue conflicting international interests as aggression toward China, increasing emotion and distance instead of reason and compromise. Contrary to what some Americans believe, China is not "behind" and destined to "catch up" to Western democratic norms. Authoritarian education does not teach students autonomy and responsibility, but obedience and fear.

A related issue is seen in the comments of the Communist monitor, who is responsible, among other things, for student indoctrination into Communist Party orthodoxy. She suggested that some unidentified moral rule be violated so she could do something positive for the university. Hence, even though an important part of her job was to inculcate Communist values, she was acting on behalf of local organizational interests. In authoritarian systems, the central "value" is power.[67] In China, power has been significantly decentralized through the reforms (in an effort by the Communist Party to regain legitimacy), leading many times to undermining of central government policies by local bureaucratic self-interests. The students realized that the monitor was allowing local interests to trump general values and in this case, having a choice, did not buy into her plea for money. Usually, however, students do not have a choice.[68] The lack of choice is an important part of student "education," and what they take away from it is fatalism and conformity, not personal growth and development.

3. *Ethics, Magic, and Economic Change.* The introduction of markets into China presents challenges to Confucian ethics, one of which is a lack of a procedural ethics. My graduate students debated the Enron case:

> Tang argued that if Enron had not gotten caught and had been able to repay the money, then there would have been no ethical problem because no one would have been hurt. This happens all the time in business, but this time Enron got caught. The stealing by executives was *personal* stealing and was something different. Tang does not believe a

---

[66] Their legitimacy already in question, the last thing the Communists are willing to do is review their cruel and destructive record (Wei-ming 1994).

[67] Rieff 1985.

[68] These same students, for example, were told to donate blood. Even though they believed rumors that high-quality student blood was used only for high-level Communist Party officials and their families, they "volunteered" their blood anyway.

word she hears from companies on the Shanghai stock exchange. Someone joked that the only thing they believe in the newspaper is the date. Deng said he would definitely do what Enron did because he wants to get rich and he would do what he can to get rich. The class voted on Tang's position that it is okay to cheat if you repay the money and do not get caught. The vote was eight to eight.

(Feldman 2007c)

This debate, in which half of the students claim that an unfair process will produce fair outcomes, highlights their lack of a procedural ethics, a reliance on a fair process to lead to fair outcomes.[69]

In regard to the position that an act is ethical if no one gets hurt, the students are dealing with problems of dishonesty and manipulation simply by denying them, a thought process that has an almost magical quality to it (if I ignore it, it will go away). According to Weber's[70] analysis, Confucian ethics, with its emphasis on piety in key relationships and its belief in the possibility of worldly perfection, removes any tension between reality and abstract ideals, promoting magical thinking. The relationship emphasis is seen here in the students' loyalty to the company and, by implication, to the boss, a loyalty that leads to a common characteristic of Chinese business, the ease by which rules are broken and agreements ignored. Magical thinking is also inherent in the possibility of worldly perfection: It is a short step from thinking it is possible to thinking it is real.

Thus there is a contradiction in the students' position: They agree that hurting others is bad but approve of activities that increase the chances of hurting others. Their ultimate justification is that this is simply the way the world works. No one follows a procedural ethics, so why should they?

Half the class supported the cheating-without-hurting-others option. These students are caring, but not principled. They live in a society where they do not believe much of what their government tells them, with cynicism as the inevitable result. Stir this into a huge population with a history of economic deprivation in the context of one of the largest economic expansions in world history, and the institution of business ethics has its challenges indeed.

---

[69] To work effectively, a procedural ethics must have an independent criterion that determines the meaning of fairness and a procedure capable of producing it (Rawls 1971).

[70] Weber 1951.

For my American students, the context is different. Even though they have decreasing trust in their institutions,[71] they live in a society of considerable competition between political parties and information sources. Many of them search for information and choose their preferred providers. Their confidence in the ethics of big business has been battered, but they still believe in capitalism and democracy as the best systems, and most of them are at least willing to obey the law.

The Chinese students do not believe in capitalism as a way of life, even though they do seek to benefit from the current economic expansion.[72] Where this tremendous economic transformation will lead, no one knows. For now, the Confucian heritage remains the moral context of many direct relationships.

In summary, in 2007, when the data for this section were collected, the opening of the economy to domestic and foreign competition was 29 years old, but development of a business culture lagged behind economic development. Different generations of Chinese were trying to find their way in the new situation with new opportunities and threats, while the past, meaning different things to different generations, undoubtedly also influenced them in different ways. Corruption was found to be pervasive, though some Chinese denied it. There were signs of Western rationalization in Chinese business, but these were minor. The cultural middle was less a factor for the Chinese than for the Americans because the government remained the central institution in their work lives, both consciously and unconsciously, and here there was no cultural middle, only one authoritarian system and its shadow.

The Cultural Middle

This section explores the cultural middle in regard to American-Chinese business relations. The cultural middle can be a no-man's-land, where misunderstanding and conflict exist and integrity is lost, or a creative space, where new knowledge is created (including self-understanding), compromise is

---

[71] According to a 2011 Gallop poll survey, Americans' trust in their institutions is strongly down from historical averages: Trust in banks is down by 19 percent, Congress -14, church -9, Supreme Court -8, public schools -7, big business -6 (Jones 2011). The only significant positive is the U.S. military, +11 percent. Small business scored +2.

[72] Gates (1996) finds this attitude generally among government officials, businesspeople, and the broader society. A remark made by an entrepreneur during an interview on business-government relations captures the context for private business in Chinese society: "As long as we are not called 'capitalists,' things will be fine for us" (Tsai 2007: 102).

worked out, and integrity is maintained. The concept of the cultural middle is relevant to American (mis)understanding of Chinese culture via the "Wild West" metaphor, to the relationship between gift giving and bribery, to the use/misuse of historical knowledge, and to the role of the middleman.

1. *Misunderstanding of Chinese Culture.* Americans have a long history of misunderstanding the Chinese by seeing them as potential Americans, only lagging far behind and in need of American help.[73] Whether in relation to Christianity, democracy, capitalism, human rights, or all of the above, at many points in Chinese history over the past 200 years, Americans have stood ready, with various levels of coercion, to midwife the "modernization" of Chinese society. The "Wild West" metaphor used by American executives to describe the rough-and-tumble world of Chinese "market socialism" fits neatly into this tendency to Americanize the internal meaning and future development of China. As one CEO of a Fortune 500 company told me,

> The genie is out of the bottle with freedom. The Chinese government is plenty smart enough to know they can't stop it, too much momentum. The flywheel will not stop. . . . They know what they started and where it will end up.
>
> (Mr. Am27)

Maybe so, maybe not. As I write today in 2009, Chinese troops are cracking down hard on Tibetan protesters.

American executives using the "Wild West" trope do not mean to refer to Chinese relations with minority groups, though the trope itself easily goes in that direction to relations with the American Indian, one of the significant moral failures in American history. What the executives do mean to imply, with a smile, is each man for himself, where no law or institution constrains the individual's unadulterated pursuit of his self-interest. Americans still use the "Wild West" image as a symbol of freedom to tell themselves who and what they are. In exporting it to China, they express their belief in China's long march toward individual freedom and opportunity. The "genie is out of the bottle." America's present is China's future. The feeling that "deep down they are like us" triggers the warmth in the smile.

But the "Wild West" metaphor distorts Chinese reality. It tells us more about the American executives who use it than about the Chinese. Americans apply the "Wild West" image to China to denote the unreliability of agreements, the lack of

---

[73] Jespersen 1996.

standardization, the disregard for the rule of law, and the obliviousness to private property. Even though the image can be accompanied by a smile, it is not an expression of brotherly acceptance. The American executives are not in China to develop Chinese society or even to develop goodwill. American business executives are focused competitors seeking profit. The problem is that they are accustomed to pursuing profit within a Western legal system. It is the irrelevance of Western legal traditions in China that creates the anxiety hidden behind the smile.

The "Wild West" metaphor reveals American businesspeople's ambivalence toward the Chinese. On the one hand, they admire China's economic success and are excited to have the opportunity to participate in it; on the other, they are exceedingly frustrated by the Chinese utter disregard for Western moral and legal traditions. Knowing "the Chinese are smart" (a racially biased expression commonly used by American executives[74]), they expect the Chinese to eventually evolve toward "international legal standards." Americans expect this evolution because they want it. They know they can never reach their full profit potential in a market that does not operate under a consistently defined and universally applied legal system. It is the uncertainty that hurts.

The American view of China's future, based more on American business goals than Chinese reality, assumes that cultural and political change is determined by economic change. Ironically, this rather Marxian perspective presupposes that culture and politics are secondary to and dependent on the primary structure of economic production. If the assumption is changed, and culture and politics are seen as related to but partially independent of economics, American history becomes a questionable model for predicting China's future behavior. Of course, American executives are not in the metaphor business and certainly do not care if their metaphors do not stand up to close analysis. But as they pour billions of dollars of investment into China, they are assuming they will be able to make money. For this to happen, they will need to understand China, which, as I have tried to show, in multiple ways they do not. Just as it is misguided to think that America's past is China's present, it is also misguided to think that America's present is China's future.

Chinese executives do not see themselves as living in the "Wild West" or as moving toward an American social system. Although many Chinese

---

[74] The image of Chinese as highly intelligent is an on-again, off-again theme in American perceptions of China going back 200 years (Isaacs 1958). Americans alternate these images as easily as changing their shirt. Spence (1990a) argues that Americans do not want to understand China because the opaqueness is the attraction, the easier to project their own emotional needs onto the Chinese.

businessmen admire American business efficiency and technological prowess, what they are most focused on is wealth creation. Unlike many Chinese students who do not trust the government despite years of Communist indoctrination through the education system, Chinese executives tend to have a positive view of the central government; while acknowledging terrible corruption on the municipal and provincial levels, they say the central government "is trying to do the right thing." They do not think they are living in chaos. On the contrary, many Chinese executives are very impressed with China's economic growth and see it as proof that the central government's intentions are good. Most Chinese executives see less corruption in their daily lives than previously, and are aware of the government's attempts at professionalizing its agencies. Many Chinese executives are proud of what China is accomplishing.

The "Wild West" metaphor misses the mark of Chinese experience. The Chinese have known chaos that makes the Wild West look like a weekend camping trip. Either their parents or they as children suffered through the Cultural Revolution. One executive reported that her parents were beaten to death simply because they were teachers. This is chaos. Making money beyond one's wildest dreams is not chaos.

Focusing only on their own goals, having little interest in the past and little historical understanding, mentally geared toward business operations, most American executives miss this picture. The "Wild West" metaphor makes sense to them because it seems to capture what they see: disregard for the rule of law and business custom as they know it. But while the metaphor captures the behavior, it misses the cause, the brutal history of dictatorship that makes networks, not institutions, the basis for action.

2. Misunderstanding the Gift-Bribe Relationship. The personalism ethic of the Chinese and the impersonalism (bureaucratic rationalism) ethic of the Americans constitute two different systems of social relations.[75] This difference

---

[75] The Chinese have had a unified bureaucracy since the second century AD (Weber 1951). But Chinese bureaucracy was encapsulated in a particular social class, the Mandarins, separated from the general population as heaven is from earth (Redding 1995). Indeed, the personalism ethic was developed as a defense against a strict and all-too-often cruel bureaucracy (Gates 1996). Today, China's personalism ethic and impersonal bureaucracy are so merged that it is impossible to clearly separate them. American government bureaucracy is little more than a century old. Though it is often ineffective and inefficient, it has reached a higher level of impersonal rationality than Chinese bureaucracy because political interference is limited by the rule of law, by checks and balances in the distribution of power, and by a societal culture that views family relations as separate from professional relations.

leads to much misunderstanding in discerning the difference between gifts and bribes. When is a "gift" a bribe? It depends on whose values are used to answer the question. American executives usually use their own values and rules, ignoring the Chinese understanding of the difference between gifts and bribes. They thus tend to see all large gifts as bribes. In terms of American culture, they are right, but in terms of Chinese culture, they are wrong.

The way to determine whether a gift is a bribe in China is to look at the *intention*. If the gift is intended to show respect to the recipient and enhance the relationship between the giver and the recipient, then the gift is legitimate in terms of Chinese culture,[76] though it may still violate American rules if it is too large, say a Rolex watch. A "gift" is a bribe in Chinese culture if the giver's intention is simply to make a short-term financial gain.[77] For example, kick-backs are common in China, but the intention is purely financial, so they are unethical. Indeed, they are impersonal, falling outside the personalism ethic.

Hierarchy complicates Chinese gift giving. Snell and Tseng, as well as Hwang, point out that the strict hierarchical nature of Chinese society makes gift giving prone to degeneration because obligations to people in authority are so high.[78] One cannot give a cheap gift to a high-status individual, so the floodgates are open to temptation. For example, subordinates can give bosses extravagant gifts in hopes of preferential treatment. The mixture of relationship building and self-interest is such that moral intent disappears into a sea of ambiguity.

American executives at MNEs trying to navigate the relationship-building ethic of Chinese gift giving usually do not have to contend with the hierarchy

---

[76] Snell and Tseng (2001) state that gifts are given to express respect to the recipient and boost "face" (status) for the giver. A gift is an act of friendship. Hwang (1987) argues that face is a form of power because it enhances the giver's position in a social network. If the recipient accepts the gift, he is agreeing to a reciprocal obligation, which also enhances the giver's power. In this sense, Bell (2000) likens a gift to a premium for fire insurance, a kind of IOU for future needs. Steidlmeier (1999) stresses the moral side of reciprocal obligation, ideals of mutuality and right relationships. Reciprocity cultivates the self by defining the self in relation to the other, thereby building trust, cooperation, and caring. Consistent with this line of thinking, Smart (1993) describes Chinese gift giving as an art, bringing moral and cultural imperatives into the pursuit of social and instrumental ends.

[77] In this sense, it is outside the Confucian moral universe based in right relationships with significant others (Bell 2000). Bribery creates a conflict of interest between self and public duties (Steidlmeier 1999). The whole relationship- and community-building aspect is missing. A bribe does not create a reciprocal obligation (Smart 1993).

[78] Snell and Tseng 2001; Hwang 1987.

dimension because of their own high status or their outsider status, which cuts them slack for trying to fit in. Thus they can ethically use the Chinese relationship-building ethic to justify giving an expensive gift as long as it does not violate their core beliefs or involve government officials, which would violate U.S. law. They may view giving such a gift as showing respect for the culture in the host country.

My position can be contrasted with that of Donaldson and Dunfee, who argued that foreign companies should use "hypernorms"—basic human values that are common to all cultures, such as "fundamental human rights"— as the basic moral standard for decision making in different cultures.[79] But cultures are too diverse to share the same fundamental values, except on the most abstract level, which, in effect, destroys the idea of culture.[80] My position is that each culture has core values that should not be violated. For example, American companies should not participate in business activities that use child labor because to do so would violate fundamental American attitudes toward children. But outside core cultural values, American companies have the moral right to use host-country values while working in the host country. My position encourages the possibility of cultural compromise that shows respect for the host culture. Showing respect for the host culture is a moral positive because it increases trust, cooperation, and understanding. The only limit to compromise and the creation of shared values is the home country's core moral commitments, which would be unethical to violate. Sharing is good on the margins of culture, as long as it does not undermine core moral commitments, which are the first and last defense against moral transgression.

A second aspect of the gift-bribe puzzle that leads to American misunderstanding of Chinese behavior is the role of law in Chinese society. As mentioned, according to U.S. law, it is illegal to bribe foreign government officials.[81] American public companies worry a lot about legal prosecution for violating this law. In addition, they have their own policies limiting the value of gifts. Executives can be fired for violating these policies. Executive attention often focuses completely on these laws and policies.

---

[79] Donaldson and Dunfee 1999.

[80] Geertz 1973.

[81] Some American executives are confused about what the Foreign Corrupt Practices Act applies to. Several of my interviewees thought it disallows all bribery in general, but in reality it permits bribery of low-level officials to speed up government action (Sanyal 2005).

In China, one must use both legal and cultural criteria to determine whether a gift is a bribe. Americans are often off-base by relying solely on U.S. legal definitions. In China, as noted previously, the interpretation and application of laws can be driven by government preference. Hence court decisions can be acts of government power or the power of officials. Even lying in court, which is a violation of an almost sacred custom in the American system, can be a political act in China, constituting resistance to unwarranted government power. This is one reason why Chinese executives can so easily say they will lie for a friend in court: They have little confidence in the fairness of the legal system.

Given China's political and cultural orientation, Americans are unrealistic to expect the Chinese to follow American legal norms. Cross-cultural management skills and cross-cultural compromise are required, starting with learning about the other from the other's point of view.

3. Ethics and Historical Context. Many American executives complain about the Chinese lack of respect for rules. As was shown, the China-as-Wild-West trope used by American executives distorts Chinese reality, telling us more about the Americans than the Chinese. The American Wild West had a minimal government; China has a quasi-totalitarian government. Seen in more accurate historical perspective, is Chinese "rulelessness" unethical? The question must take into account what effect the brutal decade-long Cultural Revolution had on the current generation of Chinese executives. The fact that memory of the Cultural Revolution has been suppressed by the Chinese government and ignored by American executives makes understanding the role of history that much more difficult.

Should the brutality of the Cultural Revolution have any effect on how we evaluate the ethics of current Chinese business behavior, particularly bribe seeking, corner cutting, and profit-by-any-means activities? I think it should affect our understanding of the situation, though it cannot make unethical behavior ethical. The problem is that the Chinese are not discussing in any meaningful way the history of Communism in China. The Mao-era Communists tried to destroy moral traditions, cultural heritage, religious beliefs, and even family bonds. Eventually, by the end of the Cultural Revolution, they had destroyed themselves or at least their legitimacy and turned to markets, their ideological nemesis, to save them. Lucky for them, Chinese culture is comfortable with contradictions.[82] Be that as it may,

---

[82] Nisbett 2003; Pye 1988.

Chinese moral groundings have been and are under considerable strain. Without reflection on their recent history and a reconnection with their cultural traditions, the Chinese exist in a state of rootlessness.[83] It is not surprising that these conditions contribute to extreme self-serving behavior.

Most American executives coming into this situation, focused on their own business goals, care little about cultural history. But ignorance of Chinese history compounds relationship problems for the Americans because they end up distorting and demonizing the Chinese instead of understanding them. At the very least, historical understanding might lessen American anger and increase empathy and patience, providing a better basis for relationships. A broader dialogue in China on business ethics and history is not possible because the government will not allow it, given that it would require a review of the government's historical record. Hence, the government's insecurity and lack of legitimacy is a major block to improving business ethics in China. It is also a key reason government economic regulatory efforts are lax: The perks of economic freedom and bureaucratic corruption lighten the chains of political repression.[84]

In this context, the cultural middle is more than a conflicted space between two established cultures. It is as if the cultural "middle" extends into Chinese culture itself. Years of conflict and failed ideological purity have had their cost. In China, negotiating the cultural middle goes beyond negotiations between two foreign cultures: It has to account for the lack of moral consensus within China itself. Government power substitutes for moral consensus, and the "cultural middle" is permeated with a high degree of politics—good, bad, and corrupt. Such is the case when the political exterior remains after a 30-year attempt to make the ideal the real inevitably destroys itself.

4. The Ethics of Middlemen. American companies, as discussed earlier, use "middlemen" to pay bribes in China. They make sure there is no paper trail linking these bribes back to them, especially back to corporate headquarters in the United States. In other words, the Americans are playing by Chinese rules, not vice versa as they so often claim. They meet the letter of the law but not the spirit of their own policies. Unfortunately, there is probably no other way to do business in China at this point. It creates an ethical dilemma, however, that most American executives do not recognize. Assuming "ethical" behavior is the same as legal behavior, they do not see a problem.

[83] K. Yu 2009; Erikson 1964.
[84] Pei 2006.

In other words, for many American executives business "ethics" means avoiding penalties from violating legal statutes. Business is about profit and loss, and the only way "ethics" makes sense to many businesspeople is in terms of profit and loss. Violating legal statutes can be costly. Of course, violating ethical norms can be costly too, but apparently not in the case of using middlemen to pay bribes in China. But this "Don't ask, don't tell" approach to bribery has another kind of cost. It undermines moral culture. American companies work continuously to develop ethical employees. Delegating the bribery function to Chinese middlemen can hardly be considered a model exercise in character building.

Another problem with China's culture of bribery is that it puts some American companies at a competitive disadvantage. Mr. Am17 states,

> Ninety percent of purchasing managers ask for gifts in China. It is the most corrupt place where we have a presence. And this in our industry where products are differentiated! We can't win with gifts. It can put us at a competitive disadvantage.

If bribery undermines competitiveness in an industry where products are differentiated, it must do so even more where products are undifferentiated. Mr. Am17 works for a medium-size company. His company does not have the cash position to compete in the bribery market. Hence, American companies are in a dilemma: If they do not use middlemen to pay bribes, they lose business; if they do use middlemen to pay bribes, they make their products less competitive. As usual, pressure for short-term results leads them to use middlemen.

Are American companies unethical for using middlemen who pay bribes? Yes, for at least three reasons. First, the practice contradicts their professed claim of rejecting bribery. They cannot ethically (rationally) be against bribery *and* participate in actions that lead to bribery.[85] Second, it does not achieve a just balance of stakeholder interests.[86] It increases the income of the bribe taker but raises prices generally for the bribe giver's employer, the bribe taker's employer, and the end user.[87] Third, Americans are against bribery because it is inefficient. By participating in bribery or acquiescing to it, American companies are participating in actions that do not lead to the greatest good

---

[85] Bowie 1999.
[86] Freeman 1984.
[87] Warren, Dunfee, and Li 2004.

for the greatest number.[88] The "greatest good" principle is one of the moral justifications for capitalism, so it is hard to see how American companies can ethically ignore it in this case. Bribery in China is different than American behavior during the apartheid era in South Africa, when American companies hired blacks and paid them the same wages as whites, thus having a basis for claiming their presence in the country was ethical and in fact might lead to positive change. By using middlemen in China to pay bribes, Americans are not resisting crime, only avoiding being charged with it.

Finally, even though the middleman has a moral function inside Chinese culture—for example, mediating conflict, promoting harmony—in the Chinese-American relationship the middleman easily veers off into unethical terrain, becoming a purely instrumental agent created to resolve and exploit gaps in the social, legal, and cultural machinery between two very different business systems. These gaps or holes arise from incongruities in values and practice between the two systems. The middleman exposes a sometimes over-looked side of international business, the cultural margin, where rules and values are compromised to reach across cultural divides. The middleman is an essential part of international business, creating a bridge through cultural conflict for self-interest to achieve its goal, sometimes creating a moral consensus, other times destroying the moral content of one or both sides. The right amount of compromise provides learning and moral growth; too much and integrity is lost.

Conclusion

This study of business-to-business corruption in China supports the conclusion that "international" business ethics requires cultural compromise between the different societies engaged in economic exchange. The idea that companies should practice the business ethics of their home country when they are abroad, without regard to the ethics of the local society, is not practicable because of miscommunication, incommensurate values, distrust, and perceptions of unfairness. Participants from different cultures need to manage a "cultural middle," where value incongruities can be addressed through "cultural compromise," that is, the creation of shared values.[89]

---

[88] Rachels 2003.

[89] To be clear, "cultural compromise" is not a search for universal values; it is a local arrangement between two companies from different cultures.

The idea of cultural compromise is, of course, fraught with difficulty. If too little compromise exists, it is difficult to develop long-term, stable relationships; if too much compromise is forthcoming from either party, that party either takes on the values of the other or loses its moral integrity and it becomes liable to moral transgressions. Thus the options are an inability to cooperate, moral disintegration by one party or domination by the other, or compromise and the creation of new (shared) cultural forms.

Compromise means cultural change. Such a change can be morally sound if it leads to moral development, more trusting relationships, and better communications. It can be a creative experience that widens and deepens both parties' moral orientation. Searching for and finding shared values requires an explicit and sincere examination of one's own moral values, commitments, and priorities, as well as the same aspects of the other. This exercise in itself is a positive addition to business responsibilities.

The cultural margin can be useful for maintaining one's integrity while simultaneously attempting to understand another and work toward shared values through cultural compromise. The cultural margin is the part of one's cultural commitments that is most open to change. For example, American companies many times have dollar limits for gift giving. These limits, while culturally sensible in the United States, could be harmful or even insulting in China. Permitting more expensive gifts in China would not undermine core American values and would help start relationships with Chinese (assuming the gift is intended to help develop a long-term relationship, not gain an immediate financial benefit). In this case, an American would be reaching across the "cultural middle" to share Chinese gift-giving practices. It could be the beginning of compromises from both sides that lead to shared moral culture.

In this study, however, the data show the Chinese "middleman" is often being used in the China market to circumvent the moral requirements of one or both parties. The cultural middle can be a space where ethical violations take place and cultural differences are exploited. Or the cultural middle can be used for good. Given the intense focus of all parties on profit, as opposed to the time-consuming requirements of using the cultural middle creatively, middlemen quickly become bagmen. In this case, the middleman separates the two parties for the purpose of removing moral and legal conflicts that obstruct the pursuit of profit. Alternatively, the middleman could, and sometimes does, help the two parties resolve ethical conflicts.

One can only hope the middleman is a temporary phenomenon and as the Chinese marketplace becomes more familiar to both Chinese and foreigners, more effort will be made toward creating shared moral commitments. The central role of the Chinese government in the Chinese marketplace, however, will be crucial in any progress since it is the primary source of corruption and control.

PART

INTELLECTUAL PROPERTY

9

Clear as Mud

The Ethics of Intellectual Property in China

One of the central differences between American and Chinese cultures is in their attitudes toward contradiction.[1] Americans have a contradiction phobia, always seeking to order reality in terms of logical principles. The Chinese do not rely so heavily on abstract logic, instead being more inclined to accept contradiction and use compromise to make their way between irreconcilable positions. This attitude leaves the Chinese much better positioned than Americans to deal with conflicts over intellectual property (IP). The differences over IP between the two countries are complex and irresolvable, at least for the foreseeable future. While the Americans feel righteous in their demands that principles stated explicitly in international agreements clearly define IP rights and obligations, the Chinese, facing American pressure, use a "rope-a-dope" strategy, compromising on some IP obligations while ignoring many others.

The situation is a classic case of "trouble in the middle," though the trouble goes far beyond cultural incompatibility. Disagreements in principle and practice over IP involve economic, political, and historical, as well as cultural, issues. The result is a range of disagreements wherein conflicts on particular IP issues, as well as compromises between IP issues and other matters, leave IP disagreements in a state of moderate to low-grade conflict, improving and deteriorating simultaneously. For all practical purposes, the trouble in the middle is a permanent condition requiring continuous management. Contradictions and tensions abound, with the Chinese in the catbird seat for now, as they gain enormously through intellectual property rights (IPR) infringements and seem content to draw the situation out indefinitely.

[1] Nisbett 2003.

This chapter describes and analyzes American and Chinese IP activities, with special attention to the ethical aspects of disagreements over principles and practices. The situation is very complex, far from the simple story of Chinese unethical behavior commonly presented by American business executives and politicians.

The analysis will unfold over three main sections, the first examining Chinese IP behavior in terms of the role of the government's IP strategy and enforcement; the courts; and domestic interests, actions, and challenges. The second will examine American IP behavior in terms of the Chinese business environment, the effects of Chinese infringement on different sectors of the American economy, and the role of the American government in addressing the conflict. The third will explore the influence of Chinese and American cultures on the conflict over IP, examine the differences in economic development between the United States and China, review the West's dominant position in terms of its conflicting interests with China in regard to IP, and present an ethical evaluation of the two sides' positions and practices. Finally, the conclusion will highlight the political, economic, and cultural complexity of the situation and the challenges in determining moral responsibility for the conflict.

Intellectual Property in China

I. Infringement in China

1. The Context of Infringement Worldwide. The Organisation for Economic Co-operation and Development (OECD) estimates cross-border trade in counterfeit goods at $200 billion per year worldwide.[2] This estimate does not include counterfeit goods produced and traded within national borders. Perhaps pirated software is the largest component of counterfeit goods. In 2011, worldwide pirated software was estimated at 42 percent of usage, valued at $63.4 billion.[3] More disconcerting is the prevalence of counterfeit medicines. The World Health Organization estimates that up to 1 percent of medicines in developed countries are counterfeited, but the number goes to 10 percent in developing countries, with the worst countries reaching above 30 percent.[4]

[2] Vargo 2009.
[3] Business Software Alliance 2012.
[4] Vargo 2009.

2. Infringement in China. China is generally regarded in the West to be the largest source of counterfeit goods worldwide, by some estimates responsible for 80 percent of worldwide trade in counterfeit goods.[5] China is also thought to be the number one source of counterfeit medicines.[6] Estimates for counterfeit trade *inside* China are even more staggering. It is estimated that around 90 percent of all copyrighted materials sold in China in 2006 were pirated;[7] more than 80 percent of "Yamaha" motorcycles are counterfeit;[8] software piracy, though declining from above 90 percent, stubbornly remains at 77 percent;[9] and generally, in addition to software, pirated products in music, film, and textbooks are practically the whole market.[10]

The general sense among American business and government leaders is that the unauthorized use of IP, counterfeiting, and piracy are increasing worldwide,[11] with perhaps the main reason being the Internet,[12] which can be used to distribute huge quantities of pirated material quickly and cheaply.[13] The growing threat to IP is also seen in the continuously improving technological and manufacturing capabilities in Asia, low barriers to entry, and the opportunity for huge profits.[14]

In this context, the combination of China's manufacturing infrastructure and export capacities is unique and has led to significant though restrained efforts by the American government to pressure the Chinese government to control or reduce IPR infringement in China. Although these efforts will be discussed in more detail below, for now it can be said that the extent of infringement activities in China is large.[15] Chinese government efforts have had little impact. For example, Baidu, the largest Internet search service

---

[5] Chow 2005.

[6] Ritter 2007.

[7] Conyers 2007.

[8] Anand and Galetovic 2006.

[9] Business Software Alliance 2012.

[10] McCoy 2009; Schroeder 2007. On a visit to China, Professor Paul Schroeder saw widespread pirating of textbooks, including ones published by "Similar Press" (personal communication 2012).

[11] Stoll 2009; Holleyman 2009.

[12] Weinstein 2009.

[13] Espinel 2007.

[14] Yager 2007.

[15] As of 2012, most of the Western reporting coming out of China concludes that Chinese IP theft remains at a very high level or is getting worse (Weisman 2012; Perkowski 2012; Wines 2012a; Riley and Vance 2012).

in China, is responsible for 50 percent of illegal Internet downloads in China.[16]

In addition to the obvious lost profits to the original IP creator, there are four other problems associated with Chinese infringement. First, recall expense: In 2007, 288 (61 percent) of the 473 product recalls in the United States were for products made in China,[17] some portion of which were counterfeit. Recalls are expensive and their cost is borne by industry and in some cases the United States government. Second, danger to consumers: Some of these recalls were for medicines and other products whose use led to deaths and serious illnesses before the products were recalled. Hence, counterfeit goods can create health problems in addition to economic costs. Third, disruption in the supply chain: In one case, counterfeit cancer drugs had lot numbers identical to cancer drugs in the legitimate supply chain, leading to a massive recall.[18] The domino effect was that of shortages and confusion in the use of legitimate products vital to the well-being of society.

Fourth, firms using counterfeit products gain an unfair competitive advantage. For example, Chinese firms using pirated software for their CAD/CAM machines are not paying the required $80,000 or so in license fees,[19] enabling them to undercut the prices of firms that do pay the fees. The resulting disruption of competition will in the long run raise prices for consumers and decrease innovation as makers of CAD/CAM technology and license-paying firms are weakened.

II. The Chinese Government's IP Strategy

1. Attitudes toward IP Protection. The Chinese government is concerned that enforcement of IPR could hinder economic development by blocking access to information and technology, allowing foreign firms who own the IP to dominate the China market and creating a trade imbalance that favors the West.[20] Starting out so far behind economically and technologically, China does not feel it can afford to allow developed economies to dominate the market. Moreover, IP enforcement seems to offer few advantages. In addition, given foreign domination of China for the 100 years preceding the

[16] Smith 2007.
[17] Santoro 2009.
[18] Weinstein 2009.
[19] Miner 2005.
[20] Burrell 1998.

Communist Revolution in 1949, the Chinese do not trust the intentions of foreigners.[21] Protection of the Chinese market, which it does have control over, is much more important to the government than protection of IP, which it does not have control over. The bottom line is that the Chinese desperately want and need technology.

In any case, China's behavior is completely consistent with the historical behavior of Singapore, Taiwan, and South Korea. Singapore was a pirate's haven in the 1980s.[22] It did not start enforcing IPR until 1987, when it signed a foreign trade agreement. Even then, piracy of business software remained near 40 percent. In the 1980s, Taiwan was considered the "Counterfeit Capital of Asia."[23] In 1984, the United States said Taiwan was responsible for 60 percent of counterfeiting worldwide.[24] As late as 1991, Taiwan accounted for 70 percent of U.S. customs seizures for counterfeit computers and electronics. But in the late 1990s piracy rates fell dramatically after Taiwan passed laws criminalizing piracy[25] and specifying jail time for violators. At that time, Taiwan had the highest per capita foreign currency reserves in the world.[26] China's behavior fits right in with this history, except that it has not yet reached a significant level of enforcement, and when or if it will remains unknown.

2. Accessing Foreign IP. Over time, the Chinese government has issued numerous rules to require foreign companies to transfer technology to Chinese firms. These rules have gone by various names and have applied to a variety of contexts. Some of the most contested are the "indigenous

---

[21] In recently declassified speeches, Zhu Rongji, premier from 1998 to 2003, expressed fears that the West would use international agreements to undermine the Communist Party, Westernize Chinese culture, and break up the country (*Economist* December 10, 2011b). Indeed, as Yu Keping (2009: 155) put it, "Chinese leaders make sovereignty the basis upon which all political and economic activities take place, including economic globalization."

[22] Smith 2007. So it appears lacking IPR is no deterrent to economic development, as is often promulgated during testimony on IP to the American Congress.

[23] Smith 2007: 48.

[24] Alford 1995.

[25] Smith 2007.

[26] Hence, Taiwan and Singapore ignored IPR until they reached an advanced level of economic development (Alford 1995). The same can be said for Japan and South Korea (Riley and Vance 2012). Indeed, during the eighteenth century, the United States was the worst IP infringer in the Western world, not enforcing IP laws for 100 years until it, too, reached a significant level of economic development. Copying products and stealing IP, therefore, seems to be the normal developmental pattern of nations.

innovation" policies, which require that products sold in China be conceived, designed, and made there.[27] Rules covering licenses to sell in and export from China, contracts for government procurement, "safety certifications," monopolistic practices, and mergers with or purchases of Chinese companies, for example, all result in the transfer of foreign technology to Chinese firms.[28] Naturally, this leads to a drop in sales at American firms. On a number of occasions, some of these rules have been rescinded or revised, not least because of various forms of pushback from foreign trading partners.

Another way Chinese firms gain access to American IP is through the U.S. FDA's drug approval process, which requires applicants to submit test data demonstrating the drug's effectiveness. Immediately following the U.S. filing, multiple Chinese companies will file for approval for the same or a similar drug in China, referencing the same test data and thereby sidestepping the expensive testing.[29] Despite protests from the American pharmaceutical industry, the Chinese government has not acted to stop this practice, even though China agreed to follow rules prohibiting such tactics when accepting admission to the WTO.

Actually, the Chinese patent filing process is a general IP problem; so-called trolls file patents in China based on foreign technology.[30] Foreign patents are not valid in China, so when foreign companies come to China, they can be sued in Chinese courts for violating a patent on their own technology.[31] The "trolls" seek to be paid off to go away. To be sure, in the United States "trolls" or even major American corporations use lawsuits in similar ways with similar results. In China, however, the problem is worse because of a less sophisticated and more biased court system. In addition, even if foreign companies file patents in China, Chinese companies have much more freedom to use patented IP to develop products.

New Chinese patent rules imposed in February 2010 take another approach to foreign IP, allowing the government to demand that foreign drug companies license their manufacturing to local Chinese companies at

---

[27] Leonhardt 2011.

[28] Vargo 2009; Holleyman 2009; Miner 2005; *New York Times* December 23, 2010.

[29] Ritter 2007.

[30] Wadhwa 2011.

[31] According to *The Economist* (April 21, 2012), a recent change in Chinese law makes it more difficult to file dubious patents to rip off foreign technologies. On the other hand, because of the language barrier and the sheer number of Chinese patent filings, it is difficult for foreign companies to know if patents even exist for their technologies (Wadhwa 2011).

state-set prices.[32] This system not only turns IP over to the Chinese but does so independently of the market pricing mechanism. Since the pharmaceutical industry in China is dominated by state-owned enterprises (SOEs), foreign drug manufacturers worry that the new rules are part of a government plan for state domination of the industry. Another provision in the same rules requires foreign companies to pay Chinese employees at least two percent of the profit derived from innovations in China. In this case, it is not the IP that is being turned over but the profit it generates. In either case, foreign firms lose advantages they enjoy in the United States.

3. Barriers to Entry. In industry after industry, China has erected barriers to entry, either to gain access to foreign IP or to allow Chinese-made counterfeit products to dominate the market. Perhaps the paradigm case is that of the film industry. The WTO agreement states that China must allow 20 American movies per year into China. China lets in 14. But 2,000–3,000 American titles on pirated DVDs are widely available throughout China. Hence, there is a connection between the severe restrictions on market access for film, music, software, and book publishing and the dominance of pirated products in these markets in China.[33] It is difficult to imagine there is not an intended relationship between government import restrictions and local piracy operations.[34] To make matters worse, these same pirated DVDs are also exported, including to the United States.

Similar strategies are used in other industries. Western companies are no longer allowed to meet purchasing directors in Chinese hospitals, resulting in a significant drop in sales growth.[35] In 2009, the government banned foreign investment in domestic online games.[36] Even before the ban, Nintendo estimated it was losing more than $700 million a year to Chinese pirates.[37] Foreign insurance companies have only 4.7 percent of the life insurance market and 1 percent of the property and casualty market because of regulatory barriers.[38]

---

[32] Browne and Dean 2010.

[33] Smith 2007.

[34] In addition to restricting films, the government applies demanding regulations and high taxes on foreign home video and television content. These rules makes it impossible for U.S. firms to export this content to China, creating a vacuum that is, again, filled by pirated copies (Glickman 2005).

[35] *Economist* November 11, 2006.

[36] Ye 2010.

[37] Anand and Galetovic 2004.

[38] Browne and Dean 2010.

In a similar vein, China has established a 40 percent nontariff barrier on clean-coal technologies. Given that coal is the primary source of pollution in China, this barrier puts pressure on the U.S. government to include American environmental technologies as part of any environmental agreement with China.[39] In other environmental technologies, foreign makers of wind turbines and solar panels say they are denied access to big renewable-energy projects in China.[40]

On the other hand, China caps its tariffs at 10 percent on average, compared with more than 30 percent in Brazil and around 14 percent in India.[41] It is also more open to imports than Japan was at a similar level of development and more open to foreign direct investment than South Korea was until the 1990s. So although China aggressively pursues its interests, no small number of foreign firms still profit in China.

4. Government IP Strategy. According to Richard McGregor's study of the Chinese Communist Party, the Party never intended to "privatize" state assets in a Western sense but instead to use the market to discipline SOEs to become more efficient and produce more wealth.[42] The fundamental point is that the Party had to make money to survive. McGregor's conclusion is consistent with Yasheng Huang's research that shows the government moving away from the private entrepreneurial model of the 1980s toward the "Shanghai model," that is, economic growth through building efficient state-controlled enterprises.[43] By developing and controlling wealth-producing SOEs, so central to the Chinese economy, the Party is solidifying its own power base.[44] This is, after all, what the Party has always done. The only difference now is that the SOEs would be profitable.

Tying this political point in with the previous points about barriers to entry and gaining access to foreign IP, it can be seen that the government's

---

[39] Rapidly industrializing nations, led by China and India, insist that given the global nature of environmental challenges, environmental technologies should be exempt from IP agreements and subject to compulsory licensing (Vargo 2009). India and other developing nations have long argued, on human rights and utilitarian grounds, that basic needs like clean air and water should take precedence over private property claims (Steidlmeier 1993).

[40] Browne and Dean 2010.

[41] *Economist* December 10, 2011.

[42] R. McGregor 2010.

[43] Huang 2008.

[44] The move away from private entrepreneurs to SOEs came after the Tiananmen Square massacre, when the Party was almost thrown out of power (R. McGregor 2010).

IP strategy is to focus SOEs on key industries—oil, petrochemicals, mining, banks, insurance, telecommunications, steel, aluminum, electricity, aviation, airports, railways, ports, highways, automobiles, health care, education, and civil service—get them access to foreign IP in the cheapest way possible, and restrict competition inside China so they become the dominant players. Since the 2008–09 Western-centered economic crisis, there has been an upsurge of economic nationalism inside China and self-confidence that the Chinese economic model is sound, indeed superior to that of the West. Given the continuing high levels of GDP growth in China and the fact that the country came through the economic crisis better than the West, the Chinese are in a strong position to negotiate the myriad issues pending with the West, including IP relations. The Chinese have much less need for foreign funds than they did even a decade ago. Foreign investment as a percentage of GDP dropped from 6 percent in 1994 to 1.8 percent in 2009.[45]

Another aspect of the government's IP strategy is to stimulate innovation inside China, as can be seen in the government's 2009 procurement rules making only products that contain Chinese proprietary IP eligible for Chinese government procurement.[46] The government has also recently created new incentives to stimulate patent applications. Successful applicants can receive cash bonuses, win tenure for professors, earn residence permits in preferred cities for workers and students, have their corporate tax rate lowered from 25 percent to 15 percent, gain access to lucrative government contracts, and so on.[47]

Clearly, China has been growing more innovative. In 1999, Chinese firms won 90 patents in the United States; in 2008 that number was 1,225.[48] Inside China, the patent office took in a world-leading 800,000 patent applications in 2008.[49] The government's goal is to have 1 million invention patents by 2015.[50] Most of these patents are not impressive, but the trend toward increasing patents and innovation is clear, and most likely quality will eventually improve as well.

---

[45] Browne and Dean 2010.
[46] Watson 2009.
[47] Wadhwa 2012.
[48] *Economist* April 25, 2009.
[49] *Economist* April 25, 2009.
[50] Wadhwa 2012. In the United States, about 500,000 patents are filed in a year.

All in all, accessing foreign IP, restricting foreign firms, creating industry-dominant SOEs, and increasing indigenous innovation are central to the government's development of the Chinese economy concerning IP.[51]

III. Government IPR Enforcement

The full complexity of IP in China can be seen in its enforcement of IP laws and rules.

1. Reluctance to Criminalize Infringement. The enforcement of IP laws through the courts will be discussed in detail below. For now it will suffice to say that enforcement rates drop as low as 20 percent in the courts,[52] and most cases never even make it to the courts, in part because the threshold to define counterfeiting as a criminal act is set very high. For example, in a single year 150 million pirated DVDs are confiscated and 52,000 trademark violations are identified, but fewer than 600 arrests are made.[53] In 2005, only about 2 percent of trademark violations were prosecuted under China's revised Criminal Law.[54] American business associations complain that even when the infringement is very serious, like the uncovering of a ring of optical disk manufacturers, criminal sanctions are still not employed.[55] American business executives and government officials assert that criminal sanctions are the only remedies that will stop counterfeiting.

When China joined the WTO in 2001, its government made commitments to increase criminal prosecutions of IPR violations. Indeed, in 1998 an official at the American embassy in Beijing put together an informal coalition of businesses whose principal aim was to push for increased criminalization of counterfeiting in China.[56] It has not done much good, however.

---

[51] There is also growing concern that Chinese spy agencies and industrial organizations are carrying out extensive and effective industrial espionage activities (Riley and Vance 2012). For example, American Superconductor Corporation (AMSC) had been selling highly sophisticated electronic technology for the control of wind turbines in China, but it now accuses its Chinese buyer, Sinovel, a Chinese SOE, of having stolen its IP (Riley and Vance 2012). In November 2011, the United States, Europe, and Japan filed a complaint with the WTO about Chinese corporate spying.

[52] Mertha 2005. Reports of court rulings swayed by politics, personal relationships, and other factors are still common in 2012 (Wines 2012a; *Economist* April 21, 2012).

[53] Hillbery 2005.

[54] Mertha 2005.

[55] Smith 2007.

[56] Mertha 2005.

Between 2001, when China joined the WTO, and 2007, it is estimated that only six criminal cases were brought against violators of U.S. copyrights.[57] In 2008, the United States filed a complaint with the WTO arguing that China's numerical thresholds for criminal prosecution of counterfeiting and piracy actually function to provide a "safe harbor" for violators.[58] According to the complaint, more than 80 percent of Chinese government seizures of counterfeit goods do not meet the criminal prosecution threshold, demonstrating that violators are able to manage inventory to avoid criminal prosecution.[59]

There are several reasons the Chinese are reluctant to prosecute counterfeiting criminally. Chinese culture resists the idea of IP as private property (discussed in more detail below). For now, it is important to note that for cultural reasons the Chinese tend to see IP conflicts as civil issues, not criminal ones. Although the West has succeeded in getting China to develop IP laws, China has dragged its feet on enforcement. The same is true for criminalization; if criminalization is not consistent with Chinese culture, criminal cases will either be undermined, be transferred to administrative channels, or arrive at results that continue to frustrate Americans.

2. Ineffective Administrative Enforcement. Given the difficulty in receiving satisfactory results in the courts, Western businesses fight counterfeiting through administrative means. Even though the administrative channels are simpler and faster, requiring a lower burden of proof than legal proceedings,[60] here too American businesses tend to meet with frustration.

Despite the fact that the government has greatly increased its raids on suspected counterfeiting operations and its seizure of counterfeit goods, the penalties assessed to the counterfeiters are so minimal as to be absorbed as a normal cost of doing business.[61] For example, fines for trademark violations are capped at either three times the illegal revenue or $14,622, whichever is less; however, most fines are far less than the maximum allowed.[62] Practically all IPR enforcement in China follows this pattern and is therefore nondeterrent. Many

---

[57] Smith 2007.

[58] United States Government January 30, 2008.

[59] In 2009, the WTO concluded that there was not enough evidence to find Chinese thresholds for criminal prosecution in violation of WTO regulations (Office of the United States Trade Representative January 2009).

[60] Mertha 2005.

[61] Smith 2007.

[62] Ong 2009. Mertha (2005) reports that out of 23 raids, 10 fines were assessed, with a $990 average.

times shops open up again a few hours after being raided, or the counterfeit products move to a new location, often close by, and selling resumes.

Americans say it does not have to be this way. They point out that the Chinese government visibly and aggressively protected its Olympic logo,[63] demonstrated effective enforcement once it was informed of the milk tainting scandal,[64] and does a pretty effective job of regulating the Internet, a Herculean challenge.[65] But it does not even stop university piracy, which should be relatively easy since the government owns the universities.[66]

3. Local Protectionism. Another set of reasons the Chinese government does not do a better job of reducing counterfeiting has to do with the government itself. Business-government relations in China operate largely through interpersonal networks called *guanxi*. These networks operate in a parallel universe to laws and regulations, much of the time functioning as the definitive avenue for decision and action. Inside these networks joint operations and shared financial interests between government and business work to shield IPR infringement from legal and regulatory constraints.[67] Either local regulators do not enforce laws or they inform violators about planned enforcement operations, allowing them to take defensive action.[68] Even when enforcement actions are taken, it is often difficult to know what actions were taken, what results obtained.[69] Intentional vagueness and arbitrariness are used to keep the system unknowable and unpredictable. In Mertha's words, it is "still very tricky to prosecute 'local boys.' "[70]

Part of the problem is that counterfeiting and pirating operations are themselves owned by local governments, remnants of the People's Liberation Army, or Communist Party cadres.[71] In fact, many wholesale markets in counterfeit goods are established by local governments. Chow describes one in Yiwu with 100,000 different products and 200,000 shoppers per day purchasing some 2,000 tons of products, almost all counterfeit.[72]

---

[63] Glickman 2007.
[64] Vargo 2009.
[65] Smith 2005.
[66] Schroeder 2007.
[67] S. Li 2004.
[68] Ostergard 2003.
[69] Smith 2005.
[70] Mertha 2005.
[71] Glickman 2007.
[72] Chow 2005.

Beyond outright ownership of IPR-violating operations, municipal and provincial officials have interests different than those of central government agencies in Beijing who may want to reduce counterfeiting. Local officials are more focused on local employment and local economic development than on national priorities. Counterfeiting and piracy can be an important part of their region's economy. Beijing, in turn, has not made stopping IPR infringement a priority,[73] holding local officials accountable for economic development but not for IPR enforcement. In the same way that low penalties for counterfeiting do not stop counterfeiting, no penalties for not enforcing counterfeiting laws leaves the laws unenforced.

4. *The Regulatory System.* Separate from local governments are the national regulatory agencies with units operating across the country. The principal agencies responsible for anticounterfeiting enforcement are the Administration for Industry and Commerce (AIC) and the Quality Technical Supervisors Bureau (QTSB), both of which have enforcement arms that can assess fines and confiscate goods. Early in the reform process, control over these organizations was given to local governments, but more recently control has moved back to Beijing.

Originally both agencies either failed to carry out their anticounterfeiting mandate or did it half-heartedly. One reason is that the confiscation of counterfeit goods is costly, time-consuming, and potentially dangerous.[74] In one village where practically the whole population was organized into a counterfeiting operation, the residents attacked the inspectors with clubs and stones, and then blocked their exit.

In addition, the cost of destroying confiscated goods is so prohibitive that the regulatory agencies tend to ignore investigating counterfeiting altogether. When they do investigate and confiscate goods, American executives often complain that neither the goods nor the manufacturing equipment confiscated are destroyed; American companies have tried to get the U.S. government to make destruction a requirement in trade agreements.[75] For the Chinese, the cost of such enforcement would be triple: the costs of training and fielding inspectors, the costs of destroying goods, plus the increased

---

[73] Vargo 2009.

[74] Mertha 2005.

[75] Vargo 2009. When they confiscate goods, the Chinese prefer to take the counterfeit trademarks off and sell the goods as "generic" (Mertha 2005). Trademark holders often pay for this practice in lost sales.

unemployment and decreased wealth creation that their very success would produce.

Anticounterfeiting operations are also curtailed by a lack of cooperation between the regulatory agencies. In fact, AIC and QTSB have been known to engage in direct competition,[76] and their inability to cooperate extends to their relationships with government ministries.[77] Prosecution of repeat offenders, those pirates and counterfeiters who move from province to province, would require coordination among multiple bureaucracies at different levels in the administrative hierarchy in different provinces, an accomplishment nearly unthinkable.[78]

What led individual agencies to accept their anticounterfeiting mandates in the first place was the expectation of enormous revenues from case handling fees, side payments, and bribes.[79] Actually the situation is even more grim in that both AIC and QTSB are in the counterfeiting business themselves, deriving illicit income from enterprise registration, retail operations, or collusion and kickbacks.[80] Fighting counterfeiting was just one more revenue source. It had nothing to do with responsibility or mission, let alone justice. Ultimately, fighting counterfeiting proceeded because levying fines bolstered the agencies' public images and operating budgets at the same time. These incentives more than anything else led to significant improvement in their enforcement activities. Once enforcement became profitable, QTSB worked to educate higher-ups in Beijing about the downside to the economy from piracy and counterfeiting, offer their expertise, help develop laws and regulations, and push for more prosecutions.

The same opportunities for revenue, however, led QTSB to avoid working with the courts to pursue criminal convictions for violators. Criminal convictions meant revenue losses from enterprise registration and management fees that QTSB would normally collect from counterfeiters.[81] It also meant a loss of future revenue from skimming off the top of fines levied. The agency's reputation would suffer, too, because once it handed over case files to prosecutors, it would no longer have evidence of its investigations or any

---

[76] Mertha 2005.
[77] Toloken 2008.
[78] Mertha 2005.
[79] Mertha 2005.
[80] Mertha 2005.
[81] Mertha 2005.

enforcement actions it undertook. So cooperation would lead QTSB to appear in the system as less productive and less effective.

5. *Regulators and Foreign Business.* Andrew C. Mertha has carried out extensive fieldwork involving the working relationships between AIC, QTSB, foreign businesses, and private Chinese investigative firms hired by the foreigners to track down IPR violators.[82] Foreign-funded investigative firms do the groundwork and absorb the costs of anticounterfeiting operations, including sorting out jurisdictional conflicts between AIC and QTSB. Ironically, the funds made available by foreign businesses stimulate conflicts between AIC and QTSB as both agencies compete for the many rewards foreign businesses offer for help in stopping counterfeiting.

The actual raids on counterfeiting operations conducted by AIC and QTSB can cost $8,000 or so and involve dozens of inspectors—in one case, 100 inspectors were involved. In addition to covering these costs, foreign businesses incentivize the Chinese authorities with trips to conferences; costly postraid dinners, lunches, and karaoke bar outings (often involving prostitutes); and reimbursement for lodging, trucks to carry away counterfeit goods, storage facilities, and handling fees. In addition to foreign funds, regulatory agencies generate revenues from confiscated cash as well as goods, machinery, equipment, and cars they sell at auctions. There is also the revenue from fines levied, mentioned earlier, plus government bonuses paid to the agency for successful raids. It is within this financial windfall that regulatory agencies are moved to action.

Importantly, the process of foreign-funded, regulator-implemented raids on pirates and counterfeiters shows that foreign businesses are changing the incentives of national and local government actors, bringing their interests in line with those of foreign businesses. The foreigners are changing government operating procedures and the way the Chinese enforce the law. In other words, foreign businesses are in fact influencing Chinese domestic governance. Thus, they are hardly the helpless victims of Chinese IPR infringement often portrayed by industry leaders in testimony before the U.S. Congress.

Similar to bribery, foreign funding of regulatory action shows the important role of money and power in the cultural middle. In this case, money tips the interaction in favor of American interests and values. Here Chinese lack

---

[82] Mertha 2005.

of administrative development is ripe for influence. The fact that the Americans also try to induce American government intervention shows not only the depth of the IP problem but the many levers used by American business in pursuit of profit. In China, often the cultural middle, the use of political power, and the pursuit of profit are indistinguishable.

IV. IP and the Legal System

1. Historical Background. In the West, there are direct linkages between individualism, respect for individual human rights, and copyright/patent/trademark law that are not found in Chinese cultural development.[83] Rather than regarding invention as a private right, the Chinese regard public duplication of creative objects as the proper approach to the value of such objects because all creativity comes from a public repository and should contribute back to it. As mentioned previously, sharing is one of the most important human virtues in Confucianism, and the Chinese are much more collective in their thinking and institutions than the West. The ideas of private rights, private property, and intellectual property are much less developed in China, if at all.

Under Communism, respect for private property and IP diminished even further. Mao believed private ownership of property to be tantamount to theft.[84] There was a continuous attack on private property between 1949 and 1976, until eventually exclusive rights to trademarks ceased to exist. This was the backdrop in 1978 when Deng Xiaoping opened up China to markets and international trade.

2. IP Reform. Laws for private property did not exist in China until 1985[85] and were not enforced until 2001, when China gained entry into the WTO. The process China went through in the 1980s and 1990s to create IP laws can be characterized as ambivalent and complex. Neither Chinese nor foreign scholars fully appreciated the cultural, historical, and institutional context into which new IP laws would have to fit.[86] Transplanting legal forms from the West into the Chinese context proved particularly problematic. Legal codes were thought of in the West in terms of their formal properties, as if they were sufficient unto themselves. But Chinese lawmakers altered them to

---

[83] M. Hamilton 1997.
[84] *Economist* April 12, 2008.
[85] *Economist* April 12, 2008.
[86] Alford 1995.

meet their own objectives and they were further contorted as they were implemented inside Chinese institutions. The idea of "rights" was perhaps at the center of this tangle, and it took a good hammering.

Trademark law, established in 1982, restricted ownership rights simultaneously with establishing them.[87] Conflicts were to be handled administratively rather than through the courts, but it was unclear how administrators should apply and enforce the law. Patent law, created in 1984, was the result of heated debates inside the Communist Party between those who wanted to move away from Communism and those who feared doing so would allow the West to control technology in China.[88] The result was a bifurcated patent law that gave foreigners more patent rights than Chinese citizens, in order to encourage the former to bring their latest technology to China, which they were reluctant to do. For Chinese citizens, the law opened the door to financial rewards to stimulate innovation, but not so far as to allow monopolistic profits. In any case, the law gave ultimate control to the government to arbitrate conflicts as it saw fit.

Copyright law, established in 1990, was also the product of heated debate within the Party with the inevitable result that, like patent law, it was bifurcated, giving more rights to foreigners than to Chinese citizens.[89] Ironically, the publication explaining the new copyright law was itself pirated from Western legal scholars by the agency responsible for enforcing IP laws. As with the other laws, the bold announcement of a new copyright law was not lived up to in its actual implementation. Again conflicts would be handled administratively rather than through the court system, focusing more on ensuring government power than on protecting private property.

Finally, the software regulations, published in 1991, require that those seeking protection of their proprietary software must provide the government with detailed documentation explaining the software.[90] In other words, the regulations undermine the rights they are supposedly designed to protect. When one reflects on the above laws, created over the course of a decade, and notes the conflicted process the government went through to create them, it seems fair to say that while progress toward the protection of IP was made, the laws demonstrate a deep ambivalence toward private property and a

[87] Alford 1995.
[88] Alford 1995.
[89] Alford 1995.
[90] Alford 1995.

powerful drive to create laws that first and foremost maintain and enhance government control.

3. Political Power and the Law. The citizenry's confidence in the rule of law remains questionable[91] for a number of reasons, most of them centering on the role of the Communist Party. The legal system continues to function as an enforcement arm of the Party.[92] It is not independent; it is not above the Party. On the contrary, it is liable to interference to meet Party objectives. In addition, because the Party uses the law for its own ends and because power continually shifts within the Party, application of the law continually shifts as well.[93] Hence, the citizenry focuses on Party behavior and communications much less than on the continually changing and uncertain system of laws.[94]

Despite this uncertainty, Santoro reports that tens of thousands of Chinese have used China's Administrative Litigations Law (ALL) to sue the government and bemoans the fact that Western multinational corporations (MNCs) do not.[95] In fact, Santoro reports that MNCs rely primarily on developing relationships with government officials to have their needs addressed. In other words, Western MNCs support the system that undermines the rule of law to suppress its own people. Santoro argues that MNCs have an ethical responsibility to use the legal system and pressure the government to move toward an independent, rights-based, Western-style legal system. After all, individual Chinese with far fewer resources than MNCs and much more to lose press their rights through the court system every day.

[91] As of 2012, lack of confidence in the rule of law seems to be getting worse, judging by the increasing desire of wealthy Chinese to emigrate (Page 2012). The government's arbitrary power is a key factor in the decision to leave China.

[92] This role of the legal system continues an ancient legal tradition in China (Butterton 2001). Chinese law has always been fundamentally penal; civil law is generally neglected.

[93] S. Li 2004.

[94] There are also cultural reasons for this attitude. The Chinese do not like to be bound by the law, preferring to remain flexible in order to adjust to changing circumstances in the context of rising and declining personal relationships (Butterton 2001). The legal system is a local process involving deep local knowledge of the issues and disputants as well as participation by local others offering advice, opinions, criticism, and mediation. The whole process is more or less hemmed in by a powerful drive to maintain community harmony.

[95] Santoro 2009. However, ALL can be used only to challenge specific acts taken by a government agency. It cannot be used to question the appropriateness or reasonableness of an agency decision, nor can it challenge an agency's rule-making authority. The law is quite limited.

However, Santoro also points out that the chances of getting a court to even accept a lawsuit against a government agency are "almost zero."[96] The Chinese courts have even refused to review the case of the tainted baby formula, which poisoned 290,000 infants. This is a routine example of the Party's putting its interests above the law. As Santoro states, the most effective means to pursue justice in a court of law is to use authoritative legal principles developed over time through an independent judicial appeals process.[97] In China, there is no possibility of an independent judicial review. In fact, it is often impossible even to tell who has jurisdiction over a case.

This leads to a related matter, the continuing vagueness of laws in China, IP law being no exception.[98] The practical result, and almost certainly the intent, is to give those interpreting the law maximum discretion in applying it in any particular case. Ultimately, vagueness is used as a tool of power, allowing the government to change the interpretation of the law as its interests change over time or in particular cases. From the viewpoint of a litigant, then, it is difficult to predict or even guess how the law will be applied.

Another troubling practice that was seen in the 1980s legal reforms and that continues today is the use of *secret* laws and regulations[99]—those that exist and are enforced but are not made public. As with vague laws, secret laws are tools of power, making the law the government's prerogative as opposed to a public standard applied consistently to each and all to achieve a just order. And as with vague laws, secret laws make it impossible to argue for or against any course of action in the face of unknown rules and values regulating a situation.

In summary, the Communist Party continues to dominate the legal system, maintaining control over the law in a way somewhat similar to the way it controls economic policy or land management.

4. IP Law and the Courts. As with criminal law, civil penalties are not a deterrent to infringement. For example, the American adhesives manufacturer ABRO Industries filed suit against the Chinese firm Hunan Magic Power for counterfeiting ABRO products and representing itself as ABRO. ABRO prevailed in the Trademarks Office and in federal court but was

---

[96] Santoro 2009: 113.

[97] Santoro 2009.

[98] Zimmerman 2005.

[99] According to *The Economist* (December 10, 2011a), there have been some improvements in transparency because of China's WTO membership.

awarded only $64,000, a small fraction of its losses.[100] Hunan Magic Power continues to openly produce counterfeit products.

More positively, foreign firms generally win 60–80 percent of IP cases.[101] In 2007, the court gave its first $1 million award. Recently, a German company won a $3 million award for infringement of its bus design and a Wuhan company won $7 million for infringement.[102] Some observers think these changes reflect China's continuing economic development and the government's desire to increase innovation.

There certainly is no shortage of IP cases in the courts: in 2010, they numbered 43,000.[103] Since 2006, more patent lawsuits have been filed in China than anywhere else in the world. This is of course both progress and a measure of the problem. The majority of these cases, perhaps up to 90 percent, are brought by Chinese companies against Chinese companies,[104] a fact that could pressure the government to act more strongly against infringement.

Some observers report improvements in the training and functioning of judges, especially in the larger cities. Protectionism is more likely in local or provincial courts. New courts specializing in IP law have been established, staffed by judges with specialized training in IP law. How much these developments have helped is unclear, given the challenges of interpreting vague, secret, subject to political pressure, and changing laws. Other writers think the laws themselves are fine and the problem is with their newness and the new roles the court is expected to play. The courts have simply been slow to come up to speed, at least in the eyes of some American observers. A less generous view is that the courts remain distant, inexperienced, lacking in prestige, and more or less powerless.[105] Many efforts have been made to

---

[100] Barancy 2007. To be sure, *The Economist* (April 21, 2012) reports that the average award for damages in cases won by the plaintiff is less than $30,000, an amount that does not justify the cost of litigation.

[101] Toloken 2008.

[102] *Economist* October 16, 2010.

[103] Areddy 2011. The number of lawsuits over patent violations and infringement have grown by double digits since then (*Economist* April 21, 2012).

[104] Toloken 2008; Zimmerman 2005.

[105] The *Economist* (April 21, 2012) argues that the biggest problem with the courts is that they seldom publish detailed rulings. Because it is not public knowledge why the court ruled the way it did, what factors it considered, and what criteria it used, it is impossible to evaluate the decision in a particular case or learn from cases in general, a situation that considerably handicaps business decision making.

improve IP protection, but it is far from clear what effect they will have and to what extent they will lead to judicial independence. The question itself is not encouraging.

V. Infringement and the Domestic Market

It is certainly true that the Chinese suffer more from IP theft than do foreigners.[106] Yet in a 2008 survey, the Chinese expressed their top concerns as the rising prices of consumer goods, income inequality, and government corruption.[107] Only a small minority were concerned about product safety.[108] Clearly, the Chinese software, music, film, and publishing industries have been hit hard by piracy, for example.[109] But in the big scheme of things, IPR enforcement has yet to register as a major problem.

The landscape could change. Even though there are very few well-known Chinese brands, some are emerging, particularly in the automotive and appliance industries. As noted above, the numbers of Chinese patent applications and patent infringement lawsuits are up sharply. The government is keen to increase Chinese trademarks and patents. Chinese firms are investing heavily to develop and protect new technologies,[110] and some are eager to expand overseas.

The government finds itself between a rock and a hard place in regard to IPR violations. The economies of whole villages, towns, and even some cities are dependent on counterfeiting and piracy. To shut down IPR infringement in these areas would decimate these economies, leading to spiking unemployment and social unrest. The government is not eager to take this on, yet not to prosecute violations contradicts its own goals and efforts.

The problem will not go away by itself. The markup on pirated DVDs, for example, is estimated at 1,150 percent, a little above the margin on cocaine and entailing much less risk.[111] The Colombian government has not been

---

[106] Mertha 2005.

[107] Santoro 2009.

[108] This result is rather surprising in light of incidents like the poisoning of 290,000 infants by contaminated formula.

[109] McCoy 2009; Schroeder 2007.

[110] Some Chinese companies, like electronics giants Lenovo and Huawei, are advocating for better IP protection.

[111] Smith 2007.

able to shut down cocaine production with a full-scale military assault backed by funding and training from the United States. The Chinese government would need an even greater effort to make a sizable reduction in counterfeiting, given its magnitude, decentralization, and institutional support; not to mention that doing so would create even worse problems for the government itself. Ultimately, the Party will address the issue based on its own power interests.

American Intellectual Property Experience in China

I. American IP Culture in China

1. Attitudes Toward IP. Americans care a lot about IPR, and rightly so. IP is 50 percent of American exports and 40 percent of economic growth.[112] The piracy rate inside the United States is the lowest in the world.[113] Victoria A. Espinel, appointed to the newly minted position of intellectual property enforcement coordinator in 2009, said the United States model for protecting IP is the "world's gold standard."[114] This statement expresses the widely held American belief, also assumed in U.S. law, that IP rights are universal.[115] China is generally seen by American politicians and businessmen as corrupt and deplorable in the area of enforcing IPR. It is common for Americans to see China as backward, as yet to enter the modern era in terms of both IPR and the rule of law.

Americans are gung ho about IPR because, as noted above, it is in their self-interest to be so, but also because they believe it advances economic growth through the protection of innovation and, more basically, it is integral to private property, the ground of individual freedom. But though Americans have always been gung ho about their freedom, they have not always been so about IPR. The United States did not even pass laws for the protection of foreign copyrighted material until 1891, after it had passed through the developing-economy stage.[116] During the eighteenth century, American companies were notorious for violating European copyrights.

---

[112] Toohey 2009.

[113] Holleyman 2009.

[114] Espinel 2007: 24.

[115] Burrell 1998. It also expresses the centrality of technology in American life and a Fort Knox approach to protecting it.

[116] Alford 1995.

Still, American leaders today mention that IPR is the only right contained in the Constitution, as if to imply that IPR is written deep into our heritage. But even the writers of the Constitution were quite practical about IP, using language not about universal rights but about promoting innovation for "limited times."[117] Actually, American behavior concerning IP is far from perfect. The more patents and copyrights American firms receive, the more they end up in court trying to protect their property.[118] IP law is thus more a reflection of disregard for IPR than a testament to it as a cherished ideal.

Even the argument that IPR promotes innovation is not so cut and dried. By increasing the number of ideas and inventions that are off-limits to prospective innovators, IPR can actually reduce innovation. It is important to have a robust public domain, where knowledge and technology are available to everyone, to supply the materials for future innovators. This is why the Constitution restricts IPR to "limited times." Otherwise, market power can be concentrated, competition undermined, and innovation reduced.

2. Going to China. Over the last three decades, China has been the fastest-growing market in the world. American corporations, especially MNCs, have little choice but to enter the China market. The market is potentially so big, the cost savings so significant, and above all the competitive implications so substantial that the consequences of not entering it could be severe.[119]

In 2010, China exported $283 billion worth of goods to the United States.[120] Because of China's low-cost labor and operating environment, these imports significantly lowered prices for American consumers, resulting in increased purchasing power. It also increased the United States' trade deficit because the United States was buying more from China than China was buying from the United States—though the trade deficit is significantly offset by the fact that 60 percent of Chinese exports are from foreign companies using foreign components.[121] Exports of American manufactured goods out of China grew from $9.3 billion in 1994 to $41.8 billion in 2005. Some American companies have built extensive R&D facilities in China.

---

[117] Boyle 1996.

[118] Lawsuits plague Silicon Valley, for example (Wadhwa 2012). Microsoft, Hewlett-Packard, IBM, Oracle, Apple, and many others have recently been involved in legal battles over infringement.

[119] Perkowski 2012.

[120] The U.S.-China Business Council 2012b.

[121] Herger 2007.

Since 2001, when China joined the WTO, American exports to China have grown from $19.2 billion to $103.9 billion in 2011.[122] China is the fourth-largest export market for the United States. Top American exports to China are machinery, aircraft, medical instruments, agricultural goods and services, and numerous other services such as professional, technical, educational, and transportation services. U.S. copyright industries' sales abroad in 2007 were $125 billion.[123] Particular American products like software have an enormous future potential in China, though they currently face widespread piracy and counterfeiting. American firms receive about $2 billion per year in licensing fees and royalties from Chinese companies.[124]

3. Profit and Loss. Some estimates of losses to American industry from worldwide counterfeiting go as high as $250 billion.[125] The key industries hurt are IT, life sciences, digital content, pharmaceuticals, defense, and entertainment. By all accounts, China is the worst violator. In a 2010 American Chamber of Commerce survey, 58 percent of American firms operating in China said they suffer "material damage" from Chinese counterfeiting.[126] Generally, the situation in China has not improved despite receiving continuous attention from both the American government and business for more than a decade.[127] Smith stated in 2007 that outside of software, losses are 80–90 percent of the market in most copyright-based industries, "making it almost impossible to do business there."[128]

The lone IP improvement, software, resulted from Chinese government action. As noted earlier, software piracy dropped from above 90 percent to 77 percent in 2010. Practically the whole improvement was from preloading legitimate software on computers sold in China and from the government's installing legitimate software on its own computers.[129] In 2006, sales of legitimate software were $1.2 billion, a 358 percent increase from 2003.

---

[122] The U.S.-China Business Council 2012b.

[123] Holleyman 2009.

[124] *Economist* April 25, 2009.

[125] Watson 2009.

[126] Areddy 2011.

[127] In his January 2012 State of the Union Address, President Obama announced the creation of a "Trade Enforcement Unit" (Weisman 2012). He specifically mentioned investigating China for unfair trade practices.

[128] Smith 2007: 32.

[129] Leonhardt (2011b), however, reports government agencies are still downloading software updates illegally.

With that said, Microsoft reported in 2011 that its revenue in China will be only 5 percent of its United States revenue, even though sales of personal computers in the two countries are about the same.[130]

For many American businesses that depend on IP, China is the most frustrating market in the world. Yet there is the odd fact that American companies are loath to criticize China's IP practices. They fear retaliation from the Chinese government or SOE sector in the form of lost business or inability to get government approvals, licenses, and so forth. Some firms, in the auto industry for example, are afraid to speak out about counterfeit components because doing so would raise questions about the quality of their products back in the United States. This reluctance to openly discuss the issue has taken pressure off the Chinese government to address IP problems.

American companies try to develop relationships with government officials "off the record" to get help with IP problems. Both Li and Santoro have criticized this approach because it will raise costs, reinforce the "back-door" system, and delay development of the rule of law.[131] Other companies, in order to remain anonymous, have encouraged the American government and the American Chamber of Commerce to speak out on their behalf. The success of the U.S. government in addressing IP problems in China will be discussed below.

Microsoft has tried both the behind-the-scenes approach with Chinese officials and lawsuits.[132] The latter approach generated resentment among Chinese, perhaps because Microsoft was seen as a big, powerful (foreign) corporation taking advantage of poor China, which is just an emerging economy. This view has echoes of Western exploitation that is still a sensitive issue in China. The Chinese are quick to feel the West is trying to hold back Chinese development. Yet Microsoft is also criticized in the United States for not speaking out more forthrightly, for seeking short-term profits at the expense of its own and the United States' long-term interests in a level playing field in China.[133] The fact that Microsoft CEO Steve Ballmer publicly

---

[130] Fletcher and Dean 2011. Microsoft's revenue per personal computer in China is only about one-sixth of what it gets in India.

[131] S. Li 2004; Santoro 2009.

[132] Fletcher and Dean 2011.

[133] Coburn 2005.

criticized China's IP record in 2011 suggests the company has come around to the latter view.[134]

4. Winners and Losers. As discussed above, the number of Chinese government raids and seizures has increased, but because of light penalties, deterrence has not. In addition to the loss of sales and revenues for American companies, counterfeiting has two other insidious effects. In the pharmaceutical industry it results in harmful, sometimes deadly, medicines. Santoro argues that MNCs in search of lower and lower costs have put the public at grave risk.[135] Because the Chinese government is not capable of regulating the manufacture of medicines and component compounds in China, and because it will be decades before Chinese manufacturers are able to meet global safety standards, MNCs, it is argued, have an ethical responsibility to make sure their production pipelines using Chinese manufacturers are safe. So far the record is disconcerting at best. When Baxter International's blood thinner heparin caused illness and death in the United States, Baxter at first refused even to identify its Chinese suppliers.[136]

As discussed earlier, counterfeiting gives a competitive advantage to the firms not paying the true cost of IP, weakening the more efficient but honest firms and raising prices for consumers. Given the extent of piracy and counterfeiting in China, and the size of the Chinese economy, this mechanism leads to a substantial loss in social welfare. In terms of the American market, large firms that source from Chinese suppliers using pirated technology gain unfair advantages over small American firms that cannot afford either to go to China or to risk their IP once there.[137] Given that small firms are some of the most innovative and job creating in the United States, this unfairness creates a loss for American society as a whole.

When trying to evaluate the United States–China IP relationship, it is important to look at what parts of American society win in China and what parts lose. Many U.S. companies are making enormous amounts of money by manufacturing or sourcing their products in China and then shipping them back to the United States, but IP-dependent industries

---

[134] General Electric CEO Jeffrey Immelt also said publicly in 2012 that China is a "hard" place to do business due to government investment restrictions and support for state-owned national champions (Linebaugh 2012).

[135] Santoro 2009.

[136] Santoro 2009.

[137] Fishman 2005.

like software, entertainment, and pharmaceuticals are losing large amounts of profit through IPR infringement. One would think the latter group would speak out, but as discussed, they have been reluctant to do so, either because they are trying to protect the business they do have or because they hope to have more business in the future. Take for example DVD players, which sold for around $30 in 2005 at places like Wal-Mart and Target. How is this possible given that the license fee on the chip needed to run a DVD player was around $14?[138] In this case, retailers and consumers are benefiting at the expense of chipmakers, who are losing sales to counterfeit chips.

If IP were to be protected in China, prices would rise for consumers and profits would drop for some American companies. But since Chinese counterfeiting benefits a majority of Americans in terms of lower prices, the democratic process works such that the American government is not inclined to act too strenuously against IPR infringement. The fact that American manufacturing workers have been big losers in the outsourcing process does not fundamentally change the math, though the situation is far from simple. Ostergard, for example, mentions that the Chinese have had an influence on America's democratic process.[139] China threatened sanctions against the American aerospace industry, which was not (yet) IP-threatened, to stop that industry from supporting other high-tech American industries that *were* IP-threatened in China. Thus the American aerospace industry is a winner because it did *not* lobby the U.S. government to stop IPR infringement in China. From a purely (domestic) utilitarian perspective, the American government's mild efforts to stop IPR infringement in China may very well reflect an accurate reading of American interests, at least in the short and medium terms.

One last point about the ethics of outsourcing before moving on to the American government's record on fighting IPR infringement in China: Another reason Wal-Mart can sell DVD players for $30, for example, is that it puts constant pressure on Chinese manufacturers to continuously lower prices. How to continuously lower prices is left up to the Chinese. The result is that Chinese workers absorb the losses one way or another. Wages are not paid, benefits are nonexistent, safety is forgone, and living standards are

[138] Miner 2005.
[139] Ostergard 2003.

good only compared with conditions of poverty in rural areas.[140] Government officials look the other way as they are rewarded for creating jobs or because they are bribed. The abuse of Chinese workers is an essential factor, in addition to IP theft, enabling the American consumer to pay $30 for the DVD player. There are many invisible hands in that price, and many of them are not ethically justifiable.

II. IP, China, and the United States Government

China is the Somalia of the intellectual world.

> Diane E. Watson
> Committee on Oversight and
> Government Reform
> U.S. House of Representatives
> December 9, 2009

We reported . . . weaknesses at local levels, but also highlighted positive efforts, innovative initiatives for fighting Internet piracy in Beijing, pilot programs on enforcement in Shanghai, and deeper engagement with international rights holders in Jiangsu province.

> Victoria A. Espinel
> Assistant U.S. Representative for
> Intellectual Property and Innovation
> Office of U.S. Trade Representative
> October 18, 2007

As of this writing in 2012, IPR violations in China still abound, but as can be seen from the above two quotes, beauty is in the eye of the beholder, at least as far as the American government is concerned. The only significant improvement has been in the software area mentioned above, and that only lowered the piracy rate to 77 percent of software usage.

The most powerful tool the U.S. government has to fight foreign IPR violations is the Special 301 Report. The Special 301 Report, compiled

---

[140] Harney 2008. A 2012 report on Foxconn, China's largest electronics manufacturer, found "43 percent of workers had experienced or witnessed accidents, and almost two-thirds said their compensation 'does not meet their basic needs' " (Duhigg and Greenhouse 2012).

annually by the U.S. Trade Representative (USTR), requires the USTR to identify "priority" countries that fail to protect American IP, notify Congress, and take protective measures.[141] Out of 77 countries reviewed in 2009, 46 were named in the report.[142] Generally, the report shows growing and more sophisticated theft of American IP. The report is important because once countries are listed, retaliatory action can be taken against them. China is currently listed in the Special 301 Report.

Importantly, once China, with American support, entered the WTO in 2001, the United States was forbidden from exercising unilateral retaliation against China. Along with membership in the WTO and the granting of most-favored-nation status, tariffs on Chinese goods coming into the United States dropped from 40 percent to 2.5 percent.[143] China, however, continues to stop many American products from entering China, such as books, music, videos, journals, and other publications. So there is an inconsistency wherein China is named in the Special 301 Report as a major violator of American IPR but at the same time is given privileged access to American markets.[144] Indeed, the number of counterfeit Chinese products entering the United States increased after China was admitted to the WTO.[145]

In April 2007, the USTR used the WTO Dispute Settlement Body to file the first of several complaints against China for violations of IP agreements. Each complaint involved multiple issues. Between August 2008 and August 2009, the WTO ruled against China three times. The process took more than two years. The Chinese might appeal the decisions, requiring even more time. If the verdicts are upheld, it is not obvious how compliance will be enforced.[146]

---

[141] Alford 1995.

[142] McCoy 2009.

[143] Mulloy 2005. China, for its part, had to relax more than 7,000 tariffs, quotas, and other trade barriers (*Economist* December 10, 2011a).

[144] China benefits under other preferential treatment programs like the Generalized System of Preferences Program and the Caribbean Basin Economic Recovery Act of 1983.

[145] China accounted for 81 percent of the total domestic value of IP seizures by U.S. Customs in 2008 (Vargo 2009).

[146] Use of the WTO to prosecute trade violations presents other problems for the United States. As noted earlier, American companies are reluctant to provide evidence of Chinese violations for fear of retaliation from the Chinese government. Also, often Chinese practices fall in a gray area that is difficult to prosecute under the rules of the WTO. For these reasons, the United States often retaliates bilaterally rather than through the WTO (*Economist* December 10, 2011a). Indeed, in 2011, the WTO ruled that the United States had illegally imposed antidumping and antisubsidy duties on some Chinese exports (Miller 2011). So goes the legal trade war.

According to WTO rules, once damage is demonstrated and the case won, the damaged country has the right to implement tariffs in the amount of the damage.

Several of the WTO rulings found that China was in violation of the TRIPS (Trade-Related Intellectual Property Rights) agreement administered under the WTO. TRIPS states that IP owners must be given property rights, the rights must be clear, and they must have an effective means of enforcement.[147] TRIPS has been criticized for lax enforcement. In addition, some American executives feel TRIPS requirements are too minimal. Hamilton, however, argues that TRIPS assumes Western individualism and attempts to remake international copyright law according to Western values and interests.[148] In the debate over the rights of the individual creator versus the community free-use zone, TRIPS, he asserts, is biased in favor of the former. In Hamilton's view, it is unjustifiable to obliterate differences in cultural orientations by standardizing political relations, a practice that will only benefit the developed nations and MNCs that control most of the advanced IP. Given the lax enforcement of TRIPS by developing nations, apparently they agree with this view.

The U.S. government is under pressure to address increasing IPR violations. Its response has been to create increasing numbers of policies, organizations, and operations for IPR enforcement. In addition to what has been discussed above, there is the Anti-Counterfeiting Trade Agreement (ACTA) for Internet piracy, the Office of International Intellectual Property Enforcement in the State Department (created in 2005), Operation Summer Solstice (an American-Chinese joint criminal enforcement operation), the Foreign Relations Authorization Act (H.R. 2410) that seeks to put 10 new IP attachés in key embassies, and the Prioritizing Resources and Organizations for Intellectual Property Act of 2008 that seeks to staff an office of coordination for the eight government agencies with responsibility for IP. The latter is to include dedicated FBI agents and prosecutors specializing in IP enforcement. This is far from a complete list.[149] Yet the government's efforts to combat IP theft in China have been ineffective; in fact, Chinese IPR infringement appears to be growing.

---

[147] Toohey 2009.

[148] M. Hamilton 1997.

[149] In 2012, President Obama asked Congress for 50 people and $26 million in funding for the new Trade Enforcement Unit mentioned above (Martin and Elmquist 2012).

The lack of progress is a reflection of the enormity and complexity of the problem. It is also a reflection of the government's conflicting goals and pressures. In addition to reducing IPR infringement, the government is trying to increase access to the Chinese marketplace;[150] keep the Chinese buying American government debt; and secure its help around the world, including with the North Koreans, Iranians, and others. Human rights in China also do not receive the attention of the American government to the extent its proponents would like. Given that IPR enforcement is a threat not only to economic growth but also to public health, consumer safety, and national security, the government must manage very difficult tradeoffs indeed.

IP, Culture, Profits, and Ethics

I. The Importance of Culture

1. Chinese Cultural Background. The Confucian cultural heritage makes a distinction between *yi*, "justice," and *li*, "profit," the former the foundation of moral thought, the latter a selfish desire, for the most part outside of one's control.[151] The idea of IP clearly falls under *li* and thus is outside the moral center of Chinese culture, a concern for respectful, harmonious, and stable relationships. Traditionally, relationships become and remain respectful, harmonious, and stable by following the Way, documented and taught in Chinese classic thought. The idea that intellectual work should be private property as opposed to communal identity is unthinkable in the traditional world view. In this system, stability is valued over originality.

Thus China's traditional approach to IP, like its approach to so many other things, is collective. Not the individual but the group is privileged. The individual is obliged to share his creations with others. Since society as a whole is privileged in Chinese thought, not only is the individual obligated to society but his creations are seen as ultimately springing from the cultural heritage more than from his own creativity.[152] Diffusion of new ideas is an obligation. Confidentiality and privacy are foreign concepts.

---

[150] According to Santoro (2009), the American government bartered away safety demands involving counterfeit drugs to get access to the banking and securities industry in China.

[151] R. Wang 2002.

[152] Alford 1995.

With this background, China lacks the cultural orientation to support IPR. The government has passed laws to protect IP, but without cultural change, these laws will struggle for legitimacy.[153] The laws are not morally persuasive and indeed may be seen as morally wrong. "Piracy" may be more in tune with Chinese culture.

From the cultural perspective, two possibilities for change are apparent. First, Confucianism could evolve from within. Wang mentions that Confucian ethics do not rule out a creative synthesis between collectivism and personal well-being.[154] Hence, rewards for individual creativity that lead to societal benefit are justifiable. Evolutionary change takes time and, in this case, to work must include a satisfactory solution to the West's dominance over advanced technology.

The second possibility stems from external influences on Chinese culture that encourage an increased desire for more personal space or privacy. At least three sources are leading to an increase in individualism in China. The family, the bedrock of Chinese culture, is under pressure from the myriad opportunities marketization is opening up in China. Perhaps even more apparent, the Internet is creating a space that was not available to previous generations where private conversations take place. Fifty percent of Chinese Internet users are under the age of 25.[155] In other words, technology is providing a new generation the means to develop their thoughts and beliefs individually or in small groups, a phenomenon that will most likely lead to social change. Finally, ironically, as Western popular culture spreads throughout China through counterfeit reproductions, Western antiauthoritarianism could seep into Chinese thought.[156] If any one of these influences, or a combination of them, encourages the development of more individualistic preferences, the culture could become more hospitable to the idea of IPR.

2. American Cultural Background. In the United States, individual freedom is emphasized over society as a whole. The founding value of liberty has become "individualism" and has grown more dominant in the twentieth century.[157] In the area of IP, it has led to an emphasis on the private ownership of individual creative production.[158]

---

[153] Burrell 1998.
[154] R. Wang 2002.
[155] *China's Internet Network Information Center 2012.*
[156] M. Hamilton 1997.
[157] Shils 1997.
[158] Swinyard, Rinne, and Kau 1990.

In any case, individual rights are presupposed in the American rights-based legal system and thus in IP law. The individual rights approach to IP originated in the Western world. For many in the West, especially in the United States, this is the natural course of events. A person has a natural right to the fruits of his own labor.[159]

Lynn Paine maps out the moral presuppositions underlying IPR, arguing they are intimately related to core American commitments to individual autonomy, personality, privacy, liberty, and freedom of thought and expression.[160] Legal justifications for IPR grew out of and are based on these basic value commitments.

Critics of the individual rights approach to IP make several points. First, there is a contradiction in positing freedom of thought and expression to justify IPR but then giving control over IP to individuals.[161] Either thought and expression are free and open, or they are private and controlled. Second, most patents and copyrights in the United States are owned by organizations.[162] So even if IPR are based on individual rights, individuals gain only limited benefit from IP law.

Perhaps an even more basic question about the validity of IPR arises from the fact that such rights do not receive widespread support in practice. Even in the United States, there is some public resistance to the enforcement of IPR laws, as can be seen in pirated downloading off the Internet and illegal software copying.[163] When we look worldwide, the problem gets much worse. More than 42 percent of installed software programs worldwide are pirated, more than 67 percent in emerging markets.[164] Even Canada does not comply with the 1996 World Intellectual Property Organization (WIPO) copyright treaty and has not made IP enforcement a high priority.[165] Given widespread, worldwide violation of IPR, it is difficult to conclude that the IPR system is the best approach to manage IP globally. Certainly the diversity of cultural contexts and economic development in which IPR must be enforced does not make for universal support.

---

[159] Hettinger 1997.

[160] Paine 1997.

[161] Hettinger 1997.

[162] Hettinger 1997. In fact, almost without exception American businesses require individual employees to cede their IP claims to the corporation as a condition of employment (Steidlmeier 1993).

[163] Burrell 1998.

[164] Business Software Alliance 2012.

[165] Smith 2007.

II. Interests and Ethics

1. Profits and Losses. The United States is the world's leading producer of advanced technology products. As such, it demands a strong IPR regime to protect its competitive advantage. China, on the other hand, seeks to develop its economy, needs advanced technology to do so, but cannot develop what it needs on its own. It also does not want to pay American companies the prices they seek for their products. So the Chinese copy and steal American technology, violating copyrights, patents, trademarks, and trade secrets. Hence, there is a fundamental conflict between the American desire to protect its IP's profit-making potential and the Chinese desire to develop its economy without paying the full costs for the foreign technology needed to do so.

The situation is indeed lopsided. The world's high-income economies, wherein reside 16 percent of the world's population, contain almost 100 percent of the world's top 300 companies in terms of R&D spending.[166] Given this lopsidedness, Miner believes the Chinese are forced to pirate advanced technology to bootstrap themselves up the economic development ladder.[167] It is not that the advanced economies do not benefit from China. They have all benefited from the growth of China's economy. The problem is that China is forced to compete with the advanced economies before it is fully able to do so. If it obeyed WTO IP rules, its development would be much slower. With 1.3 billion people—many of them poor—considerable social unrest, and great ambition, China pirates technology to increase its economic growth as fast as possible.

Under other conditions, foreign firms might withhold investment and technology transfer in response to Chinese piracy, but while some foreign firms do so, foreign investment in China has been enormous. In other words, foreign businesses pour into China despite the piracy. Hence, they calculate that even with the piracy there are gains to be made (or losses to be avoided). In any case, the problem is more general than China. As was noted, IP theft is a worldwide phenomenon. Less-developed countries steal technology from more-developed countries. Indeed, as we saw, the United States did it in its earlier development.

The problem intensifies when at some point the balance of profits and losses, which was always unclear and unsatisfactory for the developed economies, gets worse. What was once a developing economy struggling to meet

---

[166] Redding and Witt 2007.
[167] Miner 2005.

basic needs, build infrastructure, and develop advanced capacities starts producing competitive businesses that take market share, directly or indirectly through infringements, from developed-country businesses worldwide. For example, the Chinese firm Huawei pirated the products of the American firm Cisco Systems and is now the number two telecom equipment vendor in the world—ahead of Cisco.[168] It used profits from the pirated products to buy legitimate patents from Qualcomm and now legitimately competes with Cisco in world markets. What at one point was piracy to avoid foreign domination becomes piracy to dominate foreigners. It is a survival-of-the-fittest conflict, wherein piracy is just one more means in the power competition between two peoples. The "rule of law" sounds nice but early in the conflict it functions to slow the developing economy's growth, just as its antithesis, infringement, functions to negatively affect the advanced economy.

2. The Ethics of IP. Many ethical issues arise in the battle between nations over IP. If enforcing IPR in China on the one hand primarily benefits foreign MNCs and on the other hand holds back economic development, puts very poor sections of the population at risk, or leads to foreign control over the most advanced technology, is it ethical for the Chinese government to enforce IPR, and is it ethical for foreign governments, through threats or sanctions, to try to force the Chinese to do so? In practice, the situation is quite messy. A crude sort of social contract seems to be in play. All parties remain in the system as long as they more or less benefit. They agree to play by the rules but cheat often until forced not to by another party. If the balance of benefits gets too one-sided, the cheating intensifies, the sanctions increase, or the system breaks down. It is far from an ethically-based system because the interests are too strongly in conflict and the relations too impersonal for the social contract to truly hold.

It seems fair to argue that a country has a right to development because human dignity requires the exercise of one's capacities.[169] So if IPR undermine development, an ethical argument can be made to ignore them. One key question is, do IPR impede economic development or stimulate it? This question is difficult to answer due to the complexity of the situation, involving such a great many variables. Depending on the time frame considered and other factors like the rate of economic development, the distribution of benefits would likely change. Focusing only on the short term, not only would the majority of

---

[168] Fishman 2005; Chao and Raice 2011.
[169] Sen 2000.

economic benefits go to MNCs, but control over technology, also a political issue, would remain with foreign companies, limiting Chinese use of technology for self-sufficiency, national security, and other political ends. In other words, foreigners would control what technology China gained access to, at what price, and when—a politically unacceptable position for any nation.

As to the issue of IPR enforcement, the literature is split. Some argue enforcement would lead to increased foreign investment, thus stimulating the economy; others argue that increased enforcement would restrict the flow of information, thus undermining technological innovation. Even this dichotomy assumes a single society and a single government. Given that in this case one country controls the technology and the other country needs it, additional factors enter the discussion, like cultural differences and political sovereignty. The situation is further complicated by the historical dimension, which in this case involves a context of foreign exploitation.[170] It is thus impossible to reduce the IPR enforcement question to that of innovation maximization. Questions about fit between IPR law and cultural context, effects on political goals and the distribution of power, and effects on different social classes over different time frames, cannot be ignored.

The literature is also split in regard to the importance of the public domain as a source for innovation. The "I made it, I own it" argument is criticized for grossly underestimating the innovator's dependence on past innovations. This is a sociologically sound line of reasoning[171] and interestingly has much in common with the traditional Chinese view. The other side of the argument is that the public domain does not innovate by itself. It takes a motivated individual to synthesize previous work and create something new. But if IPR are too strong, the public domain is constricted and future innovators have less material from which to work, thus reducing future innovation.

Since both the public domain and the motivated innovator are needed to innovate, IPR must be constructed so as to assure the contributions of both factors. Given that American individualism and Chinese collectivism address these issues from and toward different directions, it is difficult to see how one universal system of IPR is the most appropriate way to address IP.[172]

---

[170] Alford 1995. The Chinese believe the West created IPR to maintain a monopoly over the production and distribution of knowledge and knowledge products.

[171] Shils 1981.

[172] *The Economist* (April 21, 2012) asserts that as Chinese companies develop technology, they will naturally want IPR. Even if this is so, it does not make it right. It is a one-sided view of the matter and merely restarts the original problem over who benefits all over again.

The situation is further complicated by the fact that IPR are not addressed internationally as a single issue. IPR are a part of the WTO. When China joined the WTO it agreed to follow a whole slew of agreements and rules involving many aspects of trade. Presumably what China lost in terms of IPR preferences it gained in terms of tariff reductions, for example. Yet it drags its feet on IPR enforcement. One can understand the often-expressed American frustration, even alarm.

Another ethical aspect of IPR is their effect on competition. It is not uncommon for patents to be purchased by large firms to suppress competition by using the patent as a barrier to entry.[173] When applied to American-Chinese relations in China, the IPR-are-needed-to-stimulate-innovation argument thus falls apart because it implies suppressing the development of Chinese industry. Hence, IPR create a double problem: They can reduce competition generally and undermine Chinese economic development specifically.

The other side to this argument is that in a competitive system, fairness requires some limitation on access to the ideas of others.[174] It would be both unfair and self-defeating if one's competitors have unimpeded access to one's ideas. The benefits of competition would be destroyed and innovative activity would come to a halt. When applied to American-Chinese relations, however, the problem arises that China is not in a position to compete with American technological development. The competition argument assumes a marketplace of more or less equal competitors. Until it can be said that American and Chinese firms compete on a more or less equal basis, IPR enforcement would provide American firms with domination of central aspects of the Chinese economy for the foreseeable future. Thus, full enforcement of IPR are unfair at this point in China's development.

Related to the competition argument in favor of IPR enforcement is the efficiency argument. If there is not IPR enforcement, trust in business will become problematic. Businesses will more naturally hire family members or close associates in order to limit losses of IP. Businesses will have difficulty expanding in size or geographic coverage because of an inability to secure trusted employees. Interestingly, this situation actually exists in China, and

---

[173] Hettinger 1997. Sometimes the barrier is even erected by withdrawing the patent from use (D. Hamilton 2005).

[174] Paine 1997.

for more profound reasons than the lack of IPR enforcement. It is the result of unchecked government power. So the efficiency argument for IP enforcement does not apply in China because of the country's different political and cultural configuration. The rights-based IP model in the WTO is thus a specific cultural form, coinciding with more or less decentralized, individualistic cultures with democratic political systems. China is not one of these.

III. Political Change

For China to truly embrace a rights-based IP system, it will require radical change in political and economic rights. Santoro believes that until this happens—until economic rights are respected, the government is effective in enforcing regulations, and the rule of law protects the rights and interests of citizens—foreign investment will not be secure in China.[175] Santoro argues that Western firms can help bring about the rule of law in China by using the WTO dispute mechanism to push for uniform application of laws and independent judicial review.

Alternatively, William P. Alford thinks much more fundamental change in Chinese institutions is required and the West can and should have only limited influence on this level.[176] China does not have a rights-based political culture; it has an authoritarian political culture. It has changed many laws to protect rights, but the government does not always enforce the new laws because it holds its own interests and goals above the law. Without fundamental change in the political culture, the legal system will not protect rights, let alone IPR, which are primarily for foreigners.

It is true that the government needs the legal system for legitimacy and social control; to encourage foreigners to invest resources, especially technology; and to move away from central planning. But its idea of control includes control over the law. Its goals are thus contradictory. Furthermore, political leaders use the law to punish opponents within the government and between the central government and the provinces. In other words, the law is politicized. Factions use means other than voting or elections to settle political conflicts. Unless fundamental political reform takes place and political rights are established, no other rights will be secure. As of 2012, the

---

[175] Santoro 2009.
[176] Alford 1995.

government is increasing its control over ideas. IPR can never blossom in this environment.

Perhaps Taiwan can be seen as a comparison. Democratization stimulated interest in justice beyond the maintenance of order, which is still the court's primary role in China. In Taiwan, explosive economic growth, the need for its own technology, growing political and intellectual pluralism, internationalization, and growing respect for independent legal processes led to the acceptance of IPR.[177] Still it took plenty of external pressure and the development of its largest industries to the point where they sought trademark protection. China is very far away from meeting these conditions because of its enormous size, its geographic diversity, its political decentralization, its huge population, the percentage of the population in poverty, the educational level of the population, and the government's dictatorial control.

Conclusion

The American-Chinese disagreements over IPR are clear examples of "trouble in the middle," though the problems go far beyond cultural incompatibility to include political, economic, and historical conflicts. The problems are so broad, numerous, and contradictory that it is difficult to ethically evaluate the legitimacy of IPR in the China context. On the one hand, it seems simple enough. The Chinese voluntarily agreed to provide IP protection as part of seeking and accepting WTO membership. But once they were accepted into WTO membership and began to benefit from membership privileges, they provided little IP enforcement. This would seem to be wrong, and certainly many American executives say so.

But there is more to the story. For one, all developing countries tend to be IPR violators. Certainly this applied to Taiwan, Singapore, and South Korea before they reached more advanced stages of economic development. Indeed, the United States was a major violator in its earlier development. The fact is that developing nations cannot compete with developed nations in most areas of IP; if they follow international accords, which were created by developed nations, they would be agreeing to forgo access to much IP, the wealth it generates, and the economic development it makes possible. This would have significant implications for their self-sufficiency, national security, and level of

[177] Alford 1995.

economic growth. Developing nations need an extended period of "transition," during which they do not have to meet international IPR enforcement standards, to secure their legitimate economic development requirements.[178]

This is an all-the-more-sensitive issue for the Chinese because of the military and economic aggression they suffered at the hands of the West in previous centuries. They rightfully do not trust the West, given their experience.

The Chinese also understand IP differently than the West. Their collective social orientation leads them to put a lower value on individual rights than does the West. The economic argument for IPR is not cut and dried. A balance is always required between the motivated entrepreneur and his access to public information. Reasonable people can disagree as to where exactly the line should be drawn. American culture, history, and institutions lead American policy makers to emphasize the role of the individual in innovation.

There is also the suggestive fact that American executives are mostly silent on the issue of IPR violations in China. If the problem is so bad, which it is, why is there not loud and consistent protest about it? The answer is fear of retaliation and fear of losing access to China. In other words, American companies are either making money in China or have other reasons to be there. In addition to lowering costs and accessing a booming market, many firms must attack Chinese competitors in China before bigger, stronger versions show up in their home markets. Foreigners go to China voluntarily. So even with significant IP risks, there are reasons to go there.

This brings up the utilitarian question: Who is benefiting in the China market? American retailers and consumers are benefiting from continually decreasing prices. This benefit accrues to millions of American consumers and the American businesses that use low-cost manufacturing in China to supply them and other global markets with low-priced goods. Also, American companies in China are selling into Chinese consumer, manufacturing, industrial, and other markets, providing raw materials, components, and finished goods. Hence, while American workers are losing jobs and American firms are losing business to manufacturing in China, American firms and consumers are benefiting from the same phenomenon. The situation is far from a clear loss for Americans.

---

[178] While such a transition period seems fair on the level of relations between countries, it would create devastating results for some companies whose IP is forfeited. Without some adjustment mechanism for individual companies, correcting one wrong would just create another.

This is one reason why the American government's response to Chinese IPR violations is restrained. America is gaining considerably from China's economic development. The Chinese are also funding American debt through the purchase of Treasury bonds. For these and other reasons, the United States government's response has been somewhat contradictory, reflecting the complex economic and political relations between the two countries. China was named as an IPR violator in the feared U.S. Special 301 list, but it also received American support to join the WTO, thus receiving most-favored-nation status and other benefits from the United States. It is an ambivalent, competitive relationship with strong positives and negatives for both countries.

In fact, probably the weakest stakeholder in the American-Chinese relationship and the one who has been subjected to the greatest hardship is the Chinese worker—though even here there are significant positives. Impoverished rural workers have voluntarily flocked to urban areas by the millions to take higher-paying jobs. These jobs, however, are often carried out in harsh work environments, where long hours, monotonous work, poor-to-nonexistent health and safety standards, nonexistent health and pension benefits, and abusive and uncaring management are common. The continuously falling price of goods that benefits American consumers and firms is made possible by the low pay and benefits given to Chinese workers.[179] Counterfeit products also contribute to low prices that benefit American firms and consumers. IPR infringement is a good example of the complexity of the American-Chinese business relationship, providing both positive and negative outcomes. So while many Americans decry Chinese IPR infringement, they also benefit from it. They have much less to say about harm to the Chinese worker, but from this too they benefit.

In this context of significant American benefits, the legitimate development needs of a developing country, the lopsidedness of international IP laws that favor developed countries, legitimate cultural differences as to how to value the innovator rights–community rights dichotomy, legitimate policy differences as to how much rights protection is required to stimulate innovation, and the fact that the low price of goods from which Americans benefit is dependent on the mistreatment of Chinese workers, it is clear that the

---

[179] Because of public pressure on MNCs to ensure adequate treatment of workers in their supply chains, wages for Chinese workers have risen by up to 30 percent in some cases (Oster 2011). Due to social unrest, the Chinese government too has raised the minimum wage level, though poor treatment of workers is still common (Duhigg and Greenhouse 2012).

ethics of Chinese IPR infringement is a complex and multifaceted problem. Indeed, even if the Chinese government is committed to reducing infringement, it is not clear it could do so, or do so without harm to the country. To reduce infringement would definitely reduce employment, hinder growth, and present risks to the economic reforms. Not only does the government face extensive costs to try to curtail widespread counterfeiting in such a huge population, but if successful the likely rise in social unrest could destabilize the country. The government faces a dilemma; whatever decision it makes has problematic consequences. So to simply say the Chinese are unethical for not curtailing infringement is not persuasive.

Finally, there is a basic problem with the Communist Party itself. The Communist Party is above the law; it uses the law to pursue its power interests and social goals. Private property, let alone IP, does not depend on a system of laws and individual rights; it depends on the fluid and conflicting interests of the Communist Party leadership. So ultimately there cannot be IP in China until there is fundamental political change in China. Infringement is inseparable from the Party's dictatorship. Just as the government is intimately involved in businesses of all types and government officials are privately involved in private businesses, the government is involved in infringement. Indeed, the anti-infringement officials participate in infringement. So the question of infringement in China cannot be separated from the structure of its political system.

American-Chinese conflicts over IP present a paradigm case of trouble in the middle. The middle is characterized by a complex array of interests, powers, benefits and costs, and cultural orientations. Including but well beyond cultural incompatibility, the difficulties involved in addressing IPR infringement present a complex thicket of mutually created and contradictory constraints and entanglements. No simple solution is possible to resolve the IP problem; any solution necessarily affects other important issues, benefits, and costs.

The result is an inability of either side alone, or the two together, to resolve the IP problem. The IP situation is not so much a problem as a part in a complex. This is why it is not resolved but functions as a slow-moving compromise, wherein changes in other issues present some opportunities for improvement, some worsening developments, and new constraints on action. It is trouble in the middle that will stay that way for the foreseeable future. Managing the process more than resolving the problem is the key task.

10

Power, Property, and Culture

American-Chinese Conflicts over Intellectual Property in China

In the study of American-Chinese conflicts over intellectual property (IP) in China, the question arises whether the conflicts are rooted in China's developing-country status and therefore, through development, will eventually resolve themselves, as Americans commonly predict, or whether the very nature of China's culture provides limited support for private property, which poses a very different situation. Plenty of evidence can be marshaled in support of each view, making the answer far from clear. On the one hand, Taiwan and Hong Kong, two communities that share China's cultural history and both once world-class intellectual property rights (IPR) infringers, evolved into respectable citizens of the IP world. On the other hand, China is vastly bigger than Taiwan or Hong Kong, with very different institutions and populations. If it is just a matter of economic growth, then there should be some signs that infringements are declining; on the contrary, such evidence is far from forthcoming.

This chapter analyzes the perceptions and experiences of IP in China by American and Chinese executives. These parties are the closest to the matter, so it is important to hear what they say about it. They agree on some things but have some important differences in how they see the conflicts over IP and how they think conflicts should be addressed, or not. In the end, the Chinese government, as in so many other issues in Chinese-American business relations, will be found to be the central player in the drama, controlling the key levers of power to which the other stakeholders—namely the array of Chinese business organizations, American business organizations, and the American government—have to react.

The chapter begins with an analysis of American perception of IP in China, including how Americans perceive Chinese attitudes toward IP, Chinese government attitudes toward IPR violations, types of IPR violations,

American attitudes toward IP, and American protection of IP. The next section will analyze Chinese perceptions of IP in China: justifications for product copying, how to stop product copying, why product copying cannot be stopped, imitation and competition, and IP and Chinese business culture. An extended conclusion will focus on fleshing out the two general themes arising from the analysis, the roles of the Chinese government and of Chinese culture in IPR infringement.

American Perceptions of Intellectual Property in China

1. American Perceptions of Chinese Attitudes toward IP. American executives have varying perceptions of how the Chinese view IP. Some believe the Chinese do not grasp IP as property, do not understand that using someone else's technology is theft, and do not understand that copying someone else's products is unethical. American executives have a variety of explanations for these perceived Chinese views.

Chinese lack of recognition of IP as property has some basis in fact. Confucian philosophy encourages sharing of material goods and does not provide a strong moral basis for private property. In fact, Confucius was antibusiness, encouraging instead a focus on internal life and the cultivation of virtue, which meant, among other things, respect for others and social harmony. Business, in contrast, is driven by self-interest and the accumulation of profit.

The disregard for private property was intensified during the Communist era and retains significant support today:

> When we are interested in buying a Chinese company, we are required to do due diligence. We are a public company. Due diligence is not understood in China. It is resisted. They think you will steal their secrets, their business. They are afraid because stealing secrets is common business practice in China. For example, you pirate their chief technical person. I can't describe how they justify it. It is justifiable to them in some ways. They had 57 years of Communist rule. For the first 35–40 years, everyone was equal. So if you steal someone's business, they are still doing okay because of social supports.
>
> (Mr. Am22)

Mr. Am22's comments bring up the decades of Mao's rule, when the rules of the game were different than they are now, involving a continuous effort to destroy private property in fact and even in thought. Mr. Am22 concludes that in those days, stealing someone's property did that person no harm because everyone received similar economic benefits anyway. He wonders if this explains current attitudes toward IP. He notes that stealing IP is rampant in China, making it difficult to do business in keeping with Western traditions such as due diligence. In other words, Mr. Am22 understands rampant IP theft as an anachronism. It is now dysfunctional in the competitive business system, but the Chinese persist in it anyway.

Another explanation referring to the Communist era focuses on the relations between state-owned enterprises (SOEs):

> They do not grasp IP as property. . . . This is from the SOEs. Competition did not matter. The notion you "can't use this" is foreign to them. This is the best picture.
>
> (Mr. Am30)

Mr. Am30 takes a view similar to that of Mr. Am22 but laced with more suspicion. He calls the explanation based on lack of competition among SOEs the "best picture," implying a worst picture: The Chinese have no ethics. The latter view is indeed common among American executives. Most American executives have little interest in historical explanation and are not inclined to struggle to put themselves in Chinese shoes in an effort to understand the culture. Mr. Am22 is unusual in that he attempts to understand Chinese history and apply it to explain Chinese attitudes toward IP; his effort is empathetic and laudable. The typical American conclusion that Americans have ethics and Chinese lack them is, of course, without basis in historical fact and insensitive to the considerable differences between the two cultures and contexts. More understanding might help American businesses by putting them more in touch with reality.

Some American executives think the problem with IPR is part of a bigger problem, the nationalistic nature of the Chinese:

> We sell a product used in construction in China. Sales are $10 million. They can't make it themselves. India and China want to do joint ventures with us on this product. But once the genie is out of the bottle, earnings drop by 90 percent from new competitors. . . . The Chinese do not see it as unethical. They say, "It's my market, I know the people and language." It's their business style. We would lose everything: brands, property, intellectual property. These are the challenges. You

need to go in with eyes wide open. You need Party muscle, it's the only way to get recourse.

(Mr. Am19)

There are deep historical reasons for the justification based on ownership of market that Mr. Am19 perceives. The Chinese have been exploited by foreigners, are still angry about it, and have no intention of allowing it to happen again.[1]

Mr. Am19's comments also highlight American dependence on the Chinese. The Chinese know their "people and language," whereas foreigners do not. Some Chinese claim this knowledge confers a right of access to foreign property. They see no reason why they should restrict themselves to specific roles or even contractual relations. The opportunity is before them, so they take it. The government and the courts, for the most part, do not stop them, so the opportunity itself is reason enough to ignore IPR.

Mr. Am19 sees this attitude as "their business style," a perception that is not strictly accurate. The Chinese are in a momentous social and economic transition, the government having loosened the yoke of control over the economy and society after decades of strict Communist rule. The Chinese "business style" is therefore in the making. It is far from settled. Chinese businesspeople are more rushing toward opportunities after years of hardship and suffering than enacting a settled cultural pattern that can be labeled a "style."

Mr. Am19's recognition of the need for "Party muscle" to protect IP shows that the transition going on in China, despite its magnitude, does have its limits; not everything is changing, and some things, such as the arbitrary power of the Communist Party, have hardly changed at all. It is impossible to get much done without going through the government, and IP protection is no exception. Moreover, it is not laws, rules, and regulations that are the primary controls on behavior, but interpersonal connections. If one knows a key government official, much can be accomplished.

Several American executives interviewed believe that violating IPR is an overt business strategy of the Chinese:

I talked to a high-level purchasing manager at [Chinese company]. I asked about Cisco's lawsuit against them for IP copyright violations. They had to pay $2 million. I said, "I see you have a lot of benefits." He

[1] There is a continuous drumbeat on this issue in the state-controlled press (R. McGregor 2010), used to stimulate patriotism and thus support for the Communist Party.

says, "The lawsuit shows the whole world we can supply everything Cisco supplies. The lawsuit is much cheaper than advertisement cost." They eat much of Cisco's market, worldwide. Big headache for Cisco. Suddenly they become famous.

(Mr. Am7)

In Mr. Am7's example of IPR infringement as an explicit business strategy, the company even calculates that the court fine for IPR violations will be less expensive than advertising costs. Interestingly, Mr. Am7 specifically asked me not to mention the Chinese company by name, an unusual request. Importantly, the only other time this happened concerned the *same* company. It appeared to me that the two interviewees, both Chinese natives working for American companies, feared this company. It is generally known that this company has close ties with the Chinese military. There is a blurred line between the private and public sectors in China. The fact that the military is closely involved in this company's business implies that the military is also associated with using IPR violations as a business strategy.

Mr. Am7 appeared very proud of this company's success. He described in some detail the enormous new headquarters the company had built in China, where he once attended a sales meeting. He walked down an enormous hallway and was ushered into a cavernous meeting room filled with tables for the company's purchasing managers to meet with salespeople. A young woman escorted him to a table and brought him tea while he waited for the purchasing manager. The purchasing manager arrived and intense negotiations took place, focused primarily on price. No deal was struck. As the salesman went to leave, the young woman reappeared with, to his astonishment, a bill for the tea. To him, the meaning was clear: This company will overlook no opportunity, no matter how small, to make a profit. He painted a picture of Chinese business as successful, on the move, and enormously hungry. IPR violations are a central part of the broader picture of intense competitive drive.

Other American executives expressed the view that the Chinese have little choice but to copy foreign IP. An American consulate official in China put it this way: "The Chinese say, 'We do not want to be creative, just replicate'" (Feldman 2007a). Some American executives say the Chinese must replicate because they do not have the ability to innovate.

A related American view is that the Chinese imitate and copy because, despite the efforts of the Mao-era Communists, they have not been able to modernize their economy and remain decades behind developed countries in technological expertise and innovative capacities. Thus, they have few options but to imitate and copy if they desire to jump-start their economy. If they cannot copy the products of their superior foreign competitors, they will be condemned to a much slower rate of economic growth. Given the low economic base from which they started, it seems almost self-defense to steal IP to remove themselves from such a low level of economic development. If much of a whole generation's life has been destroyed by the Cultural Revolution or, spared that, is now surrounded by considerable wealth of which they have none and little chance to gain it, stealing foreign IP would be tempting indeed.

2. American Perceptions of the Chinese Government's Attitudes toward IPR Violations. American executives interviewed felt the Chinese government does little to prevent IPR violations:

> We found a Chinese company making our product and selling it under our name. We followed the product to Thailand where a plant received the fraudulent products for resale. We easily got the Thai police to raid the plant. The father, son, and daughter are now in jail. We are also working against the Chinese manufacturer, but it is in process. It is very hard to stop IP fraud in China; the government is not putting its weight behind it. The government is afraid of high unemployment. Unemployment is currently in double figures and it is a problem.
>
> (Mr. BD1)

Mr. BD1's company aggressively pursues IPR violators of its products. Once it finds them, it turns the information over to the government. In this case, the government of Thailand moved quickly to arrest the offenders while the government of China dragged its feet. Mr. BD1 believes the Chinese government is not aggressively pursuing IP fraud because unemployment is high and the government does not want to increase it.

Unemployment is high in China due in part to the reform of the economy. Millions of workers have been laid off from SOEs. The Chinese government faces a difficult balancing act: Increasing SOE efficiency strengthens the economy but increases unemployment. IP fraud is a safety net in this situation in that it allows noncompetitive businesses to earn a profit, protecting income and employment levels in this transition period of declining incomes and increasing unemployment for millions of workers. The problem is this "safety net" undermines innovation and other forms of competition that lead to improved efficiency, not to mention the enormous conflict it creates with IP owners. The Chinese government for now is trying to have it both ways, increase efficiency and permit IP theft. This strategy leads to conflicts with foreign governments, who are under pressure from their own corporations to get the Chinese government to stop IP theft. This saga has gone on for decades with no clear resolution in sight. All sides are continually evaluating their gains and losses and refining their strategies in a game of threat, penalty, and counter-penalty. Clearly, some companies have thrown in the towel and pulled out of China, but overall the number of companies involved increases and, like governments, companies continuously shift their strategies as they evaluate their gains and losses in response to changing contexts.

The Chinese government does not make this game easy to play. American executives often cite Shanghai's large retail "knockoff mall," a hugely visible symbol of IP theft, to explain how the government manages IPR violations. The Chinese government at one point shut down the mall as evidence of its tough stance against IPR violators. The mall retailers, however, merely reopened a short distance away, and have remained untouched by authorities. It is inconceivable that the government does not know about the new site, since everyone else does. Hence, the government explicitly uses a two-tiered strategy: It continually proclaims its intolerance of IP theft; creates laws, commissions, and programs against it; and selectively and visibly prosecutes IPR violators, while at the same time it ignores vast operations of IP fraud across the country.

An American consulate official adds this view:

> The Chinese government has done a lot of work against counterfeiting. They created new laws and provided training. But it has done no good. It is not a deterrent. Penalties are ridiculous. There is a lot of corruption. They don't even know what IP rights are. It's a local protection issue, too. There are economic interests involved.
>
> (Feldman 2007a)

According to this official, for the few who are prosecuted by the Chinese government, the penalties are so light that the offender pays the fine and goes right back to counterfeiting. The penalty is seen by the counterfeiter as an acceptable cost of doing business.[2]

---

[2] The government uses value thresholds to determine if criminal prosecution is warranted. The thresholds are set significantly high that much infringement cannot be prosecuted criminally (Ong 2009).

The consulate official's second point is even more important. There is a great deal of corruption in the system. Not only can counterfeiters bribe officials to receive protection from prosecution, but some officials, such as those in the police and army, have investments in and indeed run counterfeiting operations. This situation is much more serious than that of officials turning a blind eye toward IP fraud to help their citizens remain employed. If unemployment is the cause, IP fraud will decline as the economy grows. If, however, corruption is the cause of IP fraud—corruption institutionalized in the system of government—then there is no reason why it cannot go on indefinitely as long as the system does not change.

Inside the government system, there is an additional complication. The central government, responsible for the whole economy and for developing international relationships, is often at odds over corruption with local governments that have more limited interests. In fact, local governments often ignore central-government anti-counterfeiting efforts, perhaps for one of several reasons: because at some level the central government is involved in the corruption, because the central government is waiting until employment levels and capital structures improve, or because it simply is not able to control local governments. It is probably a combination of all three. How these forces will play out and over what time frame is unknown. In any case, it can be concluded that IP theft is entrenched in China's institutional structure and will not be disappearing any time soon.

Some American executives, however, feel there have been improvements. They mention that when the Chinese government moved aggressively to open up the economy in the early 1990s, there was an explosion of corruption. American executives were asked for bribes on a daily basis at that time. This level of open, visible corruption has declined. Nonetheless, there is still systemic corruption of a less visible but deep-rooted nature.

Some American executives believe that IPR enforcement is "getting better because the government has worked hard to improve IPR, but the problem is China is too big and there are too many violators to catch everything" (Mr. Am7). This view ignores the ambivalence and dysfunction in the Chinese government's anti-counterfeiting efforts. China is not "too big" if local governments are committed to anti-counterfeiting efforts in local areas. Mr. Am7 is a sales manager, his career dependent on selling his company's products in China, so he needs to take an optimistic view of the China market. Many other executives said that government corruption is much less widespread in large cities like Beijing and Shanghai, but this view, too, is suspect when it comes to IP because IPR violations are visibly rampant in these cities.

Thus there is a tendency among some executives whose careers are dependent on the China market to downplay IPR infringement in China to protect the benefits they are receiving. Likewise, at the corporate level, public criticism of China is withheld to protect the company against retaliation from the Chinese government and the SOE sector. When the rule of law is absent, self-protection rules.

3. Types of IPR Violations. American executives reported many different ways in which IP rights are violated in China. In one ploy, Chinese manufacturers buy the product legally, reverse engineer it, and then mass produce it. In another, a Chinese supplier is contracted to produce a patented product for an American manufacturer. The supplier has a second tooling assembly made, produces the product on the illicit equipment, and sells it under the original name.

Product manufacturing processes and specifications may be "leaked" by Chinese employees of American firms to Chinese firms. This information can be crucial because knowing how to do small things can significantly improve product quality. In other cases, Chinese employees of American companies quit and open up competing businesses producing patented products belonging to the American manufacturer. An American executive described his experience:

> We have a product used in building construction. It's a great product. We do $140 million in the U.S. We started in Beijing in 1998. We did a joint venture with a Chinese company. They were so excited. The product is perfect for new building codes in China. Now there are 65 manufacturers of this product in China. Five of our employees created businesses.
>
> (Mr. Am19)

Some American firms have Chinese employees sign noncompete agreements, but most have not found them to be effective.

Chinese manufacturers will sometimes make a product that appears from the outside to be identical to a product made by an American company, right down to the American company's name on the product. Inside, however, the quality is not the same as that of the American product. One executive said his company found a customer in Venezuela who, when ordering the product from China, could request any trademark in the industry be put on the product. Problems his company has with product counterfeiting around the world originate in China. In his industry there are 3,000 manufacturers in China. Under these circumstances, it is impossible to stop counterfeiting.

In another tactic, American-company product packaging material is stolen and Chinese products are shipped using this packaging. One American company began auditing its cardboard orders to combat the practice but then found plain brown wrappers to be a better solution.

Products are copied but not exactly. The product is basically the same, but the American name is slightly altered. For example, American products marketed under the name Gema find they are competing with Chinese products with similar features under the name Jema.[3]

Finally, copyrights may simply be ignored:

> We had our artwork copyrighted. We also held a license with the City of New York Museum. But at trade shows, we see this stuff. We have licensed Norman Rockwell and the *Saturday Evening Post.* We see this stuff, too, at shows.

(Mr. Am20)

American firms thus face product counterfeiting in many different forms. American companies still have superior technology to that of the Chinese 30 years after the beginning of reforms, though there is no doubt that Chinese economic development has made huge strides. Americans insist on IPR because it is in their interest to do so. The Chinese ignore these rights to a large extent because it is in their interest to do so. They need technology to develop, and the easiest way to get it is to just take it, which they do.

The Chinese government does not enforce its laws too strictly because that would hurt both economic growth and social stability, certainly in the short run. The theory goes that as China develops, it will develop its own IP and at that point the government will be more inclined to enforce the laws to protect it. Indeed, some argue that the developed nations should be patient with the government's lax enforcement because it will allow China to develop faster, to the benefit of everyone.

Unfortunately, this is not how capitalism works. Foreign firms come to China to make money. For many of them, it is hard enough without IPR violations. They do not come to China for the greater good of everyone or for

---

[3] A similar development can be seen in the creation of the Chinese Chery Automobile Group in imitation of General Motors' Chevy brand.

success in an unspecified future. They seek to make profit as soon as they can. So IPR violations appear offensive and unfair to them. According to Adam Smith, the invisible hand works through self-interest, not trading for the public good.[4]

This leaves it to the United States government to take the long-term view and not pressure China in the area of IPR enforcement so it can more quickly reach higher levels of economic development. This strategy does not seem to work, either, for several reasons. First, the U.S. government, through the election process, is subject to pressure from American businesses to force China to enforce IPR. Business and politics are far from separate in the United States. Second, the government does not have a benevolent view of China for its own reasons. It sees China as a competitor at least, and possibly a political, economic, and military threat. It wants China to be a source of profit for American firms, but it does not want it to be too powerful. Third, the U.S. government wants to maintain leadership in key areas of technology for economic, political, and military reasons—and that requires pressing China for IPR enforcement. Fourth, how long is the "long run"? It has been 30 years. How much patience is it reasonable to expect from the American people?

Inevitably, then, the United States and China are locked in a struggle over IPR enforcement. If the Chinese government wants to continue to pull large numbers of its citizens out of poverty, it will not want to pursue IPR violations too strictly. It cannot anger the Americans and others too much, but it is in the Chinese government's interest to drag its feet as long as possible. Likewise, American firms see considerable promise in the China market. This is why they flock there in large numbers despite the fact that many of them suffer IPR infringements upon entering the market. But as long as they can make a profit, have the hope of making a profit, or at least assuage their fears that their competitors will gain competitive advantages, they will go to China.

It is worth noting that even though IPR infringements produce rents and in that sense help China, these offenses and the attitudes they inculcate are used not only against foreigners but against Chinese too. Training in theft digs China into a deeper moral hole. The government will not be able to change this mind-set just when it so decides. It will probably take a genera- tion at least to correct, assuming the government puts its shoulder into the

---

[4] A. Smith 1974.

effort and assuming many other factors are favorable, such as positive relations between government levels, improved court capacities, continuing economic growth, and so on—some big assumptions indeed.

4. *American Views of American Attitudes toward IP.* Some American executives note that their countrymen do not always respect IPR either:

> If I buy a counterfeit watch in China, how can I complain about the Chinese counterfeiting my products? I cannot respect IP rights and buy the watch. The Chinese have less sense of IP as property. But Americans do the same with music, with Napster. Americans can be just as dense about IP. Americans do better in the industrial setting. Our patents are longer standing. We understand this as valuable, but we divorce consumer stuff from industrial. We are bad with consumer stuff. The Chinese are the same with the industrial.
>
> (Mr. Am30)

Mr. Am30, who is in charge of fighting IP fraud for his company, has done some soul searching in regard to his own as well as others' attitudes toward IP corruption in China and at home. He knows Americans search out and buy counterfeit products in China. He knows ethically and logically one cannot condemn the Chinese for producing counterfeits and then buy them. He says the Chinese violate IPR, but he notes Americans do the same with music and other consumer products, blurring the moral divide that American executives typically draw between China and the United States. Instead of viewing the Chinese as unethical and the Americans as ethical, Mr. Am30 points out that both countries share the same moral failures to some extent. This is a completely different story than one usually hears from American executives. More typically, self-interest and the tunnel vision it creates drive American attitudes toward Chinese IPR violations specifically and Chinese corruption generally.

In this context, it is interesting to note that despite the numerous legal battles over Napster in the United States, many in the United States question the ethical right of companies to charge for music. Indeed, there is a worldwide debate in the academic literature as to the moral validity of current international IP laws. If IP laws as they have been established in the General Agreement on Tariffs and Trade (GATT), for example, result in immense benefits to foreign firms in China with little going to the Chinese, are they fair? Certainly IP laws can be written many different ways. Certainly the distributional results of IP laws over different time frames are a relevant consideration for establishing fair laws. Certainly the establishing of laws such as GATT is a political process wherein political power contributes to the final outcome. So when the Chinese say, as Mr. Am19 reported earlier, "It's my market, I know the people and language," they are arguing they should have a bigger piece of the pie than GATT and the WTO allow them.

By dispensing with the myth that the Chinese are unethical and we are ethical, Mr. Am30 exposes the central role of self-interest in the battle over IP and its obfuscation behind the power politics of international agreements and the self-righteousness of those who benefit from them. Despite the agreements and the plethora of arbitration mechanisms they provide, conflicts over IP in China are not going away because just as the West dominates the creation of international trade agreements, the Chinese dominate the treatment of IP in China. At the end of the day, the only solution is to bring the conflicting interests into better alignment.

5. How Americans Protect IP in China. American companies use multiple means to try to protect IP in China. One is to develop reliable partnerships:

> Companies must do their homework. The main thing is to find reliable partners. It's not always easy; they could be after technology or money. You must have the same goals, vision, and strategy. It's good not to have too many hidden cards.
>
> (Mr. Am23)

Finding Chinese companies with the same goals, vision, and strategy is not easy. It is certainly possible and executives do report excellent relationships, but there are some challenges. There are vast differences between the American and Chinese cultures, making communication difficult. The problem can be exacerbated by using translators, but even if the parties speak the same language, cultural misunderstandings are common.

Many Chinese are socially cautious, indirect, and not quick to trust, especially people they do not know well. Even with people they do know well, sensitivity to others leads them not to state their preferences directly. Agreeableness is increased by the centrality of hierarchical relationships, where deference and subordination are required toward superiors. In addition, the lack of privacy in China leads people to guard their true feelings in order to stake out a private self. For these reasons employees often express agreement with superiors but then do exactly what they themselves want. Hierarchical relations are more commonly found in the *form* of relationships than in the *substance*. Thus, finding out what Chinese really think is not a direct affair of just asking them.

The high level of distrust found in Chinese society can be intensified with foreigners. I have seen several situations in which Chinese openly disparaged foreigners. Some Chinese seem to look down on other cultures. Part of this attitude is related to the history of the last 200 years, when foreign powers exploited Chinese weakness. There is also an insecurity born out of how far the Chinese have fallen behind economically and technologically. Despite their extensive economic growth, insecurity can still be discerned. From both the history and the insecurity, Chinese can be quick to feel slighted. There also sometimes seems to be an ethnic bias toward non-Chinese. One American executive was telling a group of Chinese executives about his diverse ethnic heritage when a Chinese executive (in Chinese) cracked that the American was like a mixed-breed dog. Hence, for historical, sociological, psychological, and ethnic reasons the Chinese can be disinclined to trust foreigners.

Personal networks in China can be pervasive, strong, and unknowable to outsiders. Chinese executives might be influenced by these commitments unbeknownst to the Americans with whom they are negotiating. At some later point, Americans may find out that what they understood as a shared commitment actually involved additional side commitments on the part of the Chinese that completely changed the intent of the original agreement. Network ties can be primary, and an agreement with an American company can easily be less important. Hence, self-interest is not always a foolproof way to predict Chinese behavior because "self-interest" need not always boil down to maximizing personal economic benefit; network commitments might lead a Chinese executive to do what is good for his network even at some cost to himself. So it may be desirable not to have "too many hidden cards," but it will take a lot of "homework" to bring that about. Americans, too, must develop networks of Chinese relationships over time that can be useful to help with the "homework" of evaluating prospective partners. Moving fast with investments in this social environment carries high risk.

Another way of protecting American IP is to require majority ownership:

> The key is having a majority stake and knowing the business and market. You might think you know the business, but you must know the business in China and know the Chinese. With majority ownership, we controlled the technology.

> (Mr. Am23)

Mr. Am23's point on majority ownership assumes some type of joint venture. Earlier in the reform process, American companies could not enter the Chinese market without a Chinese joint venture partner. But this is no longer the case and many American companies set up their own operations or buy a Chinese company.

Another strategy is to do everything possible to keep employees:

> If you lose an employee, he takes some information with him. It's just a fact of life. The only defense is to keep employees.
>
> (Mr. Am2)

As Mr. Am2 points out, owning the company hardly protects one from IPR violations. Employees can leave with IP. Keeping employees[5] raises labor costs; low labor costs were the central reason to manufacture in China to begin with. In any case, as noted earlier, employees do not need to quit to leak product and market information to family and friends. So ownership and employee retention are necessary but not sufficient to stop IP theft.

Many American companies safeguard key technological product components:

> We are sensitive to reverse engineering. One percent of our product is unique so we keep it offshore out of China. We also divide up assembly among different facilities. Some of our products have software and are harder to reverse engineer. There is a lot of know-how in any manufacturing. The Chinese are well educated and an industrious culture.
>
> (Mr. Am26)

Mr. Am26's comments show the vulnerability of many American manufacturers: Only one percent of his product is unique. Keeping the one percent offshore and dividing product assembly between multiple locations[6] certainly

---

[5] Gupta and Wang (2011) recommend building employee commitment by making work exciting, developing a culture of lifelong jobs, and providing opportunities for regional and international responsibility for top performers.

[6] Gupta and Wang (2011) recommend that companies know their landlord. They warn of government-owned buildings that are filled with electronic listening devices that relay confidential information to state-owned competitors. They also recommend developing relations with government officials and media representatives to enlist their help when things do go wrong. Ultimately, these authors say the key to IP protection is continuous innovation. China is no different than Silicon Valley, they say. One can take measures to slow down IP theft, but it cannot be stopped. Only continuous innovation will keep one safe from infringement. Unfortunately, this strategy applies to some products more than others.

does not stop reverse engineering, but at least it does not allow product assembly to become an advanced course on reverse engineering. Mentioning that products involving software are more difficult to reverse engineer, Mr. Am26 implies that complex products with moderate profit potential are less at risk for counterfeiting. Complex products with high profit potential, however, would signify high risk in a country with a well-educated, industrious, and IP-insensitive work force.

Mr. Am26 is polite, or at least indirect, when he leaves willingness to violate IPR out of his description of the Chinese work force as "well educated and an industrious culture." One can read between the lines, however, and take his meaning to be that the Chinese are good at product counterfeiting. Indeed, China is generally considered to produce more counterfeit products than any other country in the world. The key to Chinese counterfeiting, however, is not the citizens' education and industriousness but their willingness and orientation to replicate the work of others.

Mr. Am26 relies on a stereotype when he associates IP theft in China with education and industriousness. India, for instance, is educated and industrious but does not have the level of IP fraud found in China. It is important to address the IP problem directly, that is, morally. There are moral arguments on both sides, not just the American side. The debate should take place between these differing value systems and contexts. The idea that IP theft in China takes place because the Chinese are industrious implies that the Chinese are some sort of intellectually superior race without moral character. Nothing could be further from the truth, and in implying so Mr. Am26 unconsciously repeats an American racial stereotype. The IP problem in China is enormously difficult even without such distortion.

Understanding the China market is difficult for many executives:

> We are one of the largest industrial suppliers of a chemical product used in construction. We are doing a JV in China. We provide the chemical in concentrated form from the U.S. Our partner finishes the product and sells it in China. Otherwise, we would create 10 competitors. There is no legal recourse. It's a huge problem.
>
> (Mr. Am19)

Both Mr. Am26 and Mr. Am19 describe the extra costs American companies bear in trying to protect themselves from product counterfeiting. Both manufacture parts of their products offshore, raising transportation costs. Indeed, Mr. Am19 is shipping his product all the way from the United States.

Likewise, breaking product assembly up between different facilities raises communication, organization, and transportation costs. This is all in addition to the cost of IP theft. The costs of defending against IP theft are seldom noted because the costs of the theft itself are so much higher.

Mr. Am19 wants to settle his IP problems in China in court, as he does in the United States. He believes "no legal recourse" is a "huge problem." This is a common attitude among American executives. Yet improvements in the legal system are moving at glacial speed in China. It is possible that improvements will remain inadequate during the lifetimes of these executives. Perhaps it would be better to accept the cultural differences, since those are reality, and reevaluate the China market more in terms of what it is than what it might be. This approach would lead to a more realistic evaluation of the costs and benefits of doing business in China. Mr. Am19 says one must go into China with "eyes wide open." But despite all his losses, he is still emotionally invested in business and legal practices that China is unlikely to offer any time soon.[7]

Another tactic of American firms is to avoid taking their best technology to China:

> Because of technology theft, we do not want to take our high-end over there. At first it was *no*; now it's baby steps. We're studying how to protect it, e.g., computers with locking mechanisms and limited information, so technology is not taken off the computer. We keep the blueprints in the U.S.
>
> (Mr. Am30)

Mr. Am30's company has extensive operations in China and is optimistic about its potential in China, but the IP problem is ever looming. Either business optimism or confidence in protecting IP, or both, keep the company moving forward.[8] Nonetheless, the fact that some American companies do not manufacture or sell their most advanced technological products in China leads to yet another cost of Chinese IP theft. Both American and Chinese societies lose.

---

[7] In 2011, Mr. Am19's company pulled out of China and was making major investments in India.

[8] During a 2010 interview, representatives said the company had moved its best technology to China because China had become its most profitable division and because executives believe the Chinese are unable to copy it due to the sophisticated level of manufacturing required.

Many American companies are careful even with information available in the United States:

> Technical details are not on our products made in China, but they are on products made in the U.S. Over time, this information makes its way to China. Our products are capital intensive to manufacture, so they are not so easy to copy.

(Mr. Am24)

Interestingly, Mr. Am24, who works for the same company as Mr. Am30, says keeping technical information out of China does not help if that information is available in the United States. Hence, this company would need to shut down information availability worldwide to defend against IP theft in China. Restricting product information would negatively impact product use and sales, indirectly creating even more costs from counterfeiting. Mr. Am24 says that the company's best defense against IP theft is the huge capital investment needed to manufacture its products. Apparently, there is no direct threat in China to this company's high-end technical products; the problems are more with low-end technical products or counterfeit use of the company's brands. But the company's fear for its advanced technical information implies that the information could be used. Hence, as China industrializes, the threat to IP for companies with capital or knowledge-intensive manufacturing may increase. The old ramparts may not hold.[9]

Chinese Perceptions of Intellectual Property

1. Justification for Product Copying. Chinese executives interviewed mentioned numerous justifications for product copying. One is that product copying is not unique to China; it happens everywhere. This statement is true, but Americans claim that 80 percent of product counterfeiting worldwide comes from China. In the United States, the Chinese claim, copying is not nonexistent, just more subtle. Again, the claim is undoubtedly true, as can be seen in the pronounced similarity between products in the United States. The difference comes down to legal definition and legal prosecution. Since the Chinese

---

[9] Three years later, in 2010, Mr. Am 35 said the company's high-end products discussed in this paragraph are still safe from counterfeiting because the Chinese do not have the manufacturing "know-how" to reproduce them. The problem remains the reproduction of low-end products sold with the high-end name on them, a misrepresentation that causes public safety issues.

for the most part are not legally prosecuted, they do not bother with "subtle" product changes that can be used as a defense in court.

American business customs overlook some types of copying but not others. These lines are crossed often in the United States; this is one reason there are so many lawsuits. But China takes it to another level by not only counterfeiting identical products but pirating copyrighted works. This is one thing the Americans mean when referring to the China market as the "Wild West." Not only is American business custom violated but American law is violated, and the Americans are exceedingly frustrated that their defense of choice, the lawsuit, is of little use in China. Differences in both legal philosophy and business custom contribute to the differences seen in product copying. It is not merely a matter of the Americans being ethical while the Chinese are not, nor is it true that counterfeiting goes on everywhere equally.

A second argument is that product copying is not typical in China. General Motors, Motorola, Volkswagen, and Nokia are making huge profits in China, so product copying must not be too bad, the reasoning goes. But the argument is simply not credible. In some industries—apparel, film, and software, for example—it is systemic. In many other industries it is significant.

Yet another justification for IP theft is that Americans mistreat Chinese employees:

> In one company, Americans have one salary; Chinese have lower salary. I have friend, he is very skilled. He gets one-fiftieth or one-twentieth of [the salary of] his American colleagues. This causes problems. My friend finds out. He's very angry. It's unfair, he thinks. He said, "The only way I can make up for this is to open up my own plant." He knows the technology and production. He's now very successful.
>
> (Ms. Ch14)

The argument that American companies underpay Chinese employees, causing them to leave and become competitors, is plausible. It is unlikely American firms pay American and Chinese executives the same. For one thing, the labor markets are different. Chinese employees in China are abundant, while American executives are in short supply.[10] Americans demand

---

[10] In a 2010 interview, an American executive said he pays Chinese middle managers the same salaries he pays his workers in the United States. Skilled and experienced middle and upper-level Chinese managers are in short supply and command salaries equal to or higher than workers in the United States.

higher salaries to work in China and are therefore making higher salaries than equivalent American workers in the United States.

In addition, American executives have more business experience than their Chinese counterparts, especially at high executive levels. Because of China's Communist history, business management talent is in short supply there. American companies recruit many top executives from Taiwan and Hong Kong. Moreover, the pronounced distrust between the two cultures puts a premium on hiring American or "Westernized" executives. Finally, it is likely that American executives cannot easily judge entrepreneurial talent among Chinese employees. It is difficult to do so even with American employees in the United States. Add in language, culture, and context differences, and the task becomes much more difficult. Given the Chinese sensitivity to the way they are treated—the idea of "face" is central in Chinese culture—and American insensitivity to Chinese culture, misunderstandings can easily arise. Hence, for many reasons American salaries for Chinese executives might not be what the Chinese feel they deserve.

Even Americans come to China and buy counterfeit products, it is argued. An executive tells this "funny story":

> Polo Ralph Lauren licensed underwear in China. The Polo people arrive from Winston-Salem and want to go to the market to buy Polo fakes for themselves, 80 to 95 percent off the original price. They can't tell the difference on quality, it is so close.
>
> (Mr. Ch20)

It is certainly true that Americans buy a lot of knockoffs while visiting China. A high-level official at an American consulate office in China, whose job includes protecting American industry from IPR violations, mentioned that he buys pirated DVDs for his personal use. Likewise, Mr. Ch20 reports Polo managers cannot stop themselves from buying Polo counterfeits because the deal is so good, despite the fact that the company they work for sustains huge losses from just such products. The Chinese say counterfeits must not be so bad if Americans buy so many. Americans clearly lose their credibility if they criticize counterfeiting and at the same time benefit from it. Earlier a similar argument was made by an American executive: By buying pirated brands, Americans are giving the Chinese an incentive to make them. So they share in the responsibility for counterfeiting and can no longer complain about it.

Mr. Ch20 is also implying in the "funny story" that since American managers are buying the same counterfeits for themselves that hurt their own company, inexpensive counterfeits must be irresistible. Thus there is something natural and good about them. Surely counterfeits cannot be all bad and Americans are making too much of a fuss about them, he seems to imply.

Another argument is that it is the Taiwanese who are behind the counterfeiting:

> Hong Kong and Taiwanese taught the Chinese how to make DVDs. DVDs are controlled by the Taiwanese mafia. They run the Taiwanese factories in China; they are still a big part today. Even karaoke comes from the Taiwanese. Taiwanese businesspeople are most flexible. There are at least 500,000 Taiwanese in Shanghai. There is no difference between Chinese and Taiwanese. They are the same species. . . . In the U.S., you think everything is made in China, but it is not true. Hong Kong and Taiwanese factories moved here. Management of product design is Taiwanese.
>
> (Mr. Ch24)

It is apparently true that Hong Kong and Taiwanese companies taught the Chinese how to manufacture DVDs and still control a big part of the market. It is also true that not everything "made in China" is made by the Chinese. The Chinese do not have the product design skills to carry out all the counterfeiting that goes on in China. Hong Kong and Taiwanese factories do have these skills. One problem with Mr. Ch24's argument, however, is that the Chinese distribute the products. Without distribution by Chinese, the Hong Kong and Taiwanese factories would have much less incentive to produce pirated DVDs.

2. How to Stop Product Copying. Chinese executives had many suggestions for ways in which American companies could protect themselves against product copying. One area has to do with stopping employees from quitting, becoming competitors, and copying products. First, the higher the salary, the less likely employees will leave their position. Second, American managers must treat employees properly, which means creating an environment where employees feel comfortable and secure. Third, part of building a good organizational culture is hiring the right people. Not all Chinese are the same; American firms must be selective. Fourth, high-ranking managers should be given ownership shares, an incentive for them to stay with the company and do their best to grow the company.

As will be discussed below, the primary threat to American IP is the loss of high-level Chinese employees, not reverse engineering, which takes longer and gives American companies a chance to protect themselves through innovation. One can tell from three of the Chinese suggestions on how to stop product copying—increased salary, better treatment, and ownership shares—that they think they are not treated very well. The salary issue is particularly important. Chinese employees leave an American company because they can make more money starting their own businesses, which Americans complain are often based on stolen IP. Americans cannot possibly pay their Chinese employees enough to compensate them for not stealing IP, given that the activity carries little risk from criminal penalties. Ownership shares would seem to hold out some promise, but it is not just top Chinese executives who start their own companies; it is also midlevel engineers. So the distribution of ownership shares would have to be quite broad and thus probably too costly. Nonetheless, some type of incentive structure would probably improve what has been an untreatable problem.

The two comments about better treatment and more careful selection point to cultural issues. On the surface, better treatment is a surprising request because large multinationals usually treat their employees the same worldwide in terms of policies and procedures. Indeed, many Chinese want to work for American companies because the opportunities and rewards are better than those at Chinese companies. But at the American multinationals I visited in Shanghai, American executives expressed much bitterness, disrespect, and distrust toward Chinese employees. These attitudes put the American executives in the unworkable situation of disliking the very people they are charged with integrating into their organizations. It is not surprising if the integration is not coming along very well. This suggests that American companies must improve their intercultural training for American executives and more carefully select the ones they send to China.[11]

These same issues apply in selecting Chinese employees to work at American companies. If Americans do not understand Chinese culture or are insensitive to it, they hardly will be well positioned to select the best Chinese employees. Because of the dynamic nature of the Chinese market and the job opportunities it creates, turnover rates can reach 30 percent or more. As

---

[11] A pattern apparent in 2007 had developed further by 2010. American firms are increasingly using Chinese managers for top management positions. This practice goes a long way toward removing cultural conflict from top management–employee relations, and from company-government and company-community relations as well. The problem is qualified executives are in short supply.

discussed in Chapter 8, the high turnover rate among Chinese managers results in part from a lack of career planning skills. This puts American managers in the frustrating position of hiring, training, and losing employees. So it is difficult to develop a stable organizational culture that instills loyalty. But managing the different, unexpected, and frustrating is exactly what is expected of a skilled international manager.

A second set of suggestions the Chinese managers gave for protecting IP also focuses on employees but in a more defensive way. Some tactics are also similar to those suggested by American executives: divide departments into different sections managed by different people, keep key technological components out of the country, and have employees sign noncompete agreements. Two suggestions not mentioned by American executives are to concentrate key technological components in a few people's hands and, in the case of a design department, to have employees date, sign, and file designs so they can be tracked. If a design turns up in the marketplace, the tracking system can help determine what went wrong.

The fact that the Americans did not mention the option of keeping IP in as few Chinese hands as possible demonstrates the level of American distrust. For the Chinese, some Chinese can be trusted; for the Americans it is not so clear that any of them can. The idea of having product designers sign and date their designs was offered by the president of a company in the apparel industry, where product design is constant and continuous, and where counterfeiting is also constant and continuous. Design leakage is just one type of IP theft, but it is a problem across many industries. Signing and dating product designs is most applicable where individuals or small teams work on products and new designs are a continuous part of the business.

A third set of suggestions for protecting IP focuses on product copying by Chinese firms. First, sign contracts only with companies you know well. Chinese companies usually do business with another firm only after they know a lot about it. Second, speed up innovation so counterfeiters must expend a lot of energy for short-lived gain. Some executives believe this is the most important way to deal with counterfeiting.

The first point, sign contracts only with companies one knows well, was echoed by some American executives, while others indicated they had paid a steep price for not heeding it. The point is that the China market is treacherous for reasons that lie deep in Chinese history and culture. It is not a new phenomenon; it is not just how Americans are treated or foreigners are treated. The sociopolitical system produces and has long produced a disregard for strangers. The Chinese invest huge amounts of time and energy in developing relationships—and not just because they enjoy it or have been habituated to it. They do it because without relationships, one will "get it in the shorts," to quote an American executive who speaks from experience. Hence, doing business in China requires constant and continuous relationship building.

The other point, about speeding up innovation, makes more sense for some businesses than for others. The Chinese executive who made this comment works for a consumer products company where product changes can be yearly or even seasonal. For a classic product like Levi's jeans, innovation is less relevant. This executive's company loses a lot of money competing with copycats in the unprotected Chinese marketplace. It simply cannot innovate fast enough, and the innovations cannot improve the product enough to remove the economic rationale for purchasing the lower-priced copycat products. Innovation as a strategy against IP fraud is only a partial solution and then only for some products.

One Chinese firm, established in New York to connect American retailers with Chinese manufacturers, opened up a second office in Shanghai to be closer to manufacturers in order to better monitor and educate them:

> We set up a company in Shanghai to protect our clients. We educate the manufacturers to protect copyrights. It's difficult to control. If our designs are copied, we tell our clients and redesign. In apparel, everybody is copying everybody, but you have to change 30 percent. But in China they make exact copies. Our job is to protect American retail stores so their products are unique. We educate manufacturers to be cautious about copyrights. We tell them the consequences, a lawsuit. But if they buy from a store and copy it, we don't know. We can only focus on the design process.
>
> (Ms. Ch6)

Ms. Ch6 is a Chinese middleman but has worked for many years in the United States, starting out with American companies before opening her own company. As China opened its economy, she opened a second office in Shanghai and moved there. Since she is Chinese, speaks Chinese, has worked in the industry for two decades, and has many Chinese contacts, she tries to work directly with Chinese apparel manufacturers to reduce IP fraud. But the number of apparel manufacturers in China is huge and the copyright fraud is impossible to stop. By concentrating on careful control of her own and her clients' designs, she tries to limit the damage to American retailers. This gives American retailers some lead time before counterfeiters can buy the product in retail stores and bring copies to market. A key part of Ms. Ch6's middleman function, then, is to slow down product counterfeiting while still providing American customers with access to low-cost Chinese manufacturing.

The fourth set of recommendations to protect IP concerns working with the government and courts. First, several executives believe the courts are becoming more effective in addressing IP issues. In contract disputes, it is important that the contract specify each party's responsibilities in detail. Some executives at large private manufacturers said they had developed strong legal teams to aggressively pursue patent theft. One said patent theft had decreased because "people are afraid of us" (Mr. Ch2). After the interview, however, his assistant mentioned it is not so simple. She said, "If we sue them, we can win but this is not always easy to do and even when we do the penalties are so small it does not stop them" (Ms. Ch28).

Mr. Ch2 also commented on the Chinese government's attitude toward patent theft:

> Part of the government is not fair. They can be bribed. But if we talk about patent, it's not that difficult. The government does not protect the little patent stealer. The government faces pressure from other governments. There is the 301 Act.[12] The government will lean to protect foreign companies. You need a professional legal team. The Chinese are getting better at working with lawyers. . . . We are the number two patent owner in China. We suffer, too. It's a fact here. If you want to manufacture here, you must deal with it. You must decide if it's a good place to manufacture.

Both American and Chinese executives say the court system in China has been improved. Mr. Ch2's point that all the contract details should be spelled out is valid because the Chinese courts like written evidence, particularly evidence certified (stamped) by some agency or person in a position of formal authority.[13] However, it is unclear to what extent justice is served in the Chinese court system. American executives still complain mightily about the

---

[12] The U.S. Special 301 report discussed in Chapter 9.

[13] Ong (2009) reports that evidence must be notarized to be admitted in court which is time consuming. More importantly, there is no formal discovery process, making it difficult to obtain evidence from the accused infringer.

lack of legal recourse for IP fraud. For one thing, 80 percent of IP cases are between Chinese companies. There is evidence that American companies are reluctant to get too involved in legal battles for fear of government retaliation, even though new laws have been created. There is also evidence that judges are better trained and there is less government protection of Chinese companies in the big cities.[14] But, as mentioned, there is strong evidence that in cases where convictions are won, penalties are so light they have no deterrent effect. And outside a handful of big cities, judges can be bribed and local governments regularly protect local companies from legal prosecution, sometimes local officials themselves having ownership stakes in companies committing IP fraud.

Mr. Ch2 says he has developed a strong legal team and prosecutes IP fraud aggressively with good results. But his assistant says that picture is too rosy, that it is not always easy to win court cases. In fact, she says, IP fraud is a significant problem for their business and it hurts their bottom line. Why would Mr. Ch2 exaggerate his success in prosecuting IP fraud? Mr. Ch2 is a vice-president at a large Chinese manufacturer. His largest market is the United States, so as costly as IP fraud in China is to his company, a much bigger threat is trade sanctions from the U.S. government in retaliation for IPR violations by Chinese companies. This situation probably is the reason he exaggerates the effectiveness of the court system in fighting IP fraud in China.

The same exaggeration can be seen in Mr. Ch2's description of the Chinese government's attitude toward patent theft. He acknowledges that some government officials can be bribed, but he says this is not the case in the area of patent theft. The Chinese government is under pressure from other governments. He specifically mentions the American "301" investigation that can lead to trade sanctions. He says all that is needed is a professional legal team. The rule of law is growing in importance. The Chinese government will "lean to protect foreign companies."

---

[14] Judges, however, often rely on the opinions of outside "experts," but it is unclear how the experts are chosen and what their qualifications are (Ong 2009). In addition, data from 2010 interviews contradicts the assertion that judges are now better trained. An American lawyer living in Shanghai said, "Many judges are retired army generals. They are not well educated. It is said that the standards for judges have been raised because only 15 percent of lawyers pass the bar exam in Shanghai, while 98 percent of judges pass the exam. But it is a different and much easier exam" (Mr. Am41).

None of this description is exactly true. For many reasons the Chinese government has not stopped patent theft in China. One reason is that it is not in the government's interests to do so. Moreover, it is not clear that it can do so. In any case, the relation between the American and Chinese governments is complex. It is not in the interests of the American government to aggressively fight IPR infringement in China. Infringement is just one of many issues on which the U.S. government wants the Chinese government's help. This is why negotiations on IP issues go on for decades. There is change, but change in the form of reducing IPR violations is glacial.

Mr. Ch2's comments do not accurately portray the actions of the Chinese government, nor do they accurately portray the record of prosecutions of patent violators. Instead, they reflect Mr. Ch2's anxieties that if a trade war breaks out between the two countries his company will be terribly hurt.[15] In other words, he seeks to contribute to a view of patent enforcement that will stave off American trade sanctions. This is an important point. Mr. Ch2 says his company is the number two patent holder in China. By misrepresenting patent enforcement in China, Mr. Ch2 exposes his concern over the vastly bigger threat of trade sanctions. IP fraud may be more than nipping at his heels, but trade sanctions from the United States would be a body blow.

Mr. Ch2 wants the Americans to stop whining about IP theft. It is a fact of life in China, like its huge population. It is not going to change in the foreseeable future. He has more or less accepted it as a cost of doing business. He wants the Americans to accept it too and to put Band-Aids on it because, although the disease is currently incurable, one can make money in spite of it. But many American businesses do not see it this way. For them, it is a crippling, even fatal, disease. And, it is just wrong. If they have to play by China's rules, they are at a disadvantage because they have neither the social position nor the cultural disposition to make interpersonal networks the engine of competition. They insist, wish, and threaten China to play by Western rules, but China has neither the institutional processes nor the cultural traditions to do so. Adjustments are made by both sides, but the conflict continues.

Companies like Mr. Ch2's are caught between conflicting interests. They want product copying to stop, but at what price? If the government attacks

---

[15] In the 2010 interviews, other Chinese executives expressed concern over growing trade tensions with the United States and the likelihood of a trade war.

IPR violators, what will be the result of a significant increase in unemployment? Likewise, if the government attacks bribery, what effect will it have on the government's own internal structure of authority? Mr. Ch2 does not want to see a significant rise in social unrest. For these reasons IPR enforcement can only improve along with changes in the broader system of government and society. So change in IPR enforcement will continue to be slow, probably very slow, and why not? It is working for China. It is the Americans who have the most technology to lose.

The final recommendation for protection of IP comes from a Chinese consultant who helps American firms invest in China:

> The way to deal with IP threats is to keep cautious, preventive way. Don't focus on one strategy. You can be hurt by other people. Keep good relations with partners. It's not simple to do business in China.
>
> (Mr. Ch13)

Mr. Ch13's coy advice is to be careful in every way one can. Not only is Mr. Ch13 a traditional Chinese middleman, but he has also taken an ownership stake and managerial responsibility in an American-Chinese joint venture. He mentions keeping good relations with partners. He found himself, however, mediating one conflict after another between the American and Chinese joint venture partners, between whom there was considerable distrust. The Americans wanted many precautions taken so financial accounts could be monitored daily from the United States. The Chinese resisted having their normal practices altered. Mr. Ch13 was in the middle, trying not only to resolve the problems but also to keep the peace. In the quote above, he seems to be implying that conflict between partners in a joint venture can lead to IPR violations as the Chinese, unsatisfied with or offended by the relationship, use IP belonging to the joint venture for themselves to get what they feel they are due. Mr. Ch13 seems to be implying that one needs relationships to protect one's IP in China, and managing the relationships is the central task.

3. Product Copying as Unstoppable. Chinese executives gave many reasons as to why IPR violations are very difficult to stop.

First, there simply is no effective way to stop employees from becoming competitors. Surprisingly, the same executives who made this point also recommended having employees sign noncompete agreements. This inconsistency reflects different situations in different parts of China. Local conditions and local relationships are decisive. General knowledge is often invalid.

Management in China is local management. In one court IP theft can be prosecuted, in another it cannot.

Second, poor people must make a living:

> The government is not dealing with it. The key is to keep people employed. The government has one eye closed and one eye open in a developing country. They are cracking down, but they must let them live. Chinese do not take this seriously. It's China. China just really opened up 10–15 years ago. It will take time to get them off knockoffs. When struggling for life, they will do anything. People in that business are born for that. If they are caught by the police, they do it again. There is nothing else they can do. First it was excess production; now it's an industry.
>
> (Mr. Ch24)

Mr. Ch24's comments illustrate how entwined IP problems are with broader social and political conditions in China. American organizations calling for immediate enforcement of trade agreements by the Chinese government are asking for the impossible. There are many poor people in China, hundreds of millions, who struggle to scratch out a living. In Mr. Ch24's view, the government is not dealing with IPR violations—or more precisely it is dealing with them by not dealing with them. He sees this situation as normal for a developing country. The government fears unemployment will lead to social unrest, so the government passes laws to satisfy some interest groups (mostly foreign businesses and governments) but does not enforce them. China did not significantly open up its economy until the mid-1990s. IP fraud followed directly upon the opening. The newly unemployed from the downsized SOE sector grasp at newly emerging opportunities made possible by access to new technologies and new markets in which to sell them. It would be wrong to close off these opportunities; many of these people are struggling for life, according to Mr. Ch24.

What would American organizations, who seek an immediate end to IP fraud in China, have the government do with the lower economic classes? Mr. Ch24 says people selling counterfeit clothes or DVDs are "born for that," by which he means their life experience prepares them for nothing else. American organizations want these people put in jail. Yet these organizations also say IP fraud is on every street in China. Are there enough jails for all these people? Is it ethical to put them in jail? No, argues Mr. Ch24, it is not ethical to put very poor people in jail for making a subsistence living when they have no other opportunity. It is a universal human right to have a minimum level of economic and social well-being. There are broader issues here, and American organizations and the American government must acknowledge them rather than merely demand their economic interests be satisfied, their values followed, and international agreements they had a hand in making be obeyed.

Finally, Mr. Ch24's last sentence says that infringement started with unauthorized selling of "excess production" and has now become an "industry" in its own right. Unauthorized selling started in the 1980s when the government created the two-track pricing system. Products with controlled prices were skimmed off production runs and illegally sold at the higher market rates. When the economy was further opened in the 1990s, unauthorized production grew into its own "industry." Hence, increased reform brought increased corruption. In other words, the opened economy created the market for fraudulent goods and the ability to supply them. From the American point of view, the Chinese did not rise to the occasion and enforce the rule of law over the economy. Nonetheless, the expansive nature of self-interest and the amoral nature of markets are on display. Without the countervailing power of government enforcement, the idea of IPR has no practical relevance.

Some executives chalk up the unstoppability of counterfeiting to simple human nature:

> The government is trying hard to stop IP [rights] violations; there are many new regulations. But people are very smart, they always find a way to do it. Even foreigners buy fake discs. How can the government stop this?
>
> (Ms. Ch14)

The picture Ms. Ch14 paints is oversimplified. Despite the many new regulations, the government is not trying particularly hard. Ms. Ch14's view is a romantic idealization of the poor classes, who scratch out a living in some cases literally on the run from police. Even though Ms. Ch14 has a graduate degree in engineering from a top university and now runs her own business, she was separated from her parents as a child during the Cultural Revolution and spent years in poverty. Her background suggests the possibility that even when executives like her have their own IP to protect, they might not all demand strict enforcement of IP laws as many in the West predict. The experience of extreme poverty and hardship during the Cultural Revolution may lead to identification with the poor who are involved in counterfeiting. This is another reason it might take a generation before the will to protect IP emerges among the business classes.

Ms. Ch14's other point—that even foreigners buy fake discs, so the government cannot stop it—implies that demand creates the IPR violations. As long as money can be made, IP counterfeiting will continue. This also oversimplifies the situation. Increased enforcement efforts would raise the costs of manufacturing fake discs—thus cutting down supply, raising prices, and reducing demand.

A CEO for a large SOE described how the government deals with IPR violations within the SOE system:

> We had a supplier take our product and apply for a patent. I fought the patent and the supplier sued us. It is rare for a supplier to sue their customer. The main reason the supplier wants the patent is to compete with another supplier of ours. But this case did not go to court. The government entered and made a ridiculous decision. They said both companies owned the IPR. But the deep reason is that both the supplier and my company are military owned. So both are owned by the government. Many IPR cases do not go to court, but are dealt with by the government. They deal with it softly. But in the future, more lawsuits will go to court. At this stage, the government is mostly involved.
>
> (Mr. Ch4)

As his remarks reveal, Mr. Ch4 also feels that product copying is an issue of development. As Chinese companies become more innovative and develop their own products, they will naturally become more concerned with IPR and disinclined to participate in product copying.

Mr. Ch4's comments describe patent infringement between two SOEs, providing another view of the Chinese government's attitude toward IPR. In this case, a supplier applied for a patent on its customer's product. As odd as this might seem, when the customer fought the proposed patent the supplier sued the customer. This shows a remarkable blurring of organizational and legal boundaries between SOEs. In an apparent logical contradiction, the supplier seems to think that anything within the state-owned system can be made one's private property, that is, patented. The ultimate resolution (or nonresolution, in Mr. Ch4's opinion) rested on both companies being owned by the government.

It is clear that employees working in a system like this will not develop a deep respect for IPR. This is important because many SOEs have been shut down, downsized, or privatized, so many SOE employees socialized in an SOE culture have entered the "private" sector. This is yet another reason it will take a generation for China to significantly reduce counterfeiting, no matter how fast the economy grows. In this case, the government blocked the conflict from going to court, which, interestingly, is where the two SOEs were headed. By its decision, the government sent the signal that it is not terribly sensitive to IPR. On the contrary, it signaled that it sees itself as a parent and insists all the toys should be shared equally by the children, a role consistent with its overall strategy of maintaining dependency in the population.[16] This mind-set suggests that the government's willingness to privatize the economy is quite limited.

Interestingly, Mr. Ch4 called the government's decision "ridiculous" and said in the future more lawsuits between SOEs will go to court, though when this interview took place in 2007 the government was still "mostly involved." Governmental involvement is all the more surprising because Mr. Ch4's SOE had been told it must earn its capital in the marketplace; it could not expect the government would continue to fund its operations.

It is odd that at the same time Mr. Ch4 is told he must compete in the marketplace, the government is giving away his IP. It is also curious that a government wanting to transform this SOE into a competitive enterprise would leave Mr. Ch4 at the helm, since his four decades of work experience have all been inside the Communist industrial structure, protected from the forces of competition. I asked the graduate student translating the interview this question and was told Mr. Ch4 cannot be removed because the workers would refuse to work. It is a self-protecting system. In any case, the government does not seem to be in a rush to transform this SOE. As Mr. Ch4 looks around for new markets in which to sell his products, he faces other obstacles too, such as American refusal to grant him a visa to enter the United States because of his SOE status. Caught between a suffocating socialism and a hostile capitalism, it is hard to find much incentive for the SOE sector to develop a deep appreciation for IPR.

Nonetheless, Mr. Ch4 went on to predict that as Chinese companies become more innovative they will want protection for their IP and will stop violating IPR; but his statement appears theoretical or more probably political. Mr. Ch4 would be one of the last to know how respect for IPR develops, since his whole work experience lacks any such notion. Ironically, his view is

---

[16] Walder 1986.

the same as those in the West whose world view assumes that respect for IPR develops out of the sheer self-interest of the business classes, since their success in creating IP requires protection. What is missing from this picture is exactly the analysis just shown in the case of Mr. Ch4: the enormous role of the government in China's economy and the many interests it has in regard to IP. The people in the West who see a new IPR regime sprouting out of China's business success implicitly assume a radical transformation of China's state apparatus. For this there is little evidence.

4. Imitation and Competition. Product imitation plays a central role in the chemical industry in China. To what extent is it ethical?

> Imitation happens all the time. A person gets a small sample, analyzes it. Little by little, they get it right. I have a friend; he's clever in the lab. He improves the product. He's very successful now. He owns two big plants. He makes two good-quality products originally from imports. It's not against the law. He didn't steal anything, only analyze and imitate it.
>
> (Ms. Ch32)

Ms. Ch32 gives an example of product copying that she argues is not illegal. Her friend starts with an American chemical product and in the process of reproducing it, improves it. It is not exactly the same product.

Is this process ethical? Imitation can be seen as a range. Certainly many types of imitation are common and commonly accepted in the United States. A company comes out with a product that sells well and soon very similar products are brought out by competitors. It is ethical because it is an accepted part of how American capitalism works. An important question: Is a patent technically violated? This is a technical and legal question that must be answered on a case-by-case basis. In general, imitation is not necessarily illegal or unethical. Reverse engineering does not have the glamour of innovation, but it is a common practice in a competitive business system. Indeed, one business strategy taught in American business schools is "follow the leader." Let the leader expend the funds and efforts to innovate, assuming the high risks of failure, but once the innovation is accepted by the market, the follower enters the market with a similar or comparable product.

Product imitation has an important influence on competition:

> All products we import have local competitors. Many people analyze imported products. Some people are very original. They change the name of the product. It's patented, so they call it "product B." They

change a few things because they must because they can't get all the foreign materials; they must use local materials and still have a good product. So, it's not against the law. They make some subtle changes.

(Ms. Ch32)

Ms. Ch32 says all products she imports as a distributor have local competitors. These local products are copies. Along with a few changes in components, names have been changed. Hence, a whole field of product imitations develops around imported products. Some of these competitors make identical products and use the names of foreign products, violating patent and trademark laws. Some make changes and possibly do not violate these laws. China is a highly competitive market, both legally and illegally.

This type of competition is related to China's status as a developing market. Many companies do not have the capacities to compete technologically with American products. In the imagined future, if Chinese companies mature, American companies will face equally intense, perhaps more intense competition from technological alternatives as opposed to imitations. American companies might lose even more from technological alternatives than from the current product imitations. Creating the country's own advanced technologies is a development goal of the Chinese government. Clearly, the government is pursuing this goal in part by means of IPR infringement, as Chinese companies accumulate capital and expertise. The tipping point to "mature" competition is still not in sight.

Ms. Ch32 is a distributor for foreign products. She too is hurt by Chinese imitations:

> From a business point of view, my company imports, so we do not want imitators to improve quality too fast, because we lose business when the imitator's product is better than the imported product.

The imitators do not require a middleman to sell in China. They sell direct. So the extensive industry of middlemen that has grown up in China to distribute foreign products is also a loser from imitation in the domestic market. The product imitations undercut the imported products on price and, according to Ms. Ch32, sometimes they improve quality too.

If the distributor sells both the imported product and the imitation, she runs the risk of a conflict of interest:

> I am a distributor for one local product that is an imitation of an imported product. It does compete with imported products I

distribute. No problem. It is good quality and lower price. We don't have the transportation costs that come with the imported product. The foreign company will find out within one year. The foreign company gives us little room for profit. The local quality is similar or the same. We will close down the relationship with the foreign producer.

(Ms. Ch32)

Ms. Ch32 seems to justify distributing a competing product because the foreign company "gives little room for profit." In other words, since the foreign company is stingy, Ms. Ch32 can be dishonest. Of course, this is not ethically justifiable. Ms. Ch32 is free to reject the foreign terms, but she cannot accept them and then violate them because she was not satisfied with them in the first place. In other parts of the interview, Ms. Ch32 made strong statements about the importance of personal integrity in the context of not paying bribes to government officials to advance her business. Yet she does not see an ethical problem in lying to the foreign company to advance her business. Why is this? One answer can be found below in the analysis of her next statement.

The Chinese distributor faces lose-lose choices in deciding whether to distribute imports or imitations of them:

Another foreign producer, Rohm and Haas, will not let us distribute even their new products, because we distribute products of a competitor. No one can prevent imitation. This happens all around the world. As a distributor, we can't do anything. We try to earn enough money from foreign imports before the imitations come. The local manufacturers distribute their own products. Normally it's not so easy to imitate. Normally imitation is done by hiring a senior person at the foreign producer.

(Ms. Ch32)

In this statement, Ms. Ch32 explains how the middleman gets squeezed between a continuous supply of imitations entering the marketplace and the foreign producer's refusal to allow the middleman to distribute imitations. If the middleman obeys the foreign producer her sales are continuously in decline from the onslaught of imitations. If, on the other hand, the middleman sells the imitations the result is even worse: She is terminated by the foreign producer and faces declining sales from the imitator, who is increasingly selling his own imitations. The only profitable position is selling both, since they are sequentially temporary. Lying is required to create the selling sequence that makes profit possible in a market without IPR.

Interestingly, Ms. Ch32 says "normally" the procedure for product imitation is not reverse engineering; it is hiring a senior person at the foreign company. Reverse engineering is a second choice because it takes too long; it is not easy.[17] Thus the American nightmare of losing both trained Chinese employees and company patents is confirmed. Reverse engineering is clearly the lesser of the two threats because it takes longer; normally does not produce an identical product; and limits the loss of IP to a single product, not the broad-ranging knowledge and access to documents, designs, and customers of a senior engineer.

5. IP and Chinese Business Culture. Perceived moral, political, and economic uncertainty in the Chinese business environment creates an obsession with present opportunity and an underinvestment in the future:

> I am worried about Chinese business. It lacks credibility. A healthy business is based on trust, credibility, and fairness. In China, the business environment does not have a long-term perspective. It is a fast-growing market. People want to get in and make money and get out. People steal ideas in many areas. I can't control it, can't prevent it. It takes time to build credibility. In the long term, we need a healthy business environment. People will realize that they need a healthy business environment for the whole system.

> (Ms. Ch7)

Ms. Ch7 runs a company to help American companies do business in China, specializing in mergers and acquisitions. One of her biggest problems is that American companies do not trust Chinese companies. Her views on Chinese business culture must be seen in this light. She says a healthy business is based on trust, credibility, and fairness. Many Chinese businesses lack these qualities. By "healthy," I assume she means economic health. Is it true that a healthy business must be based on trust, credibility, and fairness? It does not seem to be. China is the world's fastest-growing economy and, according

---

[17] The other route, however, would exclude small firms with little capital to hire away senior engineers.

to some estimates, 10–20 percent of its GDP growth is the result of IP corruption. Certainly there is plenty of corruption in the United States, where courts are filled with charges of corrupt business behavior. The problem is generally perceived to be worldwide. China, however, is considered by many to be the dominant violator of IPR. So China is not different in principle, but the world's most populous nation is different in *quantity* of violations. In any case, at this point IP theft appears to be helping China's growth, not hurting it.

When Ms. Ch7 says, "People will realize that they need a healthy business environment for the whole system," she seems to be speaking theoretically. Honesty will lead to the greatest good for the greatest number of people because the market will be more efficient. But her characterization of the facts on the ground is quite different. People are selfish; they want to get in, make money, and get out, caring little how they impact others or the long term. The concern for the whole is missing in China. Tellingly, she does not mention the government. But it is the government that must enforce the laws. Indeed, the government is responsible not only for not enforcing the IP laws but also for much of their violation.

The business system is not working as a whole or for the whole, according to Ms. Ch7. Her business is negatively impacted by the lack of trust. Yet her response to the lack of honesty is idealistic, that people should be honest for the good of the whole. Theoretically, this will be good for everyone. Ms. Ch7 does not comment on why people are dishonest. They are just dishonest and that is the problem. This is the one-eye-closed approach to business ethics in China. Ms. Ch7 implies the business system should improve its ethics independent of government corruption, independent of the government's absolute and arbitrary power. If Ms. Ch7 is concerned with the "whole system," how can she ignore the government? She ignores it out of an acceptance that it cannot be changed and a fear that it is not healthy to worry about it. It is safer to worry about "business" corruption; it is safer to talk about improving "business" honesty. This shows exactly the problem of addressing business corruption in China. It cannot be addressed because it is in the shadow of government corruption and the government's unchallenge-able power.

Importantly, Chinese businesses like Ms. Ch7's, whose interests are aligned with American interests, are not so much lobbying the Chinese government to enforce IP laws as keeping their distance from political involvement. Thus leadership for IPR enforcement is muted among those who have the most need for it.[18] Hence, as long as IP fraud pays off handsomely it may be very difficult to dislodge. In a system gorging on power and wealth, those without power have little say in how the wealth is made, distributed, and spent.

The situation, as Ms. Ch7 suggests, is very difficult for Chinese entrepreneurs. A Chinese middleman gives an example from the power-generation industry:

> I am a distributor for a product that stops transmission power swings. It is sold by a little company in Boston. The company owner is very worried about IPR issues in China. . . . I found a Chinese utility that wants us to install the product so that they can see it work. The American owner says he will not sell it for the normal $20,000 price because he risks losing the IP. He will only sell the product in China for $2 million. But the utility won't pay $2 million without knowing it works. . . . The American is worried that counterfeit products will boomerang back to the U.S. I guess the product is easy to copy. I suggested we find a local Chinese manufacturer to reduce cost. A company in Dalian wants to produce it, an SOE utility. The product can be registered with the Chinese government. But the product can be easily modified and manufactured. No deal is done.
>
> (Mr. Ch25)

In this example, all the key parties are present—private American business, private Chinese business, SOEs, and the Chinese government—with no trust to be found between them to make a deal possible. For now, the economy is expanding and the Chinese government does not seem to care, even though the power industry did not get access to potentially helpful technology and entrepreneurs like Mr. Ch25 are blocked from introducing innovations and growing their businesses. Perhaps when economic growth subsides, the government will rethink the issues of trust and credibility. When that point arrives, the question is whether the government will be able to do anything about it, given that its own power structure is permeated with corruption.

---

[18] This too is contrary to the opinions of those Americans who think the Chinese, in need of IP protection, will pressure the Chinese government to provide it. Ms. Ch7's case shows that her need for IPR has left her alienated and frustrated. In addition, Tsai's (2007) data show "China's business owners have vastly different identities, interests, and political attitudes," making class-based collective action unlikely. The diverse interests and orientations of Chinese businesspeople stem from differences in family and occupational background.

Mr. Ch25 provided another example of American feelings of distrust that led to Chinese feelings of insult:

> I almost sold a couple of jobs to a huge Chinese utility. The product was a new method for maintenance. The contract was almost signed. It was blocked by legal people on both sides. . . . The American company wants arbitration carried out according to California law. The Chinese want it by Chinese law. It sunk the deal. It reflects two different views of IPR. The Chinese side took it very serious that if you come to this country, you must play by Chinese law. It's a dignity issue. . . . So I decide it's a no-win situation. The power industry is growing greatly, but when it falls to details it's a big problem. Coca Cola is growing dramatically, but IP is not.

This example presents the interesting situation that the Chinese are sensitive to receiving their due, to having their status respected, but not sensitive to the distrust and the label of "counterfeiter" that causes the distrust. It would appear profits are more important than face, except in public. In this case, the dignity issue could be part of a power play. Face, power, profits, and IP cannot be separated. This is Chinese business; its defining feature is fluidity, the opposite of the idea of IPR.

This interplay creates a credibility problem for the Chinese in the eyes of the Americans. It affects not only the economic terms of trade but also the feelings of face the Chinese experience in the business relation. Indeed, strong emotions can be seen in both Chinese and Americans in both of Mr. Ch25's examples. Thus, IP has both economic *and* symbolic value, the latter heightened in the Chinese context because the power dynamics of face are inseparable from the power dynamics of technology. IP in this context is fraught with provocative meaning, whereas, as Mr. Ch25 notes, Coca Cola is not. The trouble in the middle for IP will be the last to be resolved not only because of the economic and political conflicts but because of its inseparability from profound cultural differences involving the relation of power to property.

Conclusion

The tendency for American executives to have little understanding of Chinese history and culture, combined with significant cultural differences between the two countries, creates particular challenges in the area of IP. The

Americans, assuming individualism and self-interest as the dominant forces in human behavior, pay scant attention to the Cultural Revolution's influence on the current leaders of Chinese organizations. The influence is complex, but the data presented in this book show a dominating drive for immediate wealth as a consolation for lost youth, forgone opportunities, and years of suffering and deprivation.

Related to the same traumatic experience, the data also show identifications by Chinese entrepreneurs with the poorer classes, many of whom are closely involved with counterfeiting. The prediction common in the West that the business classes will pressure the Chinese government for IP protection once they have IP that needs protection is not so unambiguously the case. Indeed, there are many countertrends in IPR enforcement: identification with the poor, the hundreds of millions of poor who need work, a lack of alternative work, an inability for them to do other kinds of work, fears of social unrest from rising unemployment, the lack of a notion of IP among the tens of millions socialized in the SOE sector, continued government enforcement of SOE culture, political disengagement and alienation among entrepreneurs who would benefit from IPR enforcement, government corruption, and government involvement in product counterfeiting.

Another gap in American understanding of IP in China can be seen in American government officials and business executives simultaneously criticizing China for its record of IPR violations while stating that they see progress in China toward IPR enforcement. The Chinese executives interviewed acknowledged the violations, somewhat dismissing them as a worldwide phenomenon, but interestingly never claiming they are decreasing. The difference between the American and Chinese views is the difference between American self-interest and reality. The Americans recognize the positive developments in the hope they will be followed by more positive developments. American government officials recognize the positive developments as a means to praise their own labors. Nevertheless, American business executives who are hurt the most recognize the positive developments the least.

Chinese executives do not speak about reduction in IPR violations because they know more intimately than the Americans the full extent of the problem. More importantly, they know there cannot be any improvement in IPR enforcement without the government, and they know that whether the government enforces or does not enforce IP law will have little to nothing to do with them. They know there will be no class of entrepreneurs leading the way. American executives assume Chinese entrepreneurs are like them, whereas the Chinese, unlike the Americans, live in deep fear of their government. For the most part, they do not speak about the government in public or to outsiders. Furthermore, the most successful are the most closely tied to the government. There can be no business success in China without at least tacit approval from the government.[19] American executives may fear retaliation for criticizing the Chinese government, but Chinese executives feel the same fear tenfold. In 1989, entrepreneurs were *not* on Tiananmen Square. A minority of them may not like the status quo, but this does not change the fact that their success depends on Party approval and help.

These issues are related to IPR infringement. Government corruption is one of the main causes of IP infringement. Various levels of government are directly involved in or benefit from IPR infringement. Indeed, it appears infringement is an explicit government strategy. So infringement will not decline until government corruption declines—and that would require a fundamental change in the nature of the Chinese government. There is little sign such a change is happening or will happen any time soon. In fact, when the government backpedaled out of socialism into markets, changing from creator-of-the-socialist-paradise to facilitator-of-wealth-production, one thing it did not change was keeping the population in a state of dependency. While it did lighten up on mind control, it merely changed from central planning to "commanding the heights" for control of the economy. Despite the decentralization that has taken place politically and economically, the Party still controls what it wants when it wants. It is a challenging balancing act but it has been successful for more than three decades.

The Party has never really accepted the idea of private property. There cannot be IP until there is private property. Likewise there cannot be IP law until there is the rule of law. The Party has not accepted that either. In fact, the rule of law is fundamentally at odds with the Party's very nature. The rule of law implies something above the Party. The very essence of the Party is that there is nothing above it. Party rule is the "verdict of history," as they say.

American executives tend to assume that when the Chinese introduced economic reform and markets, they would evolve toward Western capitalism or at least toward capitalism as practiced in Japan, South Korea, or Singapore.

---

[19] Indeed, "in recent years officials have increased their efforts to ensure that Party cells are set up in private firms. Several local governments have started requiring private companies to contribute about 0.5 percent of their payrolls to sponsor Party activities on their premises" (*Economist* December 10, 2011b).

That is the destination toward which the country started and it would only be a matter of time before it arrived there. These perceptions and expectations either misunderstand or overlook the Chinese government, or both. It is the government that will control economic reform in China and its primary purpose in doing so will be to remain in power.

It has long been the case that the government exercises absolute and arbitrary power in Chinese society. Because of this, personal relations are of central importance, both to work with the government and to protect oneself from it. Americans are caught between, on the one hand, their outsider status, which leaves them without intimate contacts and without the knowledge and background to fully develop them and, on the other hand, a preference for contract-based relationships. But the latter do not substitute for the former; that is, contracts do not build trust in China. On the contrary, developing and managing relationships is the central means to protect IP in China. More generally, it is the central task of management.

In terms of IP, copying the products of others is the natural state of affairs in China. To receive assistance from the government to have things otherwise, to have laws enforced or regulatory actions taken, it helps to have relationships with government officials. The key aspect of developing relationships is building trust. Building trust involves developing common interests, enjoyable relations, and an understanding that you are more committed to each other than to laws, regulations, and even profit. Without these conditions, trust will be weak and cooperation limited.

A major challenge in developing personal networks to protect IP is that IP is not just another business issue, but in addition to its financial value it is loaded with symbolic value to both the Americans and the Chinese. For the Chinese, the idea of IP is related to China's technological backwardness, the history of foreign exploitation of its markets, and more recently, foreign firms selling old technology as new. These issues relate to Chinese face, how the Chinese are respected on the world stage. Technology is power—economic power, political power, and military power. To have advanced technology is to have power, to have face among the powerful countries of the world. These issues and priorities trump IPR in China.

If China is not able to gain control over advanced technology and develop the capacity to create its own, it will be left dependent on foreign powers for key aspects of its economic growth and sustainability, military security, and self-sufficiency. This is an unacceptable position for China. This means conflicts over IP are difficult to isolate as purely legal or business issues.

Government officials are wary that how they handle IP issues with American companies can easily attract the attention of higher-level officials. They cannot be seen as giving Americans control over technology at China's expense. Managing IP relations with Americans can impact their face and thus their career prospects.

For the Americans, the situation is not vastly different. China's rise, its dominance in the area of manufacturing, the loss of American jobs, and America's serious economic challenges all make for great pride in and trepidation about its dominance of advanced technology markets. These global perceptions and feelings add to the concern over extensive IPR infringement in China and the financial losses it entails. So American identity too is closely tied to IP. America's future is seen as inseparable from its ability to maintain its lead in creating new technologies. Without it, Americans see their decline in the world.

With issues of national identity so integral to both Chinese and American perceptions of IP, the struggle over IP is intense. The future for each country seems to be riding on whether it moves ahead or falls behind in this area. Because of the heightened status of IP many business relationships are held back or hemmed in. There are delays and losses for both societies because of these problems.

However, despite the considerable conflicts of interest and the vast cultural differences the two countries bring to IP issues, there are similarities. Americans may have the highest level of respect for IPR in the world, but they also have significant IPR infringement in the areas of software and music; and the American court system is taxed with addressing alleged IPR violations of all kinds. The problem of IPR is indeed worldwide. So China's IP record is a reflection not just of cultural differences but of a very large population doing what in considerable degree is done everywhere, especially developing nations.

The relation with China over IP is further complicated by the fact that many American businesses in China either do not have IP issues or are able to protect their IP adequately. Thus the American political landscape is divided over how important IP issues are in the American-Chinese relationship. For this and other reasons, firms that face IP losses can find themselves isolated in demanding stronger government action against China for IPR violations. This division is further complicated by the fact that American firms, in general, do not want to speak out publicly about IPR violations in China for fear of retaliation from the Chinese government and, in some cases, for fear of the questions it may raise about their product quality worldwide.

The American government thus reflects these conflicting interests among its constituents and indeed has conflicting interests of its own in regard to seeking China's help or discouraging China's endeavors across the globe. China is aware of these conflicting interests and others, and both uses them to its advantage and modulates its IPR enforcement in measure with this broad array of conflicting pressures and mutating powers. For now, to the dodger go the spoils.

11

Conclusion

Notes on the Cultural Middle

In one sense, Switzerland is an apt metaphor for a constructive cultural middle. Hemmed in by fortress-like mountain ranges, Switzerland has for centuries been able to keep its distance from the wars raging around it, insisting on austere neutrality. But Switzerland is no mere metaphor in American-Chinese business relations. Alarmed by increasing pressure from the Chinese to resolve business disputes through arbitration in China, American firms literally try to move arbitration hearings to Switzerland to secure a neutral and fair environment in which to have their interests represented.[1]

Whether or not Americans are lucky enough to have their arbitration hearings moved to Switzerland, the cultural middle in American-Chinese business relations is no paradise of civility. It is characterized by difficult communications, problematic cooperation, and limited trust, if any. In fact, one of the key findings in this book concerns middlemen, mostly Chinese, who are engaged, ostensibly, to bridge the gap between the two cultures, helping them develop shared understanding. Instead, middlemen often stay in the middle, communicating with each party separately and thereby keeping them apart, largely due to the parties' incompatible moral commitments. Chinese often work through personal networks called *guanxi*, which operate outside of and many times in contradiction to formal rules and laws. Americans, on the other hand, risk severe penalties if they are caught operating in violation of the U.S. Foreign Corrupt Practices Act and company policies against bribery.

Middlemen profit from this moral gap, often paying bribes on behalf of Americans, who are afraid to do so for themselves. Based on this bribe-paying function of middlemen, their importance in communicating between

---

[1] Jones and Batson 2008.

American and Chinese executives, and their substantial role in performing a host of other functions—making connections, carrying out product and market analysis, negotiating, monitoring projects, and the like—I developed the concept of the *cultural middle* to describe, analyze, and explain how two very different business systems manage the cultural differences between them.

Middlemen can, of course, be found worldwide, and none of the above activities are unknown in other places, between other cultures. However, this applies to middleman *functions*. The role of middlemen in Chinese culture is unique. See Appendix Four for a discussion of middlemen in Chinese culture. Hence, a detailed analysis of the role of middlemen in the cultural middle between American and Chinese business cultures makes possible an examination of a unique relationship where the two cultures confront one another and attempt to manage the specific problems and issues that arise. In any case, the development of knowledge about culture is the development of knowledge about a specific culture because culture exists only in particular social circumstances, at particular times, among particular individuals.[2] A culture is always changing—sometimes slowly, sometimes dynamically—so to learn about a culture one must study it in context. When two different cultures meet and attempt to work with each other, the dimension of cultural change is intensified.

Learning how specific people make sense of their lives and the lives of others makes possible a comparison with the historical record to see how the culture has changed or not changed over time. On the one hand, in terms of this book, this means a comparison of the 2006/07 data with the 2010 data to see what changed and what did not; on the other hand, it means an examination of Chinese history and the history of American-Chinese relations in China to see what came before and how it influenced what came later. In this way, through the study of individual action in specific places at specific times, in comparison with the historical context out of which the current situation unfolded, the understanding of culture is possible.

What has been found in this study of ethical and cultural issues in American-Chinese business relations—that middlemen often act in a highly instrumental manner, exploiting the cultural and moral gap between the two business cultures, and reconciling, through secrecy, the incompatibilities between them—is novel in the literature on the middleman's functions which primarily relies on Western management theories such as transaction cost theory and agency theory.[3] In

---

[2] Geertz 1973, 1983.
[3] Peng 1998; Chintakananda et al. 2009.

American-Chinese business relations, the middleman often acts as an amoral black box through which Americans do not *pay* bribes but Chinese government officials *receive* bribes. Before going on to draw general conclusions about the cultural middle from this research, a few comments need to be made on American and Chinese cultures.

In the United States, individual rights are central to national life. Individuals are expected, to a considerable degree, to pursue their own interests within the limits of the law, and central parts of the law are designed to safeguard individual rights. Rigorous competition is the norm as individuals pursue their own interests. But for the system to work effectively, individuals must have a civil sense; they must care about moral and civil order as a whole and be able to empathize with others whose interests and beliefs are different from their own.[4] This civil sense is particularly weak in the present age, as demonstrated by a practically dysfunctional Congress[5] and morally weak business sector.[6] Achieving a civil sense is always a struggle, but the current condition of the civil sense puts the United States in peril.

Civil society in the United States is crucial for the functioning of institutions that support and provide opportunities for individual expression and action, namely democratic politics, private property, freedom of contract, the market, and private associations. By putting limits on individual action, the civil sense makes possible the autonomy of institutions as well as the social spheres—of family, religion, education, arts, and business, for example—through which they function. Most importantly, the civil sense both makes democratic politics possible and limits its role by ensuring the autonomy of other parts of society. But a weakened civil sense has imperiled the autonomy of the various parts of society, too; the state has greatly expanded its role in society and the population has increasingly looked to the state to solve social problems and provide benefits for subgroups.[7]

Chinese society differs significantly from the American scenario. First of all, collective goals, not individual ones, are supreme. Starting in the family,

---

[4] Shils 1997.

[5] Significant numbers of politicians, for example, refuse to compromise with those with different opinions.

[6] Greed and disregard for others, even their own companies, characterized management behavior during the devastating subprime mortgage crisis (McLean and Nocera 2010), the latest in a string of moral breakdowns going back decades.

[7] Shils 1997.

the Chinese child is restricted from every direction. The self is defined in relation to others; mutual dependence is the ideal.[8] The American child, in
contrast, is encouraged to increase his independence from the family at a
young age; self-reliance is the ideal. In China, family relationships often
remain paramount throughout life, especially between a son and his parents.

Opposite the family in China is the state.[9] For thousands of years, the Chinese
state has been authoritarian, often making strong demands on the population.
The current Communist government follows in this tradition; its leaders are not
chosen by the population but by a small group within the Communist Party
itself. This dichotomy between state and family or extended family has led to
intensely strong family relations but little development of civility in the American
sense, whereby empathy for equal but different others is the ideal.

Though the Chinese are capable of remarkable collective efforts due to traditions of respect for authority and a strong sense of being Chinese, the family-
state structure has left the private and voluntary nature of civil society relatively
undeveloped.[10] Whereas Americans, in their civil decline, rely increasingly on
the courts to address conflict, the Chinese either look to the state for large-scale
social organization or fall back on fortress-like family-dominated networks to
manage small-scale organizations. New large-scale "private" organizations in
China tend to have a close relationship with the government, which jealously
guards against all independent sources of power and influence.[11]

The "middle way" is an important aspect of Chinese collective culture.
Because of the strong emphasis on collective goals and harmony, individuals
are encouraged to compromise for the good of the whole. Indeed, middlemen
are often used *inside* Chinese society as arbitrators representing collective
interests. Hierarchy, too, plays a central role in maintaining Chinese collectivism; and in so doing it discourages the open expression of conflict. Given
this emphasis on the collectivity, issues of "face", the individual's public status
within the collectivity, take on great importance and middlemen are again
used to address conflicts between individuals to ensure "face" is not further
offended in the process of conflict resolution.[12]

---

[8] Hsu 1981.

[9] Gates 1996 .

[10] Tsai 2007.

[11] R. McGregor 2010.

[12] In a sense, then, the cultural middle exists also within any given society, as can be seen in
conflict resolution processes the world over.

Returning now to the discussion of the middle between two cultures, it is important to note China's unique historical background in this context. Because of its location in relation to other major power centers and the geography within China and surrounding it, China was isolated from outside influence to an unusual degree until the eighteenth century.[13] Because of the long period of isolation and the great continuity of Confucian civilization (which put the highest value on loyalty), the Chinese were little disposed towards or experienced with cultural negotiation. In this sense, the cultural middle was destined to be challenging for China.[14]

Because of this insularity and its own internal development, China fell behind the West economically, technologically, and militarily. This led the West to force its way into China in the nineteenth century, humiliating China. For a century, roughly 1850 to 1950, China lost considerable control over its own territory. So from isolation to invasion, the cultural middle went from undeveloped to overrun for the Chinese. The great paradox here is that the Chinese people have been one of the most adaptable and successful immigrant groups the world over. Nonetheless, at home, their relations with foreigners have been fraught with trouble for generations.[15]

As China tries to deal with its unfortunate legacy with foreigners, that is, to enter "modernity," advance its national interests, and ensure national security, a second paradox has emerged. In 1978, when Deng Xiaoping created an "opening" to the West, he also turned away from 30 years of Mao-led Communist ideological indoctrination. On the one hand, he introduced a period of economic development unparalleled in world history; on the other hand, with the introduction of "market socialism with Chinese characteristics," Deng introduced marketization into a Communist state with a suppressed but deep Confucian heritage. This all began immediately following the highly destructive Cultural Revolution and the resultant discrediting of the Communist state. Hence, it can be seen that the cultural environment in which China's momentous transition is taking place is anything but coherent. So while "market socialism with Chinese characteristics" continues its world-beating

---

[13] China was repeatedly invaded by the non-Chinese Inner Asians, but though they became leaders of China they allowed much of Chinese culture and institutions to continue (Fairbanks and Goldman 2006).

[14] Indeed, the Chinese thought they were the middle, referring to themselves as the "Middle Kingdom." Here "middle" denotes *center* or *central.*

[15] It is for this reason that Tu Wei-ming (1994) argues that cultural change in China must come from the Chinese periphery.

economic performance, 160 years of cultural disruption and disorientation have made defining, let alone managing, the cultural middle a bewildering task. Perhaps always a bewildering task, it is made extremely so by China's history.

Based on this history and the analysis in this book, which derives from it, three points about the cultural middle merit further discussion: its ambiguity, possible responses to it, and the role of power.

1. Ambiguity in the Middle. When two different cultures attempt to work with each other, a cultural middle is created, for it is unclear which culture's practices, standards, and rules will be used in the new relationship. At the point of contact, the cultural middle is "empty" or amoral. To add to the ambiguity, in the case of the United States and China, one business culture is well established while the other one is new, somewhat incoherent, and fragmented. Americans arrive in China with well-developed business standards, policies, and processes, while China is undergoing a vast economic transition with little clarity about or experience with markets. In this case, one might expect that the established culture would dominate, but this has not happened in China. In fact, not only do American executives complain about the ruleless "Wild West," but middlemen function to bring Americans into the orbit of Chinese "rulelessness" by paying bribes on their behalf.

Two factors help explain the dominance of the "transitional" culture in this case. One, the vast age of China's culture and especially of its *guanxi* networks provide plenty of continuity for the Chinese to keep their culture dominant on its home turf. Two, the Chinese government is the central player in the China market. Hence, China's political culture, which is *not* in transition, is dominant in China's business system because it uses its political authority to monitor and control business behavior.

2. Possible Responses to the Middle. When two cultures engage each other, each has three general options as to whose standards and rules to follow: adoption, rejection, or fusion.[16] If either culture chooses to adopt the practices and standards of the other, on the surface the problem is solved. A single culture is dominant; the cultural middle ceases to exist and the semantic field is unified. However, even in this most clear of options the deeper reality is more complex. Once the adopting culture starts learning about the new cultural forms, it must integrate them into its established cultural system. In this process, both the established culture and the new forms being adopted

---

[16] Shils 1981.

change. Both meaning and action can become ambiguous as established and adopted forms take time to integrate. Ultimately, even the dominant culture changes as the dominant and adopting cultures begin working together. The master cannot avoid being influenced by the slave.

If each culture rejects the other, the cultural middle remains empty. In some ways, this is what happens in American-Chinese business relations. Americans usually reject paying bribes and the Chinese reject not receiving bribes. Hence, the middleman comes into the cultural middle and erects a "bridge" between the two sides; however, it is a strange sort of bridge, the middleman is the only one crossing it. The two cultures do not change and do not come to an agreement. The middleman merely instrumentally resolves the stalemate. The bribes are paid even though the disagreement over bribe paying is never resolved.

This situation has been examined many times in this book and will not be repeated here. It is important to note, however, the irony in the institution of the middleman: He keeps the two cultures apart while simultaneously being viewed as a "bridge" between them. Speaking both languages and having some knowledge of both cultures, he uses this knowledge to enable both cultures *not* to learn to deal with each other. Yet a compromise is somehow worked out: The Chinese officials get the bribes. The cultural middle thereby becomes a secretive place and the middleman a bagman. Under darkness, the cultural rejection turns into a kind of cultural adoption, as the Americans play by Chinese rules while claiming they do not. Here the cultural middle is amoral but not empty. Concealment and reversal take place in it, so bribes can be paid while plausible deniability is provided for the Americans. The work of the middleman carries out cultural adoption, but instead of the cultural middle disappearing, it remains and is used to conceal the adoption.

The use of concealment in the cultural middle might be called "negative adoption". It is characterized by unacceptable behavior that is accepted to further some other end, in this case the pursuit of profit. The moral ambiguity of the cultural middle is used to conceal the violation. This use of the cultural middle is far from insignificant. It is exactly the plasticity of the cultural middle that makes it so important.

Cultural fusion, the third possible response, happens when two cultures meet in the middle and work out some compromise between their different standards and practices to create a new set of cultural forms by which to regulate their joint activities. As an example, a slow-motion form of cultural fusion is taking place in China's legal system. The Chinese legal system has traditionally been used as a policy-implementing agency of the government.

Over the last 30 years of reforms, however, the government has studied Western legal systems and has made changes in its own legal system to bring it closer to Western practices. These changes ultimately appear to be limited, but there are signs that judges are receiving more training in the law; ideas on the role of legal precedent, impartiality, and facts in legal decisions are being debated; and new lawyers are entering the system arguing that individuals have legal rights.[17]

Cultural fusion is probably the master form of intercultural relations, and this for several reasons. First, there are many different ways cultures can fuse, among them amalgamation (creating a homogeneous whole), syncretism (reconciling diverse beliefs), and compromise (partial surrender to reach agreement). In all these cases renunciations and acquisitions are required. For example, to develop social relationships with Chinese businessmen, some American executives take them to the distinctly Asian karaoke bars. While the Americans go to the bars and consume alcohol, sometimes in large amounts, some say they stop short of purchasing prostitutes for their guests or themselves, which would not be uncommon among many Chinese executives. The karaoke bar activities are examples of cultural compromise, where both acceptance and rejection take place to make a shared experience possible.

A second reason that fusion often prevails is that, as noted in the discussion of adoption, intercultural relations by their nature do not tend to lead to one culture's complete replacement by another. Fusion of one sort or another is the typical outcome. Even when one culture has developed strict rules in a particular area, fusion of some sort is often the result. For example, I observed an American executive, certainly in violation of his company's policies, giving a bracelet valued at several hundred dollars to a female Chinese executive of a state-owned enterprise. So despite this multinational corporation's rigorous ethics program, gift-giving policies were watered down in China to meet Chinese relationship-building expectations.

Third, the place of fusion as the natural result of interaction between cultures is due in part to the tacit nature of culture.[18] A culture cannot be completely altered because its cultural components receive their meaning through relations with other components, many of these components and relations subconscious. So when two cultures interact, each experiences the interaction on multiple levels. Over time, the deeper levels work on the new materials, attempting to integrate them into a range of established relations

---

[17] Kellogg and Hand 2008; Yardley 2005.

and meanings, altering them in the process. When American companies hire Chinese employees, for example, they give them training in company policies. Yet this training does not remove obligations Chinese employees feel toward family and friends. When conflicts arise between the two, some Chinese employees struggle to try to meet both sets of obligations, usually to the chagrin of their American bosses.

Finally, fusion dominates because it can be crucial for *moral* resolution of cultural conflict. For example, in the conflict over intellectual property, both the American and the Chinese side have valid arguments. Hence, some compromise must be worked out. Otherwise, one side's valid moral position must be cast aside. This can be done, but it cannot be done morally.

The role of fusion in moral resolution of cultural conflict is of particular interest to this research on ethical and cultural issues in American-Chinese business relations. The moral case for fusion in situations of cultural conflict relies on fusion's basis in the virtues of respect, tolerance, and openness.

When American businesses go to China, one behavioral option for them is simply to follow American standards, completely ignoring Chinese practices. This route would not be practical, since the Chinese would not go along with it, or civil, since it would be disrespectful to completely ignore the host country's preferences. A second option would be for the Americans to reject their own standards and simply follow Chinese practices while in China. This route would also present practical and moral problems. First of all, it would leave the Americans at odds with their headquarters' practices. Even more fundamentally, it would leave the Americans at odds with themselves. How could they be Americans if they fully reject American values? It would leave them morally empty. It would lead to moral decline generally, because changing values as easily as one changes one's shirt would remove moral commitment from its basis in feeling and belief.

Fusion is thus the option that addresses both problems. On the one hand, it allows a culture to remain committed to core beliefs, without which it simply could not maintain any moral commitments of any depth. On the other hand, it enables a culture to accept the cultural commitments of the other culture, which both expresses respect, a helpful practice when doing business in a foreign country, and creates a shared cultural orientation, with obvious advantages for communication, cooperation, and trust.

[18] Polanyi 1962.

3. The Role of Power in the Middle. Finally, notwithstanding the deeper tendencies toward fusion discussed above, the role of power is more often than not the decisive arbiter in cultural conflict, as it is often in relations between nations. Nations with expanding power tend to have their values accepted in situations of cultural conflict. Power overruns the cultural middle. This fact of politics has obvious application to the rise of China. As China continues to expand and grow, its cultural predilections should gain greater and greater influence in its relations with its trading partners. This is so because of a loss of self-confidence in groups displaced by the nation whose power is expanding, the ability of the nation with growing power to force its practices on partners, and the prestige expanding power confers.

Currently, the United States' economy is more than twice the size of China's;[19] but China is growing at a much faster rate than the United States and could overtake the United States in a decade or two. Additionally, the 2008 financial crisis hurt American prestige and at the same time decreased American self-confidence; simultaneously it significantly increased China's self-confidence and prestige. The economic competition between the two countries will have a significant impact on the management of the cultural middle. If China's success continues, its culture will undoubtedly have more and more influence in American-Chinese business relations.

The double boundary of an intact cultural middle between two cultures is far from immutable. A loss of self-confidence on one side will increase the dominance of the other side. Fusion of one sort or another will become more problematic, and forced adoption will become the default outcome. Alternatively, two nations of relatively equal power can take advantage of the cultural middle as a creative space to work out the cultural interests of both nations through amalgamation, syncretism, or compromise that fits with and is acceptable to each culture. For this to happen, double trust is needed, trust from one to the other. The middleman currently provides this trust, but often in a way that keeps the parties apart. To advance to a higher level of ethical relations, the two nations must enter the cultural middle and develop their own direct relations. Power differentials do not have to rule the day. Each side can exercise restraint, thus building trust. From trust, a constructive cultural middle is possible.

---

[19] In 2010, the U.S. economy was measured at $14.58 trillion GDP and China's at $5.87 trillion GDP (World Bank July 1, 2011).

12

Epilogue

Three Years Later – 2010

In 2010, three years after finishing my first round of data collection in Shanghai, I returned to carry out follow-up interviews, conversations, and observations with both new and old informants. This epilogue is a report on the 2010 visit, whose purpose was to evaluate continuity and change in comparison with the 2007 data. It was a much smaller data collection effort. I sought only to update key themes from the 2007 data. In 2010, I focused on stability and change in the areas of Chinese and American business behavior, American-Chinese cultural relations, the role of the middleman, the role of the Chinese government in the economy and society, and private and public corruption.

The narrative that follows tells a story from three years later, focusing on what has changed and what has not. It uses the new data to explore the analysis carried out with the 2007 data and to evaluate the conclusions reached. Has the passing of three years validated or invalidated the analysis of the 2007 data? In general, despite some important political and economic changes, the focus of the original study—ethical and cultural issues in American and Chinese business relations—saw incremental changes in various directions, but the basic patterns in the 2007 data remained intact in 2010.

Change and Stability in Chinese Business Behavior

1. Chinese Management. According to the 2010 interviews, state-owned enterprises (SOEs) have become more profitable than they were in 2007 through restructuring labor, reducing debt, and benefitting from the government's investments in infrastructure. American executives observe, however, that SOEs still have significant internal problems, including low management skill level, corruption, and inefficient use of capital and labor.

The biggest problem with SOEs is management skill level. Below the top two or three management levels, management quality drops fast, according to American executives. Managers born before 1965 have little business experience. The new class of entrepreneurs cannot run the large SOEs; the task requires different skills than what they have. Managers from Taiwan, Hong Kong, and Singapore are not fully acceptable in the SOE sector. Large "private" Chinese companies sometimes hire American executives for specific functional areas. Chinese managers born after 1970 are gaining experience and according to some Chinese executives compare favorably with those in the same age group from Taiwan and Hong Kong. But at this point, there is still a shortage of Chinese business leaders to staff large organizations.

The lack of understanding of cost accounting and capital accounting mentioned in previous chapters is still a problem. At private Chinese manufacturers, it is still common for owner-managers to use "feeling" to make pricing decisions. To these owner-managers, employment levels, business survival, relationships, and so on are still more important than a strict profit-maximization discipline. The shortage of Chinese management talent presents a major challenge for Western firms because it is crucial that they localize their management. An important reason for the failure of many Western firms in China is their inability to understand and penetrate the Chinese market. Unfortunately, Chinese executives are the key solution to this problem.

Compensation for Chinese executives has gone up considerably since 2007. Chinese middle managers at American companies are paid the same as Western executives. Mid-level salaries can reach $100,000. Private Chinese companies are paying even more, when one factors in benefits and retention bonuses.[1] In some cases, small Chinese companies are paying two or three times Western salaries for specialized skills. Business experience is in short supply and salaries can therefore be bid up considerably. Graduates from China's best business school, CEIBS, in their late 20s with three years of business experience, are receiving salaries between $50,000 and $100,000—as much as managers in their 40s with much more experience—largely because of their English skills.

As can be seen from the growth in compensation levels, Chinese companies are wealthier than they were three years earlier. Likewise, Chinese executives

---

[1] *The Economist* (April 21, 2012) reported that Chinese SOEs pay the same as multinational corporations and more than private Chinese companies.

say that Chinese companies are more mature. They are less dependent on foreign firms for managerial, technological, and marketing skills. Some Chinese companies are expanding abroad. In particular, Chinese companies have less need for foreign direct investment. They are now raising capital from retained earnings and bank loans.[2]

On the down side, Chinese companies are struggling with increasing costs, particularly labor costs, which have gone up by 10–15 percent due to new minimum wage laws.[3] Costs of materials have also gone up considerably and Chinese exporters struggle with currency appreciation.

2. Decreasing Middleman Revenues. In the natural course of events, the middleman business is precarious. If the middleman is doing a poor job of distributing American products in China, he will be fired. However, even if he is doing a good job, he may also be terminated because the manufacturer may set up its own sales office. The middleman's best position is with the new entry, but as the new entry gains experience, there are increasing odds that the middleman will be let go.

Even if the middleman is not terminated, manufacturers tend to insist on lower and lower commissions each year. Again the middleman commands the highest fees at the beginning when the American firms want to enter the market. After they get a foothold, they start to squeeze the middleman to maximize their own profits. So even if the business is growing, the middleman's revenue gets smaller and smaller.

In the case where the middleman is selling Chinese goods to an American buyer, the middleman faces the constant problem of "jump-over," whereby the American firm buys directly from the Chinese manufacturer, pushing out the middleman. When the middleman is importing American products to sell, even if the American firm does not open its own sales office, it has several other options by which to squeeze the middleman. It can open a factory in China and force the middleman to buy from the factory. Since the goal of the factory is to be self-supporting, its products can be more expensive than the same products imported from the parent company in the United States.

---

[2] In 2009, 98 percent of China's outstanding bank loans were held by SOEs (*Economist* April 21, 2012).

[3] The new minimum salary in Shanghai is 1,000 renminbi (RMB, about $147) per month. The government has mandated that it increase every year and is pressuring businesses to follow the minimum salary law and to pay overtime. Many businesses do not follow the law willingly.

The American company can also hire additional middlemen, forcing them to compete and driving down the fees they are all paid. In some cases, the American firm opens an office in China not to sell its products but to manage Chinese middlemen for cost reduction—a less expensive and less difficult solution than opening its own sales office.

There are several other ways American firms avoid the use of middlemen. One way is hiring a middleman or someone with equivalent capacities as an employee. By making middlemen salesmen, for example, the firm can bring in-house the local relationships that are key to the middleman's trade. Some problems with this approach are high employee turnover rates, the cost of continuous retraining, salesmen's taking kickbacks, other forms of self-dealing in the sales department, and the loss of proprietary knowledge and customers when salesmen depart.

One large American company created its own distribution company to try to address the lack of professional distribution in China, but it found itself still dependent on middlemen to connect to buyers. The company believes that over the next two decades, as costs rise and Chinese companies rely more on innovation and less on imitation, they will examine their supply chains to cut costs and corruption. This is the only way they will remain competitive over the long run. If this is true, many middlemen will be put out of business as a direct market develops for product purchasing. The fact that this has not happened already suggests that there are deep-seated forces against it. Is distribution in China "way behind," or does China represent a different model of socioeconomic organization?

Chinese middlemen also face the threat of the maturing Chinese economy. As Chinese firms develop, they will enter markets that currently are supplied by imports, especially markets that require advanced technology or sophisticated manufacturing processes. Sales of imported products will decline. Chinese firms will buy from Chinese firms directly, with no middlemen. In those cases where middlemen still distribute Chinese products, they will compete against many more competitors than in the earlier markets where foreign products dominated. In the new markets dominated by Chinese firms, accounts receivable problems may be significant. While the domestic market looks less appealing, competition between middlemen will also increase in the import-export market.

Middlemen respond to decreasing revenues in several ways. Those who face the jump-over problem can open their own factories and vertically integrate. This gives them much more flexibility and control over production and price in negotiations with buyers. Short of this step, they can improve their service, sourcing, quality control, delivery record, and so on. By providing added value, they attempt to compete with the price advantage of direct purchase, which has its own risks.

Under constant pressure to reduce their fees, middlemen continuously seek to find new entrants, with whom their negotiating position remains strong. New entrants are not easy to find and connect with because to maximize the middleman's take, new products must offer new value, have little existing competition, and above all offer a low price for the China market. It is very difficult to continuously find new entrants that meet these three conditions. Given all the forces aligned against them and the difficulty in finding new needs to fill, it would appear that for many middlemen the window of opportunity is closing.

On the other hand, not all American manufacturers that seek to sell direct are successful. The China market is complex and middlemen do have social, managerial, and organizational capital that is not easily duplicated. One solution is continuous renegotiation of the manufacturer-middleman contract to lower middleman costs per unit while increasing units sold. Through compromise both sides can win.

Another solution seen in the 2010 data is the expansion of middleman services. Instead of only helping American firms sell or manufacture in the China market, middlemen are helping Chinese firms expand internationally. Instead of only finding joint venture partners for American firms, middlemen are expanding their networking through the whole supply chain to assist both Chinese and American firms with multiple business needs and opportunities. Chinese companies have become bigger, wealthier, and more ambitious.[4] Middlemen are adapting to their needs by providing more information and more introductions. The latter, of course, includes access to government relationships. Some new services involve professionalization of the middleman role, since advanced business training and experience are required to provide sophisticated firm and market analysis, assistance with strategic planning, and high-level consulting.

---

[4] Even though the SOE sector in China accounts for only a third of China's GDP, the 121 biggest SOEs have increased their total assets from $360 billion in 2002 to approximately $2.9 trillion in 2010 (*Economist* April 21, 2012). Make no mistake about it, the core of China's economy is state-owned.

3. Relationships in Business. The centrality of relationships in Chinese business has not changed in the last three years despite an ever-increasing body of laws and corporate rules addressing such relationships. One Chinese executive said that the "drink culture" that had declined under Communism has returned.[5]

There have, however, been some changes. A Chinese executive said previously people became rich because they had relationships with government officials to gain control over resources such as land. This still goes on, but entrepreneurs who have control over technology are growing in importance. They have the skills to do business with foreigners. The first group (with control over resources) and the second group (with success at international business) overlap. The international executives are more market based. Both groups will remain important in the future. Relationships with the government are no longer enough by themselves. The government still has control over resources and there is still corruption in these areas, but it has declined from previous levels.

4. The Role of Face. A central and unchanging aspect of the management of relationships in China is the management of face. A Chinese purchasing manager said that to get the best price, he needs to make the supplier feel like his best friend. Businesspeople in China are very worried about survival because the business environment is highly competitive and ruthless. Finding trustworthy "friends" is key to survival. Personalizing relationships can enhance both trust and survival. Making others upon whom one is dependent feel special, personally respected, and personally liked implies the foundation for a long-term relationship, if not actually offering it. These tactics are likely to induce others to offer their best price, quality, or service. Hence, face remains crucial in Chinese business culture because it addresses status, trust, and business survival needs.

The interpersonal aspects of face create problems for American businesspeople, who are more likely to focus on business targets and goals than on relationships. The Chinese see this focus as self-interested and perceive dealing with Americans as therefore risky, so they respond defensively, not making their best offer. The Chinese want a personal relationship *before* the business relationship. If there are signs of a good relationship, the Chinese will offer a good deal to further the relationship, thinking once the relationship is firm

---

[5] Male bonding through alcohol consumption is a core behavior in the culture of relationships.

they can use it to get themselves better deals in the future. The Chinese businessman is always thinking about these issues.

Another aspect of face is reputation. Reputation is important in all societies but has particular importance in China because of the collective nature of Chinese culture. In China, it is impossible to operate independently of groups and networks. Attributions of face determine one's status within the network and thus influence how much power one has. Alternatively, if one controls resources or has the power to influence others, one receives attributions of face. This is why large American corporations are treated better than small American corporations. The Chinese attribute face to the larger company and respect it because of its power and influence. If face is lost, however, one's power and influence decrease even if there is no change in one's material or structural position, because one's network position has been weakened.

5. *Women in Business.* In 2010, women continued to enter the workforce, but old antifeminist attitudes continued to reemerge. Many Chinese men do not like to work for women superiors. Many men increasingly express the belief that women are poor managers. Women face more and more pressure to prove themselves compared with men. Men nearing the age of 50 are seen as in their prime for top management positions, whereas women the same age find it difficult to change organizations.

Similar patterns can be seen in male-female romantic relations. Professional women in China have considerable difficulty finding romantic relationships, despite the fact that the ratio of females to males is 100 to 113.[6] The problem is that Chinese men seek younger women who are comparatively less educated and more obedient. They are strongly disinclined to pursue successful women, or women who make more money or have higher status than they do.[7]

Chinese marriages display similar patterns. As in the Communist period, women who work retain full responsibility for children, parents, and home. The government does not support child care. Divorce is not common. It is also common for men to have mistresses. The phenomenon of mistresses is so widespread that there was an enormously popular Chinese TV show about it

---

[6] The ratio in most nations is 100 to 101 (R. Wang 2002).

[7] A female Chinese manager said, "Chinese guys are threatened by females with higher IQ, or higher education status, or better career, or older, so women have to act stupid sometimes. A 26 year old master's graduate from Melbourne University like me will have a really hard time to find a suitable husband in China. But a 23 year old normal college graduate with lower IQ would have a lot of options" (Personal communication 2012).

called *Hot*. Because the subject is not openly acknowledged or discussed, the government took the show off the air. One Chinese woman said the Cultural Revolution damaged men who are now over 40 years old. Because they were taken from their families and uncared for, they are now selfish and treat women badly.

Broader trends of urbanization contribute to these patterns. Husbands and wives often work in different cities, usually the husband in a more desirable city than the wife. The geographic distancing contributes to the loss of faithfulness. As men start second families, wives lose face and become distraught. Even though the significant changes in China affect everyone, many women have found them particularly disheartening.[8]

Change and Stability in American Business Behavior

1. Competitive Environment. American executives say the China market is very competitive and they expect, long term, it will be the most competitive market in the world. They feel they must be able to compete in China to compete globally. For industries where cost is important, they feel they must be cost competitive in China to compete with the Chinese globally. These attitudes assume, of course, that in the decades ahead Chinese companies will be Americans' major competitors. In some industries, like green technologies, companies are centering their product development and sales in China, using this experience to develop their global product lines. American executives express concern about their ability to compete with Chinese SOEs if the latter continue to receive free capital.[9] If China becomes a major global competitor using free, state-supplied capital, American executives worry it will undermine the nature of the global financial system as it is now constituted.[10]

---

[8] As discussed in earlier chapters, China has one of the highest female suicide rates in the world (World Health Organization 2011). "Men from farms come to cities looking for work, leaving women at home to care for children and elderly in-laws. Hopelessness can set in for the wives left behind, leading to suicide" (Powell 2003).

[9] The government supports state-owned "national champions" in multiple ways in addition to free or low-interest loans. They can receive free land, favorable tax arrangements, top personnel, and so on.

[10] As noted above, bank loans predominantly go to SOEs in China, even though SOEs are less innovative and less productive than privately-owned companies (*Economist* April 21, 2012). There is also widespread corruption and waste in SOEs. Hence, all the worry about "China Inc." may be exaggerated. It is difficult to see how corruption, waste, and inefficiency will take over the world.

Chinese executives say American companies have become more interested in the China market over the last three years. Americans are spending more time visiting Chinese companies, even small ones, in a reflection of the continuing expansion of the Chinese economy. Both American and Chinese executives mention that the Chinese are moving into higher-value-added products. Thus the Chinese are looking for the latest technology and components for their manufacturing processes. American companies in China supplying these products are still net importers of components for their own manufacturing processes because high-quality components are difficult to source in China. For example, some American companies are unable to source high-quality steel in China.

2. *Inflexibility.* Chinese executives say they continually run into American arrogance. American executives, they say, do not take Chinese business ideas seriously. They repeatedly ignore Chinese advice about the China market and use the same market and product ideas they use elsewhere. American executives, too, criticize some American companies for not adapting to the China market, not developing China-specific operations. It appears to some that these companies are wishing China would just go away. The American IT industry has been particularly ineffective. Google was losing to Baidu before it pulled out of China; eBay was decimated by Chinese competitors. The American companies did not develop products that could compete with Chinese products in China.

American executives point out that the Chinese too have been showing signs of growing arrogance as they compare their successes with American failures over the last three years. The financial crisis in 2008 was a turning point; since then, the Chinese have become less tolerant of American complaints about management of the Chinese economy and more demanding in business deals. American executives say the body language of Chinese executives has observably changed. Because of American economic problems, the Chinese have become more confident in their approach and more proud of their successes. These themes are regularly seen in the Chinese press.

3. *Lowering Costs.* The 2008 financial crisis has led Americans to redouble their efforts to seek cost savings in China. Even though cost savings were the original reason American firms flocked to China, American executives say American firms are having difficulty getting their costs as low as those of Chinese firms, and this is why it takes so long for American firms to become profitable in China. American firms are paying more for expatriate managers, Chinese employees, environmental safety, and the like, putting them at a

disadvantage compared with Chinese competitors. As mentioned above, American firms are having difficulty finding experienced Chinese managers with whom to replace American managers. American executives also complain about unhelpful American tax policy that makes expatriate managers so expensive.

Chinese suppliers, however, say American firms are cooperating more readily with Chinese suppliers to lower costs, and generally are more flexible in their efforts to reduce costs. Chinese executives purchasing from American suppliers say American firms are becoming more flexible on price and payment terms, even offering free samples, unheard of just a few years ago. In some cases, American firms are undercutting the prices of Chinese firms, which shows the extent to which they have brought their costs down.

On the other hand, other Chinese firms purchasing products from American companies complain that product availability, payment terms, and delivery times have worsened considerably since 2008. GE, for example, has told Chinese customers that it is having maintenance problems and cannot meet contracts. The Chinese do not believe the company because it is taking too long to fix the problems; they think GE is having cash flow problems and does not have the capital to keep inventory. GE is not ordering supplies until it has a purchase order in hand. Interestingly, in the 2007 interviews American executives strongly criticized Chinese manufacturers for their unreliability and dishonesty; now the shoe is on the other foot.

4. *Tax Strategies.* Another aspect of American competitive behavior that was mentioned in 2007 was reported again in 2010: the avoidance of Chinese taxes. American firms set up manufacturing facilities in China but do not apply for a license to sell in China. Instead, they use an artificially low transfer price to sell their manufactured products to their affiliates outside of China. For example, a product manufactured in China is sold to a company affiliate in Hong Kong or Taiwan, booking a 4 percent gross profit in China. The product is then resold by the affiliate back to China or to a third country at a price 300–400 percent higher than the transfer price out of China. In this way, little to no tax is paid in China.

A second tax management strategy used by American firms manufacturing in China is to relocate every five years. To incentivize foreign companies to manufacture in China, the central government offers no tax for the first two years and a 50 percent discount for the next three years before reaching the full rate of 25 percent. Local governments are even more generous to attract foreign businesses, offering no tax for the first five years. Foreign companies keep a plant for five years, shut it down, move it, and start the tax-avoiding cycle all over again.

A third way Americans try to reduce their taxes is by offering "gifts" to tax administrators. This is something Chinese businesses do too. It is a high-risk practice that opens the firm up to prosecution.

The Chinese government is well aware that these tax strategies are in use. China benefits from foreign manufacturers through the investment in facilities, the hiring and training of Chinese citizens, the transfer of technical knowledge, and in some cases, the transfer of technology. Gifts to tax administrators are punished significantly when discovered; the other loopholes will eventually be closed as well. The American-Chinese business relationship in China is an evolving set of tradeoffs for both sides. Despite all the complaints and problems, both parties benefit from the relationship.

Chinese-American Cultural Relations

1. Two Business Cultures. There are deep differences between Chinese and American business cultures, a situation that has changed little in the last three years. Some of the differences discussed in earlier chapters are presented below in the context of three more years of experience with them.

Chinese managers working for American companies say their experience is vastly different from that of their Chinese friends working for Chinese companies. First of all, American firms pay more. Second, training is much more extensive, especially in the area of quality control systems. The American systems rely more heavily on general rules, decentralization, specialization, and continuous improvement. The Chinese usually employ more people, use a single process, and rely on hierarchical relations to control it.[11]

Another difference between the two business cultures can be seen in a "joke" the Chinese tell about the role of planning in Chinese and American industrial companies:

> American industrial companies have timetables, plans, etc. We tell a joke about this. An American says, when Chinese and American executives

---

[11] These differences can partly be explained by American preferences for abstract models to control causal relationships between independent objects, while Chinese holistic preferences reject abstraction and the isolation of objects from context, instead organizing concretely through hierarchically ordered superior-subordinate relationships (Nisbett 2003).

sit down together, "What is your five-year plan?" The Chinese responds, "We will be number one in the industry." The American asks three more times what's the five-year plan, but never gets an answer.

(Ms. Ch40)

Ms. Ch40 explains the "joke":

The Chinese "plan" is just a target; it has little, if any, detail. It is a different understanding of what a plan is. The Chinese are less sophisticated. They do things based on experience and feelings. Americans are more theory-based. The Chinese executive does not want so many plans. He wants a short-term plan; he wants to know the next day. He does not plan the next three years. He does not know what will happen the next three years.

There are several dimensions to Ms. Ch40's "joke." First, the Chinese economy is changing very rapidly and dramatically. Reacting to these changes and opportunities makes long-range planning irrelevant. Second, Chinese businesspeople have little confidence in the government's commitment to free markets, also making long-range planning irrelevant. Third, Chinese culture and religion have traditionally discouraged abstract thinking, alternatively focusing attention on concrete, interpersonal relations. Instead of managing the future through plans, they do so through the development of relationships. In this way, they remain highly flexible.

Mr. Ch39 captures the Chinese lack of trust in the future in his description of what he calls the Chinese "haste gene," derived from thousands of years of civil wars and invasions. The Chinese people are always fleeing. If they do not flee in a hurry, they will get killed. This also accounts for the rudeness and loudness in Chinese behavior, according to Mr. Ch39. The "haste gene" makes them inconsiderate of others, as can be seen in driving patterns in Shanghai, where the vast majority of the drivers do not give way. It is the result of a history of societal chaos.

The Chinese find American businesspeople to be more straightforward than Chinese businesspeople. They feel Americans are more open with their ideas and feelings. The Chinese are more reserved with strangers, more apt to protect themselves. On the other hand, when Americans visit Chinese companies for the first time, they are treated like an important guest. They are accompanied around the city, given a lot of attention, told where to eat or taken to dinner, in general cared for. When Chinese visit American companies in the United States, they are not given this level of care. In China, the

Chinese are pleased to be a gracious host, to treat their guest warmly. In the United States, there is more of an expectation of autonomy for the visitor and privacy for the host.[12]

In business, the Chinese want to get to know an individual personally. American executives in China spend a lot of time socializing with important or potentially important Chinese executives, drinking alcohol, smoking cigarettes, singing karaoke, and the like. Without this social bonding, Chinese executives can have difficulty trusting American executives.

In the United States, there are accepted business roles and expectations, which are usually less personal than those in China,[13] where one does business with "friends." Trust is built through personalizing relationships. American executives share information about medical problems, wives, children, and so on with Chinese executives to develop relationships. This creates moral hazards because with the personalization of relationships, bonds can trump organizational boundaries. The Chinese do not accept impersonal roles in business as do Americans. The Chinese complain when talk is about events or business; they seek the richness of personal conversation.

American executives who do not normally smoke or drink find themselves doing rounds of Chinese grain alcohol (*biao*) at evening banquets. It takes endless patience to develop important business relationships. American executives who do not socialize in this way often limit their chances to personalize relationships and build trust. In many cases, the result will certainly be a loss of business in China.[14]

The Chinese complain that when an American business partner asks a question, the Chinese respond right away, but the Americans are not reciprocal. Even when it involves a legal document, the Chinese can still respond within an hour in some cases. The Americans are much more formal.

---

[12] The principle at play here is American equality (de Tocqueville 1969). Because the American sees others as more or less his equal, he more or less openly accepts them, assumes they are not so different from him. The Chinese, on the other hand, are socialized predominantly through immediate relationships, mostly in the family, outside of which is an uncertain social environment. Americans are neither as warm as the Chinese nor as cold.

[13] In the United States, it is common to take a business relation to a professional sporting event. The background meaning is a celebration of competition. The event can improve the relationship without personalizing it. It is as if to say, "We are self-interested, but we can be so civilly." This would not work for the Chinese. Personalization would be needed to improve the relationship. Both cultures are very competitive, but they find harbor differently: the Chinese in the group, the American in himself.

[14] This appears most often the case with executives from SOEs.

Whereas the Chinese want the document short, relying instead on the relationship, the Americans want the document detailed. In their minds, the document itself defines the relationship, spells out obligations and expectations, and protects them. For the Chinese, it does little of this; it can and probably will change completely tomorrow. The Chinese do not have a legal culture; the Americans do.

2. *Cultural Misunderstanding.* There has been little improvement in cultural misunderstanding over the last three years. The reasons seem to be the limited amount of shared world view and social orientation between the two cultures. This section puts forth new examples of themes found throughout the book.

The "haste gene" leads to cultural misunderstanding with the Americans. Mr. Ch39 says he has been at many meetings where the Chinese boss starts speaking very loudly and waving his arms or takes a cell phone call and starts screaming into the phone, and the Americans turn to Mr. Ch39, the middleman, asking if the boss is angry. The boss, especially in the country-side, talks like he is quarrelling. But this is the "haste gene," which often misleads Americans. On the other hand, Chinese often do not understand Americans. They cannot read American facial expressions or body language, and often do not know whether the Americans are in agreement or satisfied with the situation, or what they are thinking.

Mr. Am35 who has worked in China for six years and who runs the China operations for an American multinational corporation (MNC) says his main job is interpreting China "for the guys back home." One thing the "guys back home" do not understand is that negotiations "take forever." Americans are direct and want to address a problem and be done with it. The SOE executives involved in the negotiations, however, do not seem to have the "haste gene." Apparently, even the "haste gene" obeys the laws of bureaucratic risk aversion.

Mr. Am35 says his superiors back home expect to come to China and enter directly into business negotiations. But "you can't just fly in here." To do so would be foolhardy. China is not easily knowable: Either the Chinese are "inscrutable" or they themselves do not know what is going on. The American executives from "back home" do not understand the considerable change, considerable opportunities, and considerable risk that exist in China. The most important part of Mr. Am35's job is to bridge the two business systems.

Ms. Ch40 says there are very typical misunderstandings between Chinese and American executives just from the "way of talking" and facial expressions—for example, the use of the word *yes*. Chinese are quick to agree, but it does not mean agreement in the American sense of shared commitment. It means yes, they will be happy to talk about it further. Likewise when the Chinese say "no problems." There are always problems. The Chinese are being friendly, polite, and positive, but the "no problems" statement does not mean they have thought through the business proposition in detail and think there will be no problems. The Americans think they have done the latter and often become frustrated and feel that the Chinese have misled them.

Chinese executives say that the major causes of cultural misunderstanding are on the American side. The Chinese feel they do a better job understanding the Americans and point to high levels of American mistrust as proof that the Americans do not understand them. The Chinese say some people simply have "clean face," but the Americans are unable to intuitively distinguish the honest Chinese from the dishonest ones.

3. The Social Responsibility Audit. In some ways, misunderstanding between the two business cultures has increased, not because of increases in cultural differences but because of politics. Ironically, the so-called "social responsibility audit" carried out by the Americans on the Chinese is an exercise in American self-interest and cultural misunderstanding. Meant to force the Chinese to meet standards of universal human rights, the audit in its implementation is a model of self-centeredness.

American companies are under pressure from social activists, nongovernmental organizations, government officials, and the American public not to participate in abusive labor practices. American companies fear damage to their reputation and loss of sales from reports in the American media that portray their companies as doing business with foreign entities that abuse their employees or the environment.[15] To protect themselves from negative publicity, American companies carry out, or more often hire Chinese companies to carry out, "audits" of Chinese factories to make sure they are meeting ethical standards set by the Americans. A Chinese company that fails to meet the standards will be removed from the American company's supply chain, often with grave financial consequences for the Chinese firm.

---

[15] This is why Apple, for example, recently joined the Fair Labor Association, released the names of 156 of its suppliers, started posting regular reports on the number of hours worked by employees at its suppliers' factories, and has carried out and asked others to carry out investigations of its supply chain (Duhigg and Greenhouse 2012).

Chinese executives say that the audit process misconstrues China and the Chinese, is a form of cultural abuse, and is morally offensive. Chinese inspectors notify the plants that they will carry out their evaluation sometime during a two- to three-week period, calling an hour before they arrive. The result of their evaluation is a quantitative score signifying that the factory meets standards (0–8); needs improvement (9–29); is unsatisfactory, must develop and implement an action plan, and can be reevaluated up to two more times (30–499); or fails, and the business relationship is terminated (above 500).

The audit evaluates employee welfare, employee health care, and whether the minimum wage is paid. Chinese executives complain the audit inappropriately applies American values to Chinese life. For example, plants are asked if they have an antiterrorist plan, a concern Chinese executives find irrelevant and laughable. Terrorism is a problem in the United States, not in the countryside around Shanghai. Executives are asked if they investigate the background of prospective employees before hiring. This practice is never followed for minimum-wage workers in China, but if the executive answers "no," the plant gets a higher score.

The auditors inspect the workers' dormitory. The score is raised if there are 6–8 workers in a room, the toilets have no privacy doors, or soap is not provided. Chinese executives say this is cultural conflict; all three of these conditions are accepted practice in China. The Chinese executives are particularly incensed because at the same time that the American firm's audit department is raising their costs, the same firm's purchasing department is continuously demanding lower prices for their goods.

Other problems for Chinese executives are overtime pay and health care. Chinese law requires overtime pay, but many companies do not comply. As previously discussed, China is not a country governed by the rule of law. In terms of health care, there are two kinds of health care systems in China: city and rural. The two types correspond to the *hukou* system of citizen registration. The city *hukou* gets health care, the rural one does not. Employees at plants and mills in rural areas thus do not receive government health care, raising the audit scores of companies in rural areas. The audit report does not take into account nor explain the *hukou* system. Some companies buy extra insurance for their employees, but they have trouble proving this to auditors or are told it is not enough insurance.

In any case, in rural areas, and in the cities too, the Chinese rely much more than Americans on their families to provide care when they are ill. When family members go to the hospital, other members of the family traditionally stay with them to care for them. Usually insurance does not cover all the costs and the family pays the uninsured part. So the audit applies an American standard of health care that does not correspond to Chinese reality.

Chinese executives say they do not want to cheat on the audit, but it puts them in an impossible position. Audits also hurt migrant workers because rising costs from the audit reduce employment. Bribing auditors is a high-risk proposition because if a bribe is found out the result is immediate termination. According to Chinese executives, the auditors tend to be honest.

Chinese executives say that American companies that insist on audits have two personalities. The sales and sourcing departments know the audits are not realistic and the goals are not possible. But the social compliance departments and top management consider themselves "representatives of justice." The problem is that the "representatives of justice" do not understand what life is like in China. China is not America.[16]

The purpose of the audit is for American companies to protect their public image. But in so doing they unfairly and inappropriately create an impossible situation for Chinese manufacturers. The result is cheating on the audits or other tricks to avoid losing business, like falsely representing a different factory, where standards are met, as one's own.

In general, American executives living in China agree that American values do not necessarily apply in China. China has a huge population barely getting by. Construction workers in Shanghai are earning $100 a month. There is an oversupply of workers. In this context, the Chinese are not sensitive to, nor do they expect, American standards for employee benefits. To the extent that American companies seek to protect employees from abuse, their intentions are laudable. But such protection needs to be implemented in a way that makes sense to both cultures. At this point, it appears the Americans care more about protecting their own reputation than about the welfare of Chinese workers; the result is that they are creating injustice as they try to remedy it.

---

[16] As if to prove the cultural divide, Chinese statements on American cultural misunderstanding demonstrate a form of reverse bias: "A comfortable life for Americans is house and car ownership, two kids, a backyard, and a wife who does gardening" (Mr. Ch39). For the most part, Chinese do not have houses, backyards, wives who do gardening, or two kids. Mr. Ch39 seems to be associating the American one-audit policy with the Chinese one-child policy, implying that he experiences the audit process as dictatorial.

The Chinese Government

I. General Perceptions

1. Control and Change. Both Chinese and American executives agree that Chinese society is tightly controlled. Though the government has liberalized the economy in the last 30 years, cultural, social, and particularly political control remain high. Elementary and secondary education, for example, includes political indoctrination.[17] The government makes changes slowly to ensure its control. Change itself is a significant risk in that it could lead to a loss of control. The rule of Chinese history, of which the Communist dynasty is well aware, is that dynasties rise and dynasties fall.

Chinese executives say that because of China's turbulent history, the size of its population, and its level of ethnic diversity, it is imperative that the government maintain control to ensure social stability. Stability is the key value, the ultimate good. There are no license plates proclaiming "Live Free or Die." Chinese executives bring up the Soviet Union as a negative example. Change must be carefully controlled so that the country does not fragment.

The rapidly growing Internet is a dilemma, on the one hand good for the economy, but on the other bad for government control. Along with diminished travel restrictions, the Internet has brought a great deal of change to Chinese society. More than 500 million Chinese use the Internet, mostly young people. Because of the extent of online influence, the government has increased control over the Internet and increased control in general.

2. Control and Wealth. Many Chinese executives do not have any problem with the one-party dictatorship; indeed, as seen in the 2007 data, they prefer it for the stability it brings. Economic growth is the central issue for them, and since the economy is growing, everything is good. As evidence, Chinese executives repeatedly mention the large amount of money many people are making in real estate. They feel that the top government leaders care about the country as a whole and are trying to do the right things, and they reject the idea that the Party's top priority is to stay in power. Given the size of the population, control must be the government's first responsibility and main

---

[17] Indeed, Beijing has introduced a "Moral and National Education curriculum" in Hong Kong, planning to make the curriculum compulsory starting in 2015 (*Wall Street Journal* July 30, 2012). Protesters say the curriculum is designed to "brainwash children into supporting China's Communist Party."

job. There is no need for freedom, only more wealth. The solution is to keep growing the economic pie.[18]

Chinese executives point out that the government does have some elections and that Western newspapers are widely available in China.[19] They say many journalists are free to do investigations and that lawyers who fight for freedom and are put in jail are corrupt. A Chinese graduate business student said that the one-party system is actually better than a democratic system because it can do long-range planning. I repeated these comments to an American lawyer who has lived in China for 15 years and teaches business law to Chinese business students. He responded,

> It is well known that the government allows one to have any business one wants and make all the wealth that one wants, but one must stay out of politics or one will die. It is common that business students express great interest in buying a car, having a child for the grandparents, and then buying an apartment. But their aspirations stop there. They have nothing to say about politics (Mr. Am34).[20]

This statement corresponds precisely with my interviews and observations.

Many Chinese executives are very excited about Chinese economic growth and believe the government has done a fine job of encouraging and managing it. They do not think other Asian governments could have accomplished what China has. China is rising and will be a major competitor for the United States. The United States is not dynamic, but China is on the move, changing deeply and broadly, they say.

Even a Chinese lawyer whose career was ended and life upended during the Mao years said the top government leaders are very good. He added, however, that the city secretaries of the Communist Party have too much power. Their power is unchecked, he said; they are above the law.

3. Wealth Gap. The majority of Chinese citizens are feeling increasing economic pressure. They make more money than they did three years earlier, but they pay even more to live. Both Chinese and American executives said

---

[18] The same argument was made by Chinese graduate students in business in my class in Cleveland in 2011.

[19] I was unable to find widespread availability of Western newspapers in Shanghai, although I did see some available in high-end Western hotels.

[20] During a research presentation on Nike's sourcing practices in China in Cleveland in 2011, my Chinese graduate students said they were unable to find any information on the role of the Chinese government, despite the fact that the literature is full of such information.

the risk of social unrest has increased, as has crime. Wealthy Chinese are changing the family names of their children to protect them from kidnapping for ransom.

The gap between the rich and everyone else continues to grow. Even on the executive level, some receive 10,000 renminbi (RMB) per year while others receive 50,000 or even 100,000 for the same job. Even though the new law mandates overtime pay, Chinese auditors working for large American accounting firms report workers receiving two hours' pay for every six hours of overtime worked. This is in the context of 90-hour weeks during peak season.

The lower economic classes are worse off than three years ago. They hate the government because they think government policy enables a small group of people to take most of the money. Government employees do well and high-level government people do the best.[21] The average person has gained little in the last three years. In addition to their salaries, health insurance, and pension, government officials receive "invisible income" that can be anything from bribes and kickbacks to officially approved second salaries to using official roles for private gain. These inequities have made society less stable. What once would have been small conflicts in communities across the country now have the potential to lead to riots and in many cases do. Hence government policy simultaneously maintains and undermines social stability.

The government spends huge amounts of money on "face" projects like the World Expo 2010 Shanghai, which cost 400 billion RMB. Chinese executives complain that this kind of spending does not help society. An American executive who travels into poor areas where some ethnic minorities live said malnutrition among children is severe. He said the government does nothing and even blocks nonprofit organizations from trying to help. Chinese executives say extravagant, irresponsible, and incompetent spending by the government is common.[22]

---

[21] Low-level government workers, such as meter readers for the electric company, receive 8,000 RMB per month, while the average college graduate earns 2,500–3,000 RMB per month. The meter reader is the electric company's lowest pay level.

[22] Examples mentioned: China Petro spent 8 million RMB ($1.76 million) for a crystal lamp for its lobby; the Highway Department spent 40,000 RMB ($5,582) to replace a single road sign. These examples were actually not mentioned to demonstrate waste but to show incompetent government action that led to the release of this information.

Twenty years ago, many Chinese people supported the government. Some still think the government is doing a good job, but the perception is no longer widely shared. More and more, a range of opinions is developing, with many people worried about their future.

4. Housing. The biggest economic change between 2007 and 2010 was the increase in the cost of housing. In some cases prices have increased by 400 percent. The central government has given responsibility for real estate to the local governments. Beijing evaluates the local governments by GDP growth, and increasing the size of local government will increase GDP. Moreover, promotions and pay increases are significantly influenced by the amount of construction. For these reasons, local officials build as many buildings as they can.[23] The building booms lead to increasing real estate prices, but the central government claims price increases are caused by private real estate speculation. Business executives argue, however, that Beijing owns all the land and regulates the building process, so it can and should control the price.

The majority of people have been priced out of home ownership,[24] while the few have made millions of renminbi by buying and selling real estate. One group becoming wealthier is the already wealthy who have capital to invest in real estate or high salaries that enable them to access bank loans. Rising prices are seen as a "window of opportunity," so people have acted very aggressively to seize the moment. Another group that has benefitted is those older than 35 who already own a house, especially the lucky ones who are near important new building developments. Of those under 35 years old, 70–80 percent have been priced out of the market, while others have made millions of dollars, sometimes in as little as a few months. This super-fast rise to riches for a minority, simultaneous with skyrocketing apartment costs for the majority, is generating widespread animosity toward the rich.

5. Health Care. As noted above, rural workers did not participate in government run insurance programs. Interviewees in Shanghai, however, also

---

[23] All levels of government make huge investments in infrastructure (e.g., railway, highway, airport), which is also a primary cause of rising real estate values. *The Economist* (April 21, 2012) reports SOEs in Beijing "erecting giant monuments to themselves, reflecting their huge power and their vision of themselves as agents of modernization."

[24] Over 30 percent of China's urban households are without kitchens and plumbing (Areddy 2012). In Shanghai, price increases peaked in 2010, after rising 2.6 times from five years earlier. The average price for apartments in Shanghai in 2011 was $276,000; and this buys about 257 square feet or 79 square meters. In any case, most people have been priced out of the market, as average annual per capita income is $13,000.

complained about expensive and inadequate health insurance. A CEO of a manufacturing company gave the following account. On a 10,000 RMB per month salary, the cost of health insurance is 3,000 RMB for 40- to 60-year-olds. Since the average salary in Shanghai is around 7,000 RMB per month, many 40- to 60-year-olds are priced out of health insurance. On the other hand, for those under 40 years old, the cost is 125 RMB per month, but the limit on claims is 1,500 RMB per year—a wash. So for either age group, many Chinese live under the threat of crushing medical expenses.

II. Avoiding Government

1. Arbitrary Power. Many successful Chinese do not feel secure in China. Chinese executives cite the case of the richest businessman in China, who did not feel secure in China and therefore illegally transferred part of his wealth to Hong Kong.[25] The government found out and put him in jail. Executives say his crime was not serious and in fact that many people in China commit more serious crimes but are not put in jail. The government cannot put everyone in jail, so it uses individuals as examples, a strategy that seems to be working, judging by the fear this incident has prompted among other rich businesspeople, many of whom would like to move their money out of China but are afraid to. Many people fear jail so they are extra cautious in their behavior.

2. The Second Passport. The successful businessperson is in the middle between a predatory government and an angry working class. There is no doubt who is in charge. The businessperson can lose everything overnight if an official decides to put him in jail. Wealthy Chinese think the best way to protect themselves from the government is to change nationality and receive protection from a foreign embassy. One American executive said half of the middle-class Chinese he knows have a second passport.[26]

Canada, Australia, and New Zealand are the most common countries from which Chinese get a second passport, though the United States too has federal

---

[25] Numerous interviewees said they had started companies in Hong Kong to avoid the Foreign Exchange Administration and the increasing value of the renminbi.

[26] He went on to say the biggest problem is that the rich do not have sound investment opportunities in China and are not allowed to invest overseas. The second passport is used to move their money abroad. Otherwise, Chinese invest up to 40 percent of their savings in the education of their single child.

programs to attract wealthy Chinese to invest in the United States and receive a green card.[27] One Chinese executive said he had invested $550,000 in a Philadelphia industrial zone. He receives no interest on his money for 5 years before getting his capital back. The green card is good for 10 years. His reason for making the investment was in case he is arrested in China; at least his children will be safe in the United States.[28]

III. Government Involvement in Business

1. Private and Public Firms. Chinese owners of small private businesses insisted government involvement in their businesses is minimal, mostly just through taxes. That has not changed in the last three years. An American lawyer living in Shanghai, however, said one has to "go through hoops" to set up a business. A Chinese lawyer added that not only is business registration complex and difficult to understand, but so are myriad government approvals that are required for established businesses. Many documents are needed and the process can take a long time.

If a business is involved with a licensed product, import, export, alcohol, drug manufacture, foreign exchange, employment issues, banks, value-added tax for export, income tax, building purchase, building expansion, product line expansion, production increase, and so on, it must deal with the government. Many of these interactions with the government involve taking officials out to lunch or dinner and giving other gifts to receive timely cooperation. The government requires many forms and explanations. Explanations are required for the way business activities are classified because the classification affects taxes. Officials in the tax department get promoted if they find tax due. In addition, bigger companies are asked off the record to support government programs.

The government catalogs industries in terms of the level of government control. There are four areas: forbidden (e.g., banking, power, national security); restricted (joint venture required); encouraged (e.g., high-tech,

---

[27] In 2011, the United States received 2,969 applications for "investment immigration" visas, compared with 787 in 2009 (Page 2012). Chinese applications were 78 percent of the 2011 total.

[28] In 2009, this individual had been taken off the street and detained for two days by government investigators who were trying to pressure him to provide evidence that an official was taking bribes. His family did not know where he was.

agriculture, and energy efficiency); and permitted. The catalog is always changing and can be difficult to understand.

Most large Chinese firms are SOEs because the government controls access to capital through control of the banks. Companies on the Chinese stock exchange are parts of SOEs that have been "privatized," usually limited to 20–30 percent of the parent company.[29] By building the economy around large companies and limiting large companies to SOEs, the government remains in firm control of the economy. Communist Party members are an essential part of the command and control structure in each SOE.

In 2010, after the financial crisis in the West, the Chinese government spent large amounts of capital to stimulate economic growth. The vast bulk of this money went to SOEs. Because of cheap capital, their profits swelled. Many private firms, however, were forced into bankruptcy.[30] In other words, the government used the two-year worldwide financial crisis to increase its control over the economy.

Chinese private-sector executives criticize the government's use of capital. As mentioned before, spending on infrastructure is excessive, and much of it does not stimulate the economy, does not lead to economic growth. Infrastructure building is an end in itself.

A similar pattern can be seen with government purchasing. The government pays high prices for goods and does not try to lower costs. It tends to buy brand names when less expensive substitutes are available. It also uses trading companies, which are like black boxes—no one knows how much the government pays the trading company and where the money goes (see discussion of trading companies below).

2. Relationships with Officials. When an American MNC took over a Chinese SOE in the middle of China in 2010, it ran into insurmountable problems with the local government. Even though low-level employees were quite happy with their higher salaries and benefits, senior management lost its under-the-table income and "warlord" status. The MNC had to keep the local management in place because managers on the coast did not want to move inland and were too expensive in any case.

---

[29] SOEs make up 80 percent of the value of Chinese stock markets (*Economist* January 21, 2012).

[30] *The Economist* (January 21, 2012) reports an "epidemic" of suicides accompanied these bankruptcies. The Communist Party is the central force in the brutal nature of the Chinese economic system.

The local general manager was not helping to resolve the difficulties, but removing him was even more of a problem because he was backed by the local government.[31] The SOE provided energy to the local community and therefore was classified with national security importance. The local community also had large minority populations. For both of these reasons the SOE was important to the government. With this heightened political attention, the MNC was going to be seen as either "good foreigners or bad elements."

Given these issues, the local government believed it had the right to monitor the MNC. Originally the MNC had entered a joint venture with the SOE. But because the SOE operated in violation of the MNC's policies—policies that kept it in accord with New York Stock Exchange listing requirements—the MNC bought out the joint venture partner. But the problems were just getting started. When the MNC stopped under-the-table payments to local officials, new problems developed. The local government accused the MNC of mistreating the minority populations, a violation that required the local government to monitor the MNC.

The local government also demanded that the joint venture be reinstated. If it was not, they said in a letter to the MNC, they would limit any changes in senior management and limit information on company operations to the MNC, the owner. In terms of Chinese law, the local government's behavior was illegal. The acquisition of the joint venture by the MNC had been approved by the central government. But the central government was far away and, in reality, the local government had considerable power.

This story is a good example of how China functions in 2010. It has not changed much from 2007. Some Chinese executives say the top leaders of the country are trying to address the dominance of relationships in government, but the progress made is small compared with the enormous size of the problem. Some say it will take several generations to change. To be sure, it is a culture, and cultures never die, they get married. Right now, there are not any eligible partners on the scene.

Some American executives say the courts are getting better in the large coastal cities. A Chinese lawyer told me, "*guanxi* cannot turn black into white." Maybe not, but it can turn black into gray, and that is enough to undermine the law. The 2010 data show increased standardization of rules,

---

[31] The manager was a relative of one of the original owners of the SOE.

more regulations in print, and more officials following the regulations in Shanghai. Is this *significant* improvement? Only if one ignores that it takes place in a context still dominated by relationships.

One problem is the legal system itself. It is driven by code, and the codes are vague and continuously changing. They are continuously changing because they are in the service of continuously changing power interests. As long as the law does not gain some autonomy from politics, improvements will not be cumulative. Another problem is the size of the population relative to the size of the economy. If the central government creates laws that will increase unemployment, for example, local governments will not enforce them. The society is organized not around laws but around relationships. There are historical, cultural, demographic, economic, and political forces keeping it this way. China is always changing, but the centrality of relationships changes the least.

3. Stability and Instability. The business environment in China is very stable. The Chinese operate on a five-year plan that spells out the government's goals and the programs to reach the goals. The government's determination and success in accomplishing the goals is widely acknowledged and admired by many. On the other hand, the government comes out with different regulations, different policies, different incentives and disincentives at different times. The institutional environment is a moving target. Part of this variability stems from power struggles, part from officials' not understanding what they are doing, and part from their not understanding the consequences of their dictates. The result is that business-people lack trust in the institutional environment and therefore take a short-term view of business. Immediate opportunities are seized, long-term investments avoided.

Despite its concerted efforts to reform the economy, the government's involvement in business is huge. It is more running the business sector than regulating it. Yasheng Huang's analysis of Chinese capitalism up to 2007 found growing government support for the SOE sector and decreasing support for the private sector,[32] a trend that appears to be continuing in 2010. Huang referred to this policy as the "Shanghai model." American executives express concern about the consolidation going on in Chinese industry. They say it shows the government is not committed to open

[32] Huang 2008.

markets. In the market for wind turbines, for example, the government is sourcing 70 percent of the technology from SOEs outside of market competition.[33] Flush with capital, the SOEs then squeeze out foreign competitors and small, private Chinese companies in the 30 percent of the market that is left.

In the end, it appears the Chinese are headed toward an economy dominated by large SOE groups working hand in glove with government policy makers. If this is the case, American business might have already seen its best days in China, or soon will. The trade door swings both ways. Americans will react to these changes.

Corruption

I. Private-Sector Corruption

1. Overview. Chinese executives say most private-sector businesspeople prefer the free market, but vast sums of money can be made through "black" behavior. When the opportunity comes to make large amounts of money through corruption, some do it and some do not. In general, the reform period is a "bad story" because "bad guys make money." This success at illegal activities is an incentive that continues to attract people into "black" behavior.

The central government is trying hard to address the problem, according to some executives. In the past few years it has created new laws. Now a company that finds out one of its employees is taking bribes can sue him in addition to firing him. Chinese executives say the new laws aim to make honest people feel better, but they will not do much good. The country's president and party chief, Hu Jintao, wants harmony. He does not have harmony, he has corruption. So the new laws aim to cover up the problem; nonetheless, executives say, maybe there will be less corruption in the future.

---

[33] Sinovel Wind Group, China's largest manufacturer of wind turbines, is run by Han Junliang, one of China's most famous entrepreneurs (Riley and Vance 2012). American Superconductor Corporation, based in Massachusetts, filed four civil complaints against Sinovel in Chinese courts for bribing an AMSC employee and for theft of technology. Sinovel is closely related to the Chinese government.

2. Dishonesty. In 2010, many Chinese executives describe a business environment permeated by dishonesty. The most pervasive source of corruption involves taxes. Most, some say all, private Chinese companies have two sets of financial statements, one for the company and one for the tax man. The Chinese say the government has a high tolerance for cheating on taxes because if it did not, many private companies would go bankrupt. Cheating is becoming more difficult because more and more information is reported online, so the government can easily cross-check information.

The two-sets-of-books problem continues to plague American foreign direct investment. American companies seeking to purchase Chinese companies or Chinese assets continue to make investment decisions based on the wrong set of financial statements, resulting in large losses.

Similarly, Chinese executives complain that they never get accurate financial data from suppliers. When asked for a price breakdown on their products, Chinese suppliers offer little information other than to say their net is zero or one percent. If one insists on a breakdown, typically fake numbers are provided. This type of misrepresentation is common in negotiations and contracts.

Other dishonest behaviors that were seen in the 2007 data are also present in the 2010 data. An American company bought a factory from a Taiwanese company. Soon after the American company moved into the factory, a second Taiwanese company opened up an identical factory next door, with the same managers, employees, distribution system, and customers of the first Taiwanese company that had just been sold. In a second 2010 example, also seen in the 2007 data, Chinese purchasing managers making large purchases from Metro, a Wal-Mart-like German retailer, set up a shell company so their employer would pay the Metro invoices to the shell company instead of Metro.

3. Bribes and Kickbacks. The 2010 interviews found bribery and kickbacks to be as pervasive as they were in the 2007 data. Some Chinese executives said there is less bribery than in 2007, but others said it is impossible to do business without paying bribes. Similar to 2007, large American companies receive considerably fewer requests for bribes than their Chinese counterparts. However, an American lawyer living in Shanghai said he had many American clients trying to address a "culture of kickbacks" among their Chinese employees. The problem is pervasive, and there is a "wellhead of anxiety" about it because the Obama administration has increased prosecution of bribery around the world.[34] American companies have stepped up compliance measures.

Some American companies report some success, "as far as we know," at reducing kickbacks by increasing education, expressing zero tolerance, and increasing monitoring. One large American manufacturer requires multiple written quotations for all purchases, a practice that has resulted in increased competition, a drop in prices, and also a drop in bribe offers because suppliers have no money left with which to pay them.

Examples of bribes in the 2010 data are salesmen bribing purchasing managers at Wal-Mart and Carrefour to carry their products, small Chinese and American companies bribing quality control companies to approve defective products in the automobile industry, and managers at American hotels steering customers to other hotels to receive "commissions." The Wal-Mart, Carrefour, and automobile industry bribes were paid by middlemen, confirming the 2007 pattern.

4. Intellectual Property. The 2010 interviews did not focus on intellectual property (IP) issues, but two interesting points came up. First, the president of China operations for a Fortune 500 company said that the American secretary of commerce, on a trade mission to Beijing, accompanied by executives from large American MNCs, did not bring up IP issues. This supports the conclusions reached in Chapters 9 and 10, that the American government is ambivalent about IP issues in China and that there is a split in American industry between the companies hurt and those not hurt by IP violations. In the words of the informant, the "mature companies" were traveling with the secretary.

This same interviewee went on to say concerns over IP have become "passé" because the Chinese government has made "genuine efforts" in the last three years to address IP violations. IP infringement hurts Chinese companies as much as international companies. It is a problem for the Chinese government because its strategy is to build global brands, so it must protect IP. The laws are clearer now and the courts are willing to protect IP. Many of these stock arguments are not true, which the informant confirmed by ending

---

[34] The Obama administration has increased prosecution under the Foreign Corrupt Practices Act, setting a record of nearly $2 billion in fines in 2009 and 2010 (Bussey 2011). Importantly, the administration is scrutinizing suppliers and middlemen and punishing American companies if their foreign partner is paying bribes. This supports the analysis of middlemen carried out in this book.

with, "but don't bring anything to China you don't want stolen." What is true is that for some American companies, IP violations are not one of their top concerns, and they do not want IP as one of the top concerns of the American government.

Second, a Chinese lawyer specializing in IP law said that American companies "let" Chinese companies copy IP and market infringed products, and then once the market is developed and consumers are familiar with the product, they file a lawsuit against the Chinese company. In this way, the American company uses the Chinese company to develop the market. Americans get the marketing for free. Once the American company wins the lawsuit, the Chinese government confiscates the Chinese company's profits. The Americans support infringement against themselves as a marketing strategy. "What Chinese company has the power to defend itself against this strategy?," he asked.

IP lawsuits require power and money. Since Americans have money and the legal power to file lawsuits, they can protect their rights. The Chinese, without money, are defenseless. IP lawsuits are a luxury of the rich, said the lawyer interviewee. This view of the dominating Americans and the vulnerable Chinese is hard to square with the analysis carried out in Chapters 9 and 10, which found that rampant Chinese infringement is not controlled by the courts or the government, and could not be even if they wanted to, given the political and institutional systems. This seems to be one more example of an emotionally driven view of American exploitation. What is important in this story is the continuing Chinese perception of themselves as innocent victims exploited by unscrupulous foreigners—fodder for government-stoked nationalism.

II. Government Corruption

1. The Bidding Process. Corruption was found in the bidding process for government contracts in the 2010 data as in 2007. Individuals who have relationships with government officials are invited to bid. They are told what price and specifications to bid. There is a rule that there must be three bids, so the official tells the friend how to defeat the other two bids. Once the winner is chosen, the price and specifications are renegotiated, rendering the process of receiving competitive bids meaningless.

Some bidders are just "bid companies." Their function is to make noncompetitive bids in support of the prechosen winner. Some bidders do not know the process is fixed, though it is designed by the "wealthy and healthy" officials in charge, who take a cut of the action.

I described this situation to a Chinese executive who runs the sales office for an American company. He competes in the same bidding process but is forbidden by company policy to participate in corruption. He was not surprised. He said the corrupt bidders are "washing money" for the officials. For him, the main issue is that the officials are stealing from the government.[35]

2. Changes in the Bidding Process. According to Chinese executives, corruption in the bidding process has been the same since the early 1980s. There have been three notable changes, however, between 2007 and 2010. First, the power of technical people has increased. In the past, the "boss" made all the buying decisions. Now end users must approve the purchase. Relationships are no longer enough by themselves. Suppliers must offer product quality and technical support in addition to having inside relationships. This latter is the biggest change in the last three years, introducing more integrity into the process and representing a loss of power for senior administrators.

Technical people are not beyond corruption, but their demands are for paid trips abroad. For example, in 2010 a small group of technicians received a fully paid eight-day visit to the Grand Canyon, Universal Studios, and Las Vegas.[36] But their key priority is for product quality. Trips are child's play compared with the multimillion-dollar bribes demanded by senior administrators.

Second, the language used by middlemen and senior administrators to discuss kickbacks over increasingly government-monitored cell phone networks has changed in the last three years. The old language denoted bribes as "cake size." The new language refers to the bribe amount as "birthday cake." The change in language reflects two underlying material changes. Because of increased government efforts to catch and punish

---

[35] Interestingly, it was widely reported that Rio Tinto executives, jailed for stealing business secrets, had access to information on how much the government was willing to pay for contracts. According to the above scenario, it would not be surprising. The issue is not that they had the information or were using it, but that they were prosecuted for it. They were singled out for prosecution for some political reason. The arrest came right after Rio Tinto scrapped plans to accept a $19.5 billion investment from Chinalco, one of China's biggest state-owned mining groups (Barboza 2010).

[36] This trip was paid for by a Chinese middleman who facilitates the sale of American technology to Chinese research institutes.

corrupt government officials, bribe payments are often paid abroad. A common practice is to use bribe money to pay tuition and room and board for children of officials studying abroad. It is difficult for the government to discover these payments.

The third change (which is also the second reason for the change in language) is that the bribe money is not coming out of the middleman's profits. The officials are raising the price paid by the government for the product. The bribe money "paid" by the middleman is funded by the price increase. By all accounts, government budgets have swelled in the past three years and officials routinely overpay for purchases. Ironically, bribe payments are included in this largesse. In other words, there is no bribe. This is why it is now called a "birthday cake"—everyone gets a piece. The middleman is simply rewarded for "money washing." The key factor is trust: Will the middleman keep it secret?[37]

3. Relationships. As is well known, relationships between businesspeople and government officials are central to Chinese marketization. As noted in the previous section, a businessperson who has a relationship with a government official will pay for trips abroad, children's college expenses, and so on. These are considered "entertainment costs." Even many Chinese executives educated in the West do not think these payments represent corruption. They consider them part of the "business relation." In conversations, when I mention to these executives that such payments are illegal according to Chinese law, they acknowledge that society suffers from the practice but argue that it is widespread and taken for granted. They say it is difficult for me to understand; what is correct in the United States is not acceptable in China. China is a different country. In the United States, work and family are separate. China is a "relationship country." Business is built on personal relationships. Business relationships are personal relationships. Payments are made to make friends, develop bonds, and get more business. With so many people and so much competition, one needs to stand out. Friends stand out. Gifts make friends. And so their argument goes.

Even with gifts, however, it is not always easy to develop relationships with officials. In discussing changes in the middleman role, middlemen say that it has become much more difficult to set up a middleman business even if one

---

[37] As seen in footnote 28, this is not child's play. Middlemen can be taken off the street by undercover investigators, held indefinitely without trial or counsel, not given access to food, not allowed to sleep, and so forth.

is educated in the United States and sent by an American company to represent it. Relationships with government officials are key, and these are more difficult to create because officials are now wealthier and monitored more closely.

Old relationships with officials work best. Some middlemen have been paying bribes to the same officials for more than 25 years. When the middlemen started working with these officials, they were "small potatoes." The middlemen took them to expensive restaurants beyond their normal means. Now they are "big potatoes," remember the old times, and are eager to help their old friends.[38] In the same spirit, middlemen say it is smart to pay for the officials' children to study abroad. The children too will become "big potatoes." Hence, the future of middlemen's bribe paying is mixed. On the one hand, it is now more difficult to start new relationships; on the other hand, in a relationship-based society, new relationships are already developing.

4. Bribery and Kickbacks. By most accounts, requests for kickbacks and bribes have decreased from 10 years ago, perhaps even from 3 years ago. Both private companies and government organizations have implemented new processes to reduce kickbacks. There are fewer demands for kickbacks from private-company managers than from SOE managers and government officials. The worst offenders are huge government departments. The central government, it is said, is reducing corruption "step by step." Still, American executives continue to report losing sales because they do not pay bribes. One American company estimated the loss at 10–15 percent of sales. American companies complain that German and Japanese companies gain a competitive advantage by bribing government officials.

Chinese executives agree it is easier to do business if one pays kickbacks and that business is lost if kickbacks are not paid. One Chinese middleman selling American construction tools bought 100 tickets to World Expo ($18.50 each) to "improve personal relationships." He usually pays for

---

[38] The continuous references to food and food metaphors are possibly related to not having enough food during the Cultural Revolution (1966–76). After all, these relationships started a few years later. In this sense, stealing from the government can be seen as related to anger at the government. Mass corruption is payback for mass destruction during the Cultural Revolution. The connection is made ironically in an anticorruption film produced by the Chinese government. In the film, a high-level executive now in jail for corruption says, "Thirty years ago [during the Cultural Revolution] I was sent to labor camp. And now I'm sending myself back" (Areddy 2008).

dinners and gives small gifts. Not every sale needs gifts; sometimes purchasing managers just want a low price. In the worst case, purchasing managers seek kickbacks of 20–30 percent of the sale amount. His worst offenders are from large SOEs with many employees.

More seriously, bribes and kickbacks are used to get around laws. Chinese executives say environmental laws are often ignored because of bribe payments. Buildings routinely have poorly constructed interiors while sporting attractive exteriors because a chain of bribe payments leaves little money left to finish the buildings' inside or to provide ongoing maintenance. All profit is made at the front end of the building process, when bribes are paid to channel monies to connected insiders. This state of affairs creates building safety issues and considerable waste as investment funds disappear into private pockets, leaving deteriorating buildings.

5. *Enforcement.* One of the most important changes between 2007 and 2010 is the creation of a new law against bribery. The definition of bribery had formerly applied only to SOE executives, but now it applies to private businesspeople and government officials. Chinese executives say 10 years ago officials did not know bribery was wrong. Now everyone knows it is illegal. It is a duty to report knowledge of bribery. If evidence is provided, people will go to jail. The government apparently decided bribery is against its interests.

In the last three years, many people have been put in jail for bribery, including high-level executives, even though the government does not have the capacity to address the problem systematically. Chinese executives estimate that 80–90 percent of government officials in key positions take bribes, but one experienced Chinese lawyer said prosecutions are as low as 1 percent. Still, many of those not prosecuted are now fearful of being found out, and many corrupt officials have fled the country with their wealth.[39]

Punishments for government officials convicted of bribery range from merely losing their job to 10–20 years in prison. The government also goes after bribe monies. It has become quite aggressive and spends a lot of money in this effort.

[39] Two surveys carried out in 2011, show that over 50 percent of high net worth individuals in China have either arranged for or are considering emigration (Page 2012). One reason so many successful Chinese seek a second passport is that they do not feel safe. One reason they do not feel safe is that they have either paid or taken bribes. They thus feel threatened by either the government, which might put them in jail, or the poor, who might attack them for stealing society's wealth.

Simultaneous with this important change, another significant change in government activities involves the increased monitoring of e-mail, cell phones, and package delivery. These two developments are obviously related.

Chinese executives believe the government's aggressive attack on bribery is related to its reversal of support for private enterprise, instead channeling capital into the SOE sector. Significant parts of the "private" sector have been openly or secretly reverted back to SOEs or SOE control. Since the government is placing its bet on the SOE sector, it needs to get SOE corruption under control.

Three dimensions of the government's new anti-corruption laws merit further discussion: the effect on risk to engage in corrupt activities; the relation of corruption to the sociopolitical system; and the prospects for success.

a. Risk. The government's program against corruption has significantly raised the risk associated with corrupt activities. Further, because of the increased monitoring and the encouragement to report corruption, the skill level needed to carry out corrupt activities is now much higher. In this context, the Internet makes it both easier to carry out corruption and easier to get caught because of the government's diligent monitoring efforts. The latter have driven corrupt activities further underground and caused people engaged in corrupt activities to spend more time checking out their potential partners because trust is essential. For all of these reasons, corruption has decreased, though the importance and use of *guanxi* relations have simultaneously increased. *Guanxi* is an ancient Chinese institution that hides private action from the government. Hence, the government's anticorruption campaign has intensified the highly elastic *guanxi* networks, stimulating their skills in evasion and secrecy.

This is exactly where the highly plastic skills of the middleman come in. Have money, will travel. As was shown earlier, middlemen pay bribes outside the country by paying for the foreign education of an official's child or by providing the official with the password to a foreign bank account in the middleman's name. The official merely goes on vacation and taps into the bank account. His name never appears on any paper trail.

In addition to increasing the risk associated with corrupt activities, the government has also raised the salaries of officials to give them less incentive to engage in corruption. But in China's dynamic economy, the government could never raise salaries enough to offset the multimillion-dollar payouts corruption makes possible for even mid-level officials.

b. Politics. The majority of Chinese executives say the top leaders want to reduce corruption to decrease social unrest and increase economic growth.

Yet, a minority of executives feel that corruption is worse, or at least no better, than it was three years earlier despite the implementation of the new anticorruption laws. American executives say improvements have been minor at best.

Chinese and American executives agree that the reason for the limited success in reducing corruption is that corruption is an integral part of the sociopolitical system. To truly attack corruption would "cause a revolution," "change all," "destroy the whole thing." Corruption is inseparable from this dictatorship. To remove corruption would require removing the dictatorship. Highly successful businesspeople do not want the dictatorship removed. They are members of the Communist Party, part of the system, and have benefited from the system as it is.

The problem only gets worse when government officials are considered. Both American and Chinese executives point out that mid-level officials make 100,000 RMB per year ($15,300) but drive Ferraris, live in million-dollar homes, own two or three apartments, send their children abroad for school, and the like.[40] All through the structure of government—for example, import-export administration, value-added tax administration, business approvals—officials extract rents from their official duties. They represent 20 to 50 million people, less than five percent of the population. The government has always been at the center of Chinese society. Its officials will not willingly give up this position and the lifestyle it makes possible.

So how are the increasing levels of prosecutions and punishments for corruption, including death sentences, explained? Top leaders really are trying to decrease corruption. What is more interesting is the specific limits they face in this effort. Most importantly, the Communist Party has no outside checks on its power. So top corrupt officials are practically untouchable, and their family and friends are as well. This is the primary reason why some are punished and others are not. An unlimited attack on corruption would destroy the Communist Party because by its very nature its power is nearly unlimited. For this reason, the fight against corruption is the key to the role of government in China and thus to the future of China.

In addition to the power of the Party, executives cite four other reasons to explain who is punished and who is not. The first is greed. Those officials who get too greedy and do not share their rents make enemies, which can

---

[40] Importantly, this list shows that officials are not trying to hide their considerable wealth.

eventually lead to their downfall. Second, officials who anger someone more powerful, or anger a low-level person who later rises in power or who knows someone in power, can be put in jail. Corruption charges are typically brought against such a person to justify the arrest. Since most officials take bribes, the charges are usually true.

Third, jail time for corruption is often the result of competitive battles between power players wherein the loser goes to jail. It is part of the political selection process in China. Fourth, when conflicts break out between factions, the result is attacks on each other's members. One faction has one person put in jail in an area it controls; the other faction retaliates by putting a person in jail in an area it controls. Alternatively, in a transition that results in one faction's gaining the upper hand, there can be a "house cleaning with dozens, even hundreds, of people going to jail."[41]

c. *The Seesaw of History.* Some Chinese executives put the fight against corruption in historical context. During the Mao-led period, there was little corruption. Corruption increased simultaneously with the liberalization of the economy, exploding in the early 1990s when the "privatization" phase was initiated. The government has gone back and forth on fighting corruption since 1985. It is currently in an increased prosecution phase. Other Chinese executives, however, believe the problem is basically hopeless for the current generation of officials; but once they pass from the scene, institutional changes that are made now will have a chance to become ingrained in the population. This mechanism is common for developing and postsocialist countries, they say. This view sees no connection to dictatorship. Wealth, time, and socialization will resolve corruption; maybe so, maybe not. Population size, power dynamics, and history may take a different course.

Conclusion

Overall, there were not any major changes in the 2010 data that call into question the analysis of ethical and cultural issues in American-Chinese business relations based on the 2007 data. There were numerous changes, continuous change, but the focus on *culture* in the 2006/07

---

[41] The brutality of the Communist Party's management of the economy is paralleled by the political brutality inside the Communist Party itself. Perhaps the key explanation for this style is the concentration of power.

data collection and analysis meant changes would most likely be incremental at most. Indeed, according to Nisbett, fundamental cultural differences between East and West, like the different emphasis on collectivism or individualism, have been stable for thousands of years,[42] a testament to the power of origins.

One important change that did surface could be seen in incremental signs that technical expertise and market success were starting to influence business and government decision making at the expense of interpersonal relationships. This is an important point because relationships are central to Chinese culture and Chinese business. So there are some signs that impersonal criteria are gaining influence. How far this trend will continue is unknown.

Another development is that as Chinese citizens have become wealthier, they are increasingly emigrating to Western countries. There are many reasons for emigration, including safety, freedom, and investment opportunities.[43] The concern for safety has three important sources. First, wealthy citizens do not trust the Chinese government, fearing its unchecked and arbitrary power. Many fear that just as the government opened up the economy and gave opportunity to its people, it can close opportunity down.

The second reason for rising emigration among the wealthy is related to corruption. Many of the wealthy, especially government officials, gained their wealth through corrupt activities. With continuously changing government priorities, many worry that the government can turn against them, perhaps putting them jail. To remove the uncertainty and threat, they move abroad.

The other corruption-related fear is the rising social unrest among the lower and even middle classes as they lose ground in China's growing economy and find themselves on the wrong end of a widening wealth gap—so much so that they are without adequate housing, health care, and retirement savings. The wealthy fear this growing unrest and the possibility of becoming the object of its anger and potential violence.

Corruption is the primary question of Chinese marketization. It is tolerated because the priority has never been liberalization but maintaining Communist

---

[42] Nisbett 2004.

[43] Page (2012) lists the reasons for Chinese emigration as cleaner air; safer food; better education; protection of financial assets; and escape from government corruption, unchecked government power, skyrocketing living costs, poor social welfare, and high taxes.

Party control. In some ways, corruption actually contributes to Party control because it binds officials and entrepreneurs to the Party. To be sure, it is a balancing act; too much corruption leads to rising social unrest, too little to declining Party support. Power, money, and tradition hold the Party in place. There is little ideological commitment left. In any case, the Party leadership has been able to both more or less maintain control over the country and more or less manage the corruption-social stability dilemma, so far.

Both the literature and my data support the view that the Party is moving toward a control economy by reducing support for the private sector and building up the SOE sector. One can imagine an economy in 10–20 years further dominated by large SOE groups. Indeed, even while maintaining a large private sector, growing Internet usage, and broad access to international travel, simultaneously the government has increased censorship of information and monitoring of its citizens' communications. The Party continues to move boldly into this brave new world, but with a tight hand on the instruments of power. A significant disruption to economic growth would test the Party's basic strategy and capacity to maintain control.

Perhaps the most insightful change in the 2010 data is government officials' use of government money to "bribe" themselves, turning the normally bribe-paying middlemen into "money washers." The practice shows an utter disregard for the country as a whole. We already know from the 1990s that the country's "privatization" process led to an enormous increase in corruption. The 2010 data are consistent with findings from that period in showing government overspending, extravagance, and waste. But paying for one's own bribes is beyond self-interest. The "birthday cake" metaphor shows an utter disregard for society, a wasteful self-centeredness bordering on feelings of omnipotence. Even with government anticorruption activities in full swing, certain officials increase their stealing, and not just for themselves. There is both a disregard for risk and an extravagant sense of power. In this sense, there are signs of the primitiveness seen in the Cultural Revolution. Indeed, today's corruption is related to yesterday's trauma. For this reason, too, it will indeed take the passing of a generation to address corruption in Chinese society.

The major question is what effect these parents and this corruption will have on the following generation. The Cultural Revolution generation will not pass from the scene without effect. The post-Cultural Revolution generation will not be unaffected by it. It is made up of children raised by traumatized parents, in a society that has "forgotten" the past, under a government that enforces collective forgetting. Under these conditions, it is likely the seeds of trauma will be transmitted. From this perspective, the "birthday cake" generation may well give the gift of corruption to their children. Stealing as receiving is one response to emotional loss.

Appendix One: Methods

Semi-structured interviews were used as the primary data collection method for this research for a number of reasons. First, since there is very little research on ethical and cultural issues in American-Chinese business relations, the research is exploratory. Semi-structured interviews offer the flexibility to search out empirical boundaries and relationships. When new leads come up, it is easy to add new questions to the next interview or even right at the point when the new information surfaces. Second, the research focus on ethics requires investigating personal judgment and reasoning. Judgments can be quite complex as tradeoffs are evaluated and weighed.[1] Reasoning many times is not a straightforward process. Semi-structured interviews are uniquely effective at following the twists and turns, and the ambivalences, more than occasionally involving denial, of moral decision making and its rationale. Third, moral values, reasoning, and decisions involve tacit knowledge, including emotions. Semi-structured interviews allow the researcher to work with the interviewee to bring tacit knowledge and emotions to the surface and find their proper place in the stream of thought. Fourth, investigating comparative business ethics and culture many times involves sensitive areas, such as bribe paying or intellectual property violations. Semi-structured interviews allow the researcher to navigate the interview, probing sensitive areas only when the interviewee signals that an adequate level of trust has been reached.

How to get people to talk about sensitive areas such as corruption, and why the reader should be confident that what they say is true and accurate, are fair questions, which have several answers. First, perhaps surprisingly, some people are eager to talk about sensitive areas. Probably the most

---

[1] Moral judgment depends upon social understanding of the meaning of action as derived from an analysis of ends and means, consequences and intentions (Steidlmeier 1999).

sensitive area in the interviews with Chinese executives is criticism of the government. Yet a small number of interviewees spoke out on everything from the one-child policy to the Tiananmen Square massacre to bribe seeking by government officials. Second, the accuracy and depth of these accounts can be checked by comparing them with the results of other published research.

Third, once a body of mutually supporting data has emerged, new questions can be added to new interviews based on these data patterns. These informed questions will produce more data. Some of the new data might contradict the original data patterns. In these cases, the researcher must evaluate the contradictory data and determine whether they call for a reinterpretation of the original data patterns or whether the new data are false or partial. If the latter, an attempt is made to account for the biases in the new data. It is possible that the interviewees providing the new data are presenting a self-enhancing account and when understood in this light, the new data actually support the original data patterns.

Fourth, an important validation criterion of an empirical account is the level of detail that is presented. The more details, the more the account can be checked against other data. Additionally, it is difficult to concoct a detailed account that is false and also consistent and coherent, especially since the interviewee must do it on the spot, not knowing the questions in advance.

As the data are collected, a model of the social system is built up. In this case, two separate models were developed, one for American business culture and one for Chinese business culture. Each model defines the distinctive patterns and themes in the corresponding culture. The emphasis is on the whole model, not the generalizability of particular facts.[2] The goal is to create a descriptive and explanatory account of the social system.

The building of the model starts with data collection. Once the data are collected they are categorized. Once categorized, relations between categories or themes are sought. For example, the Chinese categories of "respect for superiors" and "friends" led to the theme "hidden individualism" in Chinese organizations because surface-level deferential behavior is not infrequently undercut by concealed subgroup and individual self-interest. This theme was connected to the theme of "*guanxi* as an alternative to formal hierarchy" because *guanxi* networks were found to channel subordinate and out-group

---

[2] Glaser and Strauss 1967.

interests in a strongly hierarchical society. In this way, by developing themes that connect the categories and developing relations between themes, a pattern model of Chinese business culture was built. The process is one of continuous testing, evaluation, and reformulation as new data come in that show new aspects of social reality. Once new data continue to verify the pattern model, data collection is stopped and comparison between the models begins.[3]

This research thus uses comparative methods on three different levels. First, in the study of a particular business culture, data are collected and compared to test validity and develop a pattern model of that culture. Second, the comparative method is used to identify and analyze similarities and differences between business cultures. Third, the data, interpretations, and models in this research are compared with the research materials and conclusions of other researchers whose research overlaps with this study.

An important result of the comparative process is that many times perceptions of one culture by another lead back to the perceiving culture.[4] For example, common American perceptions of the China market as the "Wild West" show that Americans' experience in China involves strong influences from their own cultural heritage. These influences, combined in many cases with little understanding of Chinese history and culture, leads to misinterpretation and misunderstanding. Through comparison of the two business cultures, these biases can be identified.

In summary, validity is determined on multiple levels. A diversity of data sources is used that cross-check each other. This includes comparing one's data and interpretations with the data and interpretations of other researchers. The more the data fit with other data, the stronger the data patterns. The more data that fit with the model of the system that is being developed, the stronger the model.[5] This is contextual validity.

---

[3] Continuous verification was not reached in the data collection process, which should be seen as one of the limitations of this research. Despite the fact that the 84 interviews plus the observational data represent 16 months of full-time data collection, there are still not enough data to fully account for the complexity of the social system under study. Business culture in Shanghai and ethical and cultural issues in American-Chinese business relations involve many thousands of people, whose relational patterns cannot be fully accounted for and explained using this methodology—indeed, using any methodology. It will take many studies to adequately address these questions. Nonetheless, this study stands on the shoulders of previous research and intends to contribute to it.

[4] Dawson 1967.

[5] Diesing 1971.

One more data source that is an important check on validity should be mentioned, that of historical context.[6] Historical knowledge is used both to inform data collection and to evaluate the data collected. For example, a theme in the American interviews is the belief some American executives hold that the Chinese are evolving toward American-style capitalism and democracy. This theme can be found in American perceptions of China going back to the nineteenth century, demonstrating that the problem of understanding China is much deeper than current American business experience. The historical context helps shed light on American culture as it displays itself in perceptions of China over generations.

More specifically, an understanding of American-Chinese business relations must be situated not only in "their" history and "our" history, but also in the history of trying to understand each other.[7] Because it is in the shared history that each culture's commitments are engaged with the other, the continuing patterns in the relationship thus expose the deeper underlying points of cooperation and conflict. This book seeks to contribute to understanding this history as it is recreated and further developed in China's dynamic present.

[6] Dilthey 1986.
[7] Madsen 1995.

Appendix Two: The Shanghai Business Environment

Shanghai is a central business hub in China, but despite the city's international image as a model of economic reform, the Shanghai government is the most authoritarian in China.[1] In the post-Tiananmen Square political atmosphere of the 1990s, Shanghai produced the country's next two top leaders. During this period Shanghai developed a model for economic growth dominated by government. Its central characteristics are an interventionist state, an antirural bias, a favoring of foreign capitalists over domestic entrepreneurs, and extensive support from the central government.[2] The result is that a dominant portion of Shanghai's GDP growth accrues to the government in the form of taxes and to state-controlled and foreign corporations in the form of profits. No other province (or, as Shanghai is properly classified, province-level municipality) in China better demonstrates the domination of the state over the market.

In addition to receiving massive funding from Beijing to build world-class infrastructure, the Shanghai government requisitions extensive areas of land from rural households at below-market prices, auctions the land at market prices, and uses the profits to finance its industrial strategies, government welfare and pension obligations, and no small amount of corruption.[3] The famous Pudong business district was the model example. It resulted in the relocation of 1.7 million people. This model—forcible evictions, below-market payments, demolition of neighborhoods, and collusion with corrupt real estate developers—has been followed by other governments all over China.

---

[1] Pan 2008. Indeed, Mao relied on radical Communists from Shanghai to start the Cultural Revolution (R. McGregor 2010).

[2] Huang 2008.

[3] Huang 2008. The amount of land development in Shanghai is enormous, about 20 million square meters between 2000 and 2005 alone (R. McGregor 2010). The skyscrapers that often elicit comparison with New York City were built mostly by SOEs.

Highly relevant to this research, the Shanghai model attracts huge foreign investment, $12.6 billion in 2011.[4] Though in 2011 Shanghai accounted for 4.1 percent of China's GDP, its share of exports, dominated by foreign firms, was 11.05 percent.[5] In 2010, foreign-invested enterprises (FIEs) accounted for a staggering 70 percent of its total exports.[6] In addition to its world-class infrastructure, its eastern location (natural for foreign trade), its deep-water port, and its pre-Communist history as a world-class (foreign-oriented) business environment, the Shanghai government offered generous incentives to foreign businesses to locate in Shanghai. Many of these incentives gave foreign businesses advantages over the Chinese private sector, for example, forbidding private Chinese firms from bidding on the huge array of government-funded infrastructure projects; allowing FIEs to deduct payroll costs from tax liabilities at a much higher rate than domestic private firms; putting tough political, regulatory, and financial restrictions on domestic private firms; and forbidding large department stores from stocking products from domestic private firms.[7]

The result of these policies is a stunted private sector in Shanghai. Shanghai's domestic private firms are fewer in number and smaller in employment, sales, and assets than those of other Chinese provinces or cities.[8] In terms of small-scale household businesses, Shanghai ranks lowest in the country. In terms of large private domestic firms, Shanghai has only 6 out of the largest 100, and 3 of these are in the politically dominated (highly corrupt) real estate sector. Indeed, 7,000 private businesses moved out of Shanghai in 2007.

The income statistics tell a more personal story. Despite the fact that Shanghai's GDP per capita is five times higher than that of the country as a whole, its nonfarm business income is only half that of the country as a whole.[9] So while Shanghai's business model produced great wealth, that wealth was heavily biased toward some parts of the population at the expense of others. On the one hand, the average wage level in Shanghai is the

---

[4] China Data Online 2012.

[5] China Data Online 2012.

[6] Hong Kong Trade Development Council 2011.

[7] Huang 2008. In 2011, China started to move toward tax parity between multinationals and domestic firms.

[8] Huang 2008.

[9] Huang 2008.

highest in the country; on the other hand, the poorest 10 percent of the city's population has lost income every year since 2001 and the lower-middle and middle-income groups have seen their incomes slow down considerably since the 1980s.[10] Hence, the bulk of the large increase in wealth went to the upper-middle and high-income groups. Another way to put this is that while Shanghai's GDP per capita increased by 5 times the national average, per capita household income increased by only 1.7 times the national average.

One last dimension of this story can be seen in the employment numbers. In the period 1992–2010, employment in China rose by 94.2 percent, while employment in Shanghai rose by only 37.2 percent.[11] This took place while the compound annual growth rate of Shanghai's GDP was 15.5 percent and foreign direct investment (FDI) increased from $1.26 billion to $11.12 billion.[12] One explanation for this under-performance in employment is the downsizing that took place in the state-owned enterprise (SOE) sector. In 2010, Shanghai's SOE employment was 31 percent of what it was in 1990. This is not to say that SOEs play a small role in Shanghai's economy. In 2010, SOEs accounted for 38.9 percent of industrial output value.[13] In fact, because of the handcuffed private sector, SOEs provide 48.8 percent of source products to private firms.[14] Outside of the influx of FDI, this is hardly evidence of a burgeoning market economy. On the contrary, this story is one of government-protected, large SOEs sharing the market with FIEs for the benefit of the government, its friends, and foreign corporations, the latter needed to jump-start the program.

[10] Huang 2008.
[11] China Data Online 2011.
[12] China Data Online 2011.
[13] China Data Online 2011.
[14] Huang 2008.

Appendix Three: Data Collection

1. Interview Data. The total number of interviews carried out was 84. I interviewed 33 American executives in American companies in Cleveland, Ohio, in 2006, and 33 Chinese executives in Chinese companies in Shanghai, China, in 2007. In Shanghai in 2010, I did 18 additional interviews, 14 with Chinese executives and 4 with American executives. The Cleveland site was chosen because it is where I live and have the ability to secure this many interviews. The advantages of using Cleveland relate to its heavy concentration of manufacturing companies. The types of industrial companies in Cleveland are good examples of the kinds of companies that have flocked to China from all over the world during the past two decades, seeking to take advantage of China's cheap labor and infrastructure as well as to position themselves to sell into China's dynamic economic growth.[1]

Shanghai was chosen because it is the city in China where the highest number of Cleveland companies do business. The Cleveland companies introduced me to 24 of the 47 Chinese interviewees; 22 of the 24 had relationships with the Cleveland companies. This first group of 24 Chinese interviews led to introductions that secured an additional 10 interviews. The U.S. consulate in Shanghai, which itself had been introduced to me by one of the Cleveland companies, introduced me to 10 additional Chinese interviewees. Two Chinese interviewees were introduced by Fulbright professors whom I knew, and one was introduced by a Chinese administrator at the university where I was teaching in Shanghai.

The American interviews were secured by a similar process to the Chinese interviews; multiple means of contact were pursued. The main differences were that nine American interviews led to interviews with other members of the same company, only three of the Chinese interviews led to other

---

[1] Twenty percent of all the manufacturing in the world takes place in China (*Economist* March 10, 2012b).

interviews in the same company;[2] the American interviews were carried out in 18 companies, while the 47 Chinese interviews were carried out in 30 companies; and one American executive was interviewed twice, while seven Chinese executives were interviewed twice and two interviewed three times.[3]

Information on the American and Chinese interviewees and their companies is provided below.

INTERVIEWEE BACKGROUND[4]

Category		American	Chinese
Interviewee rank	Owner/CEO	2	24
	CEO/COO	6	2
	Vice-president	14	3
	Manager	12	14
	Attorney	3	2
	Consultant	0	2

(Continued)

[2] There were many reasons for this difference. One is that Chinese interviewees at large companies who could have introduced me to colleagues were oriented toward the external person who had set up the interview. They saw me in terms of that external network, not their company. There is an element of secrecy in this, in that the interviewee did not want the fact of the interview to be public knowledge. American executives' concern for privacy was usually addressed by the promise not to use their names or the names of their companies in print. The way the introductions worked in China points toward the centrality of networks; a tendency to keep one's activities private, especially with foreigners; and the ever-present, highly secretive, and potentially threatening nature of the Communist government in Chinese society.

[3] The reason for this was that seven of the nine Chinese repeat interviews were of Chinese middlemen, who had unequaled insight into my research focus. Also, these Chinese were very willing to speak to me for a variety of reasons, including wanting to please the "friend" who set up the interview, appreciating the opportunity to speak freely, wanting to support research on the topic, and hoping to learn something.

[4] All 47 Chinese interviewees were Chinese nationals. All but one was interviewed in China. Of the 37 American interviewees, 33 were American nationals, three were third-country nationals having worked and lived in the United States for many years, and one was a Chinese national having worked and lived in the United States for many years. Of the American interviews, 29 were carried out in the United States, seven in China, and one in Singapore.

Category		American	Chinese
Industry	Basic materials	3	1
	Consumer goods	4	9
	Conglomerate	0	1
	Energy	0	1
	Health care	5	0
	Industrial goods	17	17
	Nonprofit	0	2
	Services	3	10
	Technology	5	6
Company size (employees)	Under 10	0	8
	10–99	4	17
	100–999	2	9
	1,000–100,000	12	8
	Over 100,000	1	5
Primary China business operations	Distribution	0	1
	Manufacturing	22	15
	Middleman—sales	0	13
	Middleman—service	0	8
	Mining	1	1
	Nonprofit	0	2
	Purchasing	5	0
	Sales	7	5
	Services	2	2
Total interviews		37	47

There are several differences between the American and Chinese companies. First, 24 of the Chinese executives were owners of or partners in their firms. Only two of the American executives owned a significant portion of the company. All of the owner-operator Chinese companies were small. Of the 18 American firms, 14 were publicly traded companies. I do not have this information for all of the Chinese companies, but it is a much smaller proportion. The upshot is that the Chinese companies on the whole were smaller than the American companies.[5] Five of the Chinese companies, however, were large state-owned enterprises (SOEs), and many of the Chinese interviewees had previously worked for large SOEs. Hence, the Chinese interviewees reflect the broader Chinese economy, where many large SOEs have been shut down or downsized, with some of their employees leaving to start or work for small companies. The American companies, too, reflected the fact that a sizable percentage of large American companies are doing business in China.[6] Thus, both the American and Chinese interviewees came from companies whose size reflected dominant trends in the China market.

Second, the largest industry group for both American and Chinese companies was industrial goods (17 in each). After that, the Americans spread out into health care (5), technology (5), consumer goods (4), basic materials (3), and services (3). After industrial goods, the Chinese clustered in services (10), consumer goods (9), and technology (6). This distribution of industries reflects the randomness of the selection given an end point of 48 companies. It also reflects the heavy concentration of manufacturing companies in Shanghai and Cleveland.[7] China's low-cost labor and low-cost materials have encouraged labor-intensive businesses, both foreign and domestic, to set up operations in China. Finally, as mentioned, my research purpose, to study the relationship between American and Chinese business executives, led me to seek out Chinese middlemen, a focus that shows up in the 21 Chinese

---

[5] One important reason for this size difference is the explicit decision, made in the middle of the fieldwork in China, to focus on Chinese middlemen, all of whom were by necessity owner-operators of their own small firms.

[6] Of the world's largest 500 companies, 95 percent have set up operations in China (Moody 2010). By the beginning of 2012, 353 multinational companies made Shanghai their regional headquarters (The American Chamber of Commerce 2012).

[7] The manufacturing concentration is also seen in the final category on the chart, showing 22 American interviewees and 15 Chinese interviewees from companies primarily in manufacturing. Manufacturing accounts for 40 percent of Shanghai's economy (Hong Kong Trade Development Council 2011).

interviewees in the "middleman" categories, 45 percent of the Chinese interviews.

2. Observational Data. During my stay in Shanghai, I collected important observational data. A principal part of the observational data came from participating in spontaneous group dynamics, which enabled me to get access to different parts of the social selves of the participants than those uncovered in the interview data. The sheer unplanned nature of these encounters was an important source of new insights. Similarly, informal interaction during conversations often brought out not only new information but aspects of how relations were managed that provided key insights about such things as status, power, networking, misunderstanding, and anxiety. The observational data are recorded in documents I call the business diary and the university diary.

The business diary contains a variety of data. An important part of these data is from visits to the Shanghai operations of Cleveland companies, during which I had conversations with executives, including multiple lunches and dinners. Some of these meals were also attended by Chinese customers of the companies. One of the American executives was an "executive guest" in my business ethics class in Shanghai, which also produced some interesting data.

General business news taking place in China was also recorded in the business diary. For example, during my stay in China it was reported that children (some of them mentally retarded) had been kidnapped from around the country and used as slaves in coal mines in one province. This event made it into numerous conversations with both Chinese and Americans that generated interesting commentary on the current state of Chinese society. I also had the opportunity to attend an American university alumni club of which I was a member, where I met international executives working for foreign companies in Shanghai. This led to numerous conversations on business in China and other activities, such as my making visits to their organizations to talk about business ethics and their participating in my business ethics classes. Finally, I had the opportunity to spend "social" time with some of the American interviewees in Shanghai. This inevitably led to rich discussions on cultural issues and business topics. This was all recorded in the business diary.

The university diary also contains a variety of data. I taught two classes on business ethics, one graduate and one undergraduate, to Chinese students in Shanghai. There were 25 students in each class, coming from all over China. Data from class discussions on business ethics topics are used in the empirical chapters. I gave lectures on business ethics at other universities and interacted with students and faculty at these events. I developed close relations with my own students, having lunch with undergraduate students and dinner with graduate students once each week. I learned much about China from my students. As part of the class assignments, students wrote up case studies on ethical issues in Chinese businesses. These case descriptions, analyses, conclusions, and discussions of them provided much insight into how these young students saw business responsibility. During my 2010 visit, I met with seven of my 2007 students, who by that time had been working in business and government for two years. It was fascinating to see how they had changed and to hear their reports from the "front."

In 2007, I was part of a community of Fulbright professors who met regularly in Shanghai. I also met with Chinese professors and administrators who worked at the university where I taught. These meetings led to significant exchanges of information and experience. In this context, I attended a Fulbright conference in Guangzhou upon my arrival in China. The conference participants included Fulbright professors, members of the U.S. Department of State, Chinese professors, and Chinese government officials. The conference was important as my first direct exposure to the views of Chinese Communist Party officials.

I will give just one example that shows how episodic data collection is in the participant observation mode, which represents a good part of the observational data. At the Fulbright conference, the following conversation took place with a Chinese professor of education whom, by happenstance, I sat down next to at lunch. He was about 65 years old. The conversation was quite friendly until, toward the end of the lunch, I brought up Mao.

> Feldman: How would you estimate Mao's legacy?
> Chinese professor: Mao was a great leader. He made some mistakes but without the Cultural Revolution we would not be where we are today.
> Feldman: But there were many deaths during this period.
> Chinese professor: Only 100.
> Feldman: Western estimates are much higher.
> Chinese professor: [growing angry] I was there. I was in the Red Guard. There were not many deaths.[8]

---

[8] Western estimates are around 400,000 dead as the result of maltreatment, with many more physically and mentally disabled, and a significant but unknown number having committed suicide (Fairbank and Goldman 2006).

This was my first encounter with the role of the Communist Party in Chinese collective memory and the level of denial to which it gives rise. The observational data record many such exchanges, wherein statements are made that contradict an abundance of other data sources. These research events were important sources of new research directions that arose periodically in the fieldwork.

3. *Written Documents.* Some Chinese and American firms provided me with written materials documenting activities the firms were undertaking. For example, an American CEO proudly gave me a plant newsletter written for the Chinese employees at a plant his company had just built in Shanghai. The newsletter was an effort to build community (loyalty) in the Chinese workforce. It showed how the CEO imagined the Chinese desire for community.

Appendix Four: The Middleman

1. Background. The 21 Chinese middlemen I interviewed ranged in age from their early 30s to their mid-60s, but a strong majority of them were in the range between the mid-30s and mid-40s. The average age for the whole group was in the early 40s. There were 15 males, 6 females. Just about all were college graduates, and 9 had graduate degrees, most of these in engineering. One had an MBA and a second was working on an MBA. Just over half of them had worked in a state-owned enterprise before going into private business.

Six of the 21 had lived in the United States, but almost all had traveled to the United States, some of them often. A little over half of them had worked for an American company before going into business for themselves. An additional 4 had extensive experience working with American companies. Three were educated in the United States.

As far as I am aware, only 5 owned other businesses besides their businesses as middlemen. Just about all of them provided additional services in conjunction with their middleman functions, such as training, product evaluation, logistics, and the like. Nine of the 21 were selling foreign products in China, and 8 were exporting products made by Chinese firms. All the middleman firms were small, none having more than 50 employees; many had around 10 employees. In 2010, the oldest middleman firm was 17 years old, the youngest, four. The average age of the firms was 8.6 years.

2. Connections. The middleman is usually in the middle between buyer and seller. In Chinese culture these triadic relations are part of the *guanxi* system, social networks through which much cooperation, trust, and exchange is accomplished. The Chinese language has special names to account for the different positions in a *guanxi* network. Hence, the middleman function was part of Chinese culture before foreigners entered the picture. Middlemen are pervasive in the domestic economy.[1]

The in-between function, connecting two others who can benefit from each other, only increases in importance when foreigners arrive with their limited information about and access to the Chinese marketplace, particularly since informal network relations are one of the middleman's central structural features. Key, then, is the middleman's connections to both Chinese and American actors. Many of the middlemen had previous relationships with American companies, which they utilized to make introductions to Chinese companies. Many times these relationships or their use by middlemen are accidents of history. No middleman starts out to become a middleman. Sometimes an American firm asks a Chinese person it knows or has worked with in the past for information or an introduction, and down the road, this happenstance leads to a middleman business.

It is essential that the middleman has access to both American and Chinese companies and the ability to introduce the two. She is there at the beginning and many times stays throughout the business relationship, should it develop. Both parties benefit from the involvement of the middleman, whose service is to make the relationship between the buyer and seller more effective. People skills, then, are very important. The middleman must be able to build relationships with a wide variety of people, including people from different cultures.[2]

The most obvious need for middlemen occurs when the foreign firm first comes to China. It is a high-cost proposition for foreign firms to develop their own sales or purchasing capacities in China, and often they face uncertain success. Middlemen are hired to find customers or suppliers. Over time, the need can change as foreign firms gain experience and relationships, and begin to create their own sales, purchasing, or manufacturing operations. Middlemen can help set up these organizations, too. But even then, local operations cannot

---

[1] Traditionally, the Chinese middleman is a peacemaker or arbitrator who settles conflicts not by determining truth, justice, right, or wrong, but by smoothing ruffled feelings (Hsu 1981). Usually each side is asked to sacrifice a little, a practice that can benefit the weaker party, who could not have achieved this outcome on his own. The process demonstrates the collective nature of Chinese society as the middleman works to maintain the social order. It also demonstrates the Confucian focus on human relations as opposed to abstract principle.

[2] The profound importance in Chinese culture of negotiating between two conflicting positions is perhaps why the Chinese have been so adaptable and successful worldwide. Middlemen are specialists in this general cultural disposition.

embrace China's huge, decentralized market. Some American companies, even after setting up their own sales, purchasing, or manufacturing organizations, still use middlemen to keep costs down, gain access to new clients, and meet a plethora of other needs. Even if a middleman is hired as an employee, other middlemen are utilized for other geographic regions or other social networks. Middlemen are talking to their contacts on a regular basis, collecting detailed information with them, having dinner with them, and building relationships with managers and workers. It is difficult to replicate these networks in-house without going to considerable expense.[3] Given the localness of social networks, middlemen are difficult to replace. They are typically paid three to five percent of a successful transaction if they provided the introduction.

3. Information. In addition to searching for, introducing the client to, and communicating with other businesses, middlemen also collect information and carry out analyses. They are hired to carry out market research for the introduction of products, to evaluate the product quality and reliability of potential suppliers, to evaluate potential joint venture partners, or to evaluate a company for outright purchase, for example. One middleman, who had worked for an American corporation, said he was paid $100 per hour for market research.

To collect information and carry out analyses, a middleman must have knowledge of a specific industry, the industry's market dynamics, the particular companies in the industry, and how these companies are run. This level of knowledge enables the middleman to provide clients with the connections and advice they seek. In some cases, it requires specialized technical knowledge to evaluate specialized technical products or processes and market demand.

Middlemen can be particularly helpful in dealing with the government. Without their knowledge of government requirements and their relationships with government officials, American companies can experience long delays in dealing with banking regulations, laws, exporting, importing, shipping, currency regulation, and a plethora of required licenses, permits, and approvals. In the context of selling to government organizations, middlemen provide information on purchasing processes and how projects are run. Typically a bidding process is used, but the number of real bids submitted can

---

[3] Some American firms try. It is not unheard of for American firms to hire Chinese middlemen as employees. One American company president only half jokingly referred to one of his Chinese employees as "the executive vice-president of banquets and receptions." This employee's only job was to make valuable introductions. His particular skills were his extensive social network, popularity and social skills, and ability to initiate positive relationships.

be as few as one or two. Middlemen help prepare the proposal by providing information on customer needs, identifying product strengths and weaknesses in regard to these needs, and providing information on the project's budget for the purchase. It is not uncommon to receive information on the proposals of other bidders if there are any (corruption in government bidding processes is discussed in Chapter 12).

4. *Trust.* The Chinese do not trust an individual unless they know him personally or unless someone whom they trust knows him and vouches for him. They do not trust a person by reputation alone because reputation can be misleading; likewise with the public record. The Chinese always look for a personal connection through networks of friends and associates. If they cannot make a personal connection, they will not be forthcoming.

Hence the middle is a fundamental position in Chinese social relations. Middlemen develop relationships and build trust to capitalize on this structural position in Chinese society. They are entrepreneurs in the relationship industry. Core competencies are truth telling, promise keeping, trustworthiness, and reliability. In this way, middlemen create social capital.

The middleman functions as a bridge.[4] Through him go enough accurate communications and reliable commitments that business deals can be completed. The middleman must build relationships with both sides. Both sides must trust the middleman enough to move ahead with the transaction, even while they neither understand nor trust each other. The middleman is a prophylactic, a protective barrier that absorbs some portion of the financial, reputational, and legal risk.

5. *Cultural Relations.* Perhaps the key contribution the middleman makes to American-Chinese business relations is improving communications. This is not an obvious or easy task. Even American executives with long experience in China still run into questions that are difficult to answer and problems that are incomprehensible. The styles and backgrounds of the two business cultures are so different that interaction seems to generate misunderstanding. Suspicion is commonplace. One middleman said 50 percent of her time is spent explaining one side to the other.

---

[4] In some cases, it is a peculiar type of bridge, one that only the middleman crosses. This is the type most interesting to the field of business ethics, because the middleman's back-and-forth is exactly for the purpose of removing ethical and cultural conflict. Is it ethical to keep the parties apart, stopping them from directly addressing their conflicts? Certainly it is not ethical to have middlemen pay bribes for American companies.

One issue is the tacit level of language. Even if the two sides use the same language, the tacit meaning is often not grasped or shared by both sides. The middleman is a specialist in both cultures; she tries to bring the "back meaning" of both cultures to the surface. She tries to explain the core concerns of each party to the other. She seeks to bring objectivity to the communications. It is a position of power and can easily be manipulative; the gap in understanding can easily be used to insert the middleman's own interests.

American and Chinese executives entering into business discussions with each other represent a wide range of reactions to each other, from respect and friendship to fear and loathing. Some American executives going to China for the first time find China overwhelming and even repulsive. One company president from New York was unable to enter an elevator with Chinese workers and had to have the elevator blocked off so she could ride it alone. The Chinese middleman told the Chinese workers the woman was ill, but the incident was embarrassing to him. Another American CEO reported being compared to a mixed-breed dog by a Chinese executive when the CEO spoke of his diverse ethnic ancestry.[5]

As has been discussed many times in this book, the Chinese are disinclined to trust even their fellow countrymen without a personal connection; they are naturally suspicious of strangers. China is a huge country, with strong regional and local differences. Even between Chinese, communications can be difficult. This difficulty is amplified with Westerners, since Chinese are all too aware that Westerners look different and think differently. One Chinese middleman said he has "learned not to let Americans look at me as a freak." His sensitivity to the cultural differences led him to study American history and culture. Though his explicit study is unusual among Chinese middlemen, all of the ones I interviewed had some experience with or interest in American culture in addition to speaking English, which contributed to their becoming middlemen.[6]

---

[5] The Chinese executive making the insults made them in Chinese and did not know one of the CEO's assistants spoke Chinese.

[6] One middleman mentioned illegally studying English as a child in the hope of making a better life for himself outside the Communist system. He was furious at the government for putting his father in a labor camp during his childhood. Another middleman participated in the Tiananmen Square protests in her university years. There is a hint of social marginality in this part of the middleman profession.

This is what makes the middleman invaluable or irreplaceable in conflict situations between American and Chinese companies. When one side will not meet with the other or a conflict develops that brings the relationship to a standstill, a middleman, with understanding of both sides, is able to take the conflict into himself, so to speak, increasing trust enough to begin or reopen discussions through him. The middleman is simultaneously near and distant, near enough to have both the knowledge to address the issues and the acceptance to communicate with both parties, yet distant enough to be seen as neutral and thus trustworthy. What cannot be done without the middleman can be done with her; both parties get enough of what they need to proceed with a deal.

6. *Management.* Middlemen can become more than conduits between key players, sometimes taking ownership positions in joint ventures or taking ownership of products as a distributor. They often become involved in negotiations over price (from which they get their fees and are often squeezed by both sides) and monitor the business arrangement once it has been agreed to. Monitoring often involves training Chinese manufacturers to meet American quality standards, preferences, and delivery dates. In some cases, American companies develop such close relationships with particular middlemen that if a Chinese firm wants to do business with an American company, it has no choice but to use the Americans' chosen middleman. Many foreign companies visit China only one to three times per year. The middleman is in effect the foreign company's representative in China, acting as a gatekeeper to the foreign firm.

7. *Difficulties and Challenges.* Middlemen, though functioning between two parties that potentially will engage in a business transaction, are paid by one side. Thus they are obligated to represent their employer's interests. These may be, certainly will be perceived to be, in opposition to the interests of the other party; but the middleman needs to persuade the second party to trust her so she can accomplish her task of bringing the two parties into a working relationship. Trying to gain the trust of both parties while representing one party presents a dilemma. It is a natural imbalance of trust.

Some middlemen address this dilemma by making considerable effort to develop a relationship with the second party. This effort can include researching the second company's business operations, culture, goals, growth history, and the like. In addition to speaking to the second party, the middleman may collect information from competitors, customers, suppliers, and other relevant parties. In this way, the middleman tries to impress upon the second party that she understands its business and seeks to satisfy its interests. The second party is naturally resistant, but the middleman works at building up trust and developing a personal relationship, all without alienating the first party.

This balancing act does not always succeed. Chinese manufacturers complain that Chinese middlemen become expansive, trying to represent their American clients on every detail, up to persuading the local government to join the discussions on the side of the American company. Using this leverage, the middleman tries to force concessions from the Chinese manufacturer, including receiving payments from the manufacturer too. If the manufacturer wants the business, then he has little choice but to add to the middleman's fees. In a sense, then, the middleman is playing both sides against the middle. This role is quite different from that of helping both sides to understand each other so that they can decide for themselves.

Another problem posed by Chinese middlemen is that they demand to know detailed information about Chinese manufacturing processes in order to negotiate lower prices for their American customers and more profit for themselves. American customers seldom ask for this level of detailed information. Some Chinese manufacturers do not let middlemen onto their factory floors but have special meeting rooms for product presentation and evaluation. The threat is actually even worse than lower prices, because with enough detailed information the middleman can open his own factory and become a competitor. Chinese manufacturers try to keep middlemen away from their employees for this reason.

Finally, even though middlemen often come recommended through networks by partners, clients, suppliers, and the like, they report that gaining the trust of new clients has become more difficult in the last few years. Confidentiality agreements help little. Some Chinese executives say China is a nation without "face," without a concern for honor. The poisoned baby formula powder and other instances of poison in food are mentioned as examples. The problem is general, but it has affected the role of the middleman. Trust has become more difficult to achieve. [7]

---

[7] This can be seen as one measure of the condition of Chinese society at this point in the "reform" process.

Bibliography

Alford, William P. 1995. *To Steal a Book Is an Elegant Offense: Intellectual Property Law in Chinese Civilization.* Stanford, CA: Stanford University Press.

American Chamber of Commerce. 2011. *2011 China Business Climate Survey.*

American Chamber of Commerce. 2012. *AmCham-China's American Business in China White Paper 2012.* http://www.amchamchina.org/whitepaper2012.

Anand, Bharat and Alexander Galetovic. 2004. How Market Smarts Can Protect Property Rights. *Harvard Business Review* December: 1–8.

Anderson, Jonathan. 2006. China's True Growth: No Myth or Miracle. *Far Eastern Economic Review* 169: 9–16.

Areddy, James T. 2008. Scandal Prisoners Star in China Film. *Wall Street Journal,* January 30.

Areddy, James T. 2009. China Slowdown Stunts Entrepreneurs. *Wall Street Journal,* March 27.

Areddy, James T. 2011. Tire Suit Treads Loudly in China. *Wall Street Journal,* May 4.

Areddy, James T. 2012. Shanghai's Real-Estate Quandary. *Wall Street Journal,* August 1.

Arendt, Hannah. 1950. *Totalitarianism.* New York: Harcourt Brace Jovanovich.

Barancy, Peter. testimony before U.S. Congress. House. Committee on Ways and Means. *Hearing on U.S. Trade With China.* 110th Cong., 1st sess., February 15, 2007.

Barboza, David. 2008. Former Party boss in China Gets 18 Years. *New York Times,* April 12.

Barboza, David. 2009. Politics Permeates Anti-Corruption Drive in China. *New York Times,* September 4.

Barboza, David. 2010. Rio Tinto Workers Admit Taking Bribes in China. *New York Times,* March 22.

Barley, Stephen R. 2007. Corporations, Democracy, and the Public Good. *Journal of Management Inquiry* 16: 201–215.

Batjargal, Bat and Mannie M. Liu. 2004. Entrepreneurs' Access to Private Equity in China: The Role of Social Capital. *Organization Science* 15: 159–172.

Baumol, William J., Robert E. Litan, and Carl J. Schramm. 2007. *Good Capitalism, Bad Capitalism, and the Economics of Growth and Prosperity.* New Haven, CN: Yale University Press.

Bell, Daniel. 1978. *The Cultural Contradictions of Capitalism.* New York: Basic Books.

Bell, Duran. 2000. *Guanxi*: A Nesting of Groups. *Current Anthropology* 41: 132–138.

Bendix, Reinhard. 1960. *Max Weber: An Intellectual Portrait.* Berkeley: The University of California Press.

Bloomberg News. 2011. GM Retains No. 1 Sales Rank, August 28.

Boatright, John R. 2000. Globalization and the Ethics of Business. *Business Ethics Quarterly* 10: 1–6.

Boisot, Max and John Child. 1996. From Fiefs to Clans and Network Capitalism: Explaining China's Emerging Economic Order. *Administrative Science Quarterly* 41: 600–628.

Bowie, Norman E. 1999. A Kantian Approach to Business Ethics. In *A Companion to Business Ethics*, ed. Robert E. Frederick, 61–70. London: Blackwell Publishers.

Boyle, James. 1996. *Shamans, Software, and Spleens: Law and the Constitution of the Information Society.* Cambridge, MA: Harvard University Press.

Brand, Vivienne and Amy Slater. 2003. Using a Qualitative Approach to Gain Insights into the Business Ethics Experiences of Australian Managers in China. *Journal of Business Ethics* 45: 167–182.

Branigan, Tania. 2011. China's Jasmine Revolution: Police but No Protestors Line Streets of Beijing. *The Guardian*, February 27.

Branigan, Tania. 2012. China Shuts Down Maoist Website Utopia. *The Guardian*, April 6.

Brenkert, George 2008. Google, Human Rights, and Moral Compromise. *Journal of Business Ethics* 85: 453–478.

Broadie, Sarah. 1991. *Ethics With Aristotle.* New York: Oxford University Press.

Browne, Andrew and Jason Dean. 2010. Business Sours on China—Foreign Executives Say Beijing Creates Fresh Barriers; Broadsides, Patent Rules. *Wall Street Journal*, March 17.

Buffett, Warren E. 2006. *Newsletter to Berkshire Hathaway Shareholders*, March 20.

Burrell, Robert. 1998. A Case Study in Cultural Imperialism: The Imposition of Copyright on China by the West. In *Intellectual Property and Ethics*, eds. Lionel Bentley and Spyros M. Maniastis, 195–224. London: Sweet & Maxwell.

Business Software Alliance. 2012. *2011 BSA Global Software Piracy Study.*

Bussey, John. 2011. The Rule of Law Finds Its Way Abroad—However Painfully. *Wall Street Journal*, June 24.

Butterton, Glenn R. 2001. Pirates, Dragons, and U.S. Intellectual Property Rights in China: Problems and Prospects of Chinese Enforcement. In *The Conflict and Culture Reader*, ed. Pat K. Chew, 261–265. New York: New York University Press.

Cavanagh, Gerald F. 2000. Political Counterbalance and Personal Values: Ethics and Responsibility. *Business Ethics Quarterly* 10: 43–52.

Chao, Loretta and Shayndi Raice. 2011. Huawei Challenges U.S. to Back Claims—After Thwarted Deal, Frustrated Chinese Firm Says It Wants Investigation of Alleged Security Risks. *Wall Street Journal*, February 25.

Chao, Loretta. 2009. China Squeezes PC Makers—Beijing is Set to Require Web Filter that Would Censor "Harmful" Internet Sites. *Wall Street Journal*, June 8.

Chassequet-Smirgel, Janine. 1985. *The Ego Ideal: A Psychoanalytic Essay on the Malady of the Ideal.* New York: W. W. Norton & Company.

Chen, Chao C., Ya-Ru Chen, and Katherine Xin. 2004. *Guanxi* Practices and Trust in Management: A Procedural Justice Perspective. *Organization Science* 15: 200–209.

Chen, Roger and Chia-Pei Chen. 2005. Chinese Professional Managers and the Issue of Ethical Behavior. *Ivey Business Journal Online*, May/June.

China Daily. 2006. Shanghai Party Chief Sacked for Graft, September 25.

China Data Online, 2011.

China Data Online, 2012.

China's Internet Network Information Center. *2009 Report on the Behavior of China's Young Internet Users*, April 26, 2010.

Chintakananda, Asada, Anne S. York, Hugh M. McNeil, and Mike W. Peng. 2009. Structuring Dyadic Relationships Between Export Producers and Intermediaries. *European Journal of International Management* 3: 302–327.

Chow, Daniel C.K. testimony before U.S. Congress. Congressional—Executive Commission on China. *Intellectual Property Protection as Economic Policy: Will China Ever Enforce Its IP Laws.* 109th Cong., 1st sess., May 16, 2005.

Chow, Irene Hau-siu and Daniel Z. Q. Ding. 2002. Moral Judgment and Conflict Handling Styles Among Chinese in Hong Kong and PRC. *The Journal of Management Development* 21: 666–679.

Coburn, Tom. statements before U.S. Congress. Senate. Committee on Homeland Security and Governmental Affairs. *Ensuring Protection of American Intellectual Property Rights for American Industries in China.* 109th Cong., 1st sess., November 21, 2005.

Conyers, John Jr., prepared statement for U.S. Congress. House. Committee on the Judiciary. *International Piracy: The Challenges of Protecting Intellectual Property in the 21st Century.* 110th Cong., 1st sess., October 18, 2007.

Cragg, Wesley. 2000. Human Rights and Business Ethics: Fashioning a New Social Contract. *Journal of Business Ethics* 27: 205–214.

Davidoff, Steven M. 2011. Actions of U.S. and China to Shape Deals to Come. *The New York Times*, February 1.

Dawson, Raymond. 1967. *The Chinese Chameleon: An Analysis of European Conceptions of Chinese Civilization.* New York: Oxford University Press.

De Kluyver, Cornelis A. 2009. *The Future of Corporate Governance.* Business Expert Press. Harvard Business Publishing.

de Tocqueville, Alexis. 1969. *Democracy in America.* New York: Anchor Books.

Dean, Jason and Jeremy Page. 2011. In Depth: Running into Trouble on the China Express—Train Wreck Has Focused Attention on Corruption and Corner-Cutting Behind the Nation's Breakneck Growth. *Wall Street Journal,* August 2.

Dickson, Bruce J. 2003. *Red Capitalists in China: The Party, Private Entrepreneurs, and Prospects for Political Change.* Cambridge: Cambridge University Press.

Diesing, Paul. 1971. *Patterns of Discovery in the Social Sciences.* New York: Aldine.

Dilthey, Wilhelm. 1986. *Dilthey: Selected Writings.* Edited by H.P. Rickman. Cambridge, England: Cambridge University Press.

Doctoroff, Tom. 2012. What the Chinese Want; Consumers in China are Increasingly Modern in Their Tastes, but They are Not Becoming "Western." How the Selling of Coffee, Cars, and Pizza Sheds Light on a Nation Racing Toward Superpower Status. *Wall Street Journal,* May 18.

Dolinar, Lou. 2011. China's Growing High-Speed-Rail Troubles. *National Review Online,* March 2.

Donaldson, Thomas and Thomas Dunfee. 1999. *Ties that Bind: A Social Contracts Approach to Business Ethics.* Boston: Harvard University Business School Press.

Donaldson, Thomas. 1996. Values in Tension: Ethics Away from Home. *Harvard Business Review.*

Duhigg, Charles and Steven Greenhouse. 2012. Electronic Giant Vowing Reforms in China Plants. *Wall Street Journal,* March 29.

Dumont, Louis. 1986. *Essays on Modern Individualism: Modern Ideology in Anthropological Perspective.* Chicago: The University of Chicago Press.

Dunn and Bradstreet 2011.

Durkheim, Emile. 1934. *Suicide: A Study in Sociology.* New York: Free Press.

Economist. 2006. A Novel Prescription; Novartis, November 11.

Economist. 2006. Survey: Coming Out, March 25.

Economist. 2008. 850,000 Lawsuits in the Making: Doing Business in China, April 12.

Economist. 2009. Battle of Ideas; Intellectual Property in China, April 25.

Economist. 2010. Chinese Business: Where are the Profits, December 9.

Economist. 2010. Patents, yes; ideas, maybe; Innovation in China, October 16.

Economist. 2011. Coming Clean: China Faces Up to the Hidden Debts of Its Local Governments, June 2.

Economist. 2011. Entrepreneurship in China: Let a Million Flowers Bloom, March 10.

Economist. 2011. How Manageable is China's Red Ink, June 28.

Economist. 2011. Privatisation in China: Capitalism Confined, September 3.

Economist. 2011a. China's Economy and the WTO, December 10.

Economist. 2011b. Chinese Politics and the WTO, December 10.

Economist. 2012a. Innovation in China: From Brawn to Brain, March 10.

Economist. 2012. Intellectual Property in China: Still Murky, April 21.

Economist. 2012. Special Report: State Capitalism, January 21.

Economist. 2012b. The End of Cheap China: What Do Soaring Chinese Wages Mean for Global Manufacturing, March 10.

Egri, Carolyn P. and David A. Ralston. 2004. Generation Cohorts and Personal Values: A Comparison of China and the United States. *Organization Science* 15: 210–221.

Enderle, Georges. 1997. Five Views on International Business Ethics: An Introduction. *Business Ethics Quarterly* 7: 1–4.

Enright, Michael J. 2005. *Successful Multinationals in China.* The Asia Case Research Center. The University of Hong Kong.

Erikson, Erik. 1964. *Insight and Responsibility: Lectures on the Ethical Implications of Psychoanalytic Insight.* New York: W.W. Norton & Company.

Espinel, Victoria A. testimony before U.S. Congress. House. Committee on the Judiciary. *International Piracy: The Challenges of Protecting Intellectual Property in the 21st Century.* 110th Cong., 1st sess., October 18, 2007.

Etzioni, Amitai. 1993. *The Spirit of Community Rights: Responsibilities and the Communitarian Agenda.* New York: Crown Publishers.

European Chamber of Commerce in China. 2009. *Overcapacity in China: Causes, Impacts, and Recommendations.*

Fairbank, John King and Merle Goldman. 2006. *China: A New History.* Cambridge: Harvard University Press.

Feldman, Steven P. 2004. *Memory as a Moral Decision.* New Brunswick, NJ: Transaction Publishers.

Feldman, Steven P. 2007a. Business Diary. Shanghai, China.

Feldman, Steven P. 2007b. Moral Memory: Why and How Moral Companies Manage Tradition. *Journal of Business Ethics* 74: 395–40.

Feldman, Steven P. 2007c. University Diary. Shanghai, China.

Firth, Michael, Phyllis L. L. Mo, and Raymond M.K. Wong. 2005. Financial Statement Frauds and Auditor Sanctions: An Analysis of Enforcement Actions in China. *Journal of Business Ethics* 62: 367–381.

Fishman, Ted. testimony before U.S. Congress. Senate. Committee on Homeland Security and Governmental Affairs. *Ensuring Protection of American Intellectual Property Rights for American Industries in China.* 109th Cong., 1st sess., November 21, 2005.

Fletcher, Owen and Jason Dean. 2011. Ballmer Bares China's Travails—Microsoft CEO Details the Software Maker's Struggles With Rampant Piracy in the Region. *Wall Street Journal,* May 27.

Foucault, Michel. 1979. *Discipline and Punish: The Birthplace of the Prison.* New York: Vintage Books.

Foucault, Michel. 1980. *Power/Knowledge*. New York: Pantheon.

Freeman, John, Glenn R. Carroll, and Michael T. Hannan. 1983. The Liability of Newness: Age-dependence in Organizational Death Rates. *American Sociological Review* 88: 1116–1145.

Freeman, R. Edward. 1984. *Strategic Management: A Stakeholder Approach*. Boston: Pitman.

Freud, Sigmund. 1963. *Jokes and Their Relation to the Unconscious*. New York: W.W. Norton & Company.

Friedman, Milton. 1970. The Social Responsibility of Business Is to Increase Its Profits. *New York Times Magazine*, September 13.

Friedman, Milton. 1972. *Capitalism and Freedom*. Chicago: The University of Chicago Press.

Friedman, Milton. 2005. Social Responsibility: "Fundamentally Subversive"? *Business Week Online*, August 15.

Fukuyama, Francis. 1995. *Trust: The Social Virtues and the Creation of Prosperity*. New York: Free Press.

Gadiesh, Orit, Philip Leung, and Till Vesting. 2007. Battle for China's Good-Enough Market. *Harvard Business Review* 85: 81–89.

Gamer, Robert E. 2002. Development Reflecting Human Values. In *Candles in the Dark: A New Spirit for a Plural World*, ed. Barbara S. Baudot, 279–294. Seattle: The University of Washington Press.

Gamer, Rober E. 2003a. Chinese Politics. In *Understanding Contemporary China*, ed. Robert E. Gamer, 65–110. Boulder, CO: Lynne Rienner Publishers.

Gamer, Robert E. 2003b. International Relations. In *Understanding Contemporary China*, ed. Robert E. Gamer, 195–226. Boulder: Lynne Rienner Publishers.

Gang, Fan. 2010. China's War on Inequality. *Chinadaily.com*, November 2.

Garnaut, John. 2012. The Revenge of Wen Jiabao. *Foreign Policy*, March 29.

Gates, Hill. 1996. *China's Motor: A Thousand Years of Petty Capitalism*. Ithaca: Cornell University Press.

Geertz, Clifford. 1973. *The Interpretation of Cultures*. New York: Basic Books.

Geertz, Clifford. 1983. *Local Knowledge: Further Essays in Interpretive Anthropology*. New York: Basic Books.

Gellner, Ernest. 1992. *Reason and Culture: New Perspectives on the Past*. Oxford: Blackwell.

Glaser, Barney G. and Anselm L. Strauss. *The Discovery of Grounded Theory: Strategies for Qualitative Research*. New York: Aldine.

Glickman, Dan. testimony before U.S. Congress. House. Committee on Ways and Means. *Hearing on U.S. Trade With China*. 110th Cong., 1st sess., February 15, 2007.

Glickman, Dan. testimony before U.S. Congress. Senate. Committee on Homeland Security and Governmental Affairs. *Ensuring Protection of American Intellectual*

Property Rights for American Industries in China. 109th Cong., 1st sess., November 21, 2005.

Goldman, Merle. 2006a. Epilogue: China at the Start of the Twenty-first Century. In *China: A New History*, John King Fairbank and Merle Goldman, 457–471. Cambridge: Harvard University Press.

Goldman, Merle. 2006b. The Post-Mao Reform Era. In *China: A New History*, John King Fairbank and Merle Goldman, 406–456. Cambridge: Harvard University Press.

Green, Ronald M. 1994. *The Ethical Manager.* New York: MacMillan Publishing Company.

Guthrie, Doug. 1999. *Dragon in a Three Piece Suit: The Emergence of Capitalism in China.* Princeton: Princeton University Press.

Habib, Mohsin and Leon Zurawicki. 2002. Corruption and Foreign Direct Investment. *Journal of International Business Studies* 33: 291–307.

Hamilton, David P. 2005. Silent Treatment: How Genentech, Novartis Stifled A Promising Drug; Biotech Firm Tried to Pursue Peanut-Allergy Injection, But Contract in Way, Zack Avoids a "Kiss of Death." *Wall Street Journal*, April 5.

Hamilton, Marci A. 1997. The TRIPS Agreement: Imperialistic, Outdated, and Overprotective. In *Intellectual Property: Moral, Legal, and International Dilemmas*, ed. Adam D. Moore, 243–263. New York: Roman and Littlefield.

Hanafin, John J. 2002. Morality and the Market in China: Some Contemporary Views. *Business Ethics Quarterly* 12: 1–18.

Harney, Alexandra. 2008. *The China Price: The True Cost of Chinese Competitive Advantage.* London: Penguin Books.

Hartman, Edwin M. 2000. Socratic Ethics and the Challenge of Globalization. *Business Ethics Quarterly* 10: 211–220.

Harvey, Brian. 1999. "Graceful Merchants": A Contemporary View of Chinese Business Ethics. *Journal of Business Ethics* 20: 85–92.

He, Ahou, Jonathan J.H. Zhu, and Shiyong Peng. 2002. Cultural Values and Cultural Resolution in Enterprises in Diverse Cultural Settings in China. In *Chinese Conflict Management and Resolution*, eds. Guo-Ming Chen and Ringo MA, 129–147. Westport CN: Ablex Publishing.

Hefner, Robert W. 1998. Introduction: Society and Morality in the New Asian Capitalisms. In *Market Cultures: Society and Morality in the New Asian Capitalisms*, ed. Robert W. Hefner, 1–38. Boulder, CO: Westview Press.

Herger, Wally. 2007. opening remarks before U.S. Congress. House. Committee on Ways and Means. *Hearing on U.S. Trade With China.* 110th Cong., 1st sess., February 15, 2007.

Heritage Foundation/Wall Street Journal. 2012. 2012 Index of Economic Freedom.

Hessler, Peter. 2006. *Oracle Bones: A Journey Through Time in China.* New York: Harper.

Hettinger, Edwin C. 1997. Justifying Intellectual Property. In *Intellectual Property: Moral, Legal, and International Dimensions*, ed. Adam D. Moore, 17–37. New York: Roman and Littlefield.

Hillberg, Loren E. testimony before U.S. Congress. Senate. Committee on Homeland Security and Governmental Affairs. *Ensuring Protection of American Intellectual Property Rights for American Industries in China.* 109th Cong., 1st sess., November 21, 2005.

Hofstede, Geert, Gert Jan Hofstede, and Michael Mindov. 2010. *Cultures and Organizations: Software of the Mind.* New York: McGraw-Hill.

Hofstede, Geert. 1984. *Culture's Consequences: International Differences in Work-Related Values.* Beverly Hills: Sage.

Hoiman, Chan and Ambrose Y.C. King. 2003. "Religion." In *Understanding Contemporary China*, ed. Robert E. Gamer, 339–376. Boulder, CO: Lynne Rienner Publishers.

Hollender, Jeffrey. 2004. What Matters Most: Corporate Values and Social Responsibility. *California Management Review* 46: 111–119.

Holleyman, Robert W. testimony before U.S. Congress. House. Committee on Oversight and Government Reform. *Protecting Intellectual Property Rights in a Global Economy: Current Trends and Future Challenges.* 111th Cong., 1st sess., December 9, 2009.

Hong Trade Development Council. *Emerging Market Research Report Series, Shanghai Municipality*, 18 October, 2011.

House of Representatives Committee on Oversight and Government Reform. 2009. *Protecting Intellectual Property Rights in a Global Economy: Current Trends and Future Challenges*, December 9.

Hsu, Francis L.K. 1981. *Americans and Chinese: Passages to Differences.* Honolulu: University of Hawaii.

Hualing, Fu and D.W. Choy. 2004. From Mediation to Adjudication: Settling Labor Disputes. *China Rights Forum* 3: 17–22.

Huang, Yasheng. 2008. *Capitalism with Chinese Characteristics: Entrepreneurship and the State.* New York: Cambridge University Press.

Hutchings, Kate and Georgina Murray. 2002. Australian Expatriates Experiences in Working Behind the Bamboo Curtain: An Examination of *Guanxi* in Post-communist China. *Asian Business and Management* 1: 373–393.

Hutchings, Kate and Georgina Murray. 2003. Family, Face, and Favours: Do Australians Adjust to Accepted Business Conventions in China. *Singapore Management Review* 25: 25–49.

Hwang, Kwang-Kuo. 1987. Face and Favor: The Chinese Power Game. *American Journal of Sociology* 92: 944–974.

Isaacs, Harold R. 1958. *Scratches on Our Minds: American Images of China and India.* New York: John & Co.

Jacobsen, Linda. 1998. *A Million Truths: A Decade in China.* New York: M. Evans and Company, Inc.

Jespersen, T. Christopher. 1996. *American Images of China.* Stanford: Stanford University Press.

Jia, Wenshan. 2002. Chinese Mediation and Its Cultural Foundation. In *Chinese Conflict Management and Resolution,* eds. Guo-Ming Chen and Ringo Ma, 289–295. Westport CN: Ablex Publishing.

Jiali, Ji, Arthur Kleinman, and Anne E. Becker. 2001. Suicide in Contemporary China: A Review of China's Distinctive Suicide Demographics in Their Sociocultural Context. *Harvard Review of Psychiatry* 9: 1–12.

Johnson, Ian. 2011. Calls for a "Jasmine Revolution" in China Persist. *The New York Times,* February 23.

Johnson, Ian. 2011. China Gets Religion. *The New York Review of Books,* December 22.

Jones, Ashby and Andrew Batson. 2008. Concerns About China Arbitration Rise. *Wall Street Journal,* May 9.

Jones, Jeffrey M. 2011. Americans Most Confidence in Military, Least in Congress. *Gallup Politics,* June 23.

Kaiman, Jonathan. 2011. China Closes Solar Plant After Protests. *Los Angeles Times,* September 20.

Kellogg, Thomas E. and Keith Hand. 2008. China Crawls Slowly Towards Judicial Reform. *Asia Times Online,* January 25.

Kleinman, Arthur. 2010. Remaking the Moral Person in China: Implications for Health. *The Lancet* 375: 1074–1075.

Knight, Frank H. 1997. *The Ethics of Competition.* New Brunswick, NJ: Transaction Publishers.

Koehn, Daryl. 2001. *Local Insights, Global Ethics For Business.* New York: Rodopi.

Krueger, David A. 2009. Ethical Reflections on the Opportunities and Challenges for International Business in China. *Journal of Business Ethics* 89: 145–156.

Lam, Kit-Chun. 2002. A Study of the Ethical Performance of Foreign-Investment Enterprises in the China Labor Market. *Journal of Business Ethics* 27: 249–365.

Lampton, David M. 2001. *Same Bed, Different Dreams: Managing U.S.-China Relations.* Berkeley: The University of California Press.

Leonhardt, David. 2011. The Real Problem with China. *New York Times,* January 11.

Li, Cheng. 2009. Introduction to *Democracy is a Good Thing,* by Yu Keping, xvii–xxxi. Washington, D.C.: Brookings Institution Press.

Li, Shaomin and L. Filer. 2004. Governance Environment and Model of Investment. Paper presented at the annual meeting for the *Academy of International Business,* July 10–13, in Stockholm, Sweden.

Li, Shaomin. 2004. Why are Property Rights Protections Lacking in China? An Institutional Explanation. *California Management Review* 46: 100–115.

Li, Shaomin. 2005. Why a Poor Governance Environment Does Not Deter Foreign Direct Investment: The Case of China and its Implications for Investment Protection. *Business Horizons* 48: 297–302.

Lieberthal, Kenneth and Geoffrey Lieberthal. 2003. The Great Transition. *Harvard Business Review*, October: 28–40.

Linebaugh, Kate. 2012. Frustrated with China, GE Turns Its Eye to Australia. *Wall Street Journal*, May 1.

Liu, Lydia H. 2004. *The Clash of Empires: The Invention of China in Modern World Making*. Cambridge: Harvard University Press.

MacIntyre, Alasdair. 1984. *After Virtue*. Notre Dame, IN: The University of Notre Dame Press.

Madsen, Richard. 1995. *China and the American Dream: A Moral Inquiry*. Berkeley: The University of California Press.

Margolis, Joshua D. and James P. Walsh. 2003. Misery Loves Companies: Rethinking Social Initiatives By Business. *Administrative Science Quarterly* 48: 268–305.

Martin, Eric and Sonja Elmquist. 2012. U.S. to File WTO Complaint Over China Rare-Earth Export Caps. *Bloomberg Businessweek*, March 13.

McCoy, Stanford K. testimony before U.S. Congress. House. Committee on Oversight and Government Reform. *Protecting Intellectual Property Rights in a Global Economy: Current Trends and Future Challenges*. 111th Cong., 1st sess., December 9, 2009.

McGregor, James. 2005. *One Billion Customers: Lessons From the Front Lines of Doing Business in China*. New York: Free Press.

McGregor, Richard. 2010. *The Party: The Secret World of China's Communist Rulers*. New York: HarperCollins Publishers.

McLean, Bethany and Joe Nocera. 2010. *All the Devils are Here: The Hidden History of the Financial Crisis*. New York: Penguin Books.

Mertha, Andrew C. 2005. Shifting Legal and Administrative Goalposts: Chinese Bureaucracies Foreign Actors, and the Evolution of China's Anti-Counterfeiting Enforcement Regime. In *Engaging the Law in China: State, Society, and Possibilities for Justice*, eds. Neil J. Diamant, Stanley B. Lubman, and Kevin J. O'Brien, 161–192. Stanford, CA: Stanford University Press.

Miller, John W. 2011. Trade Body Rules in Beijing's Favor. *Wall Street Journal*, March 12.

Millington, Andrew, Markus Eberhardt, and Barry Wilkinson. 2005. Gift Giving, *Guanxi* and Illicit Payments in Buyer-Supplier Relations in China: Analyzing the Experience of UK Companies. *Journal of Business Ethics* 57: 255–268.

Miner, Anne. testimony before U.S. Congress. Senate. Committee on Homeland Security and Governmental Affairs. *Ensuring Protection of American Intellectual Property Rights for American Industries in China*. 109th Cong., 1st sess., November 21, 2005.

Moody, Andrew. 2010. Is it too late to enter China market? *China Daily*, April 26.

Mulloy, Patrick A. testimony before U.S. Congress. Senate. Committee on Homeland Security and Governmental Affairs. *Ensuring Protection of American Intellectual Property Rights for American Industries in China.* 109th Cong. 1st sess., November 21, 2005.

Munro, Donald J. 1977. *Concept of Man in Contemporary China.* Ann Arbor: The University of Michigan Press.

National Bureau of Statistics of China 2012.

New York Times. 2010. China and Intellectual Property, December 23.

Nisbett, Richard E. 2003. *The Geography of Thought: How Asians and Westerns Think Differently . . . and Why.* New York: Free Press.

North, Douglas C. 2005. *Understanding the Process of Economic Change.* Princeton, NJ: Princeton University Press.

O'Neill, Jim. 2011. *The Growth Map: Economic Opportunities in the BRICS and Beyond.* New York: Penguin.

OECD. 2009. *State Owned Enterprises in China: Reviewing the Evidence.* OECD Working Group on Privatization and Corporate Governance of State Owned Assets. January 26.

Office of the United States Trade Representative. 2009. *United States Wins WTO Dispute Over Deficiencies in China's Intellectual Property Rights Laws,* January.

Ong, Ryan. 2009. Intellectual Property: Tackling Intellectual Property Infringement in China. *China Business Review,* March–April.

Orit, Gadiesh, Philip Leung, and Bestring Till. 2007. The Battle for China's Good-Enough Market. *Harvard Business Review* 85: 80–89.

Osnos, Evan. 2008. Angry Youth: The New Generation's Neocon Nationalists. *The New Yorker,* July 28.

Osnos, Evan. 2009. Wastepaper Queen; She's China's Horatio Alger Hero. Will her fortune survive? *The New Yorker,* March 30.

Ossinger, Joanna L. 2006. CEO Compensation Survey (A Special Report); Poorer Relations: When it Comes to Pay, Why are the British so Different? *Wall Street Journal,* April 10.

Oster, Shai. 2011. China's Rising Wages Propel U.S. Prices. *Wall Street Journal,* May 9.

Ostergard, Robert L. 2003. *The Development Dilemma: The Political Economy of Intellectual Property Rights in the International System.* New York: LFB Scholarly Publishing.

Page, Jeremy. 2011. Many Rich Chinese Consider Leaving, *Wall Street Journal,* November 2.

Page, Jeremy. 2012. China's Money Trail—Plan B for China's Wealthy: Moving to the U.S., Europe. *Wall Street Journal,* February 22.

Paine, Lynn Sharp. 1997. Trade Secrets and the Justification of Intellectual Property: A Comment of Hettinger. In *Intellectual Property: Moral, Legal, and International Dimensions*, ed. Adam D. Moore, 39–56. New York: Roman and Littlefield.

Pan, Philip P. 2008. *Out of Mao's Shadow: The Struggle for the Soul of a New China.* New York: Simon and Schuster.

Panikkar, K.M. 1953. *Asia and Western Dominance.* London: George Allen and Unwin.

Park, Seung Ho and Wilfried R. Vanhonacker. 2007. The Challenge for Multinational Corporations in China: Think Local, Act Global. *MIT Sloan Management Review* 48: 8–15.

Park, Seung Ho and Yadong Luo. 2001. *Guanxi* and Organizational Dynamics: Organizational Networking in Chinese Firms. *Strategic Management Journal* 22: 455–477.

Pavlo, Walter. 2012. Avon Vice Chairman Fired Amid Bribery Probe. *Forbes*, January 31.

Pei, Minxin. 2006. *China's Trapped Transition: The Limits of Developmental Autocracy.* Cambridge: Harvard University Press.

Peng, Heyue. 2010. *China's Indigenous Innovation Policy and Its Effects on Foreign Intellectual Property Rights Holders.* King & Wood Law Firm, September 9.

Peng, Mike W. 1998. *Behind the Success and Failure of U.S. Export Intermediaries: Transactions, Agents, and Resources.* Westport, Conn.: Quorum Books.

Peng, Mike W. and Yadong Luo. 2000. Managerial Ties and Firm Performance in a Transition Economy: The Nature of a Micro-Macro Link. *Academy of Management Journal* 43: 486–501.

Perkowski, Jack. 2012. Protecting Intellectual Property Rights in China. *Forbes*, April 18.

Polanyi, Michael. 1962. *Personal Knowledge: Toward a Post-Critical Philosophy.* Chicago: The University of Chicago Press.

Pomfret, John. 2007. *Chinese Lessons: Five Classmates and the Story of the New China.* New York: Henry Holt and Company.

Powell, Alvin. 2003. Personal Pain, National Character: Kleinman Shows How Individual Travails Reveal a Society. *Harvard University Gazette*, November 20.

Pye, Lucian W. 1988. *The Mandarin and the Cadre.* Ann Arbor: The University of Michigan Press.

Rachels, James. 2003. *The Elements of Philosophy.* New York: McGraw-Hill.

Ralston, David A. David H. Holt, Robert H. Terpstra, and Kai-Cheng Yu. 1997. The Impact of Culture and Ideology on Managerial Work Values: A Study of the United States, Russia, Japan, and China. *Journal of International Business Studies* 28: 177–208.

Ramzy, Austin. 2011. Will a Scandal Slow Down China's High Speed Trains. *Time*, February 17.

Rawls, John. 1971. *A Theory of Justice.* Cambridge, MA: Harvard University Press.

Redding, Gordon. 1995. *The Sprit of Chinese Capitalism.* New York: de Gruyter.

Redding, Gordon and Michael A. Witt. 2007. *The Future of Chinese Capitalism.* Oxford: Oxford University Press.

Rieff, Philip. 1985. *Fellow Teachers: of Culture and Its Second Death.* Chicago: The University of Chicago Press.

Rieff, Philip. 1987. *The Triumph of the Therapeutic: Uses of Faith After Freud.* Chicago: The University of Chicago Press.

Riley, Michael and Ashlee Vance. 2012. Inside the China Boom in Corporate Espionage. *Bloomberg Businessweek*, March 15.

Ritter, Geralyn. testimony before U.S. Congress. House. Committee on Ways and Means. *Hearing on U.S. Trade With China.* 110th Cong., 1st sess., February 15, 2007.

Rong, Ma. 2003. Population Growth and Urbanization. In *Understanding Contemporary China*, ed. Robert E. Gamer, 227–254. Boulder, CO: Lynne Rienner Publishers.

Ropp, Paul S. 1990. Introduction. In *Heritage of China: Contemporary Perspectives on Chinese Civilization*, ed. Paul S. Ropp, ix–xxi. Berkeley: The University of California Press.

Rusk, David. 1999. *Inside Game Outside Game.* Washington, D.C.: Brookings Institution Press.

Ryan, Leo V. 2000. Combating Corruption: The 21st Century Challenge. *Business Ethics Quarterly* 10: 331–338.

Said, Edward W. 1979. *Orientalism.* New York: Vintage Books.

Santoro, Michael A. 2009. *China 2020: How Western Business Can—and Should— Influence Social and Political Change in the Coming Decade.* Ithaca: Cornell University Press.

Sanyal, Rajib. 2005. Determinants of Bribery in International Business: The Cultural and Economic Factors. *Journal of Business Ethics* 59: 139–145.

Scherer, Andreas G. and William McKinley. 2007. The Affinity Between Free Trade Theory and Postmodernism: Implications for Multinational Enterprises. In *Focus Organization: Socialwissenschaftliche: Perspektiven und Analysen*, eds. T.S. Eberle, S. Hoidn, and K.S. Kavica, 166–187. Konstanz: UVK Verlagsqeseelschaft MbH.

Schroeder, Patricia. testimony before U.S. Congress. House. Committee on Ways and Means. *Hearing on U.S. Trade With China.* 110th Cong., 1st sess., February 15, 2007.

Schroeder, Paul. 2012. Personal Communications. Case Western Reserve University.

Sen, Amartya K. 1999. Human Rights and Economic Achievements. In *The East Asian Challenge for Human Rights*, eds. John R. Bauer and Daniel A. Bell, 88–99. New York: Cambridge University Press.

Sen, Amartya. 2000. *Development as Freedom.* New York: Anchor Books.

Sennett, Richard. 1998. *The Corrosion of Character: The Personal Consequences of Work in the New Capitalism.* New York: W.W. Norton & Company.

Shenkar, Oded and Aimin Yan. 2002. Failure as a Consequence of Partner Politics: Learning From the Life and Death of an International Cooperative Venture. *Human Relations* 55: 565–602.

Shils, Edward. 1975. *Center and Periphery: Essays in Macrosociology.* Chicago: The University of Chicago Press.

Shils, Edward. 1981. *Tradition.* Chicago: The University of Chicago Press.

Shils, Edward. 1997. *The Virtue of Civility: Selected Essays on Liberalism, Tradition, and Civil Society.* Indianapolis, IN: Liberty Fund.

Shleifer, Andrei and Rober W. Vishny. 1998. *The Grabbing Hand: Government Pathologies and Their Cures.* Cambridge: Harvard University Press.

Small Business GDP: Update 2002–2010. January 2012, No. 390.

Smart, Alan. 1993. Gifts, Bribes, and *Guanxi*: A Reconsideration of Bourdieu's Social Capital. *Cultural Anthropology* 8: 388–408.

Smith, Adam. 1974. *Wealth of Nations.* New York: Penguin Books.

Smith, Eric H. testimony before U.S. Congress. Congressional—Executive Commission on China. *Intellectual Property Protection as Economic Policy: Will China Ever Enforce Its IP Laws.* 109th Cong., 1st sess., May 16, 2005.

Smith, Eric H. testimony before U.S. Congress. House. Committee on the Judiciary. *International Piracy: The Challenges of Protecting Intellectual Property in the 21st Century.* 110th Cong., 1st sess., October 18, 2007.

Snell, Robin Stanley and Choo-sin Tseng. 2001. Ethical Dilemmas of Relation Building in China. *Thunderbird International Business Review* 43: 171–200.

Spar, Debora and Jean Oi. 2006. China: Building "Capitalism with Socialist Characteristics." *Harvard Business School Case.* Boston: Harvard Business School Publishing.

Spence, Jonathan D. 1990a. Chinese Fictions in the Twentieth Century. In *Asia in Western Fiction*, eds. Robin W. Winks and James R. Rush, 100–116. Honolulu: The University of Hawaii Press.

Spence, Jonathan. 1990b. Western Perceptions of China from the Late Sixteenth Century to the Present. In *Heritage of China: Contemporary Perspectives on Chinese Civilization*, ed. Paul S. Ropp, 1–14. Berkeley: The University of California Press.

Spence, Jonathan D. 1998. *The Chan's Great Continent: China in Western Minds.* New York: W. W. Norton & Company.

Steidlmeier, Paul. 1993. The Moral Legitimacy of Intellectual Property Claims: American Business and Developing Country Perspectives. *Journal of Business Ethics* 12: 538–545.

Steidlmeier, Paul. 1997. Business Ethics and Politics in China. *Business Ethics Quarterly* 7: 131–143.

Steidlmeier, Paul. 1999. Gift Giving, Bribery and Corruption: Ethical Management of Business Relationships in China. *Journal of Business Ethics* 20: 121–132.

Stoll, Robert L. testimony before U.S. Congress. House. Committee on Oversight and Government Reform. *Protecting Intellectual Property Rights in a Global Economy: Current Trends and Future Challenges.* 111th Cong., 1st sess., December 9, 2009.

Studwell, Joe. 2004. *The China Dream: The Quest for the Last Great Untapped Market on Earth.* New York: Grove Press.

Su, Chenting and James E. Littlefield. 2001. Entering *Guanxi*: A Business Ethical Dilemma in Mainland China. *Journal of Business Ethics* 22: 199–210.

Su Xiaokang and Wang Luxuang. 1988. *Deathsong of the River.*

Sun, Yan. 2004. *Corruption and Market in Contemporary China.* Ithaca: Cornell University Press.

Swanson, Diane L. and Dann G. Fisher, eds. 2010. *Toward Assessing Business Ethics Education.* Charlotte: Information Age Publishing.

Swinyard, W.R., H. Rinne, and A. Keng Kau. 1990. The Morality of Software Piracy: A Cross-Cultural Analysis. *Journal of Business Ethics* 9: 655–664.

Terlep, Sharon. 2012. GM Seeks Sway in China. *Wall Street Journal*, April 19.

The U.S.-China Business Council. 2012a. *Foreign Direct Investment.*

The U.S.-China Business Council. 2012b. *U.S.-China Trade Statistics and China's World Trade Statistics.*

The World Bank. 2010. *China.*

Toloken, Steve. 2008. China IP System Improving, but Pitfalls Remain. *Plastic News* 20: 7–16, May 12.

Toohey, Brian. testimony before U.S. Congress. House. Committee on Oversight and Government Reform. *Protecting Intellectual Property Rights in a Global Economy: Current Trends and Future Challenges.* 111th Cong., 1st sess., December 9, 2009.

Transparency International. 2011. *Corruption Perception Index 2011: The Perceived Level of Public-Sector Corruption in 183 Countries/Territories Around the World.*

Tsai, Kellee S. 2007. *Capitalism Without Democracy: The Private Sector in Contemporary China.* Ithaca: Cornell University Press.

Tsui, Anne S., Claudia Bird Schoonhoven, Marshall W. Meyer, Chung-Ming Lau, and George T. Milkovich. 2004. Organization and Management in the Midst of Societal Transformation: The People's Republic of China. *Organization Science* 15: 133–144.

Tu, Wei-ming. 1994. Cultural China: The Periphery as the Center. In *The Living Tree: The Changing Meaning of Being Chinese Today*, ed. Tu Wei-ming, 1–34. Stanford: Stanford University Press.

Tu, Wei-ming. 2002. Confucian Humanism and the Western Enlightenment. In *Candles in the Dark: A New Spirit for a Plural World*, ed. Barbara S. Baudot, 123–135. Seattle: The University of Washington Press.

Turnbull, C. Mary. 1990. Hong Kong: fragrant harbor, city of sin and death. In *Asia in Western Fiction*, eds. Robin W. Winks and James R. Rush, 117–136. Honolulu: The University of Hawaii Press.

Turner, Victor. 1974. *Dramas, Fields, and Metaphors: Symbolic Action in Human Society*. Ithaca, NY: Cornell University Press.

UNICEF. 2010. *China-Statistics*.

United States Government. *China—Measures Affecting the Protection and Enforcement of Intellectual Property Rights*, January 30, 2008. (First Submission WTO).

Vargo, Frank. testimony before U.S. Congress. House. Committee on Oversight and Government Reform. *Protecting Intellectual Property Rights in a Global Economy: Current Trends and Future Challenges*. 111th Cong., 1st sess., December 9, 2009.

Velasquez, Manuel. 2000. Globalization and the Failure of Ethics. *Business Ethics Quarterly* 10: 343–352.

Vogel, David. 1992. The Globalization of Business Ethics: Why Americans Remain Distinctive. *California Management Review* 35: 30–50.

Wadhwa, Vivek. 2011. China Could Game the U.S. in Intellectual Property. *Businessweek*, January 10.

Walder, Andrew G. 1988. *Communist Neo-Traditionalism: Work and Authority in Chinese Industry*. Berkeley: The University of California Press.

Wall Street Journal. 2012. Hong Kong: Thousands of People Rally Against Patriotism Classes. World Watch Section, July 30.

Wang, Robin R. 2002. Globalizing the Heart of the Dragon: The Impact of Technology on Confucian Ethical Values. *Journal of Chinese Philosophy* 29: 553–569.

Warren, Danielle E., Thomas W. Dunfee, and Naihe Li. 2004. Social Exchange in China: The Double-Edged Sword of *Guanxi*. *Journal of Business Ethics* 55: 355–372.

Watson, Diane E. opening statement before U.S. Congress. House. Committee on Oversight and Government Reform. *Protecting Intellectual Property Rights in a Global Economy: Current Trends and Future Challenges*. 111th Cong., 1st sess., December 9, 2009.

Weber, Elke U., Daniel R. Ames, and Ann-Renée Blais. 2004. "How Do I Choose Thee? Let Me Count the Ways": A Textual Analysis of Similarities and Differences in Modes of Decision-Making in China and the United States. *Management and Organization Review* 1: 87–118.

Weber, Max. 1951. *The Religion of China*. New York: Free Press.

Weinstein, Jason. testimony before U.S. Congress. House. Committee on Oversight and Government Reform. *Protecting Intellectual Property Rights in a Global Economy: Current Trends and Future Challenges*. 111th Cong., 1st sess., December 9, 2009.

Weisman, Jonathan. 2012. U.S. to Share Cautionary Tale of Trade Secret Theft With Chinese Official. *New York Times*, February 14.

Weller, Robert P. 1998. Divided Market Cultures in China. In *Market Cultures: Society and Morality in the New Asian Capitalisms*, ed. Robert P. Weller, 78–103. Boulder, CO: Westview.

Werhane, Patricia H. Exporting Mental Models: Global Capitalism in the 21st Century. *Business Ethics Quarterly* 10: 353–362.

Wines, Michael. 2010. China Fortifies State Businesses to Fuel Growth. *Wall Street Journal*, August 29.

Wines, Michael. 2012a. Inflaming Trademark Dispute, Second City in China Halts Sale of the iPad. *New York Times*, February 14.

Wines, Michael. 2012b. Majority of Chinese Now Live in Cities. *New York Times*, January 17.

Witcomb, Laura L., Carol B. Erdener, Cheng Li. 1998. Business Ethical Values in China and the U.S. *Journal of Business Ethics* 17: 839–852.

Wong, Edward. 2012. Missing Chinese Lawyer Said to Be in Remote Prison. *The New York Times*, January 1.

Wong, John. 2003. China's Economy. In *Understanding Contemporary China*, ed. Robert E. Gamer, 111–154. Boulder, CO: Lynne Rienner Publishers.

World Bank. 2011. *World Development Indicators*, July 1.

World Health Organization. 2011. *Suicide rates per 100,000 by country, year and sex.*

Xin, Zhou and Nick Edwards. 2012. China Eyes 13 Percent Rise in Minimum Wage By 2015. *Huffington Post*, April 2.

Yager, Loren. testimony before U.S. Congress. House. Committee on the Judiciary. *International Piracy: The Challenges of Protecting Intellectual Property in the 21st Century.* 110th Cong., 1st sess., October 18, 2007.

Yang, C.K. 1961. *Religion in Chinese Society: A Study of Contemporary Social Functions of Religion and Some of Their Historical Factors.* Berkeley: The University of California Press.

Yang, C.K. 1963. Introduction to *The Religion of China*, by Max Weber, xiii–xliii. New York: Free Press.

Yang, Mayfair. 2002. The Resilience of *Guanxi* and its New Deployments: A Critique of Some New *Guanxi* Scholarship. *The China Quarterly* 170: 459–476.

Yardley, Jim. 2005. A Judge Tests China's Courts, Making History. *New York Times*, November 28.

Ye, Juliet. 2010. Playing for Keeps Inside China—Game Makers Battle Bureaucrats, Pirates as They Seek to Tap Growing Market. *Wall Street Journal*, March 3.

Young, Michael N., Mike W. Peng, David Ahlstrom, Garry D. Burton, and Yi Jiang. 2008. Corporate Governance in Emerging Economies: A Review of the Principal-Principal Perspective. *Journal of Management Studies* 45: 196–220.

Yu, Keping. 2009. *Democracy is a Good Thing: Essays on Politics, Society, and Culture in Contemporary China.* Washington, D. C.: Brooking Institution Press.

Zimmerman, James M. testimony before U.S. Congress. Congressional—Executive Commission on China. *Intellectual Property Protection as Economic Policy: Will China Ever Enforce Its IP Laws.* 109th Cong., 1st sess., May 16, 2005.

Index